MRS BEETON'S
FAVOURITE
CAKES AND
PUDDINGS

MRS BEETON'S
FAVOURITE CAKES AND PUDDINGS

WARD LOCK

A WARD LOCK BOOK

First published in the UK 1995 by Ward Lock

Wellington House
125 Strand
London WC2R 0BB

A Cassell imprint

Copyright © Ward Lock 1995

Mrs Beeton's is a registered trademark of Ward Lock Ltd

Edited by Jenni Fleetwood and Donna Wood
Photography by Clive Streeter
Home Economists: Lyn Rutherford and Jacqui Hine
Illustrations by Tony Randell

British Library Cataloguing-in-Publication Data
A record of this book is available from the British Library

Printed and bound in Great Britain by Bath Press.

ISBN 07063 74061

Thanks are due to Prestige for providing information on pressure cooking,
as well as a pressure cooker for testing, and to the Tupperware Company for
supplying information on moulds.

CONTENTS

Introduction	7
Useful Weights and Measures	8
Following the Recipes	10
A Guide to Ingredients	12
Classic Dessert Ingredients	21
Equipment for Perfect Puddings	25
Equipment for Perfect Cakes	32
Basic Techniques for Cakes	37
Basic Cakes	48
Cake Coverings and Fillings	54
Basic Covering and Filling Techniques	70
Simple Cake Decorating Techniques	82
Traditional Everyday Cakes	102
All Sorts of Small Cakes	126
Special Cakes and Weekend Treats	146
Gâteaux, Trifles and Cheesecakes	164
Fruit Puddings and Jellies	189
All Sorts of Ices	211
Custards and Creamy Desserts	234
Rice Puddings	295
Pancakes and Batters	308
Steamed Puddings	325
Pastries, Cobblers and Crumbles	344
Sauces and Butters	392
Glossary	407
Index	410

INTRODUCTION

Baking cakes and creating luscious desserts have always been one of the most enjoyable aspects of cooking. In Mrs Beeton's day, sweet cookery fell into two distinct categories – there were everyday cakes and puddings, and special recipes reserved for weekends or festive occasions. Weekday cakes were for afternoon tea and were made in batches, two or three at a time, from substantial mixtures that were satisfying but not too rich. These simple family recipes were stirred up with the minimum of fuss, adding a little fruit or whatever was available by way of flavourings. Special baking required far more planning and attention; ingredients were procured in advance, and the fire stoked to ensure the oven reached – and maintained – the required temperature.

Puddings and desserts were viewed in much the same way, with simple nourishing puddings served as part of family meals often using suet pastry, rice and milk as typical ingredients, particularly in winter months when fresh fruit was scarce. For grand dinner parties Mrs Beeton's contemporaries really made the most of the dessert course, offering elaborately decorated moulds or delicate creams served with crisp biscuits and often providing a choice of dishes.

Today, of course, there is such a wide choice of fresh, frozen and canned fruits that a simple dessert course can be made throughout the year and a piece of fresh fruit or a simple fruit salad is an acceptable alternative after informal meals. Despite the convenience of contemporary cooking, for many people the sweet course remains the crowning glory of a meal and a formal meal will normally end with a delicious dessert. And although the idea of regularly baking for mid-week tea is no longer popular, there are times when a slice of cake seems essential to complement a cup of tea or a once-a-year festivity for which nothing but a home-made cake will do.

Mrs Beeton's Favourite Cakes and Puddings brings together the best of sweet cookery with recipes for plain cakes as mid-week treats that are ideal for the freezer or lunch-box. There are also lots of traditional cakes for Sunday tea and and more sophisticated confections for family occasions or when there are guests.

All the basic information on ingredients, cookware, techniques and methods are included and also useful guidance on cake decorating. From simple cakes to glorious gâteaux; from desserts and fruit puddings to hearty everyday puddings, whether you simply want to check on a recipe for an old-fashioned plain cake or are in search of inspiration for a dinner party dessert, the chapters that follow are sure to provide what you need and have lots of hints and tips to ensure success every time.

USEFUL WEIGHTS AND MEASURES

USING METRIC OR IMPERIAL MEASURES

Throughout the book, all weights and measures are given first in metric, then in Imperial. For example 100 g/4 oz, 150 ml/¼ pint or 15 ml/1 tbsp.

When following any of the recipes use either metric or Imperial – do not combine the two sets of measures as they are not interchangeable.

EQUIVALENT METRIC/IMPERIAL MEASURES

Weights   The following chart lists some of the metric/Imperial weights that are used in the recipes.

METRIC	IMPERIAL
15 g	½ oz
25 g	1 oz
50 g	2 oz
75 g	3 oz
100 g	4 oz
150 g	5 oz
175 g	6 oz
200 g	7 oz
225 g	8 oz
250 g	9 oz
275 g	10 oz
300 g	11 oz
350 g	12 oz
375 g	13 oz
400 g	14 oz
425 g	15 oz
450 g	1 lb
575 g	1¼ lb
675 g	1½ lb
800 g	1¾ lb
900 g	2 lb
1 kg	2¼ lb
1.4 kg	3 lb
1.6 kg	3½ lb
1.8 kg	4 lb
2.25 kg	5 lb

Liquid Measures   The following chart lists some metric/Imperial equivalents for liquids. Millilitres (ml), litres and fluid ounces (fl oz) or pints are used throughout.

METRIC	IMPERIAL
50 ml	2 fl oz
125 ml	4 fl oz
150 ml	¼ pint
300 ml	½ pint
450 ml	¾ pint
600 ml	1 pint

Spoon Measures   Both metric and Imperial equivalents are given for all spoon measures, expressed as millilitres and teaspoons (tsp) or tablespoons (tbsp).

All spoon measures refer to British standard measuring spoons and the quantities given are always for level spoons.

Do not use ordinary kitchen cutlery instead of proper measuring spoons as they will hold quite different quantities.

METRIC	IMPERIAL
1.25 ml	¼ tsp
2.5 ml	½ tsp
5 ml	1 tsp
15 ml	1 tbsp

Length   All linear measures are expressed in millimetres (mm), centimetres (cm) or metres (m) and inches or feet. The following list gives examples of typical conversions.

METRIC	IMPERIAL
5 mm	¼ inch
1 cm	½ inch
2.5 cm	1 inch
5 cm	2 inches
15 cm	6 inches
30 cm	12 inches (1 foot)

OVEN TEMPERATURES

Whenever the oven is used, the required setting is given as three alternatives: degrees Celsius (°C), degrees Fahrenheit (°F) and gas.

The temperature settings given are for conventional ovens. If you have a fan oven, adjust the temperature according to the manufacturer's instructions.

°C	°F	GAS
110	225	¼
120	250	½
140	275	1
150	300	2
160	325	3
180	350	4
190	375	5
200	400	6
220	425	7
230	450	8
240	475	9

MICROWAVE INFORMATION

Occasional microwave hints and instructions are included for certain recipes, as appropriate. The information given is for microwave ovens rated at 650-700 watts.

The following terms have been used for the microwave settings: High, Medium, Defrost and Low. For each setting, the power input is as follows: High = 100% power, Medium = 50% power, Defrost = 30% power and Low = 20% power.

All microwave notes and timings are for guidance only: always read and follow the manufacturer's instructions for your particular appliance. Remember to avoid putting any metal in the microwave and never operate the microwave empty.

NOTES FOR AMERICAN READERS

In America dry goods and liquids are conventionally measured by the standard 8 oz cup. When translating pints, and fractions of pints, Americans should bear in mind that the U.S. pint is equal to 16 fl oz or 2 cups, whereas the Imperial pint is equal to 20 fl oz.

EQUIVALENT METRIC/AMERICAN MEASURES

METRIC/IMPERIAL	AMERICAN
Weights	
450 g/1 lb butter or margarine	2 cups (4 sticks)
100 g/4 oz grated cheese	1 cup
450 g/1 lb flour	4 cups
450 g/1 lb granulated sugar	2 cups
450 g/1 lb icing sugar	3½ cups confectioners' sugar
200 g/7 oz raw long-grain rice	1 cup
100 g/4 oz cooked long-grain rice	1 cup
100 g/4 oz fresh white breadcrumbs	2 cups
Liquid Measures	
150 ml/¼ pint	⅔ cup
300 ml/½ pint	1¼ cups
450 ml/¾ pint	2 cups
600 ml/1 pint	2½ cups
900 ml/1½ pints	3¾ cups
1 litre/1¾ pints	4 cups (2 U.S. pints)

Terminology Some useful American equivalents or substitutes for British ingredients are listed below:

BRITISH	AMERICAN
aubergine	eggplant
bicarbonate of soda	baking soda
biscuits	cookies, crackers
broad beans	fava or lima beans
chicory	endive
cling film	plastic wrap
cornflour	cornstarch
courgettes	zucchini
cream, single	cream, light
cream, double	cream, heavy
flour, plain	flour, all-purpose
frying pan	skillet
grill	broil
minced meat	ground meat
prawn	shrimp
shortcrust pastry	basic pie dough
spring onion	scallion
sultana	golden raisin
swede	rutabaga

FOLLOWING
THE RECIPES

There are a few basic culinary rules that can be applied when following all recipes or preparing any food. Good kitchen practice, accuracy when following recipes and care when cooking food are the general principles which should be applied to all cooking processes. Certain cakes and puddings are particularly delicate and special attention should be paid to their preparation. Follow these guidelines to ensure both kitchen safety and success.

BEFORE YOU START

The starting point for making any recipe is to read it through, checking that you have all the ingredients that are listed, in the right quantities, and all the cooking utensils that are needed. As well as checking these obvious points, make sure that you will have enough time to prepare and cook the recipe; this is particularly important if you are making a cake that may require lengthy cooking.

It may seem very obvious, but do clear the work surface before you start – it is all too easy to begin a baking session in enthusiasm when the kitchen is already crowded with dishes waiting to be washed after a meal, or from a previous cooking task. The lack of space and the mess suddenly become all too apparent when the tray of red-hot cakes is removed from the oven and there is not a space anywhere to put it down.

Assemble all the ingredients, utensils and baking tins. If you want to make any adjustments to the quantities – for example preparing a large batch of cakes – then work through the ingredients list, jotting down the quantities you intend to prepare, or noting any other changes so that you will be consistent as you weigh and prepare the recipe. It is very easy to forget to double up just one item when preparing a double quantity of mixture and it can be disastrous!

Lastly, make sure the oven is empty, ready for use and that the shelves are in position.

CHOICE OF INGREDIENTS

Information on basic ingredients is given on pages 12-24, but in general all ingredients should be fresh and of good quality. The rule for baking is to have foods such as butter, margarine, eggs and milk at room temperature unless otherwise stated in the recipe. Always wash eggs under cool water before cracking them open.

KITCHEN HYGIENE

Always make sure that areas where food is prepared are thoroughly clean, that all utensils are clean and dry and that dish cloths and tea-towels are scrupulously clean. And the same applies to your hands – do not handle raw food, then cooked food without washing your hands in between. Keep all utensils for raw and cooked food separate or washed between use.

WEIGHING AND MEASURING

It is important to follow the recipes closely for success. Use only one set of measures, either metric or Imperial. Use an accurate set of scales for weighing, a measuring jug for measuring quantities of fluid and British standard spoon measures.

Weigh all the ingredients before you begin to prepare the mixture so that they are all ready to be added as they are needed. It is a good idea to weigh dry ingredients, such as flour and sugar, before softer foods, like butter or margarine, as this saves having to wash the scoop or container on the scales in between weighing the items. Keep the prepared ingredients separate until they are ready to be mixed in the right order.

PREPARING TINS AND HEATING THE OVEN

Always make sure you have the correct size and shape of tin and prepare it in advance according to the instructions given in the recipe, or by following specific advice given by the bakeware manufacturer as appropriate. If you are unsure as to exactly how to line tins, then check with the chapter that explains and illustrates all the basics.

Prepare the oven, taking care to select the right temperature, at the stage suggested in the recipe.

MIXING THE INGREDIENTS

Follow the recipe method closely, taking note of any advice on the texture or colour of the mixture so that you know what you should be aiming for. If you are unsure of any term or process, then check it in the chapter on basics or in the glossary as appropriate.

The majority of cake mixtures should be baked as soon as they are prepared unless the recipe states otherwise.

COOKING TIMES

Check the cooking time before you put the cakes or pudding into the oven, setting a timer as a reminder. Many recipes give a range of times within which the cake or pudding should be cooked, so check on the cooking progress at the first suggested time. Before opening the oven door make sure that you know what you are looking for in the finished item, then you will be able to decide quickly whether it is cooked or not.

REMOVING FOOD FROM THE OVEN

Make sure that you have a clear space on which to put the baked goods as soon as they are removed from the oven. Have a heat-proof mat or stand on the work suface and always remember to use a thick oven glove to protect your hands.

Have a wire rack ready to receive the cooked food if the recipe suggests that it ought to be transferred to one. You may need a palette knife to slide items off a baking sheet, or a small knife to loosen a cake around the sides of a tin. If you are removing a cake from a loose-bottomed tin, then have a suitable vessel ready to support the middle of the tin allowing the side to slide down. A storage jar with a heat-resistant top is ideal for this.

FINISHING THE RECIPE

Follow the advice given in the recipe for cooling and finishing the baked items. Some recipes offer guidance on storing the baked goods, otherwise follow the general instructions at the beginning of the sections.

A GUIDE TO
INGREDIENTS

The basic ingredients for making both cakes and puddings are the same but the proportions in which they are used vary greatly to produce different results. The cooked cake will only be as good as the ingredients that went into the mixture and it is important to use the right type of each ingredient to achieve the required result. The following notes outline the main ingredients which form the basis for many of the recipes, with information on the different types which are available and how they should be stored. Do take note of information supplied on packaging and take advantage of leaflets and advice which is offered by manufacturers. Remember, most manufacturers want to help you to achieve the best results when using their products and they can also be helpful in solving any particular problems which you may encounter.

FLOUR

There is a wide range of flours available and the choice depends on the purpose for which it is required. Flour is obtained by milling wheat. The wheat grain is made up of various parts: the *endosperm* which is the starchy part and which is intended to provide food for the growing plant; the *outer bran layers* which are the main source of fibre; the *aleurone* which is a layer between the bran and the endosperm, providing protein, vitamins and minerals; and the *germ*, or *wheatgerm*, which is rich in protein, oil and vitamins. (The germ is the part of the grain that will grow if it is planted.)

The grain is broken down by milling. During this process either all or part of the grain can be used to make the flour. Each type of flour has a different composition and they can be broadly grouped according to the percentage of the whole cleaned wheat grain which they contain; this is known as the extraction rate. The extraction rate is given on the packet and this is useful for checking the difference between the types of brown flour that are available.

Wholemeal or Wholewheat Flour This flour contains all the wheat grain with nothing added or taken away during processing and milling. This is known as 100% extraction flour and the preferred term is wholemeal, although both names are used. When 'whole' is included in the name of the flour it means it contains all the grain.

Brown Flour This type of flour usually contains about 85% of the wheat grain (85% extraction rate) and it is most often sold under particular brand names. The term 'wheatmeal' was at one time used for this type of flour but this was confusing and its use is now illegal.

White Flour This type of flour usually contains about 75% of the wheat grain although some white flours have a lower extraction rate. Most of the bran and wheatgerm are removed during the milling process in order to produce white flour.

81% Extraction Flour This is a flour which bridges the gap between brown and white flour and it is sold under various brand names. The extraction rate is given on the packets.

Stoneground Flour This term is used for wheat which is ground between two stones instead of by modern roller methods and it does not reflect the composition of the flour.

As well as the composition of the flour which depends on the amount of the grain which it contains, other processes go to make up the different types of flour we can buy.

Plain Flour This is flour which does not have any raising agent added. It is the common term used for plain white flour. It is used for certain types of cake mixture and for making biscuits. It is also used in pastry.

Self-raising Flour This is flour which has a raising agent added to it. When used in recipes the term usually relates to white flour but self-raising wholemeal or brown flours are also available. The amount of raising agent to flour is carefully balanced during the production process so that it gives perfect results in the majority of cake recipes. When self-raising brown flour is required this is stated in the ingredients list.

Soft Flour This is usually white. This flour has a low protein content and it is very light. It is manufactured for use in light cake or biscuit mixtures, for example Victoria sandwich cakes, Genoese sponge cake or piped Viennese biscuits, or for making pastry. It is one of the most 'modern' types of flour and many manufacturers offer guidance on its use and sample recipes.

Strong Flour This is usually white. It has a high protein content and it is used in yeast mixtures, particularly in bread making.

Malted Wheat Flour This is brown flour to which malted wheat is added to give a distinctive texture and flavour. Again the main use for this type of flour is in bread but it can be used in savoury biscuits.

STORING FLOUR

Flour should be kept in a cool, dry, airy place. The bag of flour can be placed in an airtight tin or the flour can be turned into a storage jar with a tight-fitting lid. The jar should always be thoroughly washed and dried before it is filled with a new batch of flour. Do not add new flour to the remains of an older batch.

Plain white flour can be stored for four to six months but self-raising flour does not keep as well and it should be stored for up to two or three months. Wholemeal and brown flours have a higher fat content than white flour so they may go rancid if they are not properly stored or if they are kept for too long. These should be kept for up to two months, so it is best to buy small quantities frequently. Store wholemeal and brown flours in a cool, dry place and keep them separate from white flour as they should be used sooner.

CORNFLOUR

Cornflour is produced from maize and it is quite different from wheat flour. It is very fine, almost pure starch, and it is sometimes combined with wheat flour in certain cake and biscuit recipes.

RAISING AGENTS

For the majority of cake mixtures a raising agent is added to make the cake rise during cooking. In the case of a whisked mixture, such as a whisked sponge, air is incorporated into the mixture during whisking and it acts as the raising agent since it expands as the mixture is heated in the oven. Self-raising flour is used in the majority of cake recipes and it is not usually necessary to add any additional raising agent, although there are exceptions to this rule.

A combination of acid and alkaline substances are used to make most cake mixtures rise. When they are moistened and heated in combination they produce a gas (carbon dioxide) and it is the gas bubbles which make the mixture rise. The heat of the oven sets the cake and this traps the bubbles in place. Alternatively, yeast can be used as a raising agent. Yeast ferments with sugar and moisture in the presence of warmth and it produces carbon dioxide, the bubbles of which are trapped during proving (or the rising process) and baking. Yeast is used mainly for bread making.

Baking Powder Baking powder is the most common leavening agent used in baking when self-raising flour is not used for a recipe. Baking powder is made up of bicarbonate of soda (alkaline), selected acids and a certain amount of starch. These ingredients are combined in the exact proportions required to produce a rise when the powder is both moistened and heated. It is important to use the correct amount of baking powder as suggested in the recipe because too much can cause failure just as too little will result in inadequate rising.

Bicarbonate of Soda Bicarbonate of soda is used in certain recipes, for example gingerbread. Once it is moistened the bicarbonate of soda quickly starts to produce the bubbles which result in a rise, so recipes which contain bicarbonate of soda must be cooked as soon as they are mixed.

Cream of Tartar This is an acid which can be combined with bicarbonate of soda and used instead of baking powder. To be used in this way, two parts of cream of tartar should be mixed with one part of bicarbonate of soda. This is not a common raising agent for cakes but it is used in certain recipes.

Yeast In warm conditions, when combined with moisture and sugar, yeast produces carbon dioxide to make doughs and selected cake mixtures rise. There are a few cakes which rely on yeast for their rise but it is used mainly for making bread and heavy doughs. Either fresh or dried yeast can be used successfully in cooking.

Fresh yeast is sometimes available from bakers. It should be creamy in colour, have a slightly beery smell, be cool to the touch and easy to break. It can be stored in a polythene bag in the refrigerator for up to a week or it can be frozen, well wrapped, for up to a month. Fresh yeast should be blended with warm liquid for use.

Dried yeast is available in packets and tins and it keeps very well if unopened (for up to one year). Once opened it keeps for about two to three months. Before use the dried yeast is reconstituted by sprinkling it over lukewarm liquid and leaving it, loosely covered, in a warm place until it has dissolved and the liquid is frothy. The yeast liquid should be stirred to make sure that all the grains of dried yeast have dissolved before it is mixed with other ingredients.

Easy-blend yeast is a dried yeast which must be added straight to the dry ingredients. When this is used the manufacturer's instructions should be followed closely for good results.

Storing Raising Agents All dry raising agents should be stored in an airtight container in a cool, dry place. Old, stale raising agents will not give the required results, so they should be stored for no more than two or three months, then discarded. Dried yeast should be stored in a cool, dry place in an airtight container. Fresh yeast wrapped in polythene can be kept for a short time in the refrigerator or it can be frozen.

FAT

The majority of cakes and puddings include a certain amount of fat and the richer types have a high proportion of fat added. There are various fats which can be used but the majority of cakes and puddings are made from butter or margarine.

Butter This gives an excellent flavour in cooking. If it is allowed to soften at room temperature, butter creams extremely well.

When taken straight from the refrigerator and rubbed into dry ingredients, it is ideal for making cakes and biscuits. It can also be melted with other ingredients before being added to the dry ingredients.

There are two types of butter to choose from: the first is sweet cream butter which is salted or slightly salted. The second is lactic butter which is slightly salted or unsalted and may be referred to as the continental type.

Traditionally, the sweet cream varieties are the most popular and they form the largest proportion of butter produced in the United Kingdom, the Republic of Ireland and New Zealand. This type of butter is produced by churning cream which has been allowed to stand for approximately twelve hours. The addition of salt produces the characteristic flavour and improves the keeping quality of the butter.

A certain amount of lactic butter is produced in the United Kingdom but the majority is imported. A culture of lactic acid is added to the cream before it is churned; this results in a slightly acidic flavour.

In addition a number of regional butters are produced in the United Kingdom. These have subtle individual flavour qualities that are appreciated on bread. These are not usually specified for use in recipes.

When buying butter always check the sell-by date which is given on the packet. (Remember that sell-by dates are for guidance only and they are not a compulsory feature.) Store butter in the refrigerator, neatly packed in its original wrapping. The keeping quality of butter does vary according to its type and packaging. Butter in foil packaging keeps slightly better than butter in parchment packing, and salted butter keeps nominally better than the unsalted type. The foil-wrapped butter can be kept for up to eleven weeks in the refrigerator; butter in parchment can be kept for seven weeks.

Butter can be frozen, when the unopened pack should be enclosed in a sealed polythene bag. The unsalted type will keep best in the freezer and it can be stored for up to six months. Salted butter can be frozen for up to three months.

All butter should be well wrapped during storage as it absorbs flavours and odours.

To clarify butter, heat gently until melted, then stand for 2–3 minutes. Pour off clear yellow liquid on top and allow to solidify. This is the clarified butter.

Margarine Margarine is probably the most popular fat used in baking as it is less expensive than butter and yet gives comparable results, although the flavour is not as good. Generally, it is made of 80% fat and a maximum of 16% water, with added flavouring, colouring and emulsifiers.

Margarine is produced from blended edible oils and soft fats and the type used is specified on the packet or tub. Fish oil and soft animal fats can be used in combination with vegetable oils; some margarines use vegetable oils only. There are two types, either hard, block margarine or soft, tub margarine. The texture of the margarine depends on type of oils or fats used and on the manufacturing process. For creaming, the block margarine should be allowed to soften at room temperature in the same way as butter. Soft margarine can be used straight from the refrigerator. The nature of the processing method results in soft margarine being whipped before packing so that it is particularly light and will cream easily with sugar. Soft margarine is particularly useful for making one-stage mixtures.

Lard Lard is white, melted and clarified pork fat which was once very popular for cooking. It contributes little colour or flavour and it is sometimes used with spices, treacle and syrup for making gingerbread or similar cakes. Otherwise it is not widely used in the preparation of cakes and biscuits.

Dripping This is melted down meat fat – usually beef – and it has a distinctive flavour. It is not an ingredient which is commonly used in making cakes or puddings but it is used in a handful of traditional, and very economical recipes.

When it is used in baking recipes, dripping obtained from meat should be clarified. To do this the fat is heated gently in a large saucepan with the same volume of cold water until the water just begins to boil. All scum must be removed as it rises to the surface and the dripping is allowed to simmer in the water for 5 minutes. The liquid is then strained through a muslin-lined sieve into a clean bowl. The bowl is covered and the fat allowed to solidify in a cool place. The lard is lifted off the water in one piece and any sediment on its underside is scraped off. Lastly, the lard is heated very gently until all spitting and bubbling ceases, to evaporate all the water.

Oil Some recipes are developed specifically to use oil in cake doughs but otherwise this fat is not used for baking. However, it is the most convenient form of fat for greasing baking tins.

Low-fat Spreads These spreads should not be confused with margarine. They are manufactured specifically for spreading and they are not recommended instead of margarine or butter for cooking cakes since they have a high water content and they contain little fat, as the term suggests. The fat content of the spread should be given on the container and this varies according to the product.

SUGAR

Sugar, in its many forms, is widely used in cooking and it is a vital ingredient in ensuring the success of many baking recipes. Its prime function is to sweeten, but certain types of sugar also add flavour to cake and biscuit mixtures. It is important that the correct proportion of sugar is used, as stated in the recipe, and that it is incorporated into the mixture correctly.

As well as sugar, syrup and treacle are used for certain recipes; these ingredients are derived from sugar.

Granulated Sugar This is probably the most common type of sugar and it should be used in recipes where the term 'sugar' is used in the ingredients list. It is used in recipes that contain enough liquid for it to dissolve completely or where the cooking temperature and time are adequate to ensure that it dissolves. For example, it is used in rubbed-in mixtures and for melted mixtures. It can be used for creamed mixtures but caster sugar gives better results.

Caster Sugar This is finer than granulated sugar, it dissolves more quickly and it is the most suitable sugar for creaming with fat or for use in whisked mixtures. It gives more volume and a lighter result than granulated sugar in these recipes. In addition, caster sugar can be sprinkled over cooked sponge cakes to enhance their appearance.

Soft Light Brown Sugar The term used to describe this type of sugar varies according to the manufacturer; for example it may be sold as 'light golden soft sugar'. It is a fine-grained sugar which has cane molasses added, to provide flavour as well as darkening the colour. It is used in light fruit cakes or in other baking recipes and adds flavour as well as sweetening the mixture.

Soft Dark Brown Sugar Again the term used varies according to the manufacturer and this type of sugar may be sold as 'rich dark soft sugar'. It is similar to the soft light brown sugar but it contains more cane molasses, giving it a richer flavour and darker colour. It is used in rich fruit cakes or gingerbreads and it can be used to make certain puddings.

Muscovado Sugar Muscovado sugar is very dark, moist and fairly fine-grained. It is unrefined cane sugar and it has a very dark, almost black, colour and strong flavour. It is not widely used in baking but it can be used in making rich fruit cakes to give a very dark colour and rich flavour to the mixture.

Raw Cane Sugar This is sugar which contains a certain amount of the impurities from sugar cane which are otherwise removed during the processing of white sugars. Some brown sugars are first refined, then molasses is added to contribute the characteristic flavour and colour. Raw cane sugars are not refined first – the darker varieties naturally contain the most impurities and molasses; the lighter types contain fewer impurities. The composition of the product is indicated on the packet and if the sugar has first been refined, then had molasses added (or caramel), then this will be indicated by an ingredients list.

Demerara Sugar Demerara sugar is light brown in colour, with a fairly rich flavour and large crystals. It is not widely used in baking but it can be sprinkled over the top of certain types of cakes (for example, loaf cakes) before cooking to give a crunchy topping.

Icing Sugar This is very fine, powdered sugar which is not commonly used in cake mixtures but which forms the basis for many different types of icing. It is ideal for sweetening whipped cream as it dissolves very rapidly. It is also useful for sprinkling over cooked cakes once they are cooled.

Lump Sugar This is made from granulated sugar which is moistened with syrup and moulded. The lumps or cubes of sugar are dried and packed into boxes. It does not have a role to play in baking recipes other than for crushing and sprinkling over baked cakes as decoration.

Preserving Sugar As its name implies this sugar is manufactured specifically for use in preserves. It has very large crystals and it can be sprinkled over loaf cakes before cooking.

Golden Syrup This is a blend of sugar syrup, caramel and flavourings. It is used in certain baking recipes instead of sugar. It can be used to glaze the top of light fruit cakes just before they are served.

Black Treacle This is made from molasses and sugar syrup. It has a very dark colour and strong flavour and it is used in certain baking recipes, for example gingerbread, or it is added to rich fruit cakes.

Molasses Molasses is the very dark, thick syrup which is drained from raw sugar cane. It is interchangeable with black treacle in cooking.

Storing Sugar All types of sugar, syrup and treacle should be stored in airtight containers and kept in a cool, dry place. Soft brown sugar may harden slightly during storage but it usually softens again if it is warmed briefly in a cool oven (or for a few seconds in the microwave). Icing sugar does not have a long shelf life as it does harden and it is vital that there are no lumps in it if it is used to prepare icings. Syrup and treacle tins should be wiped clean with absorbent kitchen paper after use and they must be stored in a dry place. Do not use the contents of old tins which may have rusted or been damaged.

EGGS

Eggs play a vital role in cake making. They are used to lighten cakes and to ensure that they rise and set during cooking. In some mixtures, where a high proportion of eggs are used, they are the only raising agent.

The eggs can be used whole or they may be separated before they are added to the mixture. Whisked with sugar, they may form the basis for the mixture and the other ingredients will be folded into them. For some recipes the egg yolks are incorporated first, then the whisked whites are folded into the mixture. In this case a little of the white should be stirred in first to soften the bulk of the mixture before the rest of the whites are folded in.

In some recipes just the whites or yolks are used; for example, meringues require the whites only and desserts often use just yolks. Other recipes may call for more whites than yolks in order to produce a very light mixture.

Buying eggs Eggs come in different sizes and they are also categorised by quality. Two quality grades of whole eggs are sold, either A or B quality and this is clearly stated on the box. There are regulations that have to be observed for the sale of pre-packed eggs, and certain information has to be included on the outside of the box.

Firstly, the class of eggs must be clearly marked and the number of eggs in the box indicated. The size of the eggs must also be shown along with the registered number of the packing station, the name and address of those responsible for packing and the date on which the eggs were packed. In addition there may be a sell-by date, although this is optional – always look out for this and make sure that it has not expired if it is included.

Egg Sizes Class A eggs are graded in sizes from 1-7 and the sizes most commonly available are 2-4.

Size 1 – 70 g and over
Size 2 – 65 g and under 70 g
Size 3 – 60 g and under 65 g
Size 4 – 55 g and under 60 g
Size 5 – 50 g and under 55 g
Size 6 – 45 g and under 50 g
Size 7 – under 45 g

Size 3 are the most suitable for baking unless otherwise stated; for example if large eggs are called for then size 2 should be used.

Storing Eggs Eggs should be stored in the refrigerator, preferably in their box, and the pointed end of each egg should be kept downwards to help prevent breakage, reduce evaporation and help to prevent any odours being absorbed through the shell.

Using Eggs For many recipes it is best if eggs are used at room temperature so they should be removed from the refrigerator about 30 minutes before they are to be used. However this is not essential. It is very important that eggs are clean and they should be washed under cool water and dried before they are cracked, taking care not to break them, of course. It is best to crack eggs individually into a mug, cup or small basin before adding them to mixtures and any traces of broken shell should be removed.

Eggs are a protein food and they should be treated with the same standards of hygiene that are adopted for all raw meat, fish and poultry. All utensils must be thoroughly clean before use and hands should be washed before and after breaking eggs, particularly if cooked food is handled after raw eggs. Any unused beaten egg should be kept in a tightly covered container and placed in the refrigerator. It should be used within twenty-four hours. Egg whites can be frozen in a clean, airtight, rigid container. Remember to label the container with the number of whites which it contains. Once thawed, egg whites should always be used immediately.

DRIED FRUIT

Dried fruit includes raisins, sultanas, currants, dates, glacé cherries, candied peel and other fruits such as apricots, pears, peaches and apples. The smaller dried fruits, candied peel and cherries are those which are most commonly used when making cakes and biscuits. Most dried fruit is cleaned and seeded before it is packed and sold, but any stalks that may be left should be removed.

Raisins Raisins are dried grapes and the best are those obtained by drying the varieties of muscatel grape. These have to be mechanically seeded during processing. Alternatively, seedless grapes are dried. This avoids the necessity for seeding, but the quality of the raisins is not as good.

Sultanas These are dried, seedless green grapes and they are lighter in colour than raisins. They are slightly softer than raisins, and should be plump and sweet.

Currants These are smaller, darker and more shrivelled than raisins. They are dried, small black grapes which are produced mainly in Greece. Currants are used in large quantities for rich fruit cakes.

Dates Dried stoneless dates are sold ready for cooking, either in the form of a block which should be chopped before use or ready chopped and lightly coated in sugar. Both types are more suitable for cooking than the dessert dates which are boxed whole.

Figs Whole figs are dried. They should be chopped before use, although they are not as widely used as the smaller dried fruits.

Prunes There are two main types of dried prune available, either the whole dried fruit that must be washed and soaked overnight or for several hours before use or the stoned, ready-to-eat variety that is more convenient. Prunes are obtained by drying plums and they should be dark and shiny in appearance.

Cut Mixed Peel This is the mixed peel of citrus fruits, preserved by impregnating it with sugar. Lemon, orange and citron peel is usually included. Alternatively whole pieces of candied citrus peel can be purchased and individually chopped.

Glacé Cherries These are used in a wide variety of mixtures and they may be used as decoration. If they are very sticky, then they should be washed and thoroughly dried before use. The best way to do this is by placing the cherries in a sieve to wash them, then draining them well before drying them on absorbent kitchen paper. Before they are incorporated into many cake mixtures the cherries are dusted with a little of the measured flour.

Storing Dried Fruit Always keep dried fruit in clean, dry, airtight containers. They should be kept in a cool, dark cupboard that is quite dry.

NUTS

Certain nuts are often used to flavour cakes and to give texture to certain mixtures. They are also used for decorating cakes.

Almonds These can be purchased shelled with their skins on, blanched with skins removed, split, flaked or chopped. It is often a good idea to compare supermarket prices with those in wholefood shops.

To blanch almonds, place them in a saucepan with plenty of cold water and bring them just to the boil. Drain the nuts in a sieve and rinse them under a cold running tap, then pinch off their skins. Dry the blanched nuts on absorbent kitchen paper.

To split almonds, use a small, sharp, pointed kitchen knife and slide it into the side of the warm nuts.

To brown or roast almonds place them on a piece of foil on a baking sheet or in the grill pan and cook them under the grill, turning them frequently and taking care to prevent them from burning. Alternatively, they can be roasted by placing them on a baking sheet in a warm oven.

Ground almonds are often used in cake mixtures or to make marzipan and almond paste for covering and decorating cakes.

Walnuts These are not usually blanched before use in cake or pudding mixtures. They are also used for decorating cakes. Walnuts are sold in halves or pieces, with pieces the most economical buy if the nuts are to be chopped.

Hazelnuts These can be bought with their skins on, skinned or chopped, and toasted. They are used to flavour cakes or to coat the sides of gâteaux.

To remove the skins from hazelnuts, place them under the grill or in the oven, and roast them, turning frequently, until the skins can be rubbed off. To rub the skins off, place the nuts in a paper bag or in a cloth to avoid burning your fingers.

Hazelnuts can be ground in a food processor, coffee grinder (for small amounts), blender or in a rotary grater.

Peanuts Readily available shelled, either salted or unsalted, peanuts are most often used to make biscuits.

Pistachios Delicately flavoured nuts, tinged with green. They are often sold in their shells which are split open but not removed. They are expensive, so their use is limited.

Brazils, Pecans and Other Nuts A variety of other nuts are also used in cakes and desserts. These are usually available ready shelled, particularly from wholefood shops.

Chopped Mixed Nuts These are an inexpensive alternative to chopped walnuts or hazelnuts but they can be dominated by the flavour of peanuts.

Desiccated Coconut This is finely shredded, dried coconut which is used in cakes. It is also used to coat the outside of some baked items.

Long-thread Coconut Desiccated coconut which is very coarsely shredded to give long threads. Useful for decorating purposes but not usually incorporated into mixtures.

FLAVOURING INGREDIENTS

As well as the basic ingredients which go to make up the cake and pudding mixtures, a wide variety of flavourings can be added. Here are notes on just a few of the most popular ingredients used for flavouring baked goods.

Vanilla A strong flavouring which comes from the seed pods of an orchid. The flavour develops during a period of maturation after the pods have been picked, by the action of enzymes naturally present. True vanilla essence is extracted from the black pods. Vanilla is expensive and the pods are usually sold individually or in pairs. As an alternative to real vanilla, a synthetically produced essence is readily available.

Vanilla is very strong and should be used sparingly. A vanilla pod can be placed in a jar of caster sugar to make vanilla sugar. The pod and sugar should be left to stand for at least three or four weeks. Shake the jar frequently to impart the flavour to the sugar.

Almond Essence Another strong flavouring which must be used with care. It is added to certain mixtures instead of the nuts. It can have a very synthetic flavour and must be used sparingly.

Ground Mixed Spice This mixture of spices is used to flavour cakes. It usually consists of cinnamon, cloves, ginger and nutmeg.

Ground Ginger Another spice which is often used to flavour cakes. It has a strong flavour and should only be used according to recipe directions.

Ground Cinnamon A sweet spice which is used to flavour sweet mixtures. A little ground cinnamon can be mixed with caster sugar to make cinnamon sugar and this is used to dust doughnuts.

Nutmeg This can be purchased ready ground or the whole nuts can be freshly grated on a small, tough grater as the spice is required. Freshly grated nutmeg has the best flavour.

Grated Fruit Rind The grated rind of oranges and lemons is often used to flavour cakes and puddings. The fruit should be washed and dried before the rind is grated on a fine grater. When grating the rind avoid including any of the bitter pith which lies underneath.

CLASSIC DESSERT INGREDIENTS

In addition to the range of basic ingredients which can be used for cakes and puddings, supermarket shelves and chilled cabinets are packed with an impressive array of products and produce specifically for the dessert course, from exotic fruits and many types of dried ingredients to dairy foods galore. This section offers an outline of the specialist ingredients that are available, with a brief guide to their use.

AGAR AGAR

Sold as powder, flakes and sticks, this is a setting agent, similar to gelatine but derived from a seaweed rather than from animal sources. It is ideal for vegetarian desserts.

Agar agar should be dissolved in boiling water. When substituting agar agar for gelatine in a recipe, follow the instructions on the tub or packet. You will generally require slightly more agar agar than gelatine to set 600 ml/l pint liquid. Liquids set with agar agar tend to begin to set while luke-warm rather than when they are cold, and do not require refrigeration.

ARROWROOT

A flavourless thickening ingredient which gives a clear result. The fine, white powder should be blended with cold water, stirred into hot liquid and brought to the boil. Arrowroot thickens on boiling but it tends to thin again with further cooking. It is ideal for thickening fruit juices and syrups for glazing flans or the decoration on gâteaux. Clear fruit sauces should also be thickened with arrowroot.

CHOCOLATE

There are many types of chocolate of variable quality and sweetness. True chocolate must be distinguished from chocolate-flavoured cake coverings, sometimes referred to as cooking chocolate. Dark plain bitter chocolate, paler milk chocolate and white chocolate are all useful for making desserts. Price is a good indication of quality, and for best results only good-quality chocolate should be used. Most supermarkets offer a range of chocolates but the best is obtainable from specialist chocolate shops.

Cake decorating suppliers also sell chocolate, although it may need *tempering*. Tempering is the term used for melting the chocolate and working it to distribute the cocoa fat evenly. The melted chocolate is poured on to a marble slab and a large palette knife is used to lift and fold the chocolate. The process is repeated until the chocolate is smooth and shiny when it is ready for use.

As well as using chocolate for mousses, sauces and coating, it can be made into a variety of attractive decorations (page 96).

COCOA

Cocoa powder is unsweetened and should not be confused with drinking chocolate which is a sweetened product. Cocoa is combined with flour to flavour sponge cakes and puddings. It can also be blended with cornflour and milk to make a chocolate blancmange, or it may be lightly sifted over desserts as a decoration.

CREAM

There are nine types of fresh pasteurized cream:

Half Cream	Contains 12 per cent butterfat. Half cream can be used for pouring over desserts or in place of single cream. It cannot be whipped.
Single Cream	Contains 18 per cent butterfat. Single cream is often homogenized to give a thicker consistency. It can be poured over puddings or it can be stirred into mixtures but it is not suitable for whipping.
Soured Cream	Contains 18 per cent butterfat. Soured cream is fresh cream which has had a culture added to give a slightly acidic taste. It is thicker than single cream but it is not suitable for whipping. A little lemon juice may be stirred into single cream for a similar result.
Whipping Cream	Contains 35-38 per cent butterfat. This can be poured or it can be whipped to give soft peaks. When whipped it can be piped but it does not hold its shape as well as double cream or for the same length of time. The whipped cream may be frozen.
Whipped Cream	Contains 35 per cent butterfat. This is a ready whipped dairy product, used for topping desserts. Available frozen as well as fresh.
Crème Fraîche	Contains 30-35 per cent butterfat. Richer than soured cream, this has had a culture added to give the slightly acidic taste. It is not suitable for whipping.
Double Cream	Contains 48 per cent butterfat. Double cream is suitable for pouring and it whips well to give the consistency required when filling and decorating gâteaux or piping on other desserts. Whipped double cream freezes well.
Extra Thick	Contains 35-48 per cent butterfat, this is homogenized to create a thick cream which may be spooned over desserts. It is not suitable for whipping or piping.
Clotted Cream	Contains 55 per cent butterfat. Thick enough to spoon over fruit or to spread on scones. Not suitable for whipping or piping. Clotted cream will freeze successfully.

Other fresh cream products include the following:

Aerosol Cream	Fresh cream which is ready to squirt on to desserts. Suitable only for topping, this does collapse quickly.
Long-life Cream	Half, single, whipping and double creams are available in cartons or packets. These products have been heat treated or sterilized. They have a shelf life of up to three months without refrigeration. Once opened they should be treated as fresh cream.
Frozen Cream	Single, whipping, double, clotted and ready whipped creams are all available

Frozen Cream contd
frozen. Usually frozen in small pieces for thawing in small quantities.

NON-DAIRY CREAMS

Several non-dairy creams and dessert toppings are available. These may be long-life, perishable, in the form of mixes or as aerosols. Although these are not dairy cream, they may contain buttermilk or a certain amount of butterfat. Always read the label if you are unfamiliar with a product – it may not be all it seems.

CANNED CREAM

Sterilized dairy cream is sold in cans. It is not suitable for whipping but it is thick enough to spoon over desserts. It can also be stirred into mixtures. It has a distinctive flavour which distinguishes it from fresh cream or long-life cream.

FRESH FRUIT

Fresh fruit is a prime ingredient for many types of dessert. When in season, soft fruits can be frozen. They are also available ready frozen all year round. A glossary of fruit is featured at the beginning of the chapter which covers fruit puddings (page 189).

FROMAGE FRAIS

A very soft, light cheese which is fermented for a very short time. It is creamy and has a very slight tang which is not as pronounced as that of curd cheese.

The fat content ranges from virtually nil or 1 per cent to 8 per cent. Fromage frais can be used instead of cream in set desserts; it is thick enough to spoon over desserts or to use as a filling but it cannot be piped.

Fromage frais is an excellent substitute for cream for anyone following a low-fat or calorie-reduced diet.

GELATINE

Gelatine is an animal product derived from bones. A powdered form is sold in sachets and it is also available as leaves. Gelatine leaves are long, very fine pieces of crisp, slightly yellowed material.

Gelatine is used as a setting agent. For success it must be thoroughly dissolved in hot water before it is combined with the bulk of the mixture. If the gelatine is not dissolved properly before it is added to the remaining ingredients the finished pudding will have unpleasant strings of gelatine in it.

Sprinkle powdered gelatine over a little cold water in a heatproof basin and leave for 5 minutes. This process is sometimes known as *sponging*. The gelatine absorbs the water and looks spongy. Stand the basin over a pan of hot water, until the gelatine has completely dissolved. Stir occasionally.

Leaves of gelatine should be softened in cold water, drained and placed in a bowl with a little hot water. The bowl should be placed over a saucepan of hot water until the gelatine has dissolved.

Instead of dissolving the sponged gelatine over hot water, the bowl (provided it is of suitable material) may be placed in the microwave and the gelatine heated on High for about 30 seconds, or until it has dissolved.

Do not overheat gelatine: if it is allowed to boil it will not set again properly. Significant quantities of fruit acids tend to inhibit the action of gelatine. For example, desserts that contain a lot of pineapple juice or lemon juice may require extra gelatine for a good set.

Always follow a recipe closely when using gelatine and use the amount recommended. As a guide, 15 g/½ oz gelatine sets 600 ml/1 pint of liquid. One sachet of gelatine usually contains 15 ml/3 tsp or 15 g/½ oz. Approximately 3 leaves of gelatine weigh 15 g/½ oz.

HONEY

Clear or set honey is readily available and many types of flavoured honey may be found in wholefood shops. Honey is useful for sweetening and flavouring desserts; it goes well with tart fresh fruits like raspberries, or it may be trickled over freshly cooked fritters and miniature doughnuts.

SOFT CHEESE

Soft cheeses have a variety of uses in the preparation of puddings and there are a number of different types which may be used.

Cottage cheese has a granular texture and its fat content may be low or very low. It can be used to make cheesecakes or cheese tarts but must first be sieved or blended to give it a smooth texture.

Quark is made by adding an acid-producing culture and rennet to pasteurized milk. It can be made from skimmed milk, or it can have a low or medium fat content. Quark originated in Germany where it is widely used in cooking. It is similar to curd cheese in flavour, having a slight acid tang.

Fromage frais is a soft cheese which is fermented for a very short period, resulting in a mild flavour.

Curd cheese is available with a low or medium fat content. It has a smooth texture and mild, slightly tangy flavour. It can be used in place of cream cheese in cheese cakes or other desserts.

Cream cheese, or full fat cheese, is produced from single or double cream. It is smooth and rich with a slightly buttery flavour.

Italian ricotta cheese is made from whey rather than from curds. Several types of ricotta are available. One variety, which is particularly suitable for use in sweet recipes is a soft, unsalted, light white cheese which is not matured.

SYRUP

Golden syrup is a blend of sugar syrup, caramel and flavourings. It is used in cooking or it can be poured over puddings.

Maple syrup is made from the sap of the maple tree. The thin sap is boiled until most of the liquid has evaporated to produce a sweet syrup. Good-quality maple syrup is expensive; however blended syrup is available. Synthetically flavoured maple syrup does not bear comparison with the real thing.

Maple syrup may be used in cooking or poured over desserts, particularly pancakes and waffles. It is also good trickled over vanilla ice cream.

TREACLE

Black treacle is made from cane molasses and sugar syrup to give it its strong flavour and dark colour. It is used to colour and flavour rich steamed puddings.

YOGURT

Yogurt is a dairy product produced by souring cows', sheep's or goats' milk. It varies greatly from a low-fat product which may be thickened with starch to the naturally thick, creamy variety which comes from Greece or neighbouring countries.

Plain yogurt has many uses in cooking and may be substituted for single cream in many uncooked desserts. Greek-style yogurt is delicious spooned over puddings and desserts instead of cream but it has just as high a fat content.

For a simple dessert, serve plain yogurt with chopped fresh fruit and a little honey. Bananas, oranges, soft fruit, peaches, pears or plums all taste good when served this way. When fresh fruit is not available, serve soaked dried apricots with yogurt.

EQUIPMENT FOR PERFECT PUDDINGS

There is not a great deal of specialist equipment that is essential for preparing puddings and desserts. Any well-equipped kitchen should have a supply of basins, bowls, saucepans, baking tins and sheets and dishes for general use in cooking. Small electrical appliances speed up many cooking processes but they are not essential. The following guide to kitchen equipment begins by discussing the basic utensils and moves on to more specialised items, small electrical appliances and other pieces of cooking equipment. Lastly, cooking and serving dishes and containers are listed.

BASIC UTENSILS

Baking Tins and Baking Sheets Baking tins and sheets are used for certain desserts – particularly pastries, cheesecakes and gâteaux. The choice of baking equipment is broad and price is a good indication of quality. Thin, light-weight, uncoated tins do not wear well and are likely to buckle, becoming mis-shapen with use. Heavier uncoated tins have a better finish and last longer given that they are washed, dried and stored correctly.

The quality of non-stick bakeware varies enormously and the best buys are the heavier tins with tough coatings. Always follow the manufacturer's instructions closely and avoid damaging the non-stick surface by using metal utensils.

Baking tins that are in good condition also serve as useful moulds, for example watertight ring tins and loaf tins may be used to set jelled desserts. Loose-bottomed tins are useful for cheesecakes and other turned-out desserts.

Look out for non-stick ovenproof glassware that may be used in the conventional oven, microwave or freezer: round dishes, loaf dishes and baking sheets are available in this versatile range.

Bowls and Basins Mixing bowls and small basins are used for a wide variety of purposes, from beating eggs to making cakes or pastry. It is a good idea to have at least two basins of about 900 ml/1½ pint capacity, or slightly larger. A medium mixing bowl is the most useful, and two of the same, or similar, size are practical items.

Bowls and basins are made of plastic, glass or glazed earthenware. The plastic used may be heatproof, able to withstand the temperature of boiling liquid or steaming, but always check before using, as some plastic basins and bowls withstand boiling water but may not be used for steaming or for placing over a saucepan of boiling water.

The most common, and practical, glass bowls and basins are the ovenproof type. These may be used in the conventional oven, in the microwave oven, in a steamer or pressure cooker, or over a saucepan of boiling water besides being invaluable for other kitchen purposes. Some glass basins are available which withstand hot liquids but are not specifically manufactured for use in cooking. Again, it is sensible to check the manufacturer's details before purchasing glass basins.

Glazed earthenware basins are usually suitable for steaming and pressure cooking as well as for standing over a saucepan of hot water. Large glazed bowls may not withstand these cooking temperatures. Make sure that the glaze is not damaged before purchasing this type of container. Old basins and bowls that are chipped or cracked should not be used for any food preparation as the flaws tend to trap germs and dirt. Damaged basins must not be used for steaming or for pressure cooking as they may break.

You will also need a selection of bowls for serving desserts. These need not be elaborate, as there are several ways of brightening up even everyday crockery. One or two soufflé dishes will be invaluable, as will a set of ramekins.

Grater A metal grater with different grades of serrations is the best. This may be used for coarse or fine grating – for savoury foods such as cheese or for delicate tasks such as grating citrus rind. A triangular-shaped grater with a sturdy handle across the top is easy to use.

A tiny nutmeg grater is useful for grating whole nutmegs. The freshly grated spice gives the best flavour.

Knives A round-bladed knife is useful for cutting up butter and for mixing liquid into rubbed-in mixtures. A small serrated knife may be used for cutting fruit. A good, sharp, pointed kitchen knife may be put to a multitude of uses, including cutting the cores from quartered apples, peeling fruit, cutting pastry and so on. A thin-bladed paring knife is useful for cutting very fine strips of rind from citrus fruit, but this is not essential.

Measuring Jug This is essential for measuring liquids in cooking. A heatproof glass jug is best. Always stand the jug on a level surface and check the volume of liquid at eye level. Most measuring jugs give both metric and Imperial measures; some of the

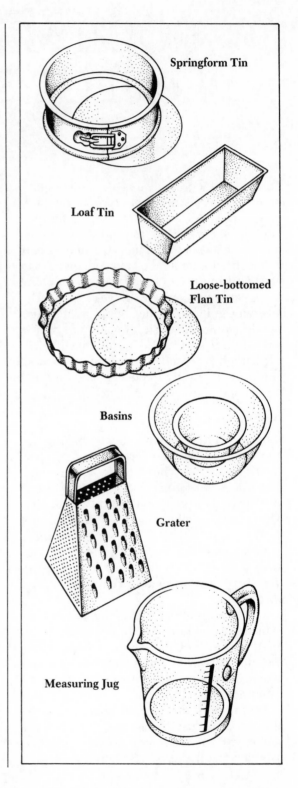

Springform Tin

Loaf Tin

Loose-bottomed Flan Tin

Basins

Grater

Measuring Jug

newer ones, however, are only marked in metric measures.

Moulds Visit a good cook's shop or hardware store for the widest choice of moulds, from expensive tinned copper moulds that give perfect definition to turned-out desserts to cheap plastic moulds. Between these extremes are good-quality glass moulds (some may be ovenproof), metal moulds and many types of plastic mould, including lidded containers or moulds with snap-on bases for easy unmoulding of set desserts.

Specialist moulds include lidded metal bombe moulds for freezing ice creams, straight-sided charlotte moulds, individual ring tins, dariole moulds or castle tins and cannon-ball moulds in various sizes for steaming Christmas puddings.

Heart-shaped china coeur à la crème moulds have perforated bottoms to allow the classic soft cheese dessert to drain and set. These are lined with scalded muslin before use so that the dessert may be unmoulded easily.

If necessary, basins, straight-sided round dishes and rigid plastic food containers may be used instead of decorative moulds. Measure the capacity of a mould by standing it on a level surface and filling it to the brim with water from a measuring jug.

Ovenproof Dishes Sweet pies and other baked puddings that are served hot look

Metal Mould

Glass Mould

Lidded Mould with Snap-on Base

Bombe Mould

Coeur à la Crème Mould

Dariole Mould

best if they are cooked in attractive dishes. Traditional, oval pie dishes finished with decorative patterns are more interesting than plain cream-coloured earthenware. Round ovenproof dishes with rims may also be used for fruit pies.

Tart plates, or pie plates, are deeper than dinner plates (similar to a traditional soup plate) and they have a rim. These are useful for fruit tarts, open tarts (such as Treacle Tart, page 355) or tarts with a lattice topping.

Ovenproof dishes for crumbles, cobblers and other baked desserts do not need a rim and plain gratin dishes may be used. However, if you do want to purchase baking dishes for making desserts, look out for patterned iron-stone ware or more expensive ovenproof china.

Ovenproof remekin dishes are useful for making individual puddings (little crumbles or fruit pies) as well as for setting baked custards or chilled desserts.

Pastry Brush A good pastry brush is a worthwhile buy. It may be used for brushing glazes of all types over cooked or uncooked foods. It is also useful for brushing away small crumbs when adding the finishing touches to gâteaux.

For a pastry brush to be hygienic and efficient it must be kept scrupulously clean and undamaged. It is best to keep a separate brush for greasing baking tins with oil. Wash brushes in very hot soapy water, rinse them in clean hot water and dry them thoroughly before putting them away.

Piping Bag A nylon piping bag is used for piping cream and uncooked mixtures such as choux pastry. This should be kept absolutely clean and it should be boiled with a little detergent, then thoroughly washed, or boiled again in fresh water, to remove all trace of the cleaning agent. Piping bags should be thoroughly dried before being stored in a clean plastic bag, tied with a wire clip.

Piping Nozzles Large nozzles are used for piping whipped cream. These may be star shaped or may have lots of slightly smaller serrations. A large plain nozzle is used for piping uncooked mixtures such as choux pastry or sponge fingers.

Scales A good set of kitchen scales is essential for all cooking. Never guess at weights when following a recipe. Always make sure that the scales register zero before weighing ingredients. Most scales offer both metric and Imperial readings; some new types are graduated only in metric measures. Always follow one set of measures only; do not mix metric and Imperial measures.

Serving Dishes The number and quality of serving dishes that you need is a matter for personal judgement. For example, you may use cereal bowls or small plates to serve the majority of puddings and desserts.

However, for a dessert to make a lasting impression it should be presented in or on an attractive dish. A glass bowl may be used for fruit salads, trifles, fruit fools or for set desserts, instead of turning them out of moulds. A well chosen dish will also double as a savoury salad bowl.

A comport is a dish with a stem. The dish may be low or tall, of fine quality crystal or plain, inexpensive glass. A comport may be used to serve fruit compotes, salads and trifles or it may be filled with an arrangement of fresh fruit as the centrepiece for a dinner party table.

Individual glass dishes are more delicate than cereal bowls for light desserts. Fruit salads, jellies, mousses or other sweets that are usually served from one large dish may be divided between individual dishes instead. Large wine glasses, cocktail glasses or small tumblers are also useful for serving individual portions.

Flat cake stands are perfect for unmoulded desserts – charlottes, custards, ice cream bombes or jellies – as well as gâteaux, cheesecakes or flans.

Remember that flat platters made of china, glass or marble also double up as good cheeseboards. Try serving a homely fruit flan or baked cheesecake on an attractive bread board (do not use a chopping board that is discoloured, marked and possibly tainted with onion or garlic).

Improvise as you wish, exercising imagination and artistic flair, when selecting serving dishes for cool desserts. Search in junk shops and jumble sales for inexpensive glassware, making sure that it is not chipped or cracked. Similarly, look out for pretty tea plates – odd plates make up a pleasing bright display. Jugs, small bowls and basins are useful for cream, yogurt or other accompaniments; they do not have to match up with other china dishes but always check that they are undamaged as cracks and breaks will harbour germs. Look out for small ladles (ideal for sweet sauces), cake forks and oddments of silver cutlery to grace the dessert trolley.

Sieve A fine metal or nylon sieve is used to sift dry ingredients, to strain liquids and to purée moist foods that are pressed through the mesh. A large sieve is the most practical and it is a good idea to keep a small sieve or tea strainer for sifting icing sugar.

Spatula A flexible plastic spatula is the best implement for scraping mixtures out of bowls or basins.

Spoons A strong white plastic spoon is more hygienic than a wooden spoon. Metal spoons are used for folding mixtures together and small metal teaspoons are useful for spooning small amounts of mixture into precise positions.

Measuring spoons are essential. A teaspoon and tablespoon measure should always be used when following a recipe. Make sure that the spoon measures include metric equivalents if you follow metric measures. Never use serving spoons or other cutlery in place of measuring spoons as they usually hold quite different quantities.

Whisks For whisking cream, egg whites and so on. A hand-held balloon whisk or coiled wire whisk is cheap and good for small amounts of light mixture. A rotary whisk makes lighter work of slightly heavier mixtures. See also *Electric Whisk* (page 30).

SPECIALIST UTENSILS

Canelle Knife A small utensil for cutting fine strips off a lemon or orange. The fine strips may be used for decoration or the aim may be to make a pattern on the outside of the fruit. The knife is pulled firmly down the length of the fruit over a plate to catch the strips of rind.

Cherry Stoner A hand-held stoner is sometimes incorporated into the handle of another implement, such as a garlic crusher. The cherry is placed in a small cup which has a hole in the middle. A spike on the opposite handle is pressed through the cherry to push the stone out through the hole in the base of the cup.

Corer A small implement with a metal ring on the end to cut the core out of apples or other fruit.

Grapefruit knife A curved knife which is serrated on both sides of the blade. It is designed to cut between the segments of halved grapefruit and to cut all the way around between the fruit's flesh and pith.

Ice Cream Scoop Available in two sizes, this usually consists of a semi-circular scoop with a metal band which flicks around the inside to release the ball of ice cream. The scoop may be made of strong metal with shallow sides but no metal band. This type gives a soft scoop of ice cream rather than a fim 'ball'.

Melon Scoop Usually a double ended implement with two semi-circular cups, one smaller than the other. Used for scooping out balls of melon flesh. Also useful for making balls of butter or for scooping vegetables into balls.

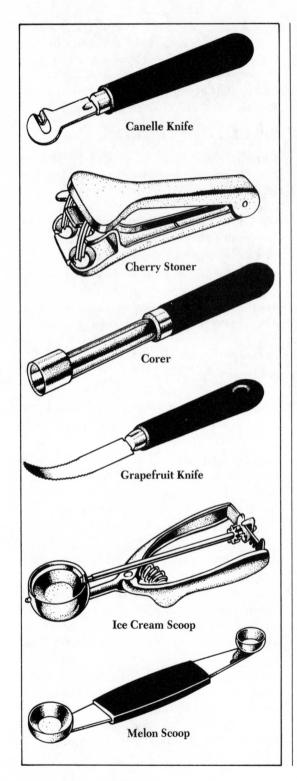

Canelle Knife

Cherry Stoner

Corer

Grapefruit Knife

Ice Cream Scoop

Melon Scoop

SMALL ELECTRIC APPLIANCES

It is essential that you read the manufacturer's instructions for any electric appliance before using it. Follow all directions, including those for cleaning.

Beater/Mixer/Electric Whisk These vary in size from small hand-held electric whisks to large appliances with a selection of complicated attachments. Useful for whisking egg whites, beating mixtures and creaming ingredients.

Blender Also known as a liquidizer, this may be a single appliance or an attachment for a large food mixer. Useful for making crumbs, for chopping nuts and for puréeing foods.

Deep Fat Fryer This has a heating element beneath a cooking container. An integral frying basket, sealed lid and filter make up the appliance. These are cleaner than using a deep frying pan. Always change the filter regularly; your instruction booklet will advise when to do this. These appliances are useful for cooking fruit fritters and other foods that require deep frying.

Food Processor A machine which can carry out a wide variety of culinary tasks, from chopping an onion to mixing a cake. It usually consists of a bowl with a lid through which ingredients may be added as the machine works, and a double-bladed knife. The knife rotates to process the food. Mixing attachments are available along with other extras, such as juice extractors.

A food processor may be used to purée foods, to mix cakes and to make pastry. Care must be taken not to overprocess foods, particularly cakes and pastry. Always observe the safety precautions when using this appliance.

Slow Cooker A cooking pot with its own heat source which operates at very low power. The food is cooked for long periods. Although slow cookers are used mainly for savoury foods, dried fruits and rice pudding cook very well by this method.

A slow cooker may also be used for cooking fruit, such as apples, until they are pulpy or for poaching them slowly so that they retain their shape and texture as they are tenderized. Christmas pudding also cooks well by this method. Always follow the manufacturer's instructions.

Waffle Iron If your family enjoys waffles, one of these appliances will be invaluable. For more information see page 309.

PRESSURE COOKER

The higher the atmospheric pressure, the longer it takes for water to boil. The water reaches a higher temperature before it boils and begins to evaporate. Because the temperature reached is higher before water boils and evaporates, the cooking process is quicker. A pressure cooker is a steam-proof vessel. The food and its cooking liquid are enclosed in the pressure cooker and the escape of steam is controlled by weight which is exerted from the outside. Therefore the temperature reached inside the pressure cooker is greater than that of normal boiling liquids. In scientific terms, the atmospheric pressure is controlled by using a weight in a pressure cooker to give higher cooking temperatures.

The traditional pressure cooker has a sealed lid and a weight which is fitted once the contents of the pan have been heated to the point where steam escapes. A choice of three weight levels are used with this type of cooker: High (15 lb), Medium (10 lb) and Low (5 lb).

Although the above type of pressure cooker is still available – and is still popular with many of those who favour this type of cooking – the design of pressure cookers has advanced significantly. Many of today's pressure cookers have a single weight of 15 lb, referred to as the cook control. Automatic controls may be set to time the cooking process and release the pressure automatically and quickly when necessary. On this type of cooker, the cook control, or weight, is fixed before cooking begins and the cooker is heated over high heat (except for milk and other foods that froth up, in which case a medium heat is used). The cooking time is taken from when the pressure cooker emits a flow of steam.

When cooking some dishes, it is important that the steam is released slowly at the end of cooking. Automatic pressure cookers have a manual setting for this purpose. At the end of the cooking time the heat is turned off (or the cooker lifted off an electric heat source) and the cooker is allowed to cool until the pressure is released. This takes some time but the food continues to cook inside the cooker and it will still be very hot when the lid is removed.

It is vital to follow the manufacturer's instructions closely, making sure that the pressure cooker contains enough liquid. Never operate a pressure cooker with less than 300 ml/½ pint water or similar liquid. Always make sure that the pressure cooker is assembled correctly and closed properly. It is important to time the cooking accurately and follow instructions for releasing the pressure exactly.

Never overfill the cooker, particularly with foods that are likely to froth up during cooking. Again, this is something that the manufacturer will include in the instruction booklet.

Keep all air vents and safety outlets clear during cooking and make sure that all parts are properly cleaned according to the manufacturer's directions.

Pressure cooking is quick, safe and fuel-saving. It is important to follow the rules set down by the manufacturer. If you have lost your instruction book, contact the manufacturer for another. Most manufacturers also provide a useful recipe book along with practical information on adapting ordinary recipes to pressure cooking.

EQUIPMENT FOR PERFECT CAKES

This section provides a brief guide to the essential and useful utensils for cake making. Specialist equipment for cake decorating is not included here but it is discussed in the relevant chapters. For preparing a simple cake, or a batch of small cakes, very little is needed in the way of equipment but if you bake regularly, or enjoy experimenting with more complicated recipes, then it is worth discovering the wide variety of utensils and baking tins which are available. One of the most important pieces of equipment for cooking perfect cakes is the oven. For good results you should have an oven which has a reliable thermostat, keeping the temperature constant and accurate, and which cooks evenly throughout the cavity. It is a good idea to have the oven professionally checked if you have doubts about its technical performance.

SMALL UTENSILS FOR PREPARING MIXTURES

Bowls and Basins One of the first items of equipment to consider has to be a container in which to mix all the ingredients. There are all sorts of mixing bowls and basins available, from glazed earthenware through to flimsy plastic. The size of bowl will depend on the amount of mixture which you are preparing and the method used to mix the ingredients; for example, if fat has to be rubbed into flour, then the bowl should be big enough to allow you to do this even if the quantities used are small. As well as the main mixing bowl you may have to use another container for beating eggs or for combining other ingredients.

Fairly heavy bowls are best for creaming ingredients together since they tend to be more stable. As well as glass and earthenware, the choice includes heavy plastic bowls which have a rubber strip on the base to prevent them from slipping on the surface. Some bowls have rims or handles to make them easy to hold with one hand while you are working.

If you bake frequently, then it is a good idea to invest in a set of basins and bowls of different sizes. Remember that those which are made of ovenproof glass can also be very useful for many other kitchen tasks, and make sure that you have some basins that will withstand the heat when placed over a saucepan of hot water.

After use wash bowls and basins in hot soapy water and rinse them under clean hot water. Drain and dry them thoroughly before storing, preferably in a closed cupboard, away from dust. Take care when stacking basins to avoid jamming them together.

Kitchen Scales More so than in any other area of cooking, when baking it is vital to weigh ingredients accurately and for this you will need a reliable set of kitchen scales. There are many types and a wide range of prices from which to select. Scales graduated in either metric or Imperial are available and many types provide the facility for measuring both.

Good quality balance scales are usually very accurate and they can be used with either metric or Imperial weights. They should always be used on a level work surface, with the correct scoop as supplied by the manufacturer.

A good beam scale also provides an accurate means of weighing ingredients. A sliding device is used to select the required weight before the ingredients are added to the scoop which should balance perfectly when the amount is correct. These tend to be more fiddly to use and they are not the most popular type of scales.

Digital scales vary in accuracy according to their type, and often according to cost. They are neat and clean, and they can be free standing or wall mounted. Always follow the manufacturer's instructions closely when using them and do make sure that batteries are replaced when necessary to ensure continued accuracy.

Spring scales indicate the weight on a dial. This is probably the least accurate type of scale but this is usually only a problem when weighing small quantities, or preparing very precise mixtures. Before buying this type of scale make sure that the dial registers small quantities as well as large ones. Instead of the traditional scoop, some scales of this type have mixing bowls, measuring jugs or neat streamlined containers to hold the ingredients. They can be free standing or wall mounted.

Whichever type you choose, always follow the manufacturer's instructions. If necessary check that the dial or digital indicator registers zero before adding ingredients. Keep the container for food scrupulously clean, washing and drying it after each use. All scales should be kept in a dry place and for convenience they are often positioned on the work surface, with the scoop (or its equivalent) inverted for cleanliness when not in use.

Measuring Spoons and Jugs It is vital to have a set of measuring spoons which comply with British Standard measures. All spoon measures given throughout the book refer to these, and serving spoons must not be used instead. Most kitchen shops, hardware stores and department stores stock spoon measures, often with metric equivalents, and these are usually quite inexpensive.

Measuring jugs are available in many shapes and sizes, and they should always be used for accuracy when using liquids.

Spoons and Spatulas A wooden spoon is used for beating fat with sugar (known as creaming) or for similar tasks. The spoon should have a handle which is long enough for the mixture to be beaten efficiently but it should not be too long for comfort. Firm, rigid plastic spoons which are as strong as wooden spoons are an alternative and these are preferable in terms of hygiene.

A large metal spoon is necessary for folding in dry ingredients, for example when making a sponge cake. Any suitable serving spoon can be used for this purpose.

A plastic spatula is useful for scraping all the mixture from the inside of a bowl; select one with a large, flexible end.

Knives A kitchen knife is used for cutting up and chopping ingredients. A round-bladed knife or small palette knife is used for smoothing mixture and easing cakes away from the edge of a tin. A large palette knife or metal spatula is used for lifting baked items off hot baking sheets.

Sieve and Sifter A fine metal or plastic sieve is used for sifting flour or a similar dry ingredient before adding it to a mixture.

A sifter is useful for sprinkling caster or icing sugar over finished cakes but it is not an essential piece of equipment.

Fine Grater A fine grater is usually used for grating lemon or orange rind which is added to mixtures. Most large graters have the facility for grating coarsely and finely. A very fine, small nutmeg grater is useful for grating whole nutmegs but the ground spice can be used for baking.

Citrus Squeezer Lemon or orange juice is sometimes added to cake mixtures and a citrus squeezer is used to extract the juice from the fruit. A wide variety of types are available, some quite inexpensive, and it is a good idea to look for one which includes a strainer to prevent the pips from dropping in when the juice is measured.

Whisk A whisk is used for whisking egg whites or similar tasks. Either a balloon or coiled whisk is ideal for light tasks; a rotary whisk can be useful for heavier work.

Cutters Pastry cutters are available in metal or plastic, in fluted or plain rounds, squares or a variety of other shapes.

Pastry Brush Useful for greasing tins with a little oil. After use the brush should be washed in very hot soapy water, rinsed and thoroughly dried.

Oil Well A handy gadget for those who often need to grease tins: a small plastic container complete with brush and cover to hold oil ready for greasing tins.

Wire Racks Most cakes are turned out of the tin and placed on a wire rack to cool. For making sandwich cakes it is wise to have two cooling racks.

ELECTRICAL APPLIANCES

Food Mixers These take the hard work out of beating and creaming cake mixtures. The smaller, hand-held mixers or beaters or those with an optional stand are ideal for making light cakes, for whisking eggs for a Swiss roll or sponge, or for whisking egg whites. The large, free-standing mixers are useful for preparing large quantities of heavy mixtures, for example fruit cakes. Although these appliances are used for creaming and beating they cannot be used for folding in.

Food Processors Most food processors have an optional attachment for mixing or beating, usually a plastic blade. They are ideal for preparing one-stage cake mixtures but it is important to avoid processing the ingredients for too long. Some food processors have the facility for whisking egg whites.

BAKING TINS

Baking Sheets These come in a variety of sizes, some with edges, others without. They can also have a non-stick coating. Many new ovens come complete with a baking sheet provided by the manufacturer. The sheets should always be cooled after cooking, then washed in hot, soapy water and dried thoroughly before storing in a dry cupboard. Do check that a large sheet will fit inside your oven before you buy one.

Plain Deep Cake Tins For baking large cakes, these can be square or round, in one piece or with a loose bottom. They are available with a variety of non-stick coatings. The loose-bottomed tins are useful for making semi-rich cakes or deep sponges which can be difficult to remove from one-piece tins. Very rich, heavy cakes are easy to remove from tins, and are often allowed to cool completely or partly cool in the tin before being transferred to a wire rack. All tins should be thoroughly washed and dried after use and before being stored in a dry cupboard. Follow the manufacturers' instructions for the treatment of specific non-stick coatings.

Springform Tins These are deep, round tins which have a spring clip to hold the side together and a loose base which is removed when the clip is loosened. They are ideal for light cakes which can be difficult to remove from tins. These tins usually have a choice of bases, including a ring-tin base.

Cake Forms Cake forms are useful for baking large, rich fruit cakes. The form consists of the sides for the tin and this is placed on a baking sheet. The 'tin' is then lined with greaseproof paper and greased before the mixture is added.

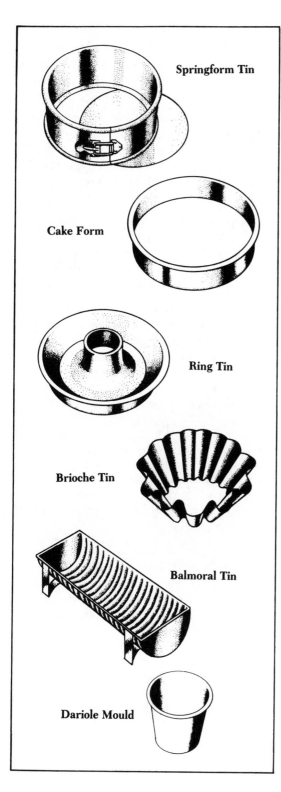

Springform Tin

Cake Form

Ring Tin

Brioche Tin

Balmoral Tin

Dariole Mould

Sandwich Tins Shallow, straight-sided tins, usually round, often with a non-stick coating, which are used to make cakes in pairs; for example Victoria sandwich. The tins can be base lined before use if the mixture is likely to stick during cooking.

Shallow Tins Available in various shapes, round, oblong or square with straight or slightly sloping sides. They can be plain or fluted, with or without a non-stick coating.

Swiss Roll Tins Large, very shallow tins, oblong in shape and usually in two sizes. They may have a non-stick coating but these tins are usually lined with greaseproof paper before use.

Loaf Tins Narrow, deep and long, these are used for making loaf cakes and semi-rich fruit cakes. They are available with non-stick coatings but are often lined before use. Tins which can have adjustable sides to make them larger or smaller are also available.

Ring Tins With rounded or square bottoms, good for making light cakes. Kugelhopf moulds are deep and highly decorated.

Brioche Tin A large, round fluted tin with sloping sides. Useful for baking light cakes as well as for the traditional rich bread.

Balmoral Tin A long, narrow tin, with a base which is semi-circular in shape and sometimes supported by metal stands at both ends. This type of tin has decorative ridges from side to side all along its length and is not as deep as a loaf tin.

Patty Tins Usually in the form of a tray of six or twelve individual hollows, these are used for baking individual cakes and tartlets. They can be deep or shallow, patterned or plain, with or without a non-stick coating.

Dariole Moulds Also known as castle tins, these are small, deep tins which are usually about 150 ml/5 fl oz in capacity or slightly less. Used to make English-style Madeleines, plain cakes coated in jam and coconut.

Shaped Tins Cake tins are available in a wide variety of different shapes, from large and small heart-shaped tins to numeral shapes, hexagonal tins, oval shapes and so on. Many of these can be hired from cook shops and hardware stores to make special, one-off cakes.

OVENPROOF CAKE DISHES

With the development of microwave cooking, and particularly combination microwave cooking, more glassware cooking dishes are available in shapes suitable for baking cakes which can withstand the temperatures in the conventional oven. As well as ordinary ovenproof glassware, some dishes are available with a non-stick coating. They are available as deep round dishes, shallow round dishes, loaf dishes and fluted dishes similar to brioche tins. If you do want certain dishes for dual purpose use then these are suitable.

DISPOSABLE ITEMS

Greaseproof Paper This is widely used in baking. It is used for lining cake tins, for rolling up in cakes which are to be cooled before filling and for making icing bags to be used for intricate icing.

Non-stick Baking Parchment This is a non-stick paper which does not need greasing and which is particularly useful for items which tend to stick during cooking, for example very delicate cakes or meringues. It can be used in place of greaseproof paper for base lining sandwich tins.

Paper Cake Cases These may be plain or patterned, and are used instead of patty tins for baking small cakes. The paper cases are stood on baking sheets or they can be placed in the patty tins for support. Large cake cases are available for putting inside tins when making semi-rich cakes or deep sponges. Small paper cake cases, of the type generally used for confectionery, may be used to make tiny cakes for small children, or petits fours.

Wax Paper This is not as widely used as greaseproof paper but it can be used for lining tins when making certain delicate cakes. It is similar to greaseproof paper but has a wax coating on one side.

Rice Paper A fine, opaque paper which is edible. It is used as a base for macaroons and similar mixtures which tend to stick during cooking. The edges are trimmed but the rice paper base bakes into the mixture and is eaten with it.

Cooking Foil Not widely used in baking but it is useful for loosely covering the top of cakes which are cooked for a long period of time, and which may begin to darken too much on top before the middle is cooked.

Brown Paper Although this is not used in direct contact with the food, it is wrapped neatly around the outside of tins when baking heavy, rich mixtures in a cool oven for long periods of time. By wrapping several thicknesses of paper around the outside of the tin the cake is prevented from forming a dry crust during cooking.

DECORATING EQUIPMENT

Specialist equipment for decorating cakes is listed in the chapter on cake decorating. A few items are useful for the preparation of certain mixtures.

Piping or Icing Bags Large piping bags are usually made of nylon or heavy cotton which is treated with a moisture-proof coating. They can be lightweight or firmer. They are useful for piping sponge fingers. Bags should always be thoroughly washed, rinsed and dried after use and they should be boiled occasionally.

Large Piping Nozzles Large plain and fluted nozzles are used for piping uncooked, soft cake mixtures; also meringue-type mixtures as well as for piping cream and other fillings for cakes.

BASIC TECHNIQUES AND METHODS OF MAKING CAKES

PREPARING TINS FOR BAKING

There is nothing quite as distressing as battling unsuccessfully to release a beautifully cooked cake in one piece from an ill-prepared tin. Difficulties with turning cakes out of tins can often be avoided if the tin is properly prepared in the first instance. Each recipe offers guidance on the size and shape of tin required and the method by which it should be prepared before the mixture is turned into it. Good cake tins are those to which the cooked mixture is not supposed to stick but this is little consolation when there is a fair chance that the tin you intend to use is quite likely to end up with the cake firmly stuck to it. So, if you have doubts about whether a particular tin is going to release the cake easily, do plan ahead and at least line the bottom of the tin. There are four main ways to prepare tins:

1 Bun tins, patty tins and baking sheets should be greased. In some instances the sheets should be dusted with flour after greasing.

2 For rubbed-in cakes each tin should be greased and the base should be lined. The lining paper should be greased before the mixture is placed in the tin.

3 For creamed mixtures it is best to line the base of each tin and in some cases, where the cake requires lengthy cooking, the sides of the tin should also be lined. The lining paper should be greased. The same preparation applies to cakes made by the melted method, for example gingerbread.

4 For whisked sponge cakes each tin should be greased and dusted with a little flour. If the tin is one to which the cake may stick on the base, then a circle of paper should be used to line the base of the tin. The floured sides of the tin provide a surface to which very light sponge mixtures may adhere as they rise during cooking.

Non-stick Tins Many non-stick tins do not have to be lined before they are used. The manufacturer's instructions should be followed carefully when preparing this type of tin.

FAT FOR GREASING

The most convenient fat for greasing is oil. A special 'oil well' gadget is designed to hold a small amount of oil with a suitable brush ready for greasing tins. Alternatively a few drops of oil can be tipped into the tin and brushed evenly over its surface. Lard or other white cooking fat is suitable for greasing tins but butter and margarine are not recommended. If butter or margarine is used it should be clarified first to remove all excess moisture and salt which it contains.

The purpose of greasing is obvious – to prevent the cake from sticking to the tin or to the lining paper. The process of lining tins is made easy if the tin itself is lightly greased first. The lining paper clings to the greased surface, allowing it to be pushed neatly up against the sides. Where the lining paper overlaps slightly, the under-piece should be lightly greased so that the top piece clings to it and stays in place.

CHOICE OF LINING PAPER

Greaseproof paper is the most common form of lining which is used when preparing tins. However non-stick baking parchment is available and this can be used instead. Follow the manufacturer's instructions when using this product as, in many cases, it does not require greasing before the cake mixture is placed on it. Heavy, re-usable non-stick baking paper is also available and this is particularly useful if you want to make a semi-permanent lining for a frequently used tin. The tin should of course be washed and the paper wiped clean between uses. Again the manufacturer's instructions should be followed for using this type of paper.

For making small cakes, paper cake cases can be used, either by standing them on a baking sheet or placing them in patty tins. If the cases are fairly flimsy, it is best to place them in tins for support. It is also possible to purchase large fluted paper cases that can be used to line full-sized cake tins. This is particularly useful if the cake is to be frozen once it is cooked.

For making rich fruit cakes, the tins are best lined with a double thickness of grease-proof paper. To protect the outside of the cake, near the sides and base of the tin, a thick piece of brown paper or newspaper can be tied securely around the outside of the tin, or a piece can be placed on a baking sheet underneath the tin. This is really only necessary when large cakes are baked for several hours and there may be a danger of the outside crust becoming dry.

LINING A SQUARE TIN

1   Place the tin flat on a single or double thickness of lining paper and draw all around the outside of the bottom. Cut out the shape as above, cutting slightly inside the pencil mark to allow for the thickness of the tin.

2   Measure a strip of paper for the sides of the tin as for lining a round tin. Make sure that there is enough to go all the way around the inside of the tin and that the strip is wide enough for a 2.5 cm/1 inch fold all around the bottom as well as to stand at least 2.5 cm/1 inch above the rim of the tin.

3   Lightly grease the tin and place one square of paper in the base if a double thickness is used; grease this lightly. Make a 2.5 cm/1 inch fold all along one side of the strip of paper.

4   Carefully lift the strip of paper into the sides of the tin. Have a pair of scissors ready to snip and fit the corners of the

paper into the tin. The overlap in the strip of paper should be positioned on one side of the tin, not at a corner.

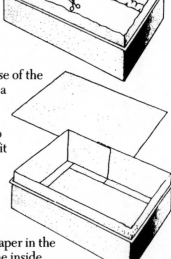

5   Press the paper against the sides of the tin and into the first corner. Snip into the corner of the strip of paper sitting in the base of the tin.

6   Overlap the paper in the base of the tin in the first corner, to make a neat squared lining. Continue to press the paper smoothly against the side of the tin up to the next corner, then cut and fit the paper as before. Fit the paper into all four corners in this way.

7   Place the square of lining paper in the base of the tin and brush all the inside evenly with a little oil.

LINING A ROUND TIN

1   Place the tin on a single or double piece of lining paper and draw around the outside edge of the bottom in pencil. Remove the tin and cut out the circle of paper, cutting slightly inside the drawn circle to allow for the thickness of the tin and to ensure that the paper will fit neatly inside the base of the tin.

2   Cut out a strip of paper which is long enough to go around the outside of the tin and overlap by 5 cm/2 inches. The paper should be at least 5 cm/2 inches wider than the depth of the tin, to allow for 2.5 cm/1 inch to sit neatly in the bottom of the tin and at least 2.5 cm/1 inch standing above the rim of the tin.

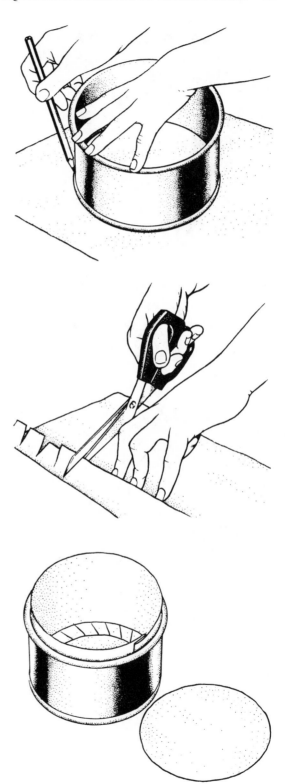

3   Make a 2.5 cm/1 inch fold all along one side of the strip of paper. Open out the fold and snip diagonally from the edge in as far as the foldline at 1-2.5 cm/½-1 inch intervals all along the length of the paper.

4   Very lightly grease the inside of the tin. If you are using a double thickness of paper, then place one circle in the base of the tin and grease it very lightly. If you are using a single thickness, then put the lining paper around the sides first. Carefully lower the strip of paper into the tin, placing the snipped folded edge downwards. The fold in the base of the strip should tuck neatly all around the inside of the bottom of the tin and the pieces of snipped paper should be overlapped. Place the circle of lining paper in the base of the tin.

5   Lightly grease the lining paper all over, making sure that it is pressed well into the shape of the tin.

LINING A SWISS ROLL TIN

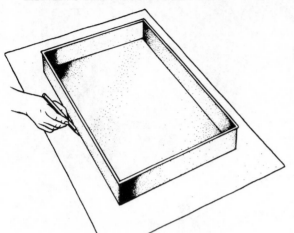

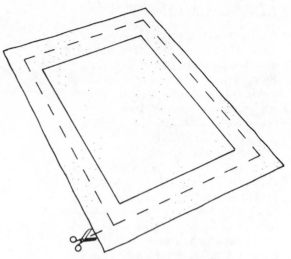

1   Stand the tin on a sheet of greaseproof paper and draw all around the outside of the bottom. Remove the tin.

2 Cut out the shape, about 5 cm/2 inches outside of the drawn shape. This is to allow enough paper to line the sides of the tin and to stand about 2.5 cm/1 inch above the rim of the tin. The paper should not stand more than 2.5 cm/1 inch above the rim as this may impair the process of browning.

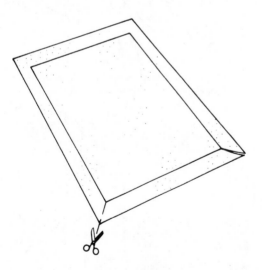

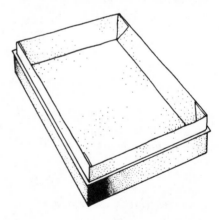

3 Cut from each outer corner of the paper into the corner of the drawn shape of the tin.

4 Lightly grease the inside of the tin. Turn the paper over so that the pencil mark is facing downwards, into the tin. Press the paper into the tin, overlapping it at the corners to make a neatly squared lining.

5 The paper will stay in place at the corners if it is greased between the overlap. Grease the lining paper evenly.

LINING A LOAF TIN

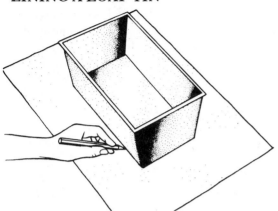

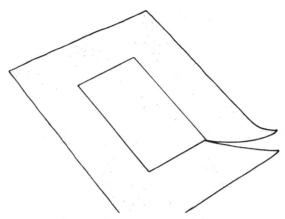

1 Cut a piece of paper large enough to cover the bottom of the tin, to come up both sides and the ends and to stand at least 2.5 cm/1 inch above the tin.

2 Stand the tin in the middle of the paper and draw all around the outside of the bottom.

3 Cut in from each outer corner of the piece of paper to the corner of the drawn shape.

4 Lightly grease the tin, then turn the paper over so that the pencil marks are downwards and lift the paper into the tin.

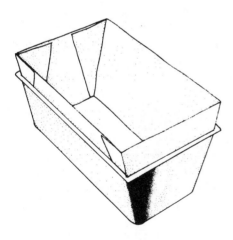

5 Press the paper neatly into the tin, overlapping the cut corners to make neat squares. Grease lightly between the overlap so that the paper clings together.

6 Grease the lining paper well.

BASE LINING TINS

If the recipe suggests that the base of the tin should be lined, then simply place the tin on a piece of paper, draw around the outside edge and cut out the shape. Lightly grease the base of the tin so that the paper will stay firmly in place. Place the piece of paper in the base of the tin, then grease the paper and the sides of the tin.

GREASING AND FLOURING TINS

Lightly grease the inside of the tin. Place a spoonful of flour in the tin. Hold the tin at an angle and turn it around and around, tapping the sides as you turn the tin, so that the flour evenly coats the inside. Tip out any excess flour.

BASIC METHODS OF MIXING CAKES

CREAMED METHOD

For this method, the fat and sugar are creamed together until they are very soft, pale in colour and light. If a brown sugar is used the mixture will not become very pale in colour but it should turn paler than it was when you started.

The fat should be warmed to room temperature if necessary so that it creams easily. Butter or margarine are the most common fats to use. Soft margarine can be creamed straight from the refrigerator.

When the creaming stage is complete the eggs are added. They should be beaten first so that they can be added gradually. The eggs should be lightly beaten in and a little of the measured flour sprinkled in if the mixture looks as though it may curdle.

When the eggs are incorporated the flour is folded in. It is important that this process is carried out correctly. A large metal spoon should be used and the mixture must not be beaten. The flour is folded in – it is sprinkled over the mixture and the spoon is used to lift the mixture and to cut the flour through it. Rather than stirring, a figure of eight motion is used. The aim is to incorporate the flour with the creamed ingredients without knocking out all the air that was beaten in during the first stage.

Dried fruit or other flavouring ingredients are folded in with the flour or immediately afterwards. Sometimes a little extra liquid is added to soften the mixture.

RUBBED-IN METHOD

The flour is sifted into a bowl and the fat is rubbed into it in the same way as for making shortcrust pastry.

For this method the fat should be chilled and all the other ingredients should be kept cool. When rubbing fat into flour it is important to use just the tips of the fingers.

Lift the mixture up and lightly rub it together, letting it fall back into the bowl. By lifting the mixture and rubbing it lightly you are incorporating air. This keeps it light.

Once the fat is incorporated the sugar and other dry ingredients are added and stirred in. The liquid is added last to bind the ingredients together.

WHISKED METHOD

The whisked method is used for making very light sponges. The eggs should be allowed to warm to room temperature. They are combined with the sugar in a bowl which is placed over a saucepan of barely simmering water. The water must not be boiling. An electric beater is best for this task but a rotary whisk can be used. It is hard work if an ordinary hand whisk of the balloon or spiral type is used and it can take a very long time with these simple utensils.

The eggs and sugar are whisked together until they are very thick, very pale and quite creamy. A common mistake with this method is to consider that the mixture is whisked sufficiently as soon as it is slightly thickened. The mixture should be thick enough to hold the trail of the whisk for at least 30 seconds. Once it is whisked sufficiently, remove the bowl from the pan of water and continue whisking for a further 5 minutes, until the mixture has cooled.

At this stage the other ingredients are folded in. Flour and a small amount of fat can be added. The fat is usually butter which is melted before it is dribbled slowly over the whisked mixture and folded in. The folding in process is vital to the success of whisked mixtures – a figure of eight motion should be used as for creamed mixtures and the whisked mixture should be gently lifted over the flour. On no account should the mixture be stirred or whisked as the air will be knocked out by the rapid movement. This type of cake relies on the air content to rise; if the air is knocked out the cake will not rise.

MELTED METHOD

For this type of mixture the fat and sugar are melted together, usually with some form of flavouring. Treacle or syrup is often used, either in place of the sugar or with it.

Once all the fat is melted the mixture should be allowed to cool very slightly before the beaten eggs are added. Do not overheat the melted ingredients; use low heat and stir the mixture frequently. Any crystals of sugar on the sides of the saucepan may be brushed down into the mixture with a pastry brush.

Lastly, the dry ingredients are beaten in. The majority of melted mixtures should be quite soft when all the ingredients are mixed and some may have the consistency of a thick batter.

ONE-STAGE METHOD

This is a modern method of cake mixing, popularised by margarine manufacturers to promote soft margarine in the early days of its availability. As well as the development of soft margarine which requires less creaming than hard fats, the growth in the ownership of electric food mixers has also helped to make this method an easy alternative to the creaming method.

All the ingredients are placed in a bowl and they are beaten together until thoroughly combined, pale and creamy. A little extra raising agent is usually added to ensure a good rise and all the ingredients should be at room temperature, the best fat to use being soft margarine.

BAKING AND TURNING OUT CAKES

For good results it is important that the oven has an even heat distribution, that it heats correctly to the temperature selected and holds that temperature steadily. The oven should stand evenly; most cookers, whether built in or free standing, have adjustable feet to compensate for any uneven floors. If the oven or shelf is not level, the cake mixture will not rise evenly.

One of the most difficult areas of cake making is deciding exactly when the cake is cooked. Firstly, follow the timing given in the recipe as a guide, checking at the first suggested time.

Open the oven door carefully – if you can see that the cake still looks raw, then shut the door quickly. Do not bang doors and cause the oven to jerk as the cake is cooking.

The appearance of the cooked cake will vary slightly according to its type. Most cakes will be well risen, the exception being very rich fruit cakes which are not intended to rise during cooking. Sponge cakes should have risen to the top of the tin; about doubled in volume. The cake should be evenly browned, not too light and not too dark. The cake should have shrunk away from the sides of the tin very slightly and when pressed lightly it should feel springy on top and the cake should bounce back. If the surface feels at all wet and if the impression of a finger-print remains on top, then the sponge cake is not cooked.

Fruit cakes should not feel spongy, they should be firm and quite well browned. For deep cakes and fruit cakes the skewer test is a good way of determining whether the cake is cooked through.

The Skewer Test Take a clean metal skewer and insert it into the middle of the cake. Leave it for a few seconds, then take it out. If the cake is cooked the skewer should not have any mixture adhering to it. The skewer will be slightly greasy and there may be sticky marks on it, particularly if the cake contains a lot of fruit. However, there should not be crumbs or any wet mixture sticking to it. Instead of a skewer, the blade of a knife can be inserted into the middle of the cake.

Protecting the Top of a Cake Some cakes that require fairly long cooking may begin to look slightly too dark on top before the middle is cooked. This may be due to the type of mixture, in which case the recipe should warn you to check the cake during cooking, or it may be due to the oven. To prevent the surface of the cake from burning while the middle of the cake cooks through, a piece of foil should be placed loosely over the top of the cake, shiny side up. This will prevent the upper crust from burning.

RELEASING CAKES FROM TINS AND COOLING

It is important that the tin is well prepared because this stage can be disastrous if the cake is stuck to the base of the tin.

Some fruit cakes should be allowed to cool in the tin for a while before being turned out and the recipe will suggest this if necessary. If this is the case, then drape a clean tea-towel over the top of the tin to absorb steam and to prevent the cake from being exposed to dust or dirt.

To turn a cake out of a tin which is not fully lined, first slide a round-bladed knife gently around the inside of the tin, between it and the cake. Place a wire rack over the top of the tin and use an oven glove to hold both rack and tin firmly. Then invert the tin on to the rack and place it on the work surface. Lift the tin off the cake and remove any lining paper. To turn the cake back up the right way, place a second rack on it and invert it yet again.

If the tin has a loose bottom, then prepare some form of stand on which to place the cake in its tin, allowing the side to fall down, away from the cake. A suitable storage jar or large upturned basin is ideal. Carefully lower the side of the tin off the cake, then lift the cake and its base to a wire rack. Slide the cake from the base of the tin on to the rack and remove any lining paper. Alternatively, simply invert the cake and tin on to the rack as before and lift off the sides and base of the tin.

Certain cakes may require special treatment, for example Swiss roll. Light sponge cakes mark very easily and they can be turned on to a wire rack covered with a clean tea towel, or on to a piece of greaseproof paper which is sprinkled with caster sugar.

The cake should be allowed to cool completely before it is stored or wrapped, unless the recipe states otherwise.

STORING AND FREEZING

The keeping quality of cakes depends on the individual mixtures. Some cakes, particularly fruit cakes, improve with keeping. Light fruit cakes often taste better a few days after they are baked and very rich fruit cakes should be allowed to mature for at least a month in order to let all the individual flavours mingle.

Fatless sponge cakes do not keep well and they quickly become very dry. Ideally they should be eaten on the same day or at least the day after they are baked.

Victoria sandwich type cakes keep quite well in an airtight container and they can be stored for about a week, although the time depends on the flavouring ingredients and any filling, covering or decoration which is added. Cakes covered in soft icings do not keep as well as plain cakes.

Most cakes should be stored in an airtight container in a cool, dry place. Fruit cakes which are to be kept for long periods are best stored with the lining paper from cooking left on. The underside is usually pierced all over and sprinkled with a little brandy or rum, then the cake is wrapped in two or three layers of greaseproof paper. To introduce the liquor, the base lining paper should be peeled back and then replaced. The cake can be stored in a clean cardboard cake box or wrapped in foil. Foil must not be placed directly on the cake as it reacts with the fruit acids and may disintegrate in places, causing the surface of the cake to be dusted with foil particles. Rich cakes of this type should not be stored in plastic containers as they may sweat. It is important to keep a rich cake in a cool, dry place and to check it occasionally during storage.

Extra brandy or rum can be used to 'feed' the cake occasionally if it is stored for a long period but it is important not to overdo the liquor feeding as the cake can become soggy.

FREEZING CAKES

Most cakes that are not decorated freeze well. There is no point in freezing a rich fruit cake as it will improve on keeping as described above. Light fruit cakes can be frozen successfully; also cakes made by the creamed or melted methods. Fatless sponges, or those with little fat added, made by the whisked method freeze particularly well and they also thaw quickly at room temperature.

Packing Plain Cakes The cake should be allowed to cool completely before it is packed for freezing. When it is completely cold, pack the cake in a polythene bag, extracting all the air from the bag, and close it tightly. Label the cake with its type and date, then place it safely in the freezer, where it will not be crushed or damaged by other items.

Layers of cake should be separated by placing double thicknesses of greaseproof paper or special interleaving freezer film between them. The layers can then be packed together in one bag and frozen.

Undecorated cakes which are sandwiched together with a filling such as jam can be frozen as one plain cake, but it is best to freeze them unfilled, ready to be sandwiched together when thawed.

Freezing Decorated Cakes Cakes which are filled and covered with fresh cream, buttercream or frosting can be frozen successfully. Although the cake can be frozen with its filling and this type of icing, any decorations should not be added before freezing. Decorated cakes should not be frozen for long periods and it is best to keep them for just two to four weeks. It is sometimes useful to be able to make a decorated cake in advance of an occasion and freeze it. Cakes covered with royal icing, glacé icing or the softer moulding icings should not be frozen as the icing will not thaw successfully.

The technique to use when packing these cakes is to open freeze them. The decorated cake should be placed on freezer film or foil on a baking sheet and frozen uncovered until it is firm. Remember that the icing will not freeze hard and that it can be easily damaged during storage, particularly if there are any piped decorations. Once the cake is frozen it can be packed loosely in a polythene bag (it is best to support the cake on a piece of card first) or, better still, it can be placed in a large rigid container. Place a little crumpled absorbent kitchen paper around the side of the cake to prevent it from slipping against the sides of the container when moved.

The cake should be unpacked and transferred to a serving plate before being allowed to thaw in the refrigerator, preferably overnight or for several hours.

Packing Individual Slices It can be useful to have slices of cake in the freezer, to be removed one piece at a time as required. Either plain or decorated cakes can be packed in this way.

The cake should be cut into slices or wedges. A piece of interleaving film should be placed carefully between each slice and the cake re-shaped. Plain cakes can be packed as above or decorated cakes should be open frozen.

The required number of slices can be removed as they are wanted – this is particularly useful for lunch boxes or hasty family teas. A piece of plain cake can be packed still frozen in a lunch box first thing in the morning and it will have thawed in time for the midday break.

Freezing Small Cakes Small cakes cooked in paper cases can be packed neatly in rigid containers or polythene bags for freezing.

Tray cakes can be cut into squares or portions and frozen in rigid containers, or interleaved with freezer film and packed in bags. They can be removed and thawed a few at a time, as required.

HINTS FOR SUCCESSFUL CAKE MAKING

■ Check that all the ingredients and equipment are ready before you begin to mix the cake.

■ Weigh and measure correctly, and prepare the tins as suggested in the recipe.

■ Follow the recipe carefully, heating the oven when necessary.

■ For cakes made by the creamed method make sure that the fat is soft before beginning to beat it with the sugar – this makes the task much easier. Have the other ingredients at room temperature.

■ For the one-stage method all the ingredients should be thoroughly warmed to room temperature.

■ When making a cake by the melting method do not overheat the ingredients. Melt them over low heat until the fat is just melted. Do not let it become too hot. Leave the melted ingredients to cool slightly, if necessary, before adding any eggs.

■ Do not open the oven door when the cake is cooking until you think it is ready for checking. By opening the door in the early stages of cooking you can cause the cake to sink.

■ Test the cake to check if it is cooked before fully removing it from the oven. Use a pair of oven gloves and slide the shelf out slightly. Check the colour and texture of the cake, and use a skewer to test if the middle is cooked if necessary.

■ Allow the cake to stand for a few minutes in the tin and there is less chance of it breaking around the edges as it turns out. A rich cake should be allowed to cool in the tin until warm; a very rich cake is best left to cool completely in the tin.

SOME COMMON FAULTS AND THEIR LIKELY CAUSES

CAKE SUNK IN THE CENTRE

1 Too much raising agent used.

2 The fat and sugar were beaten for too long or the fat was too soft (almost runny when creamed).

3 The mixture was too soft before baking – this could be due to too little flour or too much liquid.

4 The oven door was opened too early or the cake removed from the oven before the mixture had time to set.

5 The cake was removed from the oven before it was fully cooked, in which case it would have sunk on cooling slightly.

CAKE RISEN TO A PEAK AND CRACKED ON TOP

1 Fat and sugar not creamed enough.

2 Oven too hot or uneven heat distribution in oven and cake cooked too near to the top of the oven, or in too hot an area of the oven.

3 The tin was too small for the amount of mixture.

UNEVENLY RISEN CAKE

1 The mixture was not levelled out before baking.

2 The oven was not prepared before the cake was put in – this does depend on the type of oven and the time it takes to heat up.

3 The cake was placed on a far corner or to one side of the shelf.

4 Too much raising agent used.

A VERY DRY CAKE

1 Not enough liquid added to the mixture.

2 The cake was baked for too long.

3 Far too much raising agent used.

THE CAKE HAS A COARSE, OPEN TEXTURE

1 If the mixture is a rubbed-in type, then the fat was not rubbed in enough. Alternatively the fat may have been of poor quality.

2 The fat and sugar were not creamed together for long enough.

3 The oven temperature was too high.

4 Too much raising agent used.

FRUIT SUNK TO THE BOTTOM OF THE CAKE

1 The mixture was too soft and would not support the fruit.

2 Cherries are the most common offender in this example. If the cherries are added to a light fruit cake they must be washed and dried first, then dusted with a little of the measured flour. If they are left coated in syrup this will cause them to sink. The dusting of flour helps them to adhere to the surrounding mixture and this prevents them from sinking.

THE CAKE HAS A SUGARY CRUST

1 Fat and sugar not creamed together long enough.

2 Too much sugar used.

3 The sugar was too coarse.

BASIC CAKES

The essential techniques that are used in the preparation of basic cakes apply equally to the most complicated gâteaux. Once these techniques are mastered, they can be applied to the array of elaborate cake-making ideas featured in later chapters.

PLAIN CAKE

fat for greasing
200 g/7 oz self-raising flour or 200 g/7 oz
    plain flour and 10 ml/2 tsp baking
    powder
1.25 ml/¼ tsp salt
75 g/3 oz margarine or blended white
    cooking fat, diced
75 g/3 oz sugar
2 small eggs
about 125 ml/4 fl oz milk

Line and grease a 15 cm/6 inch cake tin. Set the oven at 180°C/350°F/gas 4.

Mix the flour and salt together in a mixing bowl. Rub in the margarine or cooking fat until the mixture resembles fine breadcrumbs. Add the baking powder, if used, and the sugar.

In a bowl, beat the eggs with some of the milk and stir into the flour mixture. Add a little more milk if necessary to give a consistency which just drops off the end of a wooden spoon.

Spoon the mixture into the prepared cake tin and bake for 1-1½ hours or until cooked through. Cool on a wire rack.

MAKES ONE 15 CM/6 INCH CAKE

ONE-STAGE FRUIT CAKE

fat for greasing
225 g/8 oz self-raising flour
5 ml/1 tsp mixed spice (optional)
100 g/4 oz soft margarine
100 g/4 oz glacé cherries, chopped
100 g/4 oz currants
75 g/3 oz sultanas
25 g/1 oz cut mixed peel
100 g/4 oz soft light brown sugar
2 eggs
75 ml/3 fl oz milk

Line and grease an 18 cm/7 inch round cake tin. Set the oven at 180°C/350°F/gas 4. Mix the flour and spice, if used.

Put all the ingredients in a bowl, stir, then beat until smooth, allowing 2-3 minutes by hand or 1-1½ minutes with an electric mixer. Spoon the mixture into the prepared tin and bake for 2 hours. Cool on a wire rack.

MAKES ONE 18 CM/7 INCH CAKE

> **MRS BEETON'S TIP** The cherries will be easy to chop if you use a pair of kitchen scissors whose blades have been dipped in boiling water.

SMALL RICH CAKES

fat for greasing (optional)
100 g/4 oz self-raising flour
pinch of salt
100 g/4 oz butter or margarine
100 g/4 oz caster sugar
2 eggs, beaten

Grease 12-14 bun tins or support an equivalent number of paper cases in dry bun tins. Set the oven at 180°C/350°F/gas 4. Mix the flour and salt in a bowl.

In a mixing bowl, cream the butter or margarine with the sugar until light and fluffy. Beat in the eggs, then lightly stir in the flour and salt.

Divide the mixture evenly between the prepared paper cases or bun tins, and bake for 15-20 minutes until golden brown. Cool on a wire rack.

MAKES 12 TO 14

VARIATIONS

CHERRY CAKES Add 50 g/2 oz chopped glacé cherries with the flour.
CHOCOLATE CAKES Add 30 ml/ 2 tbsp cocoa with the flour and add 15 ml/ 1 tbsp milk.
COCONUT CAKES Add 50 g/2 oz desiccated coconut with the flour and 15-30 ml/ 1-2 tbsp milk with the eggs.
COFFEE CAKES Dissolve 10 ml/2 tsp instant coffee in 5 ml/1 tsp boiling water. Add with the eggs.
QUEEN CAKES Add 100 g/4 oz currants with the flour.

RICH CAKE

fat for greasing
200 g/7 oz plain flour
1.25 ml/¼ tsp salt
2.5 ml/½ tsp baking powder
150 g/5 oz butter or margarine
150 g/5 oz caster sugar
4 eggs, beaten
15 ml/1 tbsp milk (optional)

Line and grease a 15 cm/6 inch cake tin. Set the oven at 180°C/350°F/gas 4.

Sift the flour, salt and baking powder into a bowl. Place the butter or margarine in a mixing bowl and beat until very soft. Add the sugar and cream together until light and fluffy. Add the beaten eggs gradually, beating well after each addition. If the mixture shows signs of curdling, add a little flour.

Fold in the dry ingredients lightly but thoroughly, adding the milk if too stiff.

Spoon into the prepared tin, smooth the surface and make a hollow in the centre. Bake for 30 minutes, then reduce the oven temperature to 160°C/325°F/gas 3 and bake for 50 minutes more until firm to the touch. Cool on a wire rack.

MAKES ONE 15 CM/6 INCH CAKE

VARIATIONS

CORNFLOUR CAKE Use a mixture of equal parts cornflour and plain flour.
GROUND RICE CAKE Use a mixture of 150 g/5 oz plain flour and 50 g/2 oz ground rice.
LEMON OR ORANGE CAKE Add the grated rind of 2 lemons or oranges and use fruit juice instead of milk.

VICTORIA SANDWICH CAKE

The original Victoria Sandwich was oblong, filled with jam or marmalade and cut into fingers or sandwiches. Now, the basic mixture is used with many different flavourings and fillings and is served as a single, round cake. For a softer centred cake bake the mixture in a 20 cm/8 inch round cake tin, then split and fill. All loose crumbs must be brushed off before filling. Keep the filling fairly firm – if it is too moist, it will seep into the cake.

fat for greasing
150 g/5 oz butter or margarine
150 g/5 oz caster sugar
3 eggs, beaten
150 g/5 oz self-raising flour or plain flour
    and 5 ml/1 tsp baking powder
pinch of salt
raspberry or other jam for filling
caster sugar for dredging

Line and grease two 18 cm/7 inch sandwich tins. Set the oven at 180°C/350°F/gas 4.

In a mixing bowl cream the butter or margarine with the sugar until light and fluffy. Add the eggs gradually, beating well after each addition. Sift the flour, salt and baking powder, if used, into a bowl. Stir into the creamed mixture, lightly but thoroughly, until evenly mixed.

Divide between the tins and bake for 25-30 minutes. Cool on a wire rack, then sandwich together with jam. Sprinkle the top with caster sugar or spread with Glacé Icing (page 59).

MAKES ONE 18 CM/7 INCH CAKE

ONE-STAGE VICTORIA SANDWICH

fat for greasing
150 g/5 oz self-raising flour
pinch of salt
150 g/5 oz soft margarine
150 g/5 oz caster sugar
3 eggs

Line and grease two 18 cm/7 inch sandwich tins. Set the oven at 180°C/350°F/gas 4.

Put all the ingredients in a mixing bowl and stir. Beat until smooth, allowing 2-3 minutes by hand or 1-1½ minutes with an electric mixer.

Divide the mixture evenly between the tins and level each surface. Bake for 25–30 minutes. Cool on a wire rack, then fill and top as desired.

MAKES ONE 18 CM/7 INCH CAKE

MRS BEETON'S TIP A wholemeal Victoria sandwich cake can be made by substituting self-raising wholemeal flour for white flour. If self-raising wholemeal flour is not available, then use the plain type and add 10 ml/2 tsp of baking powder. Soften the mixture with 30 ml/2 tbsp of milk or orange juice after the flour is added. The resulting cake tends to have a closer, heavier texture.

FLAVOURINGS AND FILLINGS FOR VICTORIA SANDWICH CAKES

The basic mixture for Victoria Sandwich Cake can be adapted to make a variety of cakes. For example, sweet spices or citrus rinds can be added to the mixture. Alternatively, flavourings such as vanilla essence or almond essence can be added in small quantities to slightly alter the result.

There is a wide variety of commercial preserves and sweet spreads available and many of these are ideal for filling the sandwich cake. The following ideas can be used with the traditional recipe or the one-stage recipe.

CHOCOLATE SANDWICH CAKE Substitute 60 ml/4 tbsp of cocoa for an equal quantity of the flour. Sift the cocoa with the flour and continue as in the main recipe. Sandwich the cooled cakes together with chocolate spread and sift a little icing sugar over the top of the cake.

CINNAMON AND APPLE SAND-WICH CAKE Add 10 ml/2 tsp of ground cinnamon to the flour. Continue as in the main recipe. Peel, core and slice a large cooking apple, then cook it with a little sugar until it is reduced to a pulp. Press the pulp through a sieve, return it to the saucepan and add 10 ml/2 tsp of cornflour blended with 30 ml/2 tbsp of milk. Bring to the boil, stirring, and cook until thickened. Sweeten the purée to taste, then leave it to cool. Gradually fold in 50 ml/2 fl oz of whipped double cream, then use this apple cream to sandwich the cooled cakes together.

COFFEE SANDWICH CAKE Dissolve 30 ml/2 tbsp of instant coffe in 30 ml/2 tbsp boiling water and leave to cool. Fold this into the mixture last. Whip 150 ml/¼ pint double cream with 5 ml/1 tsp of instant coffee dissolved in 15 ml/1 tbsp of boiling water and 30 ml/2 tbsp of icing sugar. Sandwich the cooled cakes with this coffee cream.

GINGER SANDWICH CAKE The combination of ground ginger and lemon rind makes a delicious cake. Add the grated rind of 1 lemon to the fat and sugar. Sift 15 ml/1 tbsp of ground ginger with the flour. Prepare and bake the cake as in the main recipe. When cool, sandwich the layers with ginger marmalade.

HARLEQUIN SANDWICH CAKE Make the cake mixture as in the main recipe, then put half in one sandwich tin. Add pink food colouring to the second portion of mixture, making it a fairly strong colour. Put the second portion in the other sandwich tin and bake the cake. When cool, cut both cakes into rings: cut a 5 cm/2 inch circle from the middle of each cake, then cut a 10 cm/4 inch circle around it. Either use plain pastry cutters or cut out circles of paper and use a pointed knife to cut round them. You should have three rings of each cake. Carefully put the rings of cake together alternating the colours to make two layers. Sandwich the layers together with raspberry jam. Spread warmed raspberry jam over the top of the cake and sift icing sugar over it. Alternatively, fill the cake with whipped cream and swirl more whipped cream over the top. When slices are cut the pattern will show.

LEMON SANDWICH CAKE Add the grated rind of 1 large lemon to the fat and sugar. Continue as in the main recipe, then sandwich the cooled cakes together with lemon curd.

MOCHA SANDWICH CAKE Substitute 30 ml/2 tbsp of cocoa for an equal quantity of flour and sift it with the flour. Prepare the mixture as in the main recipe. Dissolve 10 ml/2 tsp of instant coffee in 15 ml/1 tbsp of boiling water and add it to the mixture. Sandwich the cooled cakes together with chocolate spread.

ORANGE SANDWICH CAKE Add the grated rind of 1 large orange to the fat and sugar, then continue as in the main recipe. Sandwich the cooled cakes together with orange marmalade.

SPONGE CAKE

fat for greasing
flour for dusting
3 eggs
75 g/3 oz caster sugar
75 g/3 oz plain flour
pinch of salt
pinch of baking powder

Grease an 18 cm/7 inch round cake tin or two 15 cm/6 inch sandwich tins. Dust with sifted flour, tapping out the excess. Set the oven at 180°C/350°F/gas 4.

Whisk the eggs and sugar together in a bowl over a saucepan of hot water, taking care that the base of the bowl does not touch the water. Continue whisking for 10-15 minutes until the mixture is thick and creamy. Remove the bowl from the pan. Whisk until cold.

Sift the flour, salt and baking powder into a bowl. Add to the creamed mixture, using a metal spoon. Do this lightly, so that the air incorporated during whisking is not lost. Pour the mixture into the prepared tins.

Bake a single 18 cm/7 inch cake for 40 minutes; two 15 cm/6 inch cakes for 25 minutes. Leave the sponge in the tins for a few minutes, then cool on a wire rack. Fill and top as desired.

MAKES ONE 18 CM/7 INCH CAKE OR TWO 15 CM/6 INCH LAYERS

MRS BEETON'S TIP If an electric mixer is used there is no need to place the bowl over hot water. Whisk at high speed for about 5 minutes until thick. Fold in the flour by hand.

GENOESE SPONGE OR PASTRY

For an 18 cm/7 inch square or 15 x 25 cm/6 x 10 inch oblong cake, use 75 g/3 oz flour, pinch of salt, 50 g/2 oz clarified butter or margarine, 3 eggs and 75 g/3 oz caster sugar.

fat for greasing
100 g/4 oz plain flour
2.5 ml/½ tsp salt
75 g/3 oz Clarified Butter (page 15) or
    margarine
4 eggs
100 g/4 oz caster sugar

Line and grease a 20 x 30 cm/8 x 12 inch Swiss roll tin. Set the oven at 180°C/350°F/gas 4.

Sift the flour and salt into a bowl and put in a warm place. Melt the clarified butter or margarine without letting it get hot.

Whisk the eggs lightly in a mixing bowl. Add the sugar and place the bowl over a saucepan of hot water. Whisk for 10-15 minutes until thick. Take care that the base of the bowl does not touch the water. Remove from the heat and continue whisking until at blood-heat. The melted butter should be at the same temperature.

Sift half the flour over the eggs, then pour in half the melted butter or margarine in a thin stream. Fold in gently. Repeat, using the remaining flour and fat. Spoon gently into the prepared tin and bake for 30-40 minutes. Cool on a wire rack.

MAKES ONE 20 x 30 CM/8 x 12 INCH CAKE

MICROWAVE TIP Melt the clarified butter or margarine in a bowl on High for 45 seconds-1 minute.

GINGERBREAD

fat for greasing
200 g/7 oz plain flour
1.25 ml/¼ tsp salt
10-15 ml/2-3 tsp ground ginger
2.5 ml/½ tsp bicarbonate of soda
75 g/3 oz lard
50 g/2 oz soft light brown sugar
50 g/2 oz golden syrup
50 g/2 oz black treacle
1 egg
milk (see method)

Line and grease a 15 cm/6 inch square tin. Set the oven at 160°C/325°F/gas 3.

Sift the flour, salt, ginger and bicarbonate of soda into a mixing bowl. Warm the lard, sugar, syrup and treacle in a saucepan until the fat has melted. Do not allow the mixture to become hot.

In a measuring jug, beat the egg lightly and add enough milk to make up to 125 ml/4 fl oz. Add the melted mixture to the dry ingredients with the beaten egg and milk mixture. Stir thoroughly; the mixture should run easily off the spoon.

Pour into the prepared tin and bake for 1¼-1½ hours until firm to the touch. Cool on a wire rack.

MAKES ONE 15 CM/6 INCH SQUARE CAKE

FLAVOURINGS AND FILLINGS FOR SPONGE CAKES

Both the Sponge Cake and the Genoese Sponge cake are light in texture, with a delicate flavour, and this should be reflected in the choice of flavouring ingredients or fillings that are added. Jams and other sweet preserves can be used to fill the cakes or whipped cream is ideal for this type of cake. Fresh fruit perfectly complements the lightness of these sponges.

The following suggestions can be used for both the recipes opposite.

CHOCOLATE CREAM SPONGE Make plain sponge cakes or substitute 15 ml/1 tbsp of cocoa for an equal quantity of flour, sifting it in with the flour to flavour the cakes. For the filling, melt 100 g/4 oz of milk chocolate with 50 g/2 oz of butter in a basin over hot water. Stir well and leave to cool but do not allow to set. Carefully fold in 150 ml/¼ pint of whipped double cream, then use this chocolate cream to sandwich the cakes together.

LEMON CREAM SPONGE Add the grated rind of 1 lemon to the eggs and sugar, then continue as in the main recipe. Whip 150 ml/¼ pint of double cream and fold in 60-90 ml/4-6 tbsp of lemon curd, to taste. Use this to sandwich the cakes together.

PEACHES AND CREAM CAKE Make the cakes as in the main recipe. Finely chop peeled and stoned fresh peaches or drained canned peaches and mix them with whipped cream or soft cheese. Sweeten with icing sugar and use this to sandwich the cakes together.

STRAWBERRY CREAM CAKE Make the cakes as in the main recipe and leave to cool. Hull and halve 225 g/8 oz of strawberries. Whip 150 ml/¼ pint of double cream with icing sugar to taste, then fold in the strawberries. Sandwich the cooled cakes together with the strawberry cream.

CAKE COVERINGS
AND FILLINGS

Even a simple cake can be made extra special by adding a little icing, a golden glaze
or a nutty topping. This chapter includes recipes to complement formal cakes as well
as plain ones. In addition, a quick-reference chart provides a useful guide to
selecting the right icing for the type of cake.

GLAZES AND COATINGS

Glazes are used to give a shiny coating to
food. Pastry, cakes and biscuits may be
glazed with egg white, egg wash, sugar syrup
or warmed jam such as apricot glaze, and
then covered with crumbs, ground nuts,
coconut, marzipan, almond paste or praline.
Fruit flans or tartlets are often coated with a
sweet liquid thickened with arrowroot.

APRICOT GLAZE

*Brush this glaze over a cake before applying the
marzipan. Any yellow jam or marmalade may be
used.*

225 g/8 oz apricot jam

Warm the jam with 30 ml/2 tbsp water in a
small saucepan over a low heat until the jam
has melted. Sieve the mixture and return the
glaze to the clean saucepan. Bring slowly to
the boil. Allow to cool slightly before use.

**SUFFICIENT TO COAT THE TOP AND
SIDES OF ONE 20 CM/8 INCH CAKE**

> ☀ **MICROWAVE TIP** Melt the jam
> with the water in a bowl on High. Sieve
> into a small basin and heat the syrup on
> High. Cool slightly before use.

CHOCOLATE GLAZE

*A little oil gives this icing sugar glaze its shine. It
may be poured over chocolate cakes or it can be
used to coat plain sponge cakes or Victoria
Sandwich Cake (page 50) to provide a contrast in
flavour. Store any leftover glaze in an airtight
container in the refrigerator.*

**100 g/4 oz plain chocolate, broken into
    small pieces
5 ml/1 tsp vegetable oil
25 g/1 oz caster sugar**

Combine the chocolate, oil and caster
sugar in a heatproof bowl. Stir in 45 ml/3
tbsp boiling water. Place the bowl over hot
water and stir gently until the chocolate has
melted. Remove from the heat and cool
slightly before pouring the chocolate glaze
over the cake.

**SUFFICIENT TO COVER TOP AND SIDES
OF ONE 18 CM/7 INCH CAKE**

> ☀ **MICROWAVE TIP** Melt all the
> ingredients in a small bowl on Medium
> for 2-3 minutes.

MARASCHINO GLAZE

Unlike the apricot glaze, this one is based upon icing sugar, with milk and butter added to enhance the shiny effect.

30 ml/2 tbsp softened butter
175 g/6 oz icing sugar
30-45 ml/2-3 tbsp milk
5-10 ml/1-2 tsp maraschino liqueur or
    syrup from maraschino cherries
1-2 drops red food colouring (optional)

Put the butter into a bowl. Using a wooden spoon, gradually work in the icing sugar until thoroughly mixed. Bring the milk to the boil in a small saucepan and stir it into the mixture, with the liqueur or syrup. Add a couple of drops of colouring, if liked, to tint the icing a pale pink. The glaze should be thick enough to spread lightly, yet be able to trickle over the edge of a cake and drip down the sides.

SUFFICIENT TO COVER ONE 25 CM/10 INCH RING CAKE OR 24 SMALL CAKES

MRS BEETON'S TIP An icing sugar glaze of this kind may be used on top of an icing of a different colour and flavour. Maraschino glaze looks particularly good on chocolate icing.

GLAZE FOR SWEET FLANS

This slightly thickened glaze is useful for coating fresh or canned fruit as a decoration for light gâteaux. It can also be used with fresh fruit to top a plain cheesecake.

5 ml/1 tsp arrowroot
150 ml/¼ pint fruit syrup from canned or
    bottled fruit or 150 ml/¼ pint water
    and 25 g/1 oz sugar
1-3 drops food colouring
lemon juice

In a bowl, mix the arrowroot to a paste with a little of the cold fruit syrup or water. Pour the remaining syrup into a saucepan and bring to the boil. If using water, add the sugar and bring to the boil, stirring constantly until all the sugar has dissolved. Pour on to the arrowroot mixture, stir well, then return to the saucepan. Bring to the boil, stirring constantly. Add the appropriate food colouring, then stir in lemon juice to taste. Use at once.

SUFFICIENT TO GLAZE ONE 18 CM/7 INCH FRUIT FLAN OR 12-16 TARTLETS

MICROWAVE TIP Mix the arrowroot with a little of the syrup in a medium bowl. Add the remaining syrup and cook on High for 1 minute. Stir, then cook for 1 minute more or until the glaze clears. Add food colouring and lemon juice as above.

COOKED ALMOND PASTE

This makes a smoother and more malleable paste than the uncooked mixture. Use it for moulding decorations and for covering wedding cakes.

450 g/1 lb granulated sugar
1.25 ml/¼ tsp cream of tartar
300 g/11 oz ground almonds
2 egg whites
5 ml/1 tsp almond essence
50 g/2 oz icing sugar

Place the sugar with 150 ml/¼ pint water in a saucepan over moderate heat. Stir occasionally until all the sugar has melted, then bring the syrup to the boil.

In a cup, dissolve the cream of tartar in 5 ml/1 tsp water and stir it into the syrup. Boil, without stirring, until the syrup registers 115°C/240°F on a sugar thermometer, the soft ball stage (see Mrs Beeton's Tip).

Remove the pan from the heat and immediately stir in the ground almonds followed by the unbeaten egg whites and almond essence. Return the pan to a low heat and cook, stirring constantly, for 2 minutes. Set the pan aside until the mixture is cool enough to handle.

Sift the icing sugar on to a clean work surface, place the marzipan in the centre and knead with the fingertips until the sugar is absorbed. If the marzipan is sticky, leave to cool for longer and then add a little more icing sugar, if necessary. Cover lightly until cold, then wrap and store in a cool place, as for almond paste.

MAKES 900 G/2 LB

MRS BEETON'S TIP If you do not have a sugar thermometer, drop about 2.5 ml/½ tsp syrup into a bowl of iced water. If you can mould the syrup between your fingers to make a soft ball, the syrup is ready.

ALMOND PASTE/MARZIPAN

Quick guide to quantities required to cover fruit cakes

Round	Quantity	Square	Quantity
15 cm/6 inches	350 g/12 oz	15 cm/6 inches	500 g/18 oz
18 cm/7 inches	500 g/18 oz	18 cm/7 inches	575 g/1¼ lb
20 cm/8 inches	575 g/1¼ lb	20 cm/8 inches	800 g/1¾ lb
23 cm/9 inches	800 g/1¾ lb	23 cm/9 inches	900 g/2 lb
25 cm/10 inches	900 g/2 lb	25 cm/10 inches	1 kg/2¼ lb
28 cm/11 inches	1 kg/2¼ lb	28 cm/11 inches	1.1 kg/2½ lb
30 cm/12 inches	1.25 kg/2½ lb	30 cm/12 inches	1.4 kg/3 lb

BUTTER ICINGS AND FUDGE ICINGS

These are soft icings made with butter and icing sugar which may be used for filling or covering lighter cakes and gâteaux. On drying, an outer crust forms but the icing remains soft underneath. The iced cake should be stored away from heat or direct sunlight.

Use unsalted butter if possible and flavour the icing as required. Soften the butter before using or try using a butter mixture that spreads easily even when chilled – these usually contain vegetable oil and therefore little or no extra liquid will be required when mixing the icing.

When adding food colouring to butter-based icings, do not expect clear colours. Avoid adding blue, as the yellow in the butter will turn it green!

All these icings may be spread with a palette knife or piped using a savoy nozzle.

★ **FREEZER TIP** Buttercream can be frozen successfully, unless the recipe contains egg, in which case it may curdle. When piping with buttercream it is necessary to make slightly more than required; however any leftovers can be frozen for future use as a filling for cakes. The prepared buttercream can be flavoured before or after freezing. Pack the buttercream in a rigid container, then leave it to thaw in the refrigerator or in a cool place and beat it thoroughly before use.

RICH BUTTERCREAM

This buttercream is enriched by the addition of an egg yolk. Use only very fresh eggs and make sure that all utensils used to prepare the buttercream are perfectly clean.

1 egg yolk
200 g/7 oz icing sugar, sifted
100 g/4 oz butter, softened
flavouring

Beat the egg yolk in a mixing bowl, adding the sugar gradually until the mixture is smooth. Beat in the butter, a little at a time with the flavouring.

SUFFICIENT TO FILL AND TOP A 20 CM/8 INCH CAKE

BUTTERCREAM

100 g/4 oz butter, softened
15 ml/1 tbsp milk or fruit juice
225 g/8 oz icing sugar, sifted

In a mixing bowl, cream the butter with the milk or juice and gradually work in the icing sugar. Beat the icing until light and fluffy. Alternatively, work all the ingredients in a food processor, removing the plunger for the final mixing to allow air to enter the buttercream mixture.

SUFFICIENT TO FILL AND TOP A 20 CM/8 INCH CAKE

FLUFFY BUTTERCREAM

2 egg whites
200 g/7 oz icing sugar, sifted
100 g/4 oz butter, softened
flavouring

Whisk the egg whites in a large bowl until stiff. Add the icing sugar, a third at a time, whisking between each addition until the mixture forms peaks.

In a mixing bowl, cream the butter until light and fluffy. Gradually fold in the meringue mixture. Flavour as required.

SUFFICIENT TO FILL AND TOP A 20 CM/8 INCH CAKE

VARIATIONS

These flavourings may be used with any of the buttercreams.

CHOCOLATE BUTTERCREAM Grate 50 g/2 oz block plain chocolate. Place it in a basin over hot water with 15 ml/1 tbsp milk, stir until dissolved, then cool. Use instead of the liquid in the plain buttercream.

COFFEE BUTTERCREAM Dissolve 5 ml/1 tsp instant coffee in 15 ml/1 tbsp hot water. Cool before use. Use instead of the milk or fruit juice in the plain buttercream.

LEMON OR ORANGE BUTTERCREAM Use 15 ml/1 tbsp juice and a little grated rind.

VANILLA BUTTERCREAM Add 2.5 ml/½ tsp vanilla essence with the milk.

WALNUT BUTTERCREAM Add 25 g/1 oz chopped walnuts.

FRENCH BUTTER ICING

This resembles a frosting, in that the sugar is boiled and added as a syrup to the other ingredients. The high percentage of butter, however, assures it of a place in this section.

50 g/2 oz granulated sugar
1 egg yolk
150 g/5 oz butter, cut into small pieces

Mix the sugar with 125 ml/4 fl oz water in a small heavy saucepan. Stirring occasionally, heat gently until all the sugar has dissolved. Increase the heat and boil, without stirring, until the syrup registers 105°C/220°F on a sugar thermometer, the thread stage (see Mrs Beeton's Tip).

Place the egg yolk in a bowl, whisk lightly, then gradually whisk in the syrup. Continue whisking until cool, then add the butter, a little at a time, whisking constantly.

SUFFICIENT TO COAT THE TOP AND SIDES OF A 20 CM/8 INCH CAKE

VARIATION

CHOCOLATE FRENCH BUTTER ICING Break up 100 g/4 oz plain dark chocolate and stir into the warm syrup mixture until melted. Beat until smooth and glossy.

> **MRS BEETON'S TIP** If you do not have a sugar thermometer, test the syrup by dipping a spoon in the syrup and then pressing another spoon on to the back of it and pulling away. If a thread forms, the syrup is ready.

GLACÉ ICING

Glacé icing is mainly used as a covering for small cakes, sponge cakes or other light cakes. It is quick and easy to make and therefore ideal for simple, informal cakes. It gives a smooth, slightly crisp coating that complements piped buttercream edges. This icing can also be used to coat plain biscuits. Basically a mixture of icing sugar and warm water, it may also contain flavourings and colourings or extra ingredients as in the Chocolate Glacé Icing on page 60.

There is also a recipe for a Glacé Fondant (overleaf) which is based on the same ingredients as glacé icing but it is heated and enriched with a little butter to give a very glossy result. It should not be confused with Traditional Fondant which is a more formal icing.

The consistency of the icing is all important; it should be stiff enough to coat the back of a wooden spoon thickly, otherwise it will run off the surface of the cake and drip down the sides.

Glacé icing should be used immediately. If left to stand, even for a short while, the surface should be covered completely with damp greaseproof paper or cling film. Any crystallised icing on the surface should be scraped off before use. Because the icing sets so quickly, any additional decorations must be put on as soon as the cake is iced, or the surface will crack

The choice of decorations to use with glacé icing is important. Do not use decorations liable to melt, run or be damaged by damp. Crystallised flower petals, chocolate decorations and small sweets which will shed colour should not be used.

GLACÉ ICING

This simple, basic icing is quickly prepared and is ideal for topping a plain sponge cake or a batch of small cakes. Make the icing just before it is to be used and keep any extra decorations to the minimum.

100 g/4 oz icing sugar, sifted
food colouring, optional

Place the icing sugar in a bowl. Using a wooden spoon gradually stir in sufficient warm water (about 15 ml/1 tbsp) to create icing whose consistency will thickly coat the back of the spoon. Take care not to add too much liquid or the icing will be too runny. At first the icing will seem quite stiff, but it slackens rapidly as the icing sugar absorbs the water. Stir in 1-2 drops of food colouring, if required.

SUFFICIENT TO COVER THE TOP OF ONE 18 CM/7 INCH CAKE

VARIATIONS

LEMON OR ORANGE GLACÉ ICING Use 15 ml/1 tbsp strained lemon or orange juice instead of the water.

COFFEE GLACÉ ICING Dissolve 5 ml/1 tsp instant coffee in 15 ml/1 tbsp warm water and add instead of the water in the main recipe.

LIQUEUR-FLAVOURED GLACÉ ICING Replace half the water with the liqueur of your choice.

CHOCOLATE GLACÉ ICING

An icing that contains dessert chocolate and/or butter will thicken and set more readily than one which merely contains a liquid.

50 g/2 oz plain chocolate, broken into
    small pieces
knob of butter
100 g/4 oz icing sugar, sifted

Combine the chocolate and butter in a heatproof bowl. Add 15 ml/1 tbsp water. Place the bowl over hot water. When the chocolate has melted, stir the mixture, gradually adding the sugar. Add a little more water, if necessary, to give a smooth coating consistency. Use at once.

SUFFICIENT TO COAT THE TOP OF ONE 18 CM/7 INCH CAKE

☀ **MICROWAVE TIP** Melt the chocolate, butter and water in a bowl on Medium for 1-2 minutes.

GLACÉ FONDANT

225 g/8 oz icing sugar, sifted
2.5 ml/½ tsp lemon juice
knob of butter

Combine the icing sugar and lemon juice in a small saucepan and mix well. Add the butter and cook over a low heat, stirring with a wooden spoon, until the butter has melted and the icing is well blended. Immediately pour over the cake.

SUFFICIENT TO COVER THE TOP OF A 20 CM/8 INCH CAKE

FROSTINGS

Frosting is usually spread thickly all over a cake, covering the sides as well as the top. When set, it is crisper than glacé icing, because the sugar is heated or boiled when making it. It should have a soft, spreading consistency when applied. Have the cake ready before starting to make the frosting.

AMERICAN FROSTING

225 g/8 oz granulated sugar
pinch of cream of tartar
1 egg white
2.5 ml/½ tsp vanilla essence or a few drops
    lemon juice

Combine the sugar and cream of tartar in a small saucepan. Add 60 ml/4 tbsp water. Place over a low heat, stirring occasionally until the sugar has melted. Heat, without stirring until the syrup registers 115°C/240°F, the soft ball stage, on a sugar thermometer (see Mrs Beeton's Tip, page 56). Remove from the heat.

In a large grease-free bowl, whisk the egg white until stiff. Pour on the syrup in a thin stream, whisking continuously. Add the flavouring and continue to whisk until the frosting is thick and glossy and stands in peaks when the whisk is lifted.

Quickly spread over the cake. As the frosting cools, it may be swirled with a knife and lifted to form peaks.

SUFFICIENT TO COVER THE TOP AND SIDES OF ONE 18 CM/7 INCH CAKE

🪣 **MRS BEETON'S TIP** Make sure that both bowl and whisk are free from grease, otherwise the frosting will not whisk up well.

ROYAL ICING

Royal Icing is used for special celebration cakes, especially for wedding cakes, because the icing has sufficient strength when it sets hard to hold the tiers. The icing cannot be applied directly to the cake because it would drag the crumbs and discolour badly, so rich fruit cakes are usually covered with a layer of almond paste or marzipan before the royal icing is applied.

Traditionalists believe that royal icing can only be made successfully with egg whites and hard beating, but dried egg white or albumen powder is fast gaining in popularity because the icing can be made in a food mixer or with an electric whisk. Whichever method you choose, the secret of successful royal icing work, be it flat icing or piping, depends upon making the icing to the correct consistency. This is discussed further on page 62.

ROYAL ICING

Quick guide to quantities of Royal Icing required to cover cakes (sufficient for 3 coats)

ROUND	ROYAL ICING
15 cm/6 inch	575 g/1¼ lb
18 cm/7 inch	675 g/1½ lb
20 cm/8 inch	800 g/1¾ lb
23 cm/9 inch	900 g/2 lb
25 cm/10 inch	1 kg/2¼ lb
28 cm/11 inch	1.25 kg/2¾ lb
30 cm/12 inch	1.4 kg/3 lb

SQUARE	ROYAL ICING
15 cm/6 inch	675 g/1½ lb
18 cm/7 inch	800 g/1¾ lb
20 cm/8 inch	900 g/2 lb
23 cm/9 inch	1 kg/2¼ lb
25 cm/10 inch	1.25 kg/2¾ lb
28 cm/11 inch	1.4 kg/3 lb
30 cm/12 inch	1.5 kg/3¼ lb

ROYAL ICING (USING EGG WHITE)

It is vital to ensure that the bowl is clean and free from grease. Use a wooden spoon kept solely for the purpose and do not be tempted to skimp on the beating – insufficient beating will produce an off-white icing with a heavy, sticky texture.

2 egg whites
450 g/1 lb icing sugar, sifted

Place the egg whites in a bowl and break them up with a fork. Gradually beat in about two-thirds of the icing sugar with a wooden spoon, and continue beating for about 15 minutes until the icing is pure white and forms soft peaks. Add the remaining icing sugar, if necessary, to attain this texture. Cover the bowl with cling film and place a dampened tea towel on top. Place the bowl inside a plastic bag if storing overnight or for longer.

Before use, lightly beat the icing to burst any air bubbles that have risen to the surface. Adjust the consistency for flat icing or piping.

SUFFICIENT TO COAT THE TOP AND SIDES OF A 20 CM/8 INCH CAKE

> **MRS BEETON'S TIP** If the icing is to be used for a single cake, glycerine may be added to prevent it from becoming too brittle when dry. Add 2.5 ml/½ tsp glycerine during the final beating. Do not, however, use glycerine for a tiered cake where the icing must be hard in order to hold the tiers.

ROYAL ICING (USING DRIED EGG WHITE)

15 ml/1 tbsp dried egg white (albumen powder)
450 g/1 lb icing sugar

Place 60 ml/4 tbsp warm water in a bowl. Add the dried egg white, mix thoroughly and leave for 10-15 minutes. Whisk with a fork and strain the mixture into a mixing bowl.

Gradually beat in about two-thirds of the icing sugar and continue beating for 5 minutes in a food mixer or with a hand-held electric whisk until the icing is pure white, light and stands in soft peaks. Add extra icing sugar, if necessary.

Cover and use as for the royal icing (using egg white) except that fewer air bubbles will be present.

VARIATION

ALBUMEN SUBSTITUTE May be used in place of albumen powder. Sift it into the bowl. Beat for 5 minutes as above.

 MRS BEETON'S TIP Be careful not to beat the icing for too long or it may break when piped.

QUICK GUIDE TO CONSISTENCY OF ROYAL ICING FOR DIFFERENT APPLICATIONS

Once the required consistency has been achieved, cover the icing with a damp cloth, even during use.

CONSISTENCY	DESCRIPTION	USE
Thin Icing	Just finds its own level when gently tapped	Run-outs and flooding
Soft Peak (1)	Forms a soft peak when the spoon is lifted out but readily falls over	Embroidery work. Very fine 00 writing nozzles
Soft Peak (2)	Forms a soft peak but only tip bends over	Flat icing
Medium Peak	Firmer peak that holds its shape	Most piping except patterns using the larger nozzles
Firm Peak	Stiffer peak but still soft enough to push through a nozzle without excessive pressure	Petals for flowers, large shell and similar nozzles

CREAM FILLINGS

Fresh cream is still a prime favourite as a filling for gâteaux and afternoon tea cakes. Double cream has the best flavour and may be whipped and piped in much the same way as royal icing. Once whipped, it may be frozen on the decorated gâteaux and will not lose its shape when thawed. To reduce the risk of over-whipping, which might cause the cream to separate in hot weather, add 15 ml/1 tbsp milk to each 150 ml/¼ pint cream or replace up to one-third of the double cream with single cream. There is no need to add sugar to whipped cream.

TO WHIP THE CREAM

Choose a cool area of the kitchen in which to work and chill the bowl and whisk before use, by placing them in the refrigerator or freezer for a few minutes. A small wire balloon whisk is the best utensil, but for large quantities a hand-held electric whisk may be used with care.

Stand the bowl on a wet cloth or a non-slip surface, add the cream and tip the bowl. While whipping, incorporate as much air as possible. If using an electric whisk, start on high and reduce speed to low as the cream begins to thicken. Be very careful not to overwhip. Stop whipping as soon as the cream will stand in soft peaks and has doubled in volume.

The cream will continue to thicken slightly on standing and when piped, so stop whipping just before you think the cream is ready. It should be smooth and shiny in appearance. Overwhipped cream will 'frill' at the edges when piped.

For best results, use the whipped cream immediately, or cover and store in the refrigerator until required, giving it a gentle stir before use.

If the finished gâteau is to stand in a warm room for any length of time, whip in 5 ml/1 tsp gelatine, dissolved in 10 ml/2 tsp warm water and cooled.

FLAVOURINGS

Add any flavouring to cream when it has been whipped to soft peaks. Lemon or orange juice, liqueur or sherry may be used and should be added gradually during the final whipping. Once the cream has been whipped, finely chopped nuts, glacé fruits or grated citrus rind may be added.

REDUCING THE FAT CONTENT

For a low-fat whipped cream, replace up to one third with low or full-fat plain yogurt. This will not only make the cream less rich, but will prevent overwhipping and keep the cream smooth and shiny.

FREEZING

Cakes decorated with cream should be frozen and stored in a large domed plastic box. Alternatively, open freeze and then cocoon carefully in a dome of foil. Label well to avoid other items being inadvertently placed on top.

To thaw, remove the wrappings and thaw the cakes in a cool place, refrigerator or microwave (following the manufacturer's directions).

Small quantities of leftover cream may be whipped with a little caster sugar and piped in small stars on non-stick baking parchment for freezing. They may then be lifted off and placed, still frozen, on desserts and gâteaux for instant decoration.

CUSTARD FILLINGS

Confectioners' Custard, sometimes called Crème Patissière, makes an excellent filling for cakes. Thickened with eggs, flour or cornflour the custard sets to a thick cream when cold. Mock Cream is a simple filling based on milk thickened with cornflour and enriched with butter, while Quick Diplomat Cream is richer still, with double cream used as its base.

Unless using a double saucepan, it is easier to make these custards with yolks rather than whole eggs as the whites cook more quickly and lumps of cooked egg white may spoil the texture.

Vanilla sugar may be used instead of caster sugar in the recipes that follow. The vanilla pod or essence should then be omitted.

To prevent the formation of a skin on the cooked custard, press a dampened piece of greaseproof paper lightly on the surface. Do not use plasticised cling film for this purpose when the custard is hot.

MRS BEETON'S TIP These light fillings, thickened with eggs, go very well with light sponge cakes and gâteaux that are filled or decorated with fresh fruit. They can also be used to decorate cheesecakes. This type of filling should not be frozen as it tends to curdle.

CONFECTIONERS' CUSTARD

300 ml/½ pint milk
1 vanilla pod or a few drops of vanilla essence
2 egg yolks
50 g/2 oz caster sugar
25 g/1 oz plain flour

Place the milk and vanilla pod, if used, in a small saucepan and bring to the boil over low heat. Remove from the heat and leave to one side, adding the vanilla essence, if used.

Whisk the egg yolks with the sugar in a bowl until thick and creamy, then add the flour. Remove the vanilla pod and very gradually add the milk to the egg mixture, beating constantly until all has been incorporated. Pour the mixture back into the saucepan and stir over a low heat for 1-2 minutes to cook the flour. The custard should thickly coat the back of the wooden spoon and be smooth and shiny.

Pour the custard into a clean bowl, cover and leave to cool. Beat well then cover again and chill until required.

MAKES ABOUT 300 ML/½ PINT

VARIATIONS

CHOCOLATE CUSTARD Stir 25 g/1 oz grated chocolate into the custard while still hot.

CRÈME ST HONORE Whisk 2 egg whites with 10 ml/2 tsp of caster sugar until stiff. Fold into cold custard. Use for choux pastry or as an alternative cream for gâteaux.

CRÈME FRANGIPANE Omit the vanilla flavouring. Add 40 g/1½ oz finely chopped butter to final cooking. When cold, fold in 75 g/3 oz crushed almond macaroons or 50 g/2 oz ground almonds and a few drops of almond essence.

CONFECTIONERS' CUSTARD WITH BRANDY

25 g/1 oz cornflour
300 ml/½ pint milk
3 egg yolks
40 g/1½ oz caster sugar
2.5 ml/½ tsp brandy, rum or liqueur

In a bowl mix the cornflour with a little milk, then beat in the egg yolks and sugar. Heat the remaining milk in a saucepan until tepid and pour slowly on to the cornflour mixture, stirring constantly. Pour the mixture back into the saucepan and stir over a low heat, without boiling, until the custard thickens and thickly coats the back of the wooden spoon. Remove from the heat, stir in the brandy, rum or liqueur and pour into a clean bowl. Cover and cool, then beat well. Cover again and chill until required.

MAKES ABOUT 300 ML/½ PINT

MOCK CREAM

10 ml/2 tsp cornflour
150 ml/¼ pint milk
50 g/2 oz butter, softened
50 g/2 oz icing or caster sugar
few drops of vanilla or almond essence

Mix the cornflour with a little milk in a small saucepan. Gradually stir in the remaining milk and cook over a low heat, stirring constantly until the mixture thickens. Cover and leave until tepid.

Cream the butter and sugar together in a bowl until light and fluffy. Gradually add the custard mixture to the butter, beating well between each addition. Beat in the essence, cover and chill.

SUFFICIENT FOR 2 LAYERS IN ONE 18 CM/ 7 INCH CAKE

QUICK DIPLOMAT CREAM

15 ml/1 tbsp custard powder
10 ml/2 tsp caster sugar
150 ml/¼ pint milk
150 ml/¼ pint double cream
few drops of vanilla essence

Mix the custard powder and sugar with a little milk in a small saucepan. Gradually stir in the remaining milk and stir over a low heat for 1 minute until thick. Transfer the mixture to a bowl, cover and leave to cool. Beat well then cover again and chill.

In a clean bowl, whisk the cream with the vanilla essence until thick. Beat the custard until smooth and lightly fold in the cream until well blended. Chill until required.

MAKES ABOUT 300 ML/½ PINT

VARIATIONS

ORANGE OR LEMON Fold in 5 ml/1 tsp finely grated orange or lemon rind.

CHOCOLATE Stir 50 g/2 oz grated chocolate into the hot custard.

LIQUEUR Replace the essence with brandy or liqueur.

TOPPINGS

These simple toppings may be prepared in advance and used to quickly decorate and finish a cake or gâteau. Most toppings can be stored in a screw-topped jar or in a cardboard box for several months.

COCONUT

Coconut has an interesting texture and makes a good topping on plain cakes. Choose good-quality desiccated coconut with large strands and use plain or colour as follows: Place about 50 g/2 oz coconut in a screw top jar, leaving at least 2.5 cm/1 inch space at the top. Add a few drops of food colouring (liquid colours are best), screw on the lid and shake the jar vigorously for a few minutes until the coconut is evenly coloured. Use the same day or spread the coconut out on a piece of greaseproof paper and leave in a warm place to dry before storing in a dry screw-topped jar.

Toasted coconut is prepared in the same way as Toasted Nuts (method follows).

COLOURED SUGAR CRYSTALS

Use either granulated sugar or roughly crushed sugar lumps and colour and dry in the same way as the coloured coconut above.

TOASTED NUTS

Whole flaked or chopped nuts may be lightly toasted to improve both colour and flavour. Almonds and hazelnuts are the most commonly used varieties.

To toast nuts, remove the rack from the grill pan and line the pan with a piece of foil. Spread the nuts over the foil. Heat the grill and toast the nuts under a medium heat, stirring occasionally until evenly browned. This will only take a few seconds. Lift out the foil carefully and leave the nuts to cool. This method may also be used to remove the skins from hazelnuts. Roast them under the grill, then rub the skins off while the nuts are still hot.

Toasted nuts are best used on the same day; alternatively, store when cold in a screw-topped jar for a few days.

PRALINE

This is a fine powder of crushed nuts and caramel used to flavour creams and fillings. Crushed roughly, it may be used as a cake decoration.

oil for greasing
50 g/2 oz caster sugar
50 g/2 oz almonds, toasted

Brush a baking sheet with oil. Place the sugar and nuts in a small, heavy-bottomed saucepan and heat slowly until the sugar melts, stirring occasionally. Continue cooking until the sugar turns from pale golden in colour to deep golden. Quickly pour the caramel on to the prepared baking sheet and leave until cold.

Crush the caramel to a fine powder with a rolling pin or pestle and mortar. Alternatively, break it up roughly and crush in a blender. Store the powder in a dry screw-topped jar for up to 3 months.

MAKES ABOUT 100 G/4 OZ

FROSTED FLOWERS AND LEAVES

Suitable flowers include freshly picked small, thin-petalled flowers such as primroses, sweet peas, violets and fruit blossom. Check that the selected flower is not poisonous if eaten. Suitable leaves include rose leaves, mint, sage and French parsley.

Prepare the flowers by gently shaking them upside down. Spread them out on absorbent kitchen paper. Leave for about 20 minutes to ensure any insects have crawled out. To prepare the leaves, gently swish through cold water. Shake dry and spread the leaves out on absorbent kitchen paper to dry. Frost at least three times as many flowers or leaves as you may require as they are very fragile.

1 egg white
caster sugar

In a bowl, lightly beat the egg white with 5 ml/1 tsp water until the egg is no longer stringy but not frothy. Using a fine paint brush, paint a thin layer of egg wash over and under the petals or leaves, being careful not to miss any part. Sprinkle them lightly all over with sugar until evenly coated. Spread the frosted flowers out on greaseproof paper or non-stick baking parchment.

Leave them to dry in an airy place away from direct sunlight until dry and hard. They can be easily removed from the paper.

Store the frosted flowers and leaves between sheets of tissue paper in a small cardboard box for up to several weeks. Check them occasionally and discard any that have crumpled.

SUGARED STRANDS

The thin coloured rind of most citrus fruits may be crystallised in thin strands to sprinkle over cakes and tarts. Lemon and orange are the fruits most frequently used.

1 orange or lemon
50 g/2 oz granulated sugar

Scrub the fruit with a small brush under running water. Using a potato peeler, shave off the peel in long, thin strips. With a small sharp knife, cut the peel into long, very fine strands. Place the strands in a small saucepan with 125 ml/4 fl oz water. Simmer for 2 minutes until the peel is tender. Remove strands with a slotted spoon and drain on absorbent kitchen paper.

Stir the sugar into the water and simmer over a low heat until melted. Increase the heat and boil rapidly, without stirring, until the syrup is reduced by half. Return the peel to the pan and cook, uncovered, until well glazed. Remove the peel with a slotted spoon and leave to cool on non-stick baking parchment. When cold, store the sugared strands in a box between leaves of waxed paper or non-stick baking parchment.

☀ **MICROWAVE TIP** The whole process may be done in the microwave using a suitable small bowl. Timings will be approximately the same but take care that the sugar does not brown too much. Check every 10 seconds once the syrup is boiling.

GRILLED TOPPINGS

These toppings are used on plain and light fruit cakes instead of icing and are spread over while the cake is still warm.

GOLDEN NUT TOPPING

50 g/2 oz butter, softened
100 g/4 oz soft light brown sugar
45 ml/3 tbsp single cream
100 g/4 oz chopped mixed nuts

Cream the butter and sugar together in a bowl, then beat in the cream and fold in the mixed nuts.

Spread the topping over the cake while it is cooling. Place the cake under a preheated low grill. Heat for 2-3 minutes until the topping is bubbling and light golden in colour. Leave the cake to cool before cutting.

SUFFICIENT TO COVER TWO 15 CM/6 INCH SQUARE CAKES

VARIATION

WALNUT TOPPING Use 100 g/4 oz chopped walnuts instead of mixed nuts.

GOLDEN COCONUT TOPPING

50 g/2 oz butter, softened
100 g/4 oz soft light brown sugar
75 g/3 oz desiccated coconut
45 ml/3 tbsp single cream

Combine the butter, sugar and coconut in a bowl and work ingredients together until well blended. Stir in the cream and spread the topping over the warm cake. Place the cake under a preheated low grill for 3-4 minutes until the topping is golden brown in colour. Leave to cool before cutting.

SUFFICIENT TO COVER TWO 15 CM/6 INCH SQUARE CAKES

VARIATION

ORANGE COCONUT TOPPING Use granulated sugar and orange juice instead of the brown sugar and cream.

> MRS BEETON'S TIP Take great care when browning coconut under the grill, either on its own or in a topping. Do not have the grill too hot and watch the topping closely as it browns quickly and it may become scorched if it is left to cook unattended.

HEALTHIER ALTERNATIVES

Whether you are counting the calories or courting healthier eating habits, you may wish to use less sugar and fat in your recipes.

Sugar not only provides sweetness but also bulk, so this should be replaced with fruit, ground nuts or low-fat cream cheese. Butter may be replaced with vegetable oil-based spreads or low-fat cream cheese. Use plenty of natural flavourings or add a few drops of liqueur, and the results will be just as tasty as when conventionally made.

APRICOT SPREAD

8 apricot halves, canned in natural juice, drained
175 g/6 oz low-fat cream cheese
few drops of lemon juice

Purée or sieve the apricots. In a bowl, cream the cheese and lemon juice together and gradually beat in the apricot purée. Alternatively, place all ingredients in a blender or a food processor and work until the mixture is light and creamy. Chill the spread before use.

SUFFICIENT TO FILL A 20 CM/8 INCH CAKE

MRS BEETON'S TIP Fresh apricots or dried apricots may be substituted for canned. Soak dried apricots overnight and simmer in soaking liquor for 5-10 minutes.

APPLE AND BLACKCURRANT SPREAD

This is a thick fruit purée which may replace jam in a recipe. Because of its low sugar content, it will not keep for more than a week.

225 g/8 oz cooking apples, peeled and chopped
175 g/6 oz blackcurrants, topped and tailed
150 ml/¼ pint unsweetened apple juice
30 ml/2 tbsp apple concentrate
grated rind and juice of 1 orange

Combine the apples, blackcurrants and apple juice in a small saucepan. Cover and cook over a low heat until the fruit is soft, stirring occasionally.

Add the apple concentrate, orange rind and juice and simmer, uncovered, until the mixture is thick and pulpy. Stir occasionally to prevent the mixture from burning on the base. The purée is ready when the base of the saucepan can be seen as the mixture is stirred. Place the purée in a clean container, cover and when cold refrigerate for up to 1 week.

SUFFICIENT FOR TWO LAYERS IN ONE 18 CM/7 INCH CAKE

CITRUS CHEESE ICING

100 g/4 oz low-fat cream cheese
75 g/3 oz icing sugar, sifted
10 ml/2 tsp finely grated lemon or orange rind
30 ml/2 tbsp lemon or orange juice

Place cheese and sugar in a bowl and blend them together. Add rind and juice and beat all the ingredients together until light.

SUFFICIENT TO FILL A 20 CM/8 INCH CAKE

BASIC FILLING AND COVERING TECHNIQUES

Before progressing to piping designs of intricate detail, master the basic techniques in this chapter. From applying the first coat of glaze to achieving a perfect finish on a flat-iced cake, all the advice you need to ensure success is included here.

As with most skills, there are several ways of achieving the desired result; this is particularly true of cake decorating. In this chapter, the basic methods of filling and covering cakes are explained, using various recipes from the previous chapter. This first process of coating or covering forms the base for any decoration, simple or elaborate. Occasionally, an alternative method is given and it is a good idea to experiment with different methods to find out which suits you best.

The quality of the cake is important in determining the finished appearance. For example, the flatter the top of the cake, the better will be the final result. Make sure that you use the correct sized cake tin for the quantity of cake mixture, as peaked cakes are usually the result of using too small a tin for the mixture. Try to avoid slicing the top off a fruit cake; if this is not possible, never invert the cut side on to a cake board as this tends to draw the moisture out of the cake.

Before you begin to decorate a cake, make sure that you have all the equipment to hand and, if possible, choose a time when you are least likely to be disturbed until you have finished. Some icings set or stiffen quickly, so they need to be used efficiently without even a short break. The cake should be placed on a plate, board or wire rack, depending on the type of icing used. Use a dry pastry brush to brush away all loose crumbs which may spoil the icing.

A turntable is useful if you are coating the side of a round cake with icing. Alternatively, stand the cake on its board on a biscuit tin or upturned cake tin to raise the height of the cake and to make it easier to rotate. All the equipment must be scrupulously clean and the work surface must also be absolutely clean, dry and free of any specks of dust if the icing or cake covering is rolled out.

FILLING AND COVERING CAKES WITH APRICOT GLAZE

Apricot glaze can be used to sandwich cake layers together or it can be applied as a decorative coating. A variety of toppings can be sprinkled on to the glaze to complete the decoration. For example, try toasted, chopped or flaked nuts, toasted or coloured desiccated coconut, grated or flaked chocolate, finely chopped glacé fruits, chocolate vermicelli or praline. Before you begin, make sure that you have the following items prepared and close by ready to be used:

Apricot Glaze (page 54)
dry pastry brush
palette knife
the prepared topping (if used)
greaseproof paper or non-stick baking parchment
a plate or board for the completed cake

If not freshly prepared, re-heat the glaze with an additional 5 ml/1 tsp of water and bring it to the boil. Then leave it to cool a little but use it while still warm. Brush any loose crumbs from the top and sides of the cake. If you are adding a topping, have it prepared and spread it in a thick layer on a piece of greaseproof paper.

TO COAT THE SIDES OF THE CAKE

Quickly brush the glaze around the sides of the cake, making sure they are evenly coated. If using topping, place one hand on the top of the cake and the other under it, then lightly roll the cake in the topping until the sides are evenly covered. Press the cake down very lightly to coat the glaze thinly in topping. If too much topping is taken up at first, then the covering will be uneven and some areas will be sticky with glaze. Place the cake on a plate or board.

TO COVER THE TOP OF THE CAKE

Lightly brush the glaze over the top of the cake and sprinkle it liberally with topping. Lay a piece of clean greaseproof paper on top and press it down lightly to ensure that the coating sticks. Remove the paper.

FILLING AND TOPPING CAKES WITH BUTTERCREAM

Have the following items prepared and at hand before you begin:

the prepared cake
large serrated knife
Buttercream (page 57)
palette knife
plate or board for the completed cake

CUTTING THE CAKE INTO LAYERS

Place the cake on a flat surface and use a large serrated knife to slice horizontally through the cake, about 5 cm/2 inches in towards the centre. Slowly rotate the cake as you cut, then continue rotating and slicing the cake until it is sliced right through into two equal layers. Lift off the top layer and place it on a flat surface, top side uppermost.

TO FILL AND TOP THE CAKE

The buttercream should be of soft spreading consistency. If it was made in advance beat it to soften the mixture, adding a few drops of milk or fruit juice if necessary. Alternatively, the buttercream may be softened by warming in the microwave for 5 seconds on Defrost. Stiff icing is difficult to spread and it will drag the surface of the cake.

Use about one-third of the buttercream to sandwich the cake layers. Using a palette knife, lightly spread the buttercream evenly over the base layer of the cake, to within 5 mm/¼ inch of the edge. Carefully position the second cake layer on top. Spread the remaining buttercream on top of the cake in the same way. Finish the cake by smoothing the buttercream with the palette knife, then marking it with a fork or serrated scraper.

TO COAT THE SIDES OF THE CAKE

If the sides of the cake are covered with buttercream, divide the quantity of buttercream into four. Use one quarter for the filling, two quarters to cover the sides of the cake and the remaining quarter for the top. Spread the buttercream around the cake. The sides can be lightly rolled in a dry topping as when filling and covering with apricot glaze (see left).

If the top of the cake is to be covered in Glacé Icing (page 59), spread the buttercream up into a small ridge around the top edge of the cake to stop the icing spilling over the side.

COATING CAKES WITH GLACÉ ICING

This simple icing is not firm enough for piping or rolling. It is poured over the cake and allowed to set before any decoration is added. Glacé icing is usually only used on the top of a cake. When it dries, it is brittle and it tends to craze, especially if you move the cake before the icing is quite dry. The consistency of the icing should be similar to thick cream that will just flow to find its own level. It must not be so thin that it runs off the cake. Do not make the icing until you are ready to use it. There are two ways of coating the top of a cake with glacé icing.

Method 1 This method is used if the sides of the cake are coated with buttercream or a glaze and topping. The sides of the cake must be decorated first, taking care to extend the covering up along the top edge to form a small, even ridge.

Make up the glacé icing and pour it in a slow, steady stream starting at the centre of the cake and working in a circular movement towards the edge. The icing should find its own level but small areas may have to be teased towards the edge using the pointed end of a knife. Leave the icing to set, undisturbed, for several hours.

Method 2 If the sides of the cake are not covered, cut out a band of double-thick non-stick baking parchment to fit round the cake and extend about 1 cm/½ inch above the top edge. Place the collar in position so that it fits the cake tightly and secure it in place with a paper clip.

Make the icing and pour it on to the top of the cake as in Method 1. When the icing is dry, use a hot, dry knife to slice between the icing and the paper collar as you peel away the paper.

COATING CAKES WITH FROSTINGS OR FUDGE ICINGS

Most frostings have to be spread quickly over the cake as soon as they have been made or they will set in the bowl. It is, therefore, important to have the cake ready to ice before you begin. As they are spread on the cake, frostings and fudge icings begin to set, so it is not possible to pipe with them. Hot water is used to heat a palette knife for spreading the icing but the knife must be dried before use. It is essential to have everything organised before you begin to make the icing, so that it can be used immediately:

cake, ready-filled if required
plate or board
dry pastry brush
small palette knife
small quantity of hot water for heating the palette knife
any decorations or toppings
ingredients for frosting or fudge icing

Place the cake on a flat plate or board. Alternatively, rest it on an upturned plate so that when the icing has set, the cake can be transferred easily to its serving plate without the icing being touched and spoilt. Brush away any loose cake crumbs. Place the palette knife in the hot water. Make the icing, following the chosen recipe, and cover the cake immediately, using either of the methods that follow. Add any decorations to the cake before the icing sets.

FOR A SOFT FINISH

Pour all the icing on top of the cake and work quickly using the *dry*, hot knife. Draw the icing over the cake and down the sides, working in small circular movements from the centre outwards. Using a clean, hot knife, swirl the icing into peaks as it begins to set.

FOR A STIFFER ICING

First cover the sides of the cake. Spread about two-thirds of the icing round the sides, using the *dry*, hot knife and working quickly in small circular movements. Draw the icing up towards the top of the cake.

Spoon the remaining icing on the top of the cake and work quickly to draw the blobs of icing together to make an even coating. Use a clean, hot knife to quickly swirl the icing into soft peaks.

COVERING CAKES WITH TRADITIONAL FONDANT

Traditional fondant may be used as a cake covering when warmed and diluted with stock syrup. When dry it gives a smooth, shiny finish. It is most frequently used to coat small, fancy cakes such as petits fours. Fruit cakes must have a base coating of marzipan or almond paste before a coating of traditional fondant is applied. On a larger cake, it is essential that the surface is uncut and level, or the icing will flow away from the centre. Turn the cake upside down if necessary. Before you start, check through the following list, making sure that everything is ready:

Traditional Fondant
basin
saucepan of hot water
wooden spoon
Stock Syrup or boiled water
food colouring, if used
the prepared cake, or cakes
wire rack
baking sheet lined with non-stick baking
  parchment
dry pastry brush
Apricot Glaze (page 54)
small palette knife
small pointed knife

PREPARING THE FONDANT

Place the fondant in the basin over the saucepan of hot water and stir it occasionally until it has melted. Dilute the fondant to the consistency of thick cream by adding a little stock syrup or water. Add a few drops of food colouring at this stage, if used.

PREPARING THE CAKE

Place the cake on a wire rack and stand it over the lined baking sheet. Brush the cake with a dry brush to remove excess crumbs. Prepare the apricot glaze and brush it lightly over the cake. A small ball of marzipan may be placed in the centre of each cake when making petits fours.

COATING WITH FONDANT

When the fondant is ready, spoon it carefully over the cake and let it run down the sides to coat the cake completely. Use the pointed end of the knife to tease small areas of icing into place, if necessary, to ensure that the cake is evenly coated. Any fondant that drips through the rack can be collected and re-used, providing it is free from crumbs and glaze. Stir the fondant occasionally to prevent a skin from forming. Leave the fondant to set, then neaten the base of the cake by trimming away excess icing.

SWIRLED FONDANT

Alternatively, the icing can be applied more thickly and swirled with a knife as it sets.

COVERING CAKES WITH ALMOND PASTE OR MARZIPAN

Fruit cakes must be covered with almond paste or marzipan before they are coated with royal icing or covered with rolled-out icings or traditional fondant. The almond paste provides a flat surface for the icing and it also prevents the fruit in the cake from discolouring the icing. The cake covered with almond paste should be left in a dry place for at least a week, and up to two weeks for a wedding cake, before the icing is added. Lay a piece of greaseproof paper loosely over the top of the cake to protect it from dust. Never put the almond-paste-coated cake in an airtight tin or the paste will go mouldy.

For a professional finish, the surface must be as flat as possible. Even the flattest cake will need a little building up at the edge but if the cake is too domed, the almond paste will have to be very thick to compensate. When working, it is important to keep all crumbs away from the almond paste. Any that find their way on to the surface of the paste may discolour the icing. Assemble all the equipment and ingredients before you begin to work with the almond paste, and make sure that the work surface is scrupulously clean and dry. You will need:

the prepared cake or cakes
non-stick baking parchment
scissors
cake board
dry pastry brush
Apricot Glaze (page 54) or pure alcohol
Almond Paste (page 56) or Marzipan (page 56)
sifted icing sugar for dusting surface
rolling pin
sharp knife
small palette knife
string
small spirit level (optional)
spacers (optional)

TO COVER THE TOP OF THE CAKE

There are two methods that can be used for covering the top of the cake with almond paste or marzipan. Method 2 is suitable for small and medium-sized cakes, but you may find method 1 easier when covering larger cakes, for example, the bottom tier of a large wedding cake.

Method 1 Cut a piece of parchment to fit the top of the cake exactly. To do this either measure the cake accurately or stand the cake on a piece of parchment and draw round it, then transfer the pattern to a clean

Method 1

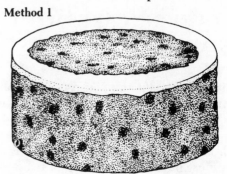

1 Press small rolls of paste around the edge of the cake to ensure the top is level.

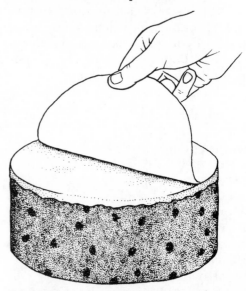

2 Invert the paper pattern and the paste on top of the cake, press lightly, then peel away the paper.

piece of parchment. Remember that if you draw round the tin in which the cake was cooked, you will need to cut slightly within the line to compensate for the thickness of the tin. Lightly dust the paper pattern with icing sugar.

Place the cake in the centre of the cake board and brush away all loose crumbs. Lightly glaze the top of the cake, around the outer edge only, with apricot glaze or alcohol.

Knead small pieces of almond paste and shape them into thin sausages. Place these all round the top outer edge of the cake. Holding the side firmly, with one hand extended to the height of the cake, press and mould the paste towards the centre of the cake to level the top. Lay a sheet of parchment on the top of the cake and roll it lightly with a rolling pin (do not use the paper pattern for this). Remove the parchment and brush the top of the cake with more glaze or alcohol.

Knead one-third of the remaining almond paste lightly into a ball and press it out on the centre of the paper pattern. Lightly dust the rolling pin with icing sugar and roll out the almond paste evenly, rotating the paper until the paste is even in thickness and the same size as the paper. If you have spacers, then use them to make sure that the paste is rolled out evenly. Trim the edges if necessary.

Lift up the paper pattern and the paste, then invert the paste on to the cake, positioning it carefully. Lightly press to stick the almond paste, then peel off the paper.

Method 2 Lightly dust the work surface with icing sugar and brush the top of the cake with apricot glaze or alcohol.

Lightly knead about one third of the paste and roll it out evenly, using spacers if available, to 2.5 cm/1 inch larger than the top of the cake. Invert the cake, glazed side downwards, on to the paste.

Using the palette knife, carefully work round the edge of the cake, pushing and easing the paste under the cake to fill the

Method 2

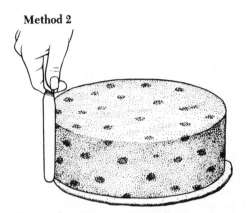

Invert the cake on to the paste, then use a palette knife to ease the edges of the paste around the cake to make a level top.

gap. This ensures that the paste will be level.

Trim off any excess paste where necessary, then carefully turn the cake over, making sure that the almond paste is not left behind on the work surface. Centre the cake, paste-side uppermost, on the cake board.

TO COVER THE SIDES OF THE CAKE

Two alternative methods are given and they can be used with either almond paste or marzipan for all shapes of cake. Method 1 is the best to use for very large cakes.

Method 1 Measure the height of the cake accurately with a piece of string. Measure the circumference with string and add on 1 cm/ ½ inch to compensate for the thickness of the almond paste. From a sheet of parchment, cut a paper pattern that measures twice the height and half the circumference of the cake. Lightly dust the pattern with icing sugar. Brush the sides of the cake to remove all crumbs.

Lightly knead the remaining almond paste and shape it into a flat sausage the same length as the pattern. Place the paste down the middle of the paper pattern. Flatten the roll, then roll it out evenly across the width to fit the pattern exactly. Trim the edges, if necessary. With the sharp knife, cut the strip of paste in half along its length to make two equal strips, then following the same cutting line made by the knife, cut the paper in half with scissors.

Small Round Cakes Brush the side of the cake with apricot glaze or alcohol. Hold the top and bottom of the cake between the palms of your hands and position the side of the cake carefully on one piece of paste, then roll the cake along its length. Repeat with the second piece. Place the cake in the middle of the cake board, carefully peel off the paper and smooth the joins with a palette knife.

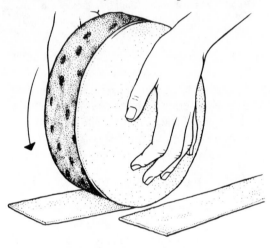

Large Round Cakes Position the cake in the middle of the cake board and brush apricot glaze or alcohol around the side. Lift up one strip of paste on the paper and place it in position around the cake. Repeat with the second piece. Carefully remove the paper and smooth the joins. Smooth around the cake with your hands to press the almond paste securely on to the cake.

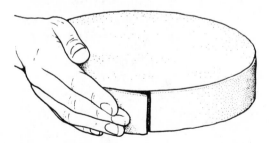

Square Cakes Attach the almond paste to a square cake as for the large round cake. It is easier if you to avoid having the joins on the corners. Mould the corners neatly once the paste is in position and when the joins have been smoothed. For very large square cakes, divide each length of paste into two for easier handling.

Method 2 Position the cake in the centre of the board. Measure the height and circumference of the cake, then lightly brush the cake with apricot glaze or alcohol.

Dust the work surface with icing sugar, then lightly knead the remaining almond paste and roll it into a long, plump sausage. Flatten the paste and roll it into a strip that measures the same height as the cake, and the same length as the circumference of the cake. Trim the edges of the paste and roll it up loosely. Place one end of the roll on the cake and unroll the paste, pressing it firmly on to the side of the cake. Smooth the join together with a palette knife.

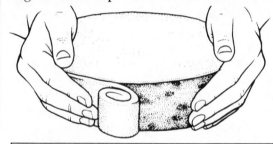

> 🥣 **MRS BEETON'S TIP** It is worth spending time on covering the cake smoothly with almond paste as it is difficult to compensate for unevenness when coating with icing. Check the level of your work surface with a spirit level before you begin – you may be surprised how much a surface can slope. Check the level of the cake when the top has been covered with paste and smooth out any uneven areas with a rolling pin, if necessary. There is no need to stick a fruit cake on to the cake board as the weight of mixture and finished icing will be sufficient to keep it in place.

COVERING CAKES WITH SUGAR PASTE AND MOULDING ICINGS

Rolled out icing can be applied directly on to a light cake. Fruit cakes should be covered with a layer of almond paste before the icing is placed on top, otherwise the icing will quickly discolour. If you dislike almond paste, try placing two layers of sugar paste over the cake, allowing the first layer to dry well before adding the second. This is not suitable for a wedding cake or any cake that is intended to be kept but for most other occasions you might get away with it.

Make sure that all your equipment is clean and free from grease. It is also a good idea to wear a large, clean apron, as small flecks of fluff from your clothing can easily fall on to the icing. Scrub the work surface and dry it thoroughly. Remove any rings from your fingers, as these would mark the icing when smoothing the surface on the cake. If you have long fingernails, take care not to mark the icing with them as you work. Impressions on the icing are difficult to eradicate.

Do not use cornflour for rolling out sugar paste that is to be placed directly on the cake as the starch will ferment. Use finely sifted icing sugar to lightly dust the work surface and the rolling pin. Cornflour can be used on the icing which is not directly in contact with a moist cake, for example to buff the top surface, for moulding flowers or making other decorations. Knead the paste lightly, using just the fingertips and use only a fine dusting of sugar. If you knead the paste too vigorously air pockets will be trapped and the surface will be uneven.

Choose a cool time of day to work and avoid using artificial light. Hairline cracks may not be seen until the morning when it will be too late to remove them. Similarly, colouring should be added to the paste in daylight. Remember, colours dry a shade or two darker.

TO COLOUR SUGAR PASTE

Remove a piece of paste about the size of a large walnut from the weighed-out quantity. Add a little paste colour to this small ball of icing and knead it in well. The ball will probably be several shades darker than required. Break off small pieces of the coloured paste and knead them lightly but thoroughly into the white paste, adding extra pieces of colour as required.

If you are matching the colour of the icing to a fabric or similar, break off a small piece, press it out thinly and leave it to dry for a few hours before checking the colour. Carefully wrap the remaining pieces of paste separately until required. When the required depth of colour has been obtained, break off a small piece and wrap it up well, keeping it, and any of the remaining deeply coloured ball, in case extra icing has to be coloured.

WORKING WITH SUGAR PASTE

Assemble all the ingredients and utensils before you begin to work on the cake:

cake, on a cake board
dry pastry brush
Apricot Glaze (page 54), alcohol or Butter-
    cream (page 57)
sifted icing sugar
rolling pin
spacers (optional)
knife
cornflour for buffing the icing

Measure the surface of the cake to be covered, including the depth of the side. Brush away all loose crumbs from the cake. If the cake is covered in almond paste, lightly coat it with apricot glaze or alcohol. Spread a thin layer of buttercream over a sponge or similar cake which is not covered in almond paste. Clean the board.

Lightly dust the work surface with icing sugar, then lightly knead the paste with the fingertips until it is smooth. Shape the ball of paste into the final shape required; for example shape a ball for a round cake, a box for a square cake or a sausage shape for a long thin strip of cake.

Lightly dust the rolling pin with icing sugar and roll out the paste evenly, using spacers, if available. The rolled out paste should be no thicker than 5 mm/¼ inch and it should be about 2.5 cm/1 inch shorter than required, as the icing will stretch and drop when it is hung over the edge of a cake. For example, if the cake to be covered is 20 cm/8 inches in diameter and 5 cm/2 inches deep, the paste should be rolled to a diameter of 28 cm/11 inches.

TO COVER A ROUND CAKE

Carefully slide the rolling pin under the paste, lift it up and position it accurately over the cake. With clean, dry hands, lightly dusted in cornflour, work the icing with the palm of your hand in a circular movement from the centre of the cake towards the edge. The icing will drop down the side and should

be lightly pressed and smoothed around the cake. Always work in a light, circular movement and avoid marking the icing with your fingernails. Trim the paste at the base of the cake, if necessary. You will probably find that you need to wash your hands again at this stage. Ensure they are well dried, dust them very lightly with cornflour and quickly but lightly buff up the surface of the cake with the palm of one hand. Using both hands, one either side of the cake, buff up the side with small circular movements, rotating the cake as necessary.

TO MAKE A SHARPER TOP EDGE FOR PIPING

Do this before the final buffing. Using both hands, one to extend the icing on the side of the cake upwards slightly and the other to smooth the paste on the top of the cake, mould a sharp edge. This step is only necessary if you intend adding a piped edge around the cake.

TO COVER A SQUARE CAKE

Follow the instructions for covering a round cake but pay attention to the corners immediately you have laid the rolled out icing over the cake. Lift the icing and work it away from the corner, not towards it. Gently ease the paste back along the sides of the cake until it is smooth. You must do this at once, otherwise thick pleats form on the corners of the cake. Continue smoothing the icing as for the round cake, trimming the edges neatly and moulding sharp edges and corners.

Leave the cake to dry out at room temperature for at least 24 hours before adding any decoration, longer if possible. Cover the top with a piece of greaseproof paper when the surface is dry to protect it from dust.

COATING CAKES WITH ROYAL ICING

This icing sets harder than any other icing and it is traditionally used for wedding cakes because it can support the weight of the tiers. Glycerine should not be added when the icing is used for tiered cakes because it softens the icing. Royal icing made with albumen or albumen substitutes tends to set harder than icing made with fresh egg white. Royal icing gives sharper edges and corners than the moulding icing or softer icings. This is better for piping a border or for adding an edging as decoration.

Royal icing can only be applied to firm cakes that are covered with almond paste or marzipan and have a firm, flat surface on which to apply icing. Make sure the almond paste or marzipan is completely dry before applying the icing. When working on a single cake, or one layer or a tiered-cake allow a minimum of 3 days to ice the cakes plus one week for the icing to dry. Allow 2 weeks or more for the icing on a tiered cake to dry.

WORKING WITH ROYAL ICING

For a good finish, three coats of royal icing should be applied; the final coat gives no thickness but makes a smooth, fine surface. Make up the full quantity of icing for all the cakes to be covered and mix the icing to a soft-peak consistency. Leave the icing to stand, covered, for 3-4 hours to dispel air bubbles.

After applying the first coat, carefully scrape the remaining icing into a clean bowl taking care that no particles of dried icing from the sides of the bowl are included. Cover the icing with a damp cloth and wrap the whole bowl in a polythene bag. The next day the icing will be a little slacker; give it a quick beat before applying it to the cake. Store the icing as before. Again, the icing will be slightly slacker for the next application.

Do not thicken the icing to the original consistency as thinner coats give a smoother finish.

It is important not to allow even one dried particle of icing to mix with the soft icing as this, when dragged across the cake, will leave a trail. If you do have particles of dried icing in the soft icing, then press it through a very fine, clean, nylon sieve. Keep the icing covered at all times with a clean, damp cloth.

Before starting, check that the work surface is level. When icing the top of the cake, the correct height is one at which you can stand with your arm bent at the elbow and your lower arm parallel to the cake.

Stand with your feet slightly apart, with one foot in front of the other. When you begin levelling the cake, start with the pressure on your front foot and gradually transfer this to the other foot as you draw the ruler across the top of the cake towards you. You will find that this enables you to complete the action with even pressure, and in one continuous movement.

Practise this position before you begin to ice the cake. Wear a large, clean apron as small flecks of fluff, hairs or specks of dust easily find their way from clothes on to the icing. If possible, ice the cake in daylight and choose a time when you are unlikely to be disturbed. Stand the cake board on a damp cloth or rubber mat to prevent it from slipping. Assemble all the equipment and ingredients that you will need before you begin to ice the cake:

marzipanned cake on board
Royal Icing (page 61), mixed to soft-peak consistency
large palette knife
small palette knife
clean damp cloth
ruler
scraper
small sharp knife (not serrated)
turntable (for a round cake)
glass-headed stainless steel pin

TO FLAT ICE THE TOP OF A ROUND OR SQUARE CAKE

Lightly beat the icing and place about half in the centre of the cake. Using the large palette knife, work the icing backwards and forwards, spreading it across the cake to cover the almond paste or marzipan. Pay particular attention to the edges and corners. Use the palette knife flat on the cake and press quite hard to break any air bubbles in the icing as you work. There is no need to use a hot knife unless your icing is too stiff. Never use a wet knife as the water will make the icing brittle.

Hold the ruler with both hands and position it at the back of the cake at an angle of 45 degrees. Ensure that the ruler is parallel to the cake at both ends. Position your feet correctly and with a firm, quick movement, draw the ruler across the cake towards you. Lift the ruler off sharply and

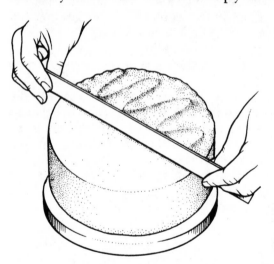

scrape the excess icing into the bowl; then cover the bowl of icing again.

If necessary, give the cake a quarter turn and repeat the process with a clean ruler. Using the sharp knife, scrape away the excess icing from the edge of the cake to give a clean sharp edge; discard this trimmed icing – do not return it to the bowl. Use a pin to prick any air bubbles that are visible on the

surface of the icing. Leave the cake to dry for 4–5 hours or more before icing the sides.

> 🥣 **MRS BEETON'S TIP** Be confident and quick with the ruler. A slow, hesitant movement will result in a ridged effect in the icing.

TO ICE THE SIDE OF THE CAKE

Round Cake Place the cake on the turntable positioning it on a damp cloth, if necessary, to ensure that the board does not slip. Using the small palette knife, spread the icing evenly around the cake, making sure that you draw it up to the top edge. Position your left hand as far round the back of the turntable as possible so that it can be fully turned in one movement. Hold the scraper in the right hand parallel to the side of the cake and at an angle of 45 degrees. Rotate the turntable at an even speed, keeping regular pressure on the scraper until just before you reach the point at which you started, when you should slightly ease the pressure, then sharply pull away the scraper. Make sure that you move the turntable, not the scraper. Repeat a second time, if necessary, with a clean scraper, then trim off excess icing at the top edge, holding the blade parallel to the top of

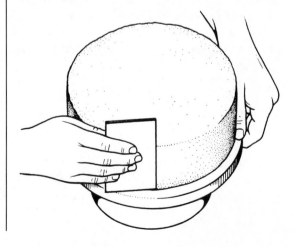

the cake. Using a pin, immediately prick any air bubbles that appear in the icing.

Square Cake Ice two opposite sides at a time, leaving them to dry for 4-6 hours before icing the remaining two sides.

Spread the icing on the side, paying particular attention to the top edge and corners. Hold the scraper parallel to the cake at an angle of 45 degrees and start at the back

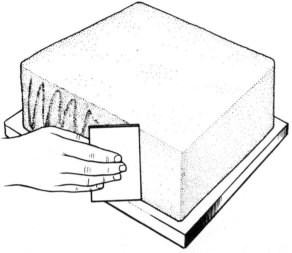

of the cake, drawing the scraper with a firm, even pressure towards you. Repeat a second time, if necessary, with a clean scraper, then scrape off the excess icing on the top edge and at the corners. Repeat this process on the opposite side.

SECOND OR THIRD COATS

Leave the first layer of icing to dry for 24 hours in a dry, cool place before adding a second layer. The same techniques should be used for each application of icing.

MRS BEETON'S TIP Royal icing will not dry in a damp atmosphere. If the room is too hot, the almond paste or marzipan may sweat and discolour the icing.

TIPS FOR SUCCESS WITH ROYAL ICING

■ Make sure that all equipment is spotlessly clean before you begin as any tiny particles of dust or dirt will spoil the icing.

■ Always thoroughly sift the icing sugar before making the icing.

■ Make sure that the icing is well beaten and free of lumps before applying it to the cake.

■ Check the consistency of the icing before use, making sure that it is neither too soft or too stiff for spreading or piping.

■ Keep the icing sealed in an airtight container to prevent it drying out when it is not being used.

■ Avoid getting any particles of dry icing into the container of soft icing.

■ Leave layers of icing to dry thoroughly before adding another coating to the cake.

SIMPLE CAKE DECORATING TECHNIQUES

Presentation is always important when serving food, sweet or savoury, to give pleasure as well as to whet the appetite. In this chapter you will find lots of clever ideas and simple designs for decorated cakes. They are all fairly quick to complete and they do not demand years of experience or highly developed skills to ensure success. The finished decorations are all attractive and tasteful – ideal for anyone who is in the early stages of learning the fulfilling craft of cake decorating.

DECORATING CAKES WITH APRICOT GLAZE OR JAM

Apricot Glaze (page 54) or warmed and sieved jam can be used as a base for adding finishing touches to light sponge cakes. There are a few quick and easy ideas.

DOILY DESIGN

Coat the sides of the cake in glaze and roll in chopped nuts, desiccated or long-thread coconut, or grated chocolate. Lay a paper doily on top of the cake (or fold a circle of paper and cut out a series of shapes to make your own pattern). Place a little icing sugar in a small sieve and gently sift it over the doily on the cake, moving the sieve all over the cake to make an even layer of sugar. Using both hands, carefully lift the doily straight upwards off the cake.

ALMOND PASTE AND APRICOT GLAZE DECORATION

Roll out a piece of almond paste to fit around the sides of the cake (page 76). Brush the sides of the cake with apricot glaze and press the almond paste into position. Cut a circle of paper to fit the top of the cake, fold it in half and roll out a piece of almond paste to fit the semi-circle, then cut the paste into four equal wedges.

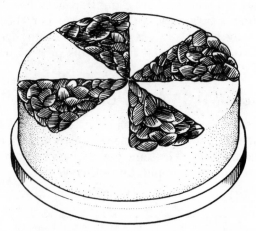

Spread the top of the cake with glaze and place the wedges of almond paste on top leaving alternate gaps of glaze. Sprinkle the wedges of glaze with toasted flaked almonds if you like.

DECORATING WITH PIPED BUTTERCREAM OR WHIPPED CREAM

Keep your hands as cool as possible when piping with buttercream or whipped fresh cream. Warm hands holding the piping bag can cause the cream to melt or become runny because of the butterfat content. Keep the kitchen cool and only fill the icing or piping bag one third full; start again with a fresh bag if the icing or cream does begin to melt. Chill the icing and cream before you start; alternatively, spoon the cream or icing into the icing bag and put the bag in the refrigerator for 10 minutes before using it.

If you want to cover a large area, for example, when decorating novelty cakes, use a large piping bag fitted with a savoy star nozzle. Avoid using a nylon bag, if possible, as these tend to make the icing or cream sweat. Do not hold the bag in the palms of your hands but squeeze it from the top. If you do need to support the bag, use only the fingers of your other hand and place them near the nozzle. If you are piping over a small area of the cake, for example around the base or the sides, use a double thickness paper icing bag with a large nozzle.

Because buttercream and whipped cream are soft, the amount of pressure used will determine the size of the decoration. Use only light pressure, otherwise the stars will be too thick and you may run out of icing or cream before you have finished. It is best to have extra buttercream or whipped cream. If you are piping small areas have about one third more than you need; allow two thirds extra when piping over large areas of cake.

DECORATING WITH BUTTERCREAM

Unless otherwise stated, these designs may be used on any shape of cake.

FORK PATTERNS

Spread the sides of the cake with buttercream and roll them in chopped nuts, desiccated coconut or grated chocolate. Cover the top of the cake with buttercream; use a palette knife to smooth it over, then use a fork to mark a decorative pattern.

STRIPED-TOP CAKE

Roll out almond paste to fit the sides of the cake (page 76). Brush the sides with glaze (page 70) and press on the almond paste. Spread the top of the cake thinly with buttercream. Divide the remaining buttercream in half, colour each portion differently with food colouring and place them in separate icing bags fitted with star nozzles. Pipe lines of one colour across the top of the cake, leaving room for another line of icing

between each row. Pipe lines of the contrasting colour between the first rows of piping.

SCRAPER DESIGN

Cover the top of the cake with buttercream; smooth it over. Spread buttercream around the sides of the cake. Mark a comb pattern

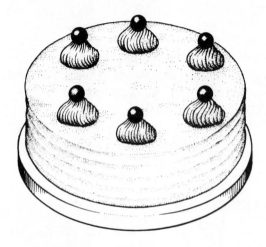

round the side, using the serrated edge of a scraper. Hold the scraper at an angle of 45 degrees and rotate the cake. If you have not got a turntable place the cake on a small biscuit tin or similar so that it is easier to rotate the cake. Use a fork or scalded, new hair comb if you do not have a scraper.

Put the remaining buttercream in a large icing bag fitted with a savoy star nozzle and pipe six or eight large swirls on the top of the cake. Alternatively, use two teaspoons to shape neat blobs of buttercream on the cake. Top each swirl with a nut, a piece of glacé cherry or a small sweet.

MUSHROOM CAKE

This is a clever idea for a round cake. Roll out a strip of almond paste to fit the side of the cake plus 1 cm/½ inch wider (page 76). Spread chocolate or pink buttercream thickly over the top of the cake and thinly around the side. Using a fork, mark the icing on the top of the cake from the edge, towards the

centre to represent the 'gills' of a mushroom. Press the almond paste on to the side of the cake and fold the top edge neatly, and loosely, down over the buttercream. Mould a small piece of almond paste to represent a stalk and dip the end in drinking chocolate powder. Position the stalk, brown end uppermost, in the centre of the cake.

For a child's birthday cake, cut out small

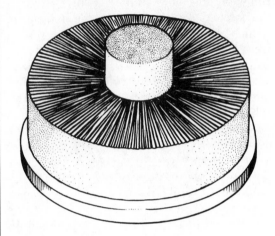

circles of red almond paste and stick them on to the side with a little jam or buttercream.

This design also works well with small cakes (page 126).

TWO-COLOUR STAR CAKE

Spread the side of a round cake thinly with buttercream and roll it in grated chocolate or chocolate vermicelli. Spread the top of the cake thinly with buttercream.

Divide the remaining buttercream between two basins and colour them as you wish; for example add melted chocolate or brown colouring to one portion and yellow to the second, or colour one portion pink and the second portion green. Place one portion in an icing bag fitted with a large star nozzle and pipe a circle of stars in the centre of the

cake. Pipe two rows of stars in the same colour round the edge of the cake. Put the second portion of buttercream in a clean bag fitted with the same size nozzle. Pipe stars to fill in the top of the cake and pipe a row of stars round the lower edge of the cake. This simple decoration can be adapted to suit a square cake by piping a square of stars in the centre, then piping the edge and filling in.

PIPED STAR DESIGN

Another idea for decorating a round cake. Spread buttercream thinly over the surface and use a palette knife to smooth it over.

Spread the sides with buttercream and draw a fork from the base upwards all round to mark a pattern in the cream on the side.

Place the remaining cream in a bag fitted with a large star nozzle and gently pipe small stars on the top of the cake to divide it into six or eight segments. Pipe a row of stars around the edge of the cake. If you like, sprinkle different, small decorations into each segment, for example hundreds and thousands, chocolate vermicelli, sprinkles or chopped nuts.

SIMPLE BIRTHDAY CAKE

Spread buttercream evenly over the top and sides of the cake and use a fork or the serrated edge of a scraper to mark a vertical pattern up the sides. Clean the scraper or fork and mark a pattern across the top of the cake. Place the remaining buttercream in a bag fitted with a large star nozzle and pipe stars around the top and bottom edges of the

cake. Place buttercream in a contrasting colour, in an icing bag fitted with a plain nozzle and write 'Happy Birthday' on top of the cake. Alternatively, bought decorations can be put on top of the cake instead of writing.

SIMPLE DESIGNS USING WHIPPED CREAM

Whipped fresh cream can be used in the same way as buttercream but take care not to over-handle the piping bag and always work in a cool place. Unless otherwise stated, these designs may be used on any shape of cake.

CHOCOLATE SCROLL CAKE

Spread cream thinly over the top of the cake and thickly around the side. Comb the side using a scraper with a serrated edge held at an angle of 45 degrees to the cake. Rotate the cake, either using a turntable or by placing the cake on a small cake tin which makes it easier to turn. Use a fork if you do not have a scraper. Cover the top of the cake with a generous pile of chocolate scrolls (page 100).

SKEWER PATTERN

Spread cream over the top and sides of the cake and use a palette knife to smooth the top as neatly as possible. Spread cocoa powder or instant coffee powder over a piece of paper and lay a long, plain metal skewer in it. Press the skewer across the cake to mark diagonals. Wash, dry and re-dip the skewer as necessary. Press chocolate curls (page 100) or chocolate finger biscuits around the side of the cake. An excellent design for square cakes.

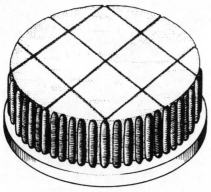

GLACÉ FRUITS AND CREAM

Spread the top of the cake thinly with cream. Spread cream thickly on the sides and use a fork or serrated scraper to mark a vertical

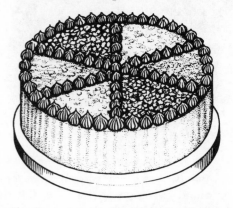

pattern in the cream. Pipe small stars of cream around the top edge and across the cake to divide it into six equal segments. Fill each segment with mixed finely chopped glacé fruits. This design works best on a round cake, but a square cake could be divided into blocks and filled in the same way.

CHOCOLATE ALMOND CAKE

Spread cream around the sides of the cake and roll it in toasted flaked almonds. Spread

cream over the top of the cake and use a palette knife to smooth it over. Drizzle melted chocolate over the top (page 98).

SIMPLE DECORATIONS USING GLACÉ ICING

FEATHER ICING

This is an attractive technique using coloured glacé icing. The colours and basic design can be varied but first follow the instructions for the basic method. Remember that the icing and decoration must be completed before the icing sets. Melted chocolate can be used instead of an icing in a contrasting colour (page 97).

Make the icing and brush any crumbs off the cake. Place 30 ml/2 tbsp of the icing in a small basin and add a few drops of food colouring to contrast with the main colour. Place the coloured icing in a paper icing bag. You do not need a nozzle.

Feather Icing

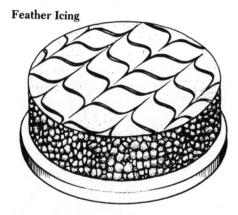

Fan Feather Icing

Use the main batch of icing to cover the top of the cake (page 72). Snip a small corner off the icing bag and immediately pipe lines of coloured icing across the cake about 1 cm/½ inch apart. Using a skewer or the point of a knife, draw lines across the piped colour icing at 1 cm/½ inch intervals. Draw the skewer alternately in opposite directions. The coloured icing will sink into the main icing and it will drag into an attractive pattern as the skewer is drawn through it, creating the feathered effect.

Circular Feather Icing

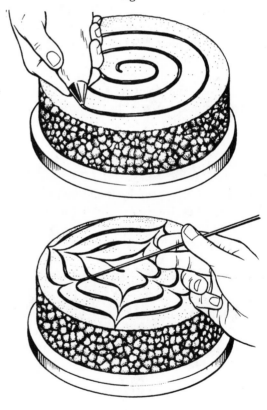

CIRCULAR FEATHER ICING

Instead of piping lines across a round cake, pipe circles at even distances out from the centre. Alternatively the circles can be piped to radiate out from one side like a fan (this works well on square cakes). Drag the icing with the skewer to create the feather effect.

SIMPLE DECORATIONS USING FONDANT

Traditional fondant thinned with stock syrup is too soft to use for elaborate piping or for swirling but it may be used as a pouring icing and can also be drizzled thinly over cakes for simple decorative effect. When decorating large cakes, the fondant should be poured over the top after the sides have been coated in another covering, for example apricot glaze and chopped nuts. Coat the sides of the cake in the chosen glaze and topping. Pour most of the fondant over the top of the cake and keep the extra warm. When the fondant on the cake is almost set, add a few drops of colouring to the warm fondant and place 30 ml/2 tbsp of it in a small, paper icing bag. Snip off just the point to make a very small hole and quickly drizzle the coloured fondant backwards and forwards across the top of the cake.

FEATHERED FONDANT

A feathered effect can be made by piping on the icing when the base coat is still wet and following the instructions for feathering glacé icing (page 87).

PLAIN FONDANT TOPPING

Coat the sides of the cake with a strip of almond paste (page 76) and pour fondant over the top of the cake. When the fondant has set, pipe small stars of whipped cream or buttercream around the edge.

FONDANT-COATED CAKE

Cover the top and sides of the cake in fondant (page 73). Piped chocolate motifs (page 98) can be added as simple decoration around the top of the cake. For a birthday cake use numerals denoting the age of the person as the shape for the chocolate motifs.

DECORATING CAKES WITH ALMOND PASTE OR MARZIPAN

Either almond paste or marzipan may be used as the main ingredient for cake decorations. Paste or marzipan may be coloured or moulded. Unless otherwise stated, the designs that follow may be used on any shape of cake.

TO COLOUR ALMOND PASTE OR MARZIPAN

Use a paste food colouring to avoid making the mixture sticky. Lightly knead the colour into the almond paste or marzipan on a work surface dusted with icing sugar. Take care not to overhandle it or it will become oily.

PLAITED-BASE CAKE

Cover the top and sides of the cake with almond paste or marzipan (page 74). Use a modelling tool or fork to press a design around the top edge of the cake. Place a plait of almond paste or marzipan around the base

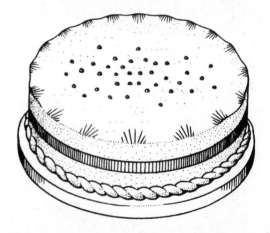

of the cake (see sugar paste ropes, twists and plaits, page 90). Sprinkle coloured sugar balls over the top of the cake and gently press them into the paste with a palette knife.

RIBBON WEAVE DESIGN

Cover the sides of the cake with roughly chopped nuts or toasted flaked almonds. Brush the top of the cake generously with apricot glaze.

Roll out almond paste or marzipan thickly and cut it into 1 cm/½ inch wide strips. Arrange two strips in a cross shape on top of the cake. Lay two more strips on the cake, one above and one below the first strip, leaving about 1 cm/½ inch between the strips.

Place two strips in the opposite direction, interweaving them with the previous two strips. Continue adding strips of paste, interweaving them until the surface of the

cake is completely covered. Trim the ends of the strips all round the edge of the cake. A colourful design can be achieved by using different coloured strips.

CRYSTAL FRUIT TOPPING

Roll out a strip of almond paste or marzipan to fit the sides of the cake. Use a modelling tool, fork or potato peeler to press out a pattern evenly over the paste. Brush the sides of the cake with apricot glaze and place the strip of almond paste in position.

Brush the top of the cake with apricot glaze, then cover it with a mixture of roughly chopped coloured glacé fruits, such as

yellow, green and red cherries, mixed peel and crystallised ginger. Roll small balls of almond paste or marzipan and place them around the top edge of the cake.

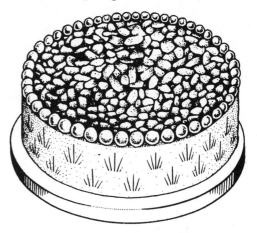

POINSETTIA CAKE

Cover the top and sides of the cake with almond paste or marzipan coloured pale green. Using red-coloured almond paste or marzipan, cut out small oval petal shapes for the sides and larger ones for the top of the cake. Use a little apricot glaze to stick the

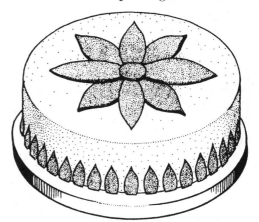

small petals in a border round the base of the cake. Overlap the large petals on the top to form a flower, again keeping them in place with a little apricot glaze. Cut a tiny circle of red almond paste to neaten the centre of the flower and place it in position.

SIMPLE DECORATIONS USING SUGAR PASTE

This is a wonderfully versatile icing which can be used to smooth-ice a cake or it can be moulded into simple decorations such as ropes, figures, plaques and flowers. It is also an invaluable ingredient for making novelty cakes. Here are some simple ideas; more complicated moulding techniques are explained later.

COVERING THE CAKE BOARD

Although cake boards are attractive, sometimes the soft line of a cake covered with sugar paste is enhanced if the icing extends to the edge of the board. The board can be covered in one operation when covering the cake but it is easier and neater to apply the icing to the board separately. The sugar paste should be rolled out and smoothed with a little cornflour. The measurements given are for a board which is 5 cm/2 inches larger than the cake. When the icing is completely dry, neaten the board by placing a strip of board edging or ribbon around it.

TO COVER A ROUND BOARD

Measure the circumference of the cake with string and divide the result by two if the cake is a small one, or by three or four if the cake is large. Centre the cake on the board.

Roll out pieces of sugar paste to the required lengths and make them 3 cm/1¼ inches wide. Place one strip on the cake board, butting one edge neatly up to the base of the cake. Gently ease the paste around the curve. Repeat with the remaining strip or strips, butting the joins together neatly, then smoothing them out with a palette knife. Trim off the excess paste at the edge of the board.

TO COVER A SQUARE BOARD

Place the square cake on the board. Roll out a strip of paste 3 cm/1¼ inches wide and the same length as one side of the board. Place the strip on the board, butting one edge neatly against the cake. Repeat with the remaining sides, loosely overlapping the paste at the corners.

Using a sharp knife, cut firmly and neatly diagonally from each corner of the cake to the corner of the board. Remove excess paste by gently lifting up the corners. Smooth the join with a palette knife or make it a feature by piping small stars or dots along it. Trim off excess paste at the edges of the board.

ROPES, TWISTS AND PLAITS

These are quick, simple edges which can be used to neaten the base of any cake; regardless of shape. They can be applied at the same time as covering the cake or later, when the paste has dried, in which case a little alcohol or cooled boiled water should be used to stick the edging to the cake.

Rope Measure the circumference of the cake and divide the total into two or four depending on the size of the cake. Small cakes can be edged with one piece of paste.

Lightly dust the work surface and your hands with cornflour and mould about 25 g/1 oz of sugar paste into a fat sausage. Place both hands over the middle of the roll, with your index fingers side by side. Using the pressure from the base of the fingers, especially the index fingers, begin rolling the paste backwards and forwards and at the same time gradually move your hands away from each other until a long, evenly thick rope is formed. The rope should be at least the required length plus 5 cm/2 inches and about 5 mm/¼ inch thick.

Twist Roll two ropes and loosely twist them together.

Twist

Plait

Plait Roll three ropes slightly thinner than 5 mm/¼ inch and loosely plait them together.

TO FIX THE EDGE ON TO THE CAKE

Lay the piece of rope around the base of the cake, taking care not to stretch it. Press it lightly on to the cake, brushing it first as you work with a little alcohol or boiled water, if necessary. Leave 2.5 cm/1 inch loose at each end. Fix any remaining pieces in place. Join the ropes by loosely twisting them together in a decorative manner; loose ends can be draped on the board or trimmed.

COLOURED EDGES

Colour the rope a contrasting colour to the main sugar paste. The twists and plaits can be made in two or more different colours.

> **MRS BEETON'S TIP** Before fixing the ropes on to the cake, decide which is be the front so that the joins can be positioned either at the side or at the back and front.

CUT OUT SHAPES

Cut out sugar paste shapes are a simple and effective means of decorating cakes coated in sugar paste. They stick well on both dried and freshly rolled paste.

Colour the sugar paste as required and use the reverse side of a laminex board as a surface for rolling, if possible. Alternatively, dust a clean, dry, smooth work surface with a little cornflour. Use a small, clean, smooth rolling pin.

Using cutters Roll out the paste evenly to about the same thickness as short crust pastry. Stamp out shapes sharply and peel away excess paste. Slide a palette knife under the paste shape and lift it on to its position on the cake. With fingertips lightly dusted with cornflour, smooth the shape on to the cake using a small, circular movement.

Using a template Draw the required shape and cut it out in thin, white card. Roll out the sugar paste and lightly dust the surface with cornflour. Lay the template on the paste and cut around it with a small pointed knife. Take care not to press too heavily on the template or it may stick to the icing. Remove the template and peel away the excess paste. Lift the shape and smooth it on to the cake as above.

USING MODELLING TOOLS

Modelling tools, available from cake decorating suppliers, can only be used on sugar paste or similar icings when still soft, so mark the pattern in the icing as soon as you have covered the cake smoothly. A variety of tools are available to create different designs. Simply press the selected tool firmly into the sugar paste, then draw it up sharply to make a neat indentation. If the tool tends to stick to the icing, lightly dust it with cornflour.

Specialist marking tools are not essential for creating patterns. With a little imagination forks, vegetable peelers, spoon handles, pointed knives and other similar objects may also be used to create attractive patterns.

PATTERNS MADE WITH CRIMPERS

Crimpers are used to press designs around the edge of the soft paste. Several different designs are available. You do need to practise the technique on a thick piece of sugar paste if you are a novice at this type of decorating. Mistakes made directly on the cake are difficult to erase. If you do make a mistake, smooth over the icing with your fingertips, working in a circular movement.

To regulate the space between the crimpers, place an elastic band about 2.5 cm/1 inch from the open end so that the ends are fixed about 5 mm/¼ inch apart. Dip the ends of the crimpers in icing sugar or cornflour during use to prevent them sticking to the paste. Before starting, use a pin to prick a line around the cake to ensure that you mark the pattern in a straight line.

Press the crimpers into the icing, then gently pinch them together until the paste between the crimpers is 3 mm/⅛ inch thick. Re-open the crimpers to the fixed gap of 5 mm/¼ inch before lifting them away. It is very important to release the pressure and open the crimpers slightly *before* lifting them away or the paste may lift away with them.

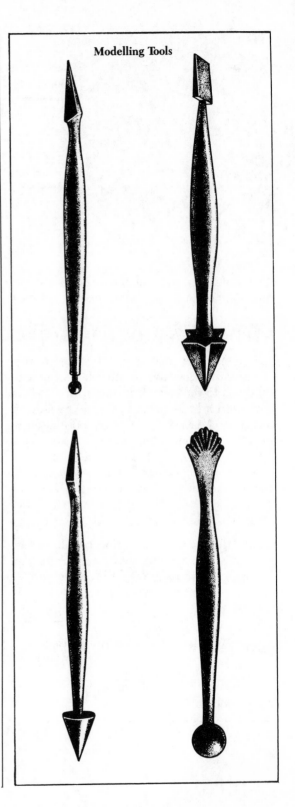

Modelling Tools

INSERTING RIBBON INTO SUGAR PASTE

The aim when attaching ribbon to a cake by this method is to give the impression that the ribbon is woven into the icing. The ribbon must be attached as soon as the cake is covered with sugar paste and while the icing is still soft. Take care not to mark the soft icing with your knuckles or fingernails as you work. If you wait until the icing has set, the ribbon will not readily stick into the slots.

Choose a narrow, satin ribbon which contrasts with the colour of the main icing. Ribbon which is a few shades darker looks best; remember that the sugar paste will be slightly darker when it is dry. Buy sufficient ribbon to go around the cake at least one and a quarter times. Cut the ribbon into 2 cm/¾ inch lengths and place these on a clean saucer.

Before you begin, cut a strip of clean greaseproof paper that equals the height of the cake and extends beyond the circumference by at least 5 cm/2 inches. Measure up from the bottom of the paper to the position where the ribbon is to be inserted and make pencil marks at 1 cm/½ inch intervals along the length of the paper. Assemble all equipment and ingredients before you start to cover the cake with paste:

cake on its board
Sugar Paste
cornflour for buffing
ribbon pieces
ribbon insertion tool or a metal nail file
2 glass-headed pins
paper pattern

Cover the marzipanned cake with sugar paste and buff the surface (page 78). Position the cake on a cake tin and sit down so that the cake is at eye level.

Lightly dust the paper pattern with cornflour and place it around the cake securing it in place with a pin at the back.

Prick out the position of the ribbon design on to the cake, then carefully remove the pattern. Smooth over any other marks which you may have made on the cake.

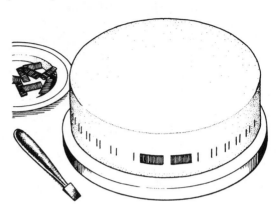

Cut vertical slits the same width as the ribbon around the cake at the marked 1 cm/½ inch intervals. Do this with a special ribbon insertion tool or the rounded, blunt end of a sterilised metal nail file. Be careful not to cut too deeply, or you will pierce right through to the almond paste or marzipan.

Start at the back of the cake and use the tool or file to press one end of a piece of cut ribbon into a slit. Leaving a small loop, insert the other end into the next slit. Leave a 1 cm/½ inch gap and insert the next piece of ribbon into the following slit. Continue around the cake.

The slits can be decorated with small piped beads or embroidery. Small narrow strips of ribbon can be used in the same way to highlight a pattern made with crimpers.

MRS BEETON'S TIP Instead of cutting all the slits around the cake at the same time you may prefer to cut each slit as you insert the ribbon, at least for the first few lengths, so that you are sure that the spacing is correct for the cake.

SIMPLE DESIGNS USING SUGAR PASTE

These simple designs (see diagrams) are suitable for round or square cakes. Any home-made or shop-bought moulding icing can be used instead of sugar paste.

MODELLING TOOL DESIGN

Cover the top and the sides of the cake with sugar paste and mark a pattern around the top edge with a modelling tool. Place a single

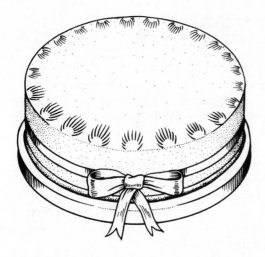

rope of sugar paste around the base of the cake and finish with a band of ribbon tied in a large bow.

CRIMPER DESIGN

Cover the top and the sides of the cake with sugar paste and use crimpers to mark a pattern around the top edge. Place a twisted rope of sugar paste around the base of the cake and a band of ribbon above. Add a bought greetings plaque or other decoration

to the top of the cake. Alternatively, cut out an appropriate numeral from rolled-out sugar paste in a contrasting colour.

BALLOON CAKE

Cover the top and the sides of the cake with sugar paste. Cover the board with paste. Cut

a template of a teddy bear, then cut out the shape in coloured sugar paste and position it on the cake. Cut balloons from paste in contrasting colours and position them around the cake. When the sugar paste is dry, use coloured icing pens to draw the string from the balloons to the teddy. Finish the cake by tying a narrow ribbon around its base.

SIMPLE SILK FLOWER CAKE

Cover the top and the sides of the cake with tinted sugar paste. Place a plaited rope of paste, tinted a slightly deeper colour, around the base of the cake. Decorate the cake with a small spray of silk flowers.

NIGHT SKY CAKE

Cover the side of the cake with apricot glaze and dark chocolate vermicelli. Cover the top

of the cake with sugar paste coloured midnight blue. Trim the edges neatly. Cut out small stars and a moon from yellow sugar paste and place them in position on the top of the cake.

SIMPLE TECHNIQUES FOR ROYAL ICING

Royal icing does not have to be smoothed over the cake to give a flat finish. It can be swirled and peaked to give a snow scene effect or it can be combed to create various designs.

PEAKED ICING

The icing should be of soft-peak consistency (page 62), so that the tip of the peak just falls. Spread the icing thickly over the cake. Using a small palette knife, press it firmly into the icing and quickly draw it towards you by about 2 cm/¾ inch before pulling it sharply away from the icing and flicking it towards the back of the cake to form a soft swirly peak of icing. Move the cake around making random peaks all over the surface.

COMBED ICING

A turntable is useful for this method of neatening the sides of the cake. Alternatively, place the cake on a cake tin to raise its height to a comfortable level.

Spread the icing over the sides of the cake making sure it comes well up to the top edge. Use a scraper with a serrated edge. Position your left hand as far around the cake as possible to hold the turntable or board. Hold the scraper in the right hand at an angle of 45 degrees to the side of the cake. Rotate the cake as the scraper sweeps over the icing in one movement. Release the pressure on the scraper slightly just as you reach the place where you started and quickly pull it away. The point where you pull off the scraper will be the back of the cake. You may have to repeat the process to get a good finish.

CHOCOLATE WORK

Dark and bitter, smooth and milky or pale and creamy – there are many types of chocolate available now and they can be put to a variety of uses. This chapter explains all about chocolate, from successful melting to creative ideas for piping, shaping and curling.

CHOCOLATE AND ITS USES

Chocolate is a blend of cocoa solids and cocoa butter to which varying quantities of vegetable fats, milk and sugar have been added. The quantity of added fat determines the hardness or softness of the chocolate.

A block of chocolate can be finely or coarsely grated, chopped, slivered and curled for decorating or coating the sides and tops of cakes.

Melted chocolate is malleable; it dries to a smooth, glossy film. It flavours and provides texture, as well as setting quality, to icings and fillings. Melted chocolate has many other uses: it can be poured over cakes or fruits or marzipan and nuts can be dipped in it. Chocolate leaves are made by coating real leaves. Chocolate curls, known as caraque, is a widely used decoration. Melted chocolate can also be set in a thin sheet, then cut into shapes, for example squares, triangles or shapes using cutters. The melted chocolate can also be piped in many ways.

Milk and Plain Chocolate Milk Chocolate has added milk products and is paler and softer in texture than plain chocolate which is darker and more brittle. The quantity of added sugar determines the sweetness. Milk chocolate contains more sugar than plain chocolate which is available as bitter, semi-sweet or plain.

Chocolate-flavoured Cake Covering This is not true chocolate. In this product the cocoa butter is replaced by other fats which make it more malleable. The resulting flavour is poor and the texture waxy. It is useful for inexpensive, everyday cakes but it should not be applied when a good result is required.

White Chocolate This is made from cocoa butter, sugar and milk and does not contain any of the cocoa solids or non-fat parts of the cocoa bean.

Carob This is manufactured from the pulp of the carob or locust bean to resemble chocolate in appearance. It is naturally sweeter than cocoa so less sugar is added; also, it is caffeine free. It is in powder form for cooking and in block form for eating. Carob can be used instead of chocolate for some of the following ideas but it is waxy in consistency and does not have such a glossy appearance.

STORING CHOCOLATE DECORATIONS

Store chocolate decorations in a cool, dry atmosphere for the shortest possible time, and no longer than seven to ten days. The chocolate will sweat if it is kept in a warm room. On very hot days keep the chocolate in the refrigerator but bring it to room temperature before melting it.

CHOCOLATE ICINGS AND DECORATIONS

Use a hard, plain dessert chocolate for the best flavour and texture. Do not be disappointed by its appearance; it will not have the same high gloss as commercial chocolates. Avoid handling the chocolate once it has set as fingermarks will readily show and the surface will become dull.

CHOPPING CHOCOLATE

Break the chocolate into pieces and place it on a chopping board. Use a sharp knife with a long blade and hold the tip of the knife on to the board with one hand. Pivot the blade, bringing it up and down with the other hand. Scrape the chocolate back to the centre of the board and continue until the pieces are even and quite small.

GRATING CHOCOLATE

Place the grater on a piece of greaseproof paper on a large plate or chopping board. Rub the block of chocolate on the coarse side of the grater. Use long, even strokes and keep your hands as cool as possible.

CHOCOLATE SLIVERS

Hold your hands under cold running water, then dry them. Hold the chocolate in the palm of the hand and shave off thin pieces of chocolate with a potato peeler, letting them fall on to a chilled plate or a sheet of greaseproof paper.

MELTING CHOCOLATE

Break up or roughly chop the chocolate and place it in a basin that fits over a saucepan. Place about 5 cm/2 inches of water in the pan and bring to the boil, then remove the pan from the heat and stand the basin over it. Leave for a few minutes, then stir the chocolate until it has melted and is smooth and glossy. If you leave the pan on the heat, the chocolate will overheat and white streaks may appear in it when it sets again.

DIPPING FOOD IN CHOCOLATE

Biscuits, choux buns, nuts, marzipan shapes, real leaves and fruits such as maraschino cherries, grapes, raisins, dates and slices of banana can all be dipped in melted chocolate. They can be part-dipped or fully dipped according to the effect required. Special dipping forks have two long prongs that are bent at the ends to stop the food falling off when dipped. Alternatively, use a corn-on-the-cob fork, cocktail stick or two fine skewers, one on either side of the food. For larger pieces of food such as choux buns, or hard foods such as almonds, it is best to use your fingers to dip the ingredients.

Melt the chocolate following the instructions left. For dipping food the consistency should be thick enough to coat the back of a spoon. If the chocolate is too thin, remove the basin from the pan and leave it to cool slightly, until the chocolate thickens. Keep the chocolate warm (over the saucepan of water), while you are working. If the chocolate becomes too thick, remove the basin, re-heat the water, then replace the basin. Stir the chocolate occasionally as you are dipping the food; this gives a glossy finish.

You will need a good depth of melted chocolate to dip food successfully; it should be at least 5 cm/2 inches deep. (When the chocolate becomes too shallow for successful dipping, do not discard it; stir the excess into buttercreams or similar icings to avoid wastage.)

Line a baking sheet or wire rack with a sheet of waxed paper or non-stick baking parchment. Have ready all the food to be dipped and start with firm items, such as nuts and marzipan. Finish with soft foods, such as fruits. Plunge the food into the chocolate to the depth required, then quickly withdraw at the same angle at which it was plunged. Do not rotate part-dipped food in the chocolate or the top line of chocolate will be uneven.

Gently shake the food to allow the excess chocolate to fall back into the basin, then place it on the prepared sheet or rack to dry.

TO DIP LEAVES

Use clean, dry leaves, such as rose leaves, and brush the underside of the leaf over the surface of the chocolate. Dry the leaves chocolate side uppermost, then carefully peel away the leaf, leaving the impression of the leaf on the chocolate.

PIPING CHOCOLATE

When adding chocolate decoration to the top of a cake, melted chocolate is difficult to pipe because it begins to set in the nozzle. Mixing a little icing sugar with it will make it more malleable; however this is not suitable for piping shapes that have to set hard.

25 g/1 oz icing sugar, sifted
100 g/4 oz chocolate, melted

Stir the icing sugar into the melted chocolate with a few drops of water to make a mixture of a thick piping consistency that drops from the spoon.

MRS BEETON'S TIP If using piping chocolate in large quantities to pipe shells around a cake, use sugar syrup instead of icing sugar to soften the chocolate.

PIPING WITH CHOCOLATE

The chocolate should be of a thin flowing consistency. Very little pressure is required to pipe with chocolate as it should flow slowly out of the bag without any encouragement.

TO DRIZZLE CHOCOLATE OVER CAKES AND BISCUITS

Place 15 ml/1 tbsp of melted chocolate into a small paper icing bag. Snip off the end and quickly move the bag backwards and forwards over the cake or biscuit. Finish by lowering the bag and quickly withdrawing it.

TO PIPE MOTIFS AND SHAPES

Prepare the pattern and piping surface as for royal icing run-outs. Alternatively, work free-hand on to the waxed paper. Make several paper icing bags out of non-stick baking parchment – greaseproof paper is not strong enough for chocolate work.

Place 30-45 ml/2-3 tbsp melted chocolate in an icing bag and snip off the end. Start with a fine hole until you have checked the size of the piping. It is a good idea to practise piping beads and buttons on the paper first. Hold the bag and pipe the shapes as for run-outs and lace. Remember to make sure that all the lines of piping are joined somewhere in the design. Shapes may be filled in using a different coloured chocolate, such as milk chocolate or white chocolate with plain chocolate. Leave the shapes to dry hard before peeling them off the waxed paper.

TO PIPE CHOCOLATE SHELLS AROUND A CAKE

Prepare piping chocolate (left). Use a strong bag made from double non-stick baking parchment and fitted with a small star nozzle. Pipe a shell pattern quickly around the cake as for royal icing. This method can also be used to pipe around home-made Easter eggs.

Outlines to Pipe in Chocolate

 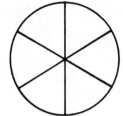 

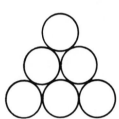  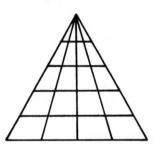

Designs to Pipe and Flood in Chocolate

TO MAKE CURLS, FRILLS AND SHAPES

Melted chocolate can be used to make a variety of different decorations without the need for piping. Here are a few examples: the key to success is to make sure that you use good quality chocolate and to leave the decorations to set firmly before using them.

CHOCOLATE CURLS OR SCROLLS (CARAQUE)

Whether you are making curls or frills the chocolate is prepared in the same way: pour melted chocolate over a clean, dry surface, such as a marble slab or a clean smooth area of work surface. Spread the chocolate backwards and forwards with a large palette knife until it is smooth, fairly thin and even. Leave to dry until almost set; do not allow the chocolate to set hard.

Hold a long, thin-bladed knife at an acute angle to the chocolate. Hold the top of the knife with the other hand and pull the knife towards you with a gentle sawing action, scraping off a thin layer of chocolate which should curl into a roll.

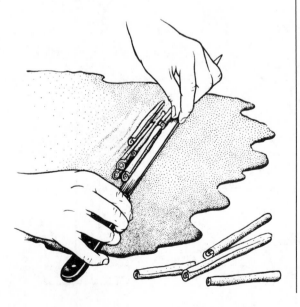

CHOCOLATE FRILLS

Starting at the edge of the chocolate, hold the tip of a small palette knife at an angle of 45 degrees or lower to the surface, and push the palette knife away from you. A thin layer of chocolate will frill as you push. Place the frills on waxed paper as you make them.

TO CUT CHOCOLATE SHAPES

Spread the melted chocolate on to waxed paper or non-stick baking parchment paper. Use petits fours cutters or small biscuit cutters, to stamp shapes out of the chocolate, cutting them as close together as possible. Leave to set hard before peeling away the paper. The excess chocolate can be finely chopped for decorations or melted for use in making more shapes.

TO CUT SQUARES, TRIANGLES OR WEDGES

Prepare a precise pattern, drawing a large square and dividing it up into smaller squares or triangles. Alternatively, draw a circle and divide it into equal wedges. In either case extend the lines beyond the square or circle so that when the pattern has been covered in chocolate, the ends of the lines will still be visible. Place the pattern under non-stick baking parchment as for royal icing run-outs.

Spread the melted chocolate over the marked shape and leave to set but not harden. Use a long-bladed knife and cut the chocolate into the shapes by holding the tip of the knife at one side of the chocolate and firmly lowering the handle so that the blade follows the cutting line. Leave the chocolate until firm, then carefully peel the shapes off the parchment.

CHOCOLATE CAKE COVERINGS

As well as chocolate-flavoured buttercreams and icings, here are two recipes for contrasting cake coverings. The Chocolate Velvet Cream recipe gives a soft and creamy, chocolate-flavoured covering that can be spread or piped on to the cake.

Alternatively, the Tipsy Chocolate Velvet is a rich, glossy and dark icing which is poured over the cake.

CHOCOLATE VELVET CREAM

150 ml/¼ pint double cream
100 g/4 oz chocolate, chopped

Combine the cream and chocolate in a small saucepan. Place over a low heat until the chocolate has melted. Continue to stir over the low heat for a further 5 minutes until the mixture is dark and creamy. Pour the cream into a bowl and chill for at least 1 hour.

Beat the cream for 5 minutes or beat it with a balloon whisk for about 10 minutes, until it has doubled in volume.

SUFFICIENT TO COVER THE TOP AND SIDES OF A 20 CM/8 INCH CAKE

TIPSY CHOCOLATE VELVET

75 g/3 oz chocolate, cut up
100 g/4 oz icing sugar, sifted
15 ml/1 tbsp dark rum
5 ml/1 tsp vegetable oil

Melt the chocolate with the 60 ml/4 tbsp water in a basin over a saucepan of hot water. Gradually beat in the icing sugar, rum and oil until the icing is smooth and coats the back of the spoon. Pour the icing over a cake and level the top and sides with a palette knife.

SUFFICIENT TO COAT THE TOP AND SIDES OF A 20 CM/8 INCH CAKE

VARIATIONS

ORANGE CHOCOLATE VELVET
Use Grand Marnier instead of rum.
MOCHA VELVET Replace the rum and water with freshly made black coffee.

TRADITIONAL EVERYDAY CAKES

This chapter progresses from the basics of cake-making to offer a selection of recipes that are suitable for everyday baking, including a variety of fruit cakes. These cakes are not over-rich, they all keep well and they are ideal for a mid-week treat. Also included are some traditional British recipes going back hundreds of years.

CHOCOLATE AND ALMOND LOAF

This tasty loaf needs no topping, but may be served with whipped cream for a special treat.

fat for greasing
200 g/7 oz plain flour
30 ml/2 tbsp cocoa
5 ml/1 tsp bicarbonate of soda
1.25 ml/¼ tsp salt
50 g/2 oz plain chocolate, broken into
    squares
100 g/4 oz butter or margarine
175 g/6 oz caster sugar
2 eggs, beaten
150 ml/5 fl oz soured cream or plain
    yogurt
30 ml/2 tbsp flaked almonds

Line and grease a 23 x 13 x 7.5 cm/9 x 5 x 3 inch loaf tin. Set the oven at 160°C/325°F/gas 3. Sift the flour, cocoa, bicarbonate of soda and salt into a bowl. Place the chocolate in a saucepan with 60 ml/4 tbsp water and melt over low heat, stirring once or twice.

In a mixing bowl cream the butter or margarine with the sugar until light. Add the beaten eggs gradually, beating well after each addition and adding a littie of the flour mixture to prevent curdling.

Fold in the rest of the flour mixture, a third at a time, alternately with the soured cream or yogurt. Finally stir in the melted chocolate and the almonds.

Spoon into the prepared tin and bake for 50-60 minutes until cooked through and firm to the touch. Cool on a wire rack.

MAKES ONE 23 x 13 x 7.5 CM/9 x 5 x 3 INCH LOAF

☀ **MICROWAVE TIP** The chocolate may be melted in the microwave. Place it in a glass measuring jug with the water and heat on High for 1-2 minutes.

---

*P*LAIN CHOCOLATE LOAF

Serve this simple loaf sliced, with a chocolate and hazelnut spread for those who like to gild the lily.

fat for greasing
175 g/6 oz plain flour
50 g/2 oz cocoa
10 ml/2 tsp baking powder
2.5 ml/½ tsp bicarbonate of soda
1.25 ml/¼ tsp salt
150 g/5 oz sugar
2 eggs, beaten
75 g/3 oz butter or margarine, melted
250 ml/8 fl oz milk

Line and grease a 23 x 13 x 7.5 cm/9 x 5 x 3 inch loaf tin. Set the oven at 180°C/350°F/gas 4. Sift the flour, cocoa, baking powder, bicarbonate of soda and salt into a mixing bowl. Stir in the sugar.

In a second bowl beat the eggs with the melted butter or margarine and milk. Pour the milk mixture into the dry ingredients and stir lightly but thoroughly.

Spoon into the prepared tin and bake for 40-50 minutes until cooked through and firm to the touch. Cool on a wire rack.

MAKES ONE 23 x 13 x 7.5 CM/9 x 5 x 3 INCH LOAF

A VARIETY OF CHOCOLATE LOAF CAKES

The recipe for Plain Chocolate Loaf can be used as a basis for making deliciously different chocolate cakes. Try some of these ideas, which include simple additional flavourings and clever ways of splitting and sandwiching the loaf cake.

CHOCOLATE LAYER LOAF The simplest way to enrich the loaf cake is to cut it horizontally into three layers and sandwich them together with chocolate and hazelnut spread. If you like, coat the top of the cake with melted chocolate softened with a knob of butter, and sprinkle toasted hazelnuts on top.

CHOCOLATE ORANGE SPLIT Add the grated rind of 1 orange to the dry ingredients, then continue as in the main recipe. Beat 225 g/8 oz curd cheese with enough orange juice to make it soft and creamy, then add icing sugar to taste. Stir in 50 g/2 oz of finely grated plain chocolate. Split the loaf vertically along its length into four slices. Sandwich the slices together with the cheese mixture and spread a thin layer over the top of the loaf. Sprinkle the top with extra grated chocolate.

CHOCOLATE WALNUT LOAF Add 100 g/4 oz of finely chopped walnuts to the dry ingredients, then continue as in the main recipe. Melt 50 g/2 oz of plain chocolate with 25 g/1 oz butter and stir in about 50 g/2 oz of chopped walnuts. Top the loaf with this nutty mixture.

CHOCOLATE BANANA LOAF Add 1 roughly chopped banana to the dry ingredients and continue as in the main recipe. Allow the loaf to cool, then spread individual slices with banana butter. To make the banana butter, cream 50 g/2 oz butter with a little icing sugar until very soft. Beat in 1 mashed banana and a little lemon juice.

MRS BEETON'S ALMOND CAKE

fat for greasing
100 g/4 oz butter or margarine
100 g/4 oz caster sugar
275 g/10 oz plain flour
10 ml/2 tsp baking powder
3 eggs
200 ml/7 fl oz milk
2.5 ml/½ tsp almond essence
50 g/2 oz flaked almonds

Line and grease a 15 cm/6 inch cake tin. Set the oven at 160°C/325°F/gas 3.

In a mixing bowl, cream the butter or margarine with the sugar until light and fluffy. Into another bowl, sift the flour and baking powder. In a measuring jug, beat the eggs with the milk.

Add the dry ingredients to the creamed mixture in 3 parts, alternately with the egg and milk mixture. Beat well after each addition. Lightly stir in the almond essence and the flaked almonds.

Spoon lightly into the prepared tin and bake for 1¼-1½ hours until cooked through and firm to the touch. Cool on a wire rack.

MAKES ONE 15 CM/6 INCH CAKE

☀ **MICROWAVE TIP** If the butter or margarine is too hard to cream readily, soften it in the mixing bowl on High for 15-30 seconds.

WEEKEND WALNUT LOAF

Illustrated on page 113

fat for greasing
275 g/10 oz plain flour
50 g/2 oz cornflour
150 g/5 oz caster sugar
5 ml/1 tsp salt
50 g/2 oz walnuts, chopped
225 g/8 oz dates, pitted and chopped
30 ml/2 tbsp oil
1 large egg
10 ml/2 tsp bicarbonate of soda

Line and grease a 23 x 13 x 7.5 cm/9 x 5 x 3 inch loaf tin. Set the oven at 180°C/350°F/gas 4.

Sift the flour, cornflour, sugar and salt into a mixing bowl. Add the walnuts and dates. In a second bowl, whisk together the oil and egg. Add to the flour, fruit and nuts and mix well. Pour 250 ml/8 fl oz boiling water into a measuring jug, add the bicarbonate of soda and stir until dissolved. Add to the mixing bowl and mix well. Beat to a soft consistency.

Pour into the prepared loaf tin and bake for about 1 hour until cooked through and firm to the touch. Leave to cool slightly before inverting on a wire rack to cool completely.

MAKES ONE 23 x 13 x 7.5 CM/9 x 5 x 3 INCH LOAF

🥄 **MRS BEETON'S TIP** Use a light unflavoured oil, such as corn oil, for the best results. Never use olive oil; its flavour is too strong.

DATE AND WALNUT CAKE

fat for greasing
200 g/7 oz self-raising flour or 200 g/7 oz
    plain flour and 10 ml/2 tsp baking
    powder
pinch of grated nutmeg
75 g/3 oz margarine
75 g/3 oz dates, stoned and chopped
25 g/1 oz walnuts, chopped
75 g/3 oz soft light brown sugar
2 small eggs
about 125 ml/4fl oz milk

Line and grease a 15 cm/6 inch tin. Set the oven at 180°C/350°F/gas 4.

Mix the flour and nutmeg in a mixing bowl, and rub in the margarine until the mixture resembles fine breadcrumbs. Add the dates and walnuts with the sugar and baking powder, if used.

In a bowl, beat the eggs with the milk and stir into the dry ingredients. Mix well.

Spoon the mixture into the cake tin and bake for 1¼-1½ hours or until cooked through and firm to the touch. Cool on a wire rack.

MAKES ONE 15 CM/6 INCH CAKE

☀ **MICROWAVE TIP** Dried dates in a compact slab are often difficult to chop. Soften them by heating for 30-40 seconds on Defrost and the job will be made much easier.

BANANA AND WALNUT CAKE

fat for greasing
200 g/7 oz plain flour
1.25 ml/¼ tsp baking powder
3.75 ml/¾ tsp bicarbonate of soda
pinch of salt
100 g/4 oz butter
150 g/5 oz caster sugar
3 large bananas, mashed
2 eggs, beaten
45 ml/3 tbsp soured milk
50 g/2 oz walnuts, finely chopped

Line and grease either a 20 cm/8 inch ring tin, or two 23 cm/9 inch sandwich tins. Set the oven at 180°C/350°F/gas 4. Sift the flour, baking powder, bicarbonate of soda and salt into a bowl.

In a mixing bowl, cream the butter and sugar until light and creamy. Mix in the mashed banana at once, blending well. Add the eggs, one at a time, beating well after each addition. Add the dry ingredients, one-third at a time, alternately with the soured milk, beating well after each addition.

Stir in the walnuts and spoon into the prepared tin. Bake the ring cake for about 40 minutes; the sandwich cakes for about 30 minutes. Cool on a wire rack.

MAKES ONE 20 CM/8 INCH RING CAKE OR TWO 23 CM/9 INCH LAYERS

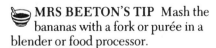 **MRS BEETON'S TIP** Mash the bananas with a fork or purée in a blender or food processor.

GOLDEN GINGERBREAD

fat for greasing
200 g/7 oz plain flour
1.25 ml/¼ tsp salt
10-15 ml/2-3 tsp ground ginger
2.5 ml/½ tsp bicarbonate of soda
grated rind of 1 orange
75 g/3 oz butter or margarine
50 g/2 oz golden granulated sugar
100 g/4 oz golden syrup
1 egg
milk (see method)

Line and grease a 15 cm/6 inch square tin.
Set the oven at 160°C/325°F/gas 3.

Sift the flour, salt, ginger and bicarbonate of soda into a mixing bowl. Stir in the orange rind. Warm the butter or margarine with the sugar and syrup in a saucepan until the fat has melted but the mixture is not hot.

In a measuring jug, beat the egg lightly and add enough milk to make up to 125 ml/ 4 fl oz. Add the melted mixture to the dry ingredients with the beaten egg and milk mixture. Stir thoroughly; the mixture should run easily off the spoon.

Pour into the prepared tin and bake for 1¼-1½ hours until firm. Cool on a wire rack.

MAKES ONE 15 CM/6 INCH SQUARE CAKE

MRS BEETON'S TIP The easiest way to measure the ingredients for melting is to weigh the empty saucepan, then add the butter or margarine until the scale registers an additional 75 g/3 oz. Add the sugar to increase the weight by a further 50 g/2 oz, then, using a spoon dipped in boiling water, ladle in syrup until the scale registers a further 100 g/4 oz.

GINGERBREAD WITH PINEAPPLE

fat for greasing
200 g/7 oz plain flour
1.25 ml/¼ tsp salt
10-15 ml/2-3 tsp ground ginger
2.5 ml/½ tsp bicarbonate of soda
50 g/2 oz crystallised ginger, chopped
50 g/2 oz crystallised pineapple, chopped
75 g/3 oz butter or margarine
50 g/2 oz soft light brown sugar
50 g/2 oz golden syrup
50 g/2 oz black treacle
1 egg
milk (see method)

Line and grease a 15 cm/6 inch square tin.
Set the oven at 160°C/325°F/gas 3.

Sift the flour, salt, ginger and bicarbonate of soda into a mixing bowl. Stir in the fruit. Warm the butter or margarine with the sugar, syrup and treacle in a saucepan until the fat has melted. Do not allow the mixture to become hot.

In a measuring jug, beat the egg lightly and add enough milk to make up to 125 ml/4 fl oz. Add the melted mixture to the dry ingredients with the beaten egg and milk mixture. Stir thoroughly; the mixture should run easily off the spoon.

Pour into the prepared tin and bake for 1¼-1½ hours until firm to the touch. Cool on a wire rack.

MAKES ONE 15 CM/6 INCH SQUARE CAKE

APPLE AND GINGER CAKE

fat for greasing
175 g/6 oz plain flour
1.25 ml/¼ tsp salt
2.5 ml/½ tsp bicarbonate of soda
5 ml/1 tsp baking powder
5 ml/1 tsp ground ginger
100 g/4 oz crystallised ginger, chopped
100 g/4 oz butter or margarine
150 g/5 oz caster sugar
2 eggs, beaten
250 ml/8 fl oz sieved apple purée

Line and grease an 18 cm/7 inch square cake tin. Set the oven at 180°C/350°F/gas 4. Sift the flour, salt, bicarbonate of soda, baking powder and ginger into a bowl. Stir in the crystallised ginger and mix well. Set aside.

Place the butter or margarine in a mixing bowl and beat until very soft. Add the sugar and cream together until light and fluffy. Add the beaten eggs gradually, beating well after each addition. If the mixture shows signs of curdling, add a little of the flour mixture. Stir in the apple purée. Fold in the dry ingredients lightly but thoroughly. Spoon into the prepared tin, smooth the surface and make a hollow in the centre.

Bake for 30 minutes, then reduce the oven temperature to 160°C/325°F/gas 3 and bake for 15 minutes more until firm to the touch. Cool on a wire rack.

MAKES ONE 18 CM/7 INCH CAKE

YEAST CAKE

fat for greasing
50 g/2 oz butter
2 eggs
125 ml/4 fl oz milk
275 g/10 oz plain flour
100 g/4 oz soft light brown sugar
25 g/1 oz fresh yeast
150 g/5 oz currants
50 g/2 oz cut mixed peel

Line and grease a 15-18 cm/6-7 inch cake tin. Melt the butter in a saucepan and leave to cool. Add the eggs and milk and whisk until frothy. Combine the flour and sugar in a large bowl. In a cup, mix the yeast with a little warm water and leave to froth.

Make a hollow in the flour mixture and pour in the yeast. Add the butter and egg mixture, and mix well. Knead on a clean work surface to a smooth, soft dough, then return to the clean mixing bowl. Cover with a damp cloth, and place in a warm, draught-free place. Leave to rise for about 1½ hours or until the dough has doubled in bulk.

Add the dried fruit and peel, and knead until it is well distributed. Form the dough into a round and place in the prepared cake tin. Leave to rise for 30 minutes.

Set the oven at 200°C/400°F/gas 6. Bake the cake for 30 minutes, then reduce the oven temperature to 160°C/325°F/gas 3 and bake for a further 1 hour or until the cake sounds hollow when rapped on the base. Cool on a wire rack.

MAKES ONE 18 CM/7 INCH CAKE

MRS BEETON'S TIP Excessive heat kills yeast so take care that the water mixed with the yeast is merely at blood temperature.

BOILED FRUIT CAKE

fat for greasing
100 g/4 oz mixed dried fruit
50 g/2 oz margarine
25 g/1 oz soft light brown sugar
grated rind of 1 orange
200 g/7 oz plain flour
2.5 ml/½ tsp mixed spice
2.5 ml/½ tsp bicarbonate of soda

Line and grease a 15 cm/6 inch cake tin. Set the oven at 180°C/350°F/gas 4.

Combine the dried fruit, margarine, sugar and orange rind in a saucepan. Add 200 ml/7 fl oz water. Bring to the boil, reduce the heat and simmer for 5 minutes. Leave to cool until tepid.

Sift the flour, spice and bicarbonate of soda into the fruit mixture and mix well. Spoon into the prepared tin. Cover with greased paper or foil and bake for 1½-2 hours or until cooked through and firm to the touch. Cool on a wire rack.

MAKES ONE 15 CM/6 INCH CAKE

MICROWAVE TIP Combine the dried fruit, margarine, sugar, water and orange rind in a mixing bowl. Cover lightly and microwave on High for 5 minutes, stirring twice. Leave to cool until tepid, then proceed as in the recipe above.

ONE-STAGE CHERRY CAKE

fat for greasing
225 g/8 oz glacé cherries
175 g/6 oz soft margarine
175 g/6 oz caster sugar
3 eggs
225 g/8 oz plain flour
12.5 ml/2½ tsp baking powder
50 g/2 oz ground almonds (optional)

Line and grease an 18 cm/7 inch round cake tin. Set the oven at 160°C/325°F/gas 3. Wash, dry and halve the cherries.

Put all the ingredients in a bowl and beat for 2-3 minutes until well mixed. Spoon the mixture into the prepared tin and bake for 1½-1¾ hours or until cooked through and firm to the touch. Cool on a wire rack.

MAKES ONE 18 CM/7 INCH CAKE.

MRS BEETON'S TIP Instead of using plain flour, self-raising flour can be substituted and the quantity of baking powder reduced to 2.5 ml/½ tsp.

CHERRY CAKE

Illustrated on page 114

fat for greasing
200 g/7 oz plain flour
1.25 ml/¼ tsp salt
2.5 ml/½ tsp baking powder
100 g/4 oz glacé cherries, quartered
150 g/5 oz butter or margarine
150 g/5 oz caster sugar
4 eggs
15 ml/1 tbsp milk (optional)

Line and grease a 15 cm/6 inch cake tin. Set the oven at 180°C/350°F/gas 4. Sift the flour, salt and baking powder into a bowl. Add the cherries and mix well. Set aside.

Place the butter or margarine in a mixing bowl and beat until very soft. Add the sugar and cream together until light and fluffy. Add the beaten eggs gradually, beating well after each addition. If the mixture shows signs of curdling, add a little of the flour mixture.

Fold in the dry ingredients lightly but thoroughly, adding the milk if too stiff.

Spoon into the prepared tin, level the surface and make a hollow in the centre, Bake for 30 minutes, then reduce the oven temperature to 160°C/325°F/gas 3 and bake for 50 minutes more until cooked through and firm to the touch. Cool on a wire rack.

MAKES ONE 15 CM/6 INCH CAKE

MRS BEETON'S TIP When adding the cherries to the flour, be sure to mix them in thoroughly. If the cherries are coated in flour they will not sink to the bottom of the cake.

FESTIVAL FRUIT CAKE

fat for greasing
200 g/7 oz plain flour
1.25 ml/¼ tsp salt
2.5 ml/½ tsp baking powder
50 g/2 oz currants
50 g/2 oz sultanas
50 g/2 oz glacé cherries, chopped
50 g/2 oz cut mixed peel
150 g/5 oz butter or margarine
150 g/5 oz caster sugar
4 eggs
15 ml/1 tbsp milk (optional)

Line and grease an 18 cm/7 inch cake tin. Set the oven at 180°C/350°F/gas 4. Sift the flour, salt and baking powder into a bowl. Stir in the dried fruit and mixed peel and mix well. Set aside.

Place the butter or margarine in a mixing bowl and beat until very soft. Add the sugar and cream together until light and fluffy. Add the beaten eggs gradually, beating well after each addition. If the mixture shows signs of curdling, add a little of the flour mixture.

Fold in the dry ingredients lightly but thoroughly, adding the milk if too stiff.

Spoon into the prepared tin, smooth the surface and make a hollow in the centre. Bake for 30 minutes, then reduce the oven temperature to 160°C/325°F/gas 3 and bake for 40 minutes more until firm to the touch. Cool on a wire rack.

MAKES ONE 18 CM/7 INCH CAKE

COUNTESS SPICE CAKE

fat for greasing
100 g/4 oz plain flour
100 g/4 oz cornflour
2.5 ml/½ tsp ground ginger
3.75 ml/¾ tsp grated nutmeg
3.75 ml/¾ tsp ground cinnamon
1.25 ml/¼ tsp salt
75 g/3 oz margarine
10 ml/2 tsp baking powder
75 g/3 oz sugar
2 small eggs
about 125 ml/4 fl oz milk
50 g/2 oz currants
50 g/2 oz seedless raisins

Line and grease a 15 cm/6 inch cake tin. Set the oven at 180°C/350°F/gas 4.

Mix the flour, cornflour, spices and salt in a mixing bowl. Rub in the margarine until the mixture resembles fine breadcrumbs. Add the baking powder and the sugar.

In a bowl, beat the eggs with 50 ml/2 fl oz of the milk and stir into the flour mixture. Add more milk, if necessary, to give a consistency which just drops off the end of a wooden spoon. Stir in the currants and raisins.

Spoon the mixture into the prepared cake tin and bake for 1-1½ hours or until cooked through. Cool on a wire rack.

MAKES ONE 15 CM/6 INCH CAKE

MIXED FRUIT LOAF

Illustrated on page 114

fat for greasing
200 g/7 oz self-raising flour
pinch of salt
100 g/4 oz margarine
100 g/4 oz caster sugar
grated rind of 1 orange
225 g/8 oz mixed dried fruit, eg 25 g/1 oz glacé cherries, 25 g/1 oz cut mixed peel, 75 g/3 oz sultanas, 75 g/3 oz seedless raisins
1 egg
milk (see method)

Grease and line a 23 x 13 x 7.5 cm/9 x 5 x 3 inch loaf tin. Set the oven at 180°C/350°F/gas 4.

Mix the flour and salt in a mixing bowl and rub in the margarine until the mixture resembles fine breadcrumbs. Stir in the sugar and orange rind. Cut the cherries, if used, into 4-6 pieces each, depending on size, and add with the remaining fruit.

In a measuring jug, beat the egg lightly and add enough milk to make up to 125 ml/4 fl oz. Add to the flour mixture, stir in, then mix well. Spoon into the prepared tin and bake for about 1 hour or until firm to the touch. Cool on a wire rack.

MAKES ONE 23 x 13 x 7.5 CM/9 x 5 x 3 INCH LOAF

☀ **MICROWAVE TIP** The dried fruit may be cleaned and plumped in a single operation in the microwave. Place the fruit in a bowl with cold water to cover. Heat on High until the water boils, allow to stand until cool enough to handle, then drain the fruit, removing any stalks.

EVERYDAY BRAN CAKE

fat for greasing
175 g/6 oz self-raising flour
25 g/1 oz natural wheat bran
1.25 ml/¼ tsp salt
100 g/4 oz margarine
100 g/4 oz caster sugar or soft light brown
  sugar
150 g/5 oz mixed dried fruit (currants,
  sultanas, seedless raisins)
2 eggs
30 ml/2 tbsp milk

Line and grease a 15 cm/6 inch cake tin.
Set the oven at 180°C/350°F/gas 4.

Mix the flour, bran and salt in a mixing
bowl and rub in the margarine until the
mixture resembles fine breadcrumbs. Stir in
the sugar and fruit.

In a bowl, beat the eggs with the milk, add
to the dry ingredients and fruit and mix well.
Spoon into the prepared tin and bake for
about 1 hour or until cooked through. Cool
on a wire rack.

MAKES ONE 15 CM/6 INCH CAKE

HOLIDAY CAKE

fat for greasing
200 g/7 oz self-raising flour
1.25 ml/¼ tsp salt
1.25 ml/¼ tsp baking powder
75 g/3 oz margarine
75 g/3 oz sugar
100 g/4 oz currants
100 g/4 oz seedless raisins
1 large egg
100 ml/3½ fl oz milk

Line and grease a 15 cm/6 inch round cake
tin. Set the oven at 180°C/350°F/gas 4.

Sift the flour, salt and baking powder into
a mixing bowl. Rub in the margarine until
the mixture resembles fine breadcrumbs.
Stir in the sugar and dried fruit.

In a small bowl, beat the egg lightly and
add the milk. Stir into the dry ingredients
and fruit and beat to a soft consistency.
Spoon into the tin and bake for 1½ hours,
until cooked through. Cool on a wire rack.

MAKES ONE 15 CM/6 INCH CAKE

SPICED SULTANA CAKE

fat for greasing
200 g/7 oz self-raising flour
10 ml/2 tsp mixed spice
100 g/4 oz margarine
225 g/8 oz sultanas
100 g/4 oz soft light brown sugar
1 egg
milk (see method)

Line and grease a 15 cm/6 inch round cake
tin. Set the oven at 180°C/350°F/gas 4. Sift
the flour and spice. Rub in the margarine
until the mixture resembles fine breadcrumbs, then stir in the sultanas and sugar.

In a measuring jug, beat the egg lightly
and add enough milk to make up to 125 ml/4
fl oz. Add to the dry ingredients, stir, then
mix well. Spoon the mixture into the prepared tin and bake for about 1¼ hours or
until cooked through and firm to the touch.
Cool on a wire rack.

MAKES ONE 15 CM/6 INCH CAKE

★ **FREEZING TIP** When the cake is
completely cold, wrap in foil, label and
freeze for up to 3 months.

LUNCH CAKE

It is always useful to have a cake ready to slice for lunchboxes. If making this with children in view you may wish to reduce the amount of spice.

fat for greasing
225 g/8 oz plain flour
1.25 ml/¼ tsp salt
10 ml/2 tsp mixed spice
2.5 ml/½ tsp ground cloves
5 ml/1 tsp ground cinnamon
5 ml/1 tsp cream of tartar
2.5 ml/½ tsp bicarbonate of soda
75 g/3 oz margarine
100 g/4 oz sugar
75 g/3 oz currants
50 g/2 oz seedless raisins
25 g/1 oz cut mixed peel
2 eggs
60 ml/2 fl oz milk

Line and grease a 15 cm/6 inch round cake tin. Set the oven at 180°C/350°F/gas 4.

Sift the flour, salt, spices, cream of tartar and bicarbonate of soda into a mixing bowl. Rub in the margarine until the mixture resembles fine breadcrumbs. Add the sugar, dried fruit and peel.

In a bowl beat the eggs lightly with the milk. Make a hollow in the dry ingredients and pour in the milk mixture. Stir, then beat lightly to a soft consistency. Spoon into the prepared tin and bake for 1¼ hours or until cooked through and firm to the touch. Cool on a wire rack.

MAKES ONE 15 CM/6 INCH CAKE

VINEGAR CAKE

fat for greasing
200 g/7 oz plain flour
1.25 ml/¼ tsp salt
75 g/3 oz margarine
75 g/3 oz soft dark brown sugar
50 g/2 oz currants
50 g/2 oz sultanas
25 g/1 oz cut mixed peel
175 ml/6 fl oz milk
5 ml/1 tsp bicarbonate of soda
15 ml/1 tbsp malt vinegar

Line and grease a 15 cm/6 inch round tin. Set the oven at 180°C/350°F/gas 4.

Mix the flour and salt in a mixing bowl and rub in the margarine until the mixture resembles fine breadcrumbs. Stir in the sugar, dried fruit and peel.

Warm half the milk in a small saucepan. Stir in the bicarbonate of soda until dissolved. Add this with the remaining milk and the vinegar to the dry ingredients and mix thoroughly.

Bake for 1 hour, then reduce the oven temperature to 160°C/325°F/gas 3 and bake for a further 30-40 minutes, or until cooked through and firm to the touch. Cool on a wire rack.

MAKES ONE 15 CM/6 INCH CAKE

Classic Madeira Cake (page 156) and Weekend Walnut Loaf (page 104)

Mixed Fruit Loaf (page 110) and Cherry Cake (page 109)

Butterfly Cakes (page 128) and English Madeleines (page 129)

Mocha Fingers (page 132) and Corkers (page 145)

Mini Christmas Cakes and Festive Log (both on page 148)

Simnel Cake (page 150)

Pineapple Upside-down Cake (page 151)

Easter Cakes (page 154)

WESTMORLAND PARKIN

This makes a dense, dark parkin with excellent keeping qualities.

fat for greasing
200 g/7 oz butter or clarified dripping
   (page 15)
450 g/1 lb black treacle
450 g/1 lb fine oatmeal
200 g/7 oz plain flour
5 ml/1 tsp ground ginger
2.5 ml/½ tsp salt
10 ml/2 tsp baking powder
200 g/7 oz demerara sugar
100 ml/3½ fl oz milk
5 ml/1 tsp bicarbonate of soda

Line and grease two 20 cm/8 inch square tins. Set the oven at 160°C/325°F/gas 3.

Heat the butter or dripping and treacle gently in a saucepan, stirring until the fat has melted. Mix all the dry ingredients, except the bicarbonate of soda, in a mixing bowl and make a well in the centre.

In a saucepan over low heat warm the milk to hand-hot. Stir in the bicarbonate of soda until dissolved. Pour into the dry ingredients and mix well. Stir in the melted butter and treacle.

Spoon the mixture into the prepared tins and bake for about 1¼ hours or until cooked through and firm to the touch. Cool in the tins, then cut into squares.

MAKES TWO 20 CM/8 INCH CAKES (ABOUT 32 SQUARES)

> **MRS BEETON'S TIP** A lighter cake may be made by substituting honey for half the treacle.

OLD ENGLISH CIDER CAKE

fat for greasing
225 g/8 oz plain flour
7.5 ml/1½ tsp grated nutmeg
1.25 ml/¼ tsp ground cinnamon
5 ml/1 tsp baking powder
pinch of salt
100 g/4 oz butter or margarine
100 g/4 oz caster sugar
2 eggs
125 ml/4 fl oz dry still cider

Line and lightly grease a shallow 20 cm/ 8 inch square cake tin. Set the oven at 180°C/350°F/gas 4.

Sift the flour into a bowl with the spices, baking powder and salt. Cream the butter or margarine with the sugar until light and fluffy, then beat in the eggs. Beat half the flour mixture into the creamed mixture. Beat in half the cider. Repeat, using the remaining flour and cider.

Spoon the mixture into the prepared tin and bake for 50-55 minutes until the cake is cooked through and firm to the touch. Cool on a wire rack.

MAKES ONE 20 CM/8 INCH CAKE

> **MRS BEETON'S TIP** A nutmeg grater is an invaluable accessory, but is difficult to clean. A child's toothbrush, kept specifically for the purpose, is ideal.

PATTERDALE PEPPER CAKE

Store this traditional British cake for at least a week before cutting.

fat for greasing
450 g/1 lb self-raising flour
15 ml/1 tbsp ground ginger
1.25 ml/¼ tsp ground cloves
2.5 ml/½ tsp freshly ground black pepper
100 g/4 oz butter
200 g/7 oz caster sugar
100 g/4 oz seedless raisins
100 g/4 oz currants
25 g/1 oz cut mixed peel
200 g/7 oz golden syrup, warmed
2 large eggs, lightly beaten
125 ml/4 fl oz skimmed milk

Line and grease a deep 18 cm/7 inch square cake tin or a somewhat shallower 20 cm/8 inch tin.

Set the oven at 160°C/325°F/gas 3. Sift the flour, spices and black pepper into a mixing bowl. Rub in the butter until the mixture resembles fine breadcrumbs. Stir in the sugar, and add the fruit and peel. Make a well in the flour mixture, pour in the syrup, eggs and milk, and beat lightly.

Spoon the mixture into the prepared tin and bake for 2½ hours or until cooked through and firm to the touch. Cool on a wire rack.

MAKES ONE 18 CM/7 INCH CAKE

☀ MICROWAVE TIP Warming the syrup will make it easier to measure. If you are using syrup in a glass jar, remove the lid and heat the jar on High for 1 minute. Do not attempt this if the syrup is in a tin.

BOODLES CAKE

fat for greasing
200 g/7 oz self-raising flour or 200 g/7 oz plain flour and 10 ml/2 tsp baking powder
2.5 ml/½ tsp mixed spice
75 g/3 oz margarine
75-100 g/3-4 oz sugar
75 g/3 oz sultanas
75 g/3 oz seedless raisins
50 g/2 oz currants
2 small eggs
about 125 ml/4 fl oz milk

Line and grease a 15 cm/6 inch cake tin. Set the oven at 180°C/350°F/gas 4.

Mix the flour and spice in a mixing bowl and rub in the margarine until the mixture resembles fine breadcrumbs. Add the sugar, dried fruit and baking powder, if used.

In a bowl, beat the eggs with the milk and add to the dry ingredients and fruit. Stir well.

Spoon the mixture into the prepared tin and bake for 45 minutes, then reduce the oven temperature to 160°C/325°F/gas 3 and bake for a further 30 minutes until cooked through and firm to the touch. Cool on a wire rack.

MAKES ONE 15 CM/6 INCH CAKE

MISS MUFFET CAKE

You don't need the whey for this traditional treat, but the curds are essential. Make them 24 hours before you intend to bake the cake.

Pastry Base, using 100 g/4 oz plain flour
   plain flour
flour for rolling out

FILLING
   500 ml/18 fl oz milk
   15 ml/1 tbsp rennet essence
   50 g/2 oz butter, melted
   1 egg, beaten
   25 g/1 oz self-raising flour
   2.5 ml/½ tsp baking powder
   pinch of salt
   75 g/3 oz sugar
   25 g/1 oz currants
   grated nutmeg

First make the curds for the filling. Pour the milk into a saucepan and heat to blood heat (about 37°C/98.6°F). Transfer the milk to a bowl and stir in the rennet. Leave to stand at room temperature for 1 hour.

Line a sieve or colander with a thin scalded damp cloth and stand it over a bowl or shallow dish. Spoon the curds carefully into the cloth. Bring the corners of the cloth together, tie securely with string and hang above the bowl for 18 hours. By this time all the whey will have run out and the curds will be firm. You should have about 75 g/3 oz.

Roll out the pastry on a lightly floured surface and use it to line an 18 cm/7 inch flan ring. Set the oven at 190°C/375°F/gas 5.

Transfer the curds to a bowl and break them down with a fork. If they are very firm, rub them through a sieve. Add the melted butter, beaten egg, flour, baking powder, salt, sugar, currants and a little grated nutmeg and mix thoroughly. Spoon the mixture into the flan case. Bake for 25-30 minutes until the pastry is lightly browned and the filling set. Serve warm or cold.

SERVES 4 TO 6

ROCK CAKES

fat for greasing
200 g/7 oz self-raising flour
1.25 ml/¼ tsp salt
1.25 ml/¼ tsp grated nutmeg
75 g/3 oz margarine
75 g/3 oz sugar
75 g/3 oz mixed dried fruit (currants,
   sultanas, mixed peel, glacé cherries)
1 egg
milk (see method)

Thoroughly grease 2 baking sheets. Set the oven at 200°C/400°F/gas 6.

Sift the flour and salt into a mixing bowl. Add the nutmeg. Rub in the margarine until the mixture resembles fine breadcrumbs. Stir in the sugar and dried fruit.

Put the egg into a measuring jug and add enough milk to make up to 125 ml/4 fl oz. Add the liquid to the dry ingredients and mix with a fork to a sticky stiff mixture that will support the fork.

Divide the mixture into 12-14 portions. Form into rocky heaps on the prepared baking sheets, allowing about 2 cm/¾ inch between each for spreading. Bake for 15-20 minutes or until each bun is firm to the touch on the base. Cool on a wire rack.

MAKES 12 TO 14

DRIPPING CAKE

Perhaps not the healthiest cake, but certainly economical.

fat for greasing
200 g/7 oz self-raising flour
pinch of salt
1.25 ml/¼ tsp mixed spice
100 g/4 oz clarified beef dripping (page 23)
75 g/3 oz sugar
75 g/3 oz seedless raisins
50 g/2 oz currants
1 egg
100 ml/3½ fl oz milk

Line and grease a 15 cm/6 inch round cake tin. Set the oven at 180°C/350°F/gas 4.

Mix the flour, salt and spice in a mixing bowl. Rub in the dripping until the mixture resembles breadcrumbs. Add the sugar and dried fruit.

In a bowl, beat the egg with the milk and add to the dry ingredients. Stir well, then beat until smooth. Spoon into the prepared tin and bake for 1 hour 10 minutes or until cooked through and firm to the touch. Cover the top with greaseproof paper after 1 hour if the cake is already brown enough.

MAKES ONE 15 CM/6 INCH CAKE

MRS BEETON'S TIP Use clarified dripping (see page 15) which does not have too strong a flavour. If it has been kept in the refrigerator, allow it to come to room temperature.

SHEARING CAKE

In Welsh this simple cake is known as 'Cacen Gneifio' and traditionally it was prepared to serve with tea for all the farm workers who gathered to help on days when the sheep were sheared and dipped.

butter for greasing
400 g/14 oz plain flour
pinch of salt
10 ml/2 tsp baking powder
200 g/7 oz butter
225 g/8 oz soft light brown sugar
grated rind of ½ lemon
20 ml/4 tsp caraway seeds
5 ml/1 tsp grated nutmeg or to taste
2 eggs
200 ml/7 fl oz milk

Line and grease a 20 cm/8 inch round cake tin. Set the oven at 180°C/350°F/gas 4.

Sift the flour, salt and baking powder into a mixing bowl. Rub in the butter until the mixture resembles breadcrumbs, then stir in the sugar, lemon rind and spices. In a second bowl, beat the eggs lightly with the milk, then stir gradually into the dry ingredients.

Spoon the mixture into the prepared tin and bake for 1½ hours or until cooked through and firm to the touch, covering the surface with a piece of greased paper or foil if it browns too quickly. Cool for 10 minutes in the tin, then invert on a wire rack to cool completely.

MAKES ONE 20 CM/8 INCH CAKE

FREEZING TIP Wrap in foil or freeze in a sealed polythene bag. Thaw the cake, still wrapped, for 3-4 hours at room temperature.

SEED CAKE

fat for greasing
200 g/7 oz plain flour
1.25 ml/¼ tsp salt
2.5 ml/½ tsp baking powder
15 ml/1 tbsp caraway seeds
150 g/5 oz butter or margarine
150 g/5 oz caster sugar
4 eggs, beaten
15 ml/1 tbsp milk (optional)

Line and grease a 15 cm/6 inch cake tin. Set the oven at 180°C/350°F/gas 4. Sift the flour, salt and baking powder into a bowl. Stir in the caraway seeds and mix well. Set aside.

Place the butter or margarine in a mixing bowl and beat until very soft. Add the sugar and cream together until light and fluffy. Add the beaten eggs gradually, beating well after each addition. If the mixture shows signs of curdling, add a little of the flour mixture.

Fold in the dry ingredients lightly but thoroughly, adding the milk if too stiff.

Spoon into the prepared tin, smooth the surface and make a hollow in the centre. Bake for 30 minutes, then reduce the oven temperature to 160°C/325°F/gas 3 and bake for 50 minutes more until firm to the touch. Cool on a wire rack.

MAKES ONE 15 CM/6 INCH CAKE

GUY FAWKES GINGERBREAD

Make this gingerbread at least a week before eating and store in an airtight tin. It is best eaten sliced and spread with butter. An excellent treat for November 5th!

fat for greasing
200 g/7 oz plain flour
1.25 ml/¼ tsp salt
15 ml/1 tsp ground ginger
50 g/2 oz soft light brown sugar
50 g/2 oz butter or margarine
100 g/4 oz black treacle
75 ml/5 tbsp milk
5 ml/1 tsp bicarbonate of soda
1 egg, beaten

Line and grease an 18 cm/7 inch square tin or a 23 x 13 x 7.5 cm/9 x 5 x 3 inch loaf tin. Set the oven at 180°C/350°F/gas 4.

Sift the flour, salt and ginger into a mixing bowl. Add the sugar. Heat the butter or margarine, treacle, and most of the milk gently in a saucepan until the fat has melted.

In a second saucepan, warm the remaining milk and stir in the bicarbonate of soda until dissolved. Pour the melted mixture into the dry ingredients. Add the beaten egg with the milk and soda mixture and beat well.

Pour into the prepared tin and bake for 20 minutes. Reduce the oven temperature to 150°C/300°F/gas 2 and bake for a further 30-40 minutes until cooked through and firm to the touch.

MAKES ONE 18 CM/7 INCH SQUARE CAKE OR ONE 23 x 13 x 7.5 CM/9 x 5 x 3 INCH LOAF

ALL SORTS OF SMALL CAKES

From Basic Buns and tray bakes to Mocha Fingers and Mayfair Cakes, this section illustrates that small cakes can be simple or special. Whether you intend to batch bake for the freezer or prepare a treat for tea, small cakes are quick to make and simple to serve.

BASIC BUNS

These small buns may be baked in paper cases or greased patty tins if preferred, in which case the consistency should be softer than when the buns are put on a baking sheet. The mixture should drop off the spoon with a slight shake, so increase the milk to about 125 ml/4 fl oz. If baked in patty tins, the mixture will make 14 to 16 buns.

fat for greasing
200 g/7 oz self-raising flour
1.25 ml/¼ tsp salt
75 g/3 oz margarine
75 g/3 oz sugar
1 egg
milk (see method)
Glacé Icing (page 59) to decorate
  (optional)

Thoroughly grease 2 baking sheets. Set the oven at 200°C/400°F/gas 6.

Sift the flour and salt into a mixing bowl. Rub in the margarine until the mixture resembles fine breadcrumbs. Stir in the sugar. Put the egg into a measuring jug and add enough milk to make up to 125 ml/4 fl oz. Add the liquid to the dry ingredients and mix with a fork to a sticky stiff mixture that will support the fork.

Divide the mixture into 12-14 portions. Form into rocky heaps on the prepared baking sheets, allowing about 2 cm/¾ inch between each for spreading. Bake for 15-20 minutes or until each bun is firm to the touch on the base. Cool on a wire rack, then coat with icing, if liked.

MAKES 12 TO 14

VARIATIONS

CHOCOLATE BUNS Add 50 g/2 oz cocoa to the flour and 5 ml/1 tsp vanilla essence with the milk.

CHOCOLATE CHIP BUNS Add 100 g/4 oz of cooking chocolate chips with the sugar.

COCONUT BUNS Add 75 g/3 oz desiccated coconut with the flour and an extra 10 ml/2 tsp milk.

FRUIT BUNS Add 75 g/3 oz mixed dried fruit with the sugar.

SEED BUNS Add 15 ml/1 tbsp caraway seeds with the sugar.

SPICE BUNS Add 5 ml/1 tsp mixed spice or 2.5 ml/½ tsp ground cinnamon and 2.5 ml/½ tsp grated nutmeg with the flour.

WALNUT ORANGE BUNS Add the grated rind of 1 orange to the flour. Stir in 100 g/4 oz finely chopped walnuts with the sugar.

MRS BEETON'S TIP Plain flour may be used for the buns, but add 10 ml/2 tsp baking powder with the sugar.

RASPBERRY BUNS

fat for greasing
200 g/7 oz self-raising flour
1.25 ml/¼ tsp salt
75 g/3 oz margarine
75 g/3 oz sugar
1 egg
milk (see method)
60-75 ml/4-5 tbsp raspberry jam
beaten egg for brushing
caster sugar for sprinkling

Thoroughly grease 2 baking sheets. Set the oven at 200°C/400°F/gas 6.

Sift the flour and salt into a mixing bowl. Rub in the margarine until the mixture resembles fine breadcrumbs. Stir in the sugar. Put the egg into a measuring jug and add enough milk to make up to 125 ml/4 fl oz. Add the liquid to the dry ingredients and mix with a fork to a sticky stiff mixture that will support the fork.

Divide the mixture into 12-14 portions. Form into 12-14 balls with lightly floured hands. Make a deep dent in the centre of each and drop 5 ml/1 tsp raspberry jam inside. Close the bun mixture over the jam. Brush with egg and sprinkle with sugar, then arrange on the prepared sheets, allowing about 2 cm/¾ inch between each for spreading. Bake for 15-20 minutes or until each bun is firm to the touch on the base. Cool on a wire rack.

MAKES 12 TO 14

GINGER BUNS

fat for greasing (optional)
150 g/5 oz self-raising flour
pinch of salt
5 ml/1 tsp ground ginger
1.25 ml/¼ tsp ground cinnamon
75 g/3 oz butter or margarine
50 g/2 oz soft light brown sugar
25 g/1 oz blanched almonds, chopped
1 egg
20 ml/4 tsp black treacle
20 ml/4 tsp golden syrup
30 ml/2 tbsp milk

Grease 18-20 bun tins or arrange an equivalent number of paper cake cases on baking sheets. Set the oven at 190°C/375°F/gas 5.

Sift the flour, salt and spices into a mixing bowl. Rub in the butter or margarine until the mixture resembles fine breadcrumbs. Stir in the sugar and almonds.

Put the egg into a measuring jug and add the treacle, syrup and milk. Mix well. Add the liquid to the dry ingredients and beat until smooth.

Divide the mixture between the prepared bun tins or paper cases. Bake for 15-20 minutes or until well risen and cooked through. Cool on a wire rack.

MAKES 18 TO 20

☼ **MICROWAVE TIP** The jug in which the egg, treacle, syrup and milk were mixed will be easy to clean if filled with water and heated in the microwave on High for 2-3 minutes. Take care when pouring the water away; it will be very hot. The steam generated in the microwave oven will have the added effect of loosening any grease on the walls, so give the cabinet a quick wipe at the same time.

HONEY BUNS

fat for greasing (optional)
200 g/7 oz self-raising flour
pinch of salt
75 g/3 oz butter or margarine
25 g/1 oz caster sugar
1 egg
30 ml/2 tbsp clear honey
30 ml/2 tbsp milk

Grease 18-20 bun tins or arrange an equivalent number of paper cake cases on baking sheets. Set the oven at 190°C/375°F/gas 5.

Sift the flour and salt into a mixing bowl. Rub in the butter or margarine until the mixture resembles fine breadcrumbs. Stir in the sugar.

Put the egg into a measuring jug and add the honey and milk. Mix well. Add the liquid to the dry ingredients and beat until smooth.

Divide the mixture between the prepared bun tins or paper cases. Bake for 15-20 minutes or until well risen and cooked through. Cool on a wire rack.

MAKES 18 TO 20

BUTTERFLY CAKES

Illustrated on page 115

fat for greasing
100 g/4 oz self-raising flour
pinch of salt
100 g/4 oz butter or margarine
100 g/4 oz caster sugar
2 eggs, beaten

DECORATION
150 ml/5 fl oz double cream
5 ml/1 tsp caster sugar
1.25 ml/¼ tsp vanilla essence
icing sugar for dusting

Grease 12-14 bun tins. Set the oven at 180°C/350°F/gas 4. Mix the flour and salt in a bowl.

In a mixing bowl, cream the butter or margarine with the sugar until light and fluffy. Beat in the eggs, then lightly stir in the flour and salt. Divide the mixture evenly between the prepared bun tins, and bake for 15-20 minutes until golden brown. Cool on a wire rack.

In a bowl, whip the cream with the caster sugar and vanilla essence until stiff. Transfer to a piping bag fitted with a large star nozzle.

When the cakes are cold, cut a round off

the top of each. Cut each round in half to create two 'butterfly wings'. Pipe a star of cream on each cake, then add the 'wings', placing them cut side down, and slightly apart. Dust with icing sugar.

MAKES 12 TO 14

ENGLISH MADELEINES

Illustrated on page 115

fat for greasing
100 g/4 oz self-raising flour
pinch of salt
100 g/4 oz butter or margarine
100 g/4 oz caster sugar
2 eggs, beaten

DECORATION
  45 ml/3 tbsp smooth apricot jam
  25 g/1 oz desiccated coconut
  glacé cherries, halved
  20 angelica leaves

Thoroughly grease 10 dariole moulds. Set the oven at 180°C/350°F/gas 4. Mix the flour and salt in a bowl.

In a mixing bowl cream the butter or margarine with the sugar until light and fluffy. Beat in the eggs, then lightly stir in the flour and salt. Divide the mixture evenly between the prepared moulds and bake for 15-20 minutes until golden brown. Cool on a wire rack.

Trim off the rounded ends of the cakes, if necessary, and stand upright. Warm the jam in a small saucepan, then brush the cakes all over. Toss in coconut. Decorate the top of each with a glacé cherry or angelica leaves or both.

MAKES 10

CHOCOLATE MOTHS

fat for greasing
100 g/4 oz self-raising flour
pinch of salt
30 ml/2 tbsp cocoa
100 g/4 oz butter or margarine
100 g/4 oz caster sugar
2 eggs, beaten
15 ml/1 tbsp milk

DECORATION
  Buttercream (page 57), using 50 g/2 oz
    butter
  chocolate vermicelli

Grease 12-14 bun tins. Set the oven at 180°C/350°F/gas 4. Mix the flour, salt and cocoa in a bowl.

In a mixing bowl, cream the butter or margarine with the sugar until light and fluffy. Beat in the eggs and milk, then lightly stir in the flour mixture. Divide the mixture evenly between the prepared bun tins, and bake for 15-20 minutes until golden brown. Cool on a wire rack.

Make the buttercream and place it in an icing bag fitted with a large star nozzle.

When the cakes are cold, cut a round off the top of each. Cut each round in half to create 2 'moth wings'. Pipe a star of buttercream on each cake, then add the 'wings', placing them cut side down, and slightly apart. Sprinkle with chocolate vermicelli.

MAKES 12 TO 14

BUTTERSCOTCH BROWNIES

*Rich, gooey and delightfully chewy, these are
bound to prove popular.*

fat for greasing
75 g/3 oz butter
175 g/6 oz soft light brown sugar
1 egg, beaten
5 ml/1 tsp vanilla essence
75 g/3 oz plain flour
5 ml/1 tsp baking powder
1.25 ml/¼ tsp salt
50 g/2 oz dates, chopped
50 g/2 oz blanched almonds, chopped

Line and grease an 18 cm/7 inch square
tin. Set the oven at 160°C/325°F/gas 3.

Combine the butter and sugar in a large
heavy-bottomed saucepan and heat gently
until all the sugar has dissolved, stirring
occasionally. Remove from the heat, cool
slightly, then blend in the egg and vanilla
essence.

Sift the flour, baking powder and salt into
a bowl. Add the dates and mix to coat in
flour. Stir the flour mixture into the saucepan
with the almonds and mix well.

Spoon the mixture into the prepared tin
and bake for 20-30 minutes. Cool in the tin.
When cold, cut into squares.

MAKES 20

CHOCOLATE SPICE SQUARES

*The combination of chocolate and cinnamon
makes these delicious tray-bake cakes just that bit
different. If you want to make them extra special,
top them with melted chocolate.*

fat for greasing
225 g/8 oz margarine
225 g/8 oz soft light brown sugar
4 eggs
225 g/8 oz self-raising flour
30 ml/2 tbsp cocoa
10 ml/2 tsp cinnamon

Base-line and grease a roasting tin,
measuring about 25 x 30 cm/10 x 12 inches.
Set the oven at 180°C/350°F/gas 4.

Cream the margarine and sugar together
until soft and light. Beat in the eggs. Sift the
flour with the cocoa and the cinnamon, then
fold these dry ingredients into the mixture.

Turn the mixture into the prepared tin
and smooth it out evenly. Bake for about 1
hour, until the mixture is evenly risen and
firm to the touch. Leave to cool in the tin for
15 minutes, then cut the cake into 5 cm/2
inch squares and transfer them to a wire rack
to cool completely.

MAKES 35

★ **FREEZING TIP** The squares of cake
freeze very well and individual portions
can be removed as required – ideal for
lunch boxes. Pack the pieces of cake in a
large rigid container leaving a very small
space between each square. Alternatively,
open freeze the squares on a baking sheet
lined with cling film. When solid, stack the
squares in polythene bags and seal.

A VARIETY OF TRAY BAKES

By baking a large quantity of cake mixture in a roasting tin or large baking tin, then cutting it into squares, you can make a good batch of individual cakes very speedily. It is a good idea to set aside a roasting tin specifically for baking cakes. Use the mixture for the Chocolate Spice Squares as a base and try some of the ideas given here.

FRUIT 'N' NUT SQUARES Omit the cocoa from the mixture. Instead, fold in 225 g/8 oz of chopped nuts – walnuts, hazelnuts or mixed nuts – and 100 g/4 oz of mixed dried fruit.

ALMOND SQUARES Omit the cocoa from the Chocolate Spice Squares. Add a few drops of almond essence to the fat and sugar. Fold in 225 g/8 oz of ground almonds with the flour. Sprinkle 100 g/4 oz of flaked almonds over the mixture once it is smoothed in the tin.

COCONUT SQUARES The chocolate can be omitted if liked, or it can be left in the mixture as its flavour is complementary to the coconut. Add 225 g/8 oz of desiccated coconut after the flour is folded in. Soften the mixture with 60 ml/4 tbsp of milk or orange juice. The cooked squares can be spread with apricot or raspberry jam and sprinkled with desiccated or long-thread coconut.

MARBLED SQUARES Prepare the mixture, omitting the cocoa. Divide it into two portions and flavour one half with cocoa. Add a little grated orange rind and juice to the second portion. Drop small spoonfuls of the mixture into the prepared tin and drag the point of a knife through just once. Do not over-swirl the two flavours or they will blend into one during cooking. Top the cooled cakes with melted chocolate.

MARMALADE SQUARES Make up the cake mixture, creaming 60 ml/4 tbsp of marmalade with the fat and sugar and omitting the cocoa. Glaze the tops of the cakes with warmed marmalade.

CRUMBLY APPLE SQUARES

fat for greasing
150 ml/¼ pint apple purée
1 Cox's Orange Pippin apple, peeled, cored and chopped
100 g/4 oz butter or margarine
100 g/4 oz sugar
1 egg
175 g/6 oz self-raising flour

TOPPING
50 g/2 oz plain flour
25 g/1 oz butter or margarine
30 ml/2 tbsp caster sugar
100 g/4 oz walnuts, chopped
1.25 ml/¼ tsp ground cloves
5 ml/1 tsp cinnamon

Line and grease an 18 cm/7 inch shallow, square tin, allowing the paper to stand above the rim of the tin by 2.5 cm/1 inch. Set the oven at 180°C/350°F/gas 4.

Make sure that the apple purée is very smooth and absolutely cold, then stir in the chopped apple. Cream the butter or margarine and sugar until pale and very soft. Beat in the egg and the apple purée. Fold in the flour. Transfer the mixture to the prepared tin, spreading it out evenly.

For the crumble topping, sift the flour into a bowl and rub in the butter or margarine until the mixture resembles fine breadcrumbs. Stir in the sugar, nuts and spices, then sprinkle this crumble lightly over the top of the cake mixture. Bake for 50-60 minutes, until the cake is evenly risen and the topping crisp and brown.

Allow to cool in the tin for 15 minutes, then cut into squares and transfer to a wire rack to cool completely. Store in an airtight container.

MAKES 16

MOCHA FINGERS

Illustrated on page 116

fat for greasing
75 g/3 oz plain flour
2.5 ml/½ tsp salt
50 g/2 oz Clarified Butter (page 15) or
    margarine
3 eggs
75 g/3 oz caster sugar

DECORATION
    Coffee Buttercream (pages 57-58)
        using 50 g/2 oz butter
    50 g/2 oz toasted almond flakes
    icing sugar for dredging

Line and grease a 15 x 25 cm/6 x 10 inch rectangular cake tin. Set the oven at 180°C/350°F/gas 4.

Sift the flour and salt into a bowl and put in a warm place. Melt the clarified butter or margarine without letting it get hot.

Whisk the eggs lightly in a mixing bowl. Add the sugar and place the bowl over a saucepan of hot water. Whisk for 10-15 minutes until thick. Take care that the bottom of the bowl does not touch the water. Remove from the heat and continue whisking until at blood-heat. The melted butter should be at the same temperature.

Sift half the flour over the eggs, then pour in half the melted butter or margarine in a thin stream. Fold in gently. Repeat, using the remaining flour and fat. Spoon gently into the tin and bake for 30-40 minutes. Cool.

Spread the top of the cold sponge with the buttercream. Cover with the toasted almonds and dredge with icing sugar. Cut into 20 2.5 cm/1 inch fingers.

MAKES 20

MAYFAIR CAKES

fat for greasing
100 g/4 oz plain flour
2.5 ml/½ tsp salt
75 g/3 oz Clarified Butter (page 15) or
    margarine
4 eggs
100 g/4 oz caster sugar

DECORATION
    300 ml/½ pint double cream
    10 ml/2 tsp caster sugar
    chocolate vermicelli

Line and grease a 20 x 30 cm/8 x 12 inch Swiss roll tin. Set the oven at 180°C/350°F/gas 4.

Sift the flour and salt into a bowl and put in a warm place. Melt the clarified butter or margarine without letting it get hot. Put to one side.

Whisk the eggs lightly in a mixing bowl. Add the sugar and place the bowl over a saucepan of hot water. Whisk for 10-15 minutes until thick. Take care that the bottom of the bowl does not touch the water. Remove from the heat. Continue whisking until the mixture is at blood-heat. The melted butter or margarine should be at the same temperature.

Sift half the flour over the eggs, then pour in half the melted butter or margarine in a thin stream. Fold in gently. Repeat, using the remaining flour and fat. Spoon gently into the prepared tin and bake for 30-40 minutes. Cool on a wire rack.

Cut the cold sponge into about eighteen 4 cm/1½ inch rounds. In a bowl, whip the cream with the sugar until fairly stiff. Use most of the cream to spread over the top and sides of each cake. Coat with chocolate vermicelli, spreading it lightly with a round-bladed knife. Using a piping bag fitted with a large rose nozzle, pipe the remaining cream on to each cake in a star.

MAKES 18

SWISS SHORTCAKES

150 g/5 oz butter
50 g/2 oz caster sugar
150 g/5 oz plain flour
few drops of vanilla essence

DECORATION
glacé cherries
angelica, cut into diamonds
smooth red jam

Place 16 paper cases in dry bun tins. Set the oven at 180°C/350°F/gas 4.

In a mixing bowl, cream the butter and sugar until light and fluffy. Work in the flour and vanilla essence, then spoon the mixture into a piping bag fitted with a large star nozzle. Pipe the mixture in whorls into the prepared paper cases.

Bake for 15-20 minutes. Cool on a wire rack. Decorate the shortcakes with glacé cherries and angelica diamonds kept in place with a tiny dab of jam.

MAKES 16

MRS BEETON'S TIP Make mini-shortcakes for a child's birthday party. Fit a small star nozzle on the piping bag and pipe the mixture into paper sweet cases instead of cupcake cases. Bake for about 10 minutes.

WHOLEMEAL ALMOND SHORTCAKES

fat for greasing
75 g/3 oz butter
40 g/1½ oz soft dark brown sugar
100 g/4 oz wholemeal flour
1.25 ml/¼ tsp salt
25 g/1 oz ground almonds

Grease a 15 cm/6 inch sandwich tin. Set the oven at 160°C/325°F/gas 3.

Cream the butter and sugar in a mixing bowl until light and fluffy. Mix the flour and salt in a second bowl, then add to the creamed mixture with the ground almonds, working the mixture with the hands until the dough is smooth. Press into the prepared sandwich tin and bake for 50 minutes. Cut into 8 wedges while still warm. Cool in the sandwich tin.

MAKES 8

COCONUT PYRAMIDS

fat for greasing
2 eggs, separated
150 g/5 oz caster sugar
150 g/5 oz desiccated coconut

Grease a baking sheet and cover with rice paper. Set the oven at 140°C/275°F/gas 1. In a clean dry bowl, whisk the egg whites until stiff, then fold in the sugar and coconut, using a metal spoon. Divide the mixture into 12 portions and place in heaps on the rice paper. Using a fork, form into pyramid shapes. Bake for 45 minutes-1 hour until pale brown in colour. Cool on the baking sheet.

MAKES 12

MUSHROOM CAKES

fat for greasing
100 g/4 oz self-raising flour
pinch of salt
100 g/4 oz butter or margarine
100 g/4 oz caster sugar
2 eggs, beaten

DECORATION
Apricot Glaze (page 54)
Almond Paste (page 56), using 75 g/3 oz
    almonds
icing sugar and ground cinnamon for
    dusting
Buttercream (page 57) using 50 g/oz
    butter

Grease 12-14 bun tins. Set the oven at 180°C/350°F/gas 4. Mix the flour and salt.

In a mixing bowl, cream the butter or margarine with the sugar until light and fluffy. Beat in the eggs, then lightly stir in the flour and salt. Divide the mixture evenly between the prepared bun tins, and bake for 15-20 minutes until golden brown. Cool.

Brush the sides and tops of the cold cakes with apricot glaze. Roll out the almond paste thinly and cut rounds to cover the top and sides of the cakes; press into position.

Mix the icing sugar and cinnamon together and place on a sheet of greaseproof paper. Holding each cake near its base, roll it in the cinnamon sugar.

Put the buttercream in an icing bag fitted with a small star nozzle and pipe threads on the surface of each cake, radiating from the centre to the edge, to represent gills. Use the almond paste trimmings to make tiny stalks and place one of these in the centre of each cake, making a small hole with a skewer.

MAKES 12 TO 14

CAULIFLOWERS

fat for greasing
100 g/4 oz plain flour
2.5 ml/½ tsp salt
75 g/3 oz Clarified Butter (page 15) or
    margarine
4 eggs
100 g/4 oz caster sugar

DECORATION
green food colouring
Almond Paste (page 142) using 200 g/7 oz
    almonds
Almond Paste (page 56) using 200 g/7 oz
    almonds
Apricot Glaze (page 54)

Line and grease a 20 x 30 cm/8 x 12 inch Swiss roll tin. Set the oven at 180°C/350°F/gas 4.

Sift the flour and salt into a bowl and put in a warm place. Melt the clarified butter or margarine without letting it get hot.

Whisk the eggs lightly in a mixing bowl. Add the sugar and place the bowl over a saucepan of hot water. Whisk for 10-15 minutes until thick. Take care that the bottom of the bowl does not touch the water. Remove from the heat and continue whisking until at blood-heat. The melted butter should be at the same temperature.

Sift half the flour over the eggs, then pour in half the melted butter or margarine in a thin stream. Fold in gently. Repeat, using the remaining flour and fat. Spoon gently into the prepared tin and bake for 30-40 minutes. Cool on a wire rack.

Cut the cold sponge into about eighteen 4 cm/1½ inch rounds. Work a few drops of green food colouring into the almond paste, roll it out thinly and cut out five 4 cm/1½ inch rounds for each cake.

Brush the sides of each cake with apricot glaze. Press the circles of almond paste round the sides of each cake, overlapping them slightly. Bend the centre top of each piece outwards to represent cauliflower leaves. In a bowl, whip the cream with the sugar until stiff. Using a piping bag fitted with a small star nozzle, pipe tiny rosettes of cream on top of each cake to represent the cauliflower florettes.

MAKES 18

CINNAMON DOUGHNUTS

150 g/5 oz self-raising flour
2.5 ml/½ tsp salt
2.5 ml/½ tsp ground cinnamon
50 g/2 oz margarine
25 g/1 oz sugar
1 egg, beaten
15-30 ml/1-2 tbsp milk
flour for rolling out
oil for deep frying
caster sugar and ground cinnamon for
    dusting

Mix the flour, salt and cinnamon together in a mixing bowl. Rub in the margarine until the mixture resembles fine breadcrumbs. Stir in the sugar. Add the beaten egg with the milk and mix to a soft, scone-like dough.

Roll out the dough to a thickness of about 1cm/½ inch on a floured board. Cut into rounds with a 5 cm/2 inch cutter, then remove the centres with an apple corer. Gather the trimmings together, roll out again and cut more rounds.

Heat the fat (see recipe right) and fry the doughnuts, turning once with a slotted spoon when brown on the underside. Drain on kitchen paper and while still hot, toss in caster sugar flavoured with cinnamon.

MAKES 8 TO 10

RING DOUGHNUTS

200 g/7 oz plain flour
1.25 ml/¼ tsp salt
pinch of ground cinnamon or nutmeg
7.5 ml/1½ tsp baking powder
40 g/1½ oz butter or margarine
45 ml/3 tbsp sugar
1 egg, lightly beaten
about 60 ml/4 tbsp milk
flour for rolling out
oil for deep frying
caster sugar for dusting

Sift the flour, salt, spice and baking powder into a mixing bowl. Rub in the butter or margarine until the mixture resembles breadcrumbs. Stir in the sugar. Make a well in the centre of the dry ingredients and add the egg. Gradually work it into the dry ingredients, adding enough milk to make a soft dough.

Roll out the dough to a thickness of 1 cm/½ inch on a floured board. Heat the oil to 180-190°C/350-375°F or until a cube of bread added to the oil browns in 30 seconds. Cut the dough into rings using a 6 cm/2½ inch and a 2 cm/¾ inch cutter. Re-roll and re-cut the trimmings.

Fry 1 or 2 doughnuts in the hot oil until light brown underneath; then carefully turn with a slotted spoon and cook the second side. Lift the doughnuts out and drain well on absorbent kitchen paper.

Put some caster sugar in a large paper bag and add the doughnuts while still hot. Toss them gently until coated. Transfer to absorbent paper dusted with sugar. Continue until all the doughnuts are fried. Bring the oil back to temperature between each batch.

MAKES ABOUT 12

APRICOT BASKETS

fat for greasing
100 g/4 oz self-raising flour
pinch of salt
100 g/4 oz butter or margarine
100 g/4 oz caster sugar
2 eggs, beaten

DECORATION
1 (425 g/15 oz) can apricot halves in syrup
¼ (142 g/5 oz) packet lemon jelly cubes
1 (15 cm/6 inch) stick angelica
150 ml/5 fl oz double cream
5 ml/1 tsp caster sugar

Grease 12-14 bun tins. Set the oven at 180°C/350°F/gas 4. Mix the flour and salt in a bowl.

In a mixing bowl, cream the butter or margarine with the sugar until light and fluffy. Beat in the eggs, then lightly stir in the flour and salt. Divide the mixture evenly between the prepared bun tins, and bake for 15-20 minutes until golden brown. Cool on a wire rack.

While the cakes are cooling, drain the apricots, reserving 125 ml/4 fl oz of the syrup in a small saucepan. Bring the syrup to the boil, then add the jelly cubes and stir until dissolved. Set aside to cool.

Soften the angelica (see Mrs Beeton's Tip), then cut it into 12-14 strips 5 mm/¼ inch wide. In a bowl, whip the cream with the sugar until stiff.

When the cakes are cold and the jelly is just on the point of setting, place half an apricot, rounded side uppermost, on the top of each cake. Coat each apricot with jelly. Using a piping bag fitted with a small star nozzle, pipe stars of cream around the apricots. Arch the strips of angelica over the cakes to form handles, pushing them in to the sides of the cakes.

MAKES 12 TO 14

> 🥣 **MRS BEETON'S TIP** Soften the angelica by placing it in a bowl of very hot water for 3-4 minutes. Pat dry on absorbent kitchen paper.

Battenburg Cake (page 155) and Swiss Roll (page 152)

Dundee Cake (page 156)

Dark Secrets Ring Cake (page 159)

Black Forest Gâteau (page 168)

Strawberry Meringue Torte (page 172)

Individual Apricot Trifles and Rum Babas (both on page 175)

Mrs Beeton's Traditional Trifle (page 178)

Knickerbocker Glory (page 233) and Neapolitan Ice (page 226)

CORKERS

Illustrated on page 116

fat for greasing
100 g/4 oz self-raising flour
pinch of salt
100 g/4 oz butter or margarine
100 g/4 oz caster sugar
2 eggs, beaten

DECORATION
    Apricot Glaze (page 54)
    15 g/½ oz pistachio nuts, blanched and
      chopped
    150 ml/5 fl oz double cream
    icing sugar for dusting

Grease 12-14 bun tins. Set the oven at 180°C/350°F/gas 4. Mix the flour and salt in a bowl.

In a mixing bowl, cream the butter or margarine with the sugar until light and fluffy. Beat in the eggs, then lightly stir in the flour and salt. Divide the mixture evenly between the prepared bun tins, and bake for 15-20 minutes until golden brown. Cool on a wire rack.

When the cakes are cold, remove a small cylindrical section about 1-2 cm/½-⅓ inch deep from the centre of each cake, using an apple corer or small cutter. Have both the apricot glaze and the chopped nuts ready.

Dip the top of each cake cork in glaze then in nuts. Spoon the rest of the glaze into the hollows in each cake.

In a bowl, whip the cream until stiff. Using a piping bag fitted with a star nozzle, pipe a cream star on top of the glaze in each cake hollow. Return the corks, pressing them down lightly, then dust with icing sugar.

MAKES 12 TO 14

BROWNIES

Brownies should be moist and chewy. Do not overbake them.

fat for greasing
150 g/5 oz margarine
150 g/5 oz caster sugar
2 eggs
50 g/2 oz plain flour
30 ml/2 tbsp cocoa
100 g/4 oz walnuts, chopped

Line and grease a shallow 15 cm/6 inch square tin. Set the oven at 180°C/350°F/gas 4.

Cream the margarine and sugar in a mixing bowl until light and fluffy. Beat in the eggs. Sift the flour and cocoa into a second bowl, then fold in. Add half the chopped walnuts to the mixture.

Spread the mixture evenly in the prepared tin and bake for 10 minutes; then sprinkle the rest of the walnuts all over the surface. Bake for 15 minutes more. Cool in the tin. When cold, cut into squares.

MAKES ABOUT 9

VARIATION

CAROB BROWNIES Follow the recipe above but substitute 45 ml/3 tbsp carob powder for the cocoa.

SPECIAL CAKES AND WEEKEND TREATS

A special cake is an essential feature of any celebration, whether the occasion is a birthday tea, an informal gathering of friends or a festival such as Christmas or Easter. Alongside seasonal cakes, this chapter includes exciting recipes that are just that bit different.

CHRISTMAS CAKE

fat for greasing
200 g/7 oz plain flour
1.25 ml/¼ tsp salt
5-10 ml/1-2 tsp mixed spice
200 g/7 oz butter
200 g/7 oz caster sugar
6 eggs, beaten
30-60 ml/2-4 tbsp brandy or sherry
100 g/4 oz glacé cherries, chopped
50 g/2 oz preserved ginger, chopped
50 g/2 oz walnuts, chopped
200 g/7 oz currants
200 g/7 oz sultanas
150 g/5 oz seedless raisins
75 g/3 oz cut mixed peel

COATING AND ICING
  Almond Paste (page 56)
  Royal Icing (page 61)

Line and grease a 20 cm/8 inch round cake tin. Use doubled greaseproof paper and tie a strip of brown paper around the outside. Set the oven at 160°C/325°F/gas 3.

Sift the flour, salt and spice into a bowl. In a mixing bowl, cream the butter and sugar together until light and fluffy. Gradually beat in the eggs and the brandy or sherry, adding a little flour if the mixture starts to curdle. Add the cherries, ginger and walnuts. Stir in the dried fruit, peel and flour mixture. Spoon into the prepared tin and make a slight hollow in the centre.

Bake for 45 minutes, then reduce the oven temperature to 150°C/300°F/gas 2 and bake for a further hour. Reduce the temperature still further to 140°C/275°F/gas 1, and continue cooking for 45 minutes-1 hour until cooked through and firm to the touch. Cool in the tin. Cover the cake with almond paste and decorate with royal icing.

MAKES ONE 20 CM/8 INCH CAKE

> **MRS BEETON'S TIP** The quickest way to complete the decoration on a Christmas cake is to apply the royal icing in rough peaks, then add bought decorations. For a change, why not bake the cake mixture in a shaped tin, for example in the shape of a star or a bell? Shaped tins can be hired from kitchen shops and cake decorating suppliers.
> To decide on the quantity of mixture which will fill the tin, pour water into the tin until it is full to the brim. Measure the quantity of water as you are pouring it into the tin. Do the same with a 20 cm/8 inch round tin. Compare the volumes and adjust the weight of ingredients accordingly.

INGREDIENTS FOR RICH FRUIT CAKE

ROUND SQUARE	15 cm/6 inch 13 cm/5 inch	18 cm/7 inch 15 cm/6 inch	20 cm/8 inch 18 cm/7 inch	23 cm/9 inch 20 cm/8 inch	25 cm/10 inch 23 cm/9 inch	28 cm/11 inch 25 cm/10 inch	30 cm/12 inch 28 cm/11 inch	33 cm/13 inch 30 cm/12 inch
Currants	225 g/8 oz	275 g/10 oz	400 g/14 oz	500 g/1 lb 2oz	575 g/1¼ lb	675 g/1½ lb	900 g/2 lb	1.25 kg/2½ lb
Raisins	100 g/4 oz	150 g/5 oz	200 g/7 oz	250 g/9 oz	300 g/11 oz	375 g/13 oz	450 g/1 lb	575 g/1¼ lb
Sultanas	100 g/4 oz	150 g/5 oz	200 g/7 oz	250 g/9 oz	300 g/11 oz	375 g/13 oz	450 g/1 lb	575 g/1¼ lb
Butter, softened	100 g/4 oz	150 g/5 oz	200 g/7 oz	250 g/9 oz	300 g/11 oz	375 g/13 oz	450 g/1 lb	575 g/1¼ lb
Moist dark brown sugar	100 g/4 oz	150 g/5 oz	200 g/7 oz	250 g/9 oz	300 g/11 oz	375 g/13 oz	450 g/1 lb	575 g/1¼ lb
Lemon, grated rind of	½	½	1	1	1½	1½	2	2
Almonds, shelled	25 g/1 oz	25 g/1 oz	40 g/1½ oz	65 g/2½ oz	75 g/3 oz	90 g/3½ oz	100 g/4 oz	100 g/4 oz
Citrus peel, chopped	25 g/1 oz	25 g/1 oz	40 g/1½ oz	65 g/2½ oz	75 g/3 oz	90 g/3½ oz	100 g/4 oz	100 g/4 oz
Glacé cherries	50 g/2 oz	50 g/2 oz	75 g/3 oz	90 g/3½ oz	100 g/4 oz	150 g/5 oz	175 g/6 oz	175 g/6 oz
Plain flour	100 g/4 oz	150 g/5 oz	200 g/7 oz	250 g/9 oz	300 g/11 oz	375 g/13 oz	450 g/1 lb	575 g/1¼ lb
Ground mixed spice	1.25 ml/¼ tsp	2.5 ml/½ tsp	2.5 ml/½ tsp	5 ml/1 tsp	5 ml/1 tsp	7.5 ml/1½ tsp	7.5 ml/1½ tsp	10 ml/2 tsp
Eggs, beaten	2	2	3	4	5	6	8	10
Black treacle	10 ml/2 tsp	10 ml/2 tsp	15 ml/1 tbsp	15 ml/1 tbsp	22.5 ml/4½ tsp	22.5 ml/4½ tsp	30 ml/2 tbsp	30 ml/2 tbsp

This chart provides at-a-glance quantities for cakes of different sizes.

Set the oven at 150°C/300°F/gas 2. Line and grease the appropriate tin. Mix the currants, raisins and sultanas. Cream the butter, sugar and lemon rind until very soft. Beat in the almonds and the citrus peel. Wash and dry the cherries, then roughly chop them and toss them with a little of the measured flour. Sift the remaining flour with the spice and toss a little with the mixed dried fruit. Beat the eggs and treacle into the creamed mixture, adding a spoonful of the flour occasionally to prevent the mixture curdling. Fold in the the remaining flour. Lastly fold in the fruit and the cherries.

Turn the mixture into the tin and smooth the top with the back of a wetted metal spoon, hollowing out the centre slightly. The cooking time depends on the size of the cake. The small cakes will take about 1½-2 hours, the cakes of between 20-23 cm/8-9 inches will need about 4-5 hours and the larger cakes take about 7-8 hours. Insert a clean metal skewer into the centre of the cake to test if it is cooked: it should come out clean when the cake is ready. If there is any sticky mixture on the skewer the cake is not cooked.

Leave the cake to cool in the tin for at least an hour, then transfer it to a wire rack to cool completely. Do not remove the lining paper. Wrap the cake, still in the lining paper, in fresh greaseproof paper and store it in an airtight tin.

MINI CHRISTMAS CAKES

Illustrated on page 117

*These small cakes make an ideal Christmas gift
for anyone who lives alone.*

20 cm/8 inch round quantity Rich Fruit
    Cake mixture (page 147)
Almond Paste (page 56)
Sugar Paste

DECORATION

    cut-out candle, holly and berries
    moulded snowman without a scarf
        scarf
    red or orange icing pen or food colouring
    red and green food colouring

You will need crimpers and a modelling
tool to decorate these cakes. Use two 10 cm/
4 inch round cake tins as containers to bake
the rich fruit cake mixture. Alternatively,
wash and dry two empty 822 g/1 lb 3 oz cans,
for example fruit cans. Bake the cakes for
about 1½ hours, leave them to cool and cover
with almond paste and sugar paste.

Using the crimpers, mark around the top
edge of one of the cakes (page 92). Roll out
a thin rope of sugar paste and place it around
the base of the cake, joining it at the back to
make a neat edge.

Place the candle, holly and berries on the
top of the cake. Use a dampened paint brush
to moisten them if they are dry. If the cut-
outs are freshly made, smooth them on to the
cake and round off the corners. Leave the
cake to dry.

Finish this first cake by painting or
drawing short lines radiating out from the
flame of the candle. Tie a ribbon around the
side of the cake, if you like, securing the join
at the back with a tiny piece of adhesive tape.

To decorate the second cake, use the
modelling tool to mark around the top edge
of the cake. Divide the remaining sugar paste
in half and colour one portion red, the other
green. Make the snowman's scarf by arranging two thin rolls of coloured paste side by
side. Place the scarf around the snowman's
neck.

Roll the remaining portions of coloured
paste separately into two long rolls, twist
these together lightly and place them around
the lower edge of the cake. Make a decorative join at the front of the cake. Place the
snowman on top of the cake.

ABOUT 10-12 PORTIONS EACH

FESTIVE LOG

Illustrated on page 117

Swiss Roll (page 152) or Chocolate Roll
(page 153)
1 quantity American Frosting (page 60)

DECORATION

    Chocolate leaves (page 98) or Marzipan
        leaves, dipped in chocolate
    small piece of marzipan or moulding
        icing, coloured red and rolled into
        berries

Place the cake on a suitable board. Make
up the frosting and quickly spread it over the
cake, making sure it comes well down on
each side. As the frosting begins to set, draw
a fork or serrated scraper down the length of
the cake. Swirl the icing on the ends of the
cake into circles. Add the leaves and berries
to complete the decoration.

ABOUT 10 PORTIONS

*I*CED PETITS FOURS

fat for greasing
75 g/3 oz plain flour
2.5 ml/½ tsp salt
50 g/2 oz Clarified Butter (page 15) or
    margarine
3 eggs
75 g/3 oz caster sugar

FILLING
    jam, lemon curd or Buttercream (page
        57), using 50 g/2 oz butter

ICING AND DECORATION
    Glacé Icing (page 59)
    food colouring
    crystallised violets
    silver balls
    glacé fruits
    angelica
    chopped nuts

Line and grease a 15 x 25 cm/6 x 10 inch rectangular cake tin. Set the oven at 180°C/350°F/gas 4.

Sift the flour and salt into a bowl and put in a warm place. Melt the clarified butter or margarine without letting it get hot. Put to one side.

Whisk the eggs lightly in a mixing bowl. Add the sugar and place the bowl over a saucepan of hot water. Whisk for 10-15 minutes until thick. Take care that the bottom of the bowl does not touch the water. Remove from the heat and continue whisking until at blood-heat. The melted butter should be at the same temperature.

Sift half the flour over the eggs, then pour in half the melted butter or margarine in a thin stream. Fold in gently. Repeat, using the remaining flour and fat. Spoon gently into the prepared tin and bake for 30-40 minutes. Cool on a wire rack.

Cut the cold cake in half horizontally, spread with the chosen filling and sandwich together again. Cut the cake into small rounds, triangles or squares and place on a wire rack set over a large dish. Brush off any loose crumbs.

Make up the icing to a coating consistency which will flow easily. Tint part of it with food colouring, if wished. Using a small spoon, coat the top and sides of the cakes with the icing or, if preferred, pour it over the cakes, making sure that the sides are coated evenly all over. Place the decorations on top and leave to set. The cakes may be served in paper cases, if liked

MAKES 18 TO 24

MRS BEETON'S TIP For perfect petits fours it is important that all loose crumbs are brushed away so that they do not spoil the appearance of the icing. The cake is easier to cut, and produces fewer crumbs, if it is chilled in the freezer for about an hour. It should be firm but not thoroughly frozen. Use a very sharp, serrated knife to cut the cakes cleanly and chill them again briefly before coating them with the icing. Any cake trimmings can be used to make trifle, or frozen for later use.

TWELFTH NIGHT CAKE

*The tradition of the Twelfth Night Cake goes back
to the days of the early Christian Church and
beyond. In the Middle Ages, whoever found the
bean in his cake became the 'Lord of Misrule' or
'King' for the festivities of Twelfth Night, with the
finder of the pea as his 'Queen'. Finding the bean
was thought to bring luck. The tradition survived
until near the end of the nineteenth century.*

fat for greasing
150 g/5 oz margarine
75 g/3 oz soft dark brown sugar
3 eggs
300 g/11 oz plain flour
60 ml/4 tbsp milk
5 ml/1 tsp bicarbonate of soda
30 ml/2 tbsp golden syrup
2.5 ml/½ tsp mixed spice
2.5 ml/½ tsp ground cinnamon
pinch of salt
50 g/2 oz currants
100 g/4 oz sultanas
100 g/4 oz cut mixed peel
1 dried bean (see above)
1 large dried whole pea (see above)

Line and grease a 15 cm/6 inch round cake
tin. Set the oven at 180°C/350°F/gas 4.

In a mixing bowl, cream the margarine
and sugar until light and fluffy. Beat in the
eggs, one at a time, adding a little flour with
each. Warm the milk, add the bicarbonate of
soda and stir until dissolved. Add the syrup.

Mix the spices and salt with the remaining
flour in a bowl. Add this to the creamed
mixture alternately with the flavoured milk.
Lightly stir in the dried fruit and peel. Spoon
half the cake mixture into the prepared tin,
lay the bean and pea in the centre, then
cover with the rest of the cake mixture. Bake
for about 2 hours. Cool on a wire rack.

MAKES ONE 15 CM/6 INCH CAKE

SIMNEL CAKE

Illustrated on page 118

fat for greasing
200 g/7 oz plain flour
2.5 ml/½ tsp baking powder
1.25 ml/¼ tsp salt
150 g/5 oz butter
150 g/5 oz caster sugar
4 eggs
100 g/4 oz glacé cherries, halved
150 g/5 oz currants
150 g/5 oz sultanas
100 g/4 oz seedless raisins
50 g/2 oz cut mixed peel
50 g/2 oz ground almonds
grated rind of 1 lemon

DECORATION
Double quantity Almond Paste (page 56)
    or 450 g/1 lb marzipan
30 ml/2 tbsp smooth apricot jam (see
    method)
1 egg, beaten
White Glacé Icing (page 59) using 50 g/
    2 oz icing sugar
Easter decorations

Line and grease an 18 cm/7 inch cake tin.
Set the oven at 180°C/350°F/gas 4.

Sift the flour, baking powder and salt into
a bowl. In a mixing bowl, cream the butter
and sugar together well and beat in the eggs,
adding a little of the flour mixture if
necessary. Fold the flour mixture, cherries,
dried fruit, peel and ground almonds into the
creamed mixture. Add the lemon rind and
mix well.

Spoon half the mixture into the prepared
tin. Cut off one third of the almond paste and
roll it to a pancake about 1 cm/½ inch thick
and slightly smaller than the circumference
of the tin. Place it gently on top of the cake
mixture and spoon the remaining cake
mixture on top.

Bake for 1 hour, then reduce the oven temperature to 160°C/325°F/gas 3 and bake for 1½ hours more. Cool in the tin, then turn out on a wire rack.

Warm, then sieve the apricot jam. When the cake is cold, divide the remaining almond paste in half. Roll one half to a round slightly narrower than the circumference of the cake. Brush the top of the cake with apricot jam and press the almond paste lightly on to it. Trim the edge neatly.

Make 11 small balls with the remaining paste and place them around the edge of the cake. Brush the balls with the beaten egg and brown under the grill. Pour the glacé icing into the centre of the cake and decorate with chickens and Easter eggs.

MAKES ONE 18 CM/7 INCH CAKE

*P*INEAPPLE UPSIDE-DOWN CAKE

Illustrated on page 119

Serve this delicious cake cold for afternoon tea.

1 (227 g/8 oz) can pineapple rings
100 g/4 oz butter
275 g/10 oz soft dark brown sugar
8 maraschino or glacé cherries
450 g/1 lb self-raising flour
5 ml/1 tsp ground cinnamon
5 ml/1 tsp ground nutmeg
2 eggs
250 ml/8 fl oz milk

Drain the pineapple rings, reserving the syrup. Melt 50 g/2 oz of the butter in a 20 cm/8 inch square baking tin. Add 100 g/4 oz of the sugar and 15 ml/1 tbsp pineapple syrup and mix well. Arrange the pineapple

rings in an even pattern on the base of the tin, and place a cherry in the centre of each ring. Set the oven at 180°C/350°F/gas 4.

Sift the flour, cinnamon and nutmeg into a mixing bowl. In a second bowl, beat the eggs with the remaining brown sugar. Melt the remaining butter in a saucepan and add to the eggs and sugar with the milk; stir into the spiced flour and mix well.

Pour this mixture carefully over the fruit in the baking tin without disturbing it. Bake for 45-50 minutes. Remove the tin from the oven and at once turn upside-down on to a plate; allow the caramel to run over the cake before removing the baking tin.

MAKES ONE 20 CM/8 INCH CAKE

VARIATIONS

APRICOT UPSIDE-DOWN CAKE Substitute canned apricot halves for the pineapple, placing them rounded-side down in the tin. Arrange the cherries between the apricots.
PLUM UPSIDE-DOWN CAKE Arrange halved and stoned fresh plums in the bottom of the tin instead of pineapple. Use orange juice instead of the pineapple syrup and place the plums cut side down. Omit the cherries.
PEAR UPSIDE-DOWN PUDDING Use canned pears instead of the pineapple. If you like, substitute ground ginger for the nutmeg.

SWISS ROLL

Illustrated on page 137

fat for greasing
3 eggs
75 g/3 oz caster sugar
75 g/3 oz plain flour
2.5 ml/½ tsp baking powder
pinch of salt
about 60 ml/4 tbsp jam for filling
caster sugar for dusting

Line and grease a 20 x 30 cm/8 x 12 inch Swiss roll tin. Set the oven at 220°C/425°F/gas 7.

Combine the eggs and sugar in a heat-proof bowl. Set the bowl over a pan of hot water, taking care that the bottom of the bowl does not touch the water. Whisk for 10-15 minutes until thick and creamy, then remove from the pan and continue whisking until the mixture is cold.

Sift the flour, baking powder and salt into a bowl, then lightly fold into the egg mixture. Pour into the prepared tin and bake for 10 minutes. Meanwhile warm the jam in a small saucepan.

When the cake is cooked, turn it on to a large sheet of greaseproof paper dusted with caster sugar. Peel off the lining paper. Trim off any crisp edges. Spread the cake with the warmed jam and roll up tightly from one long side. Dredge with caster sugar and place on a wire rack, with the join underneath, to cool.

MAKES ONE 30 CM/12 INCH SWISS ROLL

A VARIETY OF ROLLED CAKES

The classic Swiss Roll is quick and easy to make once you have mastered the technique of rolling the hot cake. The basic recipe for the light, rolled sponge can be used as a base for making cakes that are just that little bit different.

The following variations suggest combinations of flavouring ingredients, fillings and coatings.

CHOCOLATE ICE ROLL Make the Chocolate Roll following the recipe on the right. Leave the rolled cake to cool completely. Using a shallow spoon, scoop flat portions of ice cream and place them on a baking sheet lined with cling film. Replace them in the freezer so that they are firmly frozen. Just before the cake is to be served, unroll it and fill with the ice cream, pressing it down lightly with a palette knife. Quickly re-roll the cake and sprinkle with icing sugar. Serve at once, with whipped cream.

CHOCOLATE RUM ROLL Make this luscious, rich, rolled cake for special occasions. Prepare the Chocolate Roll, following the recipe on the right, and allow it to cool. Soak 50 g/2 oz of seedless raisins in 60 ml/4 tbsp of rum for 30 minutes. Drain the raisins and add the rum to 150 ml/¼ pint of double cream. Add 15 ml/1 tbsp of icing sugar to the cream and lightly whip it. Fold in the raisins and 30 ml/2 tbsp of chopped Maraschino cherries. Spread this cream over the unrolled cake and re-roll.

EASTER ALMOND ROLL Make the Swiss Roll following the recipe on the left. Leave to cool completely. Roll out 350 g/12 oz marzipan or almond paste into an oblong the same width as the length of the roll, and long enough to wrap around the roll. Brush the outside of the Swiss Roll with warmed apricot jam and place it on the rolled out marzipan or almond paste. Wrap the paste around the roll, trimming off excess and making sure that the join is underneath. Decorate the top of the roll with miniature chocolate Easter eggs.

GINGER CREAM ROLL Make the plain Swiss Roll following the recipe on the left. Place a sheet of greaseproof paper in the hot roll instead of adding the jam, then leave it to cool completely. Whip 300 ml/½ pint of double cream with 45 ml/3 tbsp of ginger wine. Mix 30 ml/2 tbsp of finely chopped crystallised ginger into half the cream and spread this over the unrolled cake, then re-roll it. Cover the outside with a thin layer of the remaining cream and pipe rosettes of cream along the top. Decorate the roll with crystallised ginger.

RASPBERRY MERINGUE ROLL Make a plain Swiss Roll as left, rolling it up with sheet of greaseproof paper instead of spreading it with jam. Whip 150 ml/¼ pint of double cream with 30 ml/2 tbsp of icing sugar, then fold in 175 g/6 oz of raspberries. Spread this over the unrolled cake and roll it up again.

Whisk 2 egg whites until stiff, then whisk in 100 g/4 oz caster sugar. Continue whisking until the mixture is smooth, stiff and glossy. Swirl or pipe this meringue all over the roll. Brown the meringue under a moderately hot grill. Decorate with a few raspberries.

ST CLEMENT'S ROLL Make a Swiss Roll as left, adding the grated rind of 1 orange to the eggs and sugar. Instead of jam, use lemon curd to fill the cake.

WALNUT AND ORANGE ROLL Make a Swiss Roll following the recipe on the left and adding the grated rind of 1 orange to the eggs and sugar. Roll the cake with a sheet of greasproof paper instead of adding the jam, then leave it to cool.

Finely chop 100 g/4 oz of fresh walnuts. Beat 15-30 ml/1-2 tbsp of honey, to taste, into 100 g/4 oz of soft cheese. Stir in the nuts and spread this mixture over the cake before re-rolling it.

CHOCOLATE ROLL

fat for greasing
3 eggs
75 g/3 oz caster sugar
65 g/2½ oz plain flour
30 ml/2 tbsp cocoa
2.5 ml/½ tsp baking powder
pinch of salt
Chocolate Buttercream (pages 57-58)
    for filling
caster sugar for dusting

Line and grease a 20 x 30 cm/8 x 12 inch Swiss roll tin. Set the oven at 220°C/425°F/gas 7.

Combine the eggs and sugar in a heatproof bowl. Set the bowl over a pan of hot water, taking care that the bottom of the bowl does not touch the water. Whisk for 10-15 minutes until thick and creamy, then remove from the pan and continue whisking until the mixture is cold.

Sift the flour, cocoa, baking powder and salt into a bowl, then lightly fold into the egg mixture. Pour into the prepared tin and bake for 10 minutes.

When the cake is cooked, turn it on to a large sheet of greaseproof paper dusted with caster sugar. Peel off the lining paper. Trim off any crisp edges. Place a second piece of greaseproof paper on top of the cake and roll up tightly from one long side, with the paper inside. Cool completely on a wire rack.

When cold, unroll carefully, spread with the buttercream and roll up again. Dust with caster sugar.

MAKES ONE 30 CM/12 INCH SWISS ROLL

*H*ARVEST CAKE

The cake can either be covered in a thin layer of marzipan or almond paste and sugar paste; a sponge cake can be covered in buttercream. The basket weave piping is done in royal icing; however buttercream can also used.
The centre of the basket is filled with a selection of moulded marzipan fruits, vegetables and leaves.

23 cm/9 inch round Rich Fruit Cake (page 147) covered in Marzipan or Almond Paste (page 56) and Sugar Paste
450 g/1 lb Royal Icing (page 61), tinted with yellow or cream food colouring

DECORATION

marzipan fruits, vegetables and leaves

NOZZLES

medium basket or ribbon nozzle
plain writing nozzle no 2
small shell or star nozzle

Centre the cake on a 28 cm/11 inch board. Cut out a 23 cm/9 inch circle of greaseproof paper and fold it in half. Draw a line parallel to the fold and 5 cm/2 inches away from it. Turn the paper over and draw another line 5 cm/2 inches from the fold. Open out the paper.

Place the pattern on top of the cake and mark the position of the two lines with a pin. Remove the pattern. Place some of the royal icing in an icing bag fitted with the basket nozzle and fill in the two end areas on top of the cake with basket weave piping. Change to an icing bag fitted with the writing nozzle and neaten the straight edges of the basket weave piping with a line of plain piping.

Pipe basket weave around the side of the cake. Using an icing bag fitted with the shell nozzle, neaten the top and bottom edges with a row of fine shells. Leave icing to dry.

Arrange the fruits, vegetables and leaves down the centre of the cake.

ABOUT 30 PORTIONS

EASTER CAKES

Illustrated on page 120

Yellow is associated with Easter and springtime and yellow almond paste or marzipan is traditionally used to cover Simnel and Easter cakes.

EASTER LOG

Cover a Swiss Roll (page 152) with yellow almond paste by first cutting out two circles to fit the ends and then enclosing in a large piece of almond paste extending slightly over the ends. Neaten the roll, then drizzle melted chocolate over the top. Decorate the board with green-coloured desiccated coconut, moulded marzipan ducks and small Easter eggs or piped spring flowers.

EASTER CROWN

Colour almond paste green. Roll it out and cut a shape to cover the side only of a round cake (page 76). Before placing the almond paste in position around the cake, pattern it by pressing a meat hammer or grater over the surface. Coat the top of the cake in Apricot Glaze (page 54); sprinkle with chopped chocolate and lay the moulded marzipan daffodils on top.

BATTENBURG CAKE

Illustrated on page 137

fat for greasing
100 g/4 oz self-raising flour
pinch of salt
100 g/4 oz butter or margarine
100 g/4 oz caster sugar
2 eggs
pink food colouring
Apricot Glaze (page 54)
200 g/7 oz Almond Paste (page 56)

Line and grease a 23 x 18 cm/9 x 7 inch Battenburg tin, which has a metal divider down the centre; or use a 23 x 18 cm/9 x 7 inch tin and cut double greaseproof paper to separate the mixture into 2 parts. Set the oven at 190°C/375°F/gas 5. Mix the flour and salt in a bowl.

In a mixing bowl, cream the butter or margarine and sugar together until light and fluffy. Add the eggs, one at a time with a little flour. Stir in, then beat well. Stir in the remaining flour lightly but thoroughly.

Place half the mixture in one half of the tin. Tint the remaining mixture pink, and place it in the other half of the tin. Smooth both mixtures away from the centre towards the outside of the tin.

Bake for 25-30 minutes. Leave the cakes in the tin for a few minutes, then transfer them to a wire rack and peel off the paper. Leave to cool completely.

To finish the Battenburg, cut each slab of cake lengthways into 3 strips. Trim off any crisp edges and rounded surfaces so that all 6 strips are neat and of the same size. Arrange 3 strips with 1 pink strip in the middle. Where the cakes touch, brush with the glaze and press together lightly. Make up the other layer in the same way, using 2 pink with 1 plain strip in the middle. Brush glaze over the top of the base layer and place the second layer on top.

Roll out the almond paste thinly into a rectangle the same length as the strips and wide enough to wrap around them. Brush it with glaze and place the cake in the centre. Wrap the paste around the cake and press the edges together lightly. Turn so that the join is underneath; trim the ends. Mark the top of the paste with the back of a knife to make a criss-cross pattern.

MAKES ONE 23 x 18 CM/9 x 7 INCH CAKE

> ☀ **MICROWAVE TIP** Almond paste that has hardened will become soft and malleable again if heated in the microwave for a few seconds on High.

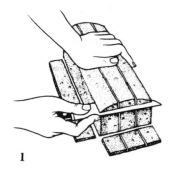

1

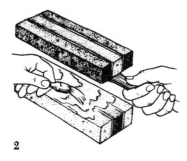

2

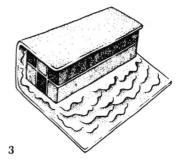

3

CLASSIC MADEIRA CAKE

Illustrated on page 113

fat for greasing
150 g/5 oz butter or margarine
150 g/5 oz caster sugar
4 eggs, beaten
200 g/7 oz plain flour
10 ml/2 tsp baking powder
pinch of salt
grated rind of 1 lemon
caster sugar for dredging
1 thin slice candied or glacé citron peel

Line and grease a 15 cm/6 inch round cake tin. Set the oven at 180°C/350°F/gas 4.

In a mixing bowl, cream the butter or margarine with the sugar until light and fluffy. Gradually add the eggs, beating well after each addition. Sift the flour, baking powder and salt together into a second bowl, then fold into the creamed mixture. Stir in the lemon rind and mix well. Spoon into the prepared tin. Dredge the top with caster sugar.

Bake for 20 minutes, then lay the slice of peel on top. Bake for a further 45-50 minutes or until cooked through and firm to the touch. Cool on a wire rack.

MAKES ONE 15 CM/6 INCH CAKE

◗ MRS BEETON'S TIP If you do not have a sugar dredger, place a small amount of sugar in a tea strainer and pass it over the top of the cake.

DUNDEE CAKE

Illustrated on page 138

fat for greasing
200 g/7 oz plain flour
2.5 ml/½ tsp baking powder
1.25 ml/¼ tsp salt
150 g/5 oz butter
150 g/5 oz caster sugar
4 eggs, beaten
100 g/4 oz glacé cherries, quartered
150 g/5 oz currants
150 g/5 oz sultanas
100 g/4 oz seedless raisins
50 g/2 oz cut mixed peel
50 g/2 oz ground almonds
grated rind of 1 lemon
50 g/2 oz blanched split almonds

Line and grease an 18 cm/7 inch round cake tin. Set the oven at 180°C/350°F/gas 4. Sift the flour, baking powder and salt into a bowl. In a mixing bowl, cream the butter and sugar together well, and beat in the eggs. Fold the flour mixture, cherries, dried fruit, peel and ground almonds into the creamed mixture. Add the lemon rind and mix well.

Spoon into the prepared tin and make a slight hollow in the centre. Bake for 20 minutes, by which time the hollow should have filled in. Arrange the split almonds on top.

Return the cake to the oven, bake for a further 40-50 minutes, then reduce the temperature to 160°C/325°F/gas 3 and bake for another hour. Cool on a wire rack.

MAKES ONE 18 CM/7 INCH CAKE

MARBLE CAKE

fat for greasing
175 g/6 oz butter or margarine
175 g/6 oz caster sugar
3 eggs, beaten
few drops of vanilla essence
225 g/8 oz self-raising flour
pinch of salt
30 ml/2 tbsp milk
30 ml/2 tbsp strong black coffee
50 g/2 oz chocolate, broken into chunks
Chocolate Buttercream (pages 57-58)
15 ml/1 tbsp grated chocolate

Line and grease a 20 cm/8 inch round cake tin. Set the oven at 180°C/350°F/gas 4.

In a mixing bowl cream the butter or margarine with the sugar until light and fluffy. Add the eggs gradually, beating well after each addition. Stir in the vanilla.

Sift the flour and salt into a bowl. Stir into the creamed mixture, lightly but thoroughly, until evenly mixed. Place half the mixture in a second bowl and beat in the milk.

Combine the coffee and chocolate in a bowl set over a saucepan of simmering water. Heat gently until the chocolate melts. Stir thoroughly, then add to the cake mixture in the mixing bowl, beating well.

Put alternate spoonfuls of plain and chocolate mixture into the prepared cake tin. Bake for 45 minutes-1 hour, until firm to the touch. Cool on a wire rack. Top with the buttercream and grated chocolate.

MAKES ONE 20 CM/8 INCH CAKE

VARIATION

THREE-TONE MARBLE CAKE This is popular with children. Divide the cake mixture into 3 equal parts, leaving one plain, flavouring one with chocolate and tinting the third pink with food colouring. Combine and bake as suggested left.

CHOCOLATE LAYER CAKE

fat for greasing
150 g/5 oz butter or margarine
150 g/5 oz caster sugar
3 eggs, beaten
few drops of vanilla essence
100 g/4 oz self-raising flour or plain flour
    and 5 ml/1 tsp baking powder
25 g/1 oz cocoa
pinch of salt
Chocolate Buttercream (pages 57-58)
    for filling
caster sugar for dredging

Line and grease two 18 cm/7 inch sandwich tins. Set the oven at 180°C/350°F/gas 4.

In a mixing bowl cream the butter or margarine with the sugar until light and fluffy. Add the eggs gradually, beating well after each addition. Stir in the vanilla essence.

Sift the flour, cocoa, salt and baking powder, if used, into a bowl. Stir into the creamed mixture, lightly but thoroughly, until evenly mixed.

Divide between the tins and bake for 25-30 minutes. Cool on a wire rack, then sandwich together with the buttercream. Sprinkle the top with caster sugar.

MAKES ONE 18 CM/7 INCH CAKE

> **MRS BEETON'S TIP** Always use eggs at room temperature. Eggs that have been kept in the refrigerator may be brought to the correct temperature by placing in warm water for a few minutes.

COFFEE CREAM CAKE

fat for greasing
15 ml/1 tbsp instant coffee
150 g/5 oz butter or margarine
150 g/5 oz caster sugar
3 eggs, beaten
150 g/5 oz self-raising flour or plain flour
    and 5 ml/1 tsp baking powder
pinch of salt

FILLING AND TOPPING
150 ml/5 fl oz whipping cream
15 ml/1 tbsp caster sugar
Coffee Buttercream (pages 57-58)

Line and grease two 18 cm/7 inch sand-wich tins. Set the oven at 180°C/350°F/gas 4. In a cup, mix the instant coffee with 10ml/2 tsp boiling water. Set aside.

In a mixing bowl, cream the butter or margarine with the sugar until light and fluffy. Add the eggs gradually, beating well after each addition.

Sift the flour, salt and baking powder, if used, into a bowl. Stir into the creamed mixture, lightly but thoroughly, until evenly mixed. Stir in the coffee mixture, mixing well. Divide between the tins and bake for 25-30 minutes. Cool on a wire rack.

Place the cream in a bowl and whip until it holds its shape. Add the caster sugar and whip until thick. Use to sandwich the cake layers together. Top with the buttercream.

MAKES ONE 18 CM/7 INCH CAKE

MRS BEETON'S TIP Spread the top layer of the cake with the buttercream before assembling the cake. This is much easier than first filling the cake with the cream and then trying to ice the top without causing the centre to ooze out!

HAZELNUT CAKE

fat for greasing
75 g/3 oz self-raising flour
2.5 ml/½ tsp salt
75 g/3 oz butter or margarine
75 g/3 oz caster sugar
15 ml/1 tbsp strong black coffee
1 egg, separated, plus 1 egg white
75 g/3 oz hazelnuts, skinned and ground

FILLING
Coffee Buttercream (pages 57-58)

ICING
Chocolate Glacé Icing (page 60)

Line and grease a 15 cm/6 inch cake tin. Set the oven at 180°C/350°F/gas 4. Sift the flour and salt into a bowl. In a mixing bowl, cream the butter or margarine and sugar until light and fluffy. Beat the coffee and egg yolk into the creamed mixture. Stir in the ground hazelnuts with the flour mixture.

In a clean, dry bowl, whisk both egg whites until stiff, and fold into the mixture. Spoon into the prepared tin and bake for 45 minutes.

When cool, split the cake in half horizon-tally, brushing off excess crumbs. Sandwich together with coffee buttercream and cover with chocolate glacé icing.

MAKES ONE 15 CM/6 INCH CAKE

DARK SECRETS RING CAKE

Illustrated on page 139

An irresistible almond-flavoured cake, soaked in maraschino syrup and coated in dark chocolate. Maraschino cherries with stalks are available, bottled in syrup, from good food shops.

150 g/5 oz butter, softened
150 g/5 oz caster sugar
3 small eggs, beaten
200 g/7 oz self-raising flour
50 g/2 oz ground almonds
a little milk
75 ml/3 fl oz maraschino syrup (from a jar of cherries, or home-made syrup flavoured with the liqueur)
fat for greasing
flour for dusting

ICING AND DECORATION

one quantity Tipsy Chocolate Velvet (page 101), omitting the rum
icing sugar for dusting
half quantity Citrus Cheese Icing (page 69)
small star nozzle
three pairs of maraschino cherries, half dipped in plain chocolate (page 97)

Grease a 1.1 litre/2 pint capacity ring tin and dust it lightly with flour. Set the oven at 160°C/325°F/gas 3.

Cream the butter and sugar in a mixing bowl until pale and soft, then beat in the eggs, a little at a time. Fold in the flour and ground almonds, adding sufficient milk to give the mixture a soft, dropping consistency.

Spread the mixture into the prepared tin and stand it on a baking sheet. Bake the cake for 1-1¼ hours, until firm to the touch and beginning to shrink from the side of the tin.

Leave the cake to rest in the tin for 5 minutes, then turn it out on to a wire rack.

Wash and dry the mould and invert the cake back into it. Prick the cake all over with a skewer. Warm the maraschino syrup and drizzle it over the warm cake. Leave the cake to cool completely in the mould. When it is cold, invert the cake on to a piece of non-stick baking parchment on a wire rack or baking sheet. Pour the chocolate icing over the cake, using a palette knife to smooth the sides if it does not coat the cake evenly. Leave it to set, then trim the base of any excess chocolate and carefully transfer the cake to a plate. Dust with icing sugar.

Place the citrus cheese icing in an icing bag fitted with a star nozzle and pipe a row of small stars around the base of the cake. Decorate with the dipped cherries.

MRS BEETON'S TIP Instead of using the cherries for decoration, this rich ring cake can be varied by adding different decorations according to the season. For example frosted or moulded flowers may be used to decorate the cake for Easter. For a quick Christmas cake add holly leaves and berries instead of the cherries. For a fun birthday cake combine moulded flowers or shop-bought decorations with a ring of birthday candles on the top of the cake.

ABOUT 20 PORTIONS

DEVIL'S FOOD CAKE

fat for greasing
plain flour for dusting
100 g/4 oz butter
350 g/12 oz sugar
5 ml/1 tsp vanilla essence
3 eggs, separated
250 g/9 oz plain flour
50 g/2 oz cocoa
7.5 ml/1½ tsp bicarbonate of soda
5 ml/1 tsp salt

FILLING AND DECORATION
American Frosting (see page 60)

Grease and lightly flour three 20 cm/8 inch sandwich tins. Set the oven at 180°C/350°F/gas 4.

Cream the butter with 225 g/8 oz of the sugar until light, then add the vanilla essence. Add the egg yolks, one at a time alternately with 250 ml/8 fl oz cold water, beating well after each addition. Beat in the flour, cocoa, bicarbonate of soda and salt.

Whisk the egg whites to soft peaks, add the remaining sugar and continue whisking until stiff peaks form. Fold the egg whites into the creamed mixture.

Gently pour one-third of the cake mixture into each prepared sandwich tin. Bake for 30-35 minutes, until the cakes are firm. When cold, fill and cover with American Frosting.

MAKES ONE 20 CM/8 INCH LAYER CAKE

☆ **FREEZING TIP** Open freeze the cake until solid, then wrap in cling film and place in a polythene bag. Seal, label and freeze for up to 3 months.

ANGEL FOOD CAKE

flour for dusting
100 g/4 oz plain flour
275 g/10 oz caster sugar
12 egg whites (measuring 300 ml/½ pint)
7.5 ml/1½ tsp cream of tartar
1.25 ml/¼ tsp salt
5 ml/1 tsp vanilla essence
1.25 ml/¼ tsp almond essence

DECORATION
American Frosting (page 60) or
Maraschino Glaze (page 55)

Sift the plain flour and 150 g/5 oz of the sugar 6 times. In a spotlessly clean bowl, whisk the egg whites with the cream of tartar, salt, vanilla and almond essence until they form soft peaks. Add the remaining sugar, 30 ml/2 tbsp at a time, whisking well; continue whisking until the whites form stiff peaks.

Sift about a quarter of the flour mixture over the egg whites; fold in. Repeat the sifting and folding in 3 more times.

Spoon the cake mixture into an ungreased 25 cm/10 inch ring tin dusted with flour and bake for 35-40 minutes, or until the cake is pale gold on top, and springs back when lightly pressed with the finger. Cool in the tin.

Decorate with American Frosting or Maraschino Glaze.

MAKES ONE 25 CM/10 INCH CAKE

🥄 **MRS BEETON'S TIP** Angel food cake is very delicate so do not cool it on a wire rack or it will mark. The traditional way to cool the cake in the tin is to invert the tin over the neck of a bottle. When the cake is completely cool, loosen it with a spatula and remove from the tin.

SACHER TORTE

This most famous of all Austrian cakes is often served as a dessert, with sweetened whipped cream.

fat for greasing
flour for dredging
125 g/4½ oz butter
125 g/4½ oz sugar
125 g/4½ oz plain chocolate
6 eggs, separated
125 g/4½ oz self-raising flour
about 50 g/2 oz apricot jam

FILLING
25 g/1 oz icing sugar
50 g/2 oz plain chocolate, grated
40 g/1½ oz softened unsalted butter

ICING
175 g/6 oz plain chocolate, grated
150 g/5 oz lump sugar
25 g/1 oz unsalted butter

Line and grease an 18 cm/7 inch loose-bottomed cake tin. Dust with flour, shaking out the excess. Set the oven at 190°C/375°F/gas 5.

In a mixing bowl, cream the butter and sugar until light and fluffy. Melt the chocolate in a bowl over a saucepan of hot water, cool slightly, then stir it into the creamed mixture. Beat in the egg yolks, one by one, until thoroughly mixed.

Sift the flour into a second bowl and in a third, whisk the egg whites to firm peaks. Fold the stiffly beaten whites into the mixture alternately with the flour, using either a metal spoon or an electric mixer on the lowest speed. Pour the mixture into the prepared tin. Set on a baking sheet. Make a slight hollow in the centre of the cake to ensure even rising.

Bake for about 1½ hours. If the cake begins to overbrown after 1 hour, lower the oven temperature to 160°C/325°F/gas 3 and continue baking until the cake is fully cooked and a skewer inserted in the centre comes out clean. Leave the cake in the tin for a few minutes, then remove from the tin and place on a wire rack to cool completely at room temperature.

Make the filling when the cake is cold. Sift the icing sugar. Melt the chocolate in a bowl over a saucepan of hot water. In another bowl cream the icing sugar and butter together. Add the melted chocolate and beat until very smooth and fully blended.

Split the cold cake in half, dusting off the crumbs, and spread the filling over the cut surfaces. Sandwich the coated halves together. Warm the apricot jam until liquid, and spread it very thinly over the top and sides of the cake.

Make the icing. Melt the chocolate in a bowl over a pan of hot water. Keep it soft over the hot water while preparing the syrup. Put the sugar in a heavy-bottomed saucepan with 175ml/6 fl oz water. Bring to the boil, and boil until the mixture forms a thread (see page 58). Gradually stir this into the melted chocolate, and beat until the icing coats a wooden spoon thickly, and can be drawn up to a point. Do not overbeat or the mixture will lose its gloss. Stir in the butter. Spread the icing quickly and smoothly over the cake.

MAKES ONE 18 CM/7 INCH CAKE

 MRS BEETON'S TIP Use a knife dipped in hot water to spread the icing.

*I*TALIAN CANDIED FRUIT GATEAU

Make this marvellous gâteau 24 hours before serving to allow the flavours to develop.

CAKE
75 g/3 oz butter or margarine
75 g/3 oz caster sugar
2 small eggs, beaten
75 g/3 oz self-raising flour
pinch of salt

FILLING AND COATING
150 ml/5 fl oz double cream
75 g/3 oz caster sugar
225 g/8 oz ricotta cheese, sieved
thinly grated rind and juice of 1 lemon
75 ml/5 tbsp orange liqueur
50 g/2 oz glacé cherries, chopped
50 g/2 oz cut mixed peel, chopped
50 g/2 oz angelica, chopped
50 g/2 oz crystallised ginger, chopped
50 g/2 oz glacé pineapple slices, chopped
50 g/2 oz bitter-sweet dessert chocolate, grated

ICING
100 g/4 oz plain chocolate
100 g/4 oz icing sugar
100 g/4 oz butter
20 ml/4 tsp rum

First make the cake. Line and grease an 18 cm/7 inch cake tin. Set the oven at 180°C/350°F/gas 4. In a mixing bowl, cream the butter or margarine with the sugar until light and fluffy. Add the eggs gradually, beating well after each addition. Sift the flour and salt into a bowl. Stir into the creamed mixture, lightly but thoroughly, until evenly mixed. Spoon into the prepared tin and bake for 30-40 minutes until cooked through. Cool on a wire rack.

Meanwhile put the double cream in a bowl and chill in the coldest part of the refrigerator for 2 hours.

Whip the chilled cream to soft peaks, adding 30 ml/2 tbsp of the caster sugar. Spoon half the whipped cream into a second bowl and set aside for decoration. To the remaining whipped cream add the sieved cheese, the lemon rind and juice, and the liqueur. Beat until very smooth and light. Add the chopped fruits, the grated chocolate and the remaining caster sugar.

Split the cake in half, brushing off excess crumbs. Fill it with about half of the cream mixture, then use the remaining mixture to coat the sides smoothly. Chill while making the icing.

Combine all the icing ingredients in the top of a double saucepan set over simmering water. Heat until both the chocolate and the butter have melted, then remove from the heat and beat until smooth. Cool until tepid, then spread over the top of the sponge. When firm, decorate with the reserved whipped cream. Chill overnight before serving.

SERVES 6

PAVLOVA

Make the pavlova shell on the day when it is to be eaten, as it does not store well. Fill it just before serving.

3 egg whites
150 g/5 oz caster sugar
2.5 ml/½ tsp vinegar
2.5 ml/½ tsp vanilla essence
10 ml/2 tsp cornflour

FILLING
250 ml/8 fl oz double cream
caster sugar (see method)
2 peaches, skinned and sliced
glacé cherries and angelica to decorate

Line a baking sheet with greaseproof paper or non-stick baking parchment. Draw a 20 cm/8 inch circle on the paper and very lightly grease the greaseproof paper, if used. Set the oven at 150°C/300°F/gas 2.

In a large bowl, whisk the egg whites until very stiff. Continue whisking, gradually adding the sugar until the mixture stands in stiff peaks. Beat in the vinegar, vanilla and cornflour.

Spread the meringue over the circle, piling it up at the edges to form a rim, or pipe the circle and rim from a piping bag fitted with a large star nozzle.

Bake for about 1 hour or until the pavlova is crisp on the outside and has the texture of marshmallow inside. It should be pale coffee in colour. When cool, carefully remove the paper and put the pavlova on a large plate.

Make the filling by whipping the cream in a bowl with caster sugar to taste. Add the sliced peaches and pile into the pavlova shell. Decorate with glacé cherries and angelica and serve as soon as possible.

SERVES 4 TO 6

VARIATIONS

FRUIT AND LIQUEUR Add 15-30 ml/ 1-2 tbsp liqueur to the cream when whipping it. Stir in the fruit of your choice (pineapple, apricots, grapes, kiwi fruit, strawberries or raspberries). Pile into the pavlova case.

BANANAS AND BRANDY Thinly slice 4 bananas into a bowl. Add 30 ml/2 tbsp brandy and chill for 1 hour, turning the fruit from time to time. In a second bowl, lightly whip 250 ml/8 fl oz double cream. Fold in the bananas and brandy and add 100 g/4 oz halved, stoned, fresh or maraschino cherries. Pile into the pavlova case and sprinkle generously with grated chocolate and nuts.

LIGHT RASPBERRY AND ALMOND Instead of using double cream as the base for the filling, why not try fromage frais as a light alternative? You will need 450 g/1 lb of fromage frais. Before stirring it, drain off any thin liquid on the surface. Sweeten the fromage frais to taste with honey, then fold in 225 g/8 oz of raspberries and spoon into the pavlova case. Sprinkle lightly toasted flaked almonds over the filling.

SOFT CHEESE AND STRAWBERRY Another alternative to a double cream filling is one based on low-fat soft cheese, for example curd cheese. You will need 225 g/ 8 oz of curd cheese. Beat it with icing sugar to taste, then work in enough thoroughly mashed strawberries to make a soft, creamy mixture. Add about 175 g/6 oz of halved strawberries, then pile the mixture into the pavlova case.

GATEAUX, TRIFLES AND CHEESECAKES

A chapter of glorious gâteaux, lusciously decorated with whipped cream or lavishly filled with chocolate concoctions. These are the perfect desserts to present on any special dinner party occasion.

A splendid gâteau always looks impressive and it is not necessarily a difficult dessert to prepare. The base may be a sponge cake, pastry or meringue, either plain or flavoured.

FREEZING

For best results, freeze the unfilled gâteau, separating the layers with sheets of freezer film. These do not have to be thawed before being filled and decorated, provided the finished gâteau is set aside for some time before it is served.

COATING THE SIDE OF A GÂTEAU

Gâteaux are often covered completely in cream, with chopped nuts, grated chocolate or vermicelli used to decorate the sides. To coat the sides, the layers must first be sandwiched together. The coating ingredient should be spread out on a sheet of greaseproof paper. Spread the side of the gâteau thinly with cream, or a similar covering. Using both hands to support the gâteau on its side, roll it in the coating.

TRIFLES

The classic British sherry trifle transforms a small amount of sponge cake into a luscious sweet by flavouring it with a fruit preserve and adding a creamy custard. A good trifle

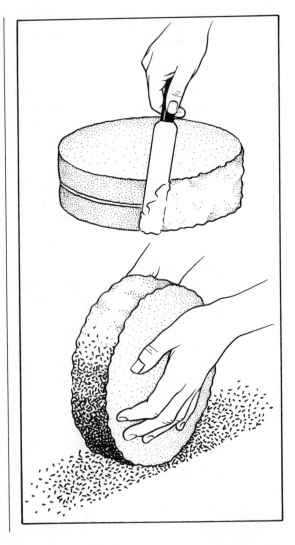

of this type has a plain, pleasing flavour that complements a rich main course. By adding fresh fruits and by varying the custard topping a wide variety of interesting trifles may be created. A selection of recipes is included in this chapter.

A good trifle is well balanced, with the right proportion of custard topping to complement the sponge base and enough fruit or other ingredients to add a contrasting flavour. If the proportions of sponge and custard topping are not balanced the trifle will not be the best.

A trifle should be chilled for a few hours so that the flavours have time to mingle; then it should be removed from the refrigerator about 30 minutes before serving so that it is not too cold. Some fruit trifles benefit from being prepared a day ahead, allowing time for the fruit juices to soak into the sponge. Leave the final decoration until the last minute.

CHARLOTTES

Charlottes are moulded desserts consisting of a light mixture set in a surround of sponge fingers. A custard-based mixture, mousse or jelled dessert usually forms the centre of a charlotte and this may be poured over a thin layer of fruit set with jelly.

Charlotte moulds are deeper than cake tins, however a straight-sided cake tin that does not have a loose bottom may be used instead.

Charlotte mixtures should be lightly set not rubbery. The charlotte must not be unmoulded too long before serving or it may loose its shape. Tying a wide ribbon around the charlotte helps to support the sponge casing as well as being a splendid way of decorating a rather special dessert.

Charlottes do not freeze well as the mixture tends to soften during freezing and the unmoulded dessert will not hold its shape. However, rich charlottes filled with creamy mousses may be served iced, or part frozen.

CHEESECAKES

The cheesecakes that are popular today tend to be American-style concoctions, with gelatine as the setting agent. However, the traditional cuisines of European countries offer alternative recipes for baked cheesecakes that are zesty with lemon and fruity with sultanas, delicate and creamy with Italian ricotta cheese, or more substantial in the tradition of British baking.

There are no rules for making cheesecakes. For uncooked recipes made with soft cheese, the cheese used may be varied according to individual requirements. Use cream cheese for a rich result or lighter curd cheese (or sieved cottage cheese) for a cheesecake with a lower fat content. Plain yogurt or fromage frais may be used instead of cream in some recipes.

Recipes for baked cheesecakes should be followed more closely as the type of cheese used may well affect the result and yogurt or fromage frais may separate out during cooking.

A CHOICE OF BASE

Which base, or case, to use to hold the cheese mixture depends on the type of cheesecake being made. Cooked cheesecakes may be set in a sweet pastry case or on a base of pastry; alternatively a sponge cake mixture may form the base. Uncooked cheesecakes are usually set in a case or on a base made of biscuit crumbs and butter.

BISCUIT BASE

Quick and easy to make, a biscuit base is ideal for uncooked cheesecakes. Although it is possible to use a biscuit base for cooked cheesecakes, the biscuits tend to become slightly overcooked and the fat which binds them seeps out during cooking.

To line the base only of a 20 cm/8 inch container you will need about 100 g/4 oz crushed biscuits combined with 50 g/2 oz butter. Digestive biscuits or other plain sweet biscuits are usually used; however chocolate-coated biscuits, gingernuts or coconut cookies may be crushed to vary the flavour of the base.

Crush the biscuits in a food processor if you have one. Otherwise, place them in a strong polythene bag and use a rolling pin to crush them. It is best to close the bag loosely with a metal tie to allow air to escape. Crush the biscuits carefully to avoid breaking the bag and making a mess.

Melt the butter in a saucepan, then stir in the crushed biscuits off the heat. Alternatively, melt the butter in a mug or small bowl in the microwave, allowing about 1 minute on High, then pour it over the biscuits in a dish and stir well.

When the mixture is pressed on to the base of the container, smooth it over with the back of a clean metal spoon. Allow the base to cool, then chill it before adding the topping.

To line the sides of the container as well as the base, double the quantity of biscuits and butter and turn all the mixture into the container. Use a metal spoon to press the mixture all over the base and up the sides. This is only practical for a shallow container, such as a flan dish or tin.

PASTRY CASE

A case of sweet pastry is often used for a baked cheesecake. The ingredients and method are included in the relevant recipes. To vary the pastry slightly, spices, a few finely chopped or ground nuts (almonds or hazelnuts), grated lemon or orange rind may be added.

CAKE BASE

This type of base is used for cooked cheesecakes. A one-stage mixture of fat, egg and flour may be used and spread in the container before the topping is added (as for Baked Coffee Cheesecake, page 182).

A cake base may be made for an uncooked cheesecake. Set the oven at 180°C/350°F/gas 4. In a mixing bowl, beat together 50 g/2 oz each of butter, caster sugar and self-raising flour with 1 egg and 5 ml/1 tsp baking powder. When all the ingredients are thoroughly combined, spread the mixture in a well-greased 20 cm/8 inch sandwich tin and bake for 20-25 minutes, until risen and golden. The cake should feel firm on top when cooked. Turn it out on to a wire rack to cool.

Trim the top of the cake level before placing it in the base of a 20 cm/8 inch deep cake tin. Set the cheesecake mixture on top. For a very thin base to a shallow cheesecake, slice through the cake horizontally and use one half. Pack and freeze the second slice for making a second cheesecake. The base may be frozen for up to 3 months.

TURNING OUT A CHEESECAKE

To remove a cheesecake from a loose-bottomed flan tin, have ready a storage jar or small soufflé dish. Make sure that the jar has a flat, heat-resistant lid if the cheesecake is fresh from the oven. Stand the tin containing the cheesecake on top of the jar, so that the loose base is well supported

and the side is free. Gently ease the side away from the cheesecake, then transfer the dessert on its base to a flat platter.

FREEZING CHEESECAKES

Baked and fairly firm uncooked cheesecakes freeze very well. Freeze the whole cheesecake before adding any decoration. A cheesecake which is decorated with piped cream should be open frozen, then put in a large, deep, rigid container.

Any leftover cheesecake may be frozen in slices. Arrange the slices in a rigid container or on a double thickness of foil, placing a piece of freezer film between each slice. Close the foil loosely around the slices or cover the container and place in a level place in the freezer.

A decorated cheesecake may be frozen successfully for 2-3 weeks ready to be served for a special dessert. Slices of cheesecake may be frozen for up to 2 or 3 months. They will not look their best but will taste good as an impromptu family pudding.

MALAKOFF GÂTEAU

150 g/5 oz butter
4 egg yolks
200 g/7 oz caster sugar
200 g/7 oz ground almonds
250 ml/8 fl oz double cream
30-32 sponge fingers

DECORATION
250 ml/8 fl oz double cream
100 g/4 oz caster sugar
1 × 410 g/14 oz can apricot halves, drained

Line a 1 kg/2¼ lb loaf tin with foil. In a mixing bowl, beat the butter until light and creamy. Stir in the egg yolks one at a time, then add the sugar and ground almonds. Bind with the double cream.

Arrange a layer of sponge fingers along the base of the prepared tin. Spread a layer of filling over them. Repeat the layers until all the ingredients have been used, finishing with a layer of sponge fingers. Cover with foil and place heavy weights evenly on top. Chill for 2-3 hours until firm.

Shortly before serving, combine the cream and sugar in a bowl and whip until stiff. Carefully turn the gâteau out on a serving dish. Remove the foil and decorate with the cream and apricot halves. Serve lightly chilled.

SERVES 8 TO 10

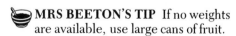 **MRS BEETON'S TIP** If no weights are available, use large cans of fruit.

*B*LACK FOREST GÂTEAU

Illustrated on page 140

fat for greasing
150 g/5 oz butter or margarine
150 g/5 oz caster sugar
3 eggs, beaten
few drops of vanilla essence
100 g/4 oz self-raising flour *or* plain flour
    and 5 ml/1 tsp baking powder
25 g/1 oz cocoa
pinch of salt

FILLING AND TOPPING
    250 ml/8 fl oz double cream
    125 ml/4 fl oz single cream
    1 × 540 g/18 oz can Morello cherries
    kirsch (see method)
    25 g/1 oz plain chocolate, grated

Line and grease a 20 cm/8 inch cake tin. Set the oven at 180°C/350°F/gas 4.

In a mixing bowl, cream the butter or margarine with the sugar until light and fluffy. Add the eggs gradually, beating well after each addition. Stir in the vanilla essence.

Sift the flour, cocoa, salt and baking powder, if used, into a bowl. Stir into the creamed mixture, lightly but thoroughly, until evenly mixed.

Spoon into the tin and bake for 40 minutes. Cool on a wire rack. When quite cold, carefully cut the cake into three layers, brushing all loose crumbs off the cut sides.

Make the filling. Combine the creams in a bowl and whip until stiff. Place half the whipped cream in another bowl.

Drain the cherries, reserving the juice. Set aside 11 whole cherries and halve and stone the remainder. Gently fold the halved cherries into one of the bowls of cream. Set aside. Strain the reserved cherry juice into a measuring jug and add kirsch to taste.

Prick the cake layers and sprinkle with the cherry juice and kirsch until well saturated. Sandwich the layers together with the whipped cream and cherries. When assembled, cover with the remaining plain cream and use the whole cherries to decorate the top. Sprinkle the grated chocolate over the cream.

SERVES 10 TO 12

*C*OFFEE GÂTEAU

fat for greasing
20 ml/4 tsp instant coffee
150 g/5 oz butter
150 g/5 oz caster sugar
3 eggs, beaten
150 g/5 oz self-raising flour

COFFEE BUTTERCREAM
    30 ml/2 tbsp instant coffee
    150 g/5 oz butter
    450 g/1 lb icing sugar

DECORATION
    50-75 g/2-3 oz walnuts, chopped
    10-12 walnut halves

Line and grease two 20 cm/8 inch sandwich tins. Set the oven at 160°C/325°F/gas 3. In a cup, mix the instant coffee with 20 ml/4 tsp boiling water. Set aside to cool.

In a mixing bowl, cream the butter with the sugar until light and fluffy. Beat in the cooled coffee. Add the eggs gradually, beating well after each addition.

Sift the flour and fold it into the creamed mixture, using a metal spoon. Divide between the tins and bake for 35-40 minutes or until well risen, firm and golden brown. Leave in the tins for 2-3 minutes, then cool on a wire rack.

Make the buttercream. In a cup, mix the instant coffee with 30 ml/2 tbsp boiling water and leave to cool. Cream the butter with half the icing sugar in a bowl. Beat in the cooled coffee, then add the rest of the icing sugar. Beat to a creamy mixture.

Using about a quarter of the buttercream, sandwich the cake layers together. Spread about half the remaining buttercream on the sides of the cake, then roll in the chopped walnuts. Spread most of the remaining buttercream on top of the cake and mark with a fork in a wavy design. Spoon any remaining buttercream into a piping bag fitted with a small star nozzle and pipe 10-12 rosettes on top of the cake. Decorate each rosette with a walnut half.

SERVES 8 TO 12

AUSTRIAN HAZELNUT LAYER

fat for greasing
200 g/7 oz hazelnuts
5 eggs, separated
150 g/5 oz caster sugar
grated rind of ½ lemon
flour for dusting

FILLING
250 ml/8 fl oz double cream
vanilla essence

DECORATION
whole hazelnuts
grated chocolate

Grease and flour two 25 cm/10 inch springform or loose-bottomed cake tins. Set the oven at 180°C/350°F/gas 4.

Spread the hazelnuts out on a baking sheet and roast for 10 minutes or until the skins start to split. While still warm, rub them in a rough cloth to remove the skins. Grind the nuts in a nut mill or process briefly in a blender.

Combine the egg yolks and sugar in a bowl and beat until light and creamy. Mix in the ground nuts and lemon rind. Whisk the egg whites in a clean, grease-free bowl, until stiff but not dry. Fold the egg whites quickly and gently into the nut mixture. Divide between the prepared tins and bake for 1 hour. Test that the cakes are cooked (see Mrs Beeton's Tip), then cool the layers on wire racks, removing the sides and bases of the tins after a few minutes.

To make the filling, whip the cream with a few drops of vanilla essence until stiff. When the cake layers are cold, sandwich them together with some of the cream, and cover the top with the remainder. Decorate with a few whole hazelnuts and a sprinkling of grated chocolate.

SERVES 12

> **MRS BEETON'S TIP** When the cakes are ready, a warmed skewer pushed into the centre of each layer should come out dry. The sides of the cake should have begun to shrink slightly from the edges of the tin.

*M*OUSSELINE CAKE

fat for greasing
caster sugar for dusting
50 g/2 oz plain flour
50 g/2 oz cornflour
4 eggs, separated
100 g/4 oz caster sugar
vanilla essence or grated rind of ½ lemon

DECORATION
125 ml/4 fl oz double cream
100 g/4 oz strawberries
100 g/4 oz icing sugar
5-10 ml/1-2 tsp orange-flavoured liqueur

Base line and grease two 18 cm/7 inch sandwich cake tins. Dust with caster sugar, tapping out the excess. Set the oven at 190°C/375°F/gas 5. Sift the flour and corn-flour together into a bowl and set aside.

In a large heatproof bowl, whisk the egg yolks with the sugar until thick, creamy and pale, adding the essence or grated lemon rind. Whisk the egg whites in a clean, grease-free bowl until they form soft peaks, then add to the yolk mixture.

Set the bowl of mixture over gently simmering water and whisk until the volume is greatly increased and the mixture is thick enough to hold the mark of a trial for 2-3 seconds. Remove the bowl from the heat and continue whisking until the mixture is cold.

Fold the sifted flours into the cold cake mixture. Divide between the prepared sandwich tins and bake for 20-25 minutes until well risen and browned. Leave in the tins for 1-2 minutes, then turn out on to wire racks to cool.

To decorate the cake, whip the cream in a bowl. Put one third of the cream into a piping bag. Set aside 4 of the best straw-berries. Chop the rest and add to the re-maining cream. Mix lightly, then spread over one layer of the cake. Add the top layer.

In a small bowl, mix the icing sugar with enough of the liqueur to form a glacé icing. Warm the icing by placing the bowl in a basin of hot water, if necessary.

Pipe whirls of whipped cream around the top edge of the cake. Carefully spoon the liqueur icing over the top of the cake to form an even coating. Cut the reserved strawberries in half or in slices and de-corate the top of the cake. Serve as soon as possible.

SERVES 6

VARIATIONS

Ring the changes with different fresh or well-drained canned fruit. Raspberries, pineapple, peaches or nectarines are good. Flavour the cream with a complementary liqueur. The exotic combination of kiwi fruit and advocaat-flavoured cream is particularly tasty.

☆ **FREEZER TIP** The cooked, cooled cakes may be frozen. Wrap them in foil or pack them in a freezer bag, placing a sheet of foil between them. Unwrap the cakes and leave at room temperature until softened before filling and decorating as above.

CHOCOLATE ROULADE

This cake is best baked the day before it is to be served.

oil and butter for greasing
150 g/5 oz bitter-sweet dessert chocolate,
    in squares
4 eggs, separated
100 g/4 oz caster sugar
15 g/½ oz icing sugar
about 175 ml/6 fl oz double cream
few drops of vanilla essence

Brush a 30 × 42 cm/12 × 17 inch Swiss roll tin with oil. Line with a piece of grease-proof paper, letting the paper overlap the edge a little. Cut out a second sheet of greaseproof paper to the same size, to cover the cooked roulade, and have ready a damp clean tea towel with which to cover the baking sheet. Set the oven at 190°C/375°F/gas 5.

Heat a saucepan of water. Place the chocolate in a heatproof bowl. When the water boils, remove the pan from the heat and set the pan over the hot water. Leave to melt, stirring occasionally.

Combine the egg yolks and caster sugar in a bowl and beat briskly until the mixture is pale and creamy. Add 45 ml/3 tbsp hot water to the melted chocolate and beat until well blended. Stir the chocolate into the egg yolk mixture, then whisk thoroughly.

In a clean, grease-free bowl, whisk the egg whites until fairly stiff. Using a metal spoon, fold them carefully into the chocolate mixture. Tip into the prepared Swiss roll tin and bake for 20 minutes until the roulade is firm on the surface.

Butter the remaining sheet of grease-proof paper. Remove the tin from the oven and immediately cover the cake with the buttered paper and the damp tea towel. Leave to stand overnight.

Next day, remove the cloth. Turn the paper buttered side up, sprinkle with icing sugar and replace sugared side down. Grip the paper and tin and invert both together so that the roulade is upside-down. Lay it down on the paper and remove the tin. Peel off the lining paper.

In a bowl, whip the cream until very stiff, stir in the vanilla essence and spread evenly over the surface of the roulade. Roll the roulade up from one long side, using the paper as a guide. Place on a serving plate, with the join underneath, dust with extra icing sugar and chill for several hours before serving.

SERVES 6

> **MRS BEETON'S TIP** Do not worry too much if cracks appear in the roulade during rolling. The mixture does not include any flour so that the baked roulade is rich and sweet with a fragile texture. Dusting with icing sugar disguises the cracks.

HAZELNUT MERINGUE GÂTEAU

75 g/3 oz hazelnuts
3 egg whites
150 g/5 oz caster sugar
2-3 drops vinegar
2-3 drops vanilla essence

FILLING AND TOPPING
125 ml/4 fl oz double cream
5-10 ml/1-2 tsp caster sugar

Reserve a few hazelnuts for decorating the gâteau. Bake the rest in a preheated 180°C/350°F/gas 4 oven for 10 minutes. Rub off the skins. Chop the nuts very finely or process briefly in a blender or food processor. Set aside. Do not turn off the oven.

Line two baking sheets with greaseproof paper or non-stick baking parchment. Draw a 15 cm/6 inch circle on each and very lightly oil the greaseproof paper, if used.

Combine the egg whites and caster sugar in a heatproof bowl. Set over a saucepan of gently simmering water and whisk until the meringue mixture is very thick and holds its shape. Add the vinegar, vanilla essence and chopped nuts.

Spread the meringue inside the marked circles or place it in a piping bag with a 1 cm/½ inch plain nozzle. Starting from the middle of one circle, pipe round and round to form a coiled, flat round 15 cm/6 inches in diameter. Pipe a similar round on the other sheet. Bake for 35-40 minutes, until each layer is crisp and lightly browned. Leave to cool.

Whip the cream in a bowl until it stands in stiff peaks, then stir in caster sugar to taste. Place one of the meringue rounds on a serving plate and spread with most of the cream. Put the second meringue round on top and decorate with the rest of the cream and the reserved hazelnuts.

SERVES 4 TO 6

STRAWBERRY MERINGUE TORTE

Illustrated on page 141

4 egg whites
pinch of salt
100 g/4 oz granulated sugar
100 g/4 oz caster sugar

FILLING
450 g/1 lb fresh strawberries, hulled
juice of 1 lemon
30 ml/2 tbsp caster sugar
125 ml/4 fl oz double cream or whipped
    cream flavoured with brandy or kirsch

Line a baking sheet with greaseproof paper or non-stick baking parchment. Draw a 15 cm/6 inch circle on the paper and very lightly oil the greaseproof paper if used. Set the oven at 110°C/225°F/gas ¼.

Combine the egg whites, salt and sugars in a heatproof bowl. Set over a saucepan of gently simmering water and whisk until the mixture is very thick and holds its shape.

Spread some of the meringue all over the circle to form the base of a meringue case. Put the rest of the mixture into a piping bag fitted with a large star nozzle. Pipe three quarters of the mixture around the edge of the ring to make a 5 cm/2 inch rim or border. Use the remaining mixture to pipe small meringue shapes. Bake the case for 3-4 hours; the small shells for 1½-2 hours. Leave to cool.

Make the filling. Put the strawberries in

a bowl and sprinkle with lemon juice and caster sugar. Chill in the refrigerator until the meringue case is cool. Reserve a few choice berries for decoration. Drain and halve the rest and put them into the meringue case. In a bowl, whip the cream lightly and cover the fruit, or simply spoon the liqueur-flavoured cream over. Decorate with the small meringues and reserved strawberries. Serve at once.

SERVES 4

RASPBERRY VACHERIN

3 egg whites
pinch of salt
150 g/5 oz caster sugar

FILLING AND TOPPING
350 g/12 oz fresh raspberries
300 ml/½ pint double cream
5 ml/1 tsp caster sugar
kirsch
a few angelica leaves

Line 2 baking sheets with greaseproof paper or non-stick baking parchment. Draw a 15 cm/6 inch circle on each and very lightly oil the greaseproof paper, if used. Set the oven at 110°C/225°F/gas ¼.

Combine the egg whites, salt and sugar in a heatproof bowl. Set over a saucepan of gently simmering water and whisk until the meringue mixture is very thick and holds its shape.

Put the meringue mixture into a piping bag fitted with a 1 cm/½ inch plain nozzle. Starting from the middle of one circle, pipe round and round until the 15 cm/6 inch circle is completely filled. Pipe a similar round on the other piece of paper. Use any remaining mixture to pipe small meringues on the paper around the circles. Bake for 1-1½ hours, then leave to cool. Meanwhile, pick over the raspberries, spread out on a large platter and leave to stand for 30 minutes.

Make the filling. Rinse the raspberries, patting them dry with absorbent kitchen paper. Reserve a few choice berries for decoration and set the rest aside in a bowl. Whip the cream in a bowl to firm peaks, then stir in the caster sugar and kirsch to taste.

Place one of the meringue rounds on a serving plate, spread with some of the cream (see Mrs Beeton's Tip) and arrange half the raspberries on it in a layer. Put the second meringue on top of the raspberries and arrange the reserved raspberries in the centre. Put the remaining cream into a piping bag fitted with a star or shell nozzle and pipe rosettes or a decorative edge of cream around the berries. Decorate the sides of the vacherin with the tiny meringues and angelica leaves.

Serve the vacherin in slices, like a cake, using a flat cake slice to transfer the slices to individual plates.

SERVES 4 TO 6

🥣 **MRS BEETON'S TIP** When filling the vacherin, do not make the cream layer too thick or it will ooze out when the vacherin is cut, making it messy to serve and eat.

S AVARIN

oil for greasing
75 ml/5 tbsp milk
10 ml/2 tsp dried yeast
150 g/5 oz strong white flour
1.25 ml/¼ tsp salt
10 ml/2 tsp sugar
75 g/3 oz butter
3 eggs, beaten

RUM SYRUP
75 g/3 oz lump sugar
30 ml/2 tbsp rum
15 ml/1 tbsp lemon juice

GLAZE
45 ml/3 tbsp apricot jam

Oil a 20 cm/8 inch savarin mould (ring tin). Set the oven at 200°C/400°F/gas 6.

Warm the milk in a saucepan until tepid. Remove from the heat and sprinkle on the dried yeast. Stir in 15 ml/1 tbsp of the flour and leave in a warm place for 20 minutes.

Sift the rest of the flour and the salt into a mixing bowl. Stir in the sugar, then rub in the butter. Add the yeast liquid to the mixture, then add the eggs. Beat well until smooth: the batter should be quite elastic. Pour the mixture into the prepared tin. Cover with a large, lightly oiled polythene bag, and leave in a warm place until the mixture has almost reached the top of the tin.

Bake for about 40 minutes or until the savarin is golden brown and fim to the touch. Check after 30 minutes and cover the savarin loosely with foil if it is becoming too dark on top.

Meanwhile make the rum syrup. Put the sugar in a saucepan with 125 ml/4 fl oz water. Heat, stirring, until the sugar has dissolved, then boil the mixture steadily for 6-8 minutes, without stirring, until it forms a syrup. Stir in the rum and lemon juice.

Turn the warm savarin on to a serving dish, prick it all over with a fine skewer and spoon the hot rum syrup over it. Use as much of the syrup as the savarin will absorb. Set aside until cold.

Make the glaze by sieving the apricot jam into a small saucepan. Add 30 ml/2 tbsp water and bring to the boil, stirring constantly. When the mixture is smooth and shiny, use a pastry brush to glaze the soaked savarin.

SERVES 6 TO 8

TYPES OF YEAST

FRESH YEAST Fresh yeast may be used for the savarin, if preferred. Simply blend it with the tepid liquid. Fresh yeast is not always easy to obtain but can often be found at health food shops, bakers or at some of the hot-bread sections of large supermarkets. It should be greyish in colour, firm and cool to the touch and have a pleasant aromatic smell. It is worth buying more than you actually need. Wrap the excess in usable amounts and freeze for up to 6 weeks. Frozen yeast may be blended straight into the tepid liquid or allowed to thaw for 20 minutes before use.

EASY-BLEND DRIED YEAST Easy-blend dried yeast is available in small sachets from supermarkets. Unlike ordinary dried yeast, this product is mixed with the flour and other dry ingredients before the liquid is added. The liquid should be warmer than that used for other types of yeast and it is important to follow the manufacturer's instructions carefully.

RUM BABAS

Illustrated on page 142

oil for greasing
75 ml/5 tbsp milk
10 ml/2 tsp dried yeast
150 g/5 oz strong white flour
1.25 ml/¼ tsp salt
10 ml/2 tsp sugar
75 g/3 oz butter
3 eggs, beaten
50 g/2 oz currants

RUM SYRUP
75 g/3 oz lump sugar
30 ml/2 tbsp rum
15 ml/1 tbsp lemon juice

Oil 12 baba tins. Set the oven at 200°C/ 400°F/gas 6. Warm the milk until tepid. Sprinkle on the dried yeast. Stir in 15 ml/ 1 tbsp of the flour and leave in a warm place for 20 minutes.

Sift the rest of the flour, the salt and the sugar into a mixing bowl. Rub in the butter. Add the yeast liquid to the mixture, then add the eggs. Beat until well mixed, then work in the currants. Half fill the prepared tins with mixture. Cover with oiled polythene, and leave in a warm place until the tins are two-thirds full. Bake for 10-15 minutes or until the babas are golden brown and springy to the touch.

Heat the sugar in a saucepan with 125 ml/4 fl oz water. Stir until the sugar has dissolved, then boil the mixture steadily for 6-8 minutes, without stirring, until it forms a syrup. Stir in the rum and lemon juice.

Remove the babas from the tins, prick all over with a fine skewer and transfer to individual dishes. Spoon hot rum syrup over each baba. Serve cold, with cream.

SERVES 12

INDIVIDUAL APRICOT TRIFLES

Illustrated on page 142

6 small rounds of sponge cake, about
    2 cm/¾ inch thick and 6 cm/2½ inches
    across
15 ml/1 tbsp sweet sherry
175 ml/6 fl oz orange juice
6 fresh apricots, halved and stoned
25 g/1 oz granulated sugar

DECORATION
125 ml/4 fl oz double cream
6 pistachio nuts

Place the sponge cake rounds in individual dishes. In a jug, mix the sherry with 30 ml/2 tbsp of the orange juice, and pour it over the sponge cakes. Place 2 apricot halves in each dish, on top of the sponge cake. Set aside.

Put the remaining orange juice in a saucepan with the sugar and heat gently until all the sugar has dissolved. Bring to the boil and boil steadily for 10 minutes until the mixture forms a thick syrup. Glaze the apricots with the syrup. Leave to cool.

In a bowl, whip the cream until thick. Blanch, skin, dry and chop the pistachios. Pipe the cream on to the trifles, surrounding the glazed apricots, and decorate with the pistachios. Chill before serving.

SERVES 6

VARIATION

Peach halves or pineapple rings may be used instead of apricots. This also works well with drained canned fruit.

APPLE TRIFLE

1 kg/2¼ lb cooking apples
grated rind and juice of ½ lemon
150 g/5 oz granulated sugar
6 trifle sponges
350 ml/12 fl oz milk
2 eggs plus 1 yolk
15 ml/1 tbsp caster sugar
few drops of vanilla essence

DECORATION
175 ml/6 fl oz double cream
25 g/1 oz flaked almonds, browned

Peel, quarter and core the apples. Put them into a saucepan with the lemon rind and juice and granulated sugar. Add 30 ml/2 tbsp water and cover the pan. Simmer the apple mixture gently until the fruit is reduced to a pulp. Purée in a blender or food processor and allow the mixture to cool slightly.

Slice the sponges and place in a large glass dish. Spread with the apple purée and set aside.

In a saucepan, bring the milk to just below boiling point. Put the eggs and caster sugar into a bowl, mix well, then stir in the scalded milk and vanilla essence. Strain the custard mixture into a heavy-bottomed saucepan or a heatproof bowl placed over a saucepan of simmering water. Alternatively, use a double saucepan, but make sure the water does not touch the upper pan.

Cook the custard over very gentle heat for 15-25 minutes, stirring all the time with a wooden spoon, until the custard thickens to the consistency of single cream. Stir well around the sides as well as the base of the pan or bowl to prevent the formation of lumps, especially if using a double saucepan. Do not let the custard boil.

As soon as the custard thickens, pour it carefully over the apple purée in the dish (see Mrs Beeton's Tip). Cover the surface of the custard with dampened greaseproof paper to prevent the formation of a skin. Cool.

In a bowl, whip the cream until stiff. Spread it on the cold custard and decorate with the almonds. Serve chilled.

SERVES 6

VARIATION

GOOSEBERRY TRIFLE Use 1 kg/2¼ lb gooseberries, topped and tailed, instead of apples.

MRS BEETON'S TIP When adding the hot custard to the glass dish, pour it over a metal spoon whose bowl rests in the dish. This will reduce the possibility of the hot liquid causing the dish to crack.

APRICOT TRIFLE

6 slices Swiss roll filled with jam
2 almond macaroons
1 × 540 g/18½ fl oz can apricot halves
30 ml/2 tbsp sherry
500 ml/17 fl oz milk
3 eggs plus 2 yolks
25 g/1 oz caster sugar
few drops of vanilla essence

DECORATION
150 ml/¼ pint double cream
25 g/1 oz blanched almonds

Cut the Swiss roll into cubes and break the macaroons into chunks. Arrange them on the base of a glass dish.

Drain the apricots, reserving 125 ml/ 4 fl oz of the juice in a measuring jug and adding the sherry. Pour the mixture over the cake in the dish. Reserve half the apricot halves, cutting the remainder into chunks and adding them to the dish.

In a saucepan, bring the milk to just below boiling point. Put the eggs and sugar into a bowl, mix well, then stir in the scalded milk. Strain the custard mixture into a heavy-bottomed saucepan or a heatproof bowl placed over a saucepan of simmering water. Alternatively, use a double saucepan, but make sure the water does not touch the upper pan.

Cook the custard over very gentle heat for 15-25 minutes, stirring all the time with a wooden spoon, until the custard thickens to the consistency of single cream. Stir well around the sides as well as the base of the pan or bowl to prevent the formation of lumps, especially if using a double saucepan.

As soon as the custard thickens, pour it carefully over the apricots in the dish (see Mrs Beeton's Tip, opposite). Cover the surface of the custard with dampened greaseproof paper to prevent the formation of a skin and set aside for 30 minutes to set.

In a bowl, whip the cream until stiff. Spread it on the cold custard and decorate with the reserved apricots and the almonds. Serve chilled.

SERVES 6

VARIATIONS

PEACH TRIFLE Use peach slices instead of apricots and add 15 ml/1 tbsp lemon juice to the syrup.
PINEAPPLE TRIFLE Use pineapple cubes instead of apricots.

PEAR AND CHOCOLATE TRIFLE

6 individual sponge cakes or trifle sponges
6 canned pear halves

SAUCE
  25 g/1 oz butter
  25 g/1 oz cocoa
  25 g/1 oz plain flour
  500 ml/17 fl oz milk
  25 g/1 oz sugar
  10 ml/2 tsp gelatine

DECORATION
  150 ml/¼ pint double cream
  angelica

Place the sponge cakes in 6 individual dishes. Drain the canned pears well on absorbent kitchen paper, then place a pear half, rounded side uppermost, on each sponge cake.

To make the sauce, melt the butter in a saucepan, add the cocoa and flour and cook for 2 minutes. Stir in the milk gradually, add the sugar and bring the mixture to the boil, stirring all the time. Lower the heat and simmer for 2 minutes, then remove from the heat.

Place 30 ml/2 tbsp water in a small heatproof bowl. Sprinkle the gelatine on to the liquid. Stand the bowl over a saucepan of hot water and stir the gelatine until it has dissolved completely. Stir it into the sauce. Leave to cool to a coating consistency.

Pour the chocolate sauce over the pears and allow some to run into the dish. Cool. In a bowl, whip the cream until stiff, and use with the angelica to decorate the trifles.

SERVES 6

MRS BEETON'S TRADITIONAL TRIFLE

Illustrated on page 143

4 individual sponge cakes or trifle sponges
60 ml/4 tbsp raspberry or strawberry jam
6 almond macaroons, crushed
12 ratafias, crushed
125 ml/4 fl oz sherry
25 g/1 oz flaked almonds
grated rind of ½ lemon
350 ml/12 fl oz milk
2 eggs plus 1 yolk
45 ml/3 tbsp caster sugar
few drops of vanilla essence
125 ml/4 fl oz double cream

DECORATION
    glacé cherries
    angelica

Cut the sponge cakes in half and spread one half of each with jam. Sandwich together and arrange in a glass dish. Add the crushed macaroons and ratafias. Pour the sherry over the top, sprinkle with the almonds and lemon rind and set aside while making the custard.

In a saucepan, bring the milk to just below boiling point. Put the eggs and 15 ml/1 tbsp caster sugar into a bowl, mix well, then stir in the scalded milk and vanilla essence. Strain the custard mixture into a heavy-bottomed saucepan or a heat-proof bowl placed over a saucepan of simmering water. Alternatively, use a double saucepan, but make sure the water does not touch the upper pan.

Cook the custard over very gentle heat for 15-25 minutes, stirring all the time with a wooden spoon, until the custard thickens to the consistency of single cream. Stir well around the sides as well as the base of the pan or bowl to prevent the formation of lumps, especially if using a double saucepan. Do not let the custard boil.

As soon as the custard thickens, pour it carefully into the glass bowl (see Mrs Beeton's Tip, page 176) and leave for about 30 minutes to cool, covering the surface of the custard with dampened greaseproof paper to prevent the formation of a skin.

In a bowl, whip together the cream and remaining sugar until stiff. Spread over the custard in the dish. Decorate with cherries and angelica.

SERVES 6

WINE TRIFLES

grated rind and juice of ½ lemon
3 eggs
100 g/4 oz caster sugar
5 ml/1 tsp cornflour
375 ml/13 fl oz sweet white wine
6 individual sponge cakes or trifle
    sponges

Put the lemon rind and juice into a heat-proof bowl. Add the eggs, sugar, and cornflour and stir the mixture well. Gradually whisk in the wine.

Place the bowl over a saucepan of hot water and heat very gently, whisking all the time until light and fluffy. The mixture must not be allowed to boil; it may be prepared in the top of a double saucepan and will take about 15 minutes to thicken.

Remove the bowl from the heat and leave to cool slightly. Place the sponge cakes in 6 individual dishes. Just before serving, pour over the sauce.

SERVES 6

MRS BEETON'S TIPSY CAKE

1 × 15 cm/6 inch sponge cake
30 ml/2 tbsp redcurrant jelly
75 ml/3 fl oz brandy
50 g/2 oz whole blanched almonds
375 ml/13 fl oz milk
125 ml/4 fl oz single cream
8 egg yolks
75 g/3 oz caster sugar
extra redcurrant jelly to decorate

Put the cake in a glass bowl or dish 16 cm/6½ inches in diameter and as deep as the cake. Spread the cake thinly with jelly, then pour over as much brandy as the cake can absorb.

Cut the almonds lengthways into spikes and stick them all over the top of the cake.

Mix the milk and cream in a bowl. In a second, heatproof, bowl beat the yolks until liquid, and pour the milk and cream over them. Stir in the sugar. Transfer the mixture to the top of a double saucepan and cook over gently simmering water for about 10 minutes or until the custard thickens, stirring all the time. Let the custard cool slightly, then pour it over and around the cake. Cover with dampened greaseproof paper. When cold, refrigerate the tipsy cake for about 1 hour, Decorate with small spoonfuls of redcurrant jelly and serve.

SERVES 4 TO 6

DEAN'S CREAM

This is a very old recipe for a dessert that was one of the forerunners of the standard modern trifle.

6 individual sponge cakes
raspberry jam
apricot jam
100 g/4 oz ratafias
250 ml/8 fl oz sherry
75 ml/5 tbsp brandy
500 ml/17 fl oz double cream
50 g/2 oz caster sugar

DECORATION
angelica
glacé cherries
crystallized pineapple

Cut the sponge cakes in half lengthways, and spread half with raspberry jam and half with apricot jam. Arrange them in a deep glass dish, jam sides upwards.

Break the ratafias into pieces and sprinkle on top of the sponge cakes. Pour the sherry over the cakes and leave to soak for about 30 minutes.

Put the brandy, cream, and sugar into a bowl and whisk until very thick. Pile into the dish and decorate with angelica, cherries, and crystallized pineapple. Chill well before serving.

SERVES 8

*M*RS BEETON'S CHARLOTTE RUSSE

45 ml/3 tbsp icing sugar, sifted
24 sponge fingers
15 ml/1 tbsp gelatine
500 ml/17 fl oz single cream
45 ml/3 tbsp any sweet liqueur
1 × 15 cm/6 inch round sponge cake,
    1 cm/½ inch thick

In a small bowl, mix 30 ml/2 tbsp of the icing sugar with a little water to make a thin glacé icing. Cut 4 sponge fingers in half, and dip the rounded ends in the icing. Line a 15 cm/6 inch soufflé dish with the halved fingers, placing them like a star, with the sugared sides uppermost and the iced ends meeting in the centre. Dip one end of each of the remaining biscuits in icing and use to line the sides of the dish, with the sugared sides outward and the iced ends at the base. Trim the biscuits to the height of the dish.

Place 45 ml/3 tbsp water in a small heatproof bowl and sprinkle the gelatine on to the liquid. Stand the bowl over a saucepan of hot water and stir the gelatine until it has dissolved completely.

Combine the cream, liqueur and remaining icing sugar in a bowl. Add the gelatine and whisk until frothy. Stand the mixture in a cool place until it begins to thicken, then pour carefully into the charlotte. Cover the flavoured cream with the sponge cake, making sure it is set enough to support the cake. Chill for 8-12 hours, until firm.

Loosen the biscuits from the sides of the dish with a knife, carefully turn the charlotte out on to a plate and serve.

SERVES 6

*C*HARLOTTE RUSSE WITH COINTREAU

250 ml/8 fl oz Clear Lemon Jelly (page 204)
20 sponge fingers
4 egg yolks or 1 whole egg and 2 yolks
50 g/2 oz caster sugar
250 ml/8 fl oz milk
thinly pared rind and juice of 1 lemon
15 ml/1 tbsp Cointreau
10 ml/2 tsp gelatine
150 ml/¼ pint double cream
150 ml/¼ pint single cream

Pour enough jelly into the base of an 18 cm/7 inch soufflé dish or charlotte mould to give a depth of 5 mm/¼ inch. Refrigerate until set. Place the remaining jelly in a heatproof bowl over hot water so that it remains liquid.

Trim one end of each sponge finger so that they will stand upright. Dip the long side of one of the sponge fingers in the liquid jelly and stand in the mould, with the cut end resting on the layer of jelly, and the sugared side outwards. Repeat with a second sponge finger, sticking it to its neighbour with the aid of the jelly coating. Repeat until the mould is lined, then chill for about 2½ hours until set.

Meanwhile make the bavarois filling. In a bowl, beat the eggs and sugar together until fluffy and pale. Warm the milk in a saucepan with the lemon rind; do not let it boil. Remove from the heat and slowly strain the flavoured milk into the egg mixture, then return the custard to the clean saucepan or to a double saucepan or heatproof bowl placed over hot water. Cook over very low heat until the custard thickens.

Strain the thickened custard into a bowl, stir in the lemon juice and Cointreau. Cool.

Put 15 ml/1 tbsp water into a small heat-proof bowl and sprinkle the gelatine on to the liquid. Stand the bowl over a saucepan and stir the gelatine until it has dissolved completely. Cool until tepid and add to the custard. Leave in a cool place until the mixture thickens at the edges, stirring from time to time to prevent the formation of a skin.

Combine the creams in a bowl and whip lightly. Fold into the custard mixture, and set aside in a cool place until on the point of setting. Pour carefully into the charlotte shell, taking care not to disturb the sponge fingers.

Chill the charlotte until the bavarois filling is completely set, then loosen the biscuits from the sides of the dish with a knife, carefully turn the charlotte out on to a plate and serve.

SERVES 6

C HARLOTTE ST JOSÉ

250 ml/8 fl oz Clear Lemon Jelly (page 204)
glacé pineapple
20 sponge fingers
1 × 127 g/4½ oz tablet pineapple jelly
1 × 376 g/13 oz can crushed pineapple
30 ml/2 tbsp custard powder
250 ml/8 fl oz milk
250 ml/8 fl oz double cream

Line a 1.25 litre/2¼ pint charlotte mould with a thin layer of the clear lemon jelly and leave to set. Decorate the jelly (see page 192) with pieces of glacé pineapple, dipping them in liquid lemon jelly before setting into place. Spoon over a very thin layer of jelly to hold them firmly, then refrigerate until set.

Trim one end of each sponge finger and use to line the sides of the mould, placing the trimmed end of each on to the jelly on the base. Chill while preparing the pineapple jelly cream filling.

Chop the pineapple jelly tablet roughly. Heat 100 ml/3½ fl oz water in a saucepan, add the jelly and stir until dissolved. Drain the crushed pineapple, stirring the juice into the jelly mixture in the pan, and reserving the fruit. Set the jelly mixture aside to cool.

Meanwhile, in a bowl, blend the custard powder with a little of the milk. Put the rest of the milk into a saucepan and bring to the boil. Pour it slowly on to the blended custard powder, stirring all the time until the custard thickens.

Cool the custard slightly, then stir into the jelly mixture. Cool again until beginning to set, then fold in the reserved crushed pineapple.

In a clean bowl, whip 125 ml/4 fl oz of the cream until it leaves a trail, then fold into the setting mixture. Spoon into the prepared mould and refrigerate for 2-3 hours until set.

Trim the sponge fingers level with the top of the mould and turn out on to a serving dish. Put the remaining cream into a bowl and whip until stiff. Use to decorate the charlotte.

SERVES 8

B AKED COFFEE CHEESECAKE

BASE

50 g/2 oz butter or margarine
50 g/2 oz caster sugar
1 egg, beaten
50 g/2 oz self-raising flour
2.5 ml/½ tsp baking powder

FILLING

75 g/3 oz butter
100 g/4 oz caster sugar
30 ml/2 tbsp instant coffee
15 ml/1 tbsp orange juice
30 ml/2 tbsp brandy
1 egg
50 g/2 oz plain flour
75 g/3 oz sultanas
450 g/1 lb full-fat soft cheese
250 ml/8 fl oz double cream

Set the oven at 160°C/325°F/gas 3. Make the base. Combine all the ingredients in a mixing bowl and beat until smooth. Spread the mixture over the base of a deep loose-bottomed 20 cm/8 inch cake tin.

For the filling, cream the butter with the sugar in a large bowl until light and fluffy. Put the coffee in a small bowl and add 15 ml/1 tbsp boiling water. Stir until dissolved, add the orange juice and leave to cool.

Beat the coffee and orange juice into the creamed mixture with the brandy and egg. Fold in the flour and sultanas.

In a separate bowl, beat the cheese until smooth. Gradually beat in the cream. Fold the cheese mixture carefully into the butter mixture and spoon into the prepared tin.

Bake for 1¼-1½ hours or until firm. Cool, then remove from the tin and transfer to a serving plate. Serve cold.

SERVES 10 TO 12

C URD CHEESECAKE

BASE

175 g/6 oz plain flour
75 g/3 oz margarine
1 egg yolk
flour for rolling out

FILLING

75 g/3 oz curd cheese
50 g/2 oz butter, melted
1 egg, beaten
pinch of salt
100 g/4 oz sugar
25 g/1 oz currants
grated nutmeg
5 ml/1 tsp baking powder

Set the oven at 190°C/375°F/gas 5. To make the pastry base, sift the flour into a bowl, then rub in the margarine until the mixture resembles fine breadcrumbs. Add the egg yolk and enough water (about 15-30 ml/1-2 tbsp) to mix the ingredients into a short pastry. Press the pastry together gently with your fingertips.

Roll out the pastry on a lightly floured

surface and use to line an 18 cm/7 inch flan ring set on a baking sheet.

Press the curd cheese through a sieve into a mixing bowl. Add the melted butter, egg, salt, sugar, currants and a little grated nutmeg. Mix well, then stir in the baking powder. Spoon the mixture into the un-cooked flan case.

Bake for 25-30 minutes until the pastry is lightly browned and the filling set. Serve warm or cold.

SERVES 4

☼ **MICROWAVE TIP** Melt the butter in a small bowl on High for 1-2 minutes.

---

*C*HEDDAR CHEESECAKE

BASE
   175 g/6 oz plain flour
   75 g/3 oz margarine
   1 egg yolk
   flour for rolling out

FILLING
   1 egg, separated, plus 1 white
   grated rind and juice of 1 lemon
   75 ml/5 tbsp plain yogurt
   25 g/1 oz self-raising flour
   75 g/3 oz caster sugar
   150 g/5 oz Cheddar cheese, grated

Set the oven at 200°C/400°F/gas 6. To make the pastry base, sift the flour into a bowl, then rub in the margarine until the mixture resembles fine breadcrumbs. Add the egg yolk and enough water (about 15-30 ml/1-2 tbsp) to mix the ingredients into a short pastry. Press the pastry together gently with your fingertips.

Roll out the pastry on a lightly floured surface and use to line a 20 cm/8 inch flan ring or dish. Bake 'blind' (see Mrs Beeton's Tip). Lower the oven temperature to 160°C/325°F/gas 3.

In a mixing bowl, combine the egg yolk, lemon rind and juice, yogurt, flour and sugar. Mix well, then fold in the grated cheese.

In a clean, grease-free bowl, whisk both egg whites until stiff. Stir 15 ml/1 tbsp of the beaten egg whites into the cheese mixture to lighten it, then gently fold in the remaining egg white. Turn into the prepared pastry case.

Bake for 35-45 minutes or until firm in the centre and lightly browned. Serve cold.

SERVES 6 TO 8

🥣 **MRS BEETON'S TIP** To bake blind, prick the base of the pastry case with a fork, then cover with a piece of greaseproof paper. Fill the pastry case with dried beans, bread crusts or rice and bake at 200°C/400°F/gas 6 for 10 minutes. Remove the paper and beans or other dry filling and return the case to the oven for 5 minutes to dry out the inside before adding the chosen filling and returning the case to the oven. If a fully cooked pastry case is required, as when a cold filling is to be added, bake the pastry case blind for 20-30 minutes, and dry out for 5-7 minutes.

ALMOND CHEESECAKE

fat for greasing
75 g/3 oz curd cheese
50 g/2 oz butter, melted
2 eggs, separated
grated rind and juice of ½ lemon
50 g/2 oz ground almonds
50 g/2 oz caster sugar
30 ml/2 tbsp self-raising flour

Line and grease an 18 cm/7 inch sandwich cake tin. Set the oven at 220°C/425°F/gas 7.

Press the curd cheese through a sieve into a mixing bowl. Add the melted butter, egg yolks, lemon rind and juice, almonds and caster sugar and mix thoroughly. Sift the flour over the mixture and fold in.

In a clean, grease-free bowl, whisk the egg whites until stiff. Fold into the almond mixture. Spoon the mixture into the prepared tin and bake for 10 minutes.

Lower the oven temperature to 180°C/350°F/gas 4 and cook for about 15 minutes more. Test to see whether the cake is cooked (see Mrs Beeton's Tip). If necessary, return the cake to the oven for a few minutes, covering the surface loosely with foil or greaseproof paper to prevent overbrowning.

SERVES 4

MRS BEETON'S TIP To test the cake, insert a thin heated skewer into the centre. If the skewer comes out dry, the cake is cooked.

LEMON CHEESECAKE

BASE
100 g/4 oz digestive biscuits
50 g/2 oz butter
25 g/1 oz caster sugar

FILLING
200 g/7 oz full-fat soft cheese
75 g/3 oz caster sugar
2 eggs, separated
125 ml/4 fl oz soured cream
15 g/½ oz gelatine
grated rind and juice of 1 lemon

Make the base. Crumb the biscuits (see page 166). Melt the butter in a small saucepan and mix in the crumbs and sugar. Press the mixture on to the base of a loose-bottomed 15 cm/6 inch cake tin. Put in a cool place until set.

Make the filling. In a mixing bowl, beat the cheese and sugar together. Add the egg yolks and beat well. Stir in the soured cream.

Place 45 ml/3 tbsp water in a small heat-proof bowl. Sprinkle the gelatine on to the liquid. Stand the bowl over a saucepan of hot water and stir the gelatine until it has dissolved completely. Stir the lemon rind, juice and dissolved gelatine into the cheese mixture.

In a clean, grease-free bowl, whisk the egg whites until stiff and fold carefully into the mixture. Pour into the prepared tin and chill for 45 minutes-1 hour until firm. When quite cold, remove from the tin, transfer to a plate and serve.

SERVES 4 TO 6

RASPBERRY YOGURT CHEESECAKE

BASE
   fat for greasing
   50 g/2 oz butter
   50 g/2 oz caster sugar
   15 ml/1 tbsp golden syrup
   25 g/1 oz walnuts, chopped
   50 g/2 oz crisp rice cereal

FILLING
   15 ml/1 tbsp gelatine
   300 g/11 oz cottage cheese
   125 ml/4 fl oz raspberry – flavoured yogurt
   15 ml/1 tbsp lemon juice
   3 eggs, separated
   225 g/8 oz caster sugar
   250 ml/8 fl oz double cream
   1 × 175 g/6 oz can raspberries

GLAZE (optional)
   syrup from canned raspberries
   10 ml/2 tsp arrowroot
   few drops of red food colouring

Grease a 20 cm/8 inch loose-bottomed cake tin. Melt the butter, sugar and syrup together in a saucepan. Add the walnuts and crisp rice cereal. Stir well and press the mixture on to the base of the prepared cake tin. Chill for 10 minutes.

Make the filling. Place 45 ml/3 tbsp water in a small bowl and sprinkle the gelatine on to the liquid. Stand the bowl over a saucepan of hot water and stir the gelatine until it has dissolved completely.

Sieve the cottage cheese into a bowl, add the yogurt and lemon juice and beat until smooth. Combine the egg yolks and 150 g/5 oz of the sugar in a saucepan and cook over low heat, stirring all the time, until the mixture thickens. Remove from the heat and pour into a mixing bowl. Add the dis-solved gelatine, mix well, then allow to cool until the mixture is beginning to thicken.

Stir the yogurt and cheese mixture into the cooled gelatine mixture. In a clean dry bowl, whisk the egg whites until stiff, then gradually whisk in the remaining sugar. In a separate bowl, whip the cream until it just holds its shape. Fold the cream into the mixing bowl, then fold in the egg whites. Pour carefully into the prepared tin. Chill the mixture for at least 4 hours.

If leaving the cake unglazed, remove from the tin, discard the syrup from the can of raspberries and arrange the fruit on top. Chill before serving. If glazing the cake, make up the can syrup to 125 ml/4 fl oz with water and blend it into the arrowroot in a small saucepan. Bring to the boil, stirring all the time, until the sauce thickens and clears. Add a few drops of red food colouring. Arrange the fruit on top of the cake and coat with the glaze. Chill in the refrigerator before serving.

SERVES 8 TO 10

VARIATIONS

Use the same quantity of canned or frozen peaches, strawberries, blackcurrants, apricots or black cherries with the appropriate yogurt and food colouring.

*P*ICNIC CHEESECAKE

As its name suggests, this is the perfect centrepiece for an afternoon picnic. The cooked cheesecake is firm so it will not disintegrate. For safety's sake, transport it in the tin, covering the top in foil.

BASE
   75 g/3 oz butter
   150 g/5 oz fine dry white breadcrumbs
   50 g/2 oz caster sugar
   7.5 ml/3 tsp ground cinnamon

FILLING
   3 eggs, separated
   100 g/4 oz caster sugar
   375 g/13 oz full-fat soft cheese
   grated rind and juice of 1 lemon
   125 ml/4 fl oz soured cream
   25 g/1 oz chopped mixed nuts
   caster sugar and cinnamon for dusting
   15 ml/1 tbsp butter

Set the oven at 180°C/350°F/gas 4. Make the base. Melt the butter in a frying pan and stir in the breadcrumbs. Cook over gentle heat, stirring until the crumbs are golden. Remove from the heat, stir in the sugar and cinnamon and leave to cool.

Press about two thirds of the crumbs over the base of a loose-bottomed 20 cm/8 inch cake tin. Reserve the remaining crumbs.

Beat the egg yolks in a mixing bowl until liquid. Set aside 15 ml/1 tbsp of the sugar in a small bowl. Add the remaining sugar to the egg yolks, beating until creamy. Press the cheese through a sieve into the bowl, then work in lightly. Add the lemon rind and juice to the mixture with the cream.

In a clean, grease-free bowl, whisk the egg whites to soft peaks. Stir 30 ml/2 tbsp into the cheese mixture, then fold in the rest lightly. Turn the mixture gently on to the prepared base in the tin. Bake for 45 minutes.

Sprinkle the reserved crumbs and the nuts on top of the partially cooked cheesecake and return to the oven for 15 minutes more.

Meanwhile, mix the cinnamon with the reserved sugar. Remove the cake from the oven and test that it is firm in the centre (see Mrs Beeton's Tip, page 184). Increase the oven temperature to 220°C/425°F/gas 7.

Sprinkle the cinnamon and sugar mixture over the top of the cheesecake and dot with butter. Return the cheesecake to the oven for 2-4 minutes or until glazed on top. Cool in the tin. Serve cold.

SERVES 8 TO 10

> ☆ **FREEZER TIP** Cooked cheesecakes freeze well. When cold, wrap in foil or greaseproof paper and freeze in a labelled polythene bag. Thaw wrapped at room temperature for 3 hours.

*M*ARIGOLD CHEESECAKE

BASE
100 g/4 oz digestive biscuits
50 g/2 oz butter
25 g/1 oz caster sugar

FILLING
25 g/1 oz gelatine
2 eggs, separated
200 g/7 oz full-fat soft cheese
25 g/1 oz caster sugar
250 ml/8 fl oz milk
pared rind of 1 orange

DECORATION
orange segments
½ glacé cherry

Make the base. Crumb the biscuits (see 166). Melt the butter in a small saucepan and mix in the crumbs and sugar. Press the mixture into a loose-bottomed 15 cm/6 inch cake tin. Chill.

Place 30 ml/2 tbsp water in a small heatproof bowl. Sprinkle the gelatine on to the liquid. Stand the bowl over a saucepan of hot water and stir the gelatine until it has dissolved completely.

Combine the egg yolks, soft cheese, sugar, milk, orange rind and gelatine mixture in the bowl of a blender or food processor. Process for 45 seconds or until smooth, then scrape into a mixing bowl with a spatula. Alternatively, beat well by hand.
In a clean, grease-free bowl, whisk the egg whites to soft peaks, then gently fold into the cheese mixture. Spoon very gently on to the base and chill until firm.

Garnish with orange pieces and cherry.

SERVES 4 TO 6

*M*ELOPITA

In Greece, this honey-flavoured dessert would be made from myzithra. Sieved cottage cheese is an acceptable substitute.

BASE
300 g/11 oz plain flour
7.5 ml/3 tsp baking powder
pinch of salt
125 g/4½ oz butter
flour for rolling out

FILLING
675 g/1½ lb cottage cheese
150 g/5 oz caster sugar
10 ml/2 tsp ground cinnamon
200 g/7 oz clear honey
5 eggs

Set the oven at 180°C/350°G/gas 4. To make the pastry base, sift the flour, baking powder and salt into a bowl, then rub in the butter until the mixture resembles fine breadcrumbs. Add enough cold water to mix the ingredients to a stiff pastry.

Roll out the pastry on a lightly floured surface and use to line a 20 cm/8 inch pie plate or a flan ring set on a baking sheet.

Press the cottage cheese through a sieve into a mixing bowl and add the sugar, half the cinnamon, and the honey. Mix lightly, then add the eggs, one at a time, beating well after each addition. Press the mixture through a sieve into a clean bowl, then turn into the pastry shell.

Bake for 45 minutes, then raise the oven temperature to 220°C/425°F/gas 7 and bake for 10-15 minutes. Test by using a skewer (see Mrs Beeton's Tip, page 184), then leave to cool in the oven. Serve cold, sprinkled with the remaining cinnamon.

SERVES 6

TORTA DI RICOTTA

BASE

100 g/4 oz butter
100 g/4 oz margarine
75 g/3 oz icing sugar
2 egg yolks
pinch of ground cinnamon
250 g/9 oz plain flour
flour for rolling out

FILLING

675 g/1½ lb ricotta cheese
25 g/1 oz grated Parmesan cheese
2 eggs, separated
25 g/1 oz plain flour
45 ml/3 tbsp plain yogurt
50 g/2 oz caster sugar
grated rind and juice of 1 lemon
pinch of salt
few drops of lemon essence

DECORATION AND SAUCE

225 g/8 oz fresh raspberries
15 ml/1 tbsp arrowroot
100 g/4 oz raspberry jam
60 ml/4 tbsp maraschino liqueur
125 ml/4 fl oz sweet red vermouth

Make the pastry. Cream the butter or margarine with the sugar in a mixing bowl until light and fluffy. Blend in the egg yolks, cinnamon and flour. Knead the mixture lightly and roll into a ball. Chill for 20 minutes.

Set the oven at 150°C/300°F/gas 2. Roll out the pastry on a lightly floured surface to a round 5 mm/¼ inch thick. Ease into an 18 cm/7 inch flan ring set on a baking sheet (see Mrs Beeton's Tip). Prick the base with a fork and chill until required.

For the filling, cream the ricotta and Parmesan in a bowl and gradually beat in the rest of the filling ingredients. Spoon into the uncooked flan case, level the surface and bake for 30 minutes.

Remove the flan from the oven and cut around the pastry edge to separate the filling from the pastry (and to prevent the filling from spilling out). Return to the oven for 30 minutes more, then leave to cool.

Decorate the cooled flan with the raspberries, and chill while making the sauce. Put the arrowroot in a small bowl and mix to a thin cream with 125 ml/4 fl oz water. Melt the jam in a saucepan. When it boils, stir in the arrowroot mixture to thicken it. Flavour with the maraschino liqueur and vermouth. Remove from the heat and when cold, pour a little of the sauce over the raspberries and serve the rest separately.

SERVES 8

> **MRS BEETON'S TIP** To line the flan ring, place on the baking sheet and roll the pastry to a round at least 5 cm/2 inches larger than the ring. The pastry should be about 3 mm/1/8 inch thick. Lift the pastry round over a rolling pin to prevent it breaking and stretching, and lay it in the flan ring. Press the pastry gently down on the baking sheet and into the base of the ring. Working from the centre outwards, press the pastry into the base and up the sides, making sure it fits snugly into the flutes, if present, and is of even thickness all round. Trim off any surplus pastry by rolling across the top of the ring with the rolling pin.

FRUIT PUDDINGS AND JELLIES

A colourful bowl of fresh fruit is the simplest of desserts. The introduction to this chapter provides a guide to some of the many exotic fruits that are available. In the recipes you will find these, and more familiar fruits used in a variety of desserts and jellies, some simple, some stunning.

A wide variety of fruit is now available throughout the country all year round, including many exotics that were unheard of in Mrs Beeton's day. Fruit salads may be as simple or as exciting as you please, offering just two or three fresh fruit, a combination of exotic fresh fruits, or some familiar fresh fruits with exotic canned fruits. A fruit salad always looks good, especially when served in an ice bowl or a container made from the shell of one of the component fruits. Pineapple and Kirsch Salad (page 194), served in pineapple half-shells, looks spectacular, as would the Red Fruit Salad (page 195), served in a hollowed-out watermelon.

The diet-conscious may prefer an unsweeted fruit salad, or a little honey may be used in place of the traditional syrup. Serve cream, yogurt or fromage frais with fruit salad and offer some plain biscuits to complete the dessert.

EXOTIC FRUITS

New fruits appear on the supermarket shelves regularly. Some sell well and soon become familiar, others are only seen once or twice. The following is a brief guide to some of the unusual fruits that are available.

Apple Bananas These are very small bananas with thin skins. Their flesh is quite dry but they taste similar to a banana with a hint of apple. They are grown in Kenya and Malaysia. Their size and good flavour make apple bananas ideal dessert fruit, for topping with vanilla ice cream or serving flamed with brandy.

Carambola The carambola is known as star fruit because of its ridged shape. The slices resemble stars. The pale yellow, waxy-looking skin may be left on unless the fruit is particularly tough. The flesh has a very delicate flavour, making the fruit ideal for decorating a wide variety of desserts, including cheesecakes, trifles and gâteaux.

Figs Purple-skinned figs should be just soft when ripe. They have a deep red coloured flesh with lots of small pale seeds. When the skin is removed thinly, the flesh will be found to have a sweet flavour. Whole figs may be quartered and served with a small scoop of orange sorbet or good ice cream to make a tempting dessert. Figs are also exceedingly good with creamy goat's cheese.

Guava An oval, yellow-skinned fruit, about the size of a large pear. The guava has slightly scented, tangy flesh with lots of small seeds in the middle. The peel should be removed before the fruit is sliced. It is best lightly poached in syrup, after which the slices may be added to cool fruit salads or used in a variety of desserts.

Kiwi Fruit A green fruit with a brown, slightly furry skin that is quite thin. When cut across, the small oval fruit has a pale core, surrounded by small dark seeds and bright green flesh. The fruit should be peeled before being sliced. It is often used for decorating desserts or for adding to fruit salads.

Kumquats These look like tiny oranges. They are citrus fruit with an slightly bitter, orange flavour. They may be poached and eaten whole but they do contain pips. If sliced, the seeds may be removed before the fruit is cooked. Kumquats may be eaten raw but they are quite sharp; their skin resembles fine, orange peel.

Mango The mango is oval and about the size of a medium potato. The skin is red when the fruit is fully ripe, by which time the mango should feel slightly soft. There is a large, thin, oval stone in the centre of the juicy orange flesh. The mango has a flavour reminiscent of peaches but it is slightly more scented and a little tangy. The fruit should be peeled and the flesh cut off the stone in long wedges or slices.

Papaya An oval fruit with a deep yellow skin which is slightly green before the fruit ripens. Cut open, the papaya has seeds in the middle and sweet apricot-coloured flesh. It is very good in fruit salads.

Passion Fruit Small, round, dimpled fruit with a hard, purple skin. When cut in half the passion fruit reveals a soft, orange-coloured, juicy flesh with small, dark, edible seeds. The flesh is scooped out with a tea-spoon, and may then be sieved and used to flavour desserts or sweet sauces.

Persimmon A small, round, orange-coloured fruit with a large stalk end. The skin is thin but tough. The soft flesh is evenly coloured and it has a slightly bitter flavour.

CANNED FRUIT

A wide variety of fruit is available canned, either in syrup or in natural juice. Peaches, pears, pineapple, mandarins, fruit salad and many other familiar fruits have long held an established place in the store cupboard. However, in addition, many exotic fruit are now available canned, including carambola, kiwi fruit, mango, cherry apples (miniature apples), guava, green figs and papaya.

STEWED FRUIT

Stewed fruit may be served hot or cold. A common mistake is to overcook stewed fruit until it is reduced to a pulp. Perfectly stewed fruit should consist of large pieces of tender fruit in a small amount of syrup.

The fruit should be washed, dried and prepared according to its type.

Apples – peel, core and quarter or cut into thick slices.

Blackberries – pick over, wash and drain.

Blackcurrants – string both red and black-currants.

Gooseberries – top and tail.

Peaches – place in a bowl, cover with boiling water and leave for 1 minute, then skin. Halve and remove stones.

Pears – peel, core and halve, quarter or slice.

Plums – leave whole or halve and stone.

Rhubarb – trim and slice into 2.5-5 cm/1-2 inch lengths. If rhubarb is old, then peel it thinly to remove any tough strings.

Fruits that discolour should be sprinkled with lemon juice or kept in brine as they are prepared. Drain and thoroughly rinse fruit soaked in brine. Prepare a syrup, allowing 50-175 g/2-6 oz sugar to 150 ml/¼ pint water, depending on the fruit and on personal taste. This quantity is sufficient for 450 g/1 lb fruit. Sharp fruits, such as blackcurrants or rhubarb may require extra sugar. Dissolve the sugar in the water over low heat, then bring the syrup to the boil. Reduce the heat before adding the fruit, then cover the pan and allow the liquid to simmer very gently so that the fruit yields its juice and flavour. There should be enough syrup to come about one-third of the way up the fruit, although this depends on the size of the cooking pan. Cook the fruit until it is tender but not mushy, turning large pieces occasionally so that they cook evenly.

Medium or dry cider, or fruit juice, may be used to make the syrup instead of water. Honey may be added instead of sugar, in which case extra liquid should be used. The cooking syrup may be flavoured with a strip of lemon or orange rind, or with whole spices such as cloves or cinnamon.

Use a large spoon to transfer the fruit to a heatproof serving dish or individual dishes and coat with the cooking syrup. Alternatively, leave the fruit to cool in the covered pan and lightly chill it before serving.

MICROWAVE STEWED FRUIT

Most types of fruit cook well in the microwave. Use a large lidded dish or mixing bowl with a plate as a cover. Prepare the syrup first, allowing about 2-3 minutes on High for 150 ml/¼ pint of liquid. The more sugar, the longer the cooking time. Stir the syrup well so that the sugar has dissolved before the fruit is added. Make sure that the fruit is well coated with syrup and cover the dish. Cook the fruit on High, stirring once or twice during cooking. The following is a guide to cooking times for 450 g/1 lb fruit:

apples	– 4-6 minutes
blackcurrants	– 8-10 minutes
blackberries	– 3-5 minutes
gooseberries	– 5-7 minutes
peaches (4)	– 4-5 minutes
pears	– 6-8 minutes
plums	– 3-5 minutes
rhubarb	– 6-8 minutes

The exact microwave cooking times depend on the size and ripeness of the fruit. Allow the fruit to stand for 2 minutes before serving.

JELLIES

Home-made fruit jelly makes a refreshing, healthy dessert. The recipes in this chapter range from sparkling jellies flavoured with wine to creamy milk jellies. An indication of the size of mould to use is given in each recipe. Always check the size of the mould before pouring the jelly into it. The mould should be full but not overflowing; if it is only half full the turned out jelly will look small and shapeless.

Allow plenty of time for a jelly to set. Stand the mould on a small baking sheet. When cool place the jelly in the refrigerator. If the jelly is strongly scented of fruit cover the mould with cling film to prevent the flavour of the jelly from tainting other foods in the refrigerator. The jelly may be set in a cool place other than the refrigerator but this usually takes longer. Cover the mould to prevent any dust or dirt from dropping on to the jelly.

A small amount of jelly may be set quickly by placing the mould in the freezer. Check that the mould is freezerproof before doing this. A larger volume of jelly may be placed in the freezer for 10 minutes to speed up the chilling process before transferring it to the refrigerator to set completely. Never place hot jellies in the refrigerator or freezer.

COATING A MOULD WITH JELLY

Pour in just enough jelly to cover the base and sides of the mould. Rotate the mould in your hands until it has a thin, even coating of jelly, then place it in the refrigerator to set completely. For speed, the jelly may be placed in the freezer to set. Keep the remaining jelly in a warm place so that it does not set.

If canned fruit is being added for decoration, drain this thoroughly before putting it into the mould. Cut pieces of fruit to fit the shape of the mould and make a decorative pattern on top of the set jelly. It is a good idea to dip each piece of fruit in the remaining liquid jelly before arranging it in the mould. When the pattern is complete, spoon a little more liquid jelly over it, taking care not to disturb the arrangement of the fruit.

Allow the lined mould to set before adding the filling. When the filling is added, it should come to the top of the mould so that when the jelly or jelled dessert is turned out, the shape is perfect. If a creamed filling is used which does not fill the mould completely, allow it to set lightly, then spoon liquid jelly on top to fill the mould.

G REEN FRUIT SALAD

A fruit salad, fresh, crisp and flavoursome, is the perfect ending for a meal. Using shades of a single colour can be most effective. Here the theme is green and white, but golden or red colours can look equally attractive (see Red Fruit Salad, page 195). There is no need to stick to the selection or the proportions of fruit in the recipe; simply remember that you will need a total of about 1 kg/2¼ lb. The fruit is traditionally served in syrup, as here, but fresh fruit juices, sometimes sparked with alcohol, are equally popular today.

175 g/6 oz green-fleshed melon, scooped
    into balls
175 g/6 oz seedless green grapes
2 Granny Smith apples
2 kiwi fruit, peeled and sliced
2 greengages, halved and stoned
2 passion fruit
mint sprigs, to garnish

SYRUP
175 g/6 oz sugar
30 ml/2 tbsp lemon juice

Make the syrup. Put the sugar in a saucepan with 450 ml/¾ pint water. Heat gently, stirring until the sugar has dissolved, then bring to the boil and boil rapidly until the syrup has been reduced by about half. Add the lemon juice, allow to cool, then pour the syrup into a glass serving bowl.

When the syrup is quite cold, add the fruit. Leave the skin on the apples and either slice them or cut them into chunks. Cut the passion fruit in half and scoop out the pulp, straining it to remove the seeds, if preferred. Serve well chilled, garnished with mint.

SERVES 4 TO 6

PLUMS WITH PORT

1 kg/2¼ lb plums
100-150 g/4-5 oz soft light brown sugar
150 ml/¼ pint port

Set the oven at 150°C/300°F/gas 2. Cut the plums neatly in half and remove the stones.

Put the plums into a baking dish or casserole, sprinkle with the sugar (the amount required will depend on the sweetness of the plums) and pour the port on top.

Cover the dish securely with a lid or foil and bake for 45-60 minutes or until the plums are tender. Serve hot, or lightly chilled.

SERVES 6

☀ **MICROWAVE TIP** Cook in a covered dish for 10-12 minutes on High, stirring gently once or twice during the cooking time.

DRIED FRUIT COMPOTE

100 g/4 oz dried apricots
100 g/4 oz prunes
100 g/4 oz dried figs
50 g/2 oz dried apple rings
30 ml/2 tbsp clear honey
2.5 cm/1 inch piece of cinnamon stick
2 cloves
pared rind and juice of ½ lemon
50 g/2 oz raisins
50 g/2 oz flaked almonds, toasted

Combine the apricots, prunes and figs in a bowl. Add water to cover and leave to soak. Put the apples in a separate bowl with water to cover and leave both bowls to soak overnight.

Next day, place the honey in a saucepan with 600 ml/1 pint water. Add the cinnamon stick, cloves and lemon rind. Bring to the boil. Stir in the lemon juice.

Drain both bowls of soaked fruit. Add the mixed fruit to the pan, cover and simmer for 10 minutes. Stir in the drained apples and simmer for 10 minutes more, then add the raisins and simmer for 2-3 minutes. Discard the cinnamon, cloves and lemon rind.

Spoon the compote into a serving dish and sprinkle with the almonds. Serve warm or cold, with cream.

SERVES 6

☀ **MICROWAVE TIP** There is no need to presoak the dried fruit if cooking the compote in a microwave oven. Make the honey syrup in a large bowl, using 450 ml/¾ pint water. Microwave on High for about 4 minutes, then stir in all the dried fruit with the cinnamon, cloves and lemon rind. Cover and cook on High for 15-20 minutes or until all the fruit is soft. Stir several times during cooking, each time pressing the fruit down into the syrup. Proceed as in the recipe above.

TROPICAL FRUIT SALAD

This fruit salad utilises both fresh and canned fruits.

1 small pineapple
1 mango
1 × 312 g/11 oz can lychees, drained
3 bananas, sliced
1 × 425 g/15 oz can guava halves, drained
250 ml/8 fl oz tropical fruit juice

Peel the pineapple, removing the eyes. Cut in half or quarters lengthways and cut out the hard core. Cut the fruit into neat chunks and place in a serving dish.

Peel and slice the mango, discarding the stone. Add the mango flesh to the bowl with the lychees, bananas and guavas. Pour over the tropical fruit juice and chill.

SERVES 8

VARIATION

Orange juice, spiked with a little rum, may be used instead of tropical fruit juice. Alternatively, try ginger ale.

PINEAPPLE AND KIRSCH SALAD

2 small pineapples
100 g/4 oz black grapes
1 banana
1 pear
15 ml/1 tbsp lemon juice
30-45 ml/2-3 tbsp kirsch
sugar

Cut the pineapples in half lengthways. Cut out the core from each then scoop out the flesh, using first a knife, then a spoon, but taking care to keep the pineapple shells intact. Discard the core, and working over a bowl, chop the flesh.

Add the pineapple flesh to the bowl. Cut the grapes in half and remove the seeds. Add to the pineapple mixture. Peel and slice the banana; peel, core, and slice the pear. Put the lemon juice in a shallow bowl, add the pear and banana slices and toss both fruits before adding to the pineapple and grapes. Mix all the fruit together, pour the kirsch over and sweeten to taste with the sugar. Pile the fruit back into the pineapple shells and chill until required.

SERVES 4

ORANGE AND GRAPEFRUIT SALAD

Ortaniques would make a delicious addition to this salad. These juicy citrus fruits are a cross between a tangerine and an orange. Their thin skins make them very easy to peel and segment.

4 oranges
2 pink grapefruit

SYRUP
225 g/8 oz granulated sugar
30 ml/2 tbsp orange liqueur

Using a vegetable peeler, remove the rind from 1 orange, taking care not to include any of the bitter pith. Cut the rind into strips with a sharp knife. Bring a small saucepan of water to the boil, add the orange strips and cook for 1 minute, then drain and set aside on absorbent kitchen paper.

Peel the remaining oranges and remove all the pith. Using a sharp knife, carefully cut between the segment membranes to remove the flesh. Work over a bowl to catch any juice, and squeeze out all the juice from the remaining pulp. Segment the grapefruit in the same way.

Make the syrup. Put the sugar in a saucepan with 200 ml/7 fl oz water. Heat gently, stirring until the sugar has dissolved, then bring to the boil and boil rapidly, without stirring, until the syrup turns golden. Remove from the heat and carefully add the fruit juice and liqueur. Set aside to cool.

Arrange the citrus segments in concentric circles in a shallow serving dish or large quiche dish. Pour the caramel syrup over the top and chill thoroughly before serving.

SERVES 6

⁂ **MICROWAVE TIP** The syrup may be made in the microwave. Mix the sugar and water in a deep bowl. Cook on High for 2 minutes, then stir to dissolve the sugar. Microwave for 7-10 minutes more, checking regularly. Remove the syrup as soon as it starts to turn pale gold. The colour will deepen during standing time.

RED FRUIT SALAD

Choose small strawberries, if possible, for this dessert, since they are juicier when left whole. Do not strip the redcurrants from the stalks.

225 g/8 oz redcurrants
6 red plums, stoned and quartered
225 g/8 oz strawberries, hulled
225 g/8 oz raspberries, hulled
100 g/4 oz slice watermelon, seeded and
  cubed

TO SERVE
**Greek yogurt or clotted cream
caster sugar**

Using a pair of kitchen scissors, neatly snip the redcurrants into small bunches.

Combine the plums, strawberries, raspberries and watermelon on a large platter. Arrange the redcurrants around or over the salad.

Serve as soon as possible, with yogurt or cream. Offer a bowl of caster sugar.

SERVES 6

🥣 **MRS BEETON'S TIP** This fruit salad has little juice and is therefore ideal for serving in a decorative ice bowl.

*F*ROSTED APPLES

oil for greasing
6 cooking apples (about 800 g/1¾ lb)
30 ml/2 tbsp lemon juice
100 g/4 oz granulated sugar
15 ml/1 tbsp fine-cut marmalade
2.5 cm/1 inch piece cinnamon stick
2 cloves
2 egg whites
100 g/4 oz caster sugar, plus extra for
    dusting

DECORATION
    125 ml/4 fl oz double cream
    glacé cherries
    angelica

Line a large baking sheet with grease-proof paper or non-stick baking parchment. Oil the lining paper. Set the oven at 180°C/350°F/gas 4. Wash, core and peel the apples, leaving them whole. Reserve the peelings. Brush the apples all over with the lemon juice to preserve the colour.

Combine the granulated sugar, marmalade, cinnamon stick, cloves and apple peelings in a large saucepan. Stir in 250 ml/8 fl oz water. Heat gently, stirring occasionally, until the sugar and marmalade have melted, then boil for 2-3 minutes without stirring to make a thin syrup.

Place the apples in a baking dish and strain the syrup over them. Cover with a lid or foil and bake for about 30 minutes or until the apples are just tender. Lower the oven temperature to 120°C/250°F/gas ¼.

Using a slotted spoon, carefully remove the apples from the syrup, dry well on absorbent kitchen paper, then place on the prepared baking sheet. Whisk the egg whites in a clean, grease-free bowl until they form stiff peaks, then gradually whisk in the caster sugar, a teaspoon at a time (see Mrs Beeton's Tip).

Coat each apple completely with the meringue, and dust lightly with caster sugar. Return to the oven and bake for about 1½ hours or until the meringue is firm and very lightly coloured. Remove from the oven and leave to cool.

In a bowl, whip the cream until it just holds its shape. Pile a spoonful on top of each apple and decorate with small pieces of cherry and angelica. Serve the apples on a bed of whipped cream in individual bowls, or with the cold baking syrup poured over them.

SERVES 6

MRS BEETON'S TIP If using an electric whisk to make the meringue, whisk in all the sugar. If whisking by hand, however, whisk in only half the sugar and fold in the rest.

---

*D*ANISH APPLE CAKE

1 kg/2¼ cooking apples
150 g/5 oz dry white breadcrumbs
75 g/3 oz sugar
100-125 g/4-4½ oz butter

DECORATION
    300 ml/½ pint whipping cream
    red jam, melted

Set the oven at 180°C/350°F/gas 4. Place the apples on a baking sheet and bake for 1 hour. When cool enough to handle, remove the peel and core from each apple; purée the fruit in a blender or food processor or rub through a sieve into a bowl.

In a separate bowl, mix the breadcrumbs with the sugar. Melt the butter in a frying pan, add the crumb mixture, and fry until golden.

Place alternate layers of crumbs and apple purée in a glass dish, starting and finishing with crumbs.

Whip the cream in a bowl and put into a piping bag fitted with a large star nozzle. Decorate the top of the apple cake with cream rosettes and drizzle a little red jam over the top. Chill lightly before serving.

SERVES 4 TO 6

T OFFEE-TOPPED GRAPE CREAM

fat for greasing
225 g/8 oz seedless grapes
250 ml/8 fl oz double cream
30 ml/2 tbsp brandy
45-60 ml/3-4 tbsp demerara sugar

Grease an ovenproof dish suitable for using under the grill. Halve the grapes, and put them into the prepared dish.

In a bowl, whip the cream until it holds its shape, then spread it over the grapes. Chill in a refrigerator for at least 8 hours.

Just before serving, sprinkle the cream topping with the brandy and sugar, put under a preheated moderately hot grill, and grill for 3-4 minutes until the sugar melts and bubbles.

Serve at once with sponge fingers or dessert biscuits.

SERVES 4

O RANGES IN CARAMEL SAUCE

6 oranges
200 g/7 oz sugar
50-125 ml/2-4 fl oz chilled orange juice

Using a vegetable peeler, remove the rind from 1 orange, taking care not to include any of the bitter pith. Cut the rind into strips with a sharp knife. Bring a small saucepan of water to the boil, add the orange strips and cook for 1 minute, then drain and set aside on absorbent kitchen paper.

Carefully peel the remaining oranges, leaving them whole. Remove the pith from all the oranges and place the fruit in a heat-proof bowl.

Put the sugar in a saucepan with 125 ml/4 fl oz water. Heat gently, stirring until the sugar has dissolved, then bring to the boil and boil rapidly, without stirring, until the syrup turns a golden caramel colour. Remove from the heat and carefully add the orange juice. Replace over the heat and stir until just blended, then add the reserved orange rind.

Pour the caramel sauce over the oranges and chill for at least 3 hours before serving.

SERVES 6

☆ **FREEZING TIP** Cool the oranges quickly in the sauce, place in a rigid container, cover and freeze for up to 12 months. Remember to allow a little headspace in the top of the container, as the syrup will expand upon freezing. Thaw, covered, in the refrigerator for about 6 hours.

BANANA BONANZA

4 bananas (about 450 g/1 lb)
15 ml/1 tbsp lemon juice
30 ml/2 tbsp soft dark brown sugar
150 ml/¼ pint soured cream
30 ml/2 tbsp top-of-the-milk
grated chocolate to decorate

Mash the bananas with the lemon juice in a bowl. Stir in the sugar, soured cream and top-of-the-milk. Serve decorated with grated chocolate.

SERVES 4

BANANA SNOW

6 bananas (about 675 g/1½ lb)
50 g/2 oz golden granulated sugar
15 ml/1 tbsp lemon juice
125 ml/4 fl oz double cream
300 ml/½ pint plain yogurt
3 egg whites
25 g/1 oz flaked almonds, toasted

Mash the bananas in a bowl with the sugar and lemon juice, or purée in a blender or food processor. Tip into a bowl. Whip the cream in a bowl until it just holds its shape, then fold it into the banana purée with the yogurt.

In a clean, grease-free bowl, whisk the egg whites until they form stiff peaks, then fold into the banana mixture. Pile into 1 large or 6 individual dishes. Sprinkle with the almonds before serving.

SERVES 6

BANANAS IN RUM

This is best when the bananas are sliced and cooked immediately before serving. Have all the ingredients ready and make the dessert in the lull after the main course.

45 ml/3 tbsp soft light brown sugar
2.5 ml/½ tsp ground cinnamon
4 large bananas
25 g/1 oz butter
45-60 ml/3-4 tbsp rum
150 ml/¼ pint double cream, to serve

Mix the sugar and cinnamon in a shallow dish. Cut the bananas in half lengthways and dredge them in the sugar and cinnamon mixture.

Melt the butter in a frying pan and fry the bananas, flat side down, for 1-2 minutes or until lightly browned underneath. Turn them over carefully, sprinkle with any remaining sugar and cinnamon and continue frying.

When the bananas are soft but not mushy, pour the rum over them. Tilt the pan and baste the bananas, then ignite the rum; baste again. Scrape any caramelized sugar from the base of the pan and stir it into the rum sauce. Shake the pan gently until the flames die down.

Arrange the bananas on warmed plates, pour the rum sauce over them and serve with the cream.

SERVES 4

SUMMER PUDDING

This delectable dessert started life with the cumbersome name of Hydropathic Pudding. It was originally invented for spa patients who were forbidden rich creams and pastries. Vary the fruit filling if you wish – blackberries or bilberries make very good additions – but keep the total quantity of fruit at about 1 kg/2 lb.

150 g/5 oz caster sugar
100 g/4 oz blackcurrants or redcurrants, stalks removed
100 g/4 oz ripe red plums, halved and stoned
1 strip lemon rind
100 g/4 oz strawberries, hulled
100 g/4 oz raspberries, hulled
8-10 slices day-old white bread, crusts removed

Put the sugar into a saucepan with 60 ml/ 4 tbsp water. Heat gently, stirring, until the sugar has dissolved. Add the black or red-currants, plums and lemon rind and poach until tender.

Add the strawberries and raspberries to the saucepan and cook for 2 minutes. Remove from the heat and, using a slotted spoon, remove the lemon rind.

Cut a circle from 1 slice of bread to fit the base of a 1.25 litre/2¼ pint pudding basin. Line the base and sides of the basin with bread, leaving no spaces. Pour in the stewed fruit, reserving about 45-60 ml/3-4 tbsp of the juice in a jug. Top the stewed fruit filling with more bread slices. Cover with a plate or saucer that exactly fits inside the basin. Put a weight on top to press the pudding down firmly. Leave in a cool place for 5-8 hours, preferably overnight.

Turn out carefully on to a plate or shallow dish to serve. If there are any places on the bread shell where the juice from the fruit filling has not penetrated, drizzle a little of the reserved fruit juice over. Serve with whipped cream or plain yogurt.

SERVES 6

☆ **FREEZER TIP** After the pudding has been weighted, pack the basin in a polythene bag, seal and freeze for up to 3 months. Thaw overnight in the refrigerator. Alternatively, line the basin completely with cling film before making the pudding. Thicker microware cooking film is stronger than ordinary film, or use a double layer. Leave plenty of film overhanging the rim of the basin. Freeze the weighted pudding, then use the film to remove it from the basin. Pack and label before storing.

CHERRY COMPÔTE

675 g/1½ lb red cherries
grated rind and juice of 1 orange
100 ml/3½ fl oz red wine
45 ml/3 tbsp redcurrant jelly
15 ml/1 tbsp sugar
pinch of ground cinnamon

Set the oven at 160°C/325°F/gas 3. Stone the cherries and put them into a shallow oven-to-table baking dish.

Add the orange rind and juice to the cherries with all the remaining ingredients. Cover securely with a lid or foil and bake for about 30 minutes. Leave to cool, and chill before serving.

SERVES 6

CHERRIES JUBILEE

This famous dish was created for Queen Victoria's Diamond Jubilee. It is often finished at the table, with the cherries and sauce kept warm in a chafing dish and the kirsch ignited and added at the last moment.

50 g/2 oz sugar
450 g/1 lb dark red cherries, stoned
10 ml/2 tsp arrowroot
60 ml/4 tbsp kirsch

Put the sugar in a heavy-bottomed saucepan. Add 250 ml/8 fl oz water. Heat gently, stirring, until the sugar has dissolved, then boil steadily without stirring for 3-4 minutes to make a syrup. Lower the heat, add the cherries, and poach gently until tender. Using a slotted spoon, remove the cherries from the pan and set them aside on a plate to cool.

In a cup, mix the arrowroot with about 30 ml/2 tbsp of the syrup to a thin paste. Stir back into the saucepan. Bring to the boil, stirring constantly, until the mixture thickens. Remove from the heat.

Pile the cherries in a heatproof serving bowl. Pour the sauce over them. Heat the kirsch in a small saucepan or ladle. Ignite it, pour it over the cherries and serve at once.

SERVES 4

PEARS IN WINE

100 g/4 oz white sugar
30 ml/2 tbsp redcurrant jelly
1.5 cm/¾ inch piece cinnamon stick
4 large ripe cooking pears (about 450 g/1 lb)
250 ml/8 fl oz red wine
25 g/1 oz flaked almonds

Combine the sugar, redcurrant jelly, and cinnamon stick in a saucepan wide enough to hold all the pears upright so that they fit snugly and will not fall over. Add 250 ml/ 8 fl oz water and heat gently, stirring, until the sugar and jelly have dissolved.

Peel the pears, leaving the stalks in place. Carefully remove as much of the core as possible without breaking the fruit. Stand the pears upright in the pan, cover, and simmer gently for 15 minutes.

Add the wine and cook, uncovered, for 15 minutes more. Remove the pears carefully with a slotted spoon, arrange them on a serving dish and keep warm.

Remove the cinnamon stick from the saucepan and add the almonds. Boil the liquid remaining in the pan rapidly until it is reduced to a thin syrup. Pour the syrup over the pears and serve warm. This dessert can also be served cold. Pour the hot syrup over the pears, leave to cool, then chill before serving.

SERVES 4

MRS BEETON'S TIP This recipe works very well in a slow cooker. Increase the amount of wine to 450 ml/¾ pint and cook the pears for 3-5 hours on High, turning the fruit occasionally so that it becomes coated in syrup.

STUFFED PEACHES IN BRANDY

100 g/4 oz sugar
150 ml/¼ pint medium-dry or slightly
    sweet white wine
30 ml/2 tbsp brandy
6 large ripe peaches
125 ml/4 fl oz double cream
50 g/2 oz cut mixed peel
25 g/1 oz blanched almonds, chopped

Put 250 ml/8 fl oz water into a saucepan and add the sugar, wine and brandy. Place over low heat, stirring, until the sugar dissolves. Skin the peaches (see Microwave Tip), then poach them gently in the brandy syrup for 15 minutes. Leave in the syrup to cool completely.

Whip the cream in a bowl until it just holds its shape. Fold in the mixed peel and almonds. With a slotted spoon, remove the peaches from the cold syrup. Cut them in half and remove the stones. Put about 15 ml/ 1 tbsp of the cream mixture in the hollow of 6 halves, then sandwich the peaches together again. Arrange in a shallow serving dish, and pour the syrup over the fruit. Chill until ready to serve.

SERVES 6

☀ **MICROWAVE TIP** Prick the peach skins, then put the fruit in a shallow dish. Cover and microwave on High for 1-1½ minutes. Allow to stand for 5 minutes. The skins will slip off easily.

GOOSEBERRY FOOL

When elderflowers are available, try adding 2 heads, well washed and tied in muslin, to the gooseberries while poaching. Discard the muslin bags when the gooseberries are cooked.

575 g/1¼ lb gooseberries, topped and
    tailed
150 g/5 oz caster sugar
300 ml/½ pint whipping cream

Put the gooseberries in a heavy-bottomed saucepan. Stir in the sugar. Cover the pan and cook the gooseberries over gentle heat for 10-15 minutes until the skins are just beginning to crack. Leave to cool.

Purée the fruit in a blender or food processor, or rub through a sieve into a clean bowl.

In a separate bowl, whip the cream until it holds its shape. Fold the cream gently into the gooseberry purée. Spoon into a serving dish or 6 individual glasses. Chill before serving.

SERVES 6

VARIATIONS

If a fruit is suitable for puréeing, it will make a creamy fool. Try rhubarb, apricots, red or blackcurrants, raspberries or blackberries. Sieve purée if necessary.

☀ **MICROWAVE TIP** Combine the gooseberries and sugar in a deep 1.2 litre/2 pint dish. Cover lightly and cook for 6 minutes on High. Proceed from step 2 of the recipe.

---

*R*HUBARB AND BANANA FOOL

450 g/1 lb young rhubarb
75 g/3 oz soft light brown sugar
piece of pared lemon rind
6 bananas
caster sugar to taste
250 ml/8 fl oz cold Cornflour Custard
    Sauce (page 395) or lightly whipped
    double cream
ratafias to decorate

Remove any strings from the rhubarb and cut the stalks into 2.5 cm/1 inch lengths. Put into the top of a double saucepan and stir in the brown sugar and lemon rind. Set the pan over simmering water and cook for 10-15 minutes until the rhubarb is soft. Remove the lemon rind.

Meanwhile peel the bananas and purée in a blender or food processor. Add the rhubarb and process briefly until mixed. Alternatively, mash the bananas in a bowl and stir in the cooked rhubarb. Taste the mixture and add caster sugar, if necessary.

Fold the custard or cream into the fruit purée and turn into a serving bowl. Decorate with ratafias.

SERVES 6 TO 8

> ⬤ **MRS BEETON'S TIP** If time permits, cook the rhubarb overnight. Lay the fruit in a casserole, add the sugar and lemon rind. Do not add any liquid. Cover and bake at 110°C/225°F/gas ¼.

*R*EDCURRANT AND RASPBERRY FOOL

225 g/8 oz redcurrants
225 g/8 oz raspberries
75-100 g/3-4 oz caster sugar
15 ml/1 tbsp cornflour
extra caster sugar for topping
25 g/1 oz flaked almonds to decorate

Put the redcurrants and raspberries in a saucepan. Add 375 ml/13 fl oz water and simmer gently for about 20 minutes or until very tender. Purée in a blender or food processor, then sieve the mixture to remove any seeds. Return the mixture to the clean pan.

Stir in caster sugar to taste. Put the cornflour into a cup and stir in about 30 ml/ 2 tbsp purée. Bring the remaining purée to the boil.

Stir the cornflour mixture into the purée and bring back to the boil, stirring all the time until the fool thickens. Remove from the heat and spoon into 6 individual serving dishes. Sprinkle the surface of each fool with a little extra caster sugar to prevent the formation of a skin. Cool, then chill thoroughly.

Top with the flaked almonds just before serving. Serve with whipped cream, Greek yogurt or fromage frais.

SERVES 6

BLACKCURRANT JELLY

250 ml/8 fl oz blackcurrant syrup, bought
    or home-made
45 ml/3 tbsp sugar
20 ml/4 tsp gelatine

Heat the syrup and sugar in a saucepan, stirring until the sugar has dissolved. Set aside to cool.

Place 125 ml/4 fl oz water in a small heat-proof bowl. Sprinkle the gelatine on to the liquid. Stand the bowl over a saucepan of hot water and stir the gelatine until it has dissolved completely. Stir in a further 125 ml/4 fl oz cold water, then add the dissolved gelatine to the cooled syrup.

Pour the blackcurrant jelly into wetted individual moulds or a 600 ml/1 pint mould and chill until set.

SERVES 4

FRESH LEMON JELLY

pared rind and juice of 4 lemons
20 ml/4 tsp gelatine
45 ml/3 tbsp caster sugar

Put the lemon rind into a saucepan. Add 175 ml/6 fl oz water and simmer for 5 minutes. Set aside until cool.

Pour 75 ml/3 fl oz water into a small heat-proof bowl. Sprinkle the gelatine on to the liquid. Stand the bowl over a saucepan of hot water and stir the gelatine until it has dissolved completely. Stir a further 75 ml/3 fl oz water into the dissolved gelatine.

Remove the lemon rind from the cool liquid and add the liquid to the gelatine mixture with the lemon juice and sugar. Stir until the sugar has dissolved.

Pour the mixture into 4 individual wetted moulds or a 750 ml/1¼ pint mould and leave for about 1 hour to set.

SERVES 4

VARIATIONS

FRESH ORANGE JELLY Use 2 oranges instead of lemons and only 10 ml/2 tsp sugar.

LEMON SMOOTHIE

pared rind and juice of 3 large lemons
750 ml/1¼ pints milk
200 g/7 oz sugar
25 g/1 oz gelatine

Combine the lemon rind, milk and sugar in a saucepan. Heat until the sugar has dissolved. Set aside to cool.

Place 60 ml/4 tbsp water in a small heat-proof bowl. Sprinkle the gelatine on to the liquid. Stand the bowl over a saucepan of hot water and stir the gelatine until it has dissolved completely.

Stir the gelatine mixture into the cooled milk mixture. Stir in the lemon juice and strain into a wetted 1.1 litre/2 pint mould. Chill until set.

SERVES 6

C LEAR LEMON JELLY

It takes time to make a perfect clear jelly, but the effort is well worth while. To create jewel-like clarity, the mixture must be filtered through a foam of coagulated egg whites and crushed egg shells.

4 lemons
150 g/5 oz lump sugar
4 cloves
2.5 cm/1 inch piece cinnamon stick
40 g/1½ oz gelatine
whites and shells of 2 eggs

Before you begin, scald a large saucepan, a measuring jug, a bowl, a whisk and a 1.1 litre/2 pint jelly mould in boiling water, as the merest trace of grease may cause cloudiness in the finished jelly.

Pare the rind from 3 of the lemons and squeeze the juice from all of them into the measuring jug. Make up to 250 ml/8 fl oz with water, if necessary.

Combine the rind, lemon juice, sugar, cloves, cinnamon stick and gelatine in the large saucepan. Add 750 ml/1¼ pints water.

Put the egg whites into the bowl; wash the shells in cold water, dry with absorbent kitchen paper and crush finely.

Add the egg whites and crushed shells to the mixture in the pan and heat, whisking constantly until a good head of foam is produced. The mixture should be hot but not boiling. When the foam begins to form a crust, remove the whisk, but continue to heat the liquid until the crust has risen to the top of the saucepan. Do not allow the liquid to boil. Lower the heat and simmer for 5 minutes.

Remove the saucepan from the heat, cover and let the contents settle in a warm place for 5-10 minutes. Scald a jelly bag in boiling water and place it on a stand (see Mrs Beeton's Tip). Scald 2 large bowls, placing one of them under the jelly bag.

Strain the settled, clear jelly through the hot jelly bag into the bowl. When all the jelly has passed through the bag, replace the bowl of jelly with the second scalded bowl and strain the jelly again, pouring it very carefully through the foam crust which covers the bottom of the bag and acts as a filter.

If the jelly is not clear when looked at in a spoon or glass, the filtering must be carried out again, but avoid doing this too many times, as repeated filtering will cool the jelly and cause some of it to stick to the cloth.

Rinse the jelly mould in cold water. When the jelly is clear, pour it into the wetted mould and chill until set.

SERVES 6

MRS BEETON'S TIP If you do not have a jelly bag and stand, improvise by tieing the four corners of a perfectly clean, scalded cloth, to the legs of an upturned stool. Alternatively, line a large, scalded, metal sieve with muslin.

ORANGE JELLY BASKETS

100 g/4 oz sugar
6 oranges
2 lemons
40 g/1½ oz gelatine

DECORATION
6 angelica strips
125 ml/4 fl oz double cream

Put 500 ml/17 fl oz water into a saucepan. Add the sugar. Pare the rind from three of the oranges. Add the rind to the pan and bring slowly to the boil. Leave to infuse for 10 minutes, keeping the pan covered.

Squeeze the juice from all the oranges and lemons; make up to 500 ml/17 fl oz with water if necessary. Reserve the unpeeled orange halves for the baskets.

Put 30 ml/2 tbsp of the mixed citrus juice in a small heatproof bowl. Sprinkle the gelatine on to the liquid. Stand the bowl over a saucepan of hot water and stir the gelatine until it has dissolved completely. Stir the remaining citrus juice and dissolved gelatine into the sugar syrup.

Remove any pulp from the 6 reserved orange halves and put the orange skins into patty tins to keep them rigid. Strain the jelly into the orange shells and chill for about 2 hours until set.

Make handles from the angelica, keeping them in place by pushing the ends into the set jelly. Whip the cream in a bowl until stiff, then spoon into a piping bag. Decorate the baskets with the cream.

SERVES 6

———————— ◆ ————————

SHAPED APPLE JELLY

1 kg/2¼ lb cooking apples
175 g/6 oz sugar
2 cloves
grated rind and juice of 2 small lemons
40 g/1½ oz gelatine

Wash the apples and cut them into pieces. Put them into a saucepan with the sugar, cloves, lemon rind and juice. Add 500 ml/17 fl oz water. Cover, and cook until the apples are soft.

Place 60 ml/4 tbsp water in a small heatproof bowl. Sprinkle the gelatine on to the liquid. Stand the bowl over a saucepan of hot water and stir the gelatine until it has dissolved completely.

Rub the cooked apples through a sieve into a bowl and stir in the dissolved gelatine. Pour into a wetted 1.1 litre/2 pint mould and chill until set.

SERVES 6

VARIATION

GOOSEBERRY JELLY Use 1 kg/2¼ lb prepared gooseberries instead of apples, and omit the cloves.

BLACK MAMBA

500 ml/17 fl oz strong black coffee
50 g/2 oz sugar
20 ml/4 tsp gelatine
15 ml/1 tbsp rum or liqueur
whipped cream to decorate

Set aside 30 ml/2 tbsp coffee in a small heatproof bowl. Put the remaining coffee into a saucepan with the sugar and heat, stirring, until the sugar has dissolved. Set aside to cool.

Sprinkle the gelatine on to the coffee in the small bowl. Stand the bowl over a saucepan of hot water and stir until the gelatine has dissolved. Add the rum or liqueur to the coffee syrup. Strain the mixture into a wetted 750 ml/1¼ pint mould and chill until set.

When ready to serve the jelly, turn out and decorate with whipped cream.

SERVES 4

MRS BEETON'S TIP To turn out, or *unmould*, a jelly, run the tip of a knife around the top of the mould. Dip the mould into hot water for a few seconds, remove and dry it. Wet a serving plate and place upside down on top of the mould. Hold plate and mould together firmly and turn both over. Check that the mould is correctly positioned on the plate, sliding it into place if necessary. Shake gently and carefully lift off the mould.

MILK JELLY

500 ml/17 fl oz milk
30 ml/2 tbsp caster sugar
grated rind of 1 lemon
20 ml/4 tsp gelatine

Put the milk, sugar and lemon rind into a saucepan. Heat, stirring, until the sugar has dissolved. Set aside to cool.

Place 60 ml/4 tbsp water in a small heat-proof bowl. Sprinkle the gelatine on to the liquid. Stand the bowl over a saucepan of hot water and stir the gelatine until it has dissolved. Stir the gelatine mixture into the cooled milk, then strain into a bowl. Stir the mixture from time to time until it is the consistency of thick cream.

Pour the milk jelly into a wetted 750 ml/1¼ pint mould and chill until set.

SERVES 4

VARIATIONS

The jelly may be flavoured with vanilla, coffee or other essence, if liked. If coffee essence is used, substitute orange rind for the lemon. Omit the rind if peppermint flavouring is used.

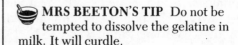**MRS BEETON'S TIP** Do not be tempted to dissolve the gelatine in milk. It will curdle.

PORT WINE JELLY

25 ml/5 tsp gelatine
50 g/2 oz sugar
30 ml/2 tbsp redcurrant jelly
250 ml/8 fl oz port
few drops of red food colouring

Place 30 ml/2 tbsp water in a small heat-proof bowl. Sprinkle the gelatine on to the liquid. Stand the bowl over a saucepan of hot water and stir the gelatine until it has dissolved completely.

Combine the sugar and redcurrant jelly in a saucepan. Add 400 ml/14 fl oz water and heat gently, stirring, until all the sugar has dissolved.

Add the gelatine liquid to the syrup and stir in the port and colouring. Pour through a strainer lined with a single thickness of scalded fine cotton or muslin into a wetted 900 ml/1½ pint mould. Chill until set.

SERVES 6

BANANA CHARTREUSE

A commercial jelly may be used as the basis of this dessert, but the flavour will be better if a fruit juice jelly is used. When filling the mould, keep the unused jelly at warm room temperature so that it does not set prematurely.

150 g/5 oz sugar
90 ml/6 tbsp lemon juice
350 ml/12 fl oz orange juice
juice of 4 oranges
30 ml/2 tbsp gelatine
5 bananas
angelica
milk (see method)
250 ml/8 fl oz double cream

Put 250 ml/8 fl oz water in a saucepan. Add 100 g/4 oz of the sugar and heat gently, stirring, until the sugar has dissolved.

Set aside 15 ml/1 tbsp lemon juice in a cup. Add the rest of the lemon juice to the saucepan with the orange juice. Dissolve 20 ml/4 tsp of the gelatine in a little of the hot liquid in a small bowl. Cool, then stir into the remaining liquid in the saucepan.

Rinse a 750 ml/1¼ pint mould and line with some of the jelly (see page 192). Chill for 10-20 minutes until set. Slice a banana thinly and arrange overlapping slices in a design on the set jelly. Cut the angelica into leaf shapes and arrange over the bananas. Carefully spoon over just enough of the remaining jelly to cover the decoration. Chill again. When all the jelly in the mould is set, add enough extra jelly to give a total depth of about 10 cm/4 inches.

Mash the remaining 4 bananas or process briefly in a blender or food processor. Pour the banana purée into a measuring jug and make up to 250 ml/8 fl oz with milk. In a bowl, whip the cream to soft peaks; fold in the banana mixture.

Put 60 ml/4 tbsp water in a small heat-proof bowl. Sprinkle the remaining gelatine on to the liquid. Stand the bowl over a saucepan of hot water and stir the gelatine until it has dissolved completely. Remove from the heat and stir in the remaining sugar, with the reserved lemon juice. Set aside.

When the gelatine mixture is cool, but not set, stir it into the banana cream. Pour into the prepared mould and chill until set. Turn out on to a wetted serving plate.

SERVES 4

VARIATIONS

250 ml/8 fl oz of any fruit purée may be used instead of bananas and milk. Apricots, strawberries and raspberries are particularly suitable.

CLARET JELLY

4 lemons
150 g/5 oz lump sugar
40 g/1½ oz gelatine
whites and shells of 2 eggs
125 ml/4 fl oz claret
few drops of red food colouring

Before you begin, scald a large saucepan, measuring jug, a bowl, a whisk and 900 ml/1½ pint jelly mould in boiling water, as the merest trace of grease may cause cloudiness in the finished jelly.

Pare the rind from 2 of the lemons and squeeze the juice from all of them into the measuring jug. Make up to 125 ml/4 fl oz with water, if necessary.

Combine the rind, lemon juice, sugar and gelatine in the large saucepan. Add 625 ml/21 fl oz water.

Put the egg whites into the bowl; wash the shells in cold water, dry with absorbent kitchen paper and crush finely.

Add the egg whites and crushed shells to the mixture in the pan and heat, whisking constantly until a good head of foam is produced. The mixture should be hot but not boiling. When the foam begins to form a crust, remove the whisk, but continue to heat the liquid until the crust has risen to the top of the saucepan. Do not allow the liquid to boil.

Pour in the claret without disturbing the foam crust. Boil the liquid again until it reaches the top of the pan. Remove the saucepan from the heat, cover and let the contents settle in a warm place for 5 minutes. Meanwhile scald a jelly bag in boiling water and place it on a stand (see Mrs Beeton's Tip, page 204). Scald 2 large bowls; place one under the jelly bag.

Strain the settled, clear jelly through the hot jelly bag into the bowl. When all the jelly has passed through the bag, replace the bowl of jelly with the second scalded bowl and strain the jelly again, pouring it very carefully through the foam crust which covers the bottom of the bag and acts as a filter.

If the jelly is not clear when looked at in a spoon or glass, the filtering must be carried out again, but avoid doing this too many times, as repeated filtering will cool the jelly and cause some of it to stick to the cloth.

When the jelly is clear, add the colouring. Rinse the jelly mould in cold water. Pour the jelly into the wetted mould and chill until set.

SERVES 6

FRUIT CHARTREUSE

4 lemons
150 g/5 oz lump sugar
4 cloves
2.5 cm/1 inch piece cinnamon stick
40 g/1½ oz gelatine
whites and shells of 2 eggs
30 ml/2 tbsp sherry
100 g/4 oz black grapes, seeded
100 g/4 oz green grapes, seeded
100 g/4 oz tangerine segments

Before you begin, scald a large saucepan, measuring jug, a bowl, a whisk and a 1.1 litre/2 pint ring mould in boiling water, as the merest trace of grease may cause cloudiness in the finished jelly.

Pare the rind from three of the lemons

and squeeze the juice from all of them into the measuring jug. Make up to 250 ml/ 8 fl oz with water, if necessary.

Combine the rind, lemon juice, sugar, cloves, cinnamon stick and gelatine in the large saucepan. Add 750 ml/1¼ pints water.

Put the egg whites into the bowl; wash the shells in cold water, dry with absorbent kitchen paper and crush finely.

Add the egg whites and crushed shells to the mixture in the pan and heat, whisking constantly until a good head of foam is produced. The mixture should be hot but not boiling. When the foam begins to form a crust, remove the whisk, but continue to heat the liquid until the crust has risen to the top of the saucepan. Do not allow the liquid to boil. Lower the heat and simmer for 5 minutes.

Remove the saucepan from the heat, cover and let the contents settle in a warm place for 5-10 minutes. Stir in the sherry.

Scald a jelly bag in boiling water and place it on a stand (see Mrs Beeton's Tip, page 204). Scald 2 large bowls, placing one of them under the jelly bag. Strain the settled, clear jelly through the hot jelly bag into the bowl. When all the jelly has passed through the bag, replace the bowl of jelly with the second scalded bowl and strain the jelly again, pouring it very carefully through the foam crust which covers the bottom of the bag and acts as a filter.

Rinse the ring mould in cold water. Pour enough of the jelly into the wetted mould to cover the base. Chill in the refrigerator until set. Arrange black grapes on the surface, pour on just enough jelly to cover, then leave to set. Add another layer of jelly, leave to set, then arrange a design of green grapes on top. Repeat the process, this time adding a layer of tangerine segments.

Continue adding layers of jelly and fruit until the mould is full, finishing with a layer of jelly. Chill until set, then turn out and decorate with whipped cream or chopped jelly.

SERVES 6 TO 8

*B*ANANA FROTH

The addition of whisked egg whites increases the volume of the jelly while boosting the nutritional value.

20 ml/4 tsp gelatine
100 g/4 oz sugar
75 ml/5 tbsp lemon juice
3 egg whites
3 bananas

Place 45 ml/3 tbsp water in a large heat-proof bowl. Sprinkle the gelatine on to the surface of the liquid. Stand the bowl over a saucepan of hot water and stir the gelatine until it has dissolved completely. Add 375 ml/13 fl oz boiling water and 100 g/4 oz sugar and stir until the sugar has dissolved. Add the lemon juice. Chill the mixture.

When the mixture is beginning to set, remove it from the refrigerator and whisk until frothy. In a clean, grease-free bowl, whisk the egg whites until just stiff; fold them into the jelly.

Slice the bananas and arrange them on the base of a glass serving dish. Pile the whipped jelly mixture on top and chill until firm.

SERVES 4 TO 6

CANDIED FRUIT CREAM JELLY

4 lemons
150 g/5 oz lump sugar
65 g/2½ oz gelatine
whites and shells of 2 eggs
125 ml/4 fl oz port
few drops of red food colouring (optional)
250 ml/8 fl oz double cream
2 strips angelica, each measuring
   5 × 1 cm/2 × ½ inch, chopped
50-75 g/2-3 oz glacé fruit (cherries,
   preserved ginger, glacé pineapple),
   chopped

Before you begin, scald a large saucepan, measuring jug, bowl, whisk and ring jelly mould in boiling water, as the merest trace of grease may cause cloudiness in the finished jelly.

Pare the rind from 2 of the lemons and squeeze the juice from all of them into the measuring jug. Make up to 125 ml/4 fl oz with water, if necessary.

Combine the rind, lemon juice and lump sugar in the large saucepan. Add 40 g/1½ oz of the gelatine and 625 ml/21 fl oz water.

Put the egg whites into the bowl; wash the shells in cold water, dry with absorbent kitchen paper and crush finely.

Add the egg whites and crushed shells to the mixture in the pan and heat, whisking constantly until a good head of foam is produced. The mixture should be hot but not boiling. When the foam begins to form a crust, remove the whisk, but continue to heat the liquid until the crust has risen to the top of the saucepan. Do not allow the liquid to boil.

Pour in the port without disturbing the foam crust. Boil the liquid again until it reaches the top of the pan. Remove the saucepan from the heat, cover and let the contents settle in a warm place for 5 minutes. Meanwhile scald a jelly bag in boiling water and place it on a stand (see Mrs Beeton's Tip, page 204). Scald 2 large bowls, placing one of them under the jelly bag.

Strain the settled, clear jelly through the hot jelly bag into the bowl. When all the jelly has passed through the bag, replace the bowl of jelly with the second scalded bowl and strain the jelly again, pouring it very carefully through the foam crust which covers the bottom of the bag and acts as a filter. Repeat, if necessary, until the jelly is clear.

A few drops of food colouring may be added to the jelly at this stage to give a rich colour. Measure 500 ml/17 fl oz of the jelly and set aside. Pour the remaining jelly into a shallow dish and chill until set.

Rinse the jelly mould in cold water. Pour in the liquid port jelly. Leave to set.

Put 15 ml/1 tbsp water in a small bowl and sprinkle the remaining gelatine on to the liquid. Set the bowl over a saucepan of hot water and stir the gelatine until it has dissolved completely.

In a bowl, whip the cream until just stiff; stir in the dissolved gelatine, angelica and glacé fruits.

Pour the cream mixture into the mould, on top of the layer of port wine jelly, then chill the dessert until set. Turn out on to a serving dish. Serve, surrounded by cubes of the reserved jelly, if liked.

SERVES 4 TO 6

ALL SORTS OF ICES

Delicate ice creams, smooth sorbets, refreshing water ices and bombes are all included in this chapter. There are also many recipes for desserts based on ice creams, including clever Baked Alaska and impressive Knickerbocker Glory.

With the increased ownership of home freezers there has been a tremendous growth in the variety of commercial ice creams that are available. The very best bought ice cream can be very good but, in general, the home-made product is superior. That is if the ice cream is smooth, well flavoured and frozen but not too hard. To achieve an excellent result, follow these guidelines:

■ The mixture should be slightly sweeter than if it is merely to be served chilled as the sweetness is lost slightly when the ice cream is frozen.

■ The mixture should have a good flavour as this tends to taste slightly weaker when the ice cream is frozen.

■ During freezing the ice cream should be beaten, whisked or churned regularly. For the very best results the mixture should be churned continuously until frozen but this is only possible if you own an ice cream maker. When working by hand, the mixture should be whisked when it is first beginning to freeze. It should be whisked at least twice more to remove all ice particles before it is allowed to freeze completely.

Ices that have been thoroughly frozen may be very hard. They should be allowed to stand in the refrigerator for up to 15 minutes before they are served. This will not only serve to soften them, but will also allow the flavours to be fully appreciated.

Lastly remember that home-made ices do not keep as well as commercial products. Most will keep for 2-3 weeks; some will keep for 6-8 weeks.

ICE CREAM MAKERS

There are a number of different ice cream making machines available. The most basic is a small container with a battery operated paddle in the middle. The ice cream mixture is placed in the container, the paddle switched on and the appliance put into the freezer. The constant churning of the mixture produces a smooth ice cream but the freezing process takes as long as for a similar mixture whisked by hand.

A more sophisticated ice cream maker is one which allows the ice cream mixture to be churned in a free-standing machine rather than in the freezer. The container of ice cream mixture is placed in an outer, insulated box which holds ice. Once the lid is fitted, the mixture is churned and frozen in about 30-45 minutes.

The most expensive and elaborate ice cream maker combines a small freezing unit in a work-top appliance. These are quite large but they produce well-frozen ice cream very quickly.

FREEZING TIMES

It is difficult to estimate the length of time necessary to freeze a mixture. This depends on the freezer as well as on the size and shape of the container. The rule is to make ice desserts at least a day ahead of when they are required to avoid having a part-frozen disaster. As a rule, freezing compartments in refrigerators will not freeze an ice cream as quickly as a separate freezer or freezing compartment of a fridge-freezer.

The recipes suggest that the fast-freeze setting, or the lowest setting on the freezer, be used to freeze the ice cream. The quicker the ice cream freezes, the fewer ice crystals are formed. Always check the manufacturer's instruction for using the fast-freeze setting and re-set the freezer to normal setting when the ice cream has frozen.

LEMON WATER ICE

Water ices are simple desserts made from fruit or flavoured syrup or a combination of fruit purée and sugar syrup. They are usually beaten halfway through the freezing process, but may be frozen without stirring, in which case they are called granités. When hot syrup is used as the basis for a water ice, it must be allowed to cool before freezing.

6 lemons
2 oranges

SYRUP
350 g/12 oz caster sugar
5 ml/1 tsp liquid glucose

Turn the freezer to the coldest setting 1 hour before making the water ice.

Make the syrup. Put the sugar in a heavy-bottomed saucepan with 250 ml/8 fl oz water. Dissolve the sugar over gentle heat, without stirring. Bring the mixture to the boil and boil gently for about 10 minutes or until the mixture registers 110°C/225°F on a sugar thermometer. Remove any scum.

Strain the syrup into a large bowl and stir in the liquid glucose. Pare the rind very thinly from the lemons and oranges and add to the bowl of syrup. Cover and cool.

Squeeze the fruit and add the juice to the cold syrup mixture. Strain through a nylon sieve into a suitable container for freezing.

Cover the container closely and freeze until half frozen (when crystals appear around the edge of the mixture). Beat the mixture thoroughly, scraping off any crystals. Replace the cover and freeze until solid. Return the freezer to the normal setting.

Transfer the water ice to the refrigerator about 15 minutes before serving, to allow it to soften and "ripen". Serve in scoops in individual dishes or glasses.

SERVES 6

> **MRS BEETON'S TIP** If an ice or ice cream is to be made by hand, rather than in a sorbetière or ice-cream churn, it is helpful to freeze it in a container which allows for it to be beaten. If there is room in your freezer or freezing compartment, use a deep bowl or box which can be securely closed. A rigid plastic bowl is ideal, since the finished ice can be stored in the same container. If your freezing compartment is shallow, or if you wish to freeze the mixture particularly quickly, use a shallow container such as an ice tray, and tip the contents into a chilled bowl for beating. Ices should not be frozen in very large quantities, since this takes too long and results in the formation of large ice crystals. Use two or more containers for freezing if necessary.

PINEAPPLE SORBET

200 g/7 oz lump sugar
250 ml/8 fl oz pineapple juice
2 egg whites

Turn the freezing compartment or freezer to the coldest setting about 1 hour before making the sorbet.

Put the sugar in a heavy-bottomed saucepan with 500 ml/17 fl oz water. Dissolve the sugar over gentle heat, without stirring. Bring the mixture to the boil and boil gently for about 10 minutes or until the mixture registers 110°C/225°F on a sugar thermometer. Remove the scum as it rises in the pan. Strain into a bowl, cover and leave to cool.

Add the pineapple juice to the syrup and pour into a suitable container for freezing (see Mrs Beeton's Tip, page 212). Cover the container closely and freeze for 1 hour.

In a clean, grease-free bowl, whisk the egg whites until stiff. Beat the sorbet mixture until smooth, scraping off any crystals. Fold in the egg whites, replace the cover on the bowl and freeze. The mixture should be firm enough to scoop; it will not freeze hard. Return the freezer to the normal setting.

Serve straight from the freezer, either in individual dishes or glasses, or in scoops in a decorative bowl.

SERVES 6

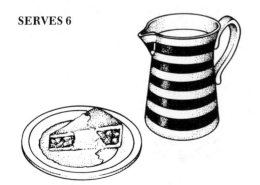

VANILLA ICE CREAM

30 ml/2 tbsp custard powder
500 ml/17 fl oz milk
100 g/4 oz caster sugar
125 ml/4 fl oz double cream
5 ml/1 tsp vanilla essence

Unless using a free-standing sorbetière or churn, turn the freezing compartment or freezer to the coldest setting about 1 hour before making the ice cream.

In a bowl, mix the custard powder to a cream with a little of the milk. Bring the remaining milk to the boil in a saucepan, then pour it into the bowl, stirring constantly.

Return the custard mixture to the clean saucepan and simmer, stirring all the time, until thickened. Stir in the sugar, cover closely with dampened greaseproof paper and set aside to cool.

In a large bowl, whip the cream to soft peaks. Add the cold custard and vanilla essence. Spoon into a suitable container for freezing (see Mrs Beeton's Tip, page 212). Alternatively, use a sorbetière or churn, following the manufacturer's instructions. Cover the container closely and freeze until half frozen (when crystals appear around the edge of the mixture). Beat the mixture until smooth, scraping off any crystals. Replace the cover and freeze until firm. Return the freezer to the normal setting.

Transfer the ice cream to the refrigerator about 15 minutes before serving, to allow it to soften and "ripen". Serve in scoops in individual dishes or in a large decorative bowl.

SERVES 6

RASPBERRY WATER ICE

450 g/1 lb ripe raspberries
juice of 2 lemons

SYRUP
225 g/8 oz caster sugar
3.75 ml/¾ tsp liquid glucose

Turn the freezing compartment or freezer to the coldest setting about 1 hour before making the water ice.

Make the syrup. Put the sugar in a heavy-bottomed saucepan with 175 ml/6 fl oz water. Dissolve the sugar over gentle heat, without stirring. Bring the mixture to the boil and boil gently for about 10 minutes or until the mixture registers 110°C/225°F on a sugar thermometer. Remove the scum as it rises in the pan.

Strain the syrup into a large bowl and stir in the liquid glucose. Cover and cool.

Purée the raspberries in a blender or food processor, or rub through a sieve into a bowl. Strain, if necessary, to remove any seeds. Stir in the lemon juice. Stir the mixture into the syrup, then pour into a suitable container for freezing (see Mrs Beeton's Tip, page 212).

Cover the container closely and freeze until half frozen (when crystals appear around the edge of the mixture). Beat the mixture thoroughly, scraping off any crystals. Replace the cover and freeze until solid. Return the freezer to the normal setting.

Transfer the water ice to the refrigerator about 15 minutes before serving, to allow it to soften and "ripen". Serve in scoops in individual dishes or glasses.

SERVES 6

MANDARIN WATER ICE

50 g/2 oz lump sugar
6 mandarins
225 g/8 oz caster sugar
3.75 ml/¾ tsp liquid glucose
2 lemons
2 oranges

Turn the freezing compartment or freezer to the coldest setting about 1 hour before making the water ice.

Rub the sugar lumps over the rind of the mandarins to extract some of the zest. Put the sugar lumps in a heavy-bottomed saucepan with the caster sugar and 300 ml/½ pint water.

Dissolve the sugar over gentle heat, without stirring. Bring the mixture to the boil and boil gently for about 10 minutes or until the mixture registers 110°C/225°F on a sugar thermometer. Remove the scum as it rises in the pan.

Strain the syrup into a large bowl and stir in the liquid glucose. Pare the rind very thinly from 1 lemon and 1 orange and add to the bowl of syrup. Cover and leave to cool.

Squeeze all the fruit and add the juice to the cold syrup mixture. Strain through a nylon sieve into a suitable container for freezing (see Mrs Beeton's Tip, page 212).

Cover the container closely and freeze until half frozen (when crystals appear around the edge of the mixture). Beat the mixture thoroughly, scraping off any crystals. Replace the cover and freeze until solid. Return the freezer to the normal setting.

Transfer the water ice to the refrigerator about 15 minutes before serving, to allow it to soften and "ripen". Serve in scoops in individual dishes or glasses.

SERVES 6 TO 8

*B*LACKCURRANT WATER ICE

450 g/1 lb blackcurrants
100 g/4 oz caster sugar
45 ml/3 tbsp white rum

Turn the freezing compartment or freezer to the coldest setting about 1 hour before making the water ice.

Prepare the fruit and put into a heavy-bottomed saucepan. Add the sugar with 350 ml/12 fl oz water. Simmer until the fruit is soft.

Purée the blackcurrant mixture in a blender or food processor or rub through a sieve into a clean bowl. Strain if necessary; the mixture should be smooth. Cool.

Pour the blackcurrant mixture into a suitable container for freezing (see Mrs Beeton's Tip, page 212). Cover the container closely and freeze until half frozen (when crystals appear around the edge of the mixture). Beat the mixture thoroughly, scraping off any crystals. Stir in the rum. Replace the cover and freeze until firm. The mixture will not freeze hard. Return the freezer to the normal setting.

Transfer the water ice to the refrigerator about 10 minutes before serving, to allow it to "ripen". Serve in scoops in individual dishes or glasses. Decorate with mint.

SERVES 6 TO 8

*L*EMON SORBET

Traditionally, sorbets were eaten between the entrée and roast courses at a formal dinner, to cleanse the palate.

10 ml/2 tsp gelatine
150 g/5 oz caster sugar
2.5 ml/½ tsp grated lemon rind
250 ml/8 fl oz lemon juice
2 egg whites

Turn the freezing compartment or freezer to the coldest setting about 1 hour before making the sorbet.

Place 30 ml/2 tbsp water in a small heat-proof bowl. Sprinkle the gelatine on to the liquid. Stand the bowl over a pan of hot water; stir the gelatine until it has dissolved.

Put the sugar in a heavy-bottomed sauce-pan with 225 ml/7 fl oz water. Dissolve the sugar over gentle heat, without stirring. Bring the mixture to the boil and boil gently for about 10 minutes. Stir the dissolved gelatine into the syrup, with the lemon rind and juice. Cover and cool.

Pour the cool syrup mixture into a suitable container for freezing (see Mrs Beeton's Tip, page 212). Cover the container closely and freeze for 1 hour.

In a clean, grease-free bowl, whisk the egg whites until stiff. Beat the sorbet mixture until smooth, scraping off any crystals. Fold in the egg whites, replace the cover on the bowl and freeze. The mixture should be firm enough to scoop; it will not freeze hard. Return the freezer to the normal setting.

Serve straight from the freezer, in dishes, glasses or lemon shells.

SERVES 6 TO 8

RICH VANILLA ICE CREAM

500 ml/17 fl oz milk
3 eggs
175 g/6 oz caster sugar
250 ml/8 fl oz double cream
5 ml/1 tsp vanilla essence

Unless using a free-standing sorbetière or churn, turn the freezing compartment or freezer to the coldest setting about 1 hour before making the ice cream.

In a saucepan, bring the milk to just below boiling point. Put the eggs into a bowl with 100 g/4 oz of the sugar. Mix well, then stir in the scalded milk. Strain the custard mixture into a heavy-bottomed saucepan or a heatproof bowl placed over a saucepan of simmering water. Alternatively, use a double saucepan, but make sure the water does not touch the upper pan.

Cook the custard over very gentle heat for 15-25 minutes, stirring all the time with a wooden spoon, until the custard coats the back of the spoon. Strain into a bowl, cover closely with dampened greaseproof paper and set aside to cool.

In a large bowl, whip the cream to soft peaks. Add the cold custard, vanilla essence and remaining sugar. Stir lightly. Spoon into a suitable container for freezing (see Mrs Beeton's Tip, page 212). Alternatively, use a sorbetière or churn, following the manufacturer's instructions.

Cover the container closely and freeze until half frozen (when crystals appear around the edge of the mixture). Beat the mixture until smooth, scraping off any crystals. Replace the cover and freeze until firm. Return the freezer to the normal setting.

Transfer the ice cream to the refrigerator about 15 minutes before serving, to allow it to soften and "ripen". Serve in scoops in individual dishes or in a large decorative bowl. The ice cream may be served in an ice bowl which should be made well in advance.

SERVES 6 TO 8

BROWN BREAD ICE CREAM

150 g/5 oz fresh brown breadcrumbs
3 egg whites
100 g/4 oz caster sugar
350 ml/12 fl oz double cream

Turn the freezing compartment or freezer to the coldest setting about 1 hour before making the ice cream.

Set the oven at 120°C/250°F/gas ½. Spread the breadcrumbs on a baking sheet and bake in the oven until golden brown, stirring occasionally. Set aside until cool.

In a clean, grease-free bowl, whisk the egg whites until stiff. Gradually whisk in the caster sugar. In a second bowl, whip the cream to soft peaks.

Fold the breadcrumbs and whipped cream into the whisked egg whites; spoon into a 1.1 litre/2 pint pudding basin. Cover and freeze for about 1½ hours or until firm. Return the freezer to the normal setting.

Invert the ice cream on a serving plate while still frozen. Allow it to soften or "ripen" in the refrigerator for about 15 minutes before serving.

SERVES 6 TO 8

TEA ICE CREAM

250 ml/8 fl oz hot strong tea
175 g/6 oz caster sugar
30 ml//2 tbsp custard powder
500 ml/17 fl oz milk
75 ml/3 fl oz single cream

Unless using a free-standing sorbetière or churn, turn the freezing compartment or freezer to the coldest setting about 1 hour before making the ice cream.

Strain the tea into a bowl, add 50 g/2 oz of the caster sugar and leave to cool.

In a bowl, mix the custard powder to a cream with a little of the milk. Bring the remaining milk to the boil in a saucepan, then pour it into the bowl, stirring constantly.

Return the custard mixture to the clean saucepan and simmer, stirring all the time, until thickened. Stir in the remaining sugar and pour the mixture into a large bowl. Cover closely with dampened greaseproof paper and set aside to cool.

Stir the custard and gradually add the cold tea and cream. Pour into a suitable container for freezing (see Mrs Beeton's Tip, page 212). Alternatively, use a sorbetière or churn, following the manufacturer's instructions. Cover the container closely and freeze until half frozen (when crystals appear around the edge of the mixture). Beat the mixture until smooth, scraping off any crystals. Replace the cover and freeze until firm. Return the freezer to the normal setting.

Transfer the ice cream to the refrigerator about 15 minutes before serving, to allow it to soften and "ripen". Serve in scoops in individual dishes or in a large decorative bowl, with sponge fingers.

SERVES 6

WALNUT ICE CREAM

750 ml/1¼ pints milk
4 eggs plus 1 yolk
150 g/5 oz caster sugar
100 g/4 oz walnuts
10 ml/2 tsp orange flower water
5 ml/1 tsp vanilla essence

Turn the freezer to the coldest setting about 1 hour before making the ice cream.

In a saucepan, bring the milk to just below boiling point. Put the eggs and egg yolk into a bowl with the sugar. Mix well, then stir in the scalded milk. Strain the custard mixture into a heavy-bottomed saucepan or a heatproof bowl placed over a saucepan of simmering water.

Cook the custard over very gentle heat for 15-25 minutes, stirring all the time with a wooden spoon, until the custard coats the back of the spoon. Strain into a bowl, cover with dampened greaseproof paper; cool.

Chop and pound the nuts on a board or in a food processor, gradually adding the orange flower water to prevent them oiling.

Stir the vanilla essence into the cold custard. Spoon into a suitable container for freezing (see Mrs Beeton's Tip, page 212). Alternatively, use a sorbetière or churn, following the manufacturer's instructions. Cover the container closely and freeze until half frozen (when crystals appear around the edge of the mixture). Beat the mixture until smooth, scraping off any crystals. Stir in the walnuts, and freeze until firm. Return the freezer to the normal setting.

Transfer the ice cream to the refrigerator about 15 minutes before serving, to allow it to soften and "ripen". Serve in scoops in individual dishes or in a large bowl.

SERVES 6

*B*LACKCURRANT ICE CREAM

15 ml/1 tbsp custard powder
250 ml/8 fl oz milk
75 g/3 oz caster sugar
200 g/7 oz ripe blackcurrants
rind and juice of 1 lemon
red food colouring
125 ml/4 fl oz double cream

Unless using a free-standing sorbetière or churn, turn the freezing compartment or freezer to the coldest setting about 1 hour before making the ice cream.

In a bowl, mix the custard powder to a cream with a little of the milk. Bring the remaining milk to the boil in a saucepan, then pour it into the bowl, stirring constantly.

Return the custard mixture to the clean saucepan and simmer, stirring all the time, until thickened. Stir in 50 g/2 oz of the sugar, cover closely with dampened grease-proof paper and set aside to cool.

Meanwhile put the blackcurrants into a saucepan with the remaining sugar. Add 125 ml/4 fl oz water, the lemon rind and juice and a few drops of red food colouring. Simmer until the fruit is tender. Purée the fruit mixture in a blender or food processor or rub through a nylon sieve into a clean bowl. Set aside to cool.

When both mixtures are cool, combine them in a suitable container for freezing (see Mrs Beeton's Tip, page 212). Alternatively, use a sorbetière or churn, following the manufacturer's instructions. Cover the container closely and freeze for 1 hour.

Whip the cream in a bowl. Beat the ice cream mixture until smooth, scraping off any crystals, then fold in the whipped cream. Replace the cover on the container and freeze until firm. Return the freezer to the normal setting.

Transfer the ice cream to the refrigerator about 15 minutes before serving, to allow it to soften and "ripen". Serve in scoops in individual dishes or in a decorative bowl.

SERVES 6

*A*PRICOT ICE CREAM

15 ml/1 tbsp custard powder
250 ml/8 fl oz milk
150 g/5 oz caster sugar
300 g/11 oz fresh apricots, halved and
    stoned
rind and juice of 1 lemon
yellow food colouring
125 ml/4 fl oz double cream

Unless using a free-standing sorbetière or churn, turn the freezing compartment or freezer to the coldest setting about 1 hour before making the ice cream.

In a bowl, mix the custard powder to a cream with a little of the milk. Bring the remaining milk to the boil in a saucepan, then pour it into the bowl, stirring constantly.

Return the custard mixture to the clean saucepan and simmer, stirring all the time, until thickened. Stir in 50 g/2 oz of the sugar, cover closely with dampened grease-proof paper and set aside to cool.

Meanwhile put the apricots into a saucepan with the remaining sugar. Add 125 ml/ 4 fl oz water, the lemon rind and juice and a few drops of yellow food colouring. Simmer until the fruit is tender. Purée the fruit mixture. Cool.

When both mixtures are cool, combine them in a suitable container for freezing (see Mrs Beeton's Tip, page 212). Alternatively, use a sorbetière or churn, following the manufacturer's instructions. Cover the container closely and freeze for 1 hour.

Whip the cream in a bowl. Beat the ice cream mixture until smooth, scraping off any crystals, then fold in the whipped cream. Replace the cover on the container and freeze until firm. Return the freezer to the normal setting.

Transfer the ice cream to the refrigerator about 15 minutes before serving. Serve in scoops in individual dishes or in a large bowl.

SERVES 6

*B*URNT ALMOND ICE CREAM

50 g/2 oz shredded almonds
12 egg yolks
175 g/6 oz caster sugar
1.1 litres/2 pints single cream
50 g/2 oz lump sugar
15 ml/1 tbsp kirsch

Unless using a free-standing sorbetière or churn, turn the freezing compartment or freezer to the coldest setting about 1 hour before making the ice cream.

Spread the shredded almonds out on a baking sheet and toast under a preheated grill until brown (see Mrs Beeton's Tip).

Combine the egg yolks and caster sugar in a deep bowl and beat together until very thick. Put 1 litre/1¾ pints of the cream in a saucepan and bring slowly to the boil. Pour the cream over the yolks and sugar, stirring well. Return the mixture to the clean pan. Cook, stirring constantly, until the custard thickens. Do not allow it to boil. Pour the thickened custard into a large heatproof bowl and keep hot over a saucepan of simmering water.

Put the lump sugar into a small heavy-bottomed saucepan. Add a few drops of water and boil until the mixture is a deep golden colour. Remove from the heat, carefully add the remaining cream and beat gently. Stir the caramel mixture into the hot custard. Cover closely with dampened greaseproof paper and set aside to cool.

When the custard is quite cold, stir in the almonds and kirch. Spoon into a suitable container for freezing (see Mrs Beeton's Tip, page 212). Alternatively, use a sorbetière or churn, following the manufacturer's instructions. Cover the container closely and freeze until half frozen (when crystals appear around the edge of the mixture). Beat the mixture until smooth, scraping off any crystals. Replace the cover and freeze until firm. Return the freezer to the normal setting.

Transfer the ice cream to the refrigerator about 15 minutes before serving, to allow it to soften and "ripen". Serve in scoops in individual dishes or in a large decorative bowl.

SERVES 8 TO 10

MRS BEETON'S TIP Shake the baking sheet frequently when cooking the almonds so that they brown evenly. Watch them closely; almonds scorch very quickly if left unattended.

CARAMEL ICE CREAM

750 ml/1¼ pints milk
3 eggs plus 12 egg yolks
175 g/6 oz caster sugar
50 g/2 oz lump sugar
100 ml/3½ fl oz single cream

Unless using a free-standing sorbetière or churn, turn the freezing compartment or freezer to the coldest setting about 1 hour before making the ice cream.

Heat the milk in a heavy-bottomed saucepan until just below boiling point. Beat the eggs and egg yolks with the caster sugar in a large bowl until thick and white, then add the hot milk, stirring well. Return the mixture to the clean saucepan and cook over gentle heat, stirring constantly, until the custard thickens. Do not allow it to boil. Pour the thickened custard into a large heatproof bowl and keep it hot over a saucepan of simmering water.

Put the lump sugar into a small heavy-bottomed saucepan. Add a few drops of water and boil until the mixture is a deep golden colour. Remove from the heat, carefully add the cream and beat gently. Return the pan to the heat. As soon as the mixture starts to rise in the pan, stir it into the hot custard. Cover closely with dampened greaseproof paper and cool.

Spoon the cold mixture into a suitable container for freezing (see Mrs Beeton's Tip, page 212). Alternatively, use a sorbetière or churn, following the manufacturer's instructions. Cover the container closely and freeze until half frozen (when crystals appear around the edge of the mixture). Beat the mixture until smooth, scraping off any crystals. Replace the cover and freeze until firm. Return the freezer to the normal setting.

Transfer the ice cream to the refrigerator about 15 minutes before serving, to allow it to soften and "ripen". Serve in scoops in individual dishes or in a large bowl.

SERVES 8 TO 10

RICH CHOCOLATE ICE CREAM

4 egg yolks
50 g/2 oz caster sugar
250 ml/8 fl oz single cream
100 g/4 oz plain chocolate, in squares
125 ml/4 fl oz double cream
5 ml/1 tsp vanilla essence

Turn the freezing compartment or freezer to the coldest setting about 1 hour before making the ice cream.

Combine the egg yolks and caster sugar in a deep bowl and beat together until very thick. Put the single cream in a saucepan and bring slowly to the boil. Pour the cream over the yolks and sugar, stirring well. Return the mixture to the clean pan. Cook, stirring constantly, until the custard thickens. Do not allow it to boil. Pour the thickened custard into a heatproof bowl and keep hot over a pan of simmering water.

Put the chocolate in a heatproof bowl and add 65 ml/2½ fl oz water. Bring a saucepan of water to the boil, remove it from the heat, and set the bowl over the hot water until the chocolate has melted. Stir, then add the chocolate mixture to the hot custard; mix lightly. Cover closely with dampened greaseproof paper and set aside to cool.

In a bowl, whip the double cream until thick. Fold it into the cool chocolate custard, with the vanilla essence. Spoon into a suitable container for freezing (see Mrs Beeton's Tip, page 212). Alternatively, use a sorbetière or churn, following the manufacturer's instructions. Cover the container closely and freeze until half frozen (when crystals appear around the edge of the mixture). Beat the mixture until smooth, scraping off any crystals. Replace the cover and freeze until firm. Return the freezer to the normal setting.

Transfer the ice cream to the refrigerator 15 minutes before serving. Serve in scoops in individual dishes or in a large bowl.

SERVES 6 TO 8

COFFEE ICE CREAM

45 ml/3 tbsp instant coffee powder
250 ml/8 fl oz double cream
75 g/3 oz caster sugar

Pour 60 ml/4 tbsp boiling water into a cup, add the instant coffee and stir until dissolved. Set aside until cool.

Whip the cream in a bowl until stiff. Stir in the sugar and fold in the dissolved coffee. Spoon into a suitable container for freezing (see Mrs Beeton's Tip, page 212). Alternatively, use a sorbetière or churn, following the manufacturer's instructions. Cover the container closely and freeze until half frozen (when crystals appear around the edge of the mixture). Beat the mixture until smooth, scraping off any crystals. Replace the cover and freeze until firm. Return the freezer to the normal setting.

Transfer the ice cream to the refrigerator about 15 minutes before serving, to allow it to soften and "ripen". Serve in scoops in individual dishes or in a large decorative bowl.

SERVES 6

MOCHA ICE CREAM

50 g/2 oz caster sugar
30 ml/2 tbsp instant coffee powder
150 g/5 oz plain chocolate, in squares
3 egg yolks
250 ml/8 fl oz double cream

Turn the freezing compartment or freezer to the coldest setting about 1 hour before making the ice cream.

Mix the sugar and coffee powder in a saucepan. Add 30 ml/2 tbsp water and bring to the boil. Boil for 1 minute, then remove from the heat and add the chocolate. When the chocolate has melted, stir lightly, then set the pan aside.

When the chocolate mixture is cool, stir in the egg yolks. In a bowl, whip the cream to soft peaks. Fold in the chocolate mixture.

Spoon into a refrigerator tray. Alternatively, use a sorbetière or churn, following the manufacturer's instructions. Cover the tray closely with foil and freeze until half frozen (when crystals appear around the edge of the mixture). Tip the mixture into a bowl and beat until smooth, scraping off any crystals. Freeze until firm. Return the freezer to the normal setting.

Transfer the ice cream to the refrigerator about 15 minutes before serving, to allow it to soften and "ripen". Serve in scoops in individual dishes or in a large bowl.

SERVES 6

 MRS BEETON'S TIP An ice cream scoop is a useful piece of equipment. Dip it into tepid water before use, and dip again after each scoop.

WHITE MAGIC

15-30 ml/1-2 tbsp freshly roasted coffee
   beans
500 ml/17 fl oz milk
2 eggs plus 8 egg yolks
100 g/4 oz caster sugar
125 ml/4 fl oz double cream

Turn the freezing compartment or freezer to the coldest setting about 1 hour before making the ice cream.

Combine the coffee beans and milk in the top of a double saucepan. Bring to just below boiling point. Place the saucepan over hot water and leave to infuse for 1 hour.

Strain the milk into a clean pan, discarding the coffee beans. Heat the flavoured milk until just below boiling point. Beat the eggs, egg yolks and sugar in a large bowl until thick and white, then add the hot milk, stirring well. Return the mixture to the clean pan and cook the custard over very gentle heat, stirring constantly, until it thickens. Do not allow it to boil. Cover the coffee-flavoured custard closely with dampened greaseproof paper and cool.

In a large bowl, whip the cream to soft peaks. Add the cold coffee custard. Spoon into a suitable container for freezing (see Mrs Beeton's Tip, page 212). Alternatively, use a sorbetière or churn, following the manufacturer's instructions. Cover the container closely and freeze until half frozen (when crystals appear around the edge of the mixture). Beat the mixture until smooth. Freeze until firm. Return the freezer to the normal setting.

Transfer the ice cream to the refrigerator about 15 minutes before serving, to allow it to soften and "ripen". Serve in scoops in individual dishes or in a large bowl.

SERVES 8 TO 10

GINGER ICE CREAM

125 ml/4 fl oz milk
3 egg yolks
75 g/3 oz caster sugar
75 g/3 oz preserved ginger in syrup
60 ml/4 tbsp ginger syrup (from the jar of
   preserved ginger)
10 ml/2 tsp ground ginger
250 ml/8 fl oz double cream

Unless using a free-standing sorbetière or churn, turn the freezing compartment or freezer to the coldest setting about 1 hour before making the ice cream.

In a saucepan, bring the milk to just below boiling point. Put the egg yolks into a bowl with 25 g/1 oz of the sugar. Mix well, then stir in the scalded milk. Return the mixture to the clean pan and cook gently, stirring constantly, until the custard coats the back of a wooden spoon. Do not allow it to boil. Cover the custard closely with dampened greaseproof paper and set aside to cool.

Dice the preserved ginger. Heat the ginger syrup in a small saucepan and stir in the ground ginger until dissolved.

In a large bowl, whip the cream until stiff. Add the custard, diced ginger, syrup mixture and remaining sugar. Mix lightly. Spoon into a suitable container for freezing (see Mrs Beeton's Tip, page 212). Alternatively, use a sorbetière or churn, following the manufacturer's instructions. Cover the container closely and freeze until half frozen (when crystals appear around the edge of the mixture). Beat the mixture until smooth, scraping off any crystals. Replace the cover and freeze until firm. Return the freezer to the normal setting.

Transfer the ice cream to the refrigerator about 15 minutes before serving, to allow it to soften and "ripen". Serve in scoops in individual dishes or in a large decorative bowl.

SERVES 6

LEMON ICE CREAM

8 egg yolks
200 g/7 oz caster sugar
juice of 2 lemons
250 ml/8 fl oz double cream

Unless using a free-standing sorbetière or churn, turn the freezing compartment or freezer to the coldest setting about 1 hour before making the ice cream.

In a bowl, beat the egg yolks until very thick. Add the sugar and beat again. Stir in the lemon juice.

Whip the cream to soft peaks in a deep bowl, then add carefully to the egg and sugar mixture. Spoon into a suitable container for freezing (see Mrs Beeton's Tip, page 212). Alternatively, use a sorbetière or churn, following the manufacturer's instructions. Cover the container closely and freeze until half frozen (when crystals appear around the edge of the mixture). Beat the mixture until smooth, scraping off any crystals. Replace the cover and freeze until firm. Return the freezer to the normal setting.

Transfer the ice cream to the refrigerator about 15 minutes before serving, to allow it to soften and "ripen". Serve in scoops in individual dishes or in a large decorative bowl.

SERVES 6

STRAWBERRY LICK

400 g/14 oz ripe strawberries, hulled
15 ml/1 tbsp granulated sugar
125 ml/4 fl oz milk
250 ml/8 fl oz double cream
2 egg yolks
150 g/5 oz caster sugar
5 ml/1 tsp lemon juice
red food colouring

Unless using a free-standing sorbetière or churn, turn the freezing compartment or freezer to the coldest setting about 1 hour before making the ice cream. Rub the strawberries through a nylon sieve into a bowl. Stir in the granulated sugar and set aside.

Combine the milk and cream in a saucepan and bring to just below boiling point. Beat the egg yolks with the caster sugar until thick and creamy, and stir in the milk and cream.

Return the custard mixture to the clean saucepan and simmer, stirring all the time, until thickened. Pour into a large bowl and stir in the strawberry purée and lemon juice. Tint pale pink with the food colouring.

Spoon the mixture into a suitable container for freezing (see Mrs Beeton's Tip, page 212). Alternatively, use a sorbetière or churn, following the manufacturer's instructions. Cover the container closely and freeze until half frozen (when crystals appear around the edge of the mixture). Beat the mixture until smooth, scraping off any crystals. Freeze until firm. Return the freezer to the normal setting.

Transfer the ice cream to the refrigerator about 15 minutes before serving, to allow it to soften and "ripen". Serve in scoops in cones, individual dishes or a large bowl.

SERVES 6

*B*OMBE CZARINE

A bombe is a moulded ice cream dessert. It usually consists of an outer shell of one flavour, with an inner core made from either a contrasting ice cream or a mousse mixture. There may be several layers, or the bombe may be made from a single flavour of ice cream, perhaps with the addition of crushed biscuits, praline or crumbled meringue.

1 quantity Vanilla Ice Cream (page 213)

FILLING
   125 ml/4 fl oz double cream
   25 g/1 oz icing sugar, sifted
   2 egg whites
   5 ml/1 tsp kummel or liqueur of own
      choice

Turn the freezing compartment or freezer to the coldest setting about 1 hour before making the bombe. Chill 2 bowls; a 1.4 litre/ 2½ pint pudding basin or bombe mould, and a smaller 600 ml/1 pint bowl.

Make the vanilla ice cream and freeze until half frozen (when crystals appear around the edge of the mixture). Beat the mixture until smooth, scraping off any crystals.

Spoon a layer of the vanilla ice cream into the chilled mould. Centre the smaller bowl inside the mould, with its rim on a level with the top of the mould. Fill the space between the outer mould and the inner bowl with vanilla ice cream. Cover the mould and freeze until firm. Reserve any remaining ice cream in the freezer.

Meanwhile prepare the filling. In a bowl, whip the cream with half the sugar. Put the egg whites in a second, grease-free bowl and whisk until stiff. Fold in the remaining sugar. Carefully mix the cream and egg whites and add the kummel. Chill lightly.

When the vanilla ice cream is firm, remove the bowl from the centre of the mould (filling it with warm water if necessary to dislodge it). Fill the centre of the ice cream mould with the kummel mixture, covering it with any remaining ice cream.

Put on the lid on the bombe mould or cover the basin with foil. Freeze for at least 4 hours. Return the freezer to the normal setting. To turn out, dip the mould or basin in cold water, and invert on to a chilled serving dish. Transfer to the refrigerator 15 minutes before serving, to allow the ice cream to soften and "ripen".

SERVES 6 TO 8

VARIATIONS
   BOMBE ZAMORA Use coffee ice cream instead of vanilla to line the mould, and flavour the filling with curaçao.
   BOMBE NESSELRODE As above, but add 60 ml/4 tbsp chestnut purée to the filling, which should be flavoured with kirsch instead of kummel.

*B*OMBE DIPLOMATE

1 quantity Vanilla Ice Cream (page 213)

FILLING
   50 g/2 oz crystallized fruit, chopped
   30 ml/2 tbsp maraschino liqueur
   125 ml/4 fl oz double cream
   25 g/1 oz icing sugar, sifted
   2 egg whites

Turn the freezing compartment or freezer to the coldest setting about 1 hour before making the bombe. Chill 2 bowls; a 1.4 litre/ 2½ pint pudding basin or bombe mould, and a smaller 600 ml/1 pint bowl.

Make the vanilla ice cream and freeze until half frozen (when crystals appear around the edge of the mixture). Beat the mixture until smooth.

Spoon a layer of the vanilla ice cream into the chilled mould. Centre the smaller bowl inside the mould, with its rim on a level with the top of the mould. Fill the space between the outer mould and the inner bowl with vanilla ice cream. Cover and freeze until firm.

Meanwhile prepare the filling. Put the chopped crystallized fruit into a shallow dish. Pour the liqueur over and set aside for 30 minutes to macerate.

In a bowl, whip the cream with half the sugar. Put the egg whites in a second, grease-free bowl and whisk until stiff. Fold in the remaining sugar. Carefully mix the cream and egg whites together, and add the crystallized fruit, with the liqueur used for soaking. Chill lightly.

When the vanilla ice cream is firm, re-move the bowl from the centre of the mould (filling it with warm water if necessary to dislodge it). Fill the centre of the ice cream mould with the maraschino and fruit mixture, covering it with any remaining ice cream.

Put the lid on the bombe mould or cover the basin with foil. Freeze for at least 4 hours. Return the freezer to the normal setting. To turn out, dip the mould or basin in cold water, and invert on to a chilled serving dish. Transfer to the refrigerator 15 minutes before serving to allow the ice cream to soften and "ripen".

SERVES 6 TO 8

B OMBE TORTONI

This is absurdly easy to make, yet it makes an impressive finale for a dinner party.

300 ml/½ pint double cream
150 ml/¼ pint single cream
50 g/2 oz icing sugar, sifted
2.5 ml/½ tsp vanilla essence
2 egg whites
100 g/4 oz hazelnut biscuits or ratafias, crushed
30 ml/2 tbsp sherry

Turn the freezing compartment or freezer to the coldest setting about 1 hour before making the bombe. Lightly oil a 1.25 litre/2½ pint bombe mould or pudding basin.

Combine the creams in a large bowl and whip until thick, adding half the icing sugar. Add the vanilla essence.

In a clean, grease-free bowl, whisk the egg whites until stiff. Fold in the remaining icing sugar.

Lightly fold the meringue mixture into the whipped cream. Stir in the hazelnut biscuits and sherry. Spoon the mixture into the prepared mould.

Put the lid on the bombe mould or cover the basin with foil. Freeze for at least 4 hours, then return the freezer to the normal setting. To turn out, dip the mould or basin in cold water, and invert on to a chilled serving dish. Transfer to the refrigerator 15 minutes before serving to allow the ice cream to soften and "ripen".

SERVES 6 TO 8

VARIATIONS

Try crushed ginger biscuits with coffee liqueur instead of sherry, or crumbled meringue with cherry brandy.

NEOPOLITAN ICE

Illustrated on page 144

250 ml/8 fl oz milk
1 egg plus 4 egg yolks
150 g/5 oz caster sugar
250 ml/8 fl oz double cream
125 ml/4 fl oz strawberry or raspberry
   purée
red food colouring (optional)
1.25 ml/¼ tsp almond or ratafia essence
green food colouring
10 ml/2 tsp vanilla essence

Turn the freezing compartment or freezer to the coldest setting about 1 hour before making the ice cream.

Heat the milk in a heavy-bottomed saucepan until just below boiling point. Beat the egg and egg yolks with 50 g/2 oz of the caster sugar in a bowl until thick and white, then add the hot milk, stirring well. Return the mixture to the clean saucepan and cook over gentle heat, stirring constantly, until the custard thickens. Do not allow it to boil. Pour the thickened custard into a large bowl. Cover with dampened greaseproof paper and allow to cool.

In a separate bowl, whip the cream to soft peaks. Fold it into the cold custard. Divide the mixture equally between 3 bowls. To one bowl add the fruit purée, with 25 g/ 1 oz of the remaining sugar and a few drops of red food colouring if necessary. Add the almond or ratafia essence to the second bowl and tint it a bright but not vivid green. Stir in half the remaining sugar. To the third bowl add the vanilla essence and the rest of the sugar.

Pour the contents of each bowl into a separate ice tray. Cover and freeze until almost firm, then pack in layers in a suitable square or oblong mould. Cover and freeze until solid. Return the freezer to the normal setting.

To serve, cut the block of ice cream in slices to reveal the coloured layers. Arrange the slices on individual plates.

SERVES 6

COTTAGE YOGURT ICE CREAM

This is a good choice for slimmers. Serve it with fresh strawberries or raspberries.

225 g/8 oz plain cottage cheese
125 ml/4 fl oz thick plain yogurt
30 ml/2 tbsp clear honey

Sieve the cheese into a bowl. Gently stir in the yogurt and honey. Spoon into a suitable container for freezing, allowing at least 2.5 cm/1 inch headspace (see Mrs Beeton's Tip, page 212). Leave to stand for 30 minutes.

Cover the container closely and freeze for 1 hour, or until crystals appear around the edge of the mixture. Beat the mixture until smooth, scraping off any crystals. Replace the cover and freeze for 2 hours until firm. Return the freezer to the normal setting.

If left in the freezer, the ice cream will get progressively harder. To obtain the right consistency it will need to be thawed for 2-4 hours at room temperature, then returned to the freezer for about 30 minutes.

SERVES 4

JAPANESE PLOMBIÈRE

A plombière is an ice cream mixture containing almonds or chestnuts. It may be frozen in a decorative mould but is more often scooped into balls and piled up to form a pyramid. It is often served with a sauce poured over the top.

50 g/2 oz apricot jam
few drops of lemon juice
8 egg yolks
100 g/4 oz caster sugar
500 ml/17 fl oz single cream
2.5 ml/½ tsp vanilla essence
100 g/4 oz ground almonds
250 ml/8 fl oz double cream
100 g/4 oz almond macaroons, crushed
12 ratafias to decorate

Unless using a free-standing sorbetière or churn, turn the freezing compartment or freezer to the coldest setting about 1 hour before making the ice cream.

Make an apricot marmalade by boiling the apricot jam in a small saucepan with a few drops of lemon juice until thick. Keep a little aside for decoration and sieve the rest into a bowl.

Combine the egg yolks and caster sugar in a deep bowl and beat together until very thick. Put the single cream in a saucepan and bring slowly to the boil. Pour the cream over the yolks and sugar, stirring well. Return the mixture to the clean pan. Cook, stirring constantly, until the custard thickens. Do not allow it to boil. Pour the thickened custard into a large bowl and stir in the sieved apricot marmalade, the vanilla essence and the ground almonds. Cover closely with dampened greaseproof paper and cool.

In a bowl, whip the double cream to the same consistency as the custard. Fold it into the custard, with the crushed macaroons.

Spoon the mixture into a suitable container for freezing (a bowl that is deep enough to allow the ice cream to be scooped is ideal). Freeze the mixture until firm.

To serve, scoop into balls, arranging these as a pyramid on a chilled plate. Drizzle the reserved apricot marmalade over the top and decorate with the ratafias.

SERVES 6 TO 8

> ☀ **MICROWAVE TIP** The apricot marmalade may be prepared in a small bowl in the microwave. It will only require about 30 seconds on High. Reheat it, if necessary, before pouring it over the ice cream pyramid.

VANILLA PLOMBIÈRE

1 quantity Vanilla Ice Cream (page 213)
125 ml/4 fl oz double cream
50 g/2 oz flaked almonds

Make the ice cream and freeze it for 1 hour in a suitable container.

In a bowl, whip the cream to soft peaks. Beat the ice cream until smooth, scraping off any crystals, then fold in the whipped cream and almonds. Cover and freeze the ice cream for 1½ hours.

If the ice cream has been made in a mould or basin, turn it out on to a chilled plate and transfer it to the refrigerator about 15 minutes before serving, to allow it to soften and "ripen". If a plastic box or bowl has been used, scoop the ice cream into balls and form these into a pyramid on a dish.

SERVES 6

SPUMA GELATA ANGELINA

30 ml/2 tbsp gelatine
250 g/9 oz caster sugar
100 ml/3½ fl oz Marsala
30 ml/2 tbsp brandy or orange liqueur
1 whole egg plus 3 yolks
finely grated rind of ½ lemon
90 ml/6 tbsp lemon juice
300 ml/½ pint double cream
3 drops orange essence
150 g/5 oz peeled orange segments

Turn the freezing compartment or freezer to the coldest setting 1 hour before making the ice cream. In a bowl, mix the gelatine with 150 g/5 oz of the caster sugar to form jelly crystals. Stir in 150 ml/¼ pint boiling water and stir until the crystals have dissolved. Cool.

Warm the Marsala and brandy gently in a small saucepan. Combine the egg and egg yolks in a large heatproof bowl. Whisk for at least 8 minutes until light and fluffy, then place over a pan of simmering water.

Add the warmed Marsala mixture to the bowl with the lemon rind, and stir in 60 ml/4 tbsp lemon juice. Cook the custard mixture, whisking constantly, until it is thick enough to coat a spoon. Stir in the cooled gelatine mixture.

Whip the cream to soft peaks. Fold in the remaining sugar, then fold into the Marsala custard. Add the orange essence with the remaining lemon juice. Spoon into a wetted 1 litre/1¾ pint mould and freeze for at least 4 hours. Return the freezer to the normal setting.

To serve, unmould on to a plate and thaw at room temperature for 15 minutes. Decorate with orange segments.

SERVES 6

CHOCOLATE FREEZER PUDDING

fat for greasing
100 g/4 oz butter
100 g/4 oz drinking chocolate powder
100 g/4 oz ground almonds
100 g/4 oz caster sugar
1 egg, beaten
100 g/4 oz Petit Beurre biscuits
whipped cream to decorate

Grease a 675 g/1½ lb baking tin. In a mixing bowl, cream the butter and chocolate powder together. Work in the ground almonds.

Put the sugar into a heavy-bottomed saucepan. Add 30 ml/2 tbsp water and heat gently until the sugar has melted. Set aside to cool.

Gradually add the syrup to the ground almond mixture, working it in well. Add the egg in the same way and beat the mixture until light and creamy.

Break the biscuits into small pieces and fold into the pudding mixture. Spoon into the prepared tin, pressing the mixture down well. Cover and freeze until firm.

To serve the pudding, thaw at room temperature for 45 minutes, then turn out on a serving dish. Decorate with whipped cream.

SERVES 6 TO 8

STRAWBERRY ICE CREAM LAYER GÂTEAU

1 litre/1¾ pints Strawberry Lick
   (page 223)
1 litre/1¾ pints Lemon Ice Cream
   (page 223)
125 g/4½ oz digestive biscuits, crushed
50 g/2 oz chopped mixed nuts
75 g/3 oz butter
25 g/1 oz soft light brown sugar
250 g/9 oz strawberry jam
60 ml/4 tbsp kirsch
100 g/4 oz whole strawberries
icing sugar to taste
200 ml/7 fl oz double cream

Line an 18 cm/7 inch loose-bottomed deep cake tin with non-stick baking parchment. Soften both ice creams. Put 25 g/1 oz of the biscuit crumbs aside in a small bowl with half the nuts.

Melt the butter in a saucepan, stir in the remaining crumbs and nuts and add the brown sugar. Press the mixture into the lined cake tin and chill until firm.

Sieve the jam into a bowl and stir in 15 ml/1 tbsp of·the kirsch. In another bowl, mix the whole strawberries with 15 ml/1 tbsp of the remaining kirsch, adding a little icing sugar if liked. Chill for at least 1 hour.

Cover the chilled biscuit crumb base with half the strawberry ice cream. Spread the top with a third of the jam. Sprinkle with a third of the reserved crumb and nut mixture. Freeze until the ice cream is firm. Repeat the process with half the lemon ice cream. Continue in this fashion, creating alternate layers of ice cream, jam, crumbs and nuts, until all the ingredients have been used, ending with a layer of lemon ice cream. Freeze each successive layer of ice cream before adding the next.

In a bowl, whip the cream with the remaining kirsch until stiff, adding icing sugar to taste. Remove the chilled gâteau from the cake tin and peel off the lining paper. Transfer the gâteau to a suitable plate and cover the top with whipped cream. Decorate with the liqueur-soaked strawberries and chill until ready to serve.

SERVES 8 TO 10

> **MRS BEETON'S TIP** Crush the digestive biscuits by working briefly in a food processor. Alternatively, put them in a strong polythene or paper bag and use a rolling pin to reduce them to crumbs.

POIRE BELLE HÉLÈNE

4 firm pears
250 ml/8 fl oz Vanilla Ice Cream
   (page 213)

CHOCOLATE SAUCE
   200 g/7 oz plain chocolate, in squares
   350 g/12 oz sugar
   salt
   2.5 ml/½ tsp vanilla essence

Make the sauce. Put the chocolate into a saucepan with the sugar, salt and vanilla essence. Add 250 ml/8 fl oz water and heat gently, stirring, until the chocolate and sugar have melted and the mixture is smooth.

Peel the pears, cut them in half and remove the cores. Place a scoop or slice of ice cream in each of 4 dishes. Top with the pear halves and mask with the hot chocolate sauce.

SERVES 4

*N*ESSELRODE PUDDING

24 chestnuts
250 ml/8 fl oz milk
4 egg yolks
150 g/5 oz caster sugar
250 ml/8 fl oz double cream
vanilla essence
50 g/2 oz glacé cherries

Unless using a free-standing sorbetière or churn, turn the freezing compartment or freezer to the coldest setting about 1 hour before making the pudding.

Using a sharp knife, make a small slit in the rounded side of the shell of each chestnut. Bring a saucepan of water to the boil, add the chestnuts and boil for 5 minutes. Drain. Peel the chestnuts while still very hot. Return them to the clean pan and add 125 ml/4 fl oz of the milk. Simmer gently until the chestnuts are tender, then rub them through a fine sieve into a bowl.

Put the egg yolks in a bowl and beat lightly. Pour the rest of the milk into a saucepan and bring to just below boiling point. Pour the milk on to the egg yolks, stirring well. Return the mixture to the clean saucepan and simmer, stirring constantly, until the custard thickens. Do not let it boil.

Remove the custard from the heat and stir in the chestnut purée and the sugar. Leave until cool.

In a bowl, whip half the cream to soft peaks. Add to the chestnut mixture with a few drops of vanilla essence. Pour into a suitable bowl for freezing, cover and freeze until half frozen (when crystals appear around the edge of the mixture).

Meanwhile rinse the cherries, pat dry on absorbent kitchen paper, and chop finely.

In a bowl, whip the remaining cream until stiff.

Beat the ice cream mixture until smooth, scraping off the crystals. Stir in the chopped cherries and fold in the whipped cream. Return to the freezer until almost set, stirring the mixture frequently. Press into a 750 ml/1¼ pint mould, cover, and return to the freezer until firm. Return the freezer to the normal setting.

Transfer the pudding to the refrigerator about 15 minutes before serving, to allow it to soften and "ripen".

SERVES 6

*O*MELETTE SOUFFLÉ EN SURPRISE

Not an omelette, but a liqueur-soaked cake whose hot soufflé topping hides a layer of ice cream.

15 ml/1 tbsp Grand Marnier or liqueur of
    own choice
1 egg, separated, plus 2 whites
50 g/2 oz caster sugar
vanilla essence
1 quantity Vanilla Ice Cream (page 213)
icing sugar for dredging
glacé cherries and angelica to decorate

CAKE
    fat for greasing
    2 eggs
    50 g/2 oz caster sugar
    few drops of vanilla essence
    50 g/2 oz plain flour, sifted
    30 ml/2 tbsp melted butter, cooled

Make the cake several hours before you intend to serve the dessert. Line and grease a 20 cm/8 inch sandwich cake tin. Set the oven at 180°C/350°F/gas 4.

Combine the eggs, sugar and vanilla essence in a heatproof bowl. Place over a saucepan of simmering water and whisk until the mixture is thick, pale lemon in colour, and has doubled in bulk. This will take 6-8 minutes. Remove the bowl from the heat and continue to beat until cooled and very thick.

Working swiftly and lightly, fold in the flour, then the butter. Spoon into the prepared tin and bake for 20-30 minutes or until cooked through and firm to the touch. Cool on a wire rack.

Set the oven at 230°C/450°F/gas 8. Place the cold cake on a silver or flameproof dish and drizzle the liqueur over the surface. Set aside to soak.

In a bowl, whisk the egg yolk and sugar until thick. Put all the egg whites in a clean, grease-free bowl and whisk until very stiff. Fold them into the yolk mixture with a few drops of vanilla essence.

Spoon the vanilla-flavoured soufflé mixture into a piping bag fitted with a large rose nozzle. Pile the ice cream on to the cake, leaving a 1 cm/½ inch clear border all around. Quickly pipe the soufflé mixture over the cake, making sure that both the ice cream and the cake are completely covered. Dredge with icing sugar.

Immediately put the dessert into the oven and bake for 3 minutes. Decorate with glacé cherries and angelica and serve at once.

SERVES 6 TO 8

P EACH MELBA

Escoffier's original recipe, created for Dame Nellie Melba consisted of fresh peaches poached in vanilla syrup and arranged in the centre of a bowl of vanilla ice cream. Cold Melba Sauce was poured over the peaches and the bowl containing the dessert was presented on a dish of crushed ice. The version that follows is the one that is more often served today.

**500 ml/17 fl oz Vanilla Ice Cream
  (page 213)
6 canned peach halves
125 ml/4 fl oz double cream**

MELBA SAUCE
  **575 g/1¼ lb fresh raspberries
  150 g/5 oz icing sugar**

Make the Melba Sauce. Put the raspberries in a sieve over a heatproof bowl. Using a wooden spoon, crush them against the sides of the sieve to extract as much of the juice as possible. Stir the sugar into the purée and place the bowl over a pan of simmering water. Stir for 2-3 minutes to dissolve the sugar. Cool the sauce, then chill until required.

Place a scoop or slice of ice cream in each of 6 sundae dishes. Cover each portion with a peach half. Coat with the Melba Sauce.

In a bowl, whip the cream until stiff. Spoon into a piping bag and pipe a large rose on top of each portion. Serve at once.

SERVES 6

BAKED ALASKA

For this popular dessert to be a success it must be assembled and cooked at the last minute. Make sure that the ice cream is as hard as possible, that the ice cream and sponge are completely coated in meringue, and that the oven has reached the recommended temperature. Watch the Baked Alaska closely as it cooks, and remove it from the oven as soon as the swirls of meringue are golden brown.

2 egg whites
150 g/5 oz caster sugar
1 quantity Vanilla Ice Cream (page 213)

CAKE
  fat for greasing
  2 eggs
  50 g/2 oz caster sugar
  few drops of vanilla essence
  50 g/2 oz plain flour, sifted
  30 ml/2 tbsp melted butter, cooled

Make the cake several hours before you intend to serve the dessert. Line and grease a 20 cm/8 inch sandwich cake tin. Set the oven at 180°C/350°F/gas 4.

Combine the eggs, sugar and vanilla essence in a heatproof bowl. Place over a saucepan of simmering water and whisk until the mixture is thick, pale lemon in colour, and has doubled in bulk. This will take 6-8 minutes. Remove the bowl from the heat and continue to beat until cooled and very thick.

Working swiftly and lightly, fold in the flour, then the butter. Spoon into the prepared tin and bake for 20-30 minutes or until cooked through and firm to the touch. Cool on a wire rack.

When almost ready to serve the Baked Alaska, set the oven at 230°C/450°F/gas 8. Put the egg whites in a clean, grease-free bowl and whisk until very stiff, gradually whisking in half the sugar. Fold in the remaining sugar.

Place the cold cake on an ovenproof plate and pile the ice cream on to it, leaving a 1 cm/½ inch clear border all around. Cover quickly with the meringue, making sure that both the ice cream and the cake are completely covered. Draw the meringue into swirls, using the blade of a knife or a palette knife.

Immediately put the Alaska into the oven and bake for 3-4 minutes until the meringue is just beginning to brown. Serve at once.

SERVES 6 TO 8

VARIATIONS

The dessert may be made with a slab of sponge cake and a family brick of bought ice cream. Fresh or drained canned fruit may be laid on the sponge base before the ice cream and meringue is added.

> **MRS BEETON'S TIP** Wash and dry half an egg shell, pop a sugar cube into it, and soak the sugar cube liberally in brandy. Just before serving the dessert, set the egg shell firmly on the top of the meringue and ignite the brandy for a spectacular effect.

KNICKERBOCKER GLORY

Illustrated on page 144

1 × 142 g/5 oz tablet orange jelly
1 × 142 g/5 oz tablet strawberry jelly
1 × 227 g/8 oz can peaches, drained and chopped
1 × 227 g/8 oz can pineapple slices, drained and chopped
1 quantity Vanilla Ice Cream (page 213)
50 g/2 oz chopped mixed nuts
150 ml/¼ pint double cream
5 ml/1 tsp caster sugar
6 maraschino cherries

MELBA SAUCE
450 g/1 lb fresh raspberries
75 g/3 oz icing sugar

Make up both jellies in separate bowls, following package directions. Leave to set.

Make the sauce. Put the raspberries in a sieve over a heatproof bowl. Using a wooden spoon, crush them against the sides of the sieve to extract as much of the juice as possible, Stir the sugar into the purée and place the bowl over a pan of simmering water. Stir for 2-3 minutes to dissolve the sugar. Cool the sauce, then chill until required.

Mix the chopped peaches and pineapple together in a bowl. Chop the set jellies. Put some chopped fruit in each of 6 tall sundae glasses. Cover with orange jelly, add a scoop of ice cream, then coat with the raspberry sauce. Repeat the process using the strawberry jelly. Sprinkle with nuts.

In a bowl, whip the cream and caster sugar until stiff. Put into a piping bag and pipe a generous swirl of whipped cream on top of each sundae. Decorate each portion with a maraschino cherry.

SERVES 6

MERINGUE GLACÉ CHANTILLY

250 ml/8 fl oz Vanilla Ice Cream (page 213)
16 small meringue shells
125 ml/4 fl oz double cream
caster sugar to taste
8 maraschino cherries, to decorate

Place a scoop or slice of ice cream in each of 8 small oval dishes. Set a meringue shell on either side of the ice cream.

In a bowl, whip the cream until stiff. Sweeten to taste, then spoon into a piping bag. Pipe a large rose of the cream on top of the ice cream. Decorate with the cherries.

SERVES 8

COUPE JACQUES

50 g/2 oz seedless grapes
1 banana
1 peach
50 g/2 oz raspberries
30 ml/2 tbsp kirsch
250 ml/8 fl oz Lemon Water Ice (page 212) or Vanilla Ice Cream (page 213)
250 ml/8 fl oz Strawberry Lick (page 223)
125 ml/4 fl oz double cream
caster sugar to taste

Chop all the fruit and mix it together in a bowl. Add the kirsch and macerate the fruit for 4 hours.

Place one portion of each ice in each of 6 sundae dishes. Cover with the macerated fruit. Whip the cream to soft peaks; sweeten to taste. Decorate with the cream.

SERVES 6

CUSTARDS AND CREAMY DESSERTS

Custards and dairy desserts may be smooth and light or rich and creamy. Made with low-fat yogurt or enriched with eggs and cream, the recipes in this chapter provide ideas for all occasions.

The section on ingredients at the beginning of the book (page 12) provides a guide to the different dairy products used to make desserts. Many of the dishes made with eggs and cream are particularly delicate and require a little extra care in the preparation. If you have experienced problems when making custards, the following notes may be of some help.

It is most important that all dairy foods are perfectly fresh. Eggs, in particular, should be purchased from a reputable source as they are only lightly cooked in some of the recipes in this chapter. Desserts that are to be served chilled should be covered and cooled quickly, then stored in the refrigerator.

MAKING PERFECT CUSTARD

A common problem when making custard is that the mixture curdles. Follow a few simple rules to ensure this never happens. Custard may be baked or cooked in a bowl over hot water to make a pouring custard. When cold and chilled a pouring custard may set, for example on the top of a trifle. The eggs in a custard curdle when the mixture has been overcooked. This may be due to cooking the custard for too long or at too high a temperature.

Pouring custards may be cooked in a double saucepan or in a heatproof bowl over a saucepan of water. The water should only just simmer; if it boils, the custard may well curdle. Stir the mixture all the time it cooks, until it thickens enough to coat the back of a spoon. A common mistake is to expect the custard to look thicker when it is cooked; remember that it will thicken on cooling and set on chilling (depending on the number of eggs used).

When the custard is cooked it should be removed from over the water and allowed to cool. To prevent the formation of a skin, the custard may be stirred as it cools or the surface may be covered with dampened greaseproof paper or microwave cling film. Alternatively, a little caster sugar may be sprinkled all over the surface to prevent a skin from forming.

BAKING CUSTARD IN A BAIN MARIE

A bain marie is simply a container of water in which to stand the dish of custard (or any other delicate mixture that requires careful cooking). A roasting tin or any fairly deep ovenproof dish that is large enough to hold the container of custard will do. Very hot, not boiling, water should be poured into the outer container. Ideally, the water in the outer container should come half way up the outside of the dish of custard.

The bain marie protects the custard from overcooking; the water barrier moderates the heat which reaches the outside of the dish. If the dessert requires very lengthy cooking the water must be topped up.

CORNFLOUR CUSTARD

An easy alternative to custard thickened solely with egg is one with a little cornflour added. When cornflour and egg yolks are combined the custard may be brought to the boil in a saucepan. This type of mixture and method is used for making crème pâtissière, a thick custard enriched with cream which is used as a filling for flans or gâteaux. It also provides a quick alternative for topping trifles or as a basis for a variety of desserts.

PRESSURE COOKING

Surprisingly, set custards cook very well in the pressure cooker and far quicker than when baked. General guidance on using pressure cookers is given in the section on equipment (page 25) and tips giving timings for pressure cooking basic custards are given below selected recipes.

MICROWAVE COOKING

Set and pouring custards both cook successfully in the microwave. Individual set custards cook more evenly than large ones. Stand the custards in a microwave-proof bain marie.

To prevent it curdling, a pouring custard must be stirred or whisked frequently during cooking. With care, custards cooked in the microwave are less likely to curdle than conventionally-cooked custards that are not watched constantly when cooking.

FREEZING

Custards and desserts thickened or lightened with eggs do not freeze successfully as they tend to separate and curdle on thawing.

H OMEMADE YOGURT

Yogurt can easily be made at home. It will not always have the consistency of the commercial product, but the results will be successful if a few simple rules are followed. The yogurt will keep for 4-5 days in a refrigerator. A new carton of commercial yogurt will be needed for the next incubation.

The yogurt can be incubated in one of three ways:

■ In an electric, thermostatically controlled incubator. These are very useful if the family eats a lot of yogurt.

■ In a wide-necked vacuum flask (a narrow-necked flask is not suitable as the yogurt is broken up when it is removed). This is suitable for smaller quantities of yogurt.

■ In a home-made incubator made from a large biscuit or cake tin with a lid. Line the base and sides with an insulating material such as woollen fabric or cotton wool and have a piece of material large enough to fit inside the top. Use 4 or 5 screw-topped glass jars that will fit inside the incubator.

METHOD

■ Sterilize all equipment to be used by immersion in boiling water for at least 3 minutes or by using a commercial sterilizing solution.

■ Heat 500 ml/17 fl oz UHT or sterilized milk to 43°C/108°F in a saucepan (use a cooking thermometer) and blend in 5 ml/1 tsp *fresh* natural yogurt. Alternatively use a yogurt starter culture (obtainable with full instructions from dairy laboratories).

■ Pour into pots or glasses, if using. Place in the prepared incubator, seal, and leave for 6-8 hours.

■ Turn the yogurt into a cold bowl and cool rapidly, standing the bowl in cold water and whisking the yogurt until creamy.

■ Cover the bowl and chill for about 4 hours when the yogurt will have thickened further.

■ When serving, gently stir in sugar. Flavour with stewed fruit or jam.

☀ **MICROWAVE TIP** Yogurt can be made in the microwave. Heat 600 ml/ 1 pint milk in a large bowl on High for 6 minutes. Cool until tepid (about 46°C/ 115°F) and stir in 15 ml/1 tbsp plain yogurt. Add 30 ml/2 tbsp dried full-cream powdered milk. Beat well. Cover the bowl and heat on Low for 70 minutes. Cool, then chill until required.

USING YOGURTS IN PUDDINGS

■ Use plain yogurt instead of soured milk when making scone toppings such as cobblers.

■ Substitute plain yogurt for cream to give a lighter texture and sharper flavour in cold desserts.

■ For a quick dessert, flavour plain yogurt with a little jam, marmalade or blackcurrant syrup or stir into fruit purée or stewed fruit.

■ Spread a thick layer of plain yogurt or Greek yogurt over drained canned apricots in a shallow gratin dish. Top with a generous coating of brown sugar and flash under a hot grill to make a wonderful fruit brûlée.

■ Stir clear honey into plain yogurt. Add toasted almonds just before serving.

■ Make a tangy fruit jelly by dissolving a jelly tablet in a half quantity of hot water. Allow the jelly to cool before stirring it into an equal quantity of plain yogurt. Pour into a mould or individual dishes and chill until set.

■ Make a quick chocolate cream dessert by stirring Greek yogurt and a little icing sugar into melted plain chocolate. Divide between glass dishes and chill lightly before serving.

■ Flavour plain yogurt with grated orange rind and sweeten to taste with honey or icing sugar. Serve with a few fresh orange segments or strawberries and crisp biscuits.

*H*OT YOGURT AND GRAPEFRUIT

2 grapefruit
150 ml/¼ pint plain yogurt
30 ml/2 tbsp brandy (optional)
30 ml/2 tbsp soft light brown sugar
2 maraschino cherries

Cut the grapefruit in half crossways and cut out the segments with a sharp knife, removing all the pith and membranes. Set the grapefruit shells aside.

Put the segments into a bowl and stir in the yogurt with the brandy if used. Return the mixture to the grapefruit shells and sprinkle with brown sugar.

Heat under a preheated hot grill for 2-3 minutes or until the sugar bubbles. Decorate with the maraschino cherries.

SERVES 4

*F*RUIT YOGURT

1 × 142 g/5 oz packet fruit jelly
300 ml/½ pint fruit yogurt
1 egg white

Put the jelly cubes in a bowl. Add 150 ml/¼ pint boiling water and stir until dissolved. When cool, stir in the yogurt.

When the jelly mixture is on the point of setting whisk the egg white in a clean, grease-free bowl until stiff. Fold it into the yogurt mixture.

Spoon the whip into glasses and put in a cool place to set.

SERVES 4

MRS BEETON'S TIP Use the same flavour for jelly and yogurt or try a blend such as lemon jelly and blackcurrant yogurt.

---

*R*ASPBERRY AND YOGURT DELIGHT

1 × 397 g/14 oz can raspberries or
    strawberries in syrup
15 ml/1 tbsp gelatine
300 ml/½ pint plain yogurt

Drain the syrup from the fruit into a measuring jug and make it up to 250 ml/8 fl oz with water. Put 60 ml/4 tbsp of the measured syrup mixture into a small heat-proof bowl and sprinkle the gelatine on to the liquid. Stand the bowl over a saucepan of hot water and stir until it has dissolved

completely. Add the rest of the syrup.

Whisk the yogurt in a bowl until the curd is broken down evenly, and gradually whisk in the syrup mixture. Put in a cool place.

When the mixture is on the point of setting, fold in the drained fruit. Spoon into a serving dish and serve cool but not chilled.

SERVES 4

*J*UNKET

The type of milk and the temperature are very important in the making of junket. The milk must not be sterilized nor must it be UHT milk, and it must be at the correct temperature; if it is too hot or too cold, it will not set. The junket should be left to set in a warm room; it should not be put in a refrigerator.

600 ml/1 pint milk
15 ml/1 tbsp sugar
few drops of vanilla essence
5 ml/1 tsp rennet essence
grated nutmeg or ground cinnamon

In a saucepan, warm the milk to blood-heat (about 37°C/98°F) with the sugar and vanilla essence. Stir in the rennet essence.

Pour the mixture into 1 large or 4 small dishes. Cover and leave to stand in a warm place for about 1 hour or until set. Do not move the junket at this stage

Sprinkle the junket with spice and serve cold but not chilled.

SERVES 4

VARIATIONS

ALMOND OR RUM JUNKET Instead

of the vanilla essence, add 2.5 ml/½ tsp almond or rum essence to the milk. Decorate with toasted almonds, if liked.

COFFEE JUNKET Stir 10 ml/2 tsp instant coffee into the warmed milk. Decorate with biscuit crumbs, if liked.

CHOCOLATE JUNKET Grate 50 g/2 oz plain chocolate into the milk, stirring until dissolved. Decorate the junket with chocolate curls.

LEMON OR ORANGE JUNKET Infuse the pared rind of 1 lemon or orange in the milk. Using a few drops of food colouring, tint the junket pale yellow or orange. Do not use any other flavouring.

RICH JUNKET Run a layer of single cream, flavoured with brandy, if liked, over the top of the junket. Flavour in any of the ways given above.

C UP CUSTARD

This is the traditional custard of nursery teas. It may be served alone, warm or cold, or used as part of a more elaborate dessert such as a trifle. For pouring custards, see the chapter on Sauces and Butters, pages 392-406.

500 ml/17 fl oz milk
3 eggs plus 2 yolks
25 g/1 oz caster sugar
few drops of vanilla essence

In a saucepan, bring the milk to just below boiling point. Put all the eggs into a bowl with the sugar, mix well, then stir in the scalded milk and vanilla essence. Strain the custard mixture into a heavy-bottomed saucepan or a heatproof bowl placed over a saucepan of simmering water. Alternatively, use a double saucepan, but make sure the water does not touch the upper pan.

Cook the custard over very gentle heat for 15-25 minutes, stirring all the time with a wooden spoon, until the custard thickens to the consistency of single cream. Stir well around the sides as well as the base of the pan or bowl to prevent lumps forming, especially if using a double saucepan. Do not let the custard boil or it may curdle.

As soon as the custard thickens, pour it into a jug to stop further cooking. Keep it warm by standing the jug in a bowl of hot water. If the custard is to be served cold, pour it into a bowl and cover with a piece of dampened greaseproof paper to prevent a skin forming. When cold, pour into a serving dish.

SERVES 4

VARIATIONS

LEMON CUP CUSTARD Infuse strips of lemon rind in the warm milk for 30 minutes, then remove before adding the milk to the eggs.

CINNAMON CUP CUSTARD Sprinkle the top of the cooked custard with ground cinnamon. Alternatively, use grated nutmeg.

RICH CUP CUSTARD Stir 30 ml/2 tbsp double cream into the custard when it is cooling.

*P*INEAPPLE CUSTARD

1 × 376 g/13 oz can crushed pineapple
25 g/1 oz cornflour
400 ml/14 fl oz milk
2 eggs, separated
25 g/1 oz caster sugar

Drain the pineapple, pouring the juice into a jug and spreading the fruit in a 750 ml/ 1¼ pint ovenproof dish.

In a bowl, blend the cornflour to a smooth paste with a little of the milk. Heat the rest of the milk in a saucepan until it is just below boiling point, then pour on to the blended cornflour. Stir in well.

Return the mixture to the clean saucepan and bring to the boil, stirring all the time. Boil gently for 1-2 minutes. Remove from the heat and stir in the reserved pineapple juice.

Add the egg yolks to the cornflour sauce. Stir well. Return to the heat and cook very gently, without boiling, stirring all the time, until the mixture thickens. Remove from the heat and leave to cool; stir from time to time to prevent the formation of a skin. Set the oven at 140°C/275°F/gas 1.

Pour the cooled custard over the crushed pineapple. In a clean, grease-free bowl, whisk the egg whites until stiff, then whisk in most of the sugar. Spread the meringue mixture over the custard, making sure that it is completely covered. Sprinkle with the rest of the sugar. Bake for 30 minutes until the meringue is crisp and browned.

SERVES 4

*Z*ABAGLIONE

4 eggs yolks
40 g/1½ oz caster sugar
60 ml/4 tbsp Marsala or Madeira

Put the egg yolks into a deep heatproof bowl and whisk lightly. Add the sugar and wine, and place the bowl over a saucepan of hot water. Whisk for about 10 minutes or until the mixture is very thick and creamy (see Mrs Beeton's Tip).

Pour the custard into individual glasses and serve at once while still warm, with sponge fingers.

SERVES 4

VARIATION

ZABAGLIONE CREAM Dissolve 50 g/ 2 oz caster sugar in 60 ml/4 tbsp water in a saucepan and boil for 1-2 minutes until syrupy. Whisk with the egg yolks until pale and thick. Add 30 ml/2 tbsp Marsala or Madeira and 30 ml/2 tbsp single cream while whisking. The finely grated rind of half a lemon can be added, if liked. Spoon into individual glasses. Chill before serving.

> **MRS BEETON'S TIP** When the whisk is lifted out of the bowl, the trail of the mixture should lie on top for 2-3 seconds.

STEAMED CUSTARD

butter for greasing
500 ml/17 fl oz milk
4 eggs or 3 whole eggs and 2 yolks
25 g/1 oz caster sugar
vanilla essence

Grease a 750 ml/1¼ pint baking dish. Prepare a steamer or half fill a large saucepan with water and bring to the boil.

In a second saucepan, warm the milk to just below boiling point. Put the eggs and sugar into a bowl, mix well, then stir in the scalded milk and vanilla essence. Strain the custard mixture into the prepared baking dish, cover with greased greaseproof paper or foil and secure with string.

Put the pudding in the perforated part of the steamer, or stand it on an old saucer or plate in the saucepan of boiling water. The water should come halfway up the sides of the basin. Cover the pan tightly and steam the pudding very gently for about 40 minutes or until just firm in the centre.

Serve hot or cold with Jam Sauce (page 402).

SERVES 4

☀ **MICROWAVE TIP** Cook individual set custards in the microwave. Pour the custard into six ramekin dishes. Stand these in a large dish and pour boiling water around them. Cook on High for 5-7 minutes, rearranging the dishes twice, until the custard is set.

BAKED CUSTARD

Egg dishes should be cooked by gentle heat. If the custard is allowed to boil, the protein will no longer be able to hold moisture in suspension and the resultant pudding will be watery. If is therefore a wise precaution to use a bain marie or water bath.

fat for greasing
500 ml/17 fl oz milk
3 eggs
25 g/1 oz caster sugar
grated nutmeg

Grease a 750 ml/1¼ pint baking dish. Set the oven at 140-150°C/275-300°F/gas 1-2.

In a saucepan, bring the milk to just below boiling point. Put the eggs and sugar into a bowl, mix well, then stir in the scalded milk. Strain the custard mixture into the prepared dish. Sprinkle the nutmeg on top.

Stand the dish in a roasting tin and add enough hot water to come halfway up the sides of the dish. Bake for 1 hour or until the custard is set in the centre.

SERVES 4

🥣 **MRS BEETON'S TIP** Do not whisk the eggs, milk and sugar until frothy or air bubbles will spoil the appearance of the baked custard.

ORANGE CUSTARD

pared rind and juice of 3 oranges
50 g/2 oz caster sugar
4 eggs
whipped cream for topping

Combine the orange rind and sugar in a

bowl. Stir in 500 ml/17 fl oz boiling water, cover and leave for 2 hours.

Strain the liquid into a saucepan and warm but do not boil it. Beat the eggs in a mixing bowl and gradually stir in the orange-flavoured liquid.

Strain the egg mixture into the clean saucepan and heat very gently, stirring all the time with a wooden spoon until the custard thickens. Do not let the custard boil or it will curdle.

Strain the orange juice into the custard, stirring constantly. Pour into 4 glasses and serve warm or chilled, topped with cream.

SERVES 4

☀ **MICROWAVE TIP** Combine the orange rind and sugar in a bowl. Add 500 ml/17 fl oz cold water and heat on High for 4 minutes. Cover and leave for 2 hours. Proceed from step 2 above.

B ANANA CUSTARD

500 ml/17 fl oz milk
3 eggs plus 2 yolks
25 g/1 oz caster sugar
few drops of vanilla essence
3 bananas (about 400 g/14 oz)

DECORATION
30 ml/2 tbsp crushed butterscotch or
    grated chocolate or toasted flaked
    almonds

In a saucepan, bring the milk to just below boiling point. Put the eggs and sugar into a bowl, mix well, then stir in the scalded milk and vanilla essence. Strain the custard mixture into a heavy-bottomed saucepan or a heatproof bowl placed over a saucepan of simmering water. Alternatively, use a double saucepan, but make sure the water does not touch the upper pan.

Cook the custard over very gentle heat for 15-25 minutes, stirring all the time with a wooden spoon, until the custard thickens to the consistency of single cream. Stir well around the sides as well as the base of the pan or bowl to prevent the formation of lumps, especially if using a double saucepan. Do not let the custard boil or it may curdle.

As soon as the custard thickens, pour it into a jug to stop further cooking. Peel and slice the bananas and stir them into the custard. Stand the jug in a bowl of hot water for 5 minutes to allow the flavours to blend. Spoon into a serving dish or individual dishes and decorate with butterscotch, grated chocolate or flaked almonds.

If the custard is to be served cold, pour it into a bowl and cover with a piece of dampened greaseproof paper to prevent the formation of a skin (see Mrs Beeton's Tip). When cold, pour into a serving dish and decorate as desired.

SERVES 4

🍯 **MRS BEETON'S TIP** If the custard is to be served cold, make sure that all the banana slices are fully submerged, and that the dampened greaseproof paper is a snug fit. This will prevent the bananas from darkening and spoiling the appearance of the dessert.

C OLD CABINET PUDDING

250 ml/8 fl oz Clear Lemon Jelly
  (page 204)
glacé cherries
angelica
10-12 sponge fingers
350 ml/12 fl oz milk
2 eggs plus 1 yolk
15 ml/1 tbsp caster sugar
25 g/1 oz ratafias, crumbled
10 ml/2 tsp gelatine
few drops of vanilla essence
125 ml/4 fl oz double cream

Make up the jelly and use half of the mixture to line a 750 ml/1¼ pint soufflé dish. Cut the cherries into quarters and the angelica into leaf shapes and decorate the jelly lining as described on page 192, dipping each piece in liquid jelly before setting it in place. Refrigerate until set. Chill the remaining jelly in a shallow tin.

Line the sides of the prepared dish with the sponge fingers, trimming one end of each so that they stand evenly on top of the jelly. Trim the fingers level with the top of the soufflé dish. Set the lined dish aside. Reserve the trimmings from the sponge fingers.

In a saucepan, bring the milk to just below boiling point. Put the eggs and caster sugar into a bowl, mix well, then stir in the scalded milk. Strain the custard mixture into a heavy-bottomed saucepan or a heatproof bowl placed over a saucepan of simmering water. Alternatively, use a double saucepan, but make sure the water does not touch the upper pan.

Cook the custard over very gentle heat for 15-25 minutes, stirring all the time with a wooden spoon, until the custard thickens to the consistency of single cream. Stir well around the sides as well as the base of the pan or bowl to prevent the formation of lumps, especially if using a double saucepan. Do not let the custard boil.

As soon as the custard thickens, remove it from the heat and whisk in the crumbled ratafias with the sponge finger trimmings.

Place 30 ml/2 tbsp water in a small bowl and sprinkle the gelatine on to the liquid. Stand the bowl over a saucepan of hot water and stir the gelatine until it has dissolved completely, then add the gelatine to the custard mixture with vanilla essence to taste.

In a bowl, whip the cream until just stiff. Fold into the crumb custard, then pour into the prepared mould. Cool, then refrigerate for 1-2 hours to set. When ready to serve, chop the reserved jelly. Turn out the mould on to a serving dish and decorate with the chopped jelly.

SERVES 6

> **MRS BEETON'S TIP** A commercial lemon jelly may be used to line the mould. Make up according to packet directions.

C ABINET PUDDING

butter for greasing
75 g/3 oz seedless raisins, halved
3-4 slices white bread, crusts removed
400 ml/14 fl oz milk
3 eggs
25 g/1 oz caster sugar
5 ml/1 tsp grated lemon rind

Grease a 1 litre/1¾ pint pudding basin.

Decorate the sides and base of the basin by pressing on some of the halved raisins. Chill.

Cut the bread slices into 5 mm/¼ inch dice. Place in a bowl. In a saucepan, warm the milk to about 65°C/150°F; do not let it come near to the boil.

Meanwhile mix the eggs and sugar in a bowl. Beat with a fork and stir in the milk, with the lemon rind and remaining raisins. Strain the custard mixture over the bread, stir, and leave to stand for at least 30 minutes. Meanwhile prepare a steamer or half fill a large saucepan with water and bring to the boil.

Pour the bread mixture into the prepared basin, cover with greased greaseproof paper or foil and secure with string.

Put the pudding in the perforated part of the steamer, or stand it on an old saucer or plate in the saucepan of boiling water. The water should come halfway up the sides of the basin. Cover the pan tightly and steam the pudding over gently simmering water for 1 hour or until firm in the centre.

Remove the cooked pudding from the steamer, leave to stand for a few minutes, then turn out on to a warmed serving dish. Serve with Jam Sauce (page 402).

SERVES 4 TO 6

☆ **FREEZER TIP** Crumb the bread crusts in a food processor and store in a polythene bag in the freezer. Next time you make a fruit pie, sprinkle a thin layer of crumbs into the pie shell before adding the fruit and they will prevent the fruit juices from making the crust soggy.

---

*B*READ AND BUTTER PUDDING

When the weather is dull and dreary, lift the spirits with this comforting old favourite.

butter for greasing
4 thin slices bread (about 100 g/4 oz)
25 g/1 oz butter
50 g/2 oz sultanas or currants
pinch of ground nutmeg or cinnamon
400 ml/14 fl oz milk
2 eggs
25 g/1 oz granulated sugar

Grease a 1 litre/1¾ pint pie dish. Cut the crusts off the bread and spread the slices with the butter. Cut the bread into squares or triangles and arrange in alternate layers, buttered side up, with the sultanas or currants. Sprinkle each layer lightly with nutmeg or cinnamon. Arrange the top layer of bread in an attractive pattern.

Warm the milk in a saucepan to about 65°C/150°F. Do not let it approach boiling point. Put the eggs in a bowl. Add most of the sugar. Beat with a fork and stir in the milk. Strain the custard mixture over the bread, sprinkle some nutmeg and the remaining sugar on top, and leave to stand for 30 minutes. Set the oven at 180°C/350°F/gas 4.

Bake for 30-40 minutes until the custard is set and the top is lightly browned.

SERVES 4

🍲 **PRESSURE COOKER TIP** Use a dish that fits in the pressure cooker. Cover the pudding with foil or greased greaseproof paper, tied down securely. Cook at 15 lb pressure for 9 minutes. Reduce the pressure slowly. Brown the pudding under the grill.

QUEEN MAB'S PUDDING

Illustrated on page 257
The pudding may be made in individual glasses.
It will require about 1 hour to set.

oil for greasing
400 ml/14 fl oz milk
pared rind of 1 lemon
3 eggs
75 g/3 oz caster sugar
few drops of almond essence
10 ml/2 tsp gelatine
50 g/2 oz glacé cherries, halved
25 g/1 oz cut mixed peel or whole citron
    peel, finely chopped
125 ml/4 fl oz double cream

DECORATION
   whipped cream
   glacé cherries

Lightly oil a 750 ml/1¼ pint mould. In a saucepan warm the milk with the lemon rind, but do not let it boil.

Beat the eggs with the sugar in a mixing bowl until fluffy and pale, and slowly stir in the warm milk. Strain the custard back into the clean pan or into a double saucepan or bowl placed over hot water. Cook over very low heat for 15-20 minutes, stirring all the time, until the custard thickens. Do not let it approach the boil. Strain the custard into a bowl, stir in the almond essence, and leave to cool.

Put 15 ml/1 tbsp water into a small heat-proof bowl, and sprinkle the gelatine on top of the liquid. Stand the bowl over a saucepan of hot water and stir the gelatine until it has dissolved completely. Cool the mixture slightly, then stir it into the custard. Leave in a cool place until it begins to set, stirring from time to time to prevent the formation of a skin.

Stir the cherries and chopped peel into the setting custard. In a separate bowl, whip the cream until it is semi-stiff, then fold it into the mixture. Pour the pudding into the prepared mould and refrigerate for about 2 hours until set. Turn out on to a flat, wetted plate. Decorate with whipped cream and glacé cherries.

SERVES 4 TO 6

MRS BEETON'S TIP Evaporated milk may be used instead of cream, if preferred, but the can should be chilled for at least 24 hours before use so that the evaporated milk may be whipped.

SHAHI TUKRA

3 medium slices white bread
2 cardamoms
2 whole unblanched almonds
4 whole unblanched pistachio nuts
40 g/1½ oz ghee or butter
250 ml/8 fl oz milk
few strands of saffron
45 ml/3 tbsp sugar
75 ml/3 fl oz double cream
30 ml/2 tbsp single cream
pinch of grated nutmeg

Cut the crusts off the bread. Cut each slice into 4 triangular pieces. Split the cardamom pods, pick out and crush the seeds, discarding the outer husk. Crush the almonds and pistachio nuts with their skins.

Heat the ghee or butter in a frying pan, and fry the bread until golden-brown on both sides. Drain on absorbent kitchen paper.

Heat the milk slowly in a shallow saucepan over moderate heat. When it begins to steam, add the saffron strands and sugar. Reduce to very low heat, and cook gently for 20 minutes.

Add the double cream to the saffron mixture and cook for a further 10 minutes. The sauce should be thickened but runny. Drop the fried bread triangles into the sauce. Turn them over after 5 minutes. Cook very slowly until the sauce is absorbed by the fried bread.

Serve hot or cold, covered with the single cream. Top each portion with a generous sprinkling of the crushed nuts and cardamom, adding a pinch of grated nutmeg.

SERVES 4 TO 5

> **MRS BEETON'S TIP** Ghee is clarified butter; it has had the water and non-fat solids removed. If the commercial product is not available, simply melt salted or unsalted butter without browning, to drive off the water, then allow to stand. The clear yellow liquid that forms on top is the clarified butter. Pour this off carefully. The milky residue may be used to enrich soups or sauces.

₿UTTERSCOTCH PUDDING

25 g/1 oz cornflour
500 ml/17 fl oz milk
2 eggs, separated
100 g/4 oz soft light brown sugar
25 g/1 oz butter
5 ml/1 tsp vanilla essence
25 g/1 oz walnuts, chopped, to decorate

In a bowl, mix the cornflour to a paste with a little of the cold milk. Bring the rest of the milk to the boil in a saucepan, and pour on to the blended cornflour, stirring to prevent the formation of lumps.

Return the mixture to the clean saucepan and bring to simmering point, stirring all the time. Simmer for 2-3 minutes. Cool for 3-4 minutes.

Add the egg yolks to the saucepan. Stir thoroughly, and cook without boiling for a further 2-3 minutes.

Melt the sugar in a heavy-bottomed saucepan and add the butter. When the butter has melted, stir the mixture into the cornflour sauce.

In a clean, grease-free bowl whisk the egg whites until fairly stiff and fold lightly into the pudding mixture. Add the essence. Pile into a serving dish and refrigerate for about 1 hour to set. Sprinkle the dessert with the walnuts before serving.

SERVES 6

*H*OUSE OF COMMONS PUDDING

50 g/2 oz seedless raisins
30 ml/2 tbsp medium sherry
butter for greasing
4 trifle sponges
9 ratafias or 2 almond macaroons
400 ml/14 fl oz milk
3 eggs
25 g/1 oz caster sugar
few drops of vanilla essence

DECORATION
  glacé cherries, halved
  angelica, cut in strips

Put the raisins in a small bowl with the sherry and macerate for 15 minutes.

Meanwhile grease a 13 cm/5 inch round cake tin and line the base with greased greaseproof paper. Decorate the base of the tin with the cherries and angelica.

Cut the sponges into 1 cm/½ inch dice and put into a bowl. Add the crumbled ratafias or macaroons and mix lightly. Drain the raisins, discarding the sherry.

Add a layer of the sponge mixture to the prepared tin, taking care not to spoil the design. Top with a few of the drained raisins. Repeat the layers until all the sponge mixture and raisins have been used.

In a saucepan, bring the milk to just below boiling point. Put the eggs and sugar into a bowl, mix well, then stir in the scalded milk. Add a few drops of vanilla essence. Slowly strain the custard mixture into the cake tin, allowing it to seep down to the base of the tin gradually, so as not to disturb the pattern on the base. Leave to stand for 1 hour.

Prepare a steamer or half fill a large saucepan with water and bring to the boil. Cover the cake tin with greased greaseproof paper or foil and secure with string.

Put the pudding in the perforated part of the steamer, or stand it on an old saucer or plate in the saucepan of boiling water. The water should come halfway up the sides of the cake tin. Cover the pan tightly and steam the pudding over gently simmering water for 1 hour.

Remove the pudding from the steamer, leave to stand for a few minutes, then turn out on to a warmed dish and peel off the lining paper. Serve with Sabayon Sauce (page 397), if liked.

SERVES 4

*C*RÈME BRÛLÉE

Illustrated on page 257
fat for greasing
15 ml/1 tbsp cornflour
250 ml/8 fl oz milk
250 ml/8 fl oz single cream
few drops of vanilla essence
3 eggs
50 g/2 oz caster sugar

Grease a 600 ml/1 pint flameproof dish. In a bowl, blend the cornflour to a smooth paste with a little of the milk. Bring the rest of the milk to the boil in a saucepan.

Pour the boiling milk on to the blended cornflour, stirring well. Return the mixture to the clean pan, bring to the boil, and boil for 1 minute, stirring all the time. Remove from the heat and set the pan aside to cool.

Combine the cream, vanilla essence and eggs in a bowl and beat well. Stir into the cooled cornflour mixture. Whisk over low heat for about 30 minutes or until the custard thickens; do not boil. Add 25 g/1 oz of the sugar and pour into the prepared dish. Sprinkle the pudding with the rest of the sugar.

Place under a preheated hot grill for 10 minutes or until the sugar has melted and turned brown. Keep the custard about 10 cm/4 inches from the heat. Serve hot or cold.

SERVES 4

> **MRS BEETON'S TIP** The brûlée may be browned in a 200°C/400°F/gas 6 oven if preferred. It will require about 15 minutes.

CRÈME BRÛLÉE À LA GRANDE CÂTELET

An ideal dinner party dish. If serving cold, tap the caramel crust sharply with the back of a spoon to break it up.

250 ml/8 fl oz single cream or milk
250 ml/8 fl oz double cream
1 vanilla pod or a few drops of vanilla essence or 15 ml/1 tbsp brandy
6 egg yolks
75 g/3 oz caster sugar

Put the cream or milk and the double cream in a double saucepan or a bowl over a saucepan of hot water. Add the vanilla pod, if used, and warm very gently. Meanwhile mix the egg yolks with 25 g/1 oz of the caster sugar in a large bowl. Beat together thoroughly.

When the cream feels just warm to the finger, remove the pod, if used. Pour the cream on to the yolks, stir, and return to the double saucepan or bowl.

Continue to cook gently for about 40 minutes, stirring all the time with a wooden spoon, until the custard thickens to the consistency of single cream (see Mrs Beeton's Tip). Do not let the custard come near to the boiling point. If a vanilla pod has not been used, add a few drops of vanilla essence or the brandy. Set the oven at 160°C/325°F/gas 3.

Strain the custard into a shallow 600 ml/1 pint flameproof dish, stand it on a baking sheet and bake for 5-10 minutes until a skin has formed on the top. Do not allow the custard to colour. Leave to cool, then refrigerate for at least 2-3 hours, or preferably overnight.

Heat the grill. Sprinkle enough caster sugar over the surface of the custard to cover it entirely with an even, thin layer. Place the dish under the hot grill for 10-15 minutes or until the sugar melts and turns to caramel. Keep the top of the custard about 10 cm/4 inches from the heat. Serve hot or cold.

SERVES 4

> **MRS BEETON'S TIP** When cooking the custard scrape down the sides of the saucepan frequently with a spatula to prevent the formation of lumps.

MARQUISE ALICE

oil for greasing
4 eggs or 1 whole egg and 2 yolks
75 g/3 oz caster sugar
250 ml/8 fl oz milk
few drops of vanilla essence
10 ml/2 tsp gelatine
50 g/2 oz Praline (see Mrs Beeton's Tip),
    crushed
5-6 sponge fingers
60 ml/4 tbsp kirsch
125 ml/4 fl oz double cream
125 ml/4 fl oz single cream

DECORATION
200 ml/7 fl oz double cream, whipped
redcurrant jelly

Oil a 750 ml/1¼ pint mould. Beat the eggs and sugar until fluffy and pale.

Warm the milk in a saucepan; do not let it boil. Slowly stir it into the egg mixture, then strain the custard into a heatproof bowl placed over hot water. Cook over very low heat until the custard thickens.

Strain the thickened custard into a bowl, stir in the vanilla essence and leave to cool.

Put 60 ml/4 tbsp water into a small heatproof bowl and sprinkle the gelatine on to the liquid. Stand the bowl over a saucepan and stir the gelatine until it has dissolved completely. Add the praline and continue to stir until the sugar in the praline has similarly dissolved. Cool until tepid and add to the custard. Leave in a cool place until the mixture thickens at the edges, stirring from time to time.

Break the sponge fingers into small pieces and put into a mixing bowl. Add the kirsch and leave to soak. In a second bowl, combine the creams and whip until soft peaks form. Fold into the setting praline custard.

Pour half the mixture into the mould and leave until thickened and beginning to set.

Arrange the soaked sponge fingers in an even layer all over the custard, leaving a 5 mm/¼ inch clear border all around so that none of the sponge finger pieces will show when the pudding is turned out. Pour the rest of the mixture over the sponge finger pieces and refrigerate until set.

Turn out on to a wetted plate and decorate with lightly whipped cream. Warm the redcurrant jelly until it runs, then drizzle it over the cream. Serve at once.

SERVES 4 TO 6

MRS BEETON'S TIP To make praline, heat 100 g/4 oz sugar with 15 ml/1 tbsp water until dissolved, then boil until golden. Stir in 100 g/4 oz toasted blanched almonds and turn the mixture on to an oiled baking sheet to cool.

FLOATING ISLANDS

3 eggs, separated
200 g/7 oz caster sugar
500 ml/17 fl oz milk
few drops of vanilla essence

In a clean, grease-free bowl whisk the egg whites until very stiff. Fold in 150 g/5 oz of the caster sugar.

Pour the milk into a frying pan and add a few drops of vanilla essence. Heat gently until the surface of the milk is just shivering. It must not boil or the milk will discolour and form a skin. Using 2 dessertspoons, mould egg shapes from the meringue and slide them into the milk. Make only a few at a time, and leave plenty of space between them in the pan as they swell when cooking.

Cook the meringue shapes slowly for 5 minutes, then turn them over, using a palette knife and a spoon, and cook for 5 minutes more. They are very delicate and must be handled with care. Remove from the milk gently and place on a cloth or absorbent kitchen paper to drain. Continue making shapes from the meringue and poaching them in the milk, until all the meringue is used. Arrange the 'islands' in a flat serving dish.

In a bowl, blend the egg yolks with the rest of the sugar. Gradually stir in the warm milk. Strain the mixture into a saucepan and cook gently, stirring all the time, until the sauce thickens slightly. Do not let it approach boiling point or it will curdle. Pour the custard around the 'islands' and serve at once.

SERVES 4

CARAMEL CUSTARD CUPS

100 g/4 oz lump or granulated sugar
300 ml/½ pint milk
100 ml/3½ fl oz single cream
2 whole eggs and 2 yolks
25 g/1 oz caster sugar
few drops of vanilla essence

Prepare 4 × 150 ml/¼ pint ovenproof moulds to receive a caramel coating (see Mrs Beeton's Tip, page 300).

Make the caramel by heating the lump sugar with 150 ml/¼ pint water in a heavy-bottomed saucepan. Stir constantly until the sugar dissolves and the mixture comes to the boil. Continue to boil, without stirring, until the mixture is golden brown. Pour a little of the caramel on to a metal plate and set aside. Immediately pour the remaining caramel into the warmed moulds, twisting and turning each mould in turn until the sides and the base are evenly coated. Leave until cold and set. Set the oven at 140-150°C/275-300°F/gas 1-2.

In a saucepan, bring the milk and cream to just below boiling point. Put the eggs and sugar into a bowl, mix well, then stir in the scalded milk. Add a few drops of vanilla essence. Strain the custard mixture into the prepared moulds.

Stand the moulds in a roasting tin and add hot water to come halfway up the sides of the moulds. Bake for 30 minutes or until the custard is set.

Remove the cooked custards and leave to stand for a few minutes, then invert each on an individual dessert plate. The caramel will run off and serve as a sauce. Break up the reserved caramel by tapping sharply with a metal spoon, and decorate the top of each custard with the pieces of broken caramel.

SERVES 4

> **MRS BEETON'S TIP** When adding the hot water to the roasting tin containing the custards it is best to use a kettle and to place the tin in the oven before adding the water. This is much safer than adding the water and then trying to move the tin without any spills.

*F*OREST PUDDING

fat for greasing
3 pieces plain cake or trifle sponges
jam
5 ml/1 tsp grated lemon rind
500 ml/17 fl oz milk
2 eggs
25 g/1 oz caster sugar

Grease a 750 ml/1¼ pint pie dish. Cut the cake vertically into 1 cm/½ inch slices and sandwich in pairs with the jam. Place the cake sandwiches in the pie dish and sprinkle with the lemon rind. Set aside.

In a saucepan, warm the milk to about 65°C/150°F; do not let it approach boiling point.

Put the eggs and sugar into a bowl, mix well, then stir in the warm milk. Strain the custard mixture into the dish and leave to stand for 1 hour. Meanwhile set the oven at 140-150°C/275-300°F/gas 1-2.

Bake the pudding for 1-1¼ hours until the custard is set and the pudding browned on top. Serve hot.

SERVES 4

*N*EWMARKET PUDDING

fat for greasing
4 individual trifle sponges
50 g/2 oz cut mixed peel
50 g/2 oz seedless raisins
25 g/1 oz currants
400 ml/7 fl oz milk
3 eggs, beaten
few drops of vanilla essence
45 ml/3 tbsp redcurrant jelly

Grease a 13 cm/5 inch round cake tin. Cut the cake vertically into 1 cm/½ inch slices. In a bowl, mix the peel, raisins and currants together. Put the cake and fruit into the prepared cake tin in alternate layers.

In a saucepan, warm the milk to about 65°C/150°F; do not let it approach boiling point. Meanwhile, mix the beaten eggs with a few drops of vanilla essence in a bowl. Stir in the warm milk.

Strain the custard mixture over the cake and fruit layers. Leave to stand for 1 hour. Prepare a steamer or half fill a large saucepan with water and bring to the boil.

Cover the top of the cake tin with greased greaseproof paper or foil and secure with string. Put the tin in the perforated part of the steamer, or stand it on an old saucer or plate in the saucepan of boiling water. The water should come halfway up the sides of the tin. Cover the pan tightly and steam the pudding over gently simmering water for 1 hour.

Remove the cooked pudding from the steamer and leave to stand for a few minutes. Meanwhile put the redcurrant jelly in a small saucepan and warm through until melted.

Turn the pudding out on to a warmed dish, pour the jelly over and serve at once.

SERVES 4 TO 6

☀ **MICROWAVE TIP** Melt the redcurrant jelly in a small bowl for a few seconds on High.

◆

RING OF PEARS

fat for greasing
3 slices plain cake or trifle sponges
400 ml/14 fl oz milk
25 g/1 oz butter
2 eggs
1 egg yolk
25 g/1 oz caster sugar
5 ml/1 tsp grated lemon rind
1 × 425 g/15 oz can pear halves in syrup
red food colouring (optional)

Grease a 600 ml/1 pint ring mould. Cut the cake vertically into 1 cm/½ inch slices and arrange these in the mould. Set the oven at 150°C/300°F/gas 2.

Warm the milk and butter in a saucepan until the butter just melts. In a bowl, mix together the whole eggs and yolk, the sugar and grated lemon rind. Stir in the warmed milk mixture and strain the mixture over the cake slices. Cover with greased greaseproof paper or foil.

Stand the pudding in a roasting tin. Add hot water to come halfway up the sides of the ring mould and bake for about 1 hour or until set.

Meanwhile drain the pears, reserving the fruit and boiling the syrup in a saucepan until slightly reduced. Add a few drops of red food colouring, if the fruit is very pale.

Leave the cooked pudding to stand for a few minutes, then carefully unmould the ring on to a warmed dish. Arrange the reserved pears in the centre, pouring the syrup over them. Serve at once.

SERVES 4

VARIATIONS

Use apricots or peaches instead of pears.

SAVOY PUDDING

fat for greasing
40 g/1½ oz cut mixed peel
125 g/4½ oz stale plain cake, finely
    crumbed
40 g/1½ oz butter, melted
300 ml/½ pint milk
45 ml/3 tbsp sweet sherry
2 eggs, separated
50 g/2 oz caster sugar

Grease a 750 ml/1¼ pint pie dish. Chop the mixed peel even more finely and put into a mixing bowl.

Add the cake crumbs, melted butter, milk and sherry to the chopped peel. Stir in the egg yolks and beat thoroughly. Leave to stand for 15 minutes. Set the oven at 160°C/325°F/gas 3.

Pour the pudding mixture into the prepared pie dish and bake for 35-40 minutes until lightly set. Remove from the oven and lower the oven temperature to 120°C/250°F/gas ½.

In a clean, grease-free bowl, whisk the egg whites until stiff. Add half the sugar and whisk again. Fold in all but 30 ml/2 tbsp of the remaining sugar, then pile the meringue on top of the pudding, making sure it is completely covered. Arrange in decorative peaks and sprinkle with the remaining sugar.

Return the pudding to the oven for 40-45 minutes until the meringue is set.

SERVES 4

> ☀ **MICROWAVE TIP** Melt the butter in a small bowl on High for 1-1½ minutes.

SAXON PUDDING

oil for greasing
glacé cherries
angelica
25 g/1 oz flaked almonds
3 slices plain cake or trifle sponges,
    crumbed
4 almond macaroons, crumbed
12 ratafias
2 eggs
100 ml/3½ fl oz single cream
25 g/1 oz caster sugar
300 ml/½ pint milk
45 ml/3 tbsp sherry

Grease a 13 cm/5 inch round cake tin and line the base with oiled greaseproof paper. Cut the cherries and angelica into small shapes and arrange in a pattern on the base of the cake tin.

Spread out the almonds on a baking sheet and place under a hot grill for a few minutes until browned. Shake the sheet from time to time and watch the nuts carefully as they will readily scorch. Use the almonds to decorate the sides of the greased cake tin.

Mix the cake and macaroon crumbs with the ratafias in a mixing bowl. In a second bowl, combine the eggs, cream and sugar. Mix lightly, then stir in the milk. Strain on to the crumb mixture and add the sherry. Stir, then leave to stand for 1 hour.

Meanwhile prepare a steamer or half fill a large saucepan with water and bring to the boil. Stir the pudding mixture again, making sure the ratafias are properly soaked. Spoon the mixture into the prepared cake tin, taking care not to spoil the decoration. Cover with greased greaseproof paper or foil and secure with string.

Put the pudding in the perforated part of the steamer, or stand it on an old saucer or plate in the saucepan of boiling water. The water should come halfway up the sides of the tin. Cover the pan tightly and steam the pudding over gently simmering water for 1-1¼ hours.

Remove the cooked pudding from the steamer, leave to stand for 5-10 minutes at room temperature to firm up, then turn out on to a warmed serving plate. Peel off the lining paper. Serve hot, with Thickened Fruit Sauce (page 399) or cold with whipped cream.

SERVES 4

PRESSURE COOKER TIP Pour 900 ml/1½ pints boiling water into the cooker. Cook the pudding at 15 lb pressure for 10 minutes. Reduce the pressure slowly.

QUEEN OF PUDDINGS

butter for greasing
75 g/3 oz soft white breadcrumbs
400 ml/14 fl oz milk
25 g/1 oz butter
10 ml/2 tsp grated lemon rind
2 eggs, separated
75 g/3 oz caster sugar
30 ml/2 tbsp red jam

Grease a 750 ml/1¼ pint pie dish. Set the oven at 160°C/325°F/gas 3. Spread the breadcrumbs out on a baking sheet and put into the oven to dry off slightly.

Warm the milk and butter with the lemon

rind in a saucepan. Meanwhile put the egg yolks in a bowl and stir in 25 g/1 oz of the sugar. Pour on the warmed milk mixture, stirring thoroughly. Add the breadcrumbs, mix thoroughly and pour into the prepared pie dish. Leave to stand for 30 minutes.

Bake the pudding for 40-50 minutes until lightly set, then remove from the oven. Lower the oven temperature to 120°C/ 250°F/gas ½. Warm the jam in a small saucepan until runny, then spread it over the top of the pudding.

In a clean, grease-free bowl, whisk the egg whites until stiff. Add half the remaining sugar and whisk again. Fold in all but 30 ml/ 2 tbsp of the remaining sugar. Spoon the meringue around the edge of the jam, drawing it up into peaks at regular intervals to resemble a crown. Sprinkle with the rest of the sugar.

Return the pudding to the oven and bake for 40-45 minutes more, until the meringue is set.

SERVES 4

☀ **MICROWAVE TIP** Warm the jam for a few seconds on High.

C USTARD TART

250 ml/8 fl oz milk
2 eggs
50 g/2 oz caster sugar
pinch of grated nutmeg

SHORT CRUST PASTRY
   100 g/4 oz plain flour
   1.25 ml/¼ tsp salt
   50 g/2 oz margarine (or half butter, half lard)
flour for rolling out

Put an 18 cm/7 inch flan ring on a heavy baking sheet, or line an 18 cm/7 inch sandwich cake tin with foil. Set the oven at 190°C/375°F/gas 5.

Make the pastry. Sift the flour and salt into a bowl, then rub in the margarine until the mixture resembles fine breadcrumbs. Add enough cold water to make a stiff dough. Press the dough together with your fingertips. Roll out on a lightly floured surface and use to line the flan ring or tin.

In a saucepan, bring the milk to just below boiling point. Put the eggs and caster sugar into a bowl, mix well, then stir in the scalded milk. Strain the mixture into the pastry case and sprinkle the top with grated nutmeg. Bake for 10 minutes.

Lower the oven temperature to 150°C/ 300°F/gas 2 and bake for 15-20 minutes more or until the custard is just set. Serve hot or cold.

SERVES 4 TO 6

SEAFOAM PUDDING

65 g/2½ oz cornflour
pared rind and juice of 2 large lemons
100-125 g/4-4½ oz sugar
3 egg whites

In a bowl, mix the cornflour to a thin cream with a little water.

Put the lemon rind into a saucepan with 750 ml/1¼ pints water. Bring to the boil, then remove the rind. Pour the water on to the blended cornflour, stirring all the time.

Return the mixture to the clean saucepan and bring to simmering point, stirring all the time. Simmer for 2-3 minutes. Add the sugar, stirring until dissolved and stir in the lemon juice.

In a clean, grease-free bowl, whisk the egg whites until stiff and, whisking all the time, gradually work in the cornflour mixture.

Pour the mixture into a wetted 1.75 litre/ 3 pint mould and refrigerate for about 2 hours to set.

When set, turn out the pudding on to a plate and serve.

SERVES 6

☀ **MICROWAVE TIP** Mix the cornflour with the measured water and lemon rind in a microwaveproof bowl. Cook on High for 7-10 minutes, whisking twice, until boiling and thickened. Continue as above.

APPLE SNOW

butter for greasing
1 kg/2¼ lb cooking apples
pared rind of 1 lemon
175 g/6 oz caster sugar
2 eggs, separated
250 ml/8 fl oz milk

Grease a 1 litre/1¾ pint pie dish. Set the oven at 160°C/325°F/gas 3.

Peel, core, and slice the apples into a saucepan. Add the lemon rind and 75 ml/ 5 tbsp water. Cover and cook until the apples are reduced to a pulp. Remove the lemon rind and beat the apple purée until smooth. Add 100 g/4 oz of the sugar.

Put the egg yolks in a bowl and beat lightly. Heat the milk with 25 g/1 oz of the remaining sugar in a saucepan. Pour on to the egg yolks. Return the mixture to the clean saucepan and cook, stirring all the time, until the mixture coats the back of the spoon. Do not allow the mixture to boil.

Put the apple purée into the prepared pie dish, pour the custard over it, and bake for 30-40 minutes.

In a clean, grease-free bowl, whisk the egg whites until stiff, fold in the remaining sugar and pile on top of the custard. Return to the oven and bake for a further 10 minutes until the meringue is just set.

SERVES 6

☀ **MICROWAVE TIP** Heat the milk and sugar for 2 minutes on High before adding to the egg yolks.

---

*P*UDDING A L'AMBASSADRICE

1 Savarin (page 174)

CUSTARD FILLING
  25 g/1 oz butter
  25 g/1 oz plain flour
  150 ml/¼ pint milk
  1 egg yolk
  45 ml/3 tbsp single cream
  15 ml/1 tbsp caster sugar
  rum or brandy essence

CARAMEL
  100 g/4 oz granulated sugar

CREAM CUSTARD
  350 ml/12 fl oz milk
  3 eggs
  150 ml/¼ pint single cream
  15 ml/1 tbsp caster sugar

Prepare and bake the savarin following the recipe instructions, then turn it out onto a wire rack to cool. Do not soak the savarin with rum syrup and do not brush it with any glaze.

Meanwhile make the custard filling. Melt the butter in a saucepan. Stir in the flour and cook for 1 minute, then gradually stir in the milk. Bring to the boil, stirring constantly to make a thick paste. Cool slightly. In a bowl, beat the egg yolk, cream and sugar together, then add to the cooled mixture. Reheat and cook, stirring all the time, until the mixture boils and thickens. Add enough essence to give a definite flavour. Set aside to cool.

Prepare a thickly folded band of news-paper long enough to encircle an 18 cm/7 inch round cake tin. Heat the tin in boiling water or in the oven and wrap the news-paper around it. Prepare the caramel by putting the sugar in a saucepan with 150 ml/¼ pint water. Heat, stirring occasionally, until the sugar has completely dissolved. Bring to the boil and boil without stirring until the syrup is golden brown. Immediately pour the caramel into the warmed, dry tin. Using the paper as a handle, tilt and turn the tin until evenly coated. Leave until the coating is cold and set.

Prepare a steamer or half fill a large sauce-pan with water and bring to the boil. Cut the savarin into 1.5 cm/¾ inch slices, spread thickly with the custard filling, and arrange in layers in the tin.

Make the cream custard. Warm the milk in a saucepan, without allowing it to approach boiling point. Stir the eggs, cream and sugar together in a bowl, then stir in the milk. Strain the custard into the prepared tin, making sure that all the pieces of savarin are covered.

Put the pudding in the perforated part of the steamer, or stand it on an old saucer or plate in the saucepan of boiling water. The water should come halfway up the sides of the tin. Cover the pan tightly and steam the pudding for 1-1¼ hours, until the custard is set and the pudding is firm.

Leave for 10 minutes at room temperature to firm up, then turn the pudding out on to a serving plate. Alternatively, the pudding may be allowed to cool completely before turning out. Serve with cream.

SERVES 4

S WISS CREAM

100 g/4 oz ratafias or sponge fingers
    or sponge cake
60 ml/4 tbsp sweet sherry
35 g/1¼ oz arrowroot
500 ml/17 fl oz milk
1.25 ml/¼ tsp vanilla essence
pinch of salt
30-45 ml/2-3 tbsp caster sugar
grated rind and juice of 1 lemon
150 ml/¼ pint double cream

DECORATION
10 ml/2 tsp flaked almonds
4 glacé cherries, halved

Break the biscuits or cake into small
pieces and place on the base of a glass dish
or individual dishes. Pour over the sherry.

Put the arrowroot in a bowl and mix to a
paste with a little of the milk. Mix the remaining milk with the vanilla essence and
salt in a heavy-bottomed saucepan. Bring to
the boil, then pour on to the blended paste,
stirring briskly to prevent the formation of
lumps.

Return the mixture to the clean saucepan and heat until it thickens and boils, stirring all the time. Stir in the caster sugar
until dissolved. Remove the pan from the
heat, cover the surface of the mixture with
greased greaseproof paper to prevent the
formation of a skin, and set aside until cold.

Stir the lemon rind and juice into the
cold arrowroot mixture. In a bowl, whip the
cream until soft peaks form, then stir lightly
into the pudding mixture. Pour over the
soaked biscuits and refrigerate for about
2 hours to set. Decorate with nuts and
cherries.

SERVES 4 TO 6

V ELVET CREAM

*This basic recipe produces one of the simplest
and most delicious of desserts, the full cream. It
lends itself to a wide range of variations and
may be served in glasses or as a decorative
mould (see Mrs Beeton's Tip). For variations on
this basic cream see page 265.*

10 ml/2 tsp gelatine
50 g/2 oz caster sugar
30 ml/2 tbsp sherry or a few drops of
    vanilla essence
250 ml/8 fl oz double cream
250 ml/8 fl oz single cream

Place 45 ml/3 tbsp water in a bowl and
sprinkle the gelatine on to the liquid. Stand
the bowl over a saucepan of hot water and
stir the gelatine until it has dissolved completely. Add the sugar and sherry or vanilla
essence and continue to stir until the sugar
has dissolved. Set aside.

Combine the creams in a mixing bowl
and whip lightly. Fold the flavoured gelatine
mixture into the cream and divide between
4 glasses or individual dishes. Refrigerate
for 1-2 hours or until set. When the cream
has set, a thin top layer of fresh fruit jelly
may be added, if liked.

SERVES 4

Queen Mab's Pudding (page 244) and Crème Brûlée (page 246)

Coffee Whip (page 269) and Cranachan (page 271)

Chocolate Dream (page 280)

Lemon Chiffon (page 290) and Fruit Soufflé (page 273)

Lemon Rice (page 300)

Everyday Pancakes (page 312/313)

Rich Christmas Pudding (page 331) with Brandy Butter (page 405)

Canary Pudding (page 337) with Jam Sauce (page 402)

VARIATIONS ON VELVET CREAM

In each of the variations below, omit the sherry or vanilla essence.

ALMOND CREAM Flavour with 1.25 ml/¼ tsp almond essence. Decorate with browned almonds.

BERRY CREAM Use 375 ml/13 fl oz double cream and fold in 125 ml/4 fl oz raspberry or strawberry purée instead of single cream. Decorate with fresh berry fruits.

CHOCOLATE CREAM Flavour with 75 g/3 oz melted chocolate. Decorate with chocolate curls.

COFFEE CREAM Flavour with 15 ml/1 tbsp instant coffee dissolved in 15 ml/1 tbsp boiling water and cooled. Add 15 ml/1 tbsp rum, if liked, and decorate with coffee beans.

HIGHLAND CREAM Flavour with 15 ml/1 tbsp whisky and serve with a whisky-flavoured apricot sauce.

LEMON AND ALMOND CREAM Flavour with 30 ml/2 tbsp lemon juice, 5 ml/1 tsp grated lemon rind and 25 g/1 oz ground almonds.

LIQUEUR CREAM Flavour with 15 ml/1 tbsp Tia Maria, curacao, kirsch or Advocaat.

PISTACHIO CREAM Blanch, skin and finely chop 100 g/4 oz pistachio nuts and fold into the mixture before adding the gelatine. Tint the cream pale green with food colouring.

MRS BEETON'S TIP The cream may be made in a mould, if preferred. Make up one quantity of Clear Lemon Jelly (page 204). Use some of the jelly to line a 750 ml/1¼ pint mould, decorating it with cut shapes of angelica and glacé cherry (see page 192). When the jelly lining has set, carefully add the prepared cream and refrigerate for 2-3 hours until set. The remaining jelly may be set in a shallow tray, then chopped for use as a decoration.

DAMASK CREAM

600 ml/1 pint single cream
1 blade of mace
10 cm/4 inch piece of cinnamon stick
20 ml/4 tsp icing sugar, sifted
triple-strength rose-water to taste
15 ml/1 tbsp rennet essence

DECORATION
deep pink rose-petals or 1 red rose

Pour 500 ml/17 fl oz of the cream into a saucepan, add the mace and cinnamon stick, and heat almost to boiling point. Remove from the heat and infuse for 20-30 minutes.

Strain the cream into a clean bowl, discarding the spices. Add 10 ml/2 tsp icing sugar to the cream with rose-water to taste. Cool to blood-heat, and stir in the rennet. Pour gently into a decorative 750 ml/1¼ pint serving bowl and leave to set in a warm room until cold and firm.

Pour the remaining cream into a jug. Flavour with rose-water and very gently pour the flavoured cream over the set cream to a depth of 5 mm/¼ inch. Sprinkle lightly all over with icing sugar.

Strew deep pink rose-petals around the edge of the dish or set one perfect red rose-bud in the centre. Serve with thin, crisp, plain or almond biscuits.

SERVES 4

VANILLA BAVAROIS

A bavarois, or Bavarian Cream, as it is sometimes known, consists of a cup custard combined with cream and flavouring, with gelatine as the setting agent.

oil for greasing
4 egg yolks or 1 whole egg and 2 yolks
50 g/2 oz caster sugar
250 ml/8 fl oz milk
2.5 ml/½ tsp vanilla essence
10 ml/2 tsp gelatine
150 ml/¼ pint double cream
150 ml/¼ pint single cream

Oil a 750 ml/1¼ pint mould. In a bowl, beat the eggs and sugar together until fluffy and pale.

Warm the milk in a saucepan; do not let it boil. Slowly stir it into the egg mixture, then strain the custard back into the clean saucepan or into a double saucepan or heat-proof bowl placed over hot water. Cook over very low heat until the custard thickens.

Strain the thickened custard into a bowl, stir in the vanilla essence and leave to cool.

Put 15 ml/1 tbsp water into a small heat-proof bowl and sprinkle the gelatine on to the liquid. Stand the bowl over a saucepan and stir the gelatine until it has dissolved completely. Cool until tepid and add to the custard. Leave in a cool place until the mixture thickens at the edges, stirring from time to time to prevent the formation of a skin.

Combine the creams in a bowl and whip lightly. Fold into the custard mixture, and pour into the prepared mould. Refrigerate for about 2 hours until set, then turn out on to a flat wetted plate to serve.

SERVES 4 TO 6

VARIATIONS

CARAMEL BAVAROIS Dissolve 100 g/4 oz granulated sugar in 15 ml/1 tbsp water and heat until the syrup turns a rich brown colour. Carefully add 60 ml/4 tbsp hot water, remove from the heat, and stir until all the caramel dissolves. Stir into the warm custard.

CHOCOLATE BAVAROIS Grate 100 g/4 oz plain chocolate and add with the milk. It will melt in the warm custard. Add 5 ml/1 tsp vanilla essence.

COFFEE BAVAROIS Dissolve 15 ml/1 tbsp instant coffee in 15 ml/1 tbsp boiling water. Cool, then stir in 15 ml/1 tbsp rum. Add this essence with the milk.

CRÈME DIPLOMATE Soak 100 g/4 oz chopped crystallized fruit in 30 ml/2 tbsp spoons kirsch. Pour the vanilla Bavarian cream into the mould to a depth of 1.5 cm/¾ inch and leave to set. Spread half the fruit over it and cover with a little of the cream. Leave to set. Continue alternating layers of fruit and cream, finishing with a layer of cream. Allow each layer to set before adding the next.

CRÈME TRICOLORE Divide the mixture into three portions. Flavour the first with vanilla essence, the second with chocolate, the third with strawberry purée. Line the mould with vanilla cream in the same way as when lining with jelly (page 192). When this is completely set, fill alternately with equal layers of the chocolate and strawberry creams, allowing each layer to set before adding the next.

GINGER BAVAROIS Reduce the sugar to 40 g/1½ oz and add 75 g/3 oz chopped preserved ginger and 45 ml/3 tbsp ginger syrup from the jar, just before folding in the cream.

ITALIAN BAVAROIS Infuse thin strips of rind from 1 lemon in the milk. Add the strained juice of the lemon to the custard with 15 ml/1 tbsp brandy, if liked.

MOCHA BAVAROIS Melt 75 g/3 oz

grated plain chocolate in the milk and add 10 ml/2 tsp instant coffee dissolved in 15 ml/1 tbsp hot water.

ORANGE BAVAROIS Infuse thin strips of rind from 2 oranges in the milk. Dissolve the gelatine in the juice from 3 oranges, make up to 250 ml/8 fl oz with water and strain it into the custard. When nearly set, fold in 125 ml/4 fl oz lightly whipped double cream.

PEACH BAVAROIS Plunge 4 ripe peaches into boiling water in a bowl. Leave the fruit for 1 minute, then drain and peel them. Halve the peaches and remove their stones. Sprinkle 4 peach halves with lemon juice, cover and set aside. Chop the remaining peaches and add to the custard before folding in the cream. Slice the reserved peaches and use as decoration.

PISTACHIO BAVAROIS Add 100 g/4 oz finely chopped skinned pistachio nuts. Tint the cream pale green.

RIBBON BAVAROIS Divide the mixture into 2 portions, and flavour and colour each half separately; for example, with vanilla and chocolate, vanilla and orange, or ginger and chocolate. Do not decorate the mould but oil it lightly. Pour in one of the creams to a depth of 1.5 cm/¾ inch, leave to set, then repeat with the second cream. Continue in this way until all the mixture is used.

MRS BEETON'S TIP It is important that the custard is not allowed to boil. If using a double saucepan, take care that the water does not come into contact with the upper pan.

QUICK JELLY CREAM

1 × 127 g/4½ oz tablet orange jelly
45 ml/3 tbsp orange juice
30 ml/2 tbsp custard powder
250 ml/8 fl oz milk
125 ml/4 fl oz double cream

Chop the jelly tablet roughly. Heat 100 ml/3½ fl oz water in a saucepan, add the jelly, and stir until dissolved. Add the orange juice and leave to cool.

Meanwhile, in a bowl, blend the custard powder with a little of the milk. Put the rest of the milk into a saucepan and bring to the boil. Pour it slowly on to the blended custard powder, stirring all the time. Return to the clean saucepan, bring to the boil and boil for 1-2 minutes, stirring all the time, until the custard thickens.

Cool the custard slightly, then stir into the jelly. Cool until beginning to set.

In a bowl, whip the cream until it leaves a trail, then fold into the setting mixture. Pour into 4 individual glasses and chill for about 1 hour. Decorate as desired.

SERVES 4

VARIATIONS

PINEAPPLE JELLY CREAM Use a pineapple jelly tablet and the juice from a 376 g/13 oz can of crushed pineapple. Fold the fruit into the setting mixture.

BERRY JELLY CREAM Use a raspberry or strawberry jelly tablet and the juice from a 219 g/7½ oz can of raspberries or strawberries. Fold the fruit into the setting mixture.

TANGERINE JELLY CREAM Use a tangerine jelly tablet and the juice from a 213 g/7½ oz can of mandarin oranges. Chop the fruit and fold into the setting mixture.

MRS BEETON'S DUTCH FLUMMERY

This is best made the day before it is to be served.

25 g/1 oz gelatine
grated rind and juice of 1 lemon
4 eggs, beaten
500 ml/17 fl oz dry sherry
50 g/2 oz caster sugar

Place 125 ml/4 fl oz water in a heatproof bowl and sprinkle the gelatine on to the liquid. Stand the bowl over a saucepan of hot water and stir the gelatine until it has dissolved completely. Pour the mixture into a measuring jug and make up to 500 ml/ 17 fl oz with cold water. Add the grated lemon rind and strain in the juice.

In a second bowl, beat the eggs, sherry and sugar together. Add to the gelatine mixture. Pour into the top of a double saucepan, place over simmering water and cook over low heat, stirring all the time, until the mixture coats the back of the spoon. Do not let the mixture boil.

Strain the mixture into a wetted 1.75 litre/ 3 pint mould and refrigerate until set. Turn out on to a plate to serve.

SERVES 4 TO 6

MRS BEETON'S TIP It is often difficult to centre a moulded dessert on a serving plate. Wet the plate first, shaking off excess moisture. When the dessert is inverted on to the plate, the thin skin of liquid on the plate will made it easy to move it into the desired position before removing the mould.

HONEYCOMB MOULD

2 eggs, separated
25 g/1 oz caster sugar
500 ml/17 fl oz milk
5 ml/1 tsp vanilla essence
20 ml/4 tsp gelatine

FILLING
375 g/13 oz chopped fresh fruit or 1 ×
425 g/15 oz can fruit, well drained

In a bowl, combine the egg yolks, sugar and milk. Mix lightly. Pour into the top of a double saucepan and cook over simmering water until the custard coasts the back of a spoon, stirring all the time. Do not allow the custard to boil. Stir in the essence.

Place 45 ml/3 tbsp water in a small heatproof bowl. Sprinkle the gelatine on to the liquid. Stand the bowl over a saucepan of hot water and stir the gelatine until it has dissolved completely. Stir the gelatine mixture into the custard. Leave to cool.

In a clean, grease-free bowl, whisk the egg whites until just stiff. When the custard is just beginning to set, fold in the egg whites.

Pour the mixture into a wetted 1 litre/1¾ pint ring mould and refrigerate for 2-3 hours until set. Turn out on to a serving plate and fill the centre with fruit.

SERVES 4 TO 6

*P*INEAPPLE BUTTERMILK WHIP

This is a very good dessert for slimmers.

400 ml/14 fl oz unsweetened pineapple or
    orange juice
15 ml/1 tbsp gelatine
150 ml/¼ pint buttermilk

Put 60 ml/4 tbsp of the fruit juice into a
heatproof bowl and sprinkle the gelatine on
to the liquid. Stand the bowl over a saucepan of hot water, and stir the gelatine until
it has dissolved completely.

Combine the gelatine mixture with the
remaining fruit juice. Pour a little of the
mixture into each of 4 stemmed glasses.

Chill the rest of the juice mixture for
about 1 hour. When it is on the point of
setting, whisk in the buttermilk until frothy.
Spoon into the glasses and chill.

SERVES 4

🥣 **MRS BEETON'S TIP** Take care
when adding the creamy mixture to
the glasses, not to disturb the jelly layer.
The two-tone effect is most attractive.

---

*B*RANDY WHIP

400 ml/14 fl oz double cream
100 ml/3½ fl oz brandy
juice of ½ lemon
caster sugar (optional)
ground nutmeg

In a large bowl, whip the cream to soft
peaks, adding the brandy and the lemon

juice gradually. Taste, and add the caster
sugar, if required.

Spoon the mixture into 4 individual
glasses. Sprinkle with a little nutmeg and
chill before serving.

Serve with sponge fingers.

SERVES 4

*C*OFFEE WHIP

Illustrated on page 258

500 ml/17 fl oz milk
15 ml//1 tbsp coffee essence
25 g/1 oz sugar
20 ml//4 tsp gelatine
1 egg white
15 ml/1 tbsp flaked almonds to decorate

In a saucepan, heat together the milk,
coffee essence and sugar. Leave for about
30 minutes to cool. Put 30 ml/2 tbsp water
in a small heatproof bowl and sprinkle the
gelatine on to the liquid. Stand the bowl
over a saucepan of hot water and stir the
gelatine until it has dissolved completely.
Stir into the cooled milk mixture.

In a clean, grease-free bowl, whisk the
egg white lightly and add to the liquid milk
jelly. Whisk very well until thick and
frothy. Pile into a serving dish and decorate
with the flaked almonds.

SERVES 4 TO 6

LEMON FLUFF

30 ml/2 tbsp lemon juice
30 ml/2 tbsp cornflour
75 ml/5 tbsp caster sugar
5 ml/1 tsp grated lemon rind
2 eggs, separated
125 ml/4 fl oz single cream

In a bowl, blend the lemon juice with the cornflour. Bring 150 ml/¼ pint water to the boil in a saucepan. Stir a little of the boiling water into the cornflour mixture, then add the contents of the bowl to the rest of the boiling water. Bring the mixture back to the boil, stirring constantly, then boil for 1-2 minutes until the mixture thickens. Stir in 45 ml/3 tbsp caster sugar with the lemon rind. Remove the pan from the heat.

Add the egg yolks to the lemon mixture, stirring them in vigorously. Cover the mixture with dampened greaseproof paper to prevent the formation of a skin, and cool until tepid.

Stir the cream into the cooled lemon custard. In a clean, grease-free bowl, whisk the egg whites until stiff, add the remaining sugar and whisk until stiff again. Fold the egg whites into the lemon mixture until evenly distributed. Spoon into 4 glasses and chill before serving.

SERVES 4

> **MRS BEETON'S TIP** When grating the lemon, be sure to remove only the outer rind and not the bitter pith.

CIDER SYLLABUB

A syllabub was originally a sweet, frothy drink made with cider or mead mixed with milk straight from the cow. Mrs Beeton's original syllabub recipe combined 600 ml/1 pint of sherry or white wine with 900 ml/1½ pints of fresh, frothy milk. Nutmeg or cinnamon and sugar was stirred in, and clotted cream may have been added. When cider was used instead of wine, brandy was added to enrich the syllabub. It is now a rich creamy dessert, often made light and frothy by the addition of egg whites.

grated rind and juice of ½ lemon
50 g/2 oz caster sugar
125 ml/4 fl oz sweet cider
15 ml/1 tbsp brandy
250 ml/8 fl oz double cream

In a large bowl, mix the lemon rind and juice with the caster sugar, cider and brandy. Stir until the sugar is dissolved.

Put the cream in a mixing bowl. Whip until it stands in stiff peaks. Gradually fold in the lemon and cider mixture.

Pour the mixture into stemmed glasses and refrigerate for about 2 hours. Remove 20 minutes before serving to allow the flavours to 'ripen'.

SERVES 4

WINE SYLLABUB

This syllabub has a frothy head, with the lemon juice and wine settling in the bottom of the glasses.

200 ml/7 fl oz double cream
2 egg whites
75 g/3 oz caster sugar
juice of ½ lemon
100 ml/3½ fl oz sweet white wine or
   sherry
crystallized lemon slices to decorate

In a large bowl, whip the cream until it just holds its shape. Put the egg whites in a clean, grease-free mixing bowl and whisk until they form soft peaks. Fold the sugar into the egg whites, then gradually add the lemon juice and wine or sherry.

Fold the egg white mixture into the whipped cream. Pour into glasses and re-frigerate for about 2 hours. Remove 20 min-utes before serving. Serve decorated with the crystallized lemon slices.

SERVES 4

WHIPPED SYLLABUB

50 ml/2 fl oz sweet red wine or ruby port
250 ml/8 fl oz double cream
50 ml/2 fl oz medium dry sherry
juice of ½ orange
grated rind of ½ lemon
50 g/2 oz caster sugar

Divide the wine or port between 4 chilled stemmed glasses, and keep chilled.

In a bowl, whip the cream, adding the remaining ingredients gradually, in order, until the mixture just holds firm peaks.

Pile the cream mixture into the chilled glasses (see Mrs Beeton's Tip). Serve as soon as possible.

SERVES 4

> **MRS BEETON'S TIP** When adding the cream mixture to the chilled wine take care not to mix the two. The wine should clearly be seen in the bottom of each glass.

CRANACHAN

Illustrated on page 258

125 g/4½ oz coarse oatmeal
400 ml/14 fl oz double cream
50 g/2 oz caster sugar
15 ml/1 tbsp rum
150 g/5 oz fresh raspberries

Toast the oatmeal under a low grill until lightly browned (see Mrs Beeton's Tip). Set aside to cool.

In a bowl, whip the cream until stiff. Stir in the toasted oatmeal and flavour with the sugar and rum.

Hull the raspberries. Stir them into the cream or layer with the Cranachan mixture, reserving 4 perfect fruit for decoration, if liked. Serve in 4 individual glass dishes.

SERVES 4

> **MRS BEETON'S TIP** When toasting the oatmeal, shake the grill pan frequently so that the mixture browns evenly.

VANILLA SOUFFLÉ

40 g/1½ oz butter
40 g/1½ oz plain flour
250 ml/8 fl oz milk
4 eggs, separated plus 1 white
50 g/2 oz caster sugar
2.5 ml/½ tsp vanilla essence
caster or icing sugar for dredging

Prepare a 1 litre/1¾ pint soufflé dish. Set the oven at 180°C/350°F/gas 4.

Melt the butter in a saucepan, stir in the flour and cook slowly for 2-3 minutes without colouring, stirring all the time. Add the milk gradually and beat until smooth. Cook for 1-2 minutes more, still stirring. Remove from the heat and beat hard until the sauce comes away cleanly from the sides of the pan. Cool slightly and put into a bowl.

Beat the yolks into the flour mixture one by one. Beat in the sugar and vanilla essence.

In a clean, grease-free bowl, whisk all the egg whites until stiff. Using a metal spoon, stir 1 spoonful of the whites into the mixture to lighten it, then fold in the rest until evenly distributed.

Spoon into the prepared dish and bake for 45 minutes until well risen and browned.

Dredge with caster or icing sugar and serve immediately from the dish, with Jam Sauce (page 402).

SERVES 4-6

VARIATIONS

ALMOND SOUFFLÉ Add 100 g/4 oz ground almonds, 15 ml/1 tbsp lemon juice and a few drops of ratafia essence to the mixture before adding the egg yolks. Reduce the sugar to 40 g/1½ oz. Omit the vanilla essence.

COFFEE SOUFFLÉ Add 30 ml/2 tbsp instant coffee dissolved in a little hot water before adding the egg yolks, or use 125 ml/4 fl oz strong black coffee and only 125 ml/4 fl oz milk. Omit the vanilla essence.

GINGER SOUFFLÉ Add a pinch of ground ginger and 50 g/2 oz chopped preserved stem ginger before adding the egg yolks. Omit the vanilla essence. Serve each portion topped with double cream and a spoonful of ginger syrup.

LEMON SOUFFLÉ Add the thinly grated rind and juice of 1 lemon before adding the egg yolks. Omit the vanilla essence. Serve with Rich Lemon Sauce (page 395).

LIQUEUR SOUFFLÉ Add 30 ml/2 tbsp Cointreau, kirsch or curaçao instead of vanilla essence and make as for Soufflé au Grand Marnier below. Serve with sweetened cream flavoured with the liqueur.

ORANGE SOUFFLÉ Thinly pare the rind of 2 oranges. Put in a saucepan with the milk and bring slowly to the boil. Remove from the heat, cover, and leave to stand for 10 minutes, then remove the rind. Make up the sauce using the flavoured milk. Reduce the sugar to 40 g/1½ oz and omit the vanilla essence. Add the strained juice of ½ orange.

PRALINE SOUFFLÉ Dissolve 30-45 ml/2-3 tbsp almond Praline (see Mrs Beeton's Tip, page 248) in the milk before making the sauce, or crush and add just before the egg yolks. Omit the vanilla essence.

SOUFFLÉ AU GRAND MARNIER Add 30-45 ml/2-3 tbsp Grand Marnier to the orange soufflé mixture. Serve with an orange sauce made by boiling 125 ml/4 fl oz orange juice and a few drops of liqueur with 50 g/2 oz caster sugar until syrupy. Add very fine strips of orange rind.

SOUFFLÉ AMBASSADRICE Crumble 2 almond macaroons; soak them in 30ml/2 tbsp rum with 50 g/2 oz chopped blanched almonds. Stir into a vanilla soufflé mixture.

SOUFFLÉ HARLEQUIN Make up 2 half quantities of soufflé mixture in different flavours, eg chocolate and vanilla, or praline and coffee. Spoon alternately into the dish.

SOUFFLÉ ROTHSCHILD Rinse 50 g/ 2 oz mixed glacé fruit in hot water to remove any excess sugar. Chop the fruit and soak it in 30 ml/2 tbsp brandy or kirsch for 2 hours. Make up 1 quantity vanilla soufflé mixture. Put half the vanilla soufflé mixture into the dish, add the fruit, and then the rest of the soufflé mixture.

SOUFFLÉ SURPRISE Crumble 3 sponge fingers or almond macaroons into a bowl. Soak the biscuits in 30 ml/2 tbsp Grand Marnier or Cointreau. Add 30 ml/2 tbsp of the same liqueur to an orange soufflé mixture. Put half the mixture into the dish, sprinkle the biscuits on top, and add the rest of the soufflé mixture.

FRUIT SOUFFLÉS

For fruit-flavoured soufflés a thick, sweet purée is added to the basic vanilla soufflé. It is important that the purée should have a strong flavour, otherwise the taste will not be discernible. If extra purée is added, the soufflé will be heavy and will not rise.

APPLE SOUFFLÉ Add 125 ml/ 4 fl oz thick sweet apple purée, 15 ml/ 1 tbsp lemon juice, and a pinch of powdered cinnamon to the soufflé before adding the egg yolks. Dust with cinnamon before serving.

APRICOT SOUFFLÉ Before adding the egg yolks, add 125 ml/4 fl oz thick apricot purée and 15 ml/1 tbsp lemon juice, if using fresh apricots. If using canned apricots (1 × 397 g/14 oz can yields 125 ml/4 fl oz purée) use half milk and half can syrup for the sauce. A purée made from dried apricots makes a delicious soufflé.

PINEAPPLE SOUFFLÉ Before adding the egg yolks, add 125 ml/ 4 fl oz crushed pineapple or 75 g/3 oz chopped fresh pineapple, and make the sauce using half milk and half pineapple juice.

RASPBERRY SOUFFLÉ Before adding the egg yolks, add 125 ml/4 fl oz raspberry purée (1 × 397 g/14 oz can yields 125 ml/4 fl oz purée) and 10 ml/ 2 tsp lemon juice.

STRAWBERRY SOUFFLÉ Before adding the egg yolks, add 125 ml/4 fl oz strawberry purée. Make the sauce using half milk and half single cream. Add a little pink food colouring, if necessary.

S WEET SOUFFLÉ OMELETTE

Soufflé omelettes are quick and easy to make – the perfect finale for the busy cook. Fill simply with 30 ml/2 tbsp warmed jam or try any of the exciting fillings that follow.

2 eggs, separated
5 ml/1 tsp caster sugar
few drops of vanilla essence
15 ml/1 tbsp unsalted butter or margarine
icing sugar for dredging

In a large bowl, whisk the yolks until creamy. Add the sugar and vanilla essence with 30 ml/2 tbsp water, then whisk again. In a clean, grease-free bowl, whisk the egg whites until stiff and matt.

Place an 18 cm/7 inch omelette pan over gentle heat and when it is hot add the butter or margarine. Tilt the pan to grease the whole of the inside. Pour out any excess.

Fold the egg whites into the yolks mixture carefully until evenly distributed, using a metal spoon (see Mrs Beeton's Tip). Heat the grill to moderate.

Pour the egg mixture into the omelette pan, level the top very lightly, and cook for 1-2 minutes over a moderate heat until the omelette is golden-brown on the underside and moist on top. (Use a palette knife to lift the edge of the omelette to look underneath.)

Put the pan under the grill for 5-6 minutes until the omelette is risen and lightly browned on the top. The texture of the omelette should be firm yet spongy. Remove from the heat as soon as it is ready, as overcooking tends to make it tough. Run a palette knife gently round the edge and underneath to loosen it. Make a mark across the middle at right angles to the pan handle but do not cut the surface. Put the chosen filling on one half, raise the handle of the pan and double the omelette over. Turn gently on to a warm plate, dredge with icing sugar and serve at once.

SERVES 1

> **MRS BEETON'S TIP** When folding the beaten egg whites into the omelette mixture, be very careful not to overmix, as it is the air incorporated in the frothy whites that causes the omelette to rise.

FILLINGS

APRICOT OMELETTE Add the grated rind of 1 orange to the egg yolks. Spread 30 ml/2 tbsp warm, thick apricot purée over the omelette.

CHERRY OMELETTE Stone 100 g/4 oz dark cherries, or use canned ones. Warm with 30 ml/2 tbsp cherry jam and 15 ml/1 tbsp kirsch. Spread over the omelette.

CREAMY PEACH OMELETTE Stone and roughly chop 1 ripe peach, then mix it with 45 ml/3 tbsp cream cheese. Add a little icing sugar to taste and mix well until softened. Spread over the omelette.

JAM OMELETTE Warm 45 ml/3 tbsp fruity jam and spread over the omelette.

LEMON OMELETTE Add the grated rind of ½ lemon to the egg yolks. Warm 45 ml/3 tbsp lemon curd with 10 ml/2 tsp lemon juice, and spread over the omelette.

ORANGE CHOCOLATE OMELETTE Warm 15 ml/1 tbsp orange mamalade and mix with 30 ml/2 tbsp chocolate spread. Spread over the omelette.

RASPBERRY OMELETTE Spread 30 ml/2 tbsp warm, thick, raspberry purée or Melba Sauce (page 398) over the omlette.

RUM OMELETTE Add 15 ml/1 tbsp rum to the egg yolks.

STRAWBERRY OMELETTE Hull 5 ripe strawberries and soak in a bowl with little kirsch. Mash slightly with icing sugar to taste. Put in the centre of the omelette.

SURPRISE OMELETTE Put ice cream into the centre of the omelette before folding. Work quickly to prevent the ice cream from melting and serve the omelette immediately.

SPECIAL EFFECTS

FLAMBÉ OMELETTE Warm 30 ml/2 tbsp rum or brandy. Put the cooked omelette on to a warm plate, pour the warmed spirit round it, ignite, and serve immediately.

BRANDED OMELETTES Soufflé omelettes are sometimes 'branded' for a special occasion. A lattice decoration is marked on the top using hot skewers. Heat the pointed ends of 3 metal skewers until red-hot. When the omelette is on the plate, dredge with icing sugar. Protecting your hand in an oven glove, quickly press the hot skewers, one at a time, on to the sugar, holding them there until the sugar caramelizes. Make a diagonal criss-cross design. Each skewer should make two marks if you work quickly.

*B*AKED SOUFFLÉ OMELETTE

fat for greasing
60 ml/4 tbsp jam or stewed fruit
4 eggs, separated
50 g/2 oz caster sugar
pinch of salt
caster or icing sugar for dredging

Grease a shallow 23 cm/9 inch ovenproof dish and spread the jam or fruit over the base. Set the oven at 190°C/375°F/gas 5.

In a mixing bowl, beat the egg yolks with the sugar and 30 ml/2 tbsp water.

In a clean, grease-free bowl, whisk the egg whites with the salt until stiff, then fold into the yolk mixture. Pour over the jam or fruit and bake for 15-20 minutes. Dredge with sugar and serve at once.

SERVES 2

MRS BEETON'S TIP A little water is often added to omelette mixtures to lighten them. Never add milk or cream, which would make the texture tough.

COLD SOUFFLÉS AND MOUSSES

MILK CHOCOLATE SOUFFLÉ

Cold soufflés are prepared in much the same way as hot ones; the difference being that gelatine is used instead of heat to set the eggs. The dish is prepared in a similar fashion, too, with a paper collar enabling the mixture to be taken above the level of the dish to simulate a risen soufflé.

10 ml/2 tsp gelatine
2 eggs, separated
50 g/2 oz sugar
150 ml/¼ pint evaporated milk, chilled
75 g/3 oz milk chocolate

DECORATION
    whipped cream
    grated chocolate

Prepare a 500 ml/17 fl oz soufflé dish and stand on a plate for easy handling.

Place 30 ml/2 tbsp water in a small bowl and sprinkle the gelatine on to the liquid. Stand the bowl over a saucepan of hot water and stir the gelatine until it has dissolved completely. Cool slightly.

Combine the egg yolks and sugar in a heatproof bowl and stand over a saucepan of hot water set over low heat. Do not let the water boil or touch the bowl. Whisk the mixture for 5-10 minutes until thick and pale, then remove from the heat.

In a bowl, whisk the chilled evaporated milk until thick, then whisk into the egg yolk mixture. Melt the chocolate on a plate over simmering water and whisk into the mixture.

Fold a little of the chocolate mixture into the cooled gelatine, then whisk this into the rest of the chocolate mixture. Put in a cool place until the mixture starts to set.

Whisk the egg whites in a clean, grease-free bowl until stiff, then fold into the mixture. Tip the soufflé gently into the prepared dish and refrigerate for about 2 hours until set.

Carefully remove the paper from the crown of the soufflé and decorate with whipped cream and grated chocolate.

SERVES 4

> **MRS BEETON'S TIP** Folding a little of the chocolate mixture into the cooled gelatine before mixing it with the yolk mixture helps to prevent the gelatine setting in lumps or forming 'ropes'.

MILANAISE SOUFFLÉ

15 ml/1 tbsp gelatine
3 eggs, separated
grated rind and juice of 2 lemons
100 g/4 oz caster sugar
125 ml/4 fl oz double cream

DECORATION
    finely chopped nuts or cake crumbs
    whipped double cream (optional)
    crystallized lemon slices
    angelica

Prepare a 500 ml/17 fl oz soufflé dish (see Mrs Beeton's Tip) and stand on a plate for easy handling.

Place 45 ml/3 tbsp water in a small bowl and sprinkle the gelatine on to the liquid. Stand the bowl over a saucepan of hot water and stir the gelatine until it has dissolved completely. Cool slightly.

Combine the egg yolks, lemon rind and juice, and sugar in a heatproof bowl and stand over a saucepan of hot water set over low heat. Do not let the water boil or touch the bowl. Whisk the mixture for 10-15 minutes until thick and pale, then remove from the heat and continue whisking until cool.

Fold a little of the yolk mixture into the cooled gelatine, then whisk this into the rest of the yolk mixture. Put in a cool place until the mixture starts to set.

In a bowl, whip the cream to soft peaks. Using a large metal spoon, fold into the yolk mixture until evenly blended. Whisk the egg whites in a clean, grease-free bowl until stiff, then fold into the mixture. Tip the soufflé gently into the prepared dish and refrigerate for about 2 hours until set.

Carefully remove the paper from the crown of the soufflé and decorate the sides with chopped nuts or cake crumbs. Pipe whipped cream on top, if liked, and decorate with crystallized lemon slices and small pieces of angelica.

SERVES 4

VARIATIONS

In each of the variations below, omit the lemon rind and juice.

CHOCOLATE SOUFFLÉ Whisk the egg yolks with 30 ml/2 tbsp water and 75 g/3 oz caster sugar. Melt 75 g/3 oz grated plain chocolate over a saucepan of hot water. Add to the yolk mixture with the dissolved gelatine and whisk well.

ORANGE SOUFFLÉ Whisk the egg yolks with the finely grated rind and juice of 2 oranges and use 75 g/3 oz caster sugar only. Add 30 ml/2 tbsp Grand Marnier or orange curaçao, if liked. Dissolve the gelatine in a mixture of 15 ml/1 tbsp water and 30 ml/2 tbsp lemon juice. Decorate the soufflé with crystallized orange slices, nuts and cream.

PRALINE SOUFFLÉ Prepare 75 g/3 oz Praline (see Mrs Beeton's Tip, page 248) and crush it. Dissolve 5 ml/1 tsp instant coffee in 30 ml/2 tbsp hot water, and add 30 ml/2 tbsp cold water. Whisk the liquid with the yolks. Add 50 g/2 oz of the crushed praline to the mixture with the whipped cream. Decorate with the remaining praline and additional cream.

FRUIT SOUFFLÉS The recipe that follows uses raspberries but fresh, frozen or canned soft fruits, such as strawberries, blackcurrants or blackberries, may be substituted to produce a strongly flavoured soufflé. Dried apricots also make a delicious soufflé. Soak 50 g/2 oz overnight in enough water to cover. Tip into a saucepan and simmer for 15-20 minutes until tender, then purée in a blender or food processor.

RASPBERRY SOUFFLÉ Soften the gelatine in 45 ml/3 tbsp of strained fruit syrup from a 440 g/15½ oz can of raspberries. And 15 ml/1 tbsp lemon juice and 150 ml/¼ pint sieved fruit to the yolk mixture (this can be made up with a little strained syrup, if necessary). Use only 75 g/3 oz sugar and 100 ml/3½ fl oz double cream. Decorate the sides with desiccated coconut, and the top with whipped cream and raspberries.

MRS BEETON'S TIP The size of the soufflé dish is crucial, since the mixture must 'rise' above it. If in doubt as to the capacity of the dish, measure by pouring in 500 ml/17 fl oz water. If the dish is slightly too small, do not worry, since the crown will merely be a little taller. A larger dish, however, will not be suitable.

CHOCOLATE MOUSSE

150 g/5 oz plain chocolate, grated
4 eggs, separated
vanilla essence

DECORATION
   whipped cream
   chopped walnuts

Put the grated chocolate into a large heat-proof bowl with 30 ml/2 tbsp water. Stand over a saucepan of simmering water until the chocolate melts. Remove from the heat and stir until smooth.

Beat the egg yolks into the chocolate with a few drops of vanilla essence. In a clean, grease-free bowl, whisk the egg whites until fairly stiff, then fold gently into the chocolate mixture until evenly blended.

Pour into 4 individual dishes and refrigerate for 1-2 hours until set. Decorate with whipped cream and chopped walnuts just before serving.

SERVES 4

VARIATIONS

MOCHA MOUSSE Dissolve 5 ml/1 tsp instant coffee in 30 ml/2 tbsp hot water and stir this liquid into the chocolate with the egg yolks and vanilla essence.
CHOC-AU-RHUM MOUSSE Add 15 ml/1 tbsp rum to the mixture. Alternatively, use brandy, Grand Marnier or Tia Maria.
WHITE MOUSSE Use white chocolate, melting it in single cream instead of water.

———————— ◇ ————————

BLACKCURRANT MOUSSE

A sweet mousse is a creamy dessert which usually has either a fruit purée or a flavoured custard sauce as its base, with beaten egg whites (and sometimes whipped cream) added to lighten the texture. Fresh, frozen or canned fruit may be used, with the amount of sugar adjusted according to the sweetness of the fruit.

250 g/9 oz fresh blackcurrants
50 g/2 oz caster sugar
10 ml/2 tsp lemon juice
10 ml/2 tsp gelatine
125 ml/4 fl oz double cream
2 egg whites
whipped cream to decorate

Reserve a few whole blackcurrants for decoration. Press the rest through a sieve into a measuring jug, then make up the purée to 150 ml/¼ pint with water.

Combine the blackcurrant purée, sugar and lemon juice in a mixing bowl. Place 30 ml/2 tbsp water in a small heatproof bowl and sprinkle the gelatine on to the liquid. Stand the bowl over a saucepan of hot water and stir the gelatine until it has dissolved completely. Cool slightly.

Fold a little of the blackcurrant purée into the cooled gelatine, then whisk this mixture into the bowl of blackcurrant purée. Leave in a cool place until the mixture starts to set.

In a deep bowl, whip the cream until it just holds its shape, then fold into the blackcurrant mixture with a metal spoon. Whisk the egg whites in a clean, grease-free bowl, and fold in. Make sure that the mixture is thoroughly and evenly blended but do not overmix.

Pour gently into a glass dish, a wetted 500 ml/17 fl oz mould or individual glasses.

Refrigerate for 1-2 hours until set, then turn out if necessary and decorate with whipped cream and the reserved blackcurrants.

SERVES 4

☆ **FREEZER TIP** Frozen blackcurrant mousse is delicious. Omit the gelatine and freeze the mixture in ice trays. Thaw for 15 minutes in the refrigerator before serving.

C HOCOLATE AND ORANGE MOUSSE

100 g/4 oz plain chocolate, grated
60 ml/4 tbsp fresh orange juice
10 ml/2 tsp gelatine
3 eggs, separated
vanilla essence
100 ml/3½ fl oz double cream

DECORATION
  whipped cream
  grated chocolate

Put the grated chocolate into a large heat-proof bowl with the orange juice. Sprinkle the gelatine on to the liquid. Stand the bowl over a saucepan of simmering water until the chocolate melts and the gelatine dissolves. Remove from the heat and stir until smooth.

Beat the egg yolks into the chocolate mixture with a few drops of vanilla essence. Whip the cream in a separate bowl until it just holds its shape, then fold into the mixture.

Finally, in a clean, grease-free bowl, whisk the egg whites until fairly stiff, then fold gently into the chocolate mixture until evenly blended. Pour into a wetted 750 ml/

1¼ pint mould or deep serving bowl and refrigerate for about 2 hours until set.

Turn out, if necessary, and decorate with whipped cream and coarsely grated chocolate.

SERVES 4

☀ **MICROWAVE TIP** Dissolve the chocolate and gelatine in the orange juice in a suitable bowl on High for 2-3 minutes.

C HOCOLATE MARQUISE

150 g/5 oz plain chocolate, coarsely grated
200 g/7 oz unsalted butter, cubed
6 eggs, separated

Put the chocolate into a large heatproof bowl and place over hot water. Heat gently until the chocolate melts.

Gradually beat the butter into the chocolate, a piece at a time. Stir in the egg yolks, one by one. When all have been added and the mixture is smooth, remove the bowl from the heat.

In a clean, grease-free bowl, whisk the egg whites until stiff. Fold them into the chocolate mixture. Pour gently into a glass bowl or 6 individual dishes and chill thoroughly before serving.

SERVES 6

☀ **MICROWAVE TIP** Melt the chocolate in a small bowl on High for 2½-3 minutes.

C HOCOLATE DREAM

Illustrated on page 259

fat for greasing
100 g/4 oz plain chocolate
400 ml/14 fl oz milk
50 g/2 oz caster sugar
50 g/2 oz plain flour
15 ml/1 tbsp butter
3 whole eggs, separated, plus 1 egg white
icing sugar for dusting

Prepare a 1.1 litre/2 pint soufflé dish. Set the oven at 180°C/350°F/gas 4.

Break the chocolate into pieces and put into a saucepan. Reserve 60 ml/4 tbsp of the milk in a mixing bowl and pour the rest into the pan with the chocolate. Add the sugar and warm over low heat until the chocolate begins to melt. Remove from the heat and leave to stand until the chocolate is completely melted, stirring occasionally.

Add the flour to the bowl containing the milk and stir to a smooth paste. Stir in the chocolate-flavoured milk, return the mixture to the clean pan and bring to the boil. Cook for 1-2 minutes, stirring all the time, then remove from the heat and add the butter. Stir well, then set aside to cool slightly.

Beat the egg yolks into the chocolate mixture one at a time. In a clean, grease-free bowl, whisk the egg whites until stiff. Stir one spoonful of the egg whites into the chocolate mixture to lighten it, then fold in the rest until evenly blended.

Spoon into the prepared dish and bake for 45 minutes. Dust with icing sugar and serve immediately, with Mocha Sauce (page 400) or Chocolate Cream Sauce (page 400).

SERVES 4

S EMOLINA SOUFFLÉ

Banish all thoughts of semolina as something thick and porridge-like. This soufflé is light and lovely.

fat for greasing
pared rind of ½ lemon
400 ml/14 fl oz milk
50 g/2 oz semolina
50 g/2 oz caster sugar
3 eggs, separated

Prepare a 1 litre/1¾ pint soufflé dish. Set the oven at 180°C/350°F/gas 4.

Combine the lemon rind and milk in a saucepan and bring to the boil. Immediately remove from the heat and leave to stand for 10 minutes. Remove the rind and sprinkle in the semolina. Cook for 2-3 minutes, stirring all the time, until the semolina mixture thickens. Stir in the sugar and leave to cool.

Beat the egg yolks into the semolina mixture one by one. In a clean, grease-free bowl, whisk the egg whites until stiff, and fold into the semolina mixture.

Put into the prepared dish and bake for 45 minutes. Serve at once, with Apricot Sauce (page 398) or Redcurrant Sauce (page 393).

SERVES 4

**Apricot and Almond Pudding (page 338) with a jug of Apricot Sauce (page 398)
and Washington Ripple (page 338) with Vanilla Custard (page 403)**

Chocolate Crumb Pudding (page 340) with Chocolate Cream Sauce (page 400)

Blackberry and Apple Pie (page 351)

A slice of Mille Feuille Gâteau (page 367) and Profiteroles (page 374)

Apple Strudel (page 377)

Nutty Plum Crumble (page 381)

Eve's Pudding (page 382)

**College Puddings (page 389) with Rich Lemon Sauce (page 395) and
Baked Jam Roll (page 391) with Vanilla Custard (page 403)**

COEUR À LA CRÈME AU CITRON

150 ml/¼ pint double cream
pinch of salt
150 g/5 oz low-fat curd cheese
50 g/2 oz caster sugar
grated rind and juice of 1 lemon
2 egg whites

Line a 400 ml/14 fl oz heart-shaped coeur à la crème mould with greaseproof paper. In a bowl whip the cream with the salt until it holds soft peaks. Break up the curd cheese with a fork, and whisk it gradually into the cream with the sugar. Do not let the mixture lose stiffness.

Fold the lemon rind and juice into the cream as lightly as possible.

In a clean, grease-free bowl, whisk the egg whites until they hold stiff peaks. Fold them into the mixture, then very gently turn the mixture into the mould, filling all the corners.

Stand the mould in a large dish or roasting tin to catch the liquid which seeps from the mixture. Chill for at least 2 hours or overnight. Turn out and serve with single cream.

SERVES 6

MRS BEETON'S TIP Individual coeur à la crème moulds may be used. If these are unavailable, clean yogurt pots, with several drainage holes punched in the base of each, make an acceptable substitute.

COCONUT CREAM PIE

PIE SHELL
100 g/4 oz digestive biscuits
50 g/2 oz butter
25 g/1 oz sugar

FILLING
40 g/1½ oz cornflour
pinch of salt
40 g/1½ oz caster sugar
300 ml/½ pint milk
1 egg yolk
25 g/1 oz butter
few drops of vanilla essence
75 g/3 oz desiccated coconut

Make the pie shell. Place the biscuits between two sheets of greaseproof paper (or in a paper or polythene bag) and crush finely with a rolling pin.

Melt the butter in a small saucepan and mix in the crumbs and sugar. Press the mixture in an even layer all over the base and sides of a shallow 18 cm/7 inch pie plate. Put in a cool place until the shell has set.

Make the filling. Put the cornflour, salt and sugar in a bowl and stir in enough of the milk to make a smooth cream. Bring the rest of the milk to the boil in a saucepan. Pour it on to the cornflour mixture, stirring constantly, then return the mixture to the pan.

Bring the filling to the boil again, stirring constantly. Cook, still stirring vigorously, for 1-2 minutes, until the sauce thickens. Beat in the egg yolk, butter, vanilla essence and coconut.

Cool the filling until tepid, then spoon into the pie shell. When cold, refrigerate for 1-2 hours before serving.

SERVES 4

COFFEE MOUSSE

250 ml/8 fl oz milk
15 ml/1 tbsp instant coffee
2 eggs, separated
50 g/2 oz caster sugar
10 ml/2 tsp gelatine
75 ml/5 tbsp double cream

DECORATION
  whipped cream
  Praline (see Mrs Beeton's Tip, page 248),
    crushed

In a saucepan, warm the milk and stir in the coffee. Set aside. Put the egg yolks into a bowl with the caster sugar and mix well, then gradually add the flavoured milk, Strain through a sieve back into the saucepan. Stir over very gentle heat for about 10 minutes until the custard starts to thicken. Cool slightly.

Place 30 ml/2 tbsp water in a small heat-proof bowl. Sprinkle the gelatine on to the liquid. Stand the bowl over a saucepan of hot water and stir the gelatine until it has dissolved completely. Cool until the gelatine mixture is at the same temperature as the custard, then mix a little of the custard into the gelatine. Stir back into the bowl of custard and leave in a cool place until beginning to set.

Whip the cream in a deep bowl until it just holds its shape. In a separate, grease-free bowl, whisk the egg whites until stiff. Fold first the cream, and then the egg whites, into the coffee custard, making sure the mixture is fully blended but not over-mixed.

Pour into a wetted 500 ml/17 fl oz mould or glass dish and refrigerate for 1-2 hours until set. Turn out, if necessary, and decorate with whipped cream and crushed praline.

SERVES 4

VARIATIONS

In each of the variations that follow, omit the instant coffee.

CARAMEL MOUSSE Before making the mousse mixture, warm 100 g/4 oz granulated sugar and 15 ml/1 tbsp water in a heavy-bottomed saucepan. Stir until the sugar dissolves. Continue heating until the syrup turns a rich brown colour. Remove from the heat and carefully add 60 ml/4 tbsp hot water, stirring quickly until all the caramel has dissolved. Cool. Add 200 ml/7 fl oz milk to the caramel and heat this with the egg yolks to make the custard for the mousse.

ORANGE PRALINE MOUSSE Before making the mousse mixture, make and crush 100 g/4 oz Praline (see Mrs Beeton's Tip, page 248). Add the finely grated rind of an orange to the custard, and use the juice to dissolve the gelatine. Fold half the crushed praline into the completed mousse mixture, and use the rest to decorate the top.

LEMON CHIFFON

Illustrated on page 260

3 eggs, separated
150 g/5 oz caster sugar
125 ml/4 fl oz lemon juice
10 ml/2 tsp gelatine
grated rind of 2 lemons

Combine the egg yolks, sugar and lemon juice in a heatproof bowl. Stand over a saucepan of gently simmering water and whisk the mixture until frothy, pale and the consistency of single cream. Remove from the heat.

Place 45 ml/3 tbsp water in a small heat-proof bowl. Sprinkle the gelatine on to the liquid. Stand the bowl over a saucepan of hot water and stir the gelatine until it has dissolved completely. Cool for 5 minutes.

Whisk the gelatine into the egg yolk mixture. Cool the mixture, then refrigerate until beginning to set. Stir in the lemon rind.

In a clean, grease-free bowl, whisk the egg whites until stiff. Fold into the lemon mixture. Spoon into 4 glasses and return to the refrigerator until completely set.

SERVES 4

*M*ANGO MOUSSE

1 kg/2¼ lb ripe mangoes
90 ml/6 tbsp fresh lime juice
100 g/3½ oz caster sugar
15 ml/1 tbsp gelatine
2 egg whites
pinch of salt
100 ml/3½ fl oz double cream
15 ml/1 tbsp light rum

Peel the fruit and cut the flesh off the stones. Purée with the lime juice in a blender or food processor (see Mrs Beeton's Tip). When smooth, blend in the sugar, then scrape the mixture into a bowl with a rubber spatula.

Place 45 ml/3 tbsp water in a small heatproof bowl. Sprinkle the gelatine on to the liquid. Stand the bowl over a saucepan of hot water and stir the gelatine until it has dissolved completely. Cool slightly, then stir into the mango purée.

In a clean, grease-free bowl, whisk the egg whites with the salt until they form fairly stiff peaks. Stir 15 ml/1 tbsp of the egg whites into the purée to lighten it, then fold in the rest.

Lightly whip the cream and rum together

in a separate bowl, then fold into the mango mixture as lightly as possible. Spoon into a serving bowl. Refrigerate for about 3 hours until set.

SERVES 6-8

MRS BEETON'S TIP If you do not have a blender or food processor, press the mango flesh through a sieve into a bowl and stir in the lime juice and sugar.

---

*M*APLE MOUSSE

It is important that genuine maple syrup be used for this dessert. If maple-flavoured syrup is used, gelatine will have to be added to set the mousse.

200 ml/7 fl oz pure maple syrup
4 egg yolks
200 ml/7 fl oz whipping cream

Pour the maple syrup into a saucepan. Beat the egg yolks lightly in a bowl, then stir them into the syrup. Cook over very low heat, stirring all the time with a wooden spoon until the mixture thickens enough to thinly coat the back of the spoon.

Remove from the heat and leave to cool, covered with dampened greaseproof paper. Stir once or twice during cooling. When the maple syrup mixture is cold, cover and refrigerate until required.

Just before serving, whip the cream in a deep bowl to the same consistency as the maple custard. Fold the cream gently into the maple custard, then chill again until required.

SERVES 4

PEPPERMINT CREAM PIE

Decorate this delectable pie with crushed peppermint crisp for a party or similar special occasion.

PIE SHELL
  100 g/4 oz gingernut biscuits
  50 g/2 oz plain chocolate
  50 g/2 oz butter

FILLING
  2 egg yolks
  75 g/3 oz caster sugar
  few drops of peppermint essence
  10 ml/2 tsp gelatine
  125 ml/4 fl oz double cream

Make the pie shell. Place the biscuits between two sheets of greaseproof paper (or in a stout polythene bag) and crush finely with a rolling pin. Alternatively, crumb the biscuits in a food processor.

Melt the chocolate and butter in a heat-proof bowl over gently simmering water. Stir in the crumbs thoroughly. Press the mixture in an even layer all over the base and sides of a shallow 18 cm/7 inch pie plate. Put in a cool place until the shell has set.

Make the filling. Combine the egg yolks and sugar in a heatproof bowl. Stir in 45 ml/3 tbsp cold water and stand the bowl over a saucepan of simmering water. Whisk the mixture until thick and pale, then whisk in the peppermint essence (see Mrs Beeton's Tip).

Place 30 ml/2 tbsp water in a small heat-proof bowl. Sprinkle the gelatine on to the liquid. Stand the bowl over a saucepan of hot water and stir the gelatine until it has dissolved completely. Cool for 5 minutes, then whisk into the peppermint mixture.

In a bowl, whisk the cream lightly. Fold it into the peppermint mixture. Turn into the chocolate crumb shell and refrigerate for about 1 hour until set.

SERVES 4

MRS BEETON'S TIP Peppermint essence is very strong, so use sparingly. The best way to do this is to use a toothpick or thin wooden skewer. Dip the toothpick into the essence, then add just one drop at a time to the mixture.

COFFEE CHIFFON PIE

PIE SHELL
  75 g/3 oz digestive biscuits
  50 g/2 oz butter
  25 g/1 oz walnuts, chopped
  25 g/1 oz sugar

FILLING
  100 g/4 oz caster sugar
  10 ml/2 tsp gelatine
  15 ml/1 tbsp instant coffee
  2 eggs, separated
  pinch of salt
  10 ml/2 tsp lemon juice
  whipped cream to decorate

Make the pie shell. Place the biscuits between two sheets of greaseproof paper (or in a paper bag) and crush finely with a rolling pin. Alternatively, crumb the biscuits in a food processor.

Melt the butter in a small saucepan and mix in the crumbs, chopped nuts and sugar. Press the mixture in an even layer all over the base and sides of a shallow 18 cm/7 inch pie plate. Put in a cool place until set.

To make the filling, mix 50 g/2 oz of the sugar with the gelatine in a cup. Put the coffee into a measuring jug, add 45 ml/ 3 tbsp boiling water, and stir until dissolved. Make up the liquid with cold water to 250 ml/8 fl oz.

Pour the coffee liquid into a heatproof bowl or the top of a double saucepan. Add the egg yolks, mix well, then place over gently simmering water. Stir in the gelatine mixture, with a pinch of salt. Cook over gentle heat for about 15 minutes, stirring constantly until the custard thickens slightly. Do not let the mixture boil. Pour into a cold bowl, cover with dampened greaseproof paper and chill until on the point of setting, then stir in the lemon juice.

In a clean, grease-free bowl, whisk the egg whites until foamy. Gradually whisk in the remaining sugar and continue whisking until stiff and glossy. Fold the coffee custard into the meringue, pour into the pie shell and chill for at least 1 hour until set. Serve decorated with whipped cream.

SERVES 4

S HERRY CREAM PIE

PIE SHELL
　　150 g/5 oz plain chocolate digestive
　　　　biscuits
　　50 g/2 oz butter

FILLING
　　125 ml/4 fl oz milk
　　2 eggs, separated
　　50 g/2 oz sugar
　　10 ml/2 tsp gelatine
　　30 ml/2 tbsp medium dry or sweet sherry
　　grated nutmeg
　　125 ml/4 fl oz double cream

Make the pie shell. Place the biscuits between two sheets of greaseproof paper

(or in a paper or polythene bag) and crush finely with a rolling pin.

Melt the butter in a small saucepan and mix in the crumbs. Press the mixture in an even layer all over the base and sides of a shallow 18 cm/7 inch pie plate. Put in a cool place until the shell has set.

To make the filling, warm the milk in a saucepan but do not let it boil. Beat the egg yolks with the sugar in a bowl, then lightly stir in the hot milk. Strain the custard into the clean pan or the top of a double saucepan. Cook over low heat, stirring, for about 15 minutes, until thickened. Do not allow the custard to boil. Cool slightly.

Meanwhile place 30 ml/2 tbsp water in a small heatproof bowl. Sprinkle the gelatine on to the liquid. Stand the bowl over a saucepan of hot water and stir the gelatine until it has dissolved completely. Remove from the heat, stir in a spoonful of the custard, then mix into the rest of the custard. Add the sherry, a little at a time to prevent the custard from curdling. Stir in nutmeg to taste, then cool until just setting.

In a deep bowl, whip the cream to soft peaks, then stir into the custard. Whisk the egg whites in a clean, grease-free bowl until stiff, and fold in. Pour the mixture gently into the pie shell and refrigerate for 1½-2 hours until set.

SERVES 4

> ☀ **MICROWAVE TIP** Dissolve the gelatine in the microwave: stir it into the water, let stand until spongy, then cook on High for 30-45 seconds.

*L*EMON CHIFFON PIE

PIE SHELL
   100 g/4 oz digestive biscuits
   50 g/2 oz butter
   25 g/1 oz sugar

FILLING
   100 g/4 oz caster sugar
   10 ml/2 tsp gelatine
   3 eggs, separated
   grated rind and juice of 2 lemons

Make the pie shell. Place the biscuits between two sheets of greaseproof paper (or in a paper or polythene bag) and crush finely with a rolling pin. Alternatively, crumb the biscuits in a food processor.

Melt the butter in a small saucepan and mix in the crumbs and sugar. Press the mixture in an even layer all over the base and sides of a shallow 18 cm/7 inch pie plate. Put in a cool place until the shell has set.

To make the filling, mix 50 g/2 oz of the caster sugar with the gelatine in a small bowl. Combine the egg yolks, lemon juice and 50 ml/2 fl oz water in a heatproof bowl or the top of a double saucepan. Mix lightly, then stir in the gelatine mixture.

Cook over very gentle heat for 10 minutes, stirring all the time, until the custard thickens. Do not let it boil. Pour into a cold bowl, cover with dampened greaseproof paper and chill until on the point of setting. Stir in the lemon rind.

In a clean, grease-free bowl, whisk the egg whites until foamy. Gradually whisk in the remaining sugar and continue to whisk until stiff and glossy. Fold the lemon custard mixture into the meringue, pile into the pie shell and chill for at least 1 hour until set.

SERVES 4

VARIATIONS

CHOCOLATE ORANGE CHIFFON PIE Make the pie shell using plain chocolate digestive biscuits. Follow the instructions for Orange Chiffon Pie (above).

LIME CHIFFON PIE Make the pie shell. For the filling substitute 3 limes for the lemons. If the limes are very small and not over juicy, add an additional 30 ml/2 tbsp lemon juice.

ORANGE CHIFFON PIE Make the pie shell. For the filling, substitute oranges for the lemons, but use the grated rind of a single fruit. Add 15 ml/1 tbsp lemon juice to the orange juice and enough water to make the liquid up to 150 ml/1/4 pint. Use this with the egg yolks, gelatine and 15 ml/1 tbsp sugar, to make a custard. When whisking the egg whites, add only 40 g/1½ oz sugar.

RICE PUDDINGS

Milk puddings are as versatile as the occasions on which they may be served are varied. You will find recipes ranging from an inexpensive, nutritious weekday pudding to a splendid fruity concoction for special occasions.

Plain milk puddings fit very well into a day-to-day diet as they are inexpensive, satisfying and nutritious. Remember that you may always use semi-skimmed or skimmed milk if you are following a low-fat diet. Although white rice is the traditional ingredient for making puddings, brown rice may be used to provide a certain amount of fibre. Between the supermarkets, ethnic shops and healthfood stores we are provided with many different types of rice, not all of which is suitable for making puddings.

TYPES OF RICE

In the first edition of her *Book of Household Management*, Mrs Beeton advises the reader on the choice of rice for making a boiled rice pudding:

'Of the varieties of rice brought to our market, that from Bengal is chiefly of the species denominated cargo rice, and is of a coarse reddish-brown cast, but peculiarly sweet and large-grained; it does not readily separate from the husk, but it is preferred by the natives to all the others. Patna rice is more esteemed in Europe, and is of very superior quality; it is small-grained, rather long and wiry, and is remarkably white. The Carolina rice is considered as the best, and is likewise the dearest in London.'

Modern supermarkets stock several varieties of rice and the choice is widened by others sold in healthfood shops and ethnic stores. Brown rice, wild rice, Basmati rice, Italian risotto rice, easy-cook rice, long-grain rice, round-grain rice, pudding rice and flaked rice are all readily available and they all have different characteristics. The greater interest in savoury dishes using rice, and the different grains that may be used for them, has detracted attention from pudding rice. The Carolina rice that Mrs Beeton favoured is still the most common type of polished, unprocessed white rice although it is now grown in other parts of America as well as Carolina. Varieties of rice that are popular for savoury dishes are not necessarily suitable for making puddings. Unprocessed long-grain rice, Patna rice, pudding rice or flaked rice should be used. Short-grain or round-grain are other terms for pudding rice and you will find brown types as well as polished rice.

Processed, or easy-cook, rice is not suitable for making puddings as the grains do not break down to give a creamy result.

Other popular ingredients used to make milk puddings include semolina, macaroni, tapioca or sago.

Baked milk puddings are easy to prepare but they require slow cooking. For a creamy result stir in the skin which forms on the top of the pudding after the first two-thirds of the cooking time has elapsed.

PRESSURE COOKING

Milk puddings may be cooked in a pressure cooker. This gives good, creamy results in a fraction of the time needed for baking or simmering. Do not use less than 600 ml/ 1 pint of milk and keep the heat at a steady temperature which is low enough to prevent the milk from rising too high in the cooker and blocking the vent. For the same reason the cooker should not be more than a quarter full when cooking a milk pudding. General guidance on the types of pressure cookers available and their use is given in the section on equipment (page 25).

MICROWAVE COOKING

The microwave oven may be used to cook milk puddings. Semolina cooks particularly well; however puddings using rice, tapioca, macaroni or semolina boil over very readily. For this reason a medium or low microwave power setting should be used and the pudding should be cooked in a very large dish – a mixing bowl covered with a suitable dinner plate or very deep casserole dish is ideal. The advantage of cooking milk puddings thickened with rice in the microwave is open to personal opinion. Since a low power setting has to be used the time saving is not enormous and this cooking method demands attention to ensure that the pudding does not boil over. As an alternative to traditional recipes, the following is an excellent microwave method for making an extravagant, deliciously creamy rice pudding.

Put 50 g/2 oz short-grain rice in a covered dish. Add 600 ml/1 pint water and cook on High for 20-25 minutes. At the end of the cooking time all the water should have been absorbed and the grains of rice should be swollen and sticky. Immediately stir in sugar to taste and 300 ml/½ pint double or single cream. The pudding may be transferred to a flameproof dish, dotted with butter and sprinkled with a little grated nutmeg, then lightly browned under a moderate grill.

*R*ICE PUDDING

This basic recipe works equally well with flaked rice, sago or flaked tapioca.

butter for greasing
100 g/4 oz pudding rice
1 litre/1¾ pints milk
pinch of salt
50-75 g/2-3 oz caster sugar
15 g/½ oz butter (optional)
1.25 ml/¼ tsp grated nutmeg

Butter a 1.75 litre/3 pint pie dish. Wash the rice in cold water, drain and put it into the dish with the milk. Leave to stand for 30 minutes.

Set the oven at 150°C/300°F/gas 2. Stir the salt and sugar into the milk mixture and sprinkle with flakes of butter, if used, and nutmeg.

Bake for 2-2½ hours or until the pudding is thick and creamy, and brown on the top. The pudding is better if it cooks even more slowly, at 120°C/250°F/gas ½ for 4-5 hours.

SERVES 4 TO 5

> **PRESSURE COOKER TIP** Bring all the ingredients to the boil in the open cooker, stirring. Reduce the heat so that the milk just bubbles. Put the lid on and bring to 15 lb pressure without increasing the heat. Cook for 12 minutes. Reduce pressure slowly.

RICE PUDDING WITH EGGS

Any suitable large grain may be used instead of pudding rice.

butter for greasing
100 g/4 oz pudding rice
1 litre/1¾ pints milk
2-3 eggs, separated
pinch of salt
50-75 g/2-3 oz caster sugar
1.25 ml/¼ tsp grated nutmeg

Butter a 1.75 litre/3 pint pie dish. Wash the rice in cold water, drain and put it into the top of a double saucepan with the milk. Cook slowly for about 1 hour, or until the grain is tender. Remove from the heat and leave to cool slightly.

Set the oven at 160°C/325°F/gas 3. Stir the egg yolks, salt, sugar and nutmeg into the rice mixture.

In a clean, grease-free bowl, whisk the egg whites to the same consistency as the pudding. Fold the egg whites into the mixture. Pour into the pie dish and bake for 40-45 minutes until creamy and browned.

SERVES 6

SEMOLINA PUDDING

Use coarsely ground rice, oatmeal, small sago or cornmeal instead of semolina, if preferred.

1 litre/1¾ pints milk
flavouring (see Mrs Beeton's Tip)
75 g/3 oz semolina
pinch of salt
50-75 g/2-3 oz caster sugar
butter for greasing (optional)

Warm the milk in a heavy-bottomed saucepan. Add any solid flavouring, if used, to the milk and infuse for about 10 minutes; then remove.

Sprinkle the semolina on to the milk, stirring quickly to prevent the formation of lumps. Bring to simmering point, stirring all the time. Continue stirring, and simmer for 15-20 minutes or until the grain is transparent and cooked through.

Stir in the salt, sugar, and any flavouring essence used. Serve the creamed semolina hot or cold or pour into a well-buttered 1.75 litre/3 pint pie dish, and bake at 180°C/350°F/gas 4, for 20-30 minutes until the top has browned.

SERVES 6

VARIATION

SEMOLINA PUDDING WITH EGGS
Cook the semolina as above, but do not add the flavouring or the salt. Leave to cool slightly. Separate 2-4 eggs. Stir the egg yolks, salt, sugar, and any flavourings into the semolina mixture. Whisk the egg whites to the same consistency as the pudding, and fold into the mixture. Pour into a well-buttered 1.75 litre/3 pint pie dish, and bake at 160°C/325°F/gas 3, for about 30 minutes until the top has browned. Sprinkle with brown sugar and/or butter flakes before baking, if liked.

MRS BEETON'S TIP Grated citrus rind, ground cinnamon, allspice or grated nutmeg may be added to the above puddings. Flavouring essences or liqueurs are equally suitable. A pinch of salt improves the flavour of all puddings.

CHOCOLATE SEMOLINA

800 ml/1⅓ pints milk
65 g/2½ oz semolina
75 g/3 oz plain chocolate
50 g/2 oz caster sugar
few drops of vanilla essence

Heat 750 ml/1¼ pints of the milk in a heavy-bottomed saucepan. Sprinkle in the semolina, stir well, and simmer for 15-20 minutes or until the semolina is cooked.

Meanwhile, grate the chocolate into a second saucepan, add the remaining milk and heat until the chocolate has melted. Stir into the semolina with the sugar and essence, and serve at once.

SERVES 4-5

BLANCMANGE MOULD

Blancmange may be made using ground rice or arrowroot instead of the cornflour given below. The quantities will be the same. Traditionally, blancmange was a white mould which was flavoured with sweet and bitter almonds. Use natural almond essence to give this mould the best flavour.

75 g/3 oz cornflour
1 litre/1¾ pints milk
50 g/2 oz sugar
a little almond essence

In a bowl, blend the cornflour to a smooth paste with a little of the cold milk. Bring the remaining milk to the boil.

Pour the boiling milk on to the cornflour mixture, stirring all the time. Pour the mixture back into the saucepan and heat gently, stirring all the time until the mixture thickens and simmers. Allow to simmer for 5-10 minutes, stirring occasionally.

Remove the pan from the heat and stir in the sugar. Add almond essence to taste, stir well, then pour the blancmange into a wetted 1.1 litre/2 pint mould. Press dampened greaseproof paper or microwave cooking film on to the surface of the blancmange and leave to cool.

Chill the cooled blancmange for at least 2 hours, or until set. Unmould the blancmange just before serving.

SERVES 6

> **MRS BEETON'S TIP** If arrowroot is used instead of cornflour, the pan should be removed from the heat as soon as the mixture has reached a full boil. If arrowroot is cooked for any length of time after boiling, it tends to thin down.

FLAVOURINGS

To keep the mould a creamy colour, vanilla, grated lemon rind or a good knob of butter with 125 ml/4 fl oz sherry may be added instead of the almond essence. However, the mixture may also be flavoured with ingredients that add colour although the result is not strictly a blancmange.

CHOCOLATE Either add 30 ml/2 tbsp cocoa to the cornflour and mix it to a paste or add 175 g/6 oz plain chocolate, broken into squares, to the cooked mixture. Stir the mixture until the chocolate has melted before pouring it into the mould.

COFFEE Dissolve 15 ml/1 tbsp instant coffee in 15 ml/1 tbsp boiling water, then stir in 30 ml/2 tbsp rum. Stir this essence into the cooked mixture.

STRAWBERRY Substitute 300 ml/½ pint fresh strawberry purée for the same volume of milk, adding it to the cornflour mixture before stirring in the boiling milk.

ARROWROOT PUDDING

The method below is suitable for all powdered grains, including cornflour, custard powder, finely ground rice or fine oatmeal.

1 litre/1¾ pints milk
flavouring (see Blancmange Mould,
    page 298)
65 g/2½ oz arrowroot
pinch of salt
50-75 g/2-3 oz caster sugar
butter for greasing (optional)

Warm the milk in a heavy-bottomed saucepan. Add any solid flavouring, if used, to the milk and infuse for 30 minutes; then remove.

Put the arrowroot in a bowl and blend with a little of the milk. In a saucepan bring the rest of the milk to boiling point with the salt, and pour on to the blended paste, stirring briskly to prevent the formation of lumps.

Return the mixture to the clean saucepan, heat until it thickens, and simmer for 2-3 minutes to cook the grain completely, stirring all the time. Add the sugar and any liquid flavouring used.

Serve the arrowroot pudding as it is, hot or cold or pour into a well-buttered 1.75 litre/3 pint pie dish, and bake for 20-30 minutes at 180°C/350°F/gas 4 until the top has browned.

SERVES 6

GENEVA PUDDING

butter for greasing
75 g/3 oz long-grain rice
750 ml/1¼ pints milk
pinch of salt
75 g/3 oz caster sugar
1 kg/2¼ lb cooking apples
50 g/2 oz butter
1.25 ml/¼ tsp ground cinnamon

Butter a 1.5 litre/2¾ pint pie dish. Wash the rice and put it into a saucepan with the milk. Add the salt and simmer for about 1 hour or until tender.

Set the oven at 180°C/350°F/gas 4. Stir 25 g/1 oz of the sugar into the rice mixture. Set aside.

Peel, core, and chop the apples. Put them into a second saucepan with the butter and cinnamon. Add 45 ml/3 tbsp water. Simmer gently until soft, then purée in a blender or food processor or push through a sieve. Stir in the rest of the sugar.

Arrange the rice and apple in alternate layers in the pie dish, with rice on the top and bottom. Bake for 20-30 minutes.

SERVES 6

CARAMEL RICE PUDDING

125 g/4½ oz long-grain rice
750 ml/1¼ pints milk
pinch of salt
75 g/3 oz lump sugar
2 eggs, beaten
40 g/1½ oz caster sugar

Wash the rice, drain thoroughly and put into a saucepan with the milk and salt. Simmer for about 1 hour or until the rice is soft and all the milk has been absorbed.

Meanwhile prepare a 1 litre/1¾ pint charlotte mould to receive a caramel coating (see Mrs Beeton's Tip). Prepare a steamer or half fill a large saucepan with water and bring to the boil.

Make the caramel by heating the lump sugar with 75 ml/5 tbsp water in a heavy-bottomed saucepan. Stir constantly until the sugar dissolves and the mixture comes to the boil. Continue to boil, without stirring, until the mixture is golden brown. Immediately pour the caramel into the warmed mould, twisting and turning it until the sides and the base are evenly coated. Leave to harden for a few minutes.

Stir the beaten eggs into the cooked rice with the caster sugar. Turn into the caramel-coated mould, cover with greased greaseproof paper or foil and secure with string.

Put the pudding in the perforated part of the steamer, or stand it on an old saucer or plate in the saucepan of boiling water. The water should come halfway up the sides of the basin. Cover the pan tightly and steam the pudding over gently simmering water for 1 hour or until firm.

Serve from the basin or turn out on to a serving plate. Serve hot or cold, with Caramel Custard Sauce (page 394), if liked.

SERVES 6

> **MRS BEETON'S TIP** Hot caramel can cause a nasty burn if it accidentally splashes on to exposed skin. The best way to safeguard yourself is by using a newspaper holder: Prepare a thickly folded band of newspaper long enough to encirle the chosen mould. Heat the mould in boiling water or in the oven, then wrap the newspaper around it, twisting the ends tightly to form a handle. Make sure that the band of paper is secure and that the ends are tightly twisted to prevent the mould from slipping. Hold the paper, not the side of the mould, when tilting it to distribute the caramel, and, as an additional safeguard, work over the sink.

LEMON RICE

Illustrated on page 261

A meringue topping gives this simple pudding a touch of class.

butter for greasing
50 g/2 oz long-grain rice
500 ml/17 fl oz milk
pinch of salt
pared rind and juice of 1 lemon
75 g/3 oz granulated sugar
2 eggs, separated
45 ml/3 tbsp smooth seedless jam
50 g/2 oz caster sugar
caster sugar for dredging

Butter a 1 litre/1¾ pint pie dish. Set the oven at 160°C/325°F/gas 3. Wash the rice and put it in a double saucepan with the milk, salt and lemon rind; simmer for about 1 hour or until tender. Remove the rind and stir in the granulated sugar. Cool slightly.

Stir the egg yolks and lemon juice into the rice. Pour into the pie dish and bake for 20-25 minutes. Lower the oven temperature to 140°C/275°F/gas 1.

Spread the jam on top of the pudding. In a clean, grease-free bowl, whisk the egg whites until stiff, and fold in the caster sugar. Pile on top of the pudding, dredge with a little extra caster sugar, and return to the oven. Bake for 20-30 minutes until the meringue is set and coloured.

SERVES 6

WINDSOR PUDDING

butter for greasing
40 g/1½ oz long-grain rice
350 ml/12 fl oz milk
450 g/1 lb cooking apples
grated rind of ½ lemon
50 g/2 oz caster sugar
3 egg whites

Butter a 1 litre/1¾ pint pudding basin or soufflé dish. Wash the rice, drain thoroughly

and place in a saucepan with the milk. Simmer for 45 minutes – 1 hour or until the rice is tender and all the milk has been absorbed. Cool slightly.

Peel, core and roughly chop the apples. Stew in a covered, heavy-bottomed saucepan until soft. Shake the pan from time to time to prevent the apples from sticking. Prepare a steamer or half fill a large saucepan with water and bring to the boil.

Purée the apples with the lemon rind in a blender or food processor. Alternatively, rub the apples through a sieve into a bowl, in which case add the grated lemon rind afterwards. Stir in the cooked rice and sugar.

In a clean, grease-free bowl, whisk the egg whites until fairly stiff and stir them into the apple mixture. Spoon the mixture into the prepared pudding basin or soufflé dish, cover with greased greaseproof paper or foil and secure with string.

Put the pudding in the perforated part of the steamer, or stand it on an old saucer or plate in the saucepan of boiling water. The water should come halfway up the sides of the basin. Cover the pan tightly and steam the pudding over gently simmering water for 45 minutes. Serve hot.

SERVES 6

> **MRS BEETON'S TIP** Windsor pudding is very light and it can be difficult to turn out. Placing a small circle on non-stick baking parchment in the bottom of the basin helps. Alternatively, serve the pudding straight from the soufflé dish.

*E*MPRESS PUDDING

butter for greasing
100 g/4 oz long-grain rice
1 litre/1¾ pints milk
pinch of salt
50 g/2 oz butter or margarine
50 g/2 oz caster sugar
200 g/7 oz jam or stewed fruit

SHORT CRUST PASTRY
75 g/3 oz plain flour
pinch of salt
40 g/1½ oz margarine (or half butter, half
    lard)
flour for rolling out

Butter the base of a 1.25 litre/2¼ pint oven-to-table baking dish. Make the pastry. Sift the flour and salt into a bowl, then rub in the margarine until the mixture resembles fine breadcrumbs. Add enough cold water to make a stiff dough. Press the dough together with your fingertips. Set the pastry aside in a cool place while preparing the filling.

Wash the rice, drain and place in a heavy-bottomed saucepan. Add the milk and salt and simmer for about 1 hour or until tender. Stir in the butter or margarine and sugar.

Set the oven at 180°C/350°F/gas 4. Roll out the pastry on a lightly floured surface and line the sides of the baking dish. Spread a layer of the rice mixture on the base of the dish and cover with jam or fruit. Repeat the layers until the dish is full, finishing with a layer of rice. Bake for 25-30 minutes. Serve with Apricot Sauce (page 398).

SERVES 6 TO 7

*P*EAR AND RICE MERINGUE

butter for greasing
75 g/3 oz long-grain rice
750 ml/1¼ pints milk
pinch of salt
1 bay leaf
40 g/1½ oz granulated sugar
25 g/1 oz butter
2 eggs, separated
6 fresh or canned pear halves
50 g/2 oz caster sugar
caster sugar for dredging

Butter a 1.5 litre/2¾ pint pie dish. Wash the rice, drain and place in a heavy-bottomed saucepan with the milk, salt and bay leaf. Simmer for about 1 hour, until the rice is tender. Remove the bay leaf.

Set the oven at 140°C/275°F/gas 1. Stir the granulated sugar and butter into the rice mixture. Cool slightly, then add the egg yolks, mixing well. Pour into the prepared pie dish and arrange the pear halves, cut side down, on top.

In a clean, grease-free bowl, whisk the egg whites until stiff and fold in the caster sugar in spoonfuls. Pile on top of the rice and pears. Dredge the meringue with a little caster sugar and bake for about 20 minutes or until the meringue is crisp and golden brown. Serve at once.

SERVES 6

MRS BEETON'S TIP Bay leaves are a valuable addition to the store cupboard. Although primarily used in stews, stocks and fish dishes, they add a subtle flavour to milk puddings.

S WEDISH RICE

300 g/11 oz long-grain rice
pinch of salt
625 g/1¼ lb cooking apples
pared rind of 1 lemon
375 ml/13 fl oz milk
75 g/3 oz caster sugar
1.25 ml/¼ tsp ground cinnamon
100 ml/3½ fl oz sweet sherry
100 g/4 oz raisins
single cream, to serve

Wash the rice, drain it and put it in a saucepan. Add boiling salted water to cover and cook for 3 minutes; drain well.

Peel and core the apples and slice them thinly into a second pan. Add the rice, lemon rind and milk and simmer gently for about 45 minutes until tender. Remove the rind.

Stir the sugar, cinnamon, sherry, and raisins into the mixture and cook for a further 4-5 minutes. Spoon into individual bowls and serve with cream.

SERVES 6

H ASTY PUDDING

750 ml/1¼ pints milk
65 g/2½ oz semolina or sago or ground
   rice
25 g/1 oz caster sugar

Heat the milk in a heavy-bottomed saucepan to just below boiling point. Sprinkle in the semolina or sago and stir briskly. Lower the heat and simmer for 10-15 minutes until the grain is cooked, and the mixture has thickened. Stir in the sugar.

Serve with cream, jam or golden syrup.

SERVES 6

H ONEY PUDDING

butter for greasing
125 ml/4 fl oz milk
25 g/1 oz semolina
2 eggs, separated
25 g/1 oz butter
100 g/4 oz honey
grated rind of ½ lemon
2.5 ml/½ tsp ground ginger
150 g/5 oz stale white breadcrumbs

Butter a 600-750 ml/1-1¼ pint pudding basin. Prepare a steamer or half fill a large saucepan with water and bring to the boil.

Heat the milk in a heavy-bottomed saucepan. Sprinkle in the semolina and cook for 10 minutes, stirring all the time.

Remove the pan from the heat and add the egg yolks, butter, honey, lemon rind, ginger and breadcrumbs. Beat well.

In a clean, grease-free bowl, whisk the egg whites until fairly stiff. Fold into the semolina mixture. Pour the mixture into the prepared basin, cover with greased greaseproof paper or foil and secure with string.

Put the pudding in the perforated part of the steamer, or stand it on an old saucer or plate in the saucepan of boiling water. The water should come halfway up the sides of the basin. Cover the pan tightly and steam the pudding over gently simmering water for 1¾-2 hours.

Serve from the basin or leave for 5-10 minutes at room temperature to firm up, then turn out on to a serving plate. Serve with Almond Sauce (page 394).

SERVES 5-6

HOT TIMBALE OF SEMOLINA

butter for greasing
500 ml/17 fl oz milk
75 g/3 oz semolina
50 g/2 oz caster sugar
few drops of vanilla essence
2 eggs, separated
30 ml/2 tbsp single cream

DECORATION
1 × 397 g/14 oz can apricot halves in
  syrup
1 strip angelica
3 glacé cherries
10 ml/2 tsp chopped almonds

Butter a 750 ml/1¼ pint timbale mould
or 6 small dariole moulds.

Heat the milk in a heavy-bottomed
saucepan, sprinkle in the semolina, stirring
all the time, and simmer for 10-15 minutes
until it is cooked. Cool slightly.

Stir the sugar and vanilla essence into the
semolina mixture, with the egg yolks. Beat
with an electric or rotary whisk until the
mixture is nearly cold. Prepare a steamer or
half fill a large saucepan with water and
bring to the boil.

In a clean, grease-free bowl, beat the
egg whites until just stiff, and fold into the
semolina mixture with the cream. Three-
quarters fill the timbale mould or small
moulds with the mixture. Cover with
greased greaseproof paper or foil and secure
with string. Put the timbale or dariole
moulds in the perforated part of the steamer
or stand on a large plate in the saucepan of
boiling water. Cover the pan tightly. Steam
the large mould for about 45 minutes and
small moulds for 30 minutes or until set.

Meanwhile, drain the apricots, reserving
250 ml/8 fl oz of the syrup in a small saucepan. Warm the fruit between 2 plates over
a pan of simmering water. Boil the apricot
syrup until well reduced. When the pudding
is cooked and set, turn out on to a hot dish
and decorate with the warmed apricot
halves, the angelica, glacé cherries and
chopped almonds. Pour the syrup around
and serve.

SERVES 6

RUM AND CHOCOLATE SEMOLINA MOULD

500 ml/17 fl oz milk
50 g/2 oz semolina
50 g/2 oz plain chocolate, grated
10 ml/2 tsp gelatine
50 g/2 oz caster sugar
2.5 ml/½ tsp rum

Bring the milk to the boil in a heavy-
bottomed saucepan. Sprinkle in the semolina and cook gently, stirring all the time,
for 15-20 minutes until soft and smooth.
Stir in the grated chocolate and mix well.

Place 30 ml/2 tbsp water in a small bowl
and sprinkle the gelatine on to the liquid.
Stand the bowl over a saucepan of hot water
and stir the gelatine until it has dissolved
completely. Stir the dissolved gelatine into
the semolina mixture with the sugar and
rum.

Leave the mixture to cool, stirring from
time to time. When tepid, pour into a wetted
600 ml/1 pint mould (see Mrs Beeton's Tip,
page 307) and leave for about 2 hours to set.
Turn out to serve.

SERVES 3 TO 4

S HEER KHURMA

Sheer Khurma is an Indian dessert, traditionally prepared at the end of the Ramadan fast. It is quite sweet and delicately spiced with cardamom.

750 ml/1¼ pints milk
1 green cardamom
15 ml/1 tbsp single cream
75 g/3 oz vermicelli
90 ml/6 tbsp sugar
100 g/4 oz desiccated coconut
30 ml/2 tbsp chopped blanched almonds
25 g/1 oz pistachio nuts, blanched,
     skinned and crushed

Put the milk, cardamom and cream into a saucepan and bring to the boil. Reduce the heat as low as possible, and cook until thickened (30-45 minutes), stirring occasionally.

Add the vermicelli to the thickened cream and stir for a few minutes. When the vermicelli is half-cooked, after about 7 minutes, add the sugar and increase the heat to give a rolling boil. Boil for 2 minutes, then reduce the heat to a simmer.

Stir the coconut, almonds and pistachios into the mixture. Simmer over low heat for 30 minutes. Remove the cardamom, pressing out any liquid from it. Serve hot or cold.

SERVES 4 TO 5

MRS BEETON'S TIP Green cardamoms are small, dry oval pods containing a cluster of dark brown or black seeds. The seeds have a strong scent and almost citrus-like flavour. The whole pod is added to this dessert and it yields the flavour of the seeds during cooking.

L OCKSHEN PUDDING

fat for greasing
2.5 ml/½ tsp salt
100 g/4 oz vermicelli
1 egg
40 g/1½ oz caster sugar
1.25 ml/¼ tsp ground cinnamon
40 g/1½ oz margarine, melted
50 g/2 oz sultanas

Grease an ovenproof dish. Set the oven at 200°C/400°F/gas 6. Bring a large saucepan of water to the boil. Add the salt and vermicelli and cook for about 8 minutes until just tender. Drain, rinse the vermicelli under hot water and drain again.

In a large bowl, beat the egg with the sugar and cinnamon. Mix in the vermicelli with the melted margarine.

Spoon half the vermicelli mixture into the prepared dish. Sprinkle with the sultanas and cover with the remaining mixture. Bake for 30 minutes.

SERVES 3 TO 4

TAPIOCA CREAM PUDDING

butter for greasing
75 g/3 oz tapioca
750 ml/1¼ pints milk
pinch of salt
15 g/½ oz butter or margarine
15 ml/1 tbsp caster sugar
1.25 ml/¼ tsp almond essence
3 eggs, separated
75 g/3 oz ratafias or small
    macaroons, crushed

Butter a 1 litre/1¾ pint pie dish. Wash the tapioca, drain and place in a saucepan with the milk and salt. Soak for 1-2 hours.

Heat the tapioca mixture and simmer for about 1 hour until the grain is soft and all the milk has been absorbed. Set the oven at 180°C/350°F/gas 4.

Remove the tapioca mixture from the heat and stir in the butter, sugar and essence. Cool slightly, then stir in the egg yolks. Pour the mixture into the prepared pie dish and bake for 15-20 minutes.

Lower the oven temperature to 140°C/275°F/gas 1. In a clean, grease-free bowl, whisk the egg whites until stiff. Fold in the crushed ratafias or macaroons. Pile on top of the tapioca mixture, return to the oven and bake for 20-30 minutes until the meringue topping is crisp and golden brown. Serve at once.

SERVES 6

AMERICAN INDIAN PUDDING

fat for greasing
750 ml/1¼ pints milk
75 g/3 oz white or yellow cornmeal
100 g/4 oz caster sugar
1.25 ml/¼ tsp ground cinnamon or
    nutmeg
25 g/1 oz butter

Grease a 1 litre/1¾ pint pie dish. Set the oven at 140-150°C/275-300°F/gas 1-2. Bring the milk to the boil in a heavy-bottomed saucepan, then pour in the cornmeal. Cook over gentle heat for 5 minutes, stirring all the time, until thickened.

Remove the saucepan from the heat and stir in the sugar, spice and butter. Pour into the prepared pie dish.

Bake the pudding for 1 hour until browned on top. Serve with maple syrup.

SERVES 4

CORNMEAL PUDDING

fat for greasing
500 ml/17 fl oz milk
75 g/3 oz white or yellow cornmeal
75 g/3 oz caster sugar
50 g/2 oz seedless raisins
grated rind and juice of ½ lemon
2 eggs, beaten

Grease a 750 ml/1¼ pint pie dish. Set the oven at 180°C/350°F/gas 4. Bring the milk to just below boiling point in a heavy-bottomed saucepan. Pour in the cornmeal.

Cook over gentle heat for 5 minutes, stirring all the time, until the mixture thickens. Remove from the heat and stir in the sugar and raisins with the lemon rind and juice. Cool slightly.

Add the beaten eggs to the mixture, transfer to the prepared pie dish and level the top.

Bake for 50-60 minutes until risen and browned on top. Serve with cream or ice cream.

SERVES 4

*O*ATMEAL FLUMMERY

150 g/5 oz fine oatmeal
juice of 1 orange
15 ml/1 tbsp caster sugar or honey

Put the oatmeal in a large bowl. Add 500 ml/17 fl oz water and soak for 24 hours.

Transfer the oatmeal mixture to a large measuring jug. Measure an equal volume of water. Place the oatmeal mixture and measured water in a large bowl, and soak for a further 24 hours.

Strain the mixture through a fine sieve into a heavy-bottomed saucepan, squeezing or pressing the oatmeal to extract as much of the floury liquid as possible. Add the orange juice and sugar or honey.

Stir over gentle heat for 15-20 minutes or until the mixture boils and is very thick. Serve warm.

SERVES 4-6

*C*HILLED RICE MOULD

150 g/5 oz pudding rice
1 litre/1¾ pints milk
75 g/3 oz sugar
vanilla essence to taste
25 g/1 oz butter

Wash the rice in cold water, drain and place in the top of a double saucepan with the milk. Cover the pan and cook the mixture gently over simmering water for 2-2½ hours until the grain is tender and the milk almost absorbed. Stir occasionally to prevent the grain from settling on the bottom of the pan.

Stir the sugar, vanilla and butter into the mixture and pour into a wetted 1 litre/ 1¾ pint mould or basin. Chill until set. Turn out and serve with stewed fruit or jam.

SERVES 4 TO 6

VARIATIONS

CREAMED RICE MOULD Fold 125 ml/4 fl oz single cream into the cooked rice.
ARABIAN NIGHTS Use 15 ml/1 tbsp rose water instead of vanilla essence. Serve with Turkish delight.

MRS BEETON'S TIP To prepare the mould, fill with cold water, tip the water out, then invert the mould for a few seconds to drain any excess.

PANCAKES AND BATTERS

Follow the techniques and recipes in this chapter to toss a perfect pancake for Shrove Tuesday or make a fruity, baked batter pudding for a hearty ending to a simple meal. Fritters and light-as-air waffles are also included.

A batter is made by combining flour with egg and liquid, usually milk or milk and water. Although some savoury batters are a simple combination of flour and liquid, a batter for pancakes and sweet puddings is enriched by the addition of eggs. These also serve to lighten the mixture.

SMOOTH BATTERS

A good batter should be perfectly smooth and light. To achieve this, a whole egg is added to a well in the flour and a little of the milk (or liquid) is poured in. A wooden spoon is used to combine the egg with the milk and the flour is gradually worked in to make a smooth, thick mixture. This mixture should be thoroughly beaten to get rid of any lumps. When the thick batter is perfectly smooth, the remaining liquid is stirred in. The batter should be used immediately for baked puddings.

Alternatively, all the ingredients may be combined in a blender or food processor and processed until smooth.

If the batter is to be used for coating fritters, the eggs are separated. The yolks are combined with the flour and liquid to make a smooth, fairly thick batter. The egg whites are whisked until stiff, then folded into the batter. The batter should be used at once. When fried this type of batter is very crisp and light.

PERFECT PANCAKES

A thin batter should be used for pancakes; it should be allowed to stand for at least 30 minutes so that all the air may escape. The batter may thicken slightly on standing and a little extra liquid may have to be added halfway through making the pancakes.

A good pan is essential for making successful pancakes. A heavy non-stick pan usually gives good results if the base is in good condition. The best pan is a heavy, cast-iron pan that has become well seasoned with years of use. It is a good idea to set aside a pan specifically for pancakes. It is possible to buy a heavy, flat, non-stick pan with a shallow rim for just this purpose.

To prevent the batter sticking, stir in a little cooking oil – about 15 ml/1 tbsp per 600 ml/1 pint of batter is sufficient. The pan should be hot and greased with oil or a mixture of butter and oil in equal proportions. Have a small bowl of oil or melted butter and oil to one side. Spoon a little into the pan and heat it, then pour out the excess and heat the pan again for a few seconds before pouring in the batter.

Use a ladle to pour the batter into the hot pan. Tilt the pan as you pour in the batter to coat the base thinly and evenly. The pan should be hot enough to set the batter immediately. Place the pan over moderate heat until the pancake has completely set and is browned underneath. Check that it is cooked underneath by lifting the edge with a palette knife or slice.

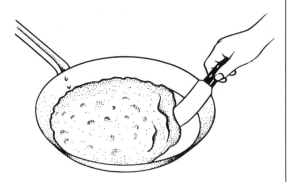

When the base of the pancake has browned and the edges are just beginning to turn crisp, slide a palette knife or slice under it and turn it over. To toss a pancake, first loosen it all around the edge, then give the pan a firm jolt upwards to flip the pancake up and over in one movement. Practice makes perfect!

As the pancakes are cooked, stack them, sprinkling each with a little caster sugar. Absorbent kitchen paper may be layered between the pancakes to prevent them sticking.

FREEZING PANCAKES

Stack cold pancakes on a double thickness of foil, layering freezer film between each one. Pack tightly, label and freeze. They keep for up to 6 months. Individual pancakes thaw quickly; if you want to thaw the whole stack quickly separate them and spread them on a clean board. Keep the pancakes covered while they are thawing. See also individual recipes.

MAKING WAFFLES

Unlike pancake batter, the mixture for waffles is made from self-raising flour. As it cooks and sets, the batter rises in the waffle iron to give a crisp, slightly spongy result.

Batter for making waffles should be the consistency of thick cream and it should be cooked as soon as it is prepared. Serve waffles freshly cooked.

WAFFLE IRONS

To shape the waffles you will need a special utensil known as a waffle iron. This is a hinged metal mould which should be greased and heated over a gas flame or electric ring. Microwave waffle irons are now available. Cordless and easy to use, these give very good results. Plug-in electric waffle cookers are also on sale, usually with non-stick plates that may be removed for easy cleaning. Always follow the manufacturer's instructions when using an electric appliance.

When using a hand-held waffle iron, pour enough batter into one side of the greased mould to cover it. Close the iron and cook the waffle on both sides until it has stopped steaming. Open the iron carefully – if the waffle is cooked it should come away from the metal plate quite easily. If you have to keep waffles hot, place them in a single layer on a wire rack in a low oven. Do not stack them or they will become soggy.

C HERRY ROLL-UPS

150 ml/¼ pint soured cream
1 × 395 g/14 oz can cherry pie filling
15 ml/1 tbsp kirsch

PANCAKES
   100 g/4 oz plain flour
   1.25 ml/¼ tsp salt
   1 egg, beaten
   250 ml/8 fl oz milk, or half milk and half
      water
   oil for frying

Make the pancakes. Sift the flour and salt into a bowl, make a well in the centre and add the beaten egg. Stir in half the milk (or all the milk, if using a mixture of milk and water), gradually working the flour down from the sides.

Beat vigorously until the mixture is smooth and bubbly, then stir in the rest of the milk (or the water). Pour into a jug. The mixture may be left to stand at this stage, in which case it should be covered and stored in the refrigerator.

Heat a little oil in a clean 18 cm/7 inch pancake pan. Pour off any excess oil, leaving the pan covered with a thin film of grease.

Stir the batter and pour about 30–45 ml/ 2–3 tbsp into the pan. There should be just enough to thinly cover the base. Tilt and rotate the pan so that the batter runs over the surface evenly.

Cook over moderate heat for about 1 minute until the pancake is set and golden brown underneath. Make sure the pancake is loose by shaking the pan, then either toss it or turn it with a palette knife or fish slice. Cook the second side for about 30 seconds or until golden.

Slide the pancake out on to a warmed plate. Keep warm over simmering water while making 7 more pancakes in the same way.

Combine the pie filling and kirsch in a saucepan. To serve, spread each pancake with soured cream, roll up and arrange in pairs on 4 individual plates. Top each portion with a spoonful of the cherry mixture. Serve the remaining cherry mixture separately.

SERVES 4

C HOCOLATE PANCAKE PIE

oil for frying
100 g/4 oz plain chocolate
50 g/2 oz icing sugar
whipped cream to serve

PANCAKES
   100 g/4 oz plain flour
   1.25 ml/¼ tsp salt
   1 egg, beaten
   250 ml/8 fl oz milk, or half milk and half
      water
   oil for frying

Make the pancakes. Sift the flour and salt into a bowl, make a well in the centre and add the beaten egg. Stir in half the milk (or all the milk, if using a mixture of milk and water), gradually working the flour down from the sides.

Beat vigorously until the mixture is smooth and bubbly, then stir in the rest of the milk (or the water). Pour into a jug. The mixture may be left to stand at this stage, in which case it should be covered and stored in the refrigerator.

Grate the chocolate into a small bowl. Have the icing sugar ready in a sifter. Heat a little oil in a clean 18 cm/7 inch pancake pan. Pour off any excess oil, leaving the pan covered with a thin film of grease.

Stir the batter and pour about 30–45 ml/ 2–3 tbsp into the pan. There should be just enough to thinly cover the base. Tilt and rotate the pan so that the batter runs over the surface evenly.

Cook over moderate heat for about 1 minute until the pancake is set and golden brown underneath. Make sure the pancake is loose by shaking the pan, then either toss it or turn it with a palette knife or fish slice. Cook the second side for about 30 seconds or until golden.

Slide the pancake out on to a warmed plate. Sprinkle generously with grated chocolate and dredge lightly with icing sugar. Cook a second pancake and stack on top of the first, adding a chocolate and icing topping as before. Continue until 8 pancakes have been made and topped. Dredge the top pancake on the stake with icing sugar only.

To serve, cut in wedges and top with whipped cream.

SERVES 4

MRS BEETON'S TIP The chocolate will be easy to grate if it is first chilled in the refrigerator. Chill the metal grater, too, if liked.

KAISERSCHMARRN

This unusual dessert depends for its success on being cooked and served swiftly. Have everything ready before you start.

75 g/3 oz plain flour
4 eggs, separated
pinch of salt
125 ml/4 fl oz milk
fat or oil for frying
60 ml/4 tbsp caster sugar
10 ml/2 tsp cinnamon

Put the flour into a mixing bowl and make a well in the centre. Mix the egg yolks, salt and half the milk in a jug, then pour into the well in the flour. Gradually work in the flour, then beat vigorously until smooth and bubbly. Stir in the rest of the milk.

In a clean, grease-free bowl, whisk the egg whites until stiff. Beat the batter again and fold in the whites.

Heat a little fat or oil in a large frying pan. Pour off the excess. Pour a quarter of the batter into the pan and fry over moderate heat for about 1 minute until light brown underneath. Turn and cook the other side for about 30 seconds until golden. Slide out on to a plate and, using two forks, tear into 6 or 8 pieces.

Immediately return the pieces to the pan and reheat for 30 seconds, turning the pieces over carefully. Turn on to a sheet of greaseproof paper, add 15 ml/1 tbsp sugar and 2.5 ml/½ tsp cinnamon and toss together. Put on to a warmed plate and keep warm over simmering water.

Cook the rest of the batter in the same way, greasing the pan when necessary. Serve with stewed fruit or jam, if liked.

SERVES 4

APPLE BATTER PUDDING

25 g/1 oz cooking fat
450 g/1 lb cooking apples
50 g/2 oz sugar
grated rind of ½ lemon

BATTER
100 g/4 oz plain flour
1.25 ml/¼ tsp salt
1 egg, beaten
250 ml/8 fl oz milk, or half milk and half
    water

Make the batter. Sift the flour and salt into a bowl, make a well in the centre and add the beaten egg. Stir in half the milk (or all the milk, if using a mixture of milk and water), gradually working in the flour.

Beat vigorously until the mixture is smooth and bubbly, then stir in the rest of the milk (or the water).

Set the oven at 220°C/425°F/gas 7. Put the fat into an 18 × 28 cm/7 × 11 inch baking tin and heat in the oven for 5 minutes.

Meanwhile peel, core and thinly slice the apples. Remove the baking tin from the oven and swiftly arrange the apples on the base. Sprinkle with the sugar and lemon rind. Pour the batter over the top and bake for 30-35 minutes until brown and risen.

Cut into 4 pieces and serve at once, with golden syrup or Rich Lemon Sauce (page 395) if liked.

SERVES 4

VARIATIONS

APRICOT BATTER PUDDING Put 100 g/4 oz dried apricots in a bowl and add water to just cover. Soak until soft, preferably overnight. Transfer the apricots and soaking liquid to a pan and simmer for 15 minutes. Drain. Make the batter as left, heat the fat, and layer the apricots on the base of the baking tin. Proceed as left. Serve with Jam Sauce (page 402), using apricot jam.

DRIED FRUIT BATTER PUDDING Make the batter and heat the fat as left, then spread 50 g/2 oz mixed dried fruit over the base of the tin. Sprinkle with 2.5 ml/½ tsp mixed spice or cinnamon. Proceed as above and serve with St. Clement's Sauce (page 395).

BLACK CAP PUDDING Make the batter as above. Grease 12 deep patty tins and divide 50 g/2 oz currants between them. Pour in enough batter to half fill each tin and bake for 15-20 minutes. Turn out to serve, and pass round Ginger Syrup Sauce (page 402).

EVERYDAY PANCAKES

Illustrated on page 262
Pancakes are much to good to be reserved exclusively for Shrove Tuesday. Simple, versatile, and always popular, they lend themselves to a wide range of fillings, some of which are suggested in the recipes that follow.

100 g/4 oz plain flour
1.25 ml/¼ tsp salt
1 egg, beaten
250 ml/8 fl oz milk, or half milk and half
    water
oil for frying

Make the batter. Sift the flour and salt into a bowl, make a well in the centre and add the beaten egg. Stir in half the milk (or all the milk, if using a mixture of milk and water), gradually working the flour down from the sides.

Beat vigorously until the mixture is

smooth and bubbly, then stir in the rest of the milk (or the water). Pour into a jug. The mixture may be left to stand at this stage, in which case it should be covered and stored in the refrigerator.

Heat a little oil in a clean 18 cm/7 inch pancake pan. Pour off any excess oil, leaving the pan covered with a thin film of grease.

Stir the batter and pour about 30-45 ml/2-3 tbsp into the pan. There should be just enough to thinly cover the base. Tilt and rotate the pan so that the batter runs over the surface evenly.

Cook over moderate heat for about 1 minute until the pancake is set and golden brown underneath. Make sure the pancake is loose by shaking the pan, then either toss it or turn it with a palette knife or fish slice. Cook the second side for about 30 seconds or until golden.

Slide the pancake out on to a warmed plate. Serve at once, with a suitable filling or sauce, or keep warm over simmering water while making 7 more pancakes in the same way. Add more oil to the pan when necessary.

MAKES 8

VARIATIONS

RICH PANCAKES Add 15 g/½ oz cooled melted butter or 15 ml/1 tbsp oil to the batter with 1 egg yolk. Alternatively, enrich the batter by adding 1 whole egg.

CREAM PANCAKES Use 150 ml/¼ pint milk and 50 ml/2 fl oz single cream instead of 250 ml/8 fl oz milk. Add 2 eggs and 25 g/1 oz cooled melted butter, then stir in 15 ml/1 tbsp brandy with caster sugar to taste. The mixture should only just coat the back of a spoon as the pancakes should be very thin.

PANCAKE FILLINGS

Lemon juice and caster sugar share the honours with warmed jam as the most common fillings for pancakes. Here are a few more ideas. Spoon the chosen filling on to the pancakes and roll up. If liked, sprinkle the rolled pancakes with caster sugar, and glaze in a very hot oven or under a hot grill.

APPLE In a bowl, mix together 250 ml/8 fl oz sweetened thick apple purée, 50 g/2 oz sultanas and a pinch of cinnamon.

APRICOT Add 15 ml/1 tbsp cinnamon to the batter when making the pancakes. Soak 50 g/2 oz dried apricots in 60 ml/4 tbsp water in a saucepan, then simmer with 50 g/2 oz sugar and a generous squeeze of lemon juice until soft and pulpy. Add 25 g/1 oz chopped toasted almonds.

BANANA In a bowl, mash 4 bananas with 50 g/2 oz softened butter, 30 ml/2 tbsp sugar and the grated rind and juice of 1 lemon.

CURD CHEESE In a bowl, beat 100 g/4 oz curd cheese with 45 ml/3 tbsp double cream, 30 ml/2 tbsp caster sugar and the grated rind of ½ lemon. Add 40 g/1½ oz sultanas.

DRIED FRUIT Put 100 g/4 oz chopped raisins, dates and cut mixed peel into a small saucepan with 100 ml/3½ fl oz apple juice. Simmer until syrupy.

GINGER AND APPLE Add 15 ml/1 tbsp ground ginger to the batter when making the pancakes, if liked. For the filling, mash 4 bananas in a bowl with 30 ml/2 tbsp double cream. Add a few pieces of chopped preserved ginger.

PINEAPPLE Drain 1 × 227 g/8 oz can crushed pineapple. Combine the fruit with 250 ml/8 fl oz soured cream in a bowl. Fill the pancakes with this mixture and serve with a sauce made by heating the fruit syrup with a few drops of lemon juice.

SURPRISE Spoon ice cream into the centre of each pancake and fold in half like an omelette. Serve with Jam Sauce (page 402) or Melba Sauce (page 398).

FRUIT AND WALNUT PANCAKE BAKE

60 ml/4 tbsp golden syrup
15 ml/1 tbsp lemon juice
50 g/2 oz glacé cherries, chopped
25 g/1 oz sultanas
25 g/1 oz walnuts, chopped
30 ml/2 tbsp demerara sugar
150 ml/¼ pint single cream, to serve

PANCAKES
100 g/4 oz plain flour
1.25 ml/¼ tsp salt
1 egg, beaten
250 ml/8 fl oz milk, or half milk and half water
oil for frying

Make the pancakes. Sift the flour and salt into a bowl, make a well in the centre and add the beaten egg. Stir in half the milk (or all the milk, if using a mixture of milk and water), gradually working the flour down from the sides.

Beat vigorously until the mixture is smooth and bubbly, then stir in the rest of the milk (or the water). Pour into a jug. The mixture may be left to stand at this stage, in which case it should be covered and stored in the refrigerator.

Set the oven at 180°C/350°F/gas 4. Heat a little oil in a clean 18 cm/7 inch pancake pan. Pour off any excess oil, leaving the pan covered with a thin film of grease.

Stir the batter and pour about 30-45 ml/ 2-3 tbsp into the pan. There should be just enough to thinly cover the base. Tilt and rotate the pan so that the batter runs over the surface evenly.

Cook over moderate heat for about 1 minute until the pancake is set and golden brown underneath. Make sure the pancake is loose by shaking the pan, then either toss it or turn it with a palette knife or fish slice. Cook the second side for about 30 seconds or until golden.

Slide the pancake out on to a warmed plate. Make 7 more pancakes in the same way.

Make the filling by combining 45 ml/3 tbsp of the golden syrup with the lemon juice, glacé cherries, sultanas and walnuts. Spoon a little of this mixture on each pancake, roll up and arrange the pancakes side by side in a shallow ovenproof dish. Drizzle with the remaining syrup, sprinkle with demerara sugar and bake for 20 minutes. Serve with the cream.

SERVES 4

PANCAKE STACK

100 g/4 oz curd cheese
1 whole egg, separated, plus 1 egg white
10 ml/2 tsp granulated sugar
grated rind of ½ lemon
45 ml/3 tbsp apricot jam
50 g/2 oz plain chocolate
50 g/2 oz almonds, chopped
100 g/4 oz caster sugar
cream, to serve

PANCAKES
100 g/4 oz plain flour
1.25 ml/¼ tsp salt
1 egg, beaten
250 ml/8 fl oz milk, or half milk and half water
oil for frying

Make the pancakes. Sift the flour and salt into a bowl, make a well in the centre and add the beaten egg. Stir in half the milk (or all the milk, if using a mixture of milk and water), gradually working the flour down from the sides.

Beat vigorously until the mixture is smooth and bubbly, then stir in the rest of the milk (or the water). Pour into a jug. The mixture may be left to stand at this stage, in which case it should be covered and stored in the refrigerator.

Set the oven at 190°C/375°F/gas 5. Heat a little oil in a clean 18 cm/7 inch pancake pan. Pour off any excess oil, leaving the pan covered with a thin film of grease.

Stir the batter and pour about 30-45 ml/ 2-3 tbsp into the pan. There should be just enough to thinly cover the base. Tilt and rotate the pan so that the batter runs over the surface evenly.

Cook over moderate heat for about 1 minute until the pancake is set and golden brown underneath. Make sure the pancake is loose by shaking the pan, then either toss it or turn it with a palette knife or fish slice. Cook the second side for about 30 seconds or until golden.

Slide the pancake out on to a warmed plate. Make 7 more pancakes in the same way, adding more oil to the pan when necessary.

Mix the curd cheese with the egg yolk in a bowl. Stir in the sugar and lemon rind. Warm the jam in a small saucepan. Grate the chocolate into another bowl and add the nuts. In a clean, grease-free bowl, whisk both egg whites until fairly stiff. Whisk in the caster sugar.

Place a pancake in a shallow pie dish and spread with a third of the curd cheese mixture. Top with a second pancake, spread with a third of the jam. Add a third pancake to the stack, this time topping with the chocolate and nut mixture. Repeat the layers until all the fulling has been used, to make a pancake pie topped in jam.

Using a spatula, coat the pancake pie completely in the meringue mixture. Bake for 15-20 minutes, until the meringue is crisp and lightly brown. To serve, cut in wedges and top with cream.

SERVES 4 TO 6

C RÊPES AU CHOIX

8 Cream Pancakes (see page 313)

TOPPINGS
   lightly whipped cream
   thick custard mixed with single cream
   Rich Lemon Sauce (page 395)
   Melba Sauce (page 398)
   smooth fruit purée

DECORATIONS AND FLAVOURINGS
   finely chopped nuts
   sweet biscuit crumbs
   Praline (see Mrs Beeton's Tip, page 248)
   grated chocolate
   3 miniature bottles of any suitable liqueur
   finely chopped glacé cherries
   mixed peel
   strained orange or lemon juice
   caster sugar

Make the pancakes in advance and re-heat just before bringing to the table. Make the toppings, pouring them into jugs or serving them in small heatproof bowls. If possible, keep the pancakes and hot fillings warm over a hot tray on the table. Guests help themselves to pancakes and add the fillings and toppings of their choice.

SERVES 4

BAKED BATTER PUDDING

The batter that is the basis of Yorkshire pudding may also be used to make a simple sweet. Try it with Jam Sauce (page 402) or Ginger Syrup Sauce (page 402)

25 g/1 oz cooking fat
caster sugar for sprinkling

BATTER
    100 g/4 oz plain flour
    1.25 ml/¼ tsp salt
    1 egg, beaten
    250 ml/8 fl oz milk, or half milk and half
      water

Make the batter. Sift the flour and salt into a bowl, make a well in the centre and add the beaten egg. Stir in half the milk (or all the milk, if using a mixture of milk and water), gradually working the flour down from the sides.

Beat vigorously until the mixture is smooth and bubbly, then stir in the rest of the milk (or the water). Pour into a jug. The mixture may be left to stand at this stage, in which case it should be covered and stored in the refrigerator.

Set the oven at 220°C/425°F/gas 7. Put the fat into an 18 × 28 cm/7 × 11 inch baking tin and heat in the oven for 15 minutes.

Stir the batter and immediately pour it into the baking tin. Return to the oven and bake for 30-35 minutes, until the pudding is brown and well risen.

Cut into squares and serve at once, sprinkled with caster sugar or with a suitable sauce.

SERVES 4

CLAFOUTI AUX CERISES

20 ml/4 tsp lard or margarine
20 ml/4 tsp butter
2 whole eggs plus 1 egg yolk
75 g/3 oz granulated sugar
250 ml/8 fl oz milk
150 g/5 oz plain flour, sifted
pinch of cinnamon
450 g/1 lb Morello cherries, stoned
25 g/1 oz caster sugar
15 ml/1 tbsp kirsch

Mix the lard or margarine with the butter in a small bowl and use to grease a fluted metal brioche tin or cake mould about 18 cm/ 7 inches in diameter narrowing to 10 cm/ 4 inches at the base. Set the oven at 200°C/ 400°F/gas 6.

In a bowl, beat the eggs and egg yolk with the sugar until light. Heat the milk in a saucepan until steaming. Gradually blend the flour into the egg mixture alternately with a little of the hot milk to make a batter. Stir in the cinnamon and remaining milk.

Pour a thin layer of the batter into the prepared mould and bake for 5-7 minutes. Meanwhile drain the cherries thoroughly on absorbent kitchen paper.

Pour the remaining batter into the mould, add the cherries and sprinkle with caster sugar. Return to the oven for 10 minutes, then lower the oven temperature to 190°C/ 375°F/gas 5 and cook for 20 minutes more.

Invert the pudding on to a warmed plate. The bottom of the batter should be crusty and the top should resemble thick custard. Serve warm, sprinkled with the kirsch.

SERVES 6

APPLE FRITTERS

450 g/1 lb apples
5 ml/1 tsp lemon juice
oil for deep frying
St Clement's Sauce (page 395) to serve

BATTER
100 g/4 oz plain flour
1.25 ml/¼ tsp salt
15 ml/1 tbsp vegetable oil
60 ml/4 tbsp milk
2 egg whites

Make the batter. Sift the flour and salt into a bowl. Make a well in the centre of the flour and add the oil and milk. Gradually work in the flour from the sides, then beat well until smooth. Stir in 75 ml/5 tbsp cold water. The mixture may be left to stand at this stage, in which case it should be covered and stored in the refrigerator.

Peel and core the apples. Cut them into 5 mm/¼ inch slices and place in a bowl of cold water with the lemon juice added.

Whisk the egg whites in a clean, grease-free bowl until stiff. Give the batter a final beat, then lightly fold in the egg whites.

Set the oven at 150°C/300°F/gas 2. Put the oil for frying in a deep wide saucepan to a depth of at least 7.5 cm/3 inches. Heat the oil to 185°F/360°C or until a bread cube immersed in the oil turns pale brown in 45 seconds. If using a deep-fat fryer, follow the manufacturer's instructions.

Drain the apples thoroughly and dry with soft absorbent kitchen paper. Coat the apple slices in batter and fry 5 or 6 pieces at a time for 2-3 minutes until golden. Lift out the fritters with a slotted spoon and dry on absorbent kitchen paper. Keep hot on a baking sheet in the oven while cooking the next batch.

When all the fritters have been cooked, sprinkle them with caster sugar and serve with St Clement's Sauce or cream.

SERVES 4

VARIATIONS

APRICOT FRITTERS Prepare batter as above. Sprinkle drained canned apricot halves with rum and leave for 15 minutes. Coat in batter, then fry. Dredge with caster sugar and serve with custard or cream.

BANANA FRITTERS Prepare batter as above. Peel 4 small bananas, cut in half lengthways, then in half across. Coat in batter, then fry. Serve with custard or liqueur-flavoured cream.

ORANGE FRITTERS Prepare batter as above. Remove the peel and pith from 4 oranges. Divide them into pieces of 2 or 3 segments each. Carefully cut into the centre to remove any pips. Coat in batter, then fry. Serve with custard or cream.

PEAR FRITTERS Prepare batter as above. Peel and core 4 pears. Cut into quarters, sprinkle with sugar and kirsch and leave to stand for 15 minutes. Finely crush 4 almond macaroons and toss the pear pieces in the crumbs. Coat in batter, then fry. Serve with Rich Lemon Sauce (page 395).

PINEAPPLE FRITTERS Prepare batter as above. Drain 1 × 556 g/19 oz can pineapple rings, pat dry on absorbent kitchen paper, and sprinkle with 20 ml/4 tsp kirsch. Leave to stand for 15 minutes. Coat in batter, then fry. Serve with the pineapple juice, thickened with arrowroot.

———————— ◆ ————————

GOOSEBERRY FRITTERS

*This recipe works with hulled
strawberries, stoned cherries, red or
blackcurrants.*

400 g/14 oz gooseberries, topped and
    tailed
oil or fat for deep frying
caster sugar for dredging

BATTER
50 g/2 oz plain flour
15 ml/1 tbsp caster sugar
2 eggs, separated
45 ml/3 tbsp milk

Make the batter. Sift the flour into a
bowl. Stir in the sugar. Add the egg yolks
and milk and beat well until smooth. Whisk
the egg whites in a clean, grease-free bowl
until stiff. Give the batter a final beat, then
lightly fold in the egg whites.

Put the oil for frying in a deep wide saucepan to a depth of at least 7.5 cm/3 inches.
Heat the oil to 185°F/360°C or until a bread
cube immersed in the oil turns pale brown
in 45 seconds.

Meanwhile add the gooseberries to the
batter. Dip a metal tablespoon into the hot
fat, then lift 3 coated gooseberries on to it.
Carefully lower the gooseberries into the
hot fat, without separating them. As the
batter cooks, the berries will fuse together.

Fry until golden brown, turning once.
Drain thoroughly and serve at once,
dredged with plenty of caster sugar.

SERVES 4

> **MRS BEETON'S TIP** Cook fritters
> completely on one side before turning
> them over, or they may disintegrate.

ALMOND FRITTERS

2 eggs, separated
25 g/1 oz caster sugar
oil or fat for deep frying
15 g/½ oz cornflour
50 g/2 oz ground almonds
15 ml/1 tbsp milk
few drops of vanilla essence
caster sugar for dredging

In a bowl, beat the egg yolks with the
sugar until pale, thick and creamy. The
mixture should have the consistency of thick
custard. Stir the cornflour, almonds, milk
and vanilla essence into the mixture to make a
smooth batter.

Whisk the egg whites in a clean, grease-
free bowl until stiff. Give the batter a final
beat, then lightly fold in the egg whites.

Put the oil for frying in a deep wide
saucepan to a depth of at least 7.5 cm/3
inches. Heat the oil to 185°F/360°C or until a
bread cube immersed in the oil turns pale
brown in 45 seconds. If using a deep-fat fryer,
follow the manufacturer's instructions.

Drop the almond batter in small spoonfuls
into the hot oil and fry until golden brown
underneath. Carefully turn the fritters over
and fry the other side. Drain well on absorbent kitchen paper and serve dredged
with caster sugar.

SERVES 4

O LADYA

Allow plenty of time when making these fritters.
They are yeast-based and must be allowed to
rise before cooking

500 ml/17 fl oz milk
25 g/1 oz fresh yeast
15 ml/1 tbsp caster sugar
450 g/1 lb plain flour
30 ml/2 tbsp cooking oil
2 eggs
5 ml/1 tsp salt
450 g/1 lb cooking apples
oil for deep frying

Put the milk in a saucepan and warm gently. It should be just hand-hot. Mash the yeast and sugar in a small bowl and stir in a little of the warm milk. Leave in a warm place until frothy.

Sift the flour into a mixing bowl, make a well in the centre and add the yeast mixture, with the remaining warm milk. Cover and leave to rise in a warm place for 30 minutes.

Meanwhile, combine the oil, eggs and salt in a bowl and mix well. Gradually add to the yeast mixture, working in well, then cover the mixture again and leave to rise for 30 minutes more.

Put the oil for frying in a deep wide saucepan to a depth of at least 7.5 cm/3 inches. Heat the oil to 185°F/360°C or until a bread cube immersed in the oil turns pale brown in 45 seconds. If using a deep-fat fryer, follow the manufacturer's instructions.

Peel and core the apples and slice into thin rings. Coat the rings in the batter and fry in the hot oil, turning once, until golden brown on both sides. Serve with sugar.

SERVES 8

P OOR KNIGHTS

'Poor Knights' originated in England, in the
Middle Ages, but soon became popular all over
Europe. Every country has its own traditional
variation, and some have more elaborate
versions called 'Rich Knights'. Some are made
with sweet bread or stale cake, others are
moistened with red wine.

4 thick slices white bread
2 eggs, beaten
200 ml/7 fl oz milk or white wine
1.25 ml/¼ tsp cinnamon
15 ml/1 tbsp sugar
oil for shallow frying
caster sugar and ground cinnamon to
    serve

Cut the crusts off the bread, then cut each slice into quarters. Put into a deep dish.

In a bowl, mix the eggs with the milk or wine, cinnamon, and sugar. Pour the liquid over the bread, cover, and leave to soak for 2-3 minutes.

Heat oil to a depth of 5 mm/¼ inch in a frying pan. Using a palette knife or fish slice, drain a piece of bread from the dish. Slide the fritter into the hot fat. Add 1 or 2 more, drained in the same way. Fry until golden-brown on both sides, turning once.

Drain the 'poor knights' on absorbent kitchen paper, then keep uncovered in a warm place until needed. Fry the rest of the bread squares in the same way. Serve sprinkled with caster sugar and cinnamon.

SERVES 4

FRIED CREAMS

butter for greasing
1 whole egg plus 4 yolks
50 g/2 oz fine cake crumbs
40 g/1½ oz plain flour
40 g/1½ oz cornflour
500 ml/17 fl oz milk
40 g/1½ oz caster sugar
pinch of salt
few drops of vanilla essence
15 ml/1 tbsp liqueur or brandy (optional)
oil for deep frying
caster sugar for dredging

Grease a shallow 600 ml/1 pint ovenproof dish. Beat the whole egg in a shallow bowl and spread the cake crumbs in a similar bowl.

Put the 4 remaining egg yolks into a bowl and beat until liquid. In a second bowl, blend the flour and cornflour with enough of the milk to make a smooth paste. Bring the rest of the milk to the boil in a saucepan. Add slowly to the blended mixture, stirring all the time. Return to the pan and bring to the boil, still stirring. Cook for 2-3 minutes (see Mrs Beeton's Tip).

Remove the pan from the heat and gradually add the sugar, salt and beaten egg yolks. The mixture will be very thick, so take care to stir thoroughly to keep it smooth. Return to the heat and warm through, but do not allow the sauce to approach boiling point. Stir in the vanilla essence and liqueur or brandy, if used. Spread the mixture in the prepared dish to a depth of about 2 cm/¾ inch. Leave until set.

Cut the set custard into neat shapes about 3 cm/1¼ inches across. Dip in the beaten whole egg and then in cake crumbs to coat. Set the coated shapes on a plate and place in the refrigerator for 15–30 minutes or until quite firm.

Put the oil for frying in a deep wide saucepan to a depth of at least 7.5 cm/3 inches. Heat the oil to 185°F/360°C or until a bread cube immersed in the oil turns pale brown in 45 seconds. If using a deep-fat fryer, follow the manufacturer's instructions.

Fry the coated shapes in the hot oil until golden brown, drain on absorbent kitchen paper and serve dredged in caster sugar.

SERVES 4

> **MRS BEETON'S TIP** Always cook the flour thoroughly or the sauce will have the flavour of raw starch.

LEXINGTON APPLES

4 cooking apples (about 675 g/1½ lb)
a little lemon juice
1 × 375 g/13 oz can pineapple pieces
10 ml/2 tsp arrowroot
25 g/1 oz plain flour
25 g/1 oz caster sugar
1 egg
25 g/1 oz cake crumbs
oil for deep frying

Peel and core the apples, leaving them whole. Brush with lemon juice. Place in the top of a steamer over simmering water and steam for about 10 minutes until half cooked. Set aside to cool.

Meanwhile drain the pineapple, reserving 125 ml/4 fl oz of the syrup in a small saucepan. Add the arrowroot to the pan and bring gently to the boil, stirring all the time until the sauce thickens and clears. Keep hot. Chop the pineapple and set aside in a saucepan.

Mix the flour and sugar in a shallow bowl. In a similar bowl, beat the egg and spread the cake crumbs in a third bowl. Roll each apple first in the flour and sugar mixture, then in egg and finally in crumbs.

Put the oil for frying in a deep wide saucepan to a depth of at least 10 cm/4 inches. Heat the oil to 185°F/360°C or until a bread cube immersed in the oil turns pale brown in 45 seconds. If using a deep-fat fryer, follow the manufacturer's instructions.

Carefully lower the apples into the hot fat, using a slotted spoon. Fry until golden brown all over. Meanwhile heat the reserved pineapple.

Drain the cooked apples on absorbent kitchen paper, place in individual bowls and fill the centres with pineapple. Pour a little of the hot pineapple syrup around each and serve at once.

SERVES 4

B EIGNETS

oil for deep frying
icing sugar for dredging

CHOUX PASTRY
    100 g/4 oz plain flour
    50 g/2 oz butter or margarine
    pinch of salt
    2 whole eggs plus 1 yolk
    vanilla essence

Start by making the choux pastry. Sift the flour on to a sheet of greaseproof paper. Put 250 ml/8 fl oz water in a saucepan and add the butter or margarine with the salt. Heat slowly until the fat melts, then bring to the boil.

As soon as the liquid boils tip in all the flour at once and remove the pan from the heat immediately. Stir until the mixture forms a smooth paste which leaves the sides of the pan clean. Cool slightly.

Add the egg yolk and beat well. Add the whole eggs one at a time, beating thoroughly between each addition (see Mrs Beeton's Tip). Continue beating the paste until smooth and glossy.

Put the oil for frying in a deep wide saucepan to a depth of at least 7.5 cm/3 inches. Heat the oil to 185°F/360°C or until a bread cube immersed in the oil turns pale brown in 45 seconds. If using a deep-fat fryer, follow the manufacturer's instructions.

Flavour the choux pastry with vanilla essence to taste. Dip a metal dessertspoon into the hot oil and use it to drop spoonfuls of the mixture gently into the hot oil, a few at a time. Fry slowly until crisp and golden, then drain on absorbent kitchen paper. Served dredged in icing sugar.

SERVES 4

MRS BEETON'S TIP The choux pastry may not accept all the egg. Add just enough to give a thick smooth paste with a glossy appearance.

⬥

SPANISH FRITTERS

oil for deep frying
caster sugar and cinnamon for dredging

CHOUX PASTRY
100 g/4 oz plain flour
50 g/2 oz butter or margarine
pinch of salt
2 whole eggs plus 1 yolk
15 ml/1 tbsp caster sugar
vanilla essence

Make the choux pastry, following the instructions in the recipe for Beignets (page 321). Stir in the caster sugar and flavour with vanilla essence to taste.

Put the oil for frying in a deep wide saucepan to a depth of at least 7.5 cm/3 inches. Heat the oil to 185°F/360°C or until a bread cube immersed in the oil turns pale brown in 45 seconds. If using a deep-fat fryer, follow the manufacturer's instructions.

Put the choux pastry into a piping bag fitted with a 1 cm/½ inch star nozzle. Press out 7.5 cm/3 inch lengths of pastry and drop carefully into the hot oil. They will form twists. Fry slowly until crisp and golden, then drain on absorbent kitchen paper. Served dredged in sugar and cinnamon.

SERVES 4

VARIATIONS

RING FRITTERS Follow the recipe above but instead of pressing out lengths of the choux pastry into the hot oil, pipe rings, about 5 cm/2 inches in diameter, on to oiled greaseproof paper. Holding the edge of the paper, slide the rings carefully into the hot fat. As the fritters cook, keep them moving with a spoon. They will rise to the surface. When drained, split the fritters and fill with jam. Serve dusted with icing sugar.

INDIAN FRITTERS Make the choux pastry in the same way as in the recipe above, but do not put it into a piping bag. Instead spoon a little into a dessertspoon, make a hollow in the centre and add about 2.5 ml/½ tsp jam. Top with more choux pastry, covering the jam completely. Slide the jam-filled shape carefully into the hot oil, using a palette knife. Make more fritters in the same way. Drain and serve, dredged in caster sugar.

BUNUELOS

These unusual deep-fried pancakes come from Mexico.

300 g/11 oz plain flour
5 ml/1 tsp baking powder
1.25 ml/¼ tsp salt
15 ml/1 tbsp soft light brown sugar
50 g/2 oz butter
200 ml/7 fl oz milk
4 eggs, lightly beaten
flour for rolling out
oil for deep frying

SAUCE
200 ml/7 fl oz runny honey
ground cinnamon

Sift the flour, baking powder and salt into

a bowl and stir in the brown sugar. Make a well in the centre of the mixture.

Melt the butter in a saucepan, stir in the milk and add to the dry ingredients with the beaten eggs. Mix well. Add enough water (about 100 ml/3½ fl oz) to make a pliable but not sticky dough.

On a floured surface, knead the dough thoroughly, then form into 2.5 cm/1 inch balls. Cover with a cloth and leave to stand for 30 minutes, then roll out each ball as thinly as possible to a round on a lightly floured surface. Leave to stand for 10 minutes.

Put the oil for frying in a deep wide saucepan to a depth of at least 7.5 cm/3 inches. Heat the oil to 185°F/360°C or until a bread cube immersed in the oil turns pale brown in 45 seconds. If using a deep-fat fryer, follow the manufacturer's instructions.

Fry the bunuelos in the hot oil, a few at a time, until light golden on both sides. Drain thoroughly on absorbent kitchen paper.

Warm the honey in a saucepan, flavour with cinnamon and serve with the bunuelos. Alternatively, break the bunuelos into soup bowls and pour the honey mixture over.

MAKES ABOUT 30

VARIATIONS

SOPAIPILLAS Instead of making balls, rest the dough in one piece, then roll out very thinly on a floured surface. Cut into small squares and fry as above. Serve with a cinnamon-flavoured hot chocolate drink instead of afternoon tea.

WAFFLES

Waffles are crisp fried wafers made from a leavened batter and cooked in a hinged waffle iron that may be electric or for use on the stove. Follow the manufacturer's instructions for use, taking care not to overfill the iron.

75 g/3 oz butter
250 g/9 oz self-raising flour
1.25 ml/¼ tsp salt
5 ml/1 tsp baking powder
2 eggs, separated
375 ml/13 fl oz milk
butter and golden syrup to serve

Melt the butter in a small saucepan. Set aside to cool. Sift the flour, salt and baking powder into a bowl. Make a well in the centre of the flour. Add the egg yolks, cooled butter and some of the milk. Gradually work in the flour from the sides and then beat well until smooth. Beat in the rest of the milk.

In a clean, grease-free bowl, whisk the egg whites until stiff, and fold into the batter. It should be the consistency of thick cream.

Heat the waffle iron, pour in some of the batter, and cook for about 5 minutes until the steaming stops.

Serve hot with butter and golden syrup.

SERVES 4–8

VARIATIONS

BUTTERMILK WAFFLES Substitute buttermilk for the milk. Add the whole eggs to the batter instead of separating them.
NUT WAFFLES Sprinkle 15 ml/1 tbsp chopped nuts over the batter as soon as it has been poured into the iron.

C RÊPES SUZETTE

100 g/4 oz unsalted butter
75 g/3 oz caster sugar
grated rind and juice of 1 orange
5 ml/1 tsp lemon juice
15 ml/1 tbsp orange liqueur
45 ml/3 tbsp brandy for flaming

CRÊPES
100 g/4 oz plain flour
1.25 ml/¼ tsp salt
1 egg, beaten
250 ml/8 fl oz milk, or half milk and half
    water
15 g/½ oz butter, melted and cooled
oil for frying

Make the crêpe batter. Sift the flour and salt into a bowl, make a well in the centre and add the beaten egg. Stir in half the milk (or all the milk, if using a mixture of milk and water), gradually working the flour down from the sides.

Beat vigorously until the mixture is smooth and bubbly, then stir in the rest of the milk (or the water). Pour into a jug. The mixture may be left to stand at this stage, in which case it should be covered and stored in the refrigerator.

Heat a little oil in a clean 18 cm/7 inch pancake pan. Pour off any excess oil, leaving the pan covered with a thin film of grease.

Stir the melted butter into the batter and pour about 30-45 ml/2-3 tbsp into the pan. There should be just enough to thinly cover the base. Tilt and rotate the pan so that the batter runs over the surface evenly.

Cook over moderate heat for about 1 minute until the crêpe is set and golden brown underneath. Make sure the crêpe is loose by shaking the pan, then either toss it or turn it with a palette knife or fish slice. Cook the second side for about 30 seconds or until golden.

Slide the crêpe out on to a plate and keep warm over simmering water while making 7 more crêpes in the same way. Add more oil to the pan when necessary.

Make the filling by creaming the unsalted butter with the sugar in a bowl. Beat in the orange rind, lemon juice and liqueur, with enough of the orange juice to give a soft, creamy consistency.

Spread the filling over the cooked crêpes, dividing it evenly between them. Fold each crêpe in half, then in half again to make a quarter circle.

Return half the crêpes to the pan and warm through for 1-2 minutes. As the orange butter melts and runs out, spoon it over the crêpes. Pour in half the brandy, tip the pan to one side and increase the heat. Ignite the brandy and serve at once, with the pan sauce. Repeat with the remaining crêpes and brandy.

SERVES 4

STEAMED PUDDINGS

The steaming-hot puddings in this chapter are perfect for winter days, from homely Treacle Layer Pudding to traditional Rich Christmas Pudding or lighter Snowdon Pudding. Treat the family to a delicious Chocolate Crumb Pudding or surprise them with a steamed Sponge Pudding cooked in minutes in the microwave.

Traditional steamed puddings take a while to cook and there are a few points to remember for safety and success. In Mrs Beeton's day steaming was a popular cooking method for both savoury and sweet puddings, fish and fowl. The food would be allowed to steam over a pot of boiling water on the kitchen fire or coal-burning stove. When gas and electric cookers became popular, they led to a decline in the use of long, hob-top cooking methods.

Recent trends in healthy eating and cooking have brought steaming right back into fashion, although this method of cooking is used primarily for savoury foods. There are many types of steamer available in the shops, from the metal saucepan-top steamer to the oriental-style bamboo steamer to fit over a wok. Here are a few key features to look out for if you are buying a steamer:

The steamer should have a large base, enabling it to hold plenty of water without needing constant topping up and it should fit neatly on top of the base to prevent steam escaping around the sides. The top of the steamer should have a tight-fitting lid to keep the steam in during cooking. The following notes outline the types of steamers available and their usefulness for cooking puddings.

SAUCEPAN AND STEAMER SET

This usually comprises a double-handled saucepan base with one, two or more steamers that fit on top. The steaming sections have perforated bases to allow the steam to pass through and they are slightly smaller in diameter at the bottom to fit neatly into the base. Usually made of stainless steel, this type of steamer may be built up to include several cooking tiers. This is ideal for cooking puddings, and the main course or vegetables for the meal may be cooked in separate tiers at the same time.

BAMBOO STEAMERS

Bamboo steamers with tight-fitting lids are available in different sizes. These are designed to fit in a wok. They are perfect for cooking vegetables, Oriental-style dishes and any suitable food which can be placed in a fairly shallow container. Some bamboo steamers are deep enough to hold pudding basins; however most woks will only hold sufficient water for comparatively short periods of steaming and need frequent topping up with boiling water. This type of steamer is not recommended for cooking puddings that require hours of steaming.

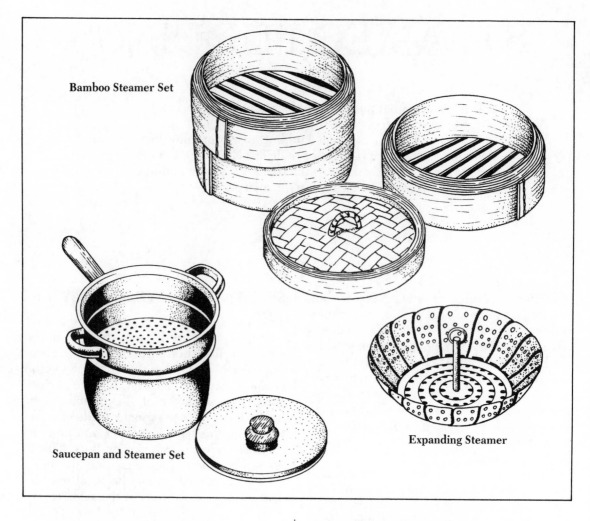

Bamboo Steamer Set

Saucepan and Steamer Set

Expanding Steamer

EXPANDING STEAMERS

This type of steamer is made from small stainless steel plates that fold up into a compact shape for storage. The steamer opens out as large as is necessary to hold the food. It stands on short legs in the base of a saucepan. The boiling water must be kept below the level of the steamer and the saucepan must have a tight fitting lid. This type of steamer is ideal for vegetables and it may be used for puddings. Since only a small amount of water may be placed in the pan beneath the steamer it is not suitable for puddings that require many hours' cooking.

ALUMINIUM STEAMERS WITH GRADUATED BASES

These are very common and are designed to fit on top of saucepans of different sizes. Ensure that the steamer has a tight-fitting lid and that it sits neatly on top of the pan.

ELECTRIC STEAMER

This is a plug-in, work-top appliance. A heating element in the base is thermostatically controlled to keep the water boiling or steaming at the right temperature. One or two tiers are supplied to fit over the base, with a tight-fitting lid for the top. In comparison with the other types of steames, this is an expensive option. However, if you intend to steam a lot of foods it may be a worthwhile purchase. Depending on the individual steamer, this types may lose a lot of steam during cooking, creating puddles on the work surface or condensation on surrounding fittings. Check the steaming layers on the base to make sure they fit neatly. Follow the manufacturer's instructions closely.

IMPROVISING

If you do not own a steamer it is possible to steam puddings by standing them in a saucepan and adding boiling water to come part of the way up the outside of the container. Place a suitable saucer or cereal bowl upside down in the bottom of the pan as a' base on which to stand the pudding, allowing for a greater depth of water. Make sure that the saucepan has a tight-fitting lid. Follow the instructions in individual recipes.

MICROWAVE COOKING

The microwave oven may be used to make excellent steamed puddings. For more information, and a sponge pudding recipe, see page 337. Here are one or two hints for safety and success:

■ Never use a metal container or dish with metal trimmings.

■ Sponge puddings rise rapidly and to a considerable height, so make sure the basin used is not more than half full before microwave steaming.

■ When cooked, sponge puddings should be slightly sticky on top.

■ Use microwave cling film or a suitable plate to cover the pudding during cooking.

PRESSURE COOKING

A pressure cooker may be used to cook steamed puddings quickly and very successfully. It may also be used to cook certain other puddings, for example set custards, and notes are given where applicable.

Detailed information on pressure cookers is included in the section on equipment (page 25). Selected recipes have been tested in a pressure cooker and timings are given in Pressure Cooker tips. The following rules should be followed when pressure cooking sponge puddings.

■ Traditional recipes for large steamed puddings should be cooked on Low (5 lb) pressure.

■ Small puddings and individual puddings may be cooked on High (15 lb) pressure.

■ Add at least 900 ml/1½ pints of water to allow for the pre-steaming time before the cooker is brought to pressure.

■ The basin used for the pudding should withstand the temperature reached in the pressure cooker; it should be watertight and not cracked or chipped.

■ Thoroughly grease the pudding basin and half or two-thirds fill it.

■ Tie down the cover securely.

■ Before bringing to pressure, all sponge puddings must be pre-steamed in boiling water with the lid on but without using weights. This allows the raising agent to work.

■ Release the pressure slowly after cooking, following the manufacturer's instructions.

APPLE PUDDING

fat for greasing
150 g/5 oz cooking apples
100 g/4 oz shredded suet
100 g/4 oz stale white breadcrumbs
100 g/4 oz soft light brown sugar
1.25 ml/¼ tsp grated nutmeg
pinch of salt
2 eggs, beaten
about 125 ml/4 fl oz milk

Peel, core and roughly chop the apples. Mix them in a large bowl with the suet, breadcrumbs, sugar, nutmeg and salt.

Add the beaten eggs with enough milk to make a soft, dropping consistency. Leave to stand for 1 hour.

Meanwhile grease a 1 litre/1¾ pint pudding basin. Prepare a steamer or half fill a large saucepan with water and bring to the boil.

Stir the pudding mixture, adding a little more milk if very stiff. Pour the mixture into the basin, cover with greased greaseproof paper or foil and secure with string.

Put the pudding in the perforated part of the steamer, or stand it on an old saucer or plate in the saucepan of boiling water. The water should come halfway up the sides of the basin. Cover the pan tightly and steam the pudding over gently simmering water for 1¾-2 hours.

Serve from the basin or leave for 5-10 minutes at room temperature to firm up, then turn out on to a serving plate.

SERVES 5-6

VARIATIONS

The recipe works equally well with a wide variety of other fruits. Try damsons, gooseberries, greengages, plums or rhubarb, adjusting the quantity of sugar as required.

PRESSURE COOKER TIP Pour 900 ml/1½ pints boiling water into the pressure cooker. Stand the pudding on the trivet and steam it with the lid on, without weights, for 10 minutes. Bring to 15 lb pressure and cook for 25 minutes. Reduce the pressure slowly.

CUMBERLAND PUDDING

fat for greasing
225 g/8 oz cooking apples
100 g/4 oz shredded suet
200 g/7 oz plain flour
10 ml/2 tsp baking powder
pinch of salt
150 g/5 oz currants
75 g/3 oz soft light brown sugar
1.25 ml/¼ tsp grated nutmeg
2 eggs, beaten
about 75 ml/5 tbsp milk
soft light brown sugar for dredging

Peel, core and roughly chop the apples. Put them in a large bowl with the suet, flour, baking powder, salt, currants, sugar and nutmeg. Mix well.

Add the beaten eggs with enough milk to make a soft, dropping consistency. Leave to stand for 1 hour.

Meanwhile grease a 750 ml/1¼ pint pudding basin. Prepare a steamer or half fill a large saucepan with water and boil.

Stir the pudding mixture, adding a little more milk if very stiff. Pour the mixture into the basin, cover with greased greaseproof paper or foil and secure with string.

Put the pudding in the perforated part of the steamer, or stand it on an old saucer or plate in the saucepan of boiling water. The water should come halfway up the sides of the basin. Cover the pan tightly and steam the pudding over gently simmering water for 1¾-2 hours.

Leave the pudding for 5-10 minutes at room temperature to firm up, then turn out on to a serving plate. Dredge with brown sugar before serving.

SERVES 5-6

*M*OUSSELINE PUDDING

It is vital to serve this lovely light pudding as soon as it is turned out of the basin. It will collapse if left to stand.

butter for greasing
50 g/2 oz butter
50 g/2 oz icing sugar
3 eggs, separated
grated rind and juice of ½ lemon or few drops of vanilla essence

Grease a 1 litre/1¾ pint pudding basin.

Prepare a steamer or half fill a large saucepan with water and heat gently.

Cream the butter with the icing sugar in a large heatproof bowl. Add the egg yolks, one at a time, beating well after each addition. Stir in the lemon rind and juice or add a few drops of vanilla essence.

Stand the bowl over a saucepan of hot water or use a double saucepan. Heat for 10-12 minutes, stirring constantly until the mixture is thick enough to hold the mark of a trail for 1-2 seconds (see Mrs Beeton's Tip). Remove from the heat and continue stirring until the mixture is cold.

In a clean, grease-free bowl, whisk the egg whites until stiff. Fold them into the egg yolk mixture, then spoon the mixture into the prepared pudding basin. Cover with greased greaseproof paper or foil and secure with string. Bring the steamer or saucepan of water to the boil.

Put the pudding in the perforated part of the steamer, or stand it on an old saucer or plate in the saucepan of boiling water. The water should come halfway up the sides of the basin. Cover the pan tightly and steam the pudding over gently simmering water for 45 minutes. Serve the pudding at once, inverting it on a serving plate.

SERVES 4

> **MRS BEETON'S TIP** When the egg yolk mixture is heated in the double saucepan, it may separate. It will also become runny as the butter melts. Persevere – it will bind again and thicken as the egg yolks cook.

BROWN BREAD PUDDING

fat for greasing
175 g/6 oz stale brown breadcrumbs
75 g/3 oz raisins
75 g/3 oz sultanas
100 g/4 oz shredded suet
75 g/3 oz caster sugar
2 eggs, beaten
milk (see method)

Grease a 750 ml/1¼ pint pudding basin. Prepare a steamer or half fill a large saucepan with water and bring to the boil.

Place the breadcrumbs, dried fruit, suet and sugar in a mixing bowl. Stir in the eggs, with enough milk to give a dropping consistency. Mix well.

Spoon the mixture into the prepared basin, cover with greased greaseproof paper or foil and secure with string.

Put the pudding in the perforated part of the steamer, or stand it on an old saucer or plate in the saucepan of boiling water. The water should come halfway up the sides of the basin. Cover the pan tightly and steam the pudding over gently simmering water for 2½-3 hours.

Serve from the basin or leave for 5-10 minutes at room temperature to firm up, then turn out on to a serving plate. Serve with Vanilla Custard (page 403) or Apricot Sauce (page 398).

SERVES 6

PRESSURE COOKER TIP Pour 1.1 litres/2 pints boiling water into the cooker. Steam the pudding without weights on the cooker for 15 minutes. Bring to 15 lb pressure and cook for 25 minutes. Reduce the pressure slowly.

DRIED FRUIT PUDDING

This pudding is boiled, not steamed, so the water in the saucepan should at all times cover the pudding basin. Top the pan up as necessary with boiling water.

fat for greasing
100 g/4 oz stale white breadcrumbs
100 g/4 oz plain flour
pinch of salt
10 ml/2 tsp baking powder
100 g/4 oz shredded suet
100 g/4 oz raisins
100 g/4 oz currants
100 g/4 oz soft light brown sugar
1.25 ml/¼ tsp ground mace
1.25 ml/¼ tsp grated nutmeg
1 egg
about 125 ml/4 fl oz milk

Grease a 1 litre/1¾ pint pudding basin. Three-quarters fill a large saucepan with water and bring to the boil.

Combine all the ingredients in a mixing bowl and beat well, adding sufficient milk to give a dropping consistency. Spoon the mixture into the basin, cover with greased greaseproof paper or foil and a floured cloth. Secure with string.

Carefully lower the basin into the pan of boiling water. Cover the pan and lower the heat so that the water is kept at a steady simmer. Cook the pudding for 4-5 hours.

Serve from the basin or leave for 5-10 minutes at room temperature to firm up, then turn out on to a serving plate. Serve with warmed golden syrup and whipped cream or with a citrus-flavoured sauce.

SERVES 6

RICH CHRISTMAS PUDDING

Illustrated on page 263

fat for greasing
225 g/8 oz plain flour
pinch of salt
5 ml/1 tsp ground ginger
5 ml/1 tsp mixed spice
5 ml/1 tsp grated nutmeg
50 g/2 oz blanched almonds, chopped
400 g/14 oz soft dark brown sugar
225 g/8 oz shredded suet
225 g/8 oz sultanas
225 g/8 oz currants
200 g/7 oz seedless raisins
175 g/6 oz cut mixed peel
175 g/6 oz stale white breadcrumbs
6 eggs
75 ml/5 tbsp stout
juice of 1 orange
50 ml/2 fl oz brandy
125-250 ml/4-8 fl oz milk

Grease four 600 ml/1 pint pudding basins. Three quarters fill four saucepans, each deep enough to hold a single pudding, with water.

Sift the flour, salt, ginger, mixed spice and nutmeg into a large mixing bowl. Add the nuts, sugar, suet, dried fruit, peel and breadcrumbs.

In a second bowl, combine the eggs, stout, orange juice, brandy and 125 ml/4 fl oz milk. Mix well.

Stir the liquid mixture into the dry ingredients, adding more milk if necessary to give a soft dropping consistency. Divide the mixture between the pudding basins, covering each with greased greaseproof paper or foil, and a floured cloth. Secure with string.

Carefully lower the basins into the pans of boiling water. Cover the pans and lower the heat so that the water is kept at a steady simmer. Cook the puddings for 6-7 hours, topping up each pan with boiling water as required. The pudding basins should be covered at all times with boiling water.

To store, cover each pudding with a clean dry cloth, wrap in greaseproof paper and store in a cool, dry place until required. To reheat, boil or steam each pudding for 1½-2 hours. Serve with Brandy Butter or Brandy and Almond Butter (both on page 405).

EACH PUDDING SERVES 6

> **PRESSURE COOKER TIP** Pour 1.5 litres/2¾ pints boiling water into the pressure cooker. Stand one pudding on the trivet and steam it, without weights, for 20 minutes. Bring to 15 lb pressure and cook for 1¾ hours. Allow the pressure to reduce slowly. To reheat, cook at 15 lb pressure for 20 minutes, reduce the pressure slowly and serve.

PLUM PUDDING

Christmas pudding became known as plum pudding in Tudor times, when dried plums (prunes) were the popular prime ingredient.

fat for greasing
100 g/4 oz cooking apples
200 g/7 oz dried figs, chopped
100 g/4 oz currants
225 g/8 oz seedless raisins
200 g/7 oz blanched almonds, chopped
25 g/1 oz shelled Brazil nuts, chopped
100 g/4 oz pine kernels
175 g/6 oz stale white breadcrumbs
5 ml/1 tsp mixed spice
100 g/4 oz soft light brown sugar
100 g/4 oz cut mixed peel
pinch of salt
grated rind and juice of 1 lemon
100 g/4 oz butter or margarine
100 g/4 oz honey
3 eggs, beaten

Grease two 750 ml/1¼ pint pudding basins. Prepare two steamers or three quarters fill two saucepans with water. Each pan should hold one pudding.

Peel, core and chop the apples. Put them in a large mixing bowl with the dried fruits, nuts, breadcrumbs, spice, sugar, peel, salt and the lemon rind and juice.

Combine the butter and honey in a saucepan and warm gently until the butter has melted. Beat in the eggs.

Stir the liquid mixture into the dry ingredients and mix well. Spoon the mixture into the basins, cover with greased greaseproof paper or foil and a floured cloth. Secure with string.

Place the basins in the steamers or carefully lower them into the pans of boiling water. Cover the pans and lower the heat so that the water is kept at a steady simmer. Boil the puddings for 3 hours or steam for 3½-4 hours, topping up each pan with boiling water as required.

To store, cover each pudding with a clean dry cloth, wrap in greaseproof paper and store in a cool, dry place until required. To reheat, boil or steam each pudding for 1½-2 hours.

EACH PUDDING SERVES 6

🥣 **MRS BEETON'S TIP** Plum puddings are traditionally flamed when served. To do this, warm 30-45 ml/ 2-3 tbsp brandy, either in a soup ladle over a low flame or in a measuring jug in the microwave for 15 seconds on High. Ignite the brandy (if warmed in a soup ladle it may well ignite spontaneously) and carefully pour over the hot pudding. Do not use holly to decorate the top of a pudding that is to be flamed.

MRS BEETON'S DELHI PUDDING

fat for greasing
400 g/14 oz cooking apples
150 g/5 oz currants
75 g/3 oz soft light brown sugar
1.25 ml/¼ tsp grated nutmeg
grated rind of 1 lemon

SUET CRUST PASTRY
400 g/14 oz plain flour
2.5 ml/½ tsp salt
10 ml/2 tsp baking powder
175 g/6 oz shredded suet

Grease a 750 ml/1¼ pint pudding basin.

Prepare a steamer or half fill a large saucepan with water and bring to the boil.

Make the pastry. Sift the flour, salt and baking powder into a mixing bowl. Add the suet and enough cold water (about 300 ml/½ pint) to make an elastic dough. Divide the dough in half.

On a floured surface, roll out one portion of the suet pastry to a round 1.5 cm/¾ inch larger than the top of the prepared pudding basin. Put the pastry into the basin and, pressing with the fingers, ease it evenly up the sides to the top. Thinly roll out the rest of the pastry and cut three rounds in graduated sizes to fit the basin at different levels.

Peel and core the apples. Slice into a bowl and mix with the remaining ingredients. Put layers of fruit and pastry into the basin, finishing with a layer of pastry. Seal the pastry edges firmly by pinching together.

Cover the pudding with greased greaseproof paper or foil and secure with string. Put the pudding in the perforated part of the steamer or stand it on an old saucer or plate in the saucepan of boiling water. The water should come halfway up the sides of the basin. Cover the pan tightly and steam the pudding over gently simmering water for 2½-3 hours.

Serve from the basin or leave for 5-10 minutes at room temperature to firm up, then turn out on to a serving plate. Serve with Vanilla Custard (page 403).

SERVES 5 TO 6

G INGER PUDDING

fat for greasing
200 g/7 oz plain flour
5 ml/1 tsp ground ginger
pinch of salt
5 ml/1 tsp bicarbonate of soda
100 g/4 oz shredded suet
75 g/3 oz caster sugar
15 ml/1 tbsp black treacle
1 egg, beaten
50-100 ml/2-3½ fl oz milk

Grease a 1 litre/1¾ pint pudding basin. Prepare a steamer or half fill a large saucepan with water and bring to the boil.

Sift the flour, ginger, salt and soda into a mixing bowl. Add the suet and sugar. Mix lightly.

In a second bowl, beat the treacle and egg with 50 ml/2 fl oz of the milk. Stir the liquid mixture into the dry ingredients, adding more milk if necessary to give a soft dropping consistency.

Spoon the mixture into the prepared basin, cover with greased greaseproof paper or foil and secure with string.

Put the pudding in the perforated part of the steamer, or stand it on an old saucer or plate in the saucepan of boiling water. The water should come halfway up the sides of the basin. Cover the pan tightly and steam the pudding over gently simmering water for 1¾-2 hours.

Serve from the basin or leave for 5-10 minutes at room temperature to firm up, then turn out on to a serving plate. Serve with Ginger Sauce (page 394) or Classic Egg Custard Sauce (page 404).

SERVES 6

*T*REACLE LAYER PUDDING

fat for greasing
65 g/2½ oz stale white breadcrumbs
grated rind of 1 lemon
200 g/7 oz treacle or golden syrup or a
    mixture

SUET CRUST PASTRY
300 g/11 oz plain flour
pinch of salt
10 ml/2 tsp baking powder
150 g/5 oz shredded suet
flour for rolling out

Grease a 1 litre/1¾ pint pudding basin. Prepare a steamer or half fill a large saucepan with water and bring to the boil.

Make the pastry. Sift the flour, salt and baking powder into a mixing bowl. Add the suet and enough cold water (about 250 ml/8 fl oz) to make an elastic dough. Divide the dough in half.

On a floured surface, roll out one portion of the suet pastry to a round 1 cm/½ inch larger than the top of the prepared pudding basin. Put the pastry into the basin and, pressing with the fingers, ease it evenly up the sides to the top.

Use half the remaining pastry to make a lid to fit the top of the basin. Thinly roll out the rest and cut two rounds in graduated sizes to fit the basin at two different levels.

In a bowl, mix the breadcrumbs and lemon rind. Put a layer of treacle or golden syrup on the base of the pastry-lined basin and sprinkle generously with the breadcrumb mixture. Cover with the smaller pastry round, moistening the edges with water and pressing them to join them to the pastry at the side of the basin. Layer the remaining ingredients and pastry, finishing with the pastry lid.

Cover the pudding with greased greaseproof paper or foil and secure with string. Put the pudding in the perforated part of the steamer or stand it on an old saucer or plate in the saucepan of boiling water. The water should come halfway up the sides of the basin. Cover the pan tightly and steam the pudding over gently simmering water for 2¼-2½ hours.

Serve from the basin or leave for 5-10 minutes at room temperature to firm up, then turn out on to a serving plate. Serve with warmed golden syrup and single cream.

SERVES 6-8

*G*OLDEN SYRUP PUDDING

fat for greasing
45 ml/3 tbsp golden syrup
150 g/5 oz plain flour
5 ml/1 tsp bicarbonate of soda
pinch of salt
5 ml/1 tsp ground ginger
150 g/5 oz stale white breadcrumbs
100 g/4 oz shredded suet
50 g/2 oz caster sugar
1 egg
15 ml/1 tbsp black treacle
75-100 ml/3-3½ fl oz milk

Grease a 1 litre/1¾ pint pudding basin and put 15 ml/1 tbsp golden syrup in the bottom. Prepare a steamer or half fill a large saucepan with water and bring to the boil.

Sift the flour, soda, salt and ginger into a mixing bowl. Add the breadcrumbs, suet and sugar and mix lightly.

In a second bowl, combine the egg, remaining syrup and treacle. Beat in 75 ml/5 tbsp of the milk. Stir into the dry ingredients, adding more milk if necessary to give a soft dropping consistency.

Spoon the mixture into the prepared basin, cover with greased greaseproof paper or foil and secure with string.

Put the pudding in the perforated part of the steamer, or stand it on an old saucer or plate in the saucepan of boiling water. The water should come halfway up the sides of the basin. Cover the pan tightly and steam the pudding over gently simmering water for 1½-2 hours.

Leave for 5-10 minutes at room temperature to firm up, then turn out on to a serving plate. Serve with additional warmed golden syrup and whipped cream.

SERVES 6-8

☆ **FREEZER TIP** Keep a bag of breadcrumbs in the freezer for sweet and savoury toppings, puddings and stuffings.

S NOWDON PUDDING

fat for greasing
25 g/1 oz glacé cherries, halved
100 g/4 oz raisins
100 g/4 oz stale white breadcrumbs
100 g/4 oz shredded suet
25 g/1 oz ground rice
grated rind of 1 lemon
100 g/4 oz caster sugar
pinch of salt
30 ml/2 tbsp marmalade
2 eggs, beaten
about 75 ml/5 tbsp milk

Grease a 1 litre/1¾ pint pudding basin and

decorate the base with some of the cherry halves and raisins. Prepare a steamer or half fill a large saucepan with water and bring to the boil.

Mix the breadcrumbs, remaining cherries and raisins, suet, ground rice, grated lemon rind, sugar, salt and marmalade in a mixing bowl. Stir in the beaten eggs with enough milk to give a dropping consistency. Spoon the mixture into the prepared basin, cover with greased greaseproof paper or foil and secure with string.

Put the pudding in the perforated part of the steamer, or stand it on an old saucer or plate in the saucepan of boiling water. The water should come halfway up the sides of the basin. Cover the pan tightly and steam the pudding over gently simmering water for 2-2½ hours.

Leave for 5-10 minutes at room temperature to firm up, then turn out on to a serving plate. Serve with Marmalade and Wine Sauce (page 403).

SERVES 6

🥣 **MRS BEETON'S TIP** Mix the cherries and raisins used in the pudding thoroughly with the dry ingredients before adding the marmalade and liquids. This will prevent the fruit from sinking to the bottom of the pudding.

⊟ **PRESSURE COOKER TIP** Pour 1.1 litres/2 pints boiling water into the cooker. Steam the pudding without weights on the cooker for 15 minutes. Bring to 15 lb pressure and cook for 25 minutes. Reduce pressure slowly.

*P*ADDINGTON PUDDING

fat for greasing
100 g/4 oz stale white breadcrumbs
100 g/4 oz sultanas
100 g/4 oz shredded suet
100 g/4 oz self-raising flour
grated rind of 1 lemon
50 g/2 oz caster sugar
pinch of salt
60 ml/4 tbsp marmalade
2 eggs, beaten
about 75 ml/5 tbsp milk

Grease a 1 litre/1¾ pint pudding basin. Prepare a steamer or half fill a large saucepan with water and bring to the boil.

Mix the breadcrumbs, sultanas, suet, flour, grated rind, sugar, salt and marmalade in a mixing bowl. Stir in the beaten eggs with enough milk to give a dropping consistency. Spoon the mixture into the prepared basin, cover with greased greaseproof paper or foil and secure with string.

Put the pudding in the perforated part of the steamer, or stand it on an old saucer or plate in the saucepan of boiling water. The water should come halfway up the sides of the basin. Cover the pan tightly and steam the pudding over gently simmering water for 1½-2 hours.

Leave for 5-10 minutes at room temperature to firm up, then turn out on to a serving plate. Serve with single cream or Marmalade and Wine Sauce (page 403).

SERVES 6

*T*ANGY LEMON PUDDING

fat for greasing
50 g/2 oz plain flour
pinch of salt
5 ml/1 tsp baking powder
175 g/6 oz stale white breadcrumbs
100 g/4 oz caster sugar
100 g/4 oz shredded suet
grated rind and juice of 2 lemons
2 eggs, beaten
150-175 ml/5-6 fl oz milk

Grease a 750 ml/1¼ pint pudding basin. Prepare a steamer or half fill a large saucepan with water and bring to the boil.

Sift the flour, salt and baking powder into a mixing bowl. Stir in the breadcrumbs, sugar, suet and lemon rind. Mix lightly.

In a second bowl, beat the eggs with the lemon juice and about 150 ml/¼ pint of the milk. Stir into the dry ingredients, adding more milk if necessary to give a soft dropping consistency. Spoon the mixture into the prepared basin, cover with greased greaseproof paper or foil and secure with string.

Put the pudding in the perforated part of the steamer, or stand it on an old saucer or plate in the saucepan of boiling water. The water should come halfway up the sides of the basin. Cover the pan tightly and steam the pudding over gently simmering water for 1½-2 hours.

Serve from the basin or leave for 5-10 minutes at room temperature to firm up, then turn out on to a serving plate. Serve with Rich Lemon Sauce (page 395).

SERVES 6

*C*ANARY PUDDING

Illustrated on page 264

fat for greasing
150 g/5 oz butter or margarine
150 g/5 oz caster sugar
3 eggs, beaten
grated rind of ½ lemon
150 g/5 oz plain flour
5 ml/1 tsp baking powder

Grease a 1 litre/1¾ pint pudding basin. Prepare a steamer or half fill a large saucepan with water and bring to the boil.

Cream the butter or margarine with the sugar in a mixing bowl until light and fluffy. Beat in the eggs gradually, adding a little of the flour if the mixture begins to curdle. Add the lemon rind.

Sift the flour and baking powder together and fold lightly into the creamed mixture. Spoon the mixture into the prepared basin, cover with greased greaseproof paper or foil and secure with string.

Put the pudding in the perforated part of the steamer, or stand it on an old saucer or plate in the saucepan of boiling water. The water should come halfway up the sides of the basin. Cover the pan tightly and steam the pudding over gently simmering water for 1¼-1½ hours.

Leave for 3-5 minutes at room temperature to firm up, then turn out on to a serving plate.

SERVES 6

VARIATIONS

COCONUT SPONGE PUDDING Add to the basic recipe 50 g/2 oz desiccated coconut. Serve with Rum and Raisin Chocolate Sauce (page 401).

DATE SPONGE PUDDING Add to the basic recipe 150 g/5 oz chopped stoned dates. Substitute orange rind for lemon rind.

DRIED FRUIT SPONGE PUDDING Add to the basic recipe 150 g/5 oz mixed dried fruit. Serve with Vanilla Custard (page 403).

CHERRY SPONGE PUDDING Add to the basic recipe 75 g/3 oz glacé cherries, stirring them into the flour.

CHOCOLATE SPONGE PUDDING Substitute 25 g/1 oz cocoa for the same quantity of the flour and stir 75 g/3 oz chocolate chips into the mixture.

GINGER SPONGE PUDDING Add 10 ml/2 tsp ground ginger with the flour and stir 50 g/2 oz chopped preserved ginger into the mixture. Serve with Ginger Sauce (page 394).

MICROWAVE TIP To make a sponge pudding in the microwave, use 50 g/2 oz each of butter or margarine, sugar and self-raising flour with 1 egg and 30 ml/2 tbsp milk. Prepare the pudding as above and put it into a greased 1.1 litre/2 pint basin. Cook on High for 3–5 minutes.

WASHINGTON RIPPLE

Illustrated on page 281

fat for greasing
150 g/5 oz butter or margarine
150 g/5 oz caster sugar
3 eggs, beaten
150 g/5 oz plain flour
5 ml/1 tsp baking powder
30 ml/2 tbsp raspberry jam or jelly

Grease a 1 litre/1¾ pint pudding basin. Prepare a steamer or half fill a large saucepan with water and bring to the boil.

Cream the butter or margarine with the sugar in a mixing bowl until light and fluffy. Beat in the eggs gradually, adding a little of the flour if the mixture begins to curdle.

Sift the flour and baking powder together and fold lightly into the creamed mixture. Add the jam or jelly, using a skewer to draw it lightly through the mixture to create a ripple effect.

Spoon the mixture into the prepared basin, cover with greased greaseproof paper or foil and secure with string. Put the pudding in the perforated part of the steamer, or stand it on an old saucer or plate in the saucepan of boiling water. The water should come halfway up the sides of the basin. Cover the pan tightly and steam the pudding over gently simmering water for 1¼-1½ hours.

Leave for 3-5 minutes at room temperature to firm up, then turn out on to a serving plate. Serve with Vanilla Custard (page 403).

SERVES 6

APRICOT AND ALMOND PUDDING

Illustrated on page 281

fat for greasing
75 g/3 oz butter or margarine
75 g/3 oz caster sugar
2 eggs, beaten
75 g/3 oz plain flour
30 ml/2 tbsp grated orange rind
2.5 ml/½ tsp baking powder
6 canned apricot halves, chopped
25 g/1 oz ground almonds
1 slice of orange, halved, to decorate

Grease a 750 ml/1¼ pint pudding basin. Prepare a steamer or half fill a large saucepan with water and bring to the boil.

Cream the butter or margarine with the sugar in a mixing bowl until light and fluffy. Beat in the eggs gradually, adding a little of the flour if the mixture begins to curdle. Add the orange rind.

Sift the flour and baking powder together and fold lightly into the creamed mixture with the chopped apricots and ground almonds. Spoon the mixture into the prepared basin, cover with greased greaseproof paper or foil and secure with string.

Put the pudding in the perforated part of the steamer, or stand it on an old saucer or plate in the saucepan of boiling water. The water should come halfway up the sides of the basin. Cover the pan tightly and steam the pudding for 1¼-1½ hours.

Leave for 5 minutes at room temperature to firm up. Turn the pudding out on to a serving plate, decorate with the orange slice and serve with Apricot Sauce (page 398).

SERVES 6

NEWCASTLE PUDDING

fat for greasing
25 g/1 oz glacé cherries, halved
100 g/4 oz butter or margarine
100 g/4 oz caster sugar
2 eggs, beaten
150 g/5 oz plain flour
pinch of salt
5 ml/1 tsp baking powder
about 45 ml/3 tbsp milk

Grease a 1 litre/1¾ pint pudding basin. With the cherries, make a pattern on the base of the basin. Prepare a steamer or half fill a large saucepan with water and bring to the boil.

Cream the butter or margarine with the sugar in a mixing bowl. Gradually beat in the eggs, adding a little flour if the mixture begins to curdle.

Sift the flour with the salt and baking powder and stir into the pudding mixture with enough milk to give a soft dropping consistency.

Spoon the mixture into the prepared basin, cover with greased greaseproof paper or foil and secure with string. Put the pudding in the perforated part of the steamer, or stand it on an old saucer or plate in the saucepan of boiling water. The water should come halfway up the sides of the basin. Cover the pan tightly and steam the pudding over gently simmering water for 1½-2 hours.

Leave for 5-10 minutes at room temperature to firm up, then turn out on to a serving plate. Serve with single cream.

SERVES 6

PATRIOTIC PUDDING

fat for greasing
45 ml/3 tbsp red jam
200 g/7 oz plain flour
pinch of salt
10 ml/2 tsp baking powder
100 g/4 oz butter or margarine
100 g/4 oz caster sugar
1 egg, beaten
about 75 ml/5 tbsp milk

Grease a 1 litre/1¾ pint pudding basin and cover the base with the jam. Prepare a steamer or half fill a large saucepan with water and bring to the boil.

Sift the flour, salt and baking powder into a mixing bowl. Rub in the butter or margarine and add the sugar. Stir in the egg and milk to give a soft dropping consistency. Spoon the mixture into the prepared basin, cover with greased greaseproof paper or foil and secure with string.

Put the pudding in the perforated part of the steamer, or stand it on an old saucer or plate in the saucepan of boiling water. The water should come halfway up the sides of the basin. Cover the pan tightly and steam the pudding over gently simmering water for 1½-2 hours.

SERVES 6

> **PRESSURE COOKER TIP** Pour 1.1 litres/2 pints boiling water into the cooker. Steam the pudding without weights on the cooker for 15 minutes. Bring to 15 lb pressure and cook for 25 minutes. Reduce the pressure slowly.

*B*ACHELOR PUDDING

fat for greasing
1 cooking apple (about 150 g/5 oz)
100 g/4 oz stale white breadcrumbs
grated rind of ½ lemon
100 g/4 oz currants
75 g/3 oz caster sugar
pinch of salt
1.25 ml/¼ tsp grated nutmeg
2 eggs, beaten
125 ml/4 fl oz milk
2.5 ml/½ tsp baking powder

Peel, core and grate the apple. Put it into a mixing bowl with the breadcrumbs, lemon rind, currants, sugar, salt and nutmeg. Add the eggs with enough of the milk to give a soft dropping consistency. Leave to stand for 30 minutes.

Grease a 1 litre/1¾ pint pudding basin. Prepare a steamer or half fill a large saucepan with water and bring to the boil.

Stir the baking powder into the pudding mixture. Spoon the mixture into the prepared basin, cover with greased greaseproof paper or foil and secure with string.

Put the pudding in the perforated part of the steamer, or stand it on an old saucer or plate in the saucepan of boiling water. The water should come halfway up the sides of the basin. Cover the pan tightly and steam the pudding over gently simmering water for 2½-3 hours.

Serve from the basin or leave for 5-10 minutes at room temperature to firm up, then turn out on to a serving plate. Serve with Redcurrant Sauce (page 393) or Cold Chantilly Apple Sauce (page 399).

SERVES 6

*C*HOCOLATE CRUMB PUDDING

Illustrated on page 282

fat for greasing
50 g/2 oz plain chocolate
125 ml/4 fl oz milk
40 g/1½ oz butter or margarine
40 g/1½ oz caster sugar
2 eggs, separated
100 g/4 oz stale white breadcrumbs
1.25 ml/¼ tsp baking powder

DECORATION
Chocolate Caraque or grated chocolate (page 100)
strawberries, halved, (optional)

Grease a 750 ml/1¼ pint pudding basin or 6 dariole moulds. Prepare a steamer or half fill a large saucepan with water and bring to the boil.

Grate the chocolate into a saucepan, add the milk and heat slowly to dissolve the chocolate.

Cream the butter or margarine with the sugar in a mixing bowl. Beat in the egg yolks with the melted chocolate mixture. Add the breadcrumbs and baking powder.

In a clean, grease-free bowl, whisk the egg whites until fairly stiff. Fold them into the pudding mixture. Spoon the mixture into the prepared basin or moulds, cover with greased greaseproof paper or foil and secure with string.

Put the pudding or puddings in the perforated part of the steamer, or stand it (them) on an old plate in the saucepan of boiling water. The water should come halfway up the sides of the basin. Cover the pan tightly and steam over gently simmering water for 1 hour for a large pudding, or 30 minutes for individual moulds.

Leave for 3-5 minutes at room temperature to firm up, then turn out. Serve with Chocolate Cream Sauce (page 400), Mocha Sauce (page 400) or whipped cream. Top the puddings with chocolate caraque or grated chocolate and decorate with fresh strawberries when in season.

SERVES 6

> **MRS BEETON'S TIP** Feather a little single cream through the sauce. Put a few drops of cream on to sauce, then drag the tip of a cocktail stick through it (see illustration, page 282).

E VERYDAY CHOCOLATE PUDDING

fat for greasing
200 g/7 oz plain flour
5 ml/1 tsp baking powder
pinch of salt
25 g/1 oz cocoa
100 g/4 oz butter or margarine
100 g/4 oz caster sugar
2 eggs
1.25 ml/¼ tsp vanilla essence
milk (see method)

Grease a 1 litre/1¾ pint pudding basin. Prepare a steamer or half fill a large saucepan with water and bring to the boil.

Sift the flour, baking powder, salt and cocoa into a mixing bowl. Rub in the butter or margarine and stir in the sugar.

In a second bowl, beat the eggs with the vanilla essence. Add to the dry ingredients with enough milk to give a soft dropping consistency.

Spoon the mixture into the prepared basin, cover with greased greaseproof paper or foil and secure with string. Put the pudding in the perforated part of the steamer, or stand it on an old saucer or plate in the saucepan of boiling water. The water should come halfway up the sides of the basin. Cover the pan tightly and steam the pudding over gently simmering water for 1¾-2 hours.

Leave for 5-10 minutes at room temperature to firm up, then turn out on to a serving plate. Serve with Mocha Sauce (page 400) or, on special occasions, with Chocolate Liqueur Sauce (page 400).

SERVES 6

> **MRS BEETON'S TIP** When rubbing the fat into the flour, use only the tips of your fingers, lifting the mixture above the surface of the bowl and letting it drop back naturally to incorporate as much air as possible.

◆

*P*RINCE ALBERT'S PUDDING

Prunes – those 'plums' so beloved of the Victorians – feature strongly in this pudding, which looks most effective when turned out.

fat for greasing
400 g/14 oz prunes, soaked overnight in
    water to cover
grated rind of 1 lemon
25 g/1 oz soft light brown sugar
100 g/4 oz butter or margarine
100 g/4 oz caster sugar
2 eggs, separated
40 g/1½ oz rice flour
100 g/4 oz brown breadcrumbs

SAUCE
5 ml/1 tsp arrowroot
250 ml/8 fl oz prune liquid (see method)
10 ml/2 tsp granulated sugar
2-3 drops red food colouring

Drain the prunes and transfer them to a saucepan. Add half the lemon rind, the brown sugar and 500 ml/17 fl oz water. Simmer gently until soft, stirring lightly from time to time to dissolve the sugar.

As soon as the prunes are soft, drain them, reserving 250 ml/8 fl oz of the cooking liquid. When the prunes are cool enough to handle, halve and stone them.

Grease a 1 litre/1¾ pint pudding basin. Use the prunes, skin side out, to line the basin. Chop any remaining prunes and set aside. Prepare a steamer or half fill a large saucepan with water and bring to the boil.

Cream the butter or margarine with the caster sugar in a mixing bowl. Beat in the egg yolks with the remaining lemon rind, the rice flour and the breadcrumbs. Stir in any remaining prunes.

In a clean, grease-free bowl, whisk the egg whites until fairly stiff. Fold into the pudding mixture. Spoon the mixture into the prepared basin, cover with greased greaseproof paper or foil and secure with string.

Put the pudding in the perforated part of the steamer, or stand it on an old saucer or plate in the saucepan of boiling water. The water should come halfway up the sides of the basin. Cover the pan tightly and steam the pudding over gently simmering water for 1½-1¾ hours.

Meanwhile make the sauce. In a bowl, mix the arrowroot to a smooth paste with some of the reserved prune liquid. Put the rest of the liquid into a saucepan and bring it to the boil. Gradually pour the hot liquid over the arrowroot paste, stirring constantly. Return the mixture to the clean saucepan and bring to the boil, stirring all the time. Lower the heat and simmer for 2-3 minutes. Add the sugar and stir until dissolved. Add the colouring.

When the pudding is cooked, leave for 5-10 minutes at room temperature to firm up, then carefully turn out on to a serving plate. Pour the sauce over the top and serve at once.

SERVES 6

☀ **MICROWAVE TIP** No time to soak the prunes overnight? Place in a suitable bowl with water or tea to cover. Cover the bowl and microwave for 6-8 minutes on High. Stand for 10 minutes before using.

*C*LOUTIE DUMPLING

300 g/11 oz self-raising flour
5 ml/1 tsp baking powder
100 g/4 oz shredded suet
5 ml/1 tsp mixed spice
5 ml/1 tsp ground ginger
5 ml/1 tsp ground cinnamon
2.5 ml/½ tsp salt
100 g/4 oz soft light brown sugar
50 g/2 oz muscatel raisins, seeded
100 g/4 oz sultanas
50 g/2 oz cut mixed peel
1 carrot, grated
100 g/4 oz black treacle
200 ml/7 fl oz milk
1 egg, beaten
flour for dusting or fat for greasing

Mix the flour, baking powder, suet, spices, salt and sugar in a mixing bowl. Stir in the raisins, sultanas and mixed peel with the carrot.

Put the treacle in a saucepan with the milk and dissolve over low heat. Stir into the dry ingredients with the egg to give a fairly soft dropping consistency. Mix thoroughly.

Put the mixture into a scalded and floured cloth and tie with string, allowing room for expansion. Place on a plate in a saucepan and add sufficient boiling water to come three-quarters of the way up the dumpling. Simmer for 3 hours.

Alternatively spoon the mixture into a greased 1.5 litre/2¾ pint basin, cover with greased greaseproof paper or foil and secure with string. Cook in a steamer or on an old saucer or plate in a saucepan of boiling water. The water should come halfway up the sides of the basin. Simmer as above.

Turn out on to a serving dish and serve hot or cold with Classic Egg Custard Sauce (page 404) or Sweet Sherry Sauce (page 402).

SERVES 4 TO 6

🍯 **MRS BEETON'S TIP** To save transferring the sticky treacle, measure it in the saucepan, weighing the empty pan first and then adding sufficient treacle to increase the weight by 100 g/ 4 oz.

PASTRIES, COBBLERS AND CRUMBLES

These hearty puddings combine seasonal fruits with sponge toppings, light crumbly coverings or delicious scones. As well as the more satisfying hot puddings, the chapter also includes Baked Apples and Apple Meringue.

When making crumbles and scone toppings for puddings, quick, light handling of the ingredients plays an important part in achieving success. Follow the notes on pastry-making given at the beginning of page 345 when rubbing fat into flour. Here are just a few additional notes and hints which apply to cobblers and crumbles.

COBBLERS

A cobbler is usually a fruit pudding with a topping of sweet scone dough. The basic scone mixture is made of self-raising flour (or plain flour with baking powder, or a mixture of bicarbonate of soda and cream of tartar) with a little fat and sugar. The dry ingredients are bound with milk.

Scone dough should be soft but not too sticky and it should be kneaded very lightly into a smooth ball before it is rolled out. It should not be handled heavily or for too long otherwise the result will be heavy.

CRUMBLES

Crumbles are quick and easy to make and the basic mixture of flour, fat and sugar may be varied in many ways. Spices, nuts and cereals may be stirred in to add texture and flavour to the cooked crumble. When served, the topping should be browned and crisp, crumbly and cooked through.

Handle the crumble mixture lightly, sprinkling it over the fruit and spreading it evenly without pressing down too firmly.

FREEZING

Both cobblers and crumbles freeze well. The scone topping for cobblers must be cooked before freezing. The complete cobbler may be frozen or prepared scone toppings may be frozen separately for thawing and reheating on a base of cooked fruit.

Crumbles may be frozen when cooked or they may be prepared ready for cooking, frozen and cooked just before serving. Alternatively, the raw crumble mix may be frozen in a suitable bag, ready to be sprinkled over the fruit before cooking.

If you are freezing a pudding in its dish do make sure that the dish is suitable.

OTHER BAKED PUDDINGS

As well as puddings with crumble or cobbler toppings, the chapter offers recipes for fruits cooked with sponge or meringue toppings. There are light mixtures baked with fruit and other flavourings or substantial puddings using bread. A recipe for a self-saucing lemon pudding is also featured: a light cake batter separates during baking to give a delicate spongy top with a tangy lemon sauce below. In addition there are a few classic British suet puddings and others that make the most of tart cooking apples.

Put your pastry-making skills to the test and sample the delights this chapter has to offer: steaming hot suet puddings, lightly layered puff pastry confections or crisply crusted fruit flans are all here for the making. If you have any doubts about basic techniques, simply read through the basic information which follows.

MAKING PASTRY

Good pastry should be light in texture. A few simple rules will help to ensure success with all types. Always weigh ingredients accurately as it is important that the correct proportions of fat, flour and liquid are used. Keep all ingredients, utensils and your hands as cool as possible.

RUBBING IN

The first stage in making several types of pastry is to rub the fat into the flour. This basic technique is used for other purposes in cookery so it is worth getting it right. Cut the fat into small pieces and mix it with the flour. Using just the tips of your fingers, lift a little of the mixture and rub the fat with the flour once or twice. Let the mixture fall back into the bowl before lifting another small portion and rubbing again. Continue in this way until the mixture has the texture of fine breadcrumbs.

It is important that you lift the mixture and rub it lightly to incorporate air into it. If you pick up too much mixture and push it back into the palms of your hands, air will not mix with it and the pastry will be heavy. Once you have mastered the technique you will find it quick and easy to perform; in fact, the quicker the process is completed, the lighter the pastry.

The mixture of flour and fat can be stored before liquid is added. It will keep in a covered container in the refrigerator for up to 3 days or it may be frozen for up to 3 months.

ADDING LIQUID TO SHORT PASTRIES

The term 'short' is used to describe pastry that is not made heavy by the addition of too much liquid. The 'melt-in-your-mouth' texture that is characteristic of good 'short' pastry is the result of using the right proportion of fat to flour and just enough liquid to hold the pastry together as it is rolled.

When making sweet pastry dishes, various types of short pastry may be used and the difference may be in the liquid added to bind the ingredients. Plain short crust pastry is bound with a little water. The water should be very cold (preferably iced) and just enough should be added to bind the rubbed in mixture into lumps. The lumps are gently pressed together so that the pastry just holds its shape. It should not be sticky.

Sweet short crust or a richer pastry for making flans may be bound with egg yolk instead of, or as well as, a little water. Egg yolk contains a high proportion of fat so the resulting pastry will be very short. Adding sugar to pastry also tends to give a short and crumbly texture. Some rich pastry is made very short by adding extra fat, usually butter, to give a good flavour as well as a short texture.

ADDING LIQUID TO PUFF PASTRY OR FLAKY PASTRY

The dough for this type of pastry has only a small proportion of the fat rubbed in, with the majority of the fat incorporated by rolling it with the pastry. A little extra liquid is added to make a dough that is just slightly sticky. This type of dough holds the fat which is added in lumps or a block during rolling. The resulting pastry is not short; it is crisp and it forms distinct layers. Puff pastry is lighter and has more layers than flaky pastry.

The layers in puff and flaky pastry trap air to make the pastry rise during cooking. A strengthening substance called *gluten* is naturally present in flour; this is developed by rolling the pastry. The process of rolling and folding actually serves to toughen the basic dough. Adding the fat each time the pastry is rolled means that the dough does not form into a solid mass but retains very fine layers. The air trapped between these layers expands as the dough is heated and so the pastry rises. Because the dough itself it toughened by the gluten, the layers set and give the finished pastry its characteristic crisp texture.

ROLLING OUT

Whatever type of pastry you are handling, you should always roll it out very lightly. Use a very light dusting of flour on the work surface. There should be just enough to prevent the pastry from sticking; short pastries usually require less than puff or flaky pastries. Too much flour at this stage may spoil the balance of ingredients.

Never turn pastry over during rolling. The pastry should be lifted occasionally and turned around to prevent it sticking to the surface. Push the rolling pin away from you in short, quick strokes. Keep the rolling pin lightly dusted with flour.

When rolling out pastry, try to establish the shape as soon as you begin. For exam-ple, if you are lining a round flan dish start with a ball of pastry which is flattened into a roughly circular shape. If you want to end up with an oblong sheet of pastry, form the pastry into an oblong lump and flatten it slightly before rolling it.

LIFTING ROLLED-OUT PASTRY

To lift a sheet of pastry, dust the rolling pin lightly with flour and place it in the middle of the pastry. Fold half the pastry over it, then use the rolling pin to lift the pastry into position.

LINING A FLAN TIN OR DISH

Roll the pastry out to a size that will cover the base and come up the sides of the dish with a little extra to spare. Lift the pastry on the rolling pin, then lower it loosely over the tin or dish.

Quickly work around the dish, lifting the edge of the pastry with one hand and pressing it down into the corner of the dish with the forefinger and knuckle of the other hand. When the pastry is pressed neatly all around the base of the dish, press the excess around the edge of the dish so that it falls backwards slightly.

Roll the rolling pin across the top of the dish to trim off excess pastry. If you are lining a tin its edge will cut off the pastry; if using a dish you will have to gently pull away the excess pastry edges.

BAKING BLIND

Pastry cases that are cooked and cooled before they are filled have a sheet of grease-proof paper and baking beans placed in them to prevent the base of the pastry from puffing up. This is known as baking blind (see Mrs Beeton's Tip, page 183). The paper and baking beans are usually removed once the pastry has cooked enough to set, and the pastry case returned to the oven to allow it to brown slightly.

In some recipes, the pastry case is partially baked before it is filled, and the cooking is completed with the filling. The technique of baking blind would be used to partially bake the pastry.

Clear instructions are given in individual recipes. Ceramic baking beans may be purchased for baking blind, or ordinary dried peas or beans may be used. These are sprinkled over the greaseproof paper to weight the pastry slightly. Dried peas or beans used for this purpose may be cooled and stored in an airtight container and used over and over again. However, they may not be cooked to be eaten in another recipe.

MAKING TURNOVERS

Turnovers may be cut in circles or squares. The size to which the pastry should be rolled depends on the quantities given in the recipe.

Use a saucer or plate to mark out circles; small turnovers are made by using large round biscuit cutters. When using a saucer or plate, place it on the pastry and cut around it with a small pointed knife.

Put the filling on one half of the pastry. Dampen all around the pastry edge, then fold the pastry over the filling. Press the pastry edges together well to seal in the filling and to give a neat semi-circular turnover.

To make triangular turnovers, roll out the pastry into a large square. Use a large, clean ruler and a small, pointed knife to trim off the pastry edges.

Cut the pastry into four squares of equal size.

Place some filling on one half of each

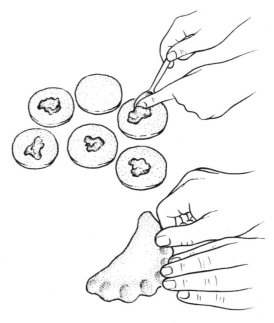

pastry square, in a corner, and dampen the edges.

Fold the corner of pastry opposite the filling over to enclose it completely and to make a neat triangle. Press the edges together to seal in the filling.

PASTRY PIES

Roll out the pastry about 5 cm/2 inches larger than the top of the dish. Cut off a strip from the edge of the pastry. Dampen the edge of the dish and press the strip of pastry on to it.

Fill the dish, dampen the pastry edge and lift the pastry lid over the top.

Press the edges of the pastry to seal in the filling. Holding the pie dish slightly raised in one hand, use a sharp knife to trim all around the edge of the dish. Keep the knife pointing outwards so that only the excess pastry is trimmed off.

KNOCKING UP

Knocking up is the term used for neatly sealing the pastry edges together. Press down and outwards on the pastry edge with the knuckle and forefinger of one hand, at the same time knocking the pastry edge inwards with the blunt edge of a round-bladed knife.

SCALLOPED EDGES

The traditional edge for a sweet pie is small scallops (large ones are used for savoury pies). Use the blunt edge of a knife to pull the pastry inwards as you push the edge out towards the rim of the dish with the finger of your other hand.

FORKED EDGE

A simple edging technique is to press all around the pastry with a fork. However, the edge does sometimes tend to become slightly too brown if the pastry is pressed very thin.

PLAITED EDGE

Re-roll leftover pastry and cut out three long, thin strips. Plait these together all around the edge of the pie.

DECORATIONS USING CUTTERS

Use small cocktail cutters to cut out pastry shapes. Dampen these and overlap them around the edge of the pie.

PASTRY LEAVES

Roll out a strip of pastry – the wider the strip, the longer the leaves – and cut it into diamond shapes. Mark veins on the leaves and pinch one end of each into a stalk.

IMAGINATIVE DESIGNS

Roll out pastry trimmings and cut out apples, pears, cherries or strawberry shapes

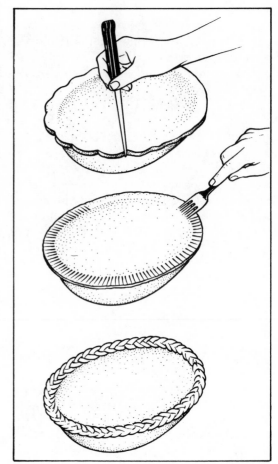

to decorate the top of the pie. Dampen the pastry to keep the decorations in place. Alternatively, cut out letters to spell 'apple', 'pear' or whichever fruit is appropriate for the filling and press them on the pie. A message, or the name of the recipient may be applied in the same way.

SUET CRUST PASTRY

Suet crust pastry is quick and easy to make. Shredded suet is combined with self-raising flour and the ingredients mixed to a soft dough with cold water. The quantity of water should give a soft but not sticky dough which may be kneaded very lightly into a smooth shape. The pastry rises to give a light, slightly spongy texture. Suet pastry is cooked by steaming, boiling or baking.

CHOUX PASTRY

Although many people shy away from making choux pastry, it is not difficult. However, it is important that all the ingredients are accurately measured and that a few rules are observed:

The water and fat must be heated together gently until the fat melts, and the mixture brought to the boil as quickly as possible. Do not bring the water to the boil before the fat melts.

The flour must be tipped into the liquid all at once, the pan removed from the heat and the mixture stirred to make a smooth paste that comes away from the sides of the pan in a clean ball. Do not beat the mixture at this stage or it will become greasy. If the mixture is too wet put the pan back on the heat and stir gently until the paste comes away from the sides of the pan. This paste must be cooled slightly before the eggs are added.

Lastly, eggs are beaten into the paste. At this stage the mixture should be thoroughly beaten until it is smooth and glossy. The paste should be soft enough to pipe but it should not be runny. Use the choux pastry at once.

FILO OR PHYLO PASTRY

This Greek pastry contains little fat. It is made with a strong flour. It is available both chilled and frozen, ready rolled in very thin sheets.

Two or three sheets are layered together before they are wrapped around a filling. Each sheet is brushed with melted butter. The pastry is very delicate to handle as it rapidly becomes brittle once unpacked. Always keep the pastry covered with cling film or under dampened tea towels when you are not working with it as it dries rapidly if exposed to the air. Make sure the work surface is perfectly dry before unrolling the pastry. Any dampness will cause the pastry to stick, soften and break up.

TIPS FOR SUCCESS WITH PASTRY

■ Work in a cool place; keep hands, utensils and all ingredients cool.

■ Weigh and measure all ingredients accurately.

■ Handle pastry as lightly as possible, and work as quickly as you can, at all stages.

■ Use the minimum amount of flour for rolling out.

■ Chill short crust, flaky and puff pastry for 20-30 minutes before rolling it out.

■ Chill finished short crust, puff or flaky pastry goods for 15 minutes before baking.

SOME COMMON FAULTS WITH PASTRY AND HOW TO AVOID THEM

Short Crust Pastry (or similar pastries)

Hard, tough pastry

■ Too little fat used

■ Too much liquid added

■ Pastry handled too much or too heavily

■ Too much flour used for rolling out

Grainy, flaky or blistered pastry

■ Fat not rubbed in sufficiently

■ Water not mixed in well

■ Pastry rolled out twice

■ Too much flour used for rolling

Pastry too short, very crumbly (collapses)

■ Too much fat used

■ Fat overworked into flour

■ Too little liquid used

Puff or Flaky Pastry

Pastry Hard and Tough

- ■ Warm fat used

- ■ Too much water used

- ■ Dough overkneaded

- ■ Oven temperature too low during cooking

Unevenly Risen

- ■ Fat not mixed in evenly during rolling

- ■ Unevenly folded and rolled

- ■ Pastry not chilled before use

Pastry flat, not light

- ■ Warm fat used

- ■ Dough not folded and rolled sufficiently

Soggy Pastry with a Hard Crust

- ■ Oven too hot; pastry browned and hardened before it had time to rise

Suet Crust Pastry

Hard and Tough

- ■ Too much water added

- ■ Cooked in a low oven for too long

Solid, Lumpy Pastry

- ■ Plain flour used in a recipe that stipulated self-raising flour or plain flour plus a raising agent

- ■ Pastry cooked too quickly (suet has not melted)

- ■ Pastry has got wet during steaming

- ■ Home-grated suet was lumpy

BLUEBERRY PIE

1 kg/2¼ lb fresh blueberries or bilberries
175 g/6 oz caster sugar
45 ml/3 tbsp plain flour
5 ml/1 tsp grated lemon rind
2.5 ml/½ tsp cinnamon
pinch of salt
15 ml/1 tbsp lemon juice
15 g/½ oz butter

SHORT CRUST PASTRY
350 g/12 oz plain flour
2.5 ml/½ tsp salt
175 g/6 oz margarine (or half butter, half lard)
flour for rolling out

Set the oven at 200°C/400°F/gas 6. To make the pastry, sift the flour and salt into a bowl, then rub in the margarine until the mixture resembles fine breadcrumbs. Add enough cold water to make a stiff dough. Press the dough together with your fingertips.

Roll out the pastry on a lightly floured surface and use just over half to line a 25 cm/10 inch pie plate. Use the remaining pastry to make a lid.

In a bowl, mix the cleaned berries with the sugar, flour, lemon rind, cinnamon and salt. Spoon the mixture into the pie case, sprinkle with lemon juice and dot with butter.

Dampen the edge of the pie and cover with the pastry lid. Seal the edge. Make 3 or 4 slits in the top of the pie to let the steam escape. Bake for 35-40 minutes or until golden. Serve hot or cold.

SERVES 6

TRADITIONAL APPLE PIE

675 g/1½ lb cooking apples
100 g/4 oz sugar
6 cloves
caster sugar for dredging

SHORT CRUST PASTRY
350 g/12 oz plain flour
4 ml/¾ tsp salt
175 ml/6 oz margarine (or half butter, half lard)
flour for rolling out

Set the oven at 200°C/400°F/gas 6. To make the pastry, sift the flour and salt into a bowl, then rub in the margarine until the mixture resembles fine breadcrumbs. Add enough cold water to make a stiff dough. Press the dough together with your fingertips.

Roll out the pastry on a lightly floured surface and use just over half to line a 750 ml/1¼ pint pie dish. Peel, core and slice the apples. Place half in the pastry-lined dish, then add the sugar and cloves. Pile the remaining apples on top, cover with the remaining pastry and seal the edges. Brush the pastry with cold water and dredge with caster sugar.

Bake for 20 minutes, then lower the even temperature to 180°C/350°F/gas 4 and bake for 20 minutes more. The pastry should be golden brown. Dredge with more caster sugar and serve hot or cold.

SERVES 6

VARIATIONS

APRICOT PIE Use two 375 g/15 oz cans apricots, drained, instead of apples. Omit the sugar and cloves.
BLACKBERRY AND APPLE PIE (*Illustrated on page 283*). Use half black-berries and half apples and replace the cloves with 2.5 ml/½ tsp grated lemon rind.
DAMSON PIE Use damsons instead of apples, increase the sugar to 150 g/5 oz and omit the cloves.
GOOSEBERRY PIE Use cleaned, topped and tailed gooseberries instead of apples. Omit the cloves.
REDCURRANT AND RASPBERRY PIE This is a winning combination. Use 450 g/1 lb redcurrants and 225 g/8 oz raspberries instead of apples. Reduce the sugar to 30 ml/2 tbsp and omit the cloves.
RHUBARB PIE Use rhubarb cut into 2 cm/¾ inch lengths instead of apples. Increase the sugar to 150 g/5 oz.

☆ FREEZER TIP The pie may be frozen cooked or uncooked. If cooked, cool completely, wrap in foil and overwrap in a polythene bag. Wrap an uncooked pie in the same way. Reheat or cook the unwrapped pie from frozen. A cooked pie will require 20 minutes at 200°C/400°F/gas 6, followed by 15-20 minutes at 180°C/350°F/gas 4. For an uncooked pie, bake at 200°C/400°F/gas 6 for 30 minutes, then at 190°C/375°F/gas 5 for about a further 40 minutes. The exact timing will depend on the depth of the pie dish. Before transferring the pie from freezer to oven, make sure that the dish will withstand the sudden change in temperature.

*M*RS BEETON'S BAKEWELL PUDDING

strawberry or apricot jam
50 g/2 oz butter
50 g/2 oz caster sugar
1 egg
50 g/2 oz ground almonds
50 g/2 oz fine cake crumbs
few drops of almond essence
icing sugar for dusting

SHORT CRUST PASTRY
    100 g/4 oz plain flour
    1.25 ml/¼ tsp salt
    50 g/2 oz margarine (or half butter, half lard)
    flour for rolling out

Set the oven at 200°C/400°F/gas 6. To make the pastry, sift the flour and salt into a bowl, then rub in the margarine until the mixture resembles fine breadcrumbs. Add enough cold water to make a stiff dough. Press the dough together lightly.

Roll out the pastry on a lightly floured surface and use to line an 18 cm/7 inch flan tin or ring placed on a baking sheet. Spread a good layer of jam over the pastry base.

In a mixing bowl, cream the butter with the sugar until pale and fluffy. Beat in the egg, then add the almonds, cake crumbs and essence. Beat until well mixed. Pour into the flan case, on top of the jam.

Bake for 30 minutes or until the centre of the pudding is firm. Sprinkle with icing sugar and serve hot or cold.

SERVES 4 TO 5

VARIATIONS

BAKEWELL TART Make as above, but use raspberry jam and only 25 g/1 oz bread or cake crumbs and 25 g/1 oz ground almonds. Bake for 25 minutes.

ALMOND TARTLETS Line twelve 7.5 cm/3 inch patty tins with the pastry. Replace the cake crumbs with an extra 50 g/2 oz ground almonds and the almond essence with 2.5 ml/½ tsp lemon juice. Bake for 12-18 minutes.

WEST RIDING PUDDING Line a 500 ml/17 oz dish with the pastry. Make as for Bakewell Pudding but substitute 75 g/3 oz plain flour and 2.5 ml/½ tsp baking powder for the cake crumbs and ground almonds. If the mixture seems stiff, add a little milk. Bake at 190°C/375°F, gas 5 for 1 hour. Serve hot or cold.

*L*EMON MERINGUE PIE

300 g/11 oz granulated sugar
45 ml/3 tbsp cornflour
45 ml/3 tbsp plain flour
pinch of salt
30 ml/2 tbsp butter
5 ml/1 tsp grated lemon rind
75 ml/5 tbsp lemon juice
3 eggs, separated
75 g/3 oz caster sugar

SHORT CRUST PASTRY
    175 g/6 oz plain flour
    2.5 ml/½ tsp salt
    75 g/3 oz margarine (or half butter, half lard)
    flour for rolling out

Set the oven at 200°C/400°F/gas 6. To make the pastry, sift the flour and salt into a bowl, then rub in the margarine until the mixture resembles fine breadcrumbs. Add enough cold water to make a stiff dough. Press the dough together lightly.

Roll out the pastry on a lightly floured surface and use to line a 23 cm/9 inch pie plate. Line the pastry with greaseproof paper and fill with baking beans. Bake 'blind' for 15 minutes; remove paper and beans. Return to the oven for 5 minutes.

Meanwhile mix the sugar, cornflour, plain flour and salt in the top of a double saucepan. In a saucepan, bring 300 ml/½ pint water to the boil. Stir the boiling water slowly into the dry mixture, then place the top of the double saucepan over gently simmering water. Cover and cook gently for 20 minutes.

Draw the pan off the heat and add the butter, lemon rind and juice. Put the egg yolks in a bowl, add a little of the cooked mixture, then add to the mixture in the pan. Beat well, replace over the heat and cook, stirring constantly until thick. Remove the pan from the heat and set aside to cool. Remove the pie from the oven and lower the oven temperature to 180°C/350°F/gas 4.

In a clean, grease-free bowl, whisk the egg whites until stiff. Fold in the caster sugar. Pour the lemon custard into the baked pastry case and cover the top with the meringue, making sure that it covers the top completely. Bake for 12-15 minutes until the meringue is lightly browned. Cool before cutting.

SERVES 6

> **MRS BEETON'S TIP** Meringue-topped pies are notoriously difficult to cut. It will simplify matters if you use a sharp knife which is dipped in warm water before each cut is made.

CRANBERRY RAISIN PIE

225 g/8 oz cranberries
175 g/6 oz raisins
150 g/5 oz sugar
30 ml/2 tbsp plain flour
1.25 ml/¼ tsp salt
25 g/1 oz butter

SHORT CRUST PASTRY
225 g/8 oz plain flour
2.5 ml/½ tsp salt
100 g/4 oz margarine (or half butter, half lard)
flour for rolling out

Set the oven at 230°C/450°F/gas 8. To make the pastry, sift the flour and salt into a bowl, then rub in the margarine until the mixture resembles fine breadcrumbs. Add enough cold water to make a stiff dough. Press the dough together with your fingertips. Roll out on a lightly floured surface and use two thirds of the pastry to line a 23 cm/9 inch pie plate.

In a bowl, combine the cranberries and raisins with the sugar, flour and salt. Mix lightly, then spoon into the pastry case. Dot with the butter.

Roll out the remaining pastry into a rectangle and cut into five 1 cm/½ inch strips. Arrange the strips in a lattice on top of the pie. Bake for 10 minutes, then lower the oven temperature to 180°C/350°F/gas 4 and bake for 30-40 minutes more.

SERVES 6

> **MRS BEETON'S TIP** When rolling out pastry, use as little flour as possible. Flour worked in at this stage toughens the pastry.

MINCEMEAT MERINGUE PIE

50 g/2 oz soft white breadcrumbs
30 ml/2 tbsp granulated sugar
2 eggs, separated
375 ml/13 fl oz milk
15 ml/1 tbsp butter
2.5 ml/½ tsp vanilla essence
225 g/8 oz mincemeat
75 g/3 oz caster sugar

SHORT CRUST PASTRY
100 g/4 oz plain flour
2.5 ml/½ tsp salt
50 g/2 oz margarine (or half butter, half lard)
flour for rolling out

Set the oven at 200°C/400°F/gas 6. To make the pastry, sift the flour and salt into a bowl, then rub in the margarine until the mixture resembles fine breadcrumbs. Add enough cold water to make a stiff dough. Press the dough together with your fingertips.

Roll out the pastry on a lightly floured surface and use to line an 18 cm/7 inch flan tin or ring placed on a baking sheet. Line the pastry with greaseproof paper and fill with baking beans. Bake 'blind' for 10 minutes, then remove the paper and beans. Return to the oven for 5 minutes, then remove. Lower the oven temperature to 180°C/350°F/gas 4.

Combine the breadcrumbs, sugar and egg yolks in a bowl and mix well. Warm the milk and butter together in a saucepan until the butter has just melted, then stir slowly into the breadcrumb mixture. Mix well, then stir in the vanilla essence. Leave to stand for 5 minutes.

Pour the breadcrumb filling into the flan case and bake for 35-45 minutes or until the custard is firm. Remove from the oven.

Raise the oven temperature to 200°C/400°F/gas 6. Spread the mincemeat over the crumb custard. Whisk the egg whites in a clean, grease-free bowl until stiff, gradually whisking in about 50 g/2 oz of the caster sugar. Pile or spoon the meringue over the pie filling, covering both the mincemeat and the pastry edge completely. Sprinkle with the remaining sugar. Bake for 5-10 minutes until the meringue is golden. Serve at once, with single cream.

SERVES 4 TO 6

JAM TART

60-90 ml/4-6 tbsp firm jam
beaten egg for glazing

SHORT CRUST PASTRY
150 g/5 oz plain flour
2.5 ml/½ tsp salt
65 g/2½ oz margarine (or half butter, half lard)
flour for rolling out

Set the oven at 220°C/425°F/gas 7. To make the pastry, sift the flour and salt into a bowl, then rub in the margarine until the mixture resembles fine breadcrumbs. Add enough cold water to make a stiff dough. Press the dough together lightly.

Roll out the pastry on a lightly floured surface and use to line a 20 cm/8 inch pie plate. Decorate the edge with any trimmings. Fill with jam and glaze the uncovered pastry with beaten egg.

Bake for 15 minutes or until the pastry is cooked. Serve hot or cold.

SERVES 6

T REACLE TART

An old favourite which is today as popular as ever. Try it with cornflakes or similar cereals for a tasty change.

45 ml/3 tbsp golden syrup
50 g/2 oz soft white breadcrumbs
5 ml/1 tsp lemon juice

SHORT CRUST PASTRY
150 g/5 oz plain flour
2.5 ml/½ tsp salt
65 g/2½ oz margarine (or half butter, half lard)
flour for rolling out

Set the oven at 200°C/400°F/gas 6. To make the pastry, sift the flour and salt into a bowl, then rub in the margarine until the mixture resembles fine breadcrumbs. Add enough cold water to make a stiff dough. Press the dough together with your fingertips.

Roll out the pastry on a lightly floured surface and use just over three quarters of it to line a 20 cm/8 inch pie plate, reserving the rest for a lattice topping.

Melt the syrup in a saucepan. Stir in the breadcrumbs and lemon juice, then pour the mixture into the prepared pastry case.

Roll out the reserved pastry to a rectangle and cut into 1 cm/½ inch strips. Arrange in a lattice on top of the tart. Bake for about 30 minutes.

SERVES 6

VARIATION

TREACLE JELLY TART Make as above, but omit the breadcrumbs and add 1 beaten egg to the syrup. Bake in a 180°C/350°F/gas 4 oven until golden brown. When cold, the filling sets like jelly.

M RS BEETON'S APPLE FLAN

6 eating apples
4 cloves
45 ml/3 tbsp medium-dry sherry
30 ml/2 tbsp soft light brown sugar
3 egg whites
45 ml/3 tbsp caster sugar

SHORT CRUST PASTRY
175 g/6 oz plain flour
2.5 ml/½ tsp salt
75 g/3 oz margarine (or half butter, half lard)

Peel and core the apples, cutting each into 8 sections. Place in a heatproof bowl, add the cloves and sherry and cover closely. Place the bowl in a deep saucepan. Add boiling water to come halfway up the sides of the bowl and cook for 20 minutes until the apple sections are tender but still intact.

Set the oven at 200°C/400°F/gas 6. Sift the flour and salt into a bowl, then rub in the margarine. Add enough cold water to make a stiff dough.

Roll out the pastry on a lightly floured surface and use to line a 23 cm/9 inch flan tin. Line the pastry with greaseproof paper and fill with baking beans. Bake for 10 minutes. Remove the paper and beans; cook for 5 minutes. Set aside.

Lower the oven temperature to 140°C/275°F/gas 1. Arrange the apples in the flan. Sprinkle with 30 ml/2 tbsp of the cooking liquid and the brown sugar.

In a clean, grease-free bowl, whisk the egg whites until stiff. Whisk in 10 ml/2 tsp of the caster sugar and spread lightly over the apples. Sprinkle the remaining sugar over. Bake for 1 hour. Serve warm or cold.

SERVES 6

PEACH FLAN

350 g/12 oz peaches
5 ml/1 tsp lemon juice
25 g/1 oz sugar
5 ml/1 tsp arrowroot

SHORT CRUST PASTRY
100 g/4 oz plain flour
1.25 ml/¼ tsp salt
50 g/2 oz margarine (or half butter, half
   lard)
flour for rolling out

Set the oven at 200°C/400°F/gas 6. To make the pastry, sift the flour and salt into a bowl, then rub in the margarine until the mixture resembles fine breadcrumbs. Add enough cold water to make a stiff dough. Press the dough together with your fingertips.

Roll out the pastry on a lightly floured surface and use to line an 18 cm/7 inch flan tin or ring placed on a baking sheet. Line the pastry with greaseproof paper and fill with baking beans. Bake 'blind' for 20 minutes, then remove the paper and beans. Return to the oven for 5-7 minutes, then leave to cool.

Skin the peaches (see Mrs Beeton's Tip), then halve and slice, discarding the stones. Put the fruit in a saucepan with 15 ml/1 tbsp water and stew gently until tender.

With a slotted spoon, carefully transfer the fruit to the cooled flan shell, shaking off as much of the liquid as possible. Make up the liquid in the saucepan to 75 ml/3 fl oz with the lemon juice and water, if necessary. Stir in the sugar. Simmer for a few minutes until the sugar has dissolved.

Meanwhile mix the arrowroot with 30 ml/2 tbsp water in a cup. Stir into the hot syrup and bring to the boil, stirring all the time until thick and smooth. Cool the mixture slightly, then spoon over the fruit. When cool, decorate the flan with piped whipped cream.

SERVES 5 TO 6

> 🥣 MRS BEETON'S TIP To skin peaches, place them in a heatproof bowl and pour over boiling water to cover. Let stand for 1-2 minutes. The skins will slip off easily.

FRESH PINEAPPLE FLAN

800 g/1¾ lb peeled fresh pineapple
250 ml/8 fl oz pineapple juice
25 g/1 oz caster sugar
10 ml/2 tsp arrowroot
lemon juice

SHORT CRUST PASTRY
225 g/8 oz plain flour
2.5 ml/½ tsp salt
100 g/4 oz margarine (or half butter, half
   lard)
flour for rolling out

Set the oven at 200°C/400°F/gas 6. To make the pastry, sift the flour and salt into a bowl, then rub in the margarine until the mixture resembles fine breadcrumbs. Add enough cold water to make a stiff dough. Press the dough together with your fingertips.

Roll out the pastry on a lightly floured surface and use to line a 20 cm/8 inch flan tin or ring placed on a baking sheet. Line the pastry with greaseproof paper and fill with baking beans. Bake 'blind' for 20 minutes, then remove the paper and beans. Return to the oven for 5-7 minutes. Set aside.

Dice the pineapple into a colander, removing the core and any remaining peel. Drain the pineapple well.

Bring the pineapple juice and sugar to the boil in a saucepan, then lower the heat and simmer for 10 minutes. In a cup, mix the arrowroot to a paste with a little lemon juice, then stir it into the syrup. Cook gently, stirring, until the sauce boils, thickens and clears.

Put the drained pineapple dice in an even layer in the cooled flan case, pour the syrup over the top and cool completely.

SERVES 8

B ANANA FLAN

1 whole egg, separated, plus 1 yolk
50 g/2 oz caster sugar
30 ml/2 tbsp plain flour
30 ml/2 tbsp cornflour
300 ml/½ pint milk
2.5 ml/½ tsp vanilla essence
3 bananas
30 ml/2 tbsp Apricot Glaze (see Savarin, page 174)

SHORT CRUST PASTRY
100 g/4 oz plain flour
1.25 ml/¼ tsp salt
50 g/2 oz margarine (or half butter, half lard)
flour for rolling out

Set the oven at 200°C/400°F/gas 6. To make the pastry, sift the flour and salt into a bowl, then rub in the margarine until the mixture resembles fine breadcrumbs. Add enough cold water (about 45 ml/3 tbsp) to make a stiff dough. Press the dough together with your fingertips.

Roll out the pastry on a lightly floured surface and use to line a 20 cm/8 inch flan tin or ring placed on a baking sheet. Line the pastry with greaseproof paper and fill with baking beans. Bake 'blind' for 20 minutes, then remove the paper and beans. Return to the oven for 5-7 minutes, then cool completely.

Make the filling. In a bowl, mix both egg yolks with the sugar. Beat until thick and pale in colour, then beat in the flours. Add enough of the milk to make a smooth paste. Pour the rest of the milk into a saucepan and bring to just below boiling point. Pour on to the yolk mixture, stirring constantly, then return the mixture to the saucepan. Cook over low heat, stirring, until the mixture boils and thickens. Remove from the heat.

Whisk the egg white in a clean, grease-free bowl until stiff. Fold it into the custard with the vanilla essence. Return to the heat and cook for a couple of minutes, then cool. Cover the surface of the custard with dampened greaseproof paper while cooling.

Spoon the cold custard into the flan case and top with sliced bananas. Glaze immediately with hot apricot glaze and leave to set. Serve cold.

SERVES 6

PUMPKIN PIE

1 × 500 g/17½ oz can pumpkin or
    450 g/1 lb cooked mashed pumpkir
150 g/5 oz soft dark brown sugar
7.5 cm/3 tsp cinnamon
2.5 ml/½ tsp salt
5 ml/1 tsp ground ginger
2.5 ml/½ tsp grated nutmeg
3 eggs
250 ml/8 fl oz milk
125 ml/4 fl oz evaporated milk

SHORT CRUST PASTRY
    225 g/8 oz plain flour
    2.5 ml/½ tsp salt
    100 g/4 oz margarine (or half butter, half
      lard)
    flour for rolling out

Set the oven at 200°C/400°F/gas 6. To make the pastry, sift the flour and salt into a bowl, then rub in the margarine until the mixture resembles fine breadcrumbs. Add enough cold water to make a stiff dough. Press the dough together with your fingertips. Roll out on a lightly floured surface and use to line a 25 cm/10 inch pie plate. Chill in the refrigerator for 30 minutes.

In a large bowl, mix the pumpkin with the sugar, cinnamon, salt, ginger and nutmeg. Beat the eggs in a second bowl, add both milks and mix well. Stir the egg mixture into the pumpkin mixture. Pour into the pastry case.

Bake for 50 minutes or until a knife inserted in the centre of the pie comes out clean. Cool before serving.

SERVES 6

SOUTHERN PECAN PIE

Pecan nuts are oval and red-shelled when whole; when shelled they resemble slim walnuts. Use unbroken halves of pecan nuts in the filling for this pie.

50 g/2 oz butter
175 g/6 oz soft light brown sugar
3 eggs
225 g/8 oz shelled pecan nuts
150 g/5 oz golden syrup
15 ml/1 tbsp dark rum
2.5 ml/½ tsp salt
double cream, to serve

SHORT CRUST PASTRY
    225 g/8 oz plain flour
    2.5 ml/½ tsp salt
    100 g/4 oz margarine (or half butter, half
      lard)
    flour for rolling out

Set the oven at 230°C/450°F/gas 8. To make the pastry, sift the flour and salt into a bowl, then rub in the margarine until the mixture resembles fine breadcrumbs. Add enough cold water to make a stiff dough. Press the dough together with your fingertips. Roll out the pastry on a lightly floured surface and use to line a 25 cm/10 inch pie plate. Prick the base well.

Bake the pie case for 5 minutes, then cool. Lower the oven temperature to 180°C/350°F/gas 4.

In a mixing bowl, cream the butter with the sugar until light. Beat in the eggs, one at a time. Stir in the rest of the ingredients. Fill the pastry case with the mixture and bake for about 40 minutes or until a knife inserted in the centre comes out clean. Serve warm or cold, with double cream.

SERVES 6

A PRICOT MERINGUE FLAN

SHORT CRUST PASTRY
    225 g/8 oz plain flour
    2.5 ml/½ tsp salt
    100 g/4 oz margarine (or half butter, half
      lard)
    flour for rolling out

FILLING
    1 × 340 g/12 oz can apricots
    25 g/1 oz margarine
    5 ml/1 tsp cornflour
    2 eggs, separated
    30 ml/2 tbsp brandy
    75 g/3 oz caster sugar

    single cream to serve (optional)

Set the oven at 200°C/400°F/gas 6. To make the pastry, sift the flour and salt into a bowl, then rub in the margarine until the mixture resembles fine breadcrumbs. Add enough cold water (about 45 ml/3 tbsp) to make a stiff dough. Press the dough together with your fingertips.

Roll out the pastry on a lightly floured surface and use to line a 20 cm/8 inch flan tin or ring placed on a baking sheet. Line the pastry with greaseproof paper and fill with baking beans. Bake 'blind' for 10 minutes, then remove the paper and beans. Return to the oven for 5 minutes.

Meanwhile make the filling. Purée the apricots with their juice in a blender or food processor. Alternatively, press through a sieve into a bowl.

Combine the margarine, cornflour and 150 ml/¼ pint water in a small saucepan. Whisking constantly over moderate heat, bring to the simmering point, then simmer gently for 2-3 minutes until thick and smooth. Cool slightly, then stir in the egg yolks, brandy and apricot purée. Spoon the mixture into the cooked flan case.

In a clean, grease-free bowl, whisk the egg whites until fairly stiff. Gradually whisk in the sugar until stiff peaks form. Pile the meringue mixture on top of the apricot filling, covering it completely. Bake for 25-35 minutes until the meringue is set and the peaks are tinged with gold.

Allow the flan to stand for at least 30 minutes before serving. It tastes best when just warm, with single cream if liked.

SERVES 4 TO 6

VARIATIONS

Other canned fruits may be substituted for the apricots. Crushed pineapple may be used, with rum instead of brandy, if preferred. Canned peaches, mango or plums work equally well. However, very delicate fruit, such as pears or gooseberries, do not contribute sufficient flavour to the filling.

——————— ◇ ———————

A LMOND AND APRICOT TARTLETS

10 ml/2 tsp apricot jam
50 g/2 oz butter or margarine
50 g/2 oz sugar
1 egg
15 ml/1 tbsp plain cake crumbs
15 ml/1 tbsp ground almonds
3 drops almond essence
10 ml/2 tsp nibbed almonds
5 ml/1 tbsp Apricot Glaze (see Savarin, page 174)
10 ml/2 tsp chopped angelica

SHORT CRUST PASTRY
100 g/4 oz plain flour
1.25 ml/¼ tsp salt
50 g/2 oz margarine (or half butter, half lard)
flour for rolling out

Set the oven at 190°C/375°F/gas 5. To make the pastry, sift the flour and salt into a bowl, then rub in the margarine until the mixture resembles fine breadcrumbs. Add enough cold water to make a stiff dough. Press the dough together lightly.

Roll out the pastry on a lightly floured surface and use to line twelve 7.5 cm/3 inch patty tins. Put a little apricot jam in each.

In a bowl, cream the butter or margarine with the sugar until pale and fluffy. Gradually beat in the egg. Stir in the cake crumbs, ground almonds and almond essence. Half fill each pastry case with the mixture and smooth the tops. Sprinkle the nibbed almonds on top.

Bake for 15 minutes or until firm to the touch. Leave the tartlets to cool. Warm the apricot glaze, brush it on top of the tartlets, then sprinkle with the chopped angelica.

MAKES 12

B ALMORAL TARTLETS

50 g/2 oz butter
50 g/2 oz sugar
1 egg, separated
15 g/½ oz glacé cherries, chopped
25 g/1 oz plain cake crumbs
15 g/½ oz cut mixed peel
5 ml/1 tsp cornflour
25 g/1 oz icing sugar

SHORT CRUST PASTRY
100 g/4 oz plain flour
1.25 ml/¼ tsp salt
50 g/2 oz margarine (or half butter, half lard)
flour for rolling out

Set the oven at 200°C/400°F/gas 6. To make the pastry, sift the flour and salt into a bowl, then rub in the margarine until the mixture resembles fine breadcrumbs. Add enough cold water to make a stiff dough. Press the dough together with your fingertips. Roll out on a lightly floured surface and use to line twelve 7.5 cm/3 inch patty tins.

In a bowl, cream the butter with the sugar until pale and fluffy. Beat in the egg yolk and add the chopped cherries with the cake crumbs, mixed peel and cornflour. Mix well.

Whisk the egg white in a clean, grease-free bowl until stiff, then fold lightly into the cherry mixture. Fill the pastry cases and bake for about 20 minutes. Cool on a wire rack.

Just before serving, sift a little icing sugar over the top of the tartlets.

MAKES 12

CHERRY ROSETTES

1 × 375 g/13 oz can red cherries in syrup
25 g/1 oz lump sugar
5 ml/1 tsp arrowroot
10 ml/2 tsp lemon juice
drop of red food colouring
125 ml/4 fl oz double cream

SHORT CRUST PASTRY
100 g/4 oz plain flour
1.25 ml/¼ tsp salt
50 g/2 oz margarine (or half butter, half lard)
flour for rolling out

Set the oven at 200°C/400°F/gas 6. To make the pastry, sift the flour and salt into a bowl, then rub in the margarine until the mixture resembles fine breadcrumbs. Add enough cold water to make a stiff dough. Press the dough together with your fingertips.

Roll out the pastry on a lightly floured surface and use to line twelve 7.5 cm/3 inch patty tins or boat-shaped moulds. Bake the tartlets blind for 10 minutes (see Mrs Beeton's Tip).

Drain and stone the cherries, reserving the syrup in a measuring jug. Make it up to 125 ml/4 fl oz with water, if necessary.

Put a layer of cherries in each pastry case. Pour the cherry syrup mixture into a saucepan, add the sugar and bring to the boil. Boil for 5 minutes.

Meanwhile mix the arrowroot to a paste with the lemon juice in a cup. Add to the syrup, stirring all the time, and bring to the boil. Add a little red food colouring. Cool the glaze slightly, then pour a little over the cherries in each tartlet. Leave to set.

In a bowl, whip the cream until stiff. Put it in a piping bag fitted with a 1 cm/½ inch nozzle and pipe a large rosette on each tartlet.

MAKES 12

VARIATIONS

BLACKCURRANT ROSETTES Use 400 g/14 oz blackcurrants stewed in 30 ml/2 tbsp water with 60 ml/4 tbsp sugar, instead of the cherries. Omit the food colouring.
RASPBERRY OR STRAWBERRY ROSETTES Fill the tartlets with fresh strawberries or raspberries. Make the glaze using 125 ml/4 fl oz water instead of fruit syrup.

> **MRS BEETON'S TIP** There is no need to line tartlet cases with greaseproof paper and baking beans when baking blind. Check the cases after 6 minutes. If any have puffed up in the middle, press the pastry down gently with the back of a spoon, then return to the oven to finish baking.

CUSTARD TARTLETS

1 egg
15 ml/1 tbsp caster sugar
125 ml/4 fl oz milk
pinch of grated nutmeg

SHORT CRUST PASTRY
100 g/4 oz plain flour
1.25 ml/¼ tsp salt
50 g/2 oz margarine (or half butter, half lard)
5 ml/1 tsp caster sugar
flour for rolling out

Set the oven at 180°C/350°F/gas 4. To make the pastry, sift the flour and salt into a bowl, then rub in the margarine until the mixture resembles fine breadcrumbs. Stir in the caster sugar. Add enough cold water to make a stiff dough. Press the dough together with your fingertips. Roll out and use to line twelve 7.5 cm/3 inch patty tins.

Beat the egg lightly in a bowl and add the sugar. Warm the milk in a saucepan, then pour it on to the egg. Strain the custard mixture into the pastry cases and sprinkle a little nutmeg on top of each.

Bake for about 30 minutes, until the custard is firm and set. Leave to cool before removing from the tins.

MAKES 12

VARIATION

CUSTARD MERINGUE TARTLETS Make as above, but omit the nutmeg and bake for 15 minutes only. Lower the oven temperature to 140°C/275°F/gas 1. Whisk 2 egg whites in a clean, grease-free bowl until stiff. Fold in 75 g/3 oz caster sugar. Pile the meringue on to the tartlets. Bake for about 30 minutes.

CANADIAN CAKES

1 egg
100 g/4 oz currants
100 g/4 oz sugar
15 g/½ oz butter
125 ml/4 fl oz whipping cream
15 ml/1 tbsp caster sugar

SHORT CRUST PASTRY
100 g/4 oz plain flour
1.25 ml/¼ tsp salt
50 g/2 oz margarine (or half butter, half lard)
flour for rolling out

Set the oven at 200°C/400°F/gas 6. To make the pastry, sift the flour and salt into a bowl, then rub in the margarine until the mixture resembles fine breadcrumbs. Add enough cold water to make a stiff dough. Press the dough together with your fingertips. Roll out on a lightly floured surface and use to line twelve 7.5 cm/3 inch patty tins.

In a bowl, beat the egg lightly and stir in the currants and sugar. Melt the butter in a saucepan and stir into the fruit mixture. Spoon the mixture into the pastry cases.

Bake for 15-20 minutes, then set aside to cool before removing from the tins. Whip the cream with the caster sugar in a bowl until stiff, put it into a piping bag and pipe a rosette on each tartlet.

MAKES 12

> **MRS BEETON'S TIP** If you do not have a pastry cutter, use an upturned glass, dipping the rim lightly in flour to prevent it sticking to the pastry.

FILBERT TARTLETS

30 ml/2 tbsp cornflour
60 ml/4 tbsp single cream or creamy milk
2 eggs
75 g/3 oz caster sugar
75 g/3 oz shelled filberts, skinned and
    chopped
25 g/1 oz ground almonds
milk and caster sugar for glazing

SHORT CRUST PASTRY
    100 g/4 oz plain flour
    1.25 ml/¼ tsp salt
    50 g/2 oz margarine (or half butter, half
      lard)
    flour for rolling out

Set the oven at 200°C/400°F/gas 6. To make the pastry, sift the flour and salt into a bowl, then rub in the margarine until the mixture resembles fine breadcrumbs. Add enough cold water to make a stiff dough. Press the dough together with your fingertips. Roll out on a lightly floured surface and use to line twelve 7.5 cm/3 inch patty tins, reserving a little pastry for decoration.

In a saucepan, mix the cornflour to a paste with the cream or milk. Stir over gentle heat until the mixture boils. Remove from the heat.

In a bowl, beat the eggs with the sugar until pale and fluffy. Add the chopped filberts, ground almonds and cornflour mixture. Spoon into the pastry cases. Cut the reserved pastry into strips and place 2 strips across each tartlet in the form of a cross.

Brush the tartlets with milk and dredge with caster sugar. Bake for about 20 minutes or until the pastry is golden brown.

MAKES 12

> **MRS BEETON'S TIP** To skin filberts (or hazelnuts), place the nuts on a baking sheet and bake at 180°C/350°F/gas 4 for 5-6 minutes. Put the nuts in a paper bag and rub against each other. The skin fibres will break down and the skins will be removed.

CREAM TARTLETS

30 ml/2 tbsp smooth apricot jam
250 ml/8 fl oz whipping cream
15 ml/1 tbsp icing sugar
30 ml/2 tbsp finely chopped pistachio nuts

SHORT CRUST PASTRY
    100 g/4 oz plain flour
    1.25 ml/¼ tsp salt
    50 g/2 oz margarine (or half butter, half
      lard)
    flour for rolling out

Set the oven at 200°C/400°F/gas 6. To make the pastry, sift the flour and salt into a bowl, then rub in the margarine until the mixture resembles fine breadcrumbs. Add enough cold water to make a stiff dough. Press the dough together with your fingertips.

Roll out the pastry on a lightly floured surface and use to line twelve 7.5 cm/3 inch patty tins. Bake blind (see Cherry Rosettes, page 361), then cool completely.

When the tartlets are quite cold, put a little apricot jam in the base of each. In a bowl, whip the cream as stiffly as possible, gradually adding the sugar. Put the cream into a piping bag fitted with a 1 cm/½ inch nozzle and pipe in swirls and peaks over the jam. Sprinkle with the chopped pistachios.

MAKES 12

COVENTRY TURNOVERS

30 ml/2 tbsp raspberry jam
15 ml/1 tbsp caster sugar

SHORT CRUST PASTRY
150 g/5 oz plain flour
1.25 ml/¼ tsp salt
65 g/2½ oz margarine (or half butter, half lard)
flour for rolling out

Set the oven at 200°C/400°F/gas 6. To make the pastry, sift the flour and salt into a bowl, then rub in the margarine until the mixture resembles fine breadcrumbs. Add enough cold water to make a stiff dough. Press the dough together with your fingertips.

Roll out the pastry on a lightly floured surface to a thickness of 3 mm/1/8 inch. Cut out 8 rounds using a 10 cm/4 inch cutter. Place spoonfuls of jam in the centre of each pastry round. Moisten the edges with water and fold the pastry over the filling. Press the edges well together and crimp or decorate with a fork.

Place the turnovers on a baking sheet, brush with water and dredge with the caster sugar. Bake for about 20 minutes or until golden brown.

MAKES 8

☆ **FREEZING TIP** When cold, open freeze on clean baking sheets, then wrap individually in freezer wrap and pack in a rigid container.

OLDBURY GOOSEBERRY TARTS

450 g/1 lb plain flour
100 g/4 oz butter, in cubes
100 g/4 oz lard, in cubes
flour for rolling out
225 g/8 oz gooseberries, topped and tailed
175 g/6 oz demerara sugar

Put the flour into a mixing bowl, make a well in the centre and add the butter and lard. Pour over 60 ml/4 tbsp boiling water. Stir until the fats melt, then mix in the flour gradually to make a warm, waxy-looking, smooth dough.

Cut off one quarter of the dough. Using just over half the piece of dough, roll out on a floured surface to a 15 cm/6 inch round. Raise the edges 3 cm/1¼ inches, moulding them to form a pastry case. Fill with a quarter of the gooseberries and sprinkle with a quarter of the sugar. Roll out the smaller piece of pastry to make a top crust for the tart. Cut a small hole in the centre, then fit the top crust on top of the gooseberries, pinching the edges together to seal firmly.

Make 3 more tarts in the same way. Carefully transfer the tarts to baking sheets and refrigerate for 3-4 hours.

Set the oven at 200°C/400°F/gas 6. Bake the tarts for 30-35 minutes. Serve hot, with clotted cream, if liked.

MAKES 4 TARTS

🥣 **MRS BEETON'S TIP** Cutting a small hole in the top of the pie helps the steam to escape and keeps the pastry crisp. If liked, a feature may be made of this vent.

*H*AMPSHIRE PIE

30 ml/2 tbsp jam
2 whole eggs plus 1 yolk
75 g/3 oz butter
75 g/3 oz caster sugar

PUFF PASTRY
150 g/5 oz plain flour
1.25 ml/¼ tsp salt
150 g/5 oz butter
2.5 ml/½ tsp lemon juice
flour for rolling out

Make the pastry. Sift the flour and salt into a mixing bowl and rub in 50 g/2 oz of the butter. Add the lemon juice and mix to a smooth dough with cold water.

Shape the remaining butter into a rectangle on greaseproof paper. Roll out the dough on a lightly floured surface to a strip a little wider than the butter and rather more than twice its length. Place the butter on one half of the pastry, fold the other half over it, and press the edges together with the rolling pin. Leave in a cool place for 15 minutes to allow the butter to harden.

Roll the pastry out into a long strip. Fold the bottom third up and the top third down, press the edges together with the rolling pin and turn the pastry so that the folded edges are on the right and left. Roll and fold again, cover and leave in a cool place for 15 minutes. Repeat this process until the pastry has been rolled out 6 times. The pastry is now ready for use. Set the oven at 200°C/400°F/gas 6.

Roll out the pastry on a lightly floured surface and use to line a deep 20 cm/8 inch pie plate. Spread the jam over the bottom.

Beat the eggs and extra yolk in a heat-proof bowl until frothy. Melt the butter in a saucepan and gradually add to the eggs with the sugar, beating well. Place the bowl over simmering water and whisk the mixture until thick. Pour it into the pie case, on top of the jam.

Bake the pie for 30 minutes or until firm and golden brown, if necessary reducing the temperature to 180°C/350°F/gas 4 after 15 minutes to prevent the pastry browning too quickly. Serve hot.

SERVES 6

☆ **FREEZER TIP** Making puff pastry is quite a fiddly job, so it is worth making a large batch when you have time and keeping a supply in the freezer. It may be frozen for up to 3 months and is best thawed overnight in the refrigerator.

———— ◇ ————

APPLE JALOUSIE

225 g/8 oz cooking apples
50 g/2 oz butter
75 g/3 oz soft light brown sugar
25 g/1 oz apricot jam
pinch of cinnamon
beaten egg and icing sugar to glaze

PUFF PASTRY
150 g/5 oz plain flour
1.25 ml/¼ tsp salt
150 g/5 oz butter
2.5 ml/½ tsp lemon juice
flour for rolling out

Make the pastry. Sift the flour and salt into a mixing bowl and rub in 50 g/2 oz of the butter. Add the lemon juice and mix to a smooth dough with cold water.

Shape the remaining butter into a rectangle on greaseproof paper. Roll out the dough on a lightly floured surface to a strip a little wider than the butter and rather more than twice its length. Place the butter on one half of the pastry, fold the other half over it, and press the edges together with the rolling pin. Leave in a cool place for 15 minutes to allow the butter to harden.

Roll the pastry out into a long strip. Fold the bottom third up and the top third down, press the edges together with the rolling pin and turn the pastry so that the folded edges are on the right and left. Roll and fold again, cover and leave in a cool place for 15 minutes. Repeat this process until the pastry has been rolled out 6 times. Rest the pastry in the refrigerator while preparing the filling.

Set the oven at 190°C/375°F/gas 5. Peel, core and slice the apples. Warm the butter and sugar in a saucepan until the butter melts, add the apple slices and turn them over until coated in butter. Increase the heat slightly and simmer for 4 minutes, or until the apple slices are partially cooked but still intact. Remove from the heat and stir in the jam and cinnamon. Leave to cool completely.

On a lightly floured surface, roll out the pastry to a rectangle measuring 18 × 15 cm/ 7 × 6 inches, and about 3 mm/1/8 inch thick. Cut in half to make two 18 × 7.5 cm/ 7 × 3 inch rectangles.

Dampen a baking sheet and lay one rectangle in the centre. Cover with the filling mixture, leaving a 1 cm/½ inch border all round. Fold the second rectangle in half lengthways, and cut 3 cm/1¼ inch slits through both thicknesses of pastry from the folded edge inwards.

Open out the pastry. It should have 6 cm/2¼ inch parallel slits across it. Dampen the edges of the base pastry and lay the slit rectangle on top. Press the edges to seal, then brush with beaten egg.

Bake for 20-25 minutes. Remove the jalousie from the oven and dust with icing sugar. Return to the oven for 5 minutes more to glaze, then cool on the baking sheet. Cut in slices to serve.

SERVES 6 TO 7

MILLE-FEUILLE GÂTEAU

Illustrated on page 284

PUFF PASTRY
200 g/7 oz plain flour
1.25 ml/¼ tsp salt
200 g/7 oz butter
2.5 ml/½ tsp lemon juice
flour for rolling out

FILLING AND TOPPING
300 ml/½ pint double cream
100 g/4 oz icing sugar, sifted
100 g/4 oz raspberry jam

Make the pastry. Sift the flour and salt into a mixing bowl and rub in 50 g/2 oz of the butter. Add the lemon juice and mix to a smooth dough with cold water.

Shape the remaining butter into a rectangle on greaseproof paper. Roll out the dough on a lightly floured surface to a strip a little wider than the butter and rather more than twice its length. Place the butter on one half of the pastry, fold the other half over it, and press the edges together with the rolling pin. Leave in a cool place for 15 minutes to allow the butter to harden.

Roll the pastry out into a long strip. Fold the bottom third up and the top third down, press the edges together with the rolling pin and turn the pastry so that the folded edges are on the right and left. Roll and fold again, cover and leave in a cool place for 15 minutes. Repeat this process until the pastry has been rolled out 6 times (see Mrs Beeton's Tip). Chill the pastry well between each rolling, wrapping it in cling film to prevent it drying on the surface. The pastry is now ready for use.

Set the oven at 230°C/450°F/gas 8. Roll out the pastry on a lightly floured surface to a thickness of 3 mm/1/8 inch. Cut into six 15 cm/6 inch rounds. If work surface space is limited, it is best to cut the pastry into portions to do this. Either cut the pastry into six portions or cut it in half and cut out three circles from each half.

Place the pastry circles on baking sheets, prick well and bake for 8-10 minutes until crisp and golden brown. Lift the rounds off carefully and cool on wire racks.

In a bowl, whip the cream until thick. Make glacé icing by mixing the icing sugar with enough cold water to form an icing that will coat the back of the spoon. Coat one pastry layer with icing and set aside for the lid. Sandwich the remaining layers together lightly with the jam and cream. Put the iced layer on top. Serve as soon as possible.

SERVES 6 TO 8

> **MRS BEETON'S TIP** Never rush the process of making puff pastry: always chill it if the fat begins to melt. It is a good idea to mark the pastry each time it is rolled, as it is is easy to lose track of the number of times this process has been carried out.

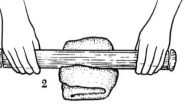

MRS BEETON'S MANCHESTER PUDDING

250 ml/8 fl oz milk
2 strips of lemon rind
75 g/3 oz soft white breadcrumbs
2 whole eggs plus 2 egg yolks
50 g/2 oz butter, softened
45 ml/3 tbsp caster sugar
45 ml/3 tbsp brandy
45-60 ml/3-4 tbsp jam
extra caster sugar for sprinkling

PUFF PASTRY
150 g/5 oz plain flour
1.25 ml/¼ tsp salt
150 g/5 oz butter
2.5 ml/½ tsp lemon juice
flour for rolling out

Heat the milk in a saucepan with the lemon rind, then remove from the heat and leave to infuse for 30 minutes. Put the breadcrumbs in a bowl, strain the flavoured milk over them and return the mixture to the clean pan. Simmer for 2-3 minutes or until the crumbs have absorbed all the milk.

Beat the eggs and yolks until liquid, then stir into the breadcrumbs with the butter, sugar and brandy. Mix thoroughly; the butter should melt in the warm mixture. Cover the surface with dampened grease-proof paper and leave to cool.

Set the oven at 200°C/400°F/gas 6. Make the pastry. Sift the flour and salt into a mixing bowl and rub in 50 g/2 oz of the butter. Add the lemon juice and mix to a smooth dough with cold water.

Shape the remaining butter into a rectangle on greaseproof paper. Roll out the dough on a lightly floured surface to a strip a little wider than the butter and rather more than twice its length. Place the butter on one half of the pastry, fold the other half over it, and press the edges together with the rolling pin. Leave in a cool place for 15 minutes to allow the butter to harden.

Roll the pastry out into a long strip. Fold the bottom third up and the top third down, press the edges together with the rolling pin and turn the pastry so that the folded edges are on the right and left. Roll and fold again, cover and leave in a cool place for 15 minutes. Repeat this process until the pastry has been rolled out 6 times.

Line a 750 ml/1¼ pint pie dish with the pastry. If liked, cut a strip out of the pastry trimmings to fit the rim of the pie dish. Dampen the rim of the lining and fit the extra strip. Wrap any remaining pastry and reserve in the refrigerator for another purpose.

Spread the jam over the base of the pastry. Turn in the cooled breadcrumb mixture and bake for 15 minutes, then lower the heat to 180°C/350°F/gas 4 and cook for 45 minutes – 1 hour more. The pudding should be set in the centre. Leave to cool. Serve cold, sprinkled with caster sugar.

SERVES 6

> **MRS BEETON'S TIP** When transferring the pastry to the pie dish, lop it over the rolling pin. Lift into the dish, easing half the pastry in first, then gently flick the rolling pin so that the other half falls into the dish.

LINZERTORTE

Linzertorte improves in flavour if kept for two to three days before cutting.

100 g/4 oz butter
75 g/3 oz caster sugar
1 egg yolk
1.25 ml/¼ tsp almond essence
grated rind of 1 small lemon
juice of ½ lemon
100 g/4 oz plain flour
5 ml/1 tsp ground cinnamon
50 g/2 oz ground almonds
flour for rolling out
200 g/7 oz raspberry jam
15 ml/1 tbsp icing sugar

In a mixing bowl, cream the butter with the sugar until pale and fluffy. Beat in the egg yolk, almond essence, lemon rind and juice. Add the flour, cinnamon and ground almonds and mix to a smooth dough. Wrap in foil and chill for 1 hour.

Set the oven at 160°C/325°F/gas 3. Roll out three quarters of the pastry on a lightly floured surface and use to line an 18 cm/7 inch flan tin. Spread the jam over the base.

Roll out the remaining pastry to a rectangle 18 cm/7 inches long and cut into strips about 5 mm/¼ inch wide. Arrange the strips in a lattice on top of the jam. Bake for about 1 hour or until the pastry is golden brown. Leave to cool.

Remove from the flan tin, dredge with icing sugar and serve cold, with whipped cream.

SERVES 5 TO 6

---◇---

STUFFED MONKEY

fat for greasing
45 ml/3 tbsp margarine
50 g/2 oz cut mixed peel
50 g/2 oz blanched almonds, chopped
50 g/2 oz sultanas
25 g/1 oz sugar
2.5 ml/½ tsp mixed spice
50 g/2 oz flaked almonds

PASTRY
150 g/5 oz plain flour
2.5 ml/½ tsp ground cinnamon
100 g/4 oz margarine
100 g/4 oz brown sugar
1 egg, beaten
flour for rolling out

Grease an 18 cm/7 inch square tin. Set the oven at 190°C/375°F/gas 5.

Make the pastry. Sift the flour and cinnamon into a bowl, then rub in the margarine until the mixture resembles fine breadcrumbs. Stir in the sugar. Add enough of the beaten egg to form a soft dough, reserving a little. Halve the dough. Roll out one portion to fit the prepared tin. Lay it in the tin.

For the filling, melt the margarine in a saucepan and stir in the mixed peel, almonds, sultanas, sugar and mixed spice. Cool. Spread the filling over the pastry, leaving a 2 cm/¾ inch clear border all around. Dampen the clear edge with water.

Roll out the second portion of pastry to the same size as the first. Lay it on the filling and press the edges together to seal. Brush with the reserved beaten egg and sprinkle with the flaked almonds. Bake for 30 minutes, then cool in the tin. Cut into squares and serve.

SERVES 9

GÂTEAU DE PITHIVIERS

225 g/8 oz plain flour
1.25 ml/½ tsp salt
225 g/8 oz butter
2.5 ml/½ tsp lemon juice
flour for rolling out
Apricot Glaze (see Savarin, page 174)
1 egg, beaten with 15 ml/1 tbsp water
icing sugar

FILLING
50 g/2 oz butter
50 g/2 oz caster sugar
1-2 drops almond essence
1 egg
20 ml/4 tsp plain flour
50 g/2 oz ground almonds

Start by making the filling. Cream the butter with the sugar in a large bowl, adding the essence. Add the egg and mix until smooth. Mix the flour and ground almonds in a bowl, then add them to the butter mixture to make a smooth pastry cream.

Make the pastry. Sift the flour and salt into a mixing bowl and rub in 50 g/2 oz of the butter. Add the lemon juice and mix to a smooth dough with cold water.

Shape the remaining butter into a rectangle on greaseproof paper. Roll out the dough on a lightly floured surface to a strip a little wider than the butter and rather more than twice its length. Place the butter on one half of the pastry, fold the other half over it, and press the edges together with the rolling pin. Leave in a cool place for 15 minutes to allow the butter to harden.

Roll the pastry out into a long strip. Fold the bottom third up and the top third down, press the edges together with the rolling pin and turn the pastry so that the folded edges are on the right and left. Roll and fold again, cover and leave in a cool place for

15 minutes. Repeat this process until the pastry has been rolled out 6 times.

Roll out the pastry again and cut 2 rounds, measuring 18 cm/7 inches and 20 cm/8 inches in diameter. Place the smaller round on a baking sheet. Cover with apricot glaze to within 1 cm/½ inch of the edge. Spread the glaze with the almond cream in an even layer. Moisten the edge of the pastry. Lay the larger round on top and press the edges to seal.

Make 5 curved cuts in the pastry lid, radiating from the centre at equal intervals. Brush the surface with the egg and water mixture. Let the pastry rest for 20 minutes.

Set the oven at 190°C/375°F/gas 5. Bake the pastry for 30 minutes or until risen and set. Dust the surface with icing sugar and return to the oven for 5 minutes to glaze. Cool on the baking sheet.

SERVES 8-10

GREENGAGE SUET PUDDING

fat for greasing
450 g/1 lb greengages
50 g/2 oz caster sugar

SUET CRUST PASTRY
200 g/7 oz plain flour
5 ml/1 tsp baking powder
pinch of salt
75 g/3 oz shredded suet
flour for rolling out

Grease a 750 ml/1¼ pint pudding basin. Prepare a steamer or half fill a large saucepan with water and bring to the boil.

Make the pastry. Sift the flour, baking powder and salt into a mixing bowl. Stir in the suet, then add enough cold water (about 150-175 ml/5-6 fl oz) to make a soft but not sticky dough. Cut off one quarter of the pastry and set aside for the lid. Roll out the rest on a lightly floured surface to a round 1 cm/½ inch larger than the top of the basin, then place the round in the basin. Pressing with the fingers, work the pastry evenly up the sides of the basin to the top.

To make the filling, halve the greengages and remove the stones. Put the fruit in a bowl and stir in the sugar. Spoon the fruit into the pastry-lined basin and add 30 ml/ 2 tbsp water. Roll out the reserved pastry to make the lid, dampen the rim and place the lid on top of the filling. Press the rim of the lid against the edge of the lining to seal the crust.

Cover the pudding with a well-floured cloth, greased greaseproof paper or foil and secure with string. Put the pudding in the perforated part of the steamer, or stand it on an old saucer or plate in the pan of boiling water. The water should come halfway up the sides of the basin. Cover the pan tightly and steam the pudding over gently simmering water for 2½-3 hours.

Remove the cooked pudding from the steamer. Serve from the basin or leave to stand for a few minutes, then turn out on to a warmed serving dish. Serve with the custard.

SERVES 6

VARIATIONS
Apples, blackberries, red and blackcurrants, cranberries, loganberries, damsons, gooseberries, plums and rhubarb may be used instead of gooseberries. Prepare the fruit according to type.

B OILED APPLE DUMPLINGS

6 cooking apples
75 g/3 oz demerara sugar
6 cloves

SUET CRUST PASTRY
150 g/5 oz plain flour
3.75 ml/¾ tsp baking powder
pinch of salt
65 g/2½ oz shredded suet
flour for rolling out

Make the pastry. Sift the flour, baking powder and salt into a mixing bowl. Stir in the suet, then add enough cold water (about 75-125 ml/3-4 fl oz) to make a soft but not sticky dough.

Divide the suet pastry into 6 portions. On a lightly floured surface, roll out each portion to a round. Core and peel the apples, and put one in the centre of each round. Work the pastry around each apple until it almost meets at the top. Fill each core hole with sugar and stick a clove upright in the middle of each apple.

Dampen the edges of the pastry, work it up to cover the apple and seal well, leaving the clove exposed. Tie each dumpling in a small well-floured pudding cloth.

Bring a large saucepan of water to the boil, add the dumplings and boil gently for 40-50 minutes. Drain well and serve with cream or custard.

SERVES 6

———————— ◇ ————————

APPLE AND BLACKBERRY PUDDING

fat for greasing
Cup Custard (page 238) to serve

SUET CRUST PASTRY
200 g/7 oz plain flour
5 ml/1 tsp baking powder
pinch of salt
75 g/3 oz shredded suet
flour for rolling out

FILLING
350 g/12 oz cooking apples
75 g/3 oz sugar
350 g/12 oz blackberries

Grease a 750 ml/1¼ pint pudding basin. Prepare a steamer or half fill a large saucepan with water and bring to the boil.

Make the pastry. Sift the flour, baking powder and salt into a mixing bowl. Stir in the suet, then add enough cold water (about 150-175 ml/5-6 fl oz) to make a soft but not sticky dough. Cut off one quarter of the pastry and set aside for the lid. Roll out the rest on a lightly floured surface to a round 1 cm/½ inch larger than the top of the basin, then place the round in the basin. Pressing with the fingers, work the pastry evenly up the sides of the basin to the top.

To make the filling, peel and core the apples and slice into a bowl. Stir in the sugar and blackberries. Spoon the fruit into the pastry-lined basin and add 30 ml/2 tbsp water. Roll out the reserved pastry to make the lid, dampen the rim and place the lid on top of the filling. Press the rim of the lid against the edge of the lining to seal the crust.

Cover the pudding with a well-floured cloth, greased greaseproof paper or foil and secure with string. Put the pudding in the perforated part of the steamer, or stand it on an old saucer or plate in the pan of boiling water. The water should come halfway up the sides of the basin. Cover the pan tightly and steam the pudding over gently simmering water for 2½-3 hours.

Remove the cooked pudding from the steamer. Serve from the basin or leave to stand for a few minutes, then turn out on to a warmed serving dish. Serve with the custard.

SERVES 6

GLAZED APPLE DUMPLINGS

6 cooking apples
1.25 ml/¼ tsp cinnamon
50 g/2 oz soft light brown sugar
12 cloves
15 ml/1 tbsp milk
25 g/1 oz caster sugar

SHORT CRUST PASTRY
175 g/6 oz plain flour
1.25 ml/¼ tsp salt
75 g/3 oz margarine (or half butter, half lard)
flour for rolling out

Set the oven at 200°C/400°F/gas 6. To make the pastry, sift the flour and salt into a bowl, then rub in the margarine until the mixture resembles fine breadcrumbs. Add enough cold water to make a stiff dough. Press the dough together with your finger-tips.

Divide the pastry into 6 portions. On a lightly floured surface roll out each portion to a round. Peel and core the apples and put one on each round of pastry. Mix the cinnamon and sugar together in a bowl and fill each apple cavity with some of the mixture. Press 2 cloves in the top of each apple. Work the pastry around each apple to enclose it, moisten the edges and press well together.

Place the dumplings on a baking sheet, brush with milk and dredge with caster sugar. Bake for 30-35 minutes or until the apples are tender. Serve with cream or custard.

SERVES 4

S TRAWBERRY TABLE DUMPLINGS

These are great fun. As their name implies, they are cooked at the table. Guests help themselves to suitable sauces.

800 g/1¾ lb fresh strawberries, hulled
100 g/4 oz caster sugar
15 ml/1 tbsp kirsch
1 whole egg, separated, plus 2 egg yolks
salt
about 225 g/8 oz plain flour
flour for rolling out
extra caster sugar to serve

Prepare the strawberries by spreading them in a shallow dish, covering them with sugar and kirsch and leaving to stand for 1 hour. Drain thoroughly, reserving any syrup. Mash the fruit lightly and put to one side.

Combine all the egg yolks in a bowl and beat lightly with a pinch of salt. Gradually add 100 ml/3½ fl oz water, then add the flour, 50 g/2 oz at a time, until a light firm dough is formed.

Roll out the dough on a lightly floured surface and cut into rounds, using a 5 cm/2 inch cutter. Brush the edges of each round with some of the egg white. Put about 2.5 ml/½ tsp strawberry filling in the centre of each round, then fold over to make small turnovers. Press the edges of each turnover with a fork, to seal.

At the table, have ready a large saucepan of lightly salted boiling water over a burner or hot tray. Lower the dumplings gently into the water, a few at a time, and cook for about 4 minutes until they rise to the surface. Lift out with a slotted spoon, drain over the pan, and serve on to the diners' plates.

A bowl of caster sugar and a sauce boat containing the strained fruit syrup should be placed by the pan so that diners may help themselves. Soured or fresh whipped cream may also be offered. The dumplings should be sprinkled with sugar before the sauce is poured over them.

SERVES 4 TO 6

*P*ROFITEROLES

Illustrated on page 284

CHOUX PASTRY PUFFS
100 g/4 oz plain flour
50 g/2 oz butter or margarine
pinch of salt
2 whole eggs plus 1 yolk

FILLING
250 ml/8 fl oz double cream, chilled
25 g/1 oz caster sugar
vanilla essence

TOPPING
200 g/7 oz icing sugar, sifted
15 ml/1 tbsp cocoa

Lightly grease 2 baking sheets. Set the oven at 220°C/425°F/gas 7.

Make the choux pastry. Sift the flour on to a sheet of greaseproof paper. Put 250 ml/8 fl oz water in a saucepan and add the butter or margarine with the salt. Heat gently until the fat melts.

When the fat has melted, bring the liquid rapidly to the boil and add all the flour at once. Immediately remove the pan from the heat and stir the flour into the liquid to make a smooth paste which leaves the sides of the pan clean. Set aside to cool slightly.

Add the egg yolk and beat well. Add the whole eggs, one at a time, beating well after each addition. Continue beating until the paste is very glossy.

Put the pastry into a piping bag fitted with a 2 cm/¾ inch nozzle and pipe it in 2 cm/¾ inch balls on the baking sheets, leaving room for them to puff up. Bake for 10 minutes, then lower the oven temperature to 180°C/350°F/gas 4 and bake for 20 minutes more until crisp, golden and

puffed.

Remove the puffs from the oven, slit them with a sharp knife, and remove any uncooked paste. If necessary, return them to the oven for a few minutes to dry out. Cool completely on a wire rack.

Just before serving, whip the cream lightly. Whip in the sugar with a few drops of vanilla essence to taste. Put into a piping bag and fill the choux buns.

Make the chocolate topping by mixing the icing sugar and cocoa in a bowl with enough warm water (about 15-30 ml/1-2 tbsp) to form an icing that will coat the back of the spoon. Glaze the tops of the choux puffs with this mixture, reserving a little for assembling the dish.

Let the icing on the puffs harden, then arrange them in a pyramid, sticking the buns together with small dabs of the remaining icing. Serve 3 or 4 buns per person, with Chocolate Cream Sauce (page 400), if liked.

SERVES 8

VARIATIONS

The filling may be varied to taste. Sweetened whipped cream, confectioners' custard or chocolate buttercream may be used. Instead of the icing, melted chocolate may simply be poured over the choux.

☆ **FREEZER TIP** When cool, the unfilled choux puffs may be packed in sealed polythene bags and frozen. Thaw in wrappings for 1-1½ hours at room temperature, then place on baking sheets and crisp in a 180°C/350°F/gas 4 oven for 5 minutes. Cool before filling and topping.

*P*ARIS-BREST

A choux pastry ring filled with praline cream, Paris-Brest is a delectable dessert.

butter for greasing
100 g/4 oz plain flour
50 g/2 oz butter or margarine
pinch of salt
2 whole eggs plus 1 yolk

TOPPING
1 egg, beaten with 15 ml/1 tbsp water
25 g/1 oz flaked almonds
icing sugar

PRALINE CREAM
50 g/2 oz hazelnuts, roasted
100 g/4 oz granulated sugar
125 ml/4 fl oz double cream
125 ml/4 fl oz single cream

Lightly grease a baking sheet. Set the oven at 190°C/375°F/gas 7.

Make the choux pastry. Sift the flour on to a sheet of greaseproof paper. Put 250 ml/8 fl oz water in a saucepan and add the butter or margarine with the salt. Heat gently until the fat melts.

When the fat has melted, bring the liquid rapidly to the boil and add all the flour at once. Immediately remove the pan from the heat and stir the flour into the liquid to make a smooth paste which leaves the sides of the pan clean. Set aside to cool slightly.

Add the egg yolks and beat well. Add the whole eggs, one at a time, beating well after each addition. Continue beating until the paste is very glossy.

Put the pastry into a piping bag fitted with a 1 cm/½ inch nozzle and pipe an 18 cm/7 inch ring on the prepared baking sheet. Brush the top of the ring with beaten egg, then sprinkle liberally with the flaked almonds. Bake for 30 minutes. Cool on the sheet.

Make the praline cream. Rub off any loose skins from the hazelnuts. Heat the sugar with 30 ml/2 tbsp water in a heavy-bottomed saucepan, stirring until the sugar dissolves. Bring to the boil and cook until the mixture is a light golden brown. Stir in the nuts. Pour on to an oiled marble or metal surface and leave to harden. When cool and hard, crush the praline finely. In a bowl, whisk the double cream until very stiff, gradually whisk in the single cream, then fold in the praline.

Split the choux ring horizontally into 2 layers, remove any soft filling inside, and fill with the praline cream. The cream will stand up above the pastry casing. Gently put the halves together so that the gâteau resembles a sandwish with a very thick filling. Dust the almond-topped surface of the cake with icing sugar. Serve at once.

SERVES 6

GÂTEAU ST HONORÉ

This gâteau is the traditional birthday cake in France.

BASE
    100 g/4 oz plain flour
    1.25 ml/¼ tsp salt
    50 g/2 oz margarine (or half butter, half lard)
    flour for rolling out
    2 eggs, beaten, for glazing

CHOUX PASTRY
    225 g/8 oz plain flour
    100 g/4 oz butter or margarine
    pinch of salt
    4 whole eggs plus 2 yolks

PASTRY CREAM
    3 eggs
    50 g/2 oz caster sugar
    35 g/1¼ oz plain flour
    25 g/1 oz cornflour
    few drops of vanilla essence
    250 ml/8 fl oz milk
    125 ml/4 fl oz double cream
    50 g/2 oz granulated sugar

DECORATION
    glacé cherries
    angelica

Set the oven at 200°C/400°F/gas 6. Make the base. Sift the flour into a bowl, then rub in the margarine until the mixture resembles fine breadcrumbs. Add enough cold water to make a stiff dough. Press the dough together with your fingertips. Rest the dough in the refrigerator while making the choux pastry.

Sift the flour for the choux on to a sheet of greaseproof paper. Put 500 ml/17 fl oz water in a saucepan and add the butter or margarine with the salt. Heat gently until the fat melts.

When the fat has melted, bring the liquid rapidly to the boil and add all the flour at once. Immediately remove the pan from the heat and stir the flour into the liquid to make a smooth paste which leaves the sides of the pan clean. Set aside to cool slightly.

Add the egg yolks and beat well. Add the whole eggs, one at a time, beating well after each addition. Continue beating until the paste is very glossy.

Roll out the chilled short crust pastry on a lightly floured surface to a 20 cm/8 inch round. Place on a baking sheet.

Put the choux pastry into a piping bag fitted with a 1 cm/½ inch nozzle; pipe a circle of it around the edge of the pastry. Brush with beaten egg.

Use the remaining choux pastry to pipe 18-20 small buns on a separate baking sheet. Bake both pastry round and buns for 15 minutes, then lower the oven temperature to 190°C/275°F/gas 5 and bake for 10-15 minutes more, until the choux ring is well risen and golden brown. Slit the buns to release the steam, then cool on wire racks.

To make the pastry cream, separate 2 of the eggs. Reserve the whites. Combine the yolks, whole egg and caster sugar in a bowl and beat well. Stir in the flour, cornflour and vanilla essence. Heat the milk in a saucepan and gradually beat it into the egg mixture. Return the mixture to the clean pan and bring to the boil, stirring all the time. Boil for 2-3 minutes. Pour the mixture into a clean bowl, cover with buttered greaseproof paper and leave until cold.

In a bowl, whip the cream until stiff. Place in a piping bag and fill the choux buns. Combine the granulated sugar and 45 ml/ 3 tbsp water in a heavy-bottomed saucepan and heat until the sugar has dissolved. Boil until the mixture turns a pale straw colour. Remove from the heat and dip the bottom of each bun quickly in the syrup. Arrange on the choux round. Spoon a little syrup over each choux bun.

Finally, in a clean, grease-free bowl, whisk the reserved egg whites until stiff. Fold into the pastry cream, adding any left-over whipped cream. Fill the centre of the gâteau with the pastry cream. Decorate with glacé cherries and angelica.

SERVES 10-12

APPLE STRUDEL

Illustrated on page 285

Anyone who has ever watched an Austrian pastrycook at work will know that the best strudel is coaxed out to the correct size by hand. Using a rolling pin is no disgrace, however, and the recipe below gives very good results.

200 g/7 oz plain flour
1.25 ml/¼ tsp salt
30 ml/2 tbsp oil
1 egg
flour for rolling out

FILLING
   450 g/1 lb cooking apples
   50 g/2 oz butter
   50 g/2 oz soft light brown sugar
   5 ml/2 tsp ground cinnamon
   50 g/2 oz sultanas

Make the pastry. Sift the flour and salt into a mixing bowl. Add the oil and egg, with 60 ml/4 tbsp warm water. Mix to a firm dough, cover with foil and leave in a warm place for about an hour. Set the oven at 190°/375°F/gas 5.

Peel and core the apples. Chop them finely and put them into a bowl. Melt the butter in a small saucepan. Have the sugar, cinnamon and sultanas ready.

Lightly flour a clean tablecloth or sheet, placed on a work surface. Place the pastry on the cloth and roll it out very thinly to a rectangle measuring 25 × 50 cm/10 × 20 inches.

Brush the strudel pastry with some of the melted butter and sprinkle with the brown sugar, cinnamon and sultanas. Top with the chopped apple. Starting from a long side, roll the strudel up like a Swiss Roll, using the sheet as a guide.

Slide the strudel on to a large baking sheet, turning it to a horseshoe shape if necessary. Position it so that the join is underneath. Brush the top with more melted butter.

Bake for 40 minutes or until golden brown. To serve, cut the strudel in wide diagonal slices. It is equally good hot or cold, with or without cream.

SERVES 8

VARIATION

Filo pastry may be used for a quick strudel. Brush each sheet generously with melted butter, covering any filo not in use with a clean damp tea towel or cling film to prevent it from drying out.

 **MRS BEETON'S TIP** Work on a table that allows clear access all round if possible, and have all the filling ingredients ready before you begin.

GERMAN APPLE TART

30–45 ml/2–3 tbsp
1 large cooking apple
25 g/1 oz butter
15 ml/1 tbsp plain flour
30 ml/2 tbsp caster sugar
grated rind of ½ lemon
30 ml/2 tbsp single cream
1 whole egg, separated, plus 1 egg white
25 g/1 oz ground almonds

PASTRY
100 g/4 oz plain flour
1.25 ml/¼ tsp salt
50 g/2 oz butter
15 ml/1 tbsp sugar
1 egg yolk
15 ml/1 tbsp milk or white wine
flour for rolling out

Set the oven at 190°C/375°F/gas 5. Make the pastry. Sift the flour and salt into a mixing bowl. Rub in the butter until the mixture resembles fine breadcrumbs, then stir in the sugar. Add the egg yolk and milk or wine and mix to a firm dough. Roll out on a lightly floured surface and line an 18 cm/7 inch flan ring set on a baking sheet.

Spread a thin layer of rolled oats on the base of the pastry case to prevent the apple juice from soaking in. Peel, core, quarter and slice the apple, and arrange in concentric circles on top of the oats.

Melt the butter in a saucepan and stir in the flour, sugar, lemon rind, cream and egg yolk. Add the ground almonds and mix well. Whisk the egg whites in a clean, grease-free bowl until stiff. Fold into the almond mixture. Pour into the flan case.

Bake the tart for 45 minutes or until the filling is well risen and the pastry is golden.

SERVES 6

APPLE AND WALNUT TART

fat for greasing
800 g/1¾ lb cooking apples
75 g/3 oz granulated sugar
30 ml/2 tbsp soft light brown sugar
5 ml/1 tsp mixed spice
50 g/2 oz sultanas
50 g/2 oz chopped walnuts
icing sugar for dusting

PASTRY
125 g/4½ oz butter
75 g/3 oz caster sugar
1 egg
5 ml/1 tsp vanilla essence
250 g/9 oz plain flour
10 ml/2 tsp baking powder
flour for rolling out

Grease an 18 cm/7 inch loose-bottomed cake tin. Set the oven at 190°C/375°F/gas 5. Peel and core the apples. Slice them into a saucepan and add the granulated sugar with 45 ml/3 tbsp water. Simmer gently until the apples are tender. Cool.

Make the pastry. Melt the butter in a large saucepan, add the caster sugar and heat gently until dissolved. Cool slightly, then stir in the egg and vanilla essence. Sift in the flour and baking powder and mix to a firm dough. Pinch off about one third of the dough, wrap in cling film and chill in the refrigerator until firm enough to grate.

Roll out the rest of the pastry on a lightly floured surface and line the cake tin.

Stir the brown sugar into the cooled apples with the mixed spice, sultanas and walnuts. Spoon the mixture into the pastry case. Grate the chilled pastry over the apples and bake the tart for 40 minutes. Dust with icing sugar and serve hot.

SERVES 6

*P*EAR AND ORANGE COBBLER

This is an excellent pudding for using up a glut of home-grown pears.

grated rind and juice of 2 large oranges
30 ml/2 tbsp clear honey
5 ml/1 tsp cornflour
8 ripe pears, peeled, cored and sliced

TOPPING
175 g/6 oz plain wholemeal flour
15 ml/1 tbsp baking powder
50 g/2 oz butter or margarine
50 g/2 oz soft light brown sugar
75 g/3 oz walnuts, chopped
about 75 ml/3 fl oz milk plus extra to glaze

Set the oven at 230°C/450°F/gas 8. Combine the orange rind and juice in a small saucepan. Stir in the honey and cornflour. Heat gently until boiling, stirring all the time. Lower the heat, add the pears and poach them for 2-5 minutes or until tender. Transfer the mixture to an ovenproof dish.

Make the topping. Mix the flour and baking powder in a bowl, then rub in the butter until the mixture resembles fine breadcrumbs. Stir in the sugar and walnuts. Mix in enough milk to make a soft dough.

Turn the dough out on to a lightly floured surface and knead it very lightly into a ball. Roll or pat out to an 18 cm/7 inch round and cut this into six equal wedges.

Arrange the scone wedges, set slightly apart, on top of the pears and brush the top of the dough with a little milk. Bake for about 15 minutes, until the scones are well risen and browned. Serve freshly cooked, with Vanilla Custard (page 403).

SERVES 6

*A*PPLE AND BANANA COBBLER

900 g/2 lb cooking apples
75-100 g/3-4 oz sugar
50 g/2 oz raisins

TOPPING
225 g/8 oz self-raising flour
5 ml/1 tsp baking powder
50 g/2 oz butter or margarine
50 g/2 oz caster sugar plus extra for
    sprinkling
1 banana
about 125 ml/4 fl oz milk plus extra for
    brushing

Peel and core the apples. Slice them into a saucepan and add the sugar, raisins and 30 ml/2 tbsp water. Cook gently, stirring occasionally, until the apples are just soft. Transfer to an ovenproof dish.

Set the oven at 230°C/450°F/gas 8. Make the topping. Sift the flour and baking powder into a bowl. Rub in the butter or margarine until the mixture resembles fine breadcrumbs, then stir in the sugar. Peel and slice the banana and add to the mixture, with enough milk to bind the dough.

Turn the dough out on to a lightly floured surface and knead it very lightly into a smooth ball. Cut the dough into quarters, then cut each piece in half to make eight scones. Flatten each portion of dough into a round about 5 cm/2 inches in diameter.

Place the scones around the edge of the dish on top of the apples, overlapping them slightly. Brush the scones with a little milk and sprinkle them with caster sugar.

Bake the cobbler for about 15 minutes, until the scones are well risen and browned.

SERVES 6 TO 8

GOOSEBERRY COBBLER

450 g/1 lb gooseberries, topped and tailed
100 g/4 oz sugar

TOPPING
100 g/4 oz self-raising flour
25 g/1 oz margarine
about 60 ml/4 tbsp milk, plus extra for
 brushing
40 g/1½ oz glacé cherries, chopped
40 g/1½ oz blanched almonds, chopped
30 ml/2 tbsp sugar

Place the gooseberries in a saucepan with the sugar. Cook gently, stirring occasionally, until the fruit is soft. Transfer to an ovenproof dish.

Set the oven at 220°C/425°F/gas 7. Sift the flour into a bowl and rub in the margarine until the mixture resembles fine breadcrumbs. Stir in enough milk to make a soft dough.

In a small bowl, mix the cherries with the almonds and sugar. Turn the dough out on to a lightly floured surface and knead it gently into a smooth ball. Roll or pat the dough to a 15 cm/6 inch square and spread the cherry mixture over the top, leaving a 1 cm/½ inch border around the edge.

Brush the edge of the dough with milk, then roll it up to enclose the filling. Press the join together. Cut the roll into eight equal pinwheels and arrange these on top of the gooseberries. Bake for about 15 minutes, until the topping is risen and cooked. Serve at once.

SERVES 4

SPICED RHUBARB COBBLER

Scones flavoured with spices and dried fruit make a hearty topping for tart stewed rhubarb.

675 g/1½ lb rhubarb, trimmed and sliced
100 g/4 oz sugar

TOPPING
175 g/6 oz self-raising flour
5 ml/1 tsp baking powder
40 g/1½ oz butter or margarine
30 ml/2 tbsp sugar
5 ml/1 tsp ground mixed spice
50 g/2 oz mixed dried fruit
grated rind of 1 orange (optional)
about 75 ml/3 fl oz milk, plus extra for
 brushing

Place the rhubarb and sugar in a heavy-bottomed saucepan and cook gently until the juice begins to run from the fruit and the sugar dissolves. Stirring occasionally, continue to cook the rhubarb gently for 15-20 minutes, until tender. Transfer to an ovenproof dish.

Set the oven at 230°C/450°F/gas 8. Make the topping. Sift the flour into a bowl with the baking powder. Rub in the butter until the mixture resembles fine breadcrumbs, then stir in the sugar, spice, dried fruit and orange rind (if used). Mix in enough of the milk to make a soft dough.

Turn the dough out on to a lightly floured surface, knead it gently into a ball and roll it out to about 1 cm/½ inch thick. Use a 5 cm/2 inch round cutter to cut out scones. Arrange the scones on top of the fruit.

Brush the scones with milk and bake for 12-15 minutes, until risen and golden.

SERVES 4

UPSIDE-DOWN COBBLER

Take the scone topping that makes a traditional cobbler and use it as the base for a fruity topping. Vary the topping to suit your taste, the season or the store cupboard, combining fresh, glacé and canned fruits.

225 g/8 oz self-raising flour
5 ml/1 tsp baking powder
50 g/2 oz butter or margarine
25 g/1 oz sugar
about 125 ml/4 fl oz milk
2 cooking apples
50 g/2 oz black grapes, halved and seeded
1 × 227 g/8 oz can peach slices, drained
30 ml/2 tbsp clear honey
15 ml/1 tbsp orange juice
25 g/1 oz flaked almonds

Grease a large baking sheet. Set the oven at 220°C/425°F/gas 7. Sift the flour and baking powder into a mixing bowl. Rub in the butter or margarine until the mixture resembles fine breadcrumbs. Stir in the sugar, then mix in enough milk to make a soft dough.

Turn the dough out on to a lightly floured surface and knead it very gently into a smooth ball. Roll or pat out the dough to a 25 cm/10 inch circle, then lift it on to the prepared baking sheet.

Peel and core the apples. Slice them into rings and arrange them, overlapping, around the outer edge of the scone base. Arrange the grapes in a circle inside the ring of apple slices. Arrange the peach slices in the middle.

Stir the honey and orange juice together in a cup, then brush a little over the apples; reserve most of the honey and orange juice glaze. Sprinkle the apples with the flaked almonds and bake for about 15-20 minutes, until the base is risen and cooked and the nuts on top are lightly browned. Remove the cobbler from the oven and brush the apples with the reserved glaze. Serve at once.

SERVES 6 TO 8

NUTTY PLUM CRUMBLE

Illustrated on page 286
Tangy plums and toasted hazelnuts make a tasty combination in this tempting pudding. Apples, rhubarb, gooseberries, or a mixture or fruit may be used instead of the plums.

675 g/1½ lb plums, halved and stoned
50 g/2 oz sugar

TOPPING
175 g/6 oz plain flour
75 g/3 oz butter or margarine
25 g/1 oz demerara sugar
5 ml/1 tsp ground cinnamon
75 g/3 oz hazelnuts, toasted and chopped

Set the oven at 180°C/350°F/gas 4. Place the plums in an ovenproof dish and sprinkle with the sugar.

Make the topping. Sift the flour into a mixing bowl and rub in the butter or margarine until the mixture resembles fine breadcrumbs. Stir in the sugar, cinnamon and hazelnuts.

Sprinkle the topping evenly over the plums, pressing it down very lightly. Bake the crumble for about 45 minutes, until the topping is golden brown and the plums are cooked. Serve with custard, cream or vanilla ice cream.

SERVES 4 TO 6

APPLE CRUMBLE

fat for greasing
675 g/1½ lb cooking apples
100 g/4 oz golden granulated sugar
grated rind of 1 lemon
150 g/5 oz plain flour
75 g/3 oz butter or margarine
75 g/3 oz caster sugar
1.25 ml/¼ tsp ground ginger

Grease a 1 litre/1¾ pint pie dish. Set the oven at 180°C/350°F/gas 4.

Peel and core the apples. Slice into a saucepan and add the granulated sugar and lemon rind. Stir in 50 ml/2 fl oz water, cover the pan and cook until the apples are soft. Spoon the apple mixture into the prepared pie dish and set aside.

Put the flour into a mixing bowl and rub in the butter or margarine until the mixture resembles fine breadcrumbs. Add the caster sugar and ginger and stir well. Sprinkle the mixture over the apples and press down lightly. Bake for 30-40 minutes until the crumble is golden-brown.

SERVES 6

VARIATIONS

Instead of apples, use 675 g/1½ lb damsons, gooseberries, pears, plums, rhubarb, or raspberries.

> ☀ **MICROWAVE TIP** Put the apple mixture in a large bowl, adding only 30 ml/2 tbsp water, cover and cook for 7 minutes on High. Add the crumble topping and cook for 4 minutes more, then brown the topping under a preheated grill.

EVE'S PUDDING

Illustrated on page 287

fat for greasing
450 g/1 lb cooking apples
grated rind and juice of 1 lemon
75 g/3 oz demerara sugar
75 g/3 oz butter or margarine
75 g/3 oz caster sugar
1 egg, beaten
100 g/4 oz self-raising flour

Grease a 1 litre/1¾ pint die dish. Set the oven at 180°C/350°F/gas 4. Peel and core the apples and slice them thinly into a large bowl. Add the lemon rind and juice, with the demerara sugar. Stir in 15 ml/1 tbsp water, then tip the mixture into the prepared pie dish.

In a mixing bowl, cream the butter or margarine with the caster sugar until light and fluffy. Beat in the egg. Fold in the flour lightly and spread the mixture over the apples.

Bake for 40-45 minutes until the apples are soft and the sponge is firm. Serve with melted apple jelly and single cream or Greek yogurt.

SERVES 4

VARIATIONS

Instead of apples use 450 g/1 lb apricots, peaches, gooseberries, rhubarb, raspberries or plums.

MARMALADE MERINGUE PUDDING

fat for greasing
75 g/3 oz soft white breadcrumbs
45 ml/3 tbsp marmalade
200 ml/7 fl oz milk
25 g/1 oz butter
2 eggs, separated
75 g/3 oz caster sugar

Grease a 750 ml/1¼ pint pie dish. Set the oven at 140°C/275°F/gas 1. Spread the breadcrumbs out on a baking sheet and put into the oven to dry off slightly.

Warm the marmalade in a small saucepan, then spread half of it over the base of the prepared pie dish. Warm the milk and butter in a second saucepan.

Meanwhile put the egg yolks in a bowl and stir in 25 g/1 oz of the sugar. Pour on the warmed milk mixture, stirring thoroughly. Add the breadcrumbs, mix thoroughly and leave to stand for 30 minutes.

Raise the oven temperature to 160°C/325°F/gas 3. Pour half the breadcrumb mixture into the prepared pie dish, spoon on another layer of marmalade, and put the rest of the crumb mixture on top. Smooth the surface, if necessary. Bake for 40-45 minutes until the pudding is lightly set.

Remove the pudding from the oven, then lower the oven temperature to 120°C/250°F/gas ½. In a clean, grease-free bowl, whisk the egg whites until stiff, add half the remaining sugar and whisk again. Fold in all but 15 ml/1 tbsp of the remaining sugar, then pile the meringue on top of the pudding mixture, making sure it is completely covered. Draw the mixture into peaks (see Mrs Beeton's Tip) and sprinkle with the reserved sugar.

Return to the oven for 40-45 minutes until the meringue is set and the tops of the peaks are brown, Serve at once.

SERVES 4

> **MRS BEETON'S TIP** To draw the meringue into peaks, use a slim spatula or flat-bladed knife, setting the blade down flat upon the meringue, then flicking it upwards.

APPLE MERINGUE

500 ml/17 fl oz thick apple purée
15 ml/1 tbsp lemon juice
3 eggs, separated
about 250 g/9 oz caster sugar

DECORATION
glacé cherries
angelica

Set the oven at 180°C/350°F/gas 4. Put the apple purée in a bowl and beat in the lemon juice and egg yolks with about 75 g/3 oz of the sugar. Spoon into a 750 ml/1¼ pint baking dish, cover, and bake for 15 minutes.

In a clean, grease-free bowl, whisk the egg whites to stiff peaks. Gradually whisk in 150 g/5 oz of the remaining sugar, adding 15 ml/1 tbsp at a time. Pile the meringue on top of the apple mixture and sprinkle with the remaining sugar. Return to the oven and bake for a further 15 minutes or until the meringue is pale golden-brown.

Serve at once with Vanilla Custard (page 403) or single cream.

SERVES 4

BAKED APPLES

6 cooking apples
75 g/3 oz sultanas, chopped
50 g/2 oz demerara sugar

Wash and core the apples. Cut around the skin of each apple with the tip of a sharp knife two-thirds of the way up from the base. Put the apples into an ovenproof dish, and fill the centres with the chopped sultanas.

Sprinkle the demerara sugar on top of the apples and pour 75 ml/5 tbsp water around them. Bake for 45-60 minutes, depending on the cooking quality and size of the apples.

Serve with Vanilla Custard (page 403), ice cream, Brandy Butter (page 405) or with whipped cream.

SERVES 6

VARIATIONS

Fill the apple cavities with a mixture of 50 g/2 oz Barbados or other raw sugar and 50 g/2 oz butter, or use blackcurrant, raspberry, strawberry or apricot jam, or marmalade. Instead of sultanas, chopped stoned dates, raisins or currants could be used. A topping of toasted almonds looks effective and tastes delicious.

MICROWAVE TIP Baked apples cook superbly in the microwave. Prepare as suggested above, but reduce the amount of water to 30 ml/2 tbsp. Cook for 10-12 minutes on High.

APPLE CHARLOTTE

butter for greasing
400 g/14 oz cooking apples
grated rind and juice of 1 lemon
100 g/4 oz soft light brown sugar
pinch of ground cinnamon
50-75 g/2-3 oz butter
8-10 large slices white bread, about
    5 mm/¼ inch thick
15 ml/1 tbsp caster sugar

Generously grease a 1 litre/1¾ pint charlotte mould or 15 cm/6 inch cake tin with butter. Set the oven at 180°C/350°F/gas 4. Peel and core the apples. Slice them into a saucepan and add the lemon rind and juice. Stir in the brown sugar and cinnamon and simmer until the apples soften to a thick purée. Leave to cool.

Melt the butter in a saucepan, than pour into a shallow dish. Cut the crusts off the bread, and dip 1 slice in the butter. Cut it into a round to fit the bottom of the mould or tin. Fill any spaces with extra butter-soaked bread, if necessary. Dip the remaining bread slices in the butter. Use 6 slices to line the inside of the mould. The slices should touch one another to make a bread case.

Fill the bread case with the cooled apple purée. Complete the case by fitting the top with more bread slices. Cover loosely with greased greaseproof paper or foil, and bake for 40-45 minutes. To serve the charlotte turn out and dredge with caster sugar. Serve with bramble jelly and cream.

SERVES 5 TO 6

MRS BEETON'S TIP The mould or tin may be lined with slices of bread and butter, placed buttered side out.

BROWN BETTY

fat for greasing
1 kg/2¼ lb cooking apples
150 g/5 oz stale wholewheat
    breadcrumbs
grated rind and juice of 1 lemon
60 ml/4 tbsp golden syrup
100 g/4 oz demerara sugar

Grease a 1 litre/1¾ pint pie dish. Set the oven at 160°C/325°F/gas 3.

Peel and core the apples. Slice them thinly into a bowl. Coat the prepared pie dish with a thin layer of breadcrumbs, then fill with alternate layers of apples, lemon rind and breadcrumbs. Put the syrup, sugar and lemon juice into a saucepan. Add 30 ml/2 tbsp water. Heat until the syrup has dissolved, then pour the mixture over the layered pudding.

Bake for 1-1¼ hours until the pudding is brown and the apple cooked. Serve with single cream or a custard.

SERVES 6

MRS BEETON'S TIP Use a tablespoon dipped in boiling water to measure the golden syrup. The syrup will slide off easily.

BAKED APPLES STUFFED WITH RICE AND NUTS

6 medium cooking apples
25 g/1 oz flaked almonds or other nuts
40 g/1½ oz seedless raisins
25-50 g/2-3 oz boiled rice (preferably
    boiled in milk)
50 g/2 oz sugar or to taste
1 egg, beaten
30 ml/2 tbsp butter
raspberry or blackcurrant syrup

Set the oven at 190°C/375°F/gas 5. Wash and core the apples but do not peel them. With a small rounded spoon, hollow out part of the flesh surrounding the core hole. Do not break the outside skin.

In a bowl, mix together the nuts, raisins and rice, using enough rice to make a stuffing for all the apples. Add the sugar, with enough egg to bind the mixture. Melt the butter and stir it into the mixture.

Fill the apples with the rice mixture. Place in a roasting tin and add hot water to a depth of 5 mm/¼ inch. Bake for 40 minutes or until the apples are tender. Remove the roasting tin from the oven and transfer the apples to a warmed serving platter, using a slotted spoon. Warm the fruit syrup and pour it over the apples.

SERVES 6

MICROWAVE TIP The rice may be cooked in the microwave. Place 50 g/2 oz pudding rice in a large bowl with 30 ml/2 tbsp sugar. Stir in 600 ml/1 pint water, cover and cook on High for 25 minutes. Stir well, then stir in 300 ml/½ pint top-of-the-milk or single cream. Use 25-50 g/1-2 oz of the cooked rice for the above pudding and reserve the remainder.

*F*RIAR'S OMELETTE

fat for greasing
1 kg/2¼ lb cooking apples
grated rind and juice of 1 lemon
75 g/3 oz butter
100 g/4 oz sugar
2 eggs, beaten
100 g/4 oz stale white breadcrumbs

Grease a 1 litre/1¾ pint pie dish. Set the oven at 220°C/425°F/gas 7.

Peel and core the apples. Slice them into a saucepan and add the lemon rind and juice, 50 g/2 oz of the butter, and sugar. Cover the pan and cook the apples until very soft. Remove the pan from the heat and cool slightly.

Stir the eggs into the apple mixture and beat well. Put half the stale breadcrumbs into the prepared pie dish, cover with the apple mixture, and sprinkle with the remaining crumbs. Dot with the remaining butter and bake for 20-25 minutes.

Serve with Vanilla Custard (page 403).

SERVES 4 TO 5

*C*HERRY PUDDING

fat for greasing
450 g/1 lb cooking cherries
75 g/3 oz soft light brown sugar
50 g/2 oz cornflour
375 ml/13 fl oz milk
50 g/2 oz caster sugar
3 eggs, separated
grated rind of 1 lemon
1.25 ml/¼ tsp ground cinnamon

Grease a 1 litre/1¾ pint pie dish. Set the oven at 200°C/400°F/gas 6.

Stone the cherries and put them into a saucepan. Add 60 ml/4 tbsp water and stir in the brown sugar. Stew very gently until the fruit is just soft. Leave to cool.

In a bowl, mix the cornflour to a paste with a little of the milk. Bring the rest of the milk to the boil in a saucepan, then pour it on to the cornflour mixture. Mix well. Return the mixture to the clean saucepan and bring to simmering point, stirring all the time. Simmer for 2-3 minutes. Stir in the caster sugar, and leave to cool.

Add the egg yolks, lemon rind and cinnamon to the cornflour sauce. In a clean, grease-free bowl, whisk the egg whites to the same consistency as the sauce and fold them in.

Arrange a layer of cherries in the base of the prepared pie dish, then add a layer of the sauce. Continue with the layers until all the sauce has been used, ending with a layer of sauce. Cover with greased paper or foil and bake for 35-45 minutes or until just set. Serve with Vanilla Custard (page 403) or single cream.

SERVES 5 TO 6

MRS BEETON'S TIP A cherry stoner makes short work of preparing the fruit. For more information about this utensil, see page 29.

---

*H*ONESTY PUDDING

fat for greasing
50 g/2 oz fine oatmeal
15 ml/1 tbsp plain flour
750 ml/1¼ pints milk
1 egg, beaten
pinch of salt
2.5 ml/½ tsp grated orange rind

Grease a 750 ml/1¼ pint pie dish. Set the oven at 180°C/350°F/gas 4. Put the oatmeal and flour in a bowl and mix to a smooth paste with a little of the milk. Bring the rest of the milk to the boil in a saucepan, then pour it over the oatmeal mixture, stirring all the time.

Return the mixture to the clean pan and cook over low heat for 5 minutes, stirring all the time. Remove from the heat, and cool for 5 minutes.

Beat the egg into the cooled oatmeal mixture. Flavour with the salt and orange rind. Pour the mixture into the prepared pie dish, and bake for 35-40 minutes.

Serve hot from the dish, with cream and brown sugar.

SERVES 4

*B*AKED SPONGE PUDDING

fat for greasing
100 g/4 oz butter or margarine
100 g/4 oz caster sugar
2 eggs, beaten
150 g/5 oz plain flour
5 ml/1 tsp baking powder
1.25 ml/¼ tsp vanilla essence
about 30 ml/2 tbsp milk

Grease a 1 litre/1¾ pint pie dish. Set the oven at 180°C/350°F/gas 4. In a mixing bowl, cream the butter or margarine with the sugar until light and fluffy. Gradually beat in the eggs. Sift the flour and baking powder together into a bowl, then fold them into the creamed mixture.

Spoon the mixture into the prepared pie dish and bake for 30-35 minutes until well risen and golden-brown.

Serve from the dish with Vanilla Custard (page 403) or any sweet sauce.

SERVES 4 TO 6

VARIATIONS

JAM SPONGE Put 30 ml/2 tbsp jam in the base of the dish before adding the sponge mixture. Serve with Jam Sauce (page 402) made with the same type of jam.

ORANGE OR LEMON SPONGE Add the grated rind of 1 orange or lemon to the creamed mixture. Serve with Rich Lemon Sauce (page 395).

SPICY SPONGE Sift 5 ml/1 tsp mixed spice, ground ginger, grated nutmeg or cinnamon with the flour. Serve with Ginger Syrup Sauce (page 402).

COCONUT SPONGE Substitute 25 g/1 oz desiccated coconut for 25 g/1 oz flour. Serve with Apricot Sauce (page 398).

CHOCOLATE SPONGE Substitute 50 g/2 oz cocoa for 50 g/2 oz flour. Serve with Chocolate Cream Sauce (page 400) or Chocolate Liqueur Sauce (page 400).

ALMOND CASTLES

fat for greasing
75 g/3 oz butter
75 g/3 oz caster sugar
3 eggs, separated
45 ml/3 tbsp single cream or milk
15 ml/1 tbsp brandy
150 g/5 oz ground almonds

Grease 8 dariole moulds. Set the oven at 160°C/325°F/gas 3.

In a mixing bowl, cream the butter and sugar until light and fluffy. Stir in the egg yolks, cream or milk, brandy and ground almonds.

In a clean, grease-free bowl, whisk the egg whites until just stiff, and fold lightly into the mixture. Three-quarters fill the dariole moulds and bake for 20-25 minutes, until the puddings are firm in the centre and golden-brown.

Turn out on to individual plates and serve with Vanilla Custard (page 403).

SERVES 4 TO 8

CASTLE PUDDINGS

fat for greasing
100 g/4 oz butter or margarine
100 g/4 oz sugar
2 eggs
1.25 ml/¼ tsp vanilla essence
100 g/4 oz plain flour
5 ml/1 tsp baking powder

Grease 6-8 dariole moulds. Set the oven at 180°C/350°F/gas 4.

In a mixing bowl, cream the butter or margarine with the sugar until light and creamy. Beat in the eggs and vanilla essence. Sift the flour and baking powder into a bowl, then fold into the creamed mixture.

Three-quarters fill the prepared dariole moulds. Bake for 20-25 minutes, until set and well risen. Serve with Vanilla Custard (page 403) or Jam Sauce (page 402).

SERVES 3-4

VARIATION

SOMERSET PUDDINGS Serve the puddings cold, with the inside of each scooped out, and the cavity filled with stewed apple or jam. Serve with whipped cream.

COTTAGE PUDDING

butter for greasing
200 g/7 oz plain flour
pinch of salt
10 ml/2 tsp baking powder
100 g/4 oz butter or margarine
75 g/3 oz soft light brown sugar
100 g/4 oz raisins
1 egg, beaten
45-75 ml/3-5 tbsp milk

Grease a 25 × 20 cm/10 × 8 inch baking dish. Set the oven at 190°C/375°F/gas 5.

Sift the flour, salt and baking powder into a mixing bowl. Rub in the butter or margarine and add the sugar and raisins. Stir in the egg, with enough milk to make a soft dropping consistency.

Spoon the mixture into the prepared

baking dish and bake for 35-40 minutes until firm in the centre and golden-brown.

Serve with Redcurrant Sauce (page 393), or Vanilla Custard (page 403).

SERVES 5 TO 6

C OLLEGE PUDDINGS

Illustrated on page 288

fat for greasing
100 g/4 oz plain flour
2.5 ml/½ tsp baking powder
pinch of salt
1.25 ml/¼ tsp mixed spice
100 g/4 oz stale white breadcrumbs
75 g/3 oz shredded suet
75 g/3 oz caster sugar
50 g/2 oz currants
50 g/2 oz sultanas
2 eggs, beaten
100-125 ml/3½-4 fl oz milk

Grease 6-8 dariole moulds. Set the oven at 190°C/375°F/gas 5.

Sift the flour, baking powder, salt and spice into a mixing bowl. Add the crumbs, suet, sugar, currants and sultanas, and mix well. Stir in the eggs with enough milk to form a soft dropping consistency.

Half fill the prepared dariole moulds with the mixture and bake for 20-25 minutes.

Turn out and serve with Rich Lemon Sauce (page 395) or Thickened Fruit Sauce (page 399).

SERVES 6 TO 8

E XETER PUDDING

butter for greasing
100 g/4 oz stale white breadcrumbs
25 g/1 oz ratafias or small almond
 macaroons
75 g/3 oz shredded suet
50 g/2 oz sago
75 g/3 oz caster sugar
grated rind and juice of 1 lemon
3 eggs
30 ml/2 tbsp milk
2 individual sponge cakes or trifle
 sponges, sliced
75 g/3 oz jam (any type)

Grease a 1 litre/1¾ pint pie dish. Coat with some of the crumbs, and cover the base with half the ratafias or macaroons. Set the oven at 180°C/350°F/gas 4.

Put the remaining crumbs into a mixing bowl with suet, sago, sugar, lemon rind and juice. In a separate bowl, beat together the eggs and milk. Stir the liquid mixture into the dry ingredients.

Spoon a layer of the suet mixture into the prepared pie dish and cover with some of the slices of sponge cake. Add a layer of jam and some of the remaining ratafias. Repeat the layers until all the ingredients are used, finishing with a layer of suet mixture.

Bake for 45-60 minutes. Serve with Jam Sauce (page 402) using the same jam as that used in the recipe.

SERVES 5 TO 6

DEVONSHIRE RUM

fat for greasing
about 225 g/8 oz cold Christmas pudding
    or rich fruit cake
10 ml/2 tsp cornflour
250 ml/8 fl oz milk
10 ml/2 tsp soft light brown sugar
1 egg, beaten
45 ml/3 tbsp rum or a few drops rum
    essence

Grease a 750 ml/1¼ pint pie dish. Set the oven at 180°C/350°F/gas 4.

Cut the pudding or cake into fingers, and arrange in the prepared pie dish. In a bowl, mix the cornflour to a paste with a little of the milk. Heat the remaining milk in a saucepan to just below boiling point, then pour it slowly on to the cornflour mixture, stirring to prevent the formation of lumps. Pour the mixture back into the pan, return the pan to the heat and cook the sauce gently for 2 minutes; then stir in the sugar, egg, and rum or rum essence.

Pour the rum sauce over the pudding or cake and bake for about 30 minutes or until firm. Serve with Fairy Butter (page 406).

SERVES 3 TO 4

LEMON DELICIOUS PUDDING

This pudding has a light spongy top with lemon sauce underneath.

butter for greasing
3 eggs, separated
75 g/3 oz caster sugar
200 ml/7 fl oz milk
15 ml/1 tbsp self-raising flour, sifted
juice and grated rind of 2 large lemons
pinch of salt
15 ml/1 tbsp icing sugar

Grease a deep 1 litre/1¾ pint ovenproof dish. Set the oven at 180°C/350°F/gas 4.

In a mixing bowl, beat the egg yolks with the caster sugar until light, pale, and creamy. Whisk the milk, flour, lemon juice, and rind into the egg yolks. In a clean, grease-free bowl, whisk the egg whites with the salt, adding the icing sugar gradually. Continue to whisk until stiff but not dry. Fold into the lemon mixture.

Pour the mixture into the prepared dish and stand the dish in a roasting tin. Add hot water to come halfway up the sides of the dish. Bake for 1 hour.

SERVES 4

MRS BEETON'S TIP If a fragment of shell drops into the egg white, use another piece of shell to remove it.

BAKED JAM ROLL

Illustrated on page 288

butter for greasing
300 g/11 oz plain flour
5 ml/1 tsp baking powder
pinch of salt
150 g/5 oz shredded suet
flour for rolling out
200-300 g/7-11 oz jam

Grease a baking sheet. Set the oven at 190°C/375°F/gas 5.

Sift the flour, baking powder and salt into a mixing bowl. Add the suet and enough cold water to make a soft, but firm dough. On a lightly floured surface, roll the dough out to a rectangle about 5 mm/¼ inch thick. Spread the jam almost to the edges. Dampen the edges of the pastry rectangle with water and roll up lightly. Seal the edges at either end.

Place the roll on the prepared baking sheet with the sealed edge underneath. Cover loosely with greased greaseproof paper or foil and bake for 50-60 minutes until golden-brown. Transfer to a warm platter, slice and serve with warmed jam.

SERVES 6

VARIATIONS

Instead of the jam, use 200-300 g/7-11 oz marmalade, or 225 g/8 oz dried fruit mixed with 50 g/2 oz demerara sugar. Serve with Vanilla Custard (page 403).

SALZBURGER NOCKERL

50 g/2 oz butter
10 ml/2 tsp caster sugar
5 eggs, separated
15 ml/1 tbsp plain flour
125 ml/4 fl oz milk
icing sugar for dredging

Set the oven at 200°C/400°F/gas 6. Beat the butter and sugar together in a mixing bowl until light and fluffy. Stir in the egg yolks one at a time.

In a clean, grease-free bowl, whisk the egg whites until stiff, and fold lightly into the egg yolk mixture with the flour.

Pour the milk into a shallow flameproof dish, and heat gently. Remove from the heat, pour in the batter, smooth it lightly, and bake for about 10 minutes until light brown in colour. Cut out spoonfuls of the nockerl, and arrange on a warmed serving plate. Serve immediately, sprinkled with icing sugar.

SERVES 4 TO 6

SAUCES AND BUTTERS

This chapter is filled with a wide variety of excellent sauces and accompaniments, from a quick custard to a rich brandy and almond butter. Use them as suggested in the recipes that follow or make up your own dessert ideas. For example, top a simple ice cream with a zesty sauce or spread simple drop scones with Orange Liqueur Butter for a dessert that is as inventive as it is easy to make.

A well-chosen, perfectly prepared sauce adds a professional touch to a dessert. Many recipes offer guidance as to the type of sauce to serve but you may wish to use a little imagination when selecting the accompaniments for a pudding. For example, a lively, cold fruit sauce contrasts well with a piping hot steamed sponge pudding; or a spicy sauce flavoured with ginger will enliven a delicate fruit mousse.

When serving a cold sauce, prepare it in advance, cool and chill it until it is needed. If you are preparing a hot sauce that requires last-minute attention weigh all the ingredients and set out all the utensils beforehand. Some hot sauces may be made and put on one side ready for last-minute reheating. To prevent the formation of a skin on a sauce, cover it with a piece of dampened greaseproof paper or microwave cooking film; alternatively, sprinkle a little caster sugar over the surface.

SAUCES THICKENED WITH EGGS

Custards and other sauces thickened with eggs need special attention. It is important that only fresh, good-quality eggs be used and that the eggs be washed just before being cracked. A double saucepan is useful for making delicate sauces or the sauce may be cooked in a bowl over a saucepan of hot, not boiling, water. If the sauce becomes too hot, or if it is cooked for too long, the eggs will curdle and the sauce will be ruined.

FREEZING

Fruit purées and sauces thickened with flour or cornflour may be frozen; however custards and sauces thickened with eggs curdle on freezing. Thaw a sauce in its container in the refrigerator, then whisk it well to make sure it is smooth before gently reheating it. Taste sauces that are to be served cold and add a little extra sweetening if necessary.

Flavoured butters also freeze well. Clean margarine or cream cheese tubs with lids are the ideal containers. Press the butter down into the tub and smooth the top, then put on the lid and pack one or more containers in a sealed polythene bag. Label the bag. To pack individual portions, form the butter into a roll by wrapping it in cling film and shaping it. Chill and slice the roll, then open freeze the slices on a baking sheet lined with freezer film. Pack the firm butter in a rigid container, with freezer film between the layers.

Decorative butter pats may be made by

piping creamy flavoured butters on to a film-lined baking sheet or by stamping out rounds using special embossed butter pats. Alternatively use a melon baller to scoop well-chilled butters before open freezing. Most flavoured butters may be frozen for up to 3 months.

MICROWAVE COOKING

The microwave oven is ideal for cooking sauces that are thickened with cornflour, flour or arrowroot. Custards and other delicate, egg-based sauces may also be cooked in the microwave but, as with conventional cooking, they require constant attention and frequent stirring or whisking. Microwave tips are included throughout the chapter.

REDCURRANT SAUCE

100 g/4 oz redcurrant jelly
45 ml/3 tbsp port

Combine the jelly and port in a small saucepan and cook over gentle heat until the jelly melts. Pour over steamed puddings or serve with hot milk puddings such as semolina. The sauce also makes a good glaze for cheesecakes topped with berry fruits.

MAKES ABOUT 150 ML/¼ PINT

MICROWAVE TIP Mix the jelly and port in a small basin. Cook on High for about 1-1½ minutes, stirring once, until the jelly has melted.

APPLE SAUCE

Rich and full of flavour, this is an ideal accompaniment to steamed fruit puddings. Cold, it makes a good filling for apple meringue pie or cake.

450 g/1 lb cooking apples
15 g/½ oz butter or margarine
grated rind and juice of ½ lemon
sugar (see method)

Peel and core the apples and slice them into a saucepan. Add 30 ml/2 tbsp water with the butter and lemon rind. Cover the pan and cook over low heat until the apple is reduced to a pulp.

Beat the pulp until smooth, then rub through a sieve. Alternatively, purée the mixture in a blender or food processor.

Return the purée to the clean pan and reheat. Stir in the lemon juice, with sugar to taste. Serve hot or cold.

MAKES 375 ML/13 FL OZ

MICROWAVE TIP Place the sliced apples in a large dish or bowl with the water, butter and lemon rind. Make sure there is room for the apples to boil up. Cover and cook on High for 5-7 minutes, stirring once. Continue as above.

MRS BEETON'S TIP Adding a little citrus rind and juice brings out the full flavour of the apples. Orange or lime may be used instead of lemon, if preferred.

CARAMEL CUSTARD SAUCE

25 g/1 oz granulated sugar
250 ml/8 fl oz milk
few drops of vanilla essence or a strip of
    lemon rind
3 egg yolks
50 g/2 oz caster sugar

Start by making the caramel. Mix the granulated sugar with 15 ml/1 tbsp water in a small saucepan. Heat gently until the sugar dissolves, then boil the syrup until it is golden brown. Remove the syrup from the heat and immediately add 30 ml/2 tbsp cold water (see Mrs Beeton's Tip). Leave in a warm place to dissolve.

Meanwhile, make the sauce. Combine the milk and chosen flavouring in a saucepan. Warm gently but do not let the liquid boil.

In a bowl, beat the egg yolks and sugar together until creamy. Remove the lemon rind, if used, from the saucepan and add the milk to the eggs.

Strain the custard into a double saucepan or a heatproof bowl placed over a saucepan of simmering water. Cook, stirring constantly, until the custard thickens and coats the back of the spoon.

Stir the caramel. Add enough to the finished custard sauce to give a good flavour and colour. Serve warm or cold.

MAKES ABOUT 300 ML/½ PINT

MRS BEETON'S TIP Take care when adding the cold water to the hot caramel. The mixture may spit, so protect your hand by wearing an oven glove.

SWEET WHITE SAUCE

20 ml/4 tsp cornflour
250 ml/8 fl oz milk
15-30 ml/1-2 tbsp sugar
vanilla essence or other flavouring

Put the cornflour in a bowl. Stir in enough of the cold milk to form a smooth, thin paste.

Heat the remaining milk in a small saucepan. When it boils, stir it into the cornflour paste, then return the mixture to the clean pan and stir until boiling.

Lower the heat and cook, stirring frequently, for 3 minutes. Stir in sugar to taste and add the chosen flavouring. Serve hot.

MAKES ABOUT 250 ML/8 FL OZ

VARIATIONS

ALMOND SAUCE Add 10 ml/2 tsp ground almonds to the cornflour when blending with the milk. When the sauce is cooked, stir in 2-3 drops of almond essence with vanilla essence to taste.
BRANDY SAUCE When the sauce is cooked, stir in 15-30 ml/1-2 tbsp brandy.
CHOCOLATE SAUCE When the sauce is cooked, stir in 15 ml/1 tbsp cocoa powder dissolved in 15 ml/1 tbsp boiling water.
COFFEE SAUCE To the cooked sauce add 10 ml/2 tsp instant coffee dissolved in 15 ml/1 tbsp boiling water.
GINGER SAUCE Stir in 10 ml/2 tsp ground ginger with the cornflour. For extra taste and texture, 50 g/2 oz crystallized ginger, finely chopped, may be added to the cooked sauce.

MICROWAVE TIP Combine all the ingredients in a bowl and cook on High for 3-5 minutes, whisking twice.

*S*WEET ARROWROOT SAUCE

The advantage in using arrowroot is that it creates a clear sauce that will not mask the pudding over which it is poured.

thinly pared rind of 1 lemon or other solid
    flavouring
100 g/4 oz sugar
lemon juice to taste
10 ml/2 tsp arrowroot

Put 125 ml/4 fl oz water in a saucepan. Add the lemon rind or other flavouring and bring to the boil. Lower the heat and simmer gently for 15 minutes.

Remove the lemon rind, if used, and stir in the sugar. Return the liquid to the boil and boil steadily for 5 minutes. Add lemon juice to taste.

In a cup, mix the arrowroot with 10 ml/ 2 tsp water until smooth. Stir into the hot liquid. Heat gently for 1-2 minutes, stirring constantly as the sauce thickens. Remove from the heat once the sauce has boiled.

MAKES ABOUT 175 ML/6 FL OZ

VARIATIONS

ST CLEMENT'S SAUCE Use the rind of ½ lemon or ½ orange and add 125 ml/ 4 fl oz lemon or orange juice.
RICH LEMON SAUCE Beat 125 ml/ 4 fl oz sherry with 1 egg yolk. Add the mixture to the thickened sauce and heat gently. Do not allow the sauce to boil once the egg yolk has been added.

> 🥣 **MRS BEETON'S TIP** A thinner sauce may be made by increasing the water in the saucepan to 250 ml/8 fl oz.

*C*ORNFLOUR CUSTARD SAUCE

15 ml/1 tbsp cornflour
250 ml/8 fl oz milk
1 egg yolk
15 ml/1 tbsp sugar
few drops of vanilla essence

Mix the cornflour with a little of the cold milk in a large bowl. Bring the rest of the milk to the boil in a saucepan, then stir into the blended mixture. Return the mixture to the clean pan.

Bring the cornflour mixture to the boil and boil for 3 minutes to cook the cornflour. Remove from the heat.

When the mixture has cooled a little, stir in the egg yolk and sugar. Return to a low heat and cook, stirring carefully, until the sauce thickens. Do not let it boil. Flavour with a few drops of vanilla essence and pour into a jug.

MAKES ABOUT 250 ML/8 FL OZ

> ☀ **MICROWAVE TIP** Mix the cornflour with all the milk in a bowl. Cook on High for 3-5 minutes, whisking twice. Whisk well, then whisk in the yolk, sugar and vanilla. Cook for a further 30-45 seconds on High.

CRÈME ANGLAISE

The classic egg custard sauce; an essential ingredient of traditional trifle.

250 ml/8 fl oz milk
few drops of vanilla essence or a strip of
    lemon rind
3 egg yolks
50 g/2 oz caster sugar

Combine the milk and chosen flavouring in a saucepan. Warm gently but do not let the liquid boil.

In a bowl, beat the egg yolks and sugar together until creamy. Remove the lemon rind, if used, from the saucepan and add the milk to the eggs.

Strain the custard into a double saucepan or a heatproof bowl placed over a saucepan of simmering water. Cook, stirring constantly, until the custard thickens and coats the back of the spoon. Serve hot or cold.

MAKES ABOUT 300 ML/½ PINT

VARIATIONS

LIQUEUR SAUCE Stir 125 ml/4 fl oz lightly whipped double cream and 30 ml/2 tbsp orange-flavoured liqueur into the completed sauce.
CHOCOLATE CUSTARD SAUCE Use vanilla essence instead of lemon rind and add 100 g/4 oz coarsely grated plain chocolate to the milk. Warm until the chocolate melts, stir, then add to the egg yolks and proceed as in the main recipe.

CREAM CUSTARD SAUCE

4 egg yolks or 2 whole eggs
50 g/2 oz caster sugar
125 ml/4 fl oz milk
grated rind of 1 orange
125 ml/4 fl oz single cream

In a mixing bowl, beat the egg yolks or the whole eggs with the sugar and milk. Stir in the orange rind and cream.

Pour into a double saucepan or into a heatproof bowl placed over a saucepan of simmering water. Cook, stirring all the time, until the sauce thickens. Serve hot or cold.

MAKES ABOUT 250 ML/8 FL OZ

 MRS BEETON'S TIP Do not allow the sauce to boil or it will curdle.

SWEET MOUSSELINE SAUCE

Serve this frothy sauce over light steamed or baked puddings, fruit desserts or Christmas pudding.

2 whole eggs plus 1 yolk
40 g/1½ oz caster sugar
75 ml/5 tbsp single cream
15 ml/1 tbsp medium-dry sherry

Combine all the ingredients in a double saucepan or in a heatproof bowl placed over a saucepan of simmering water. Cook and whisk until pale and frothy and of a thick, creamy consistency. Pour into a bowl and serve at once.

MAKES ABOUT 300 ML/½ PINT

S ABAYON SAUCE

The French version of that Italian favourite, Zabaglione, Sabayon is usually served warm as an accompaniment to steamed pudding.

3 egg yolks
25 g/1 oz caster sugar
50 ml/2 fl oz Marsala, Madeira, sweet
    sherry or sweet white wine
small strip of lemon rind

Beat the yolks and sugar together in a heatproof bowl until thick and pale. Gradually whisk in the chosen wine. Add the lemon rind.

Pour the mixture into a double saucepan or stand the bowl over a saucepan of simmering water. Cook until thick and creamy, whisking all the time. When the whisk is lifted out of the mixture it should leave a trail that lasts for 2-3 seconds. Remove the lemon rind.

Serve at once.

MAKES ABOUT 200 ML/7 FL OZ

☀ **MICROWAVE TIP** Whisk the yolks and sugar as above, in a bowl which may be used in the microwave. In a jug, heat the chosen wine on High for 30-45 seconds, until hot but not boiling, then whisk it into the yolks. Cook on High for about 1-1½ minutes, whisking thoroughly two or three times, until creamy.

C OLD SHERRY SABAYON SAUCE

50 g/2 oz caster sugar
2 egg yolks
15 ml/1 tbsp medium-sweet sherry or
    brandy
45 ml/3 tbsp double cream

Put the sugar in a saucepan with 75 ml/5 tbsp water. Warm gently until the sugar is completely dissolved, then bring to the boil and boil for 3 minutes.

Mix the egg yolks with the sherry or brandy in a bowl. Whisk in the syrup gradually, and continue whisking until the mixture is cool, thick and foamy.

In a second bowl, whip the cream lightly. Fold it gently into the egg mixture. Chill.

Pour into tall glasses and serve with ratafia biscuits. The sauce may also be served with cold desserts.

MAKES ABOUT 400 ML/14 FL OZ

C HANTILLY CREAM

250 ml/8 fl oz double cream
25 g/1 oz caster sugar
few drops of vanilla essence

Pour the cream into a mixing bowl and chill it for several hours.

Just before serving, whip the cream lightly, whip in the sugar and add a few drops of vanilla essence to taste.

MAKES ABOUT 250 ML/8 FL OZ

MELBA SAUCE

Although this sauce is principally used for Peach Melba, it is also delicious when served with meringues, sorbet or any raspberry – flavoured dessert.

225 g/8 oz fresh raspberries
45 ml/3 tbsp icing sugar
white wine (optional)

Put the raspberries in a sieve over a heat-proof bowl. Crush them lightly with the back of a wooden spoon, then add the sugar and rub the raspberries through the sieve into the bowl.

Place the bowl over a saucepan of simmering water, and stir for 2-3 minutes to dissolve the sugar.

Remove from the heat, and stir in a little white wine if a thinner consistency is preferred. The sauce should only just coat the back of a spoon. Pour into a bowl or jug and chill before use.

MAKES ABOUT 125 ML/4 FL OZ

MICROWAVE TIP Mix the fruit and sugar in a bowl. Cover and cook on High for 2 minutes, until the fruit is pulpy. Rub the sauce through a sieve. Continue as above, thinning the sauce with wine if liked.

APRICOT SAUCE

This fruity sauce may be served hot or cold, with set custards, sponge puddings, pancakes or ice cream. It also makes an unusual, lively accompaniment to plain apple pie.

225 g/8 oz fresh apricots
25-50 g/1-2 oz soft light brown sugar
15 ml/1 tbsp lemon juice
10 ml/2 tsp maraschino or apricot brandy
   (optional)
5 ml/1 tsp arrowroot

Stone the apricots, reserving the stones. Put the fruit into a saucepan with 125 ml/4 fl oz water. Cover the pan and simmer the fruit until softened. Rub through a sieve, or purée in a blender or food processor.

Crack the reserved apricot stones and remove the kernels. Cover the kernels with boiling water and leave for 2 minutes. Drain the kernels, and when cool enough to handle, skin them. Add to the apricots with sugar to taste and stir in the lemon juice with the liqueur, if used. Reheat the sauce.

In a cup, mix the arrowroot with 15 ml/1 tbsp water. Add to the sauce and bring to the boil, stirring until the sauce thickens.

MAKES ABOUT 375 ML/13 FL OZ

MRS BEETON'S TIP If time is short, substitute 1 × 425 g/15 oz can apricots for fresh fruit. Purée the drained fruit with 125 ml/4 fl oz of the can syrup. Sugar need not be added, but lemon juice and liqueur, if used, should be added before the sauce is reheated.

COLD CHANTILLY APPLE SAUCE

450 g/1 lb cooking apples
25 g/1 oz butter
50 g/2 oz sugar
150 ml/¼ pint double cream

Peel, core and slice the apples. Put them into a saucepan with 30 ml/2 tbsp water. Add the butter and sugar. Cover the pan and simmer gently until the apple is reduced to a pulp.

Beat the pulp until smooth, then rub the mixture through a sieve. Alternatively, purée in a blender or food processor. Pour into a bowl and leave to cool.

In a separate bowl, whip the cream until stiff. Fold into the apple purée. Serve cold

MAKES ABOUT 500 ML/17 FL OZ

THICKENED FRUIT SAUCE

450 g/1 lb ripe fruit (damsons, plums,
    berry fruits)
50-100 g/2-4 oz sugar
lemon juice to taste
arrowroot (see method)

Put the fruit into a saucepan with about 30 ml/2 tbsp water. Cover the pan and cook over low heat until the fruit is reduced to a pulp. Remove any stones.

Beat the pulp until smooth, then rub through a sieve. Alternatively, purée the mixture in a blender or food processor. Pour

the purée into a measuring jug; note the volume.

Return the purée to the clean pan and reheat. Stir in the sugar, with lemon juice to taste. To thicken the sauce, you will need 5 ml/1 tsp arrowroot for every 250 ml/8 fl oz fruit purée. Spoon the required amount of arrowroot into a cup or small bowl and mix to a paste with water. Add to the fruit mixture and bring to the boil, stirring constantly until the sauce thickens. Remove from the heat as soon as the sauce boils. Serve hot or cold.

MAKES ABOUT 400 ML/14 FL OZ

☆ **FREEZER TIP** It is best to freeze the fruit purée before thickening. Pour into a rigid container, cover and seal. It will keep for up to 12 months. When required, thaw for 4 hours, reheat gently and thicken the sauce as described above.

FRUIT AND YOGURT SAUCE

Any fruit purée may be used for this sauce, provided it is not too acidic. Use fresh or canned fruit – apricots are particularly good.

150 ml/¼ pint plain yogurt
250 ml/8 fl oz fruit purée
sugar to taste

Spoon the yogurt into a bowl and beat it lightly. Fold in the fruit purée. Add sugar to taste. Serve cold.

MAKES ABOUT 350 ML/12 FL OZ

CHOCOLATE CREAM SAUCE

Illustrated on page 282

Add a touch of luxury to rice pudding, poached pears or ice cream with this sauce. When cold, the sauce thickens enough to be used as a soft filling for eclairs or profiteroles.

75 g/3 oz plain chocolate, roughly grated
15 ml/1 tbsp butter
15 ml/1 tbsp single cream
5 ml/1 tsp vanilla essence

Put the grated chocolate in a heatproof bowl with the butter. Add 60 ml/4 tbsp water. Stand the bowl over a saucepan of simmering water and stir until the chocolate and butter have melted.

When the chocolate mixture is smooth, remove from the heat and immediately stir in the cream and vanilla essence. Serve at once.

MAKES ABOUT 125 ML/4 FL OZ

☀ **MICROWAVE TIP** Combine the chocolate, butter and water in a basin. Heat on High for about 1 minute, stirring once, until the chocolate has melted. Finish as above.

CHOCOLATE LIQUEUR SAUCE

75 g/3 oz plain chocolate or cooking chocolate
10 ml/2 tsp custard powder or cornflour
15 ml/1 tbsp Cointreau or Grand Marnier
15 ml/1 tbsp caster sugar

Break the chocolate into small pieces and put it in a heatproof bowl with 30 ml/2 tbsp cold water. Stand the bowl over a saucepan of simmering water and stir until the chocolate melts.

When the chocolate has melted, beat it until smooth, gradually adding 200 ml/7 fl oz water.

In a cup, mix the custard powder or cornflour with 30 ml/2 tbsp water, then stir into the chocolate sauce and cook for 3-4 minutes. Stir in the liqueur and the sugar.

MAKES ABOUT 400 ML/14 FL OZ

MOCHA SAUCE

100 g/4 oz plain chocolate
200 g/7 oz sugar
125 ml/4 fl oz strong black coffee
pinch of salt
2.5 ml/½ tsp vanilla essence

Break up the chocolate and put it into a saucepan with the other ingredients. Stir over gentle heat until the chocolate and sugar melt and the mixture becomes smooth.

Serve hot over ice cream, Profiteroles (page 374) or stewed pears.

MAKES ABOUT 150 ML/¼ PINT

RICH CHOCOLATE SAUCE

*Plain ice cream becomes a party treat with this
wickedly rich sauce. It also makes a very good
topping for a chocolate Swiss Roll.*

350 g/12 oz bitter-sweet dessert chocolate,
    roughly grated
45 ml/3 tbsp butter
30 ml/2 tbsp double cream
5 ml/1 tsp whisky

Put the grated chocolate in a saucepan
with 200 ml/7 fl oz water. Heat gently, stirring all the time, until the chocolate melts.
Do not let the sauce boil. Add the butter,
5 ml/1 tsp at a time, and continue stirring
until it melts.

Remove the sauce from the heat and stir
in the cream and whisky. Serve at once.

MAKES ABOUT 500 ML/17 FL OZ

☆ **FREEZER TIP** The sauce may be
poured into a heatproof container
with a lid, cooled quickly and then frozen
for up to 3 months. To use, thaw for 4 hours
at room temperature, then stand the
container in a saucepan of very hot water.

RUM AND RAISIN
CHOCOLATE SAUCE

25 g/1 oz cocoa
25 g/1 oz cornflour
25 g/1 oz caster sugar
175 ml/6 fl oz milk
50 g/2 oz seedless raisins, chopped
30-45 ml/2-3 tbsp rum
30-45 ml/2-3 tbsp single cream

In a bowl, mix the cocoa, cornflour and
sugar to a smooth paste with a little of the
milk. Heat the rest of the milk until boiling.
Stir it into the cocoa paste.

Return the mixture to the clean saucepan and stir until boiling. Remove from the
heat and stir in the raisins, rum and cream.
Serve hot or cold.

MAKES ABOUT 250 ML/8 FL OZ

BUTTERSCOTCH SAUCE

1 × 410 g/14 oz can evaporated milk
100 g/4 oz soft light brown sugar
100 g/4 oz caster sugar
50 g/2 oz butter
15 ml/1 tbsp clear honey
2.5 ml/½ tsp vanilla essence
pinch of salt

Put the evaporated milk, sugars, butter,
and honey into a heavy-bottomed saucepan. Stir over gentle heat until the sugar
has dissolved. Stir in the vanilla essence
and salt.

Pour into a jug and serve hot with steamed
puddings such as Ginger Pudding (page 333)
or Tangy Lemon Pudding (page 336).

MAKES ABOUT 500 ML/17 FL OZ

☀ **MICROWAVE TIP** Combine the
evaporated milk, sugars and butter in
a large jug. Add the honey (or use golden
syrup). Cook on High for 4 minutes,
stirring once during cooking time. Cool
slightly, then stir in the vanilla essence
and salt.

GINGER SYRUP SAUCE

Warm a winter's evening with this sauce poured over Ginger Pudding (page 333)

strip of lemon rind
piece of fresh root ginger
125 ml/4 fl oz ginger syrup (from jar of
    preserved ginger)
100 g/4 oz soft light brown sugar, golden
    syrup or honey
5 ml/1 tsp lemon juice
10 ml/2 tsp arrowroot
2.5 ml/½ tsp ground ginger
15 ml/1 tbsp preserved ginger, chopped

Put the lemon rind, root ginger, and syrup into a saucepan. Add 125 ml/4 fl oz water. Heat to boiling point, lower the heat and simmer gently for 15 minutes.

Remove the lemon rind and root ginger. Add the brown sugar, syrup or honey, bring the mixture to the boil and boil for 5 minutes. Stir in the lemon juice.

In a cup, mix the arrowroot and ground ginger with a little cold water until smooth. Stir the arrowroot mixture into the hot liquid. Heat gently until the liquid thickens, stirring all the time.

Add the preserved ginger to the sauce and simmer for 2-3 minutes. Serve hot.

MAKES ABOUT 300 ML/½ PINT

MRS BEETON'S TIP The syrup in a jar of preserved ginger makes a delicious addition to gingerbreads, steamed puddings and pancakes.

JAM SAUCE

Illustrated on page 264

Simple sauces can be highly successful. Try Jam Sauce on steamed or baked puddings.

60 ml/4 tbsp seedless jam
lemon juice to taste
10 ml/2 tsp arrowroot
few drops of food colouring (optional)

Put the jam in a saucepan with 250 ml/ 8 fl oz water and bring to the boil. Add lemon juice to taste.

In a cup, mix the arrowroot with a little cold water until smooth. Stir into the hot liquid and heat gently until the sauce thickens, stirring all the time. Add a little colouring if necessary. Pour into a jug and serve at once.

MAKES ABOUT 300 ML/½ PINT

VARIATION

MARMALADE SAUCE Substitute marmalade for jam and use orange juice instead of water.

SWEET SHERRY SAUCE

75 ml/5 tbsp sherry
30 ml/2 tbsp seedless jam or jelly
lemon juice to taste

Combine the sherry and jam in a saucepan. Add 75 ml/5 tbsp water with lemon juice to taste. Bring to the boil and boil for 2-3 minutes. Strain, if necessary, before serving in a jug or sauceboat.

MAKES ABOUT 150 ML/¼ PINT

MARMALADE AND WINE SAUCE

Baked puddings can be somewhat dry. This zesty sauce is the perfect accompaniment.

60 ml/4 tbsp orange marmalade
75 ml/5 tbsp white wine

Combine the marmalade and wine in a saucepan and heat gently for 5 minutes.

Transfer to a jug and serve at once.

MAKES ABOUT 125 ML/4 FL OZ

☀ **MICROWAVE TIP** Combine the ingredients in a microwave-proof jug or bowl and cook on High for 1-1½ minutes, stirring once, until the marmalade has melted.

VANILLA CUSTARD

Illustrated on page 281

Adding cornflour stabilizes the custard and makes it less inclined to curdle.

10 ml/2 tsp cornflour
500 ml/17 fl oz milk
25 g/1 oz caster sugar
2 eggs
vanilla essence

In a bowl, mix the cornflour to a smooth paste with a little of the cold milk. Heat the rest of the milk in a saucepan and when hot pour it on to the blended cornflour, stirring.

Return the mixture to the saucepan, bring to the boil and boil for 1-2 minutes, stirring all the time, to cook the cornflour. Remove from the heat and stir in the sugar. Leave to cool.

Beat the eggs together lightly in a small bowl. Add a little of the cooked cornflour mixture, stir well, then pour into the saucepan. Heat gently for a few minutes until the custard has thickened, stirring all the time. Do not boil. Stir in a few drops of vanilla essence.

Serve hot or cold as an accompaniment to a pudding or pie.

MAKES ABOUT 600 ML/1 PINT

SIMPLE CUSTARD SAUCE

The addition of cornflour makes it unnecessary to use a double saucepan to make this sauce, provided care is taken to avoid excessive heat and the custard is constantly stirred.

500 ml/17 fl oz milk
few drops of vanilla essence
6 egg yolks
100 g/4 oz caster sugar
10 ml/2 tsp cornflour

Combine the milk and vanilla essence in a saucepan. Warm gently but do not let the liquid boil.

In a bowl, beat the egg yolks, sugar and cornflour together until creamy. Add the warm milk.

Strain the mixture back into the clean pan and cook, stirring constantly, until the custard thickens and coats the back of the spoon. Serve hot or cold.

MAKES ABOUT 600 ML/1 PINT

CLASSIC EGG CUSTARD SAUCE

This recipe may be used as the basis for ice cream or for a Vanilla Bavarois (page 266).

500 ml/17 fl oz milk
few drops of vanilla essence or other flavouring
6 egg yolks
100 g/4 oz caster sugar

Put the milk in a saucepan with the vanilla or other flavouring. Warm gently but do not let the liquid boil. If a solid flavouring such as a strip of citrus rind is used, allow it to infuse in the milk for 5 minutes, then remove.

In a bowl, beat the egg yolks and sugar together until creamy. Add the warm milk to the egg mixture.

Strain the mixture into a double saucepan or a heatproof bowl placed over a saucepan of simmering water. Cook, stirring constantly with a wooden spoon for 20-30 minutes, until the custard thickens and coats the back of the spoon. Take care not to let the custard curdle. Serve hot or cold.

MAKES ABOUT 500 ML/17 FL OZ

VARIATIONS

CLASSIC LEMON CUSTARD Infuse a thin strip of lemon rind in the milk, removing it before adding to the eggs.
CLASSIC ORANGE CUSTARD Substitute orange rind for lemon rind.
CLASSIC LIQUEUR CUSTARD Add 15 ml/1 tbsp kirsch or curaçao at the end of the cooking time.
PRALINE Stir in crushed Praline (see Mrs Beeton's Tip, page 248) just before serving.

ALMOND BUTTER

100 g/4 oz butter, softened
100 g/4 oz ground almonds
about 30 ml/2 tbsp caster sugar
2.5-5 ml/½-1 tsp lemon juice
few drops of almond essence

Put the butter in a mixing bowl and work in the ground almonds thoroughly. Add the sugar, lemon juice and almond essence gradually.

Use at once or pot (see Mrs Beeton's Tip) and chill.

MAKES ABOUT 225 G/8 OZ

> **MRS BEETON'S TIP** Pots of Almond Butter make good gifts. Press the butter into small pots or cartons (mini yogurt pots are perfect) and cover with cling film. Chill in the refrigerator. Do not freeze.

CHESTNUT BUTTER

200 g/7 oz unsweetened chestnut purée
200 g/7 oz butter, softened
30-45 ml/2-3 tbsp caster sugar
15-30 ml/1-2 tbsp rum

Combine the chestnut purée and butter in a bowl and mix until thoroughly blended. Add the sugar and rum gradually, adjusting the flavour to taste. Chill until firm, then use at once, or pot and chill as for Almond Butter (above).

MAKES ABOUT 450 G/1 LB

*B*RANDY BUTTER

Illustrated on page 263

50 g/2 oz butter
100 g/4 oz caster sugar
15-30 ml/1-2 tbsp brandy

In a bowl, cream the butter until soft. Gradually beat in the sugar until the mixture is pale and light. Work in the brandy, a little at a time, taking care not to allow the mixture to curdle. Chill before using. If the mixture has separated slightly after standing, beat well before serving.

MAKES ABOUT 150 G/5 OZ

VARIATIONS

SHERRY BUTTER Make as for Brandy Butter but substitute sherry for the brandy. Add a stiffly beaten egg white, if a softer texture is preferred.
VANILLA BUTTER Make as for Brandy Butter but substitute 5 ml/1 tsp vanilla essence for the brandy.
ORANGE OR LEMON BUTTER Cream the grated rind of 1 orange or ½ lemon with the butter and sugar, then gradually beat in 15 ml/1 tbsp orange juice or 5 ml/1 tsp lemon juice. Omit the brandy.

*B*RANDY AND ALMOND BUTTER

100 g/4 oz unsalted butter
75 g/3 oz icing sugar
25 g/1 oz ground almonds
30 ml/2 tbsp brandy
few drops of lemon juice

In a mixing bowl, cream the butter until very light. Sift in the icing sugar, a little at a time, and beat in each addition lightly but thoroughly with a fork. Sift in the almonds in the same way. Lift the fork when beating, to incorporate as much air as possible.

Beat in the brandy and lemon juice, a few drops at a time, taking care not to let the mixture separate. Taste, and add extra brandy if liked.

Pile the mixture into a dish and leave to firm up before serving; or turn lightly into a jar with a screw-topped lid Cover, and store in a cool place until required. Use within one week, or refrigerate for longer storage. Bring to room temperature before serving.

MAKES ABOUT 225 G/8 OZ

*C*UMBERLAND RUM BUTTER

100 g/4 oz unsalted butter
100 g/4 oz soft light brown sugar
30 ml/2 tbsp rum
2.5 ml/½ tsp grated orange peel
grated nutmeg

Put the butter in a bowl and cream it until very soft and light-coloured. Crush any lumps in the sugar. Work it into the butter until completely blended in.

Work the rum into the butter, a few drops at a time, taking care not to let the mixture separate. Mix in the orange peel. Taste and add a little grated nutmeg.

Pile the rum butter into a dish, and leave to firm up before serving; or turn lightly into a screw-topped jar, and store in a cool place until required. Use within 4 days, or refrigerate for longer storage. Bring to room temperature before serving.

MAKES ABOUT 225 G/8 OZ

RUM BUTTER

50 g/2 oz butter
100 g/4 oz soft light brown sugar
30 ml/2 tbsp rum

In a bowl, cream the butter until soft, beating in the sugar gradually. When light and creamy, work in the rum, a little at a time. Chill before using.

MAKES ABOUT 175 G/6 OZ

ORANGE LIQUEUR BUTTER

2 oranges
4 sugar lumps
150 g/5 oz butter, softened
25 g/1 oz caster sugar
15 ml/1 tbsp orange juice, strained
20 ml/4 tsp Cointreau

Pare the rind of the oranges and grind or grate it with the sugar lumps. Put in a bowl, and work in the butter and caster sugar until well blended.

Stir in the juice and liqueur gradually, until fully absorbed. Use at once, or pot and chill as for Almond Butter (page 404).

MAKES ABOUT 175 G/6 OZ

STRAWBERRY BUTTER

100 g/4 oz butter, softened
225 g/8 oz icing sugar
175 g/6 oz fresh strawberries, hulled and
  crushed
50 g/2 oz ground almonds

In a bowl, beat the butter until light. Sift in the sugar and beat it in thoroughly.

Add the strawberries with the ground almonds. Mix thoroughly. Use at once.

MAKES ABOUT 575 G/1¼ LB

FAIRY BUTTER

Not a whipped butter, but a rich dessert composed of orange-flavoured strands. It looks very attractive and may also be used instead of whipped cream as a topping on a trifle or gâteau.

2 hard-boiled egg yolks
10 ml/2 tsp orange juice, strained
10 ml/2 tsp orange flower water
25 g/1 oz icing sugar, sifted
100 g/4 oz butter, softened
10 ml/2 tsp grated orange rind to decorate

Sieve the egg yolks into a bowl. Using an electric whisk or rotary beater, gradually add the juice, orange flower water, sugar and butter until all the ingredients form a smooth paste.

To use, press the fairy butter through a sieve on to a decorative serving plate or individual plates in a pile of thin strands. Sprinkle with grated orange rind and serve at once with almond macaroons.

MAKES ABOUT 175 G/6 OZ

 MRS BEETON'S TIP The pile of butter strands should not be pressed down. Flick any stray strands into place with a fork.

GLOSSARY

All the terms, techniques and ingredients that are used throughout this book are discussed in detail within the relevant chapter or in the introduction. This glossary can be used for quick reference, perhaps to check up on the meaning of a term.

All-in-one method A method of mixing cakes in one stage only, by combining all the ingredients in a bowl and beating them together. The fat used should be soft margarine, or softened butter or block margarine, and additional raising agent is required. Except for small quantities, it is usual to use an electric whisk or food mixer to combine the ingredients. Also known as the one-stage method.

Almond essence Very strong almond flavouring, measured in drops.

Angelica The green stems of a plant, candied and used in cakes or biscuits, or as a decoration. The plant grows easily in Britain and it can be candied at home, although this is a long, slow process.

Bake To cook by dry heat in the oven.

Beat To combine foods, using a firm, quick motion which slightly lifts and turns the food, so incorporating air. It is commonly used for batters and soft mixtures, and a wooden spoon or electric whisk is used. The mixture is 'hit' with the flat front (or back) of the spoon as it is pushed quickly through the mixture; then lifted slightly and taken back to the starting point before being pushed through the mixture again.

Bind To add moist ingredients or liquid to a dry mixture to make all the ingredients adhere to each other. Enough liquid is added to ensure that the mixture can be gathered together into one, fairly firm, mass. The term is not used when a large quantity of liquid is added to make a very soft mixture.

Blanch To cover food with, or immerse food in, boiling water, or to bring food to the boil in water, then drain and cool it quickly. This technique is used for various reasons – to preserve flavour and colour in foods that are to be frozen, to remove peel or skin, or to par-cook food. Nuts are blanched to remove their skins.

Blend To gently combine ingredients without overmixing them. Alternatively, this term is used for processing food in a blender.

Chill To cool food. This is usually carried out by placing the food in the refrigerator. Alternatively, the container of food can be immersed in a bowl of iced water. A quick method of chilling is to put the food in the freezer for a short period of time. Chilling is carried out on food which is at room temperature; hot food is cooled before it is chilled.

Chocolate cake covering An inexpensive alternative to couverture or dessert chocolate. This is useful for day-to-day cooking but its flavour cannot be compared to dessert chocolate.

Cinnamon A sweet spice, widely used in baked goods. It is the bark of a tree and is available as cinnamon sticks, which are rolled thin slivers of the spice, or ground to a fine, brown powder.

Coat To cover food with an outer coating. This can be a coating to protect foods such as fish or meat before cooking. In baking the term is applied to the use of icings and chocolate, where cakes or biscuits are covered with an even coating of one of these toppings.

Cocoa Seeds of the cocoa tree, dried,

partially fermented and roasted. They are ground to a fine powder for use as a flavouring. Cocoa is unsweetened, dark and strongly flavoured. It must not be confused with drinking chocolate which is a sweetened mixture, flavoured with cocoa.

Cochineal Natural food colouring which gives a pink, or dark pink-red colour to food. It will not give a true red colour.

Coffee Roasted coffee beans are available whole or ground. Instant coffee is the most common source of coffee flavouring for cakes and biscuits. Fresh coffee essence can be made by cooling and straining very strong fresh coffee.

Couverture Cooking chocolate which has a high cocoa fat content, giving an excellent flavour and glossy finish.

Cream This is a term used for combining ingredients, in baking usually fat and sugar. A circular motion is used and the edge of a wooden spoon cuts through the ingredients. The aim when creaming ingredients is to make them soft and light in texture by incorporating air. When fat and sugar are creamed together, the mixture gradually becomes pale in colour, soft and fluffy in texture. An electric food mixer can be used or ingredients can be creamed in a food processor.

Dariole moulds Small, straight-sided tins which are sometimes known as castle tins.

Dredge To sprinkle a fairly thick, even coating of sugar or flour over food or the work surface. If a cake is dredged with icing sugar, then it should be evenly covered in a thick coating. A sieve, sugar sifter or flour dredger (or shaker) is used to give a fine, even result.

Dust To sprinkle food or a surface with a fine, even coating of sugar or flour. Unlike dredging, dusting means that a very fine sprinkling of the dry ingredient should be evenly distributed over the surface without completely covering it.

Fold in To incorporate an ingredient into a very light mixture without knocking out any of the air. A large metal spoon is used and the mixture is gently lifted, then folded over the ingredient which has been added to it. The spoon should follow a figure of eight movement: the edge of the spoon cuts through the mixture, then the bowl of the spoon is turned to lift the mixture over in a diagonal movement. The spoon is then pushed back to the starting point. It is most important that a stirring movement is avoided as this will knock the air out of the mixture. Dry ingredients, such as flour and sugar, are folded into moist mixtures, such as whisked egg whites, beaten eggs or creamed fat and sugar. Melted fat or other liquids can be folded into light mixtures. The process of folding in should be quick, gentle and involve the minimum of 'mixing'.

Fondant A traditional icing which is made by boiling sugar and water to the soft ball stage. The mixture is then 'worked' or made pliable as it cools by turning it with the flat blade of a palette knife until it forms a soft malleable paste. Reheated and thinned, this is then poured over the cake.

Frosting The American term for 'icing'. Frosting is a soft creamy icing made by whisking egg whites and sugar over hot water.

Gâteau This term is used for creamy, light layer cakes, often filled or decorated with fruit. Instead of sponge cake, the base can be meringue.

Genoese sponge A light sponge cake, made by the whisked method, enriched with melted butter.

Glycerine This is an alcohol which is one of the ingredients used to make soap. It is a clear syrup which has a certain use as a sugar substitute or for softening mixtures. It is not widely used and should not be used in large quantities.

Knead This technique is most often used to make bread dough. One end of the dough is lifted and pulled over the middle of the piece of dough, then it is pushed back with the knuckles. As well as yeasted doughs, biscuit doughs are sometimes 'kneaded gently' but this is not a fierce movement.

When the term is applied to pastry or biscuit dough, then the fingertips are used to pull the dough, rolling it slightly and moving the hand in towards the middle of the piece of dough. Then the flat of the hand is used to lightly push the dough outwards, again slightly rolling it. This method is a combination of flattening and rolling, then pushing the dough back up again. The movement should be very light and quick, just enough to make sure that the biscuit dough is smooth.

Mocha The term used for the flavour of coffee and chocolate in combination.

Nutmeg Large, round, very hard seed of a tree. It is grated and used in sweet and savoury cooking. Available as whole nutmegs or ready grated. This is another sweet spice.

Pare To very thinly peel the rind or skin from a fruit or vegetable. The rind of citrus fruits is pared, then cut into fine strips and cooked in boiling water to be used as a decoration.

Rice Paper Rice paper has no connection with rice – it comes from a plant. It is very thin, brittle, opaque and edible. It is used as a base for mixtures such as macaroons.

Rub-in This is the term used for combining fat with dry ingredients such as flour. The fat is cut into small pieces and added to the flour. The fingertips are used to lift a portion of the dry ingredients and the fat is rubbed very lightly with the flour. As the ingredients are rubbed together, they are allowed to fall back into the bowl. The process of lifting the ingredients before and during rubbing incorporates air into the mixture. It is important that just the fingertips are used and that the hands are kept cool.

Sieve A metal or nylon fine mesh through which ingredients are passed. To sieve food means to press the food through the mesh, usually using a spoon. This term is applied to moist ingredients which are sieved to reduce them to a purée or to break down any unwanted lumps.

Sift A sieve or sifter (a container with a holed lid) is used for this purpose. Dry ingredients are shaken through the sieve, either by tapping the side of the utensil or by pressing them through with the back of a spoon. If sugar is sifted over a cake, then the sieve should be tapped gently to give a fine even sprinkling. If icing sugar or flour are sifted before they are used, they can be pushed through with a spoon.

Strain A liquid mixture is strained through a sieve to remove all unwanted solids. The liquid is the part which is retained; the food which is strained out of it may be discarded or it may be separated for another purpose.

Vanilla A flavouring ingredient which is widely used in baking.

Vanilla sugar Caster sugar which has been flavoured with a vanilla pod.

Whip The term used for whisking double cream or whipping cream.

Whisk An implement used for whisking food. Many types of whisks are available, for example, wire balloon whisks, spring whisks, rotary whisks or electric whisks. Egg whites and liquids are whisked and the result is much lighter than for mixtures which are beaten using a wooden spoon.

Zest The oils that 'spit' from citrus rind. The zest of a fruit rind is obtained by rubbing a lump of sugar over it. The sugar absorbs the oils, and therefore the flavour, of the rind.

INDEX

agar agar 21
almond
  and apricot pudding *281*, 338
  and apricot tartlets 360
  and brandy butter 405
  butter 404, 405
  cake 86, 104
  castles 388
  cheesecake 184
  and chocolate cake 86
  and chocolate loaf 102
  essence 20
  fritters 318
  ice cream 219
  junket 237-8
  and raspberry pavlova 163
  sauce 394
  shortcake 133
  soufflé 272
  squares 131
  tartlets 352
  velvet cream 265
almond paste 56, 74-6
  decorations 82, 88-9
aluminium steamers 326
ambassadrice soufflé 272-3
American frosting 60
American Indian pudding 306
angel food cake 160
apple
  baked 384
  stuffed 385
  and banana cobbler 379
  batter pudding 312
  and blackberry pie *283*, 351
  and blackberry pudding 372
  and blackcurrant spread 69
  Brown Betty 385
  Chantilly sauce 399
  charlotte 384
  and cinnamon sandwich cake 51
  crumble 382
  Danish apple cake 196-7
  dumplings
    boiled 371
    glazed 372-3
  Eve's pudding 382
  fritters 317
  frosted 196
  and ginger cake 107
  and ginger pancakes 313
  jalousie 366
  jelly 205

Lexington 320-1
  meringue 383
  Mrs Beeton's flan 355
  pancakes 313
  pie 351
  pudding 328
  sauce 393
  snow 254
  soufflé 273
  squares 131
  stewed 190
  strudel *285*, 377
  tart 378
  trifle 176
  and walnut tart 378
apple bananas 189
apricot
  and almond pudding *281*, 338
  and almond tartlets 360
  baskets 136
  batter pudding 312
  fritters 317
  glaze 54, 70-1
  decorations 82
  ice cream 218-19
  meringue flan 359
  pancakes 313
  pie 351
  sauce *281*, 398
  soufflé 273
  omelette 274
  spread 69
  trifles *142*, 175, 176-7
  upside-down cake 151
arrowroot 21
  pudding 299
  sauce 395
Austrian hazelnut layer 169

bachelor pudding 340
bain marie, making custard in 234-5
baked Alaska 232
bakewell tart 352
baking 43-4
  blind 346-7
  faults with 46-7
  hints 46
baking parchment 36, 38
baking powder 14
baking tins 25, 34-6
  lining 37-41
  preparing 11, 37
  releasing cakes from 44

Balmoral tartlets 360
bamboo steamers 325
banana
  and apple cobbler 379
  bonanza 198
  and brandy pavlova 163
  chartreuse 207
  chocolate loaf 103
  custard 241
  flan 357
  fritters 317
  froth 209
  pancakes 313
  and rhubarb fool 202
  in rum 198
  snow 198
  and walnut cake 105
basins 25-6, 32
Battenburg cake *137*, 155
batter pudding 312, 316
batters 308
Bavarian Cream 266-7
bavarois 266-7
beignets 321
bicarbonate of soda 14
birthday cakes 85, 94
black cap pudding 312
Black Forest gâteau *140*, 168
black mamba 205-6
black treacle 17, 24
blackberries
  and apple pie *283*, 351
  and apple pudding 372
  stewed 190
  velvet cream 265
blackcurrants
  and apple spread 69
  ice cream 218
  jelly 203
  mousse 278-9
  rosettes 361
  stewed 190
  water ice 215
blancmange 298
blenders 30
blueberry pie 350
bombes
  czarine 224
  diplomate 224-5
  nesselrode 224
  tortoni 225
  zamora 224
boodles cake 122

Page numbers in *italic* refer to illustrations

bowls 25-6, 32
bran cake 111
brandy
  and almond butter 405
  and banana pavlova 163
  butter *263*, 405
  sauce 394
  whip 269
bread
  and butter pudding 243
  ice cream 216
  shahi tukra 244-5
  steamed pudding 330
brown flour 12
brown paper 36
brown sugar 16
brownies 145
buns 126-8
bunuelos 322-3
butter 14-15
  flavoured 404-6
  freezing 392-3
butter icing 57-8
buttercream 57-8, 71
  decorations 83-5
butterfly cakes *115*, 128-9
buttermilk waffles 323
butterscotch
  brownies 130
  pudding 245
  sauce 401

cabinet pudding 242-3
cacen gneifio 124
Canadian cakes 362
Canary pudding *264*, 337
cane sugar 17
carambola 189
caramel
  bavarois 266
  custard cups 249
  custard sauce 394
  ice cream 220
  mousse 290
  rice pudding 300
carob 96
  brownies 145
caster sugar 16
castle puddings 388
cauliflowers 134-5
Chantilly cream 397
Chantilly sauce 399
charlottes 165
  Mrs Beeton's russe 180
  russe with Cointreau 180-1
  St José 181
Cheddar cheesecake 183

cheese 24
  cheesecake 183
  icing 69
  pancakes 313
  and strawberry pavlova 163
cheesecake 165-7, 182-7
  freezing 167
cherry
  cake 108, 109, *114*
  clafouti aux cerises 316
  compôte 199
  glacé cherries 19
  jubilee 200
  omelette soufflé 274
  pudding 386
  rich cake 49
  roll-ups (pancakes) 310
  rosettes 361
  sponge pudding 337
  stoners 29
chestnuts
  bombe nesselrode 224
  butter 404
  nesselrode pudding 230
chocolate 21, 96
  almond cake 86, 102
  banana loaf 103
  bavarois 266
  blancmange 298
  buns 126
  buttercream 58
  cake
    layer 157
    loaf 102-3
    rich 49
    sandwich 51
    scroll 86
  cream sauce *282*, 400
  cream sponge 53
  crumb pudding *282*, 340-1
  custard 64
  custard sauce 396
  decorations 96-100
  diplomat cream 65
  dipping food in 97-8
  dream *259*, 280
  freezer pudding 228
  glaze 54
  ice cream 220-1
  ice roll 152
  icing
    french butter 58
    glacé 60
  junket 238
  layer loaf 103
  liqueur sauce 400
  marquise 279

moths 129
mousse 278, 279
  orange chiffon pie 294
  orange mousse 279
  orange omelette soufflé 274
  orange split 103
  pancake pie 310-11
  and pear trifle 177
  piping 98-100
  pudding
    crumb 340-1
    everyday 341
    sponge 337
  roll 153
  roulade 171
  rum and raisin sauce 401
  rum roll 152
  sauce 394, 400, 401
  scroll cake 86
  semolina 298
    and rum 304
  soufflé 276
    Milanaise 277
    omelette 274
  spice squares 130
  sponge pudding 387
  storing 96
  types of 96
  using 97-8
  velvet cream 101, 265
  walnut loaf 103
choux pastry 349
Christmas cake *117*, 146-8
Christmas pudding *263*, 331
cider
  cake 121
  syllabub 270
cinnamon 20
  and apple sandwich cake 51
  cup custard 238
  doughnuts 135
citrus cheese icing 69
citrus squeezers 34
clafouti aux cerises 316
claret jelly 208
cloutie dumpling 343
coatings 54-6
cobblers 344, 379-81
  freezing 344
cocoa 21
coconut 20
  buns 126
  cream pie 289
  pyramids 133
  rich cakes 49
  sponge pudding 337
    baked 387

squares 131
toppings 66, 68
coeur à la crème au citron 289
coffee
    bavarois 266
    blancmange 298
    bombe zamora 224
    buttercream 58
    cake
        cream 158
        rich 49
        sandwich 51
    cheesecake 182
    chiffon pie 292-3
    gâteau 168-9
    glacé icing 59
    ice cream 221
        white magic 222
    junket 238
    mousse 290
    sauce 394
    soufflé 272
    velvet cream 265
    whip *258*, 269
college puddings *288*, 389
confectioners' custard 64
    with brandy 65
continental ovens 9
cooking foil 36
cooking times 11
corers 29
corkers *116*, 145
cornflour
    cake 49
    custard 235
    custard sauce 395
cornmeal pudding 306-7
cottage pudding 388-9
coupe Jacques 233
Coventry turnovers 364
cranachan *258*, 271
cranberry raisin pie 353
cream
    custard sauce 396
    decorations 86
    fillings 63
    pancakes 313
    and peaches cake 53
    products 22-3
    tartlets 363
    velvet cream 256, 265
cream of tartar 14
crème
    Anglaise 396
    brûlée 246-7, *257*
    diplomate 266
    fraîche 22

frangipane 64
St Honoré 64
tricolore 266
crêpes
    au choix 315
    suzette 324
crumbles 344
Cumberland pudding 328-9
Cumberland rum butter 405
curd cheesecake 182-3
currants 19
custard
    baked 240
    banana 241
    bavarois 266-7
    caramel cups 249
    confectioners' custard 64
        with brandy 65
    cup 238
    fillings 64-5
    freezing 235
    making 234-5
    orange 240-1
    pineapple 239
    steamed 240
    tart 253
    tartlets 362
    thickening 392
    vanilla *281*, *288*, 403
custard sauces 394-6, 403-4
    basic recipe 403

damask cream 265
damson pie 351
Danish apple cake 196-7
dark secrets ring cake *139*, 159
dates 19
    sponge pudding 337
    and walnut cake 105
dean's cream 179
decorations
    almond paste 82, 88-9
    apricot glaze or jam 82
    buttercream 83-5
    chocolate 96-101
    equipment for 28, 36, 70, 91-2
    fondant 88
    glacé icing 87
    marzipan 82, 88-9
    pastry 348
    royal icing 95
    sugar paste 90-5
    whipped cream 86
deep fat fryers 30
demerara sugar 17
devil's food cake 160
Devonshire rum 390

diplomat cream 65
doily design 82
doughnuts 135
dried fruit 18-19
dripping 15-16
dripping cake 124
Dundee cake *138*, 156

Easter almond roll 152-3
Easter cakes *120*, 154
eggs 17-18, 234, 392
electrical equipment 30-1, 34, 326-7
Empress pudding 302
equipment
    basic 25-9, 32-4
    decorating 28, 36, 70, 91-2
    disposable 36
    electrical 30-1, 34, 326-7
    specialist 29
    see also baking tins
Eve's pudding *287*, 382
Exeter pudding 389
expanding steamers 326

fairy butter 406
fan ovens 9
fats 14-16
feather icing 87
festive log *117*, 148
figs 19, 189
filbert tartlets 363
fillings 63-5
filo pastry 349
flaky pastry 346, 350
flans 355-7
    glaze 55
    lining a tin 346
    pastry for 345
floating islands 248-9
flour 12-13
flowers, frosted 67
fondant 60, 73
    decorations 88
food mixers 34
food processors 30, 34
forest pudding 250
fork patterns 83
freezing 44-6
    cheesecakes 167
    cobblers and crumbles 344
    cream fillings 63
    custard 235
    gâteaux 164
    ice cream 211, 212
    pancakes 309
    sauces 392-3
friar's omelette 386

fried creams 320
fritters 317-19, 322
fromage frais 23, 24
frostings 60, 67, 72-3
fruit
  buns 126
  candied cream jelly 210
  canned 190
  chartreuse 208-9
  dried 18-19
    batter pudding 312
    compote 193
    pancakes 313
    pudding 330
    sponge pudding 337
  exotic 189-90
  fresh 23, 24
  gâteau 162
  glacé and cream 96
  jellies 191-2
  and liqueur pavlova 163
  loaf 110, *114*
  mixed peel 19
  and nut squares 131
  purées 201, 392
  rinds 20
  sauce 399
  soufflé *260*, 273
    Milanaise 277
  stewed 190-1
  toppings 86, 89
  and walnut pancake bake 314
  yogurt 237
  and yogurt sauce 399
fruit cake 43, 44
  boiled 108
  Christmas cake 146-8
  festival 109
  one-stage 48
fruit salad
  green 192
  red 189, 195
  tropical 194
fudge icing 57-8, 72-3

gâteau 167-9, 172
  de Pithiviers 370
  freezing 164
  St Honoré 376
gelatine 23
Geneva pudding 299
Genoese sponge (pastry) 52
ginger 20
  and apple cake 107
  and apple pancakes 313
  bavarois 266
  buns 127

cream roll 153
  ice cream 222-3
  pudding 333
  sandwich cake 51
  sauce 394
  soufflé 272
  sponge pudding 337
  syrup sauce 402
gingerbread 53, 106
  Guy Fawkes 125
  with pineapple 106
glacé cherries 19
glacé fondant 60
glacé fruits 86
glacé icing 59-60, 72
  decorations 87
glazes 54-6
golden syrup 17, 24
  pudding 334-5
gooseberry
  cobbler 380
  fool 201
  fritters 318
  pie 351
  stewed 190
  tarts 364
  trifle 176
Grand Marnier soufflé 272
granulated sugar 16
grapefruit
  and orange salad 194-5
  yogurt 236
graters 26, 33
greaseproof paper 36, 38
greengage suet pudding 370-1
guava 189-90

Hampshire pie 365
harlequin sandwich cake 51
harlequin soufflé 273
harvest cake 154
hasty pudding 303
hazelnut
  cake 158
  meringue gâteau 172
holiday cake 111
honesty pudding 387
honey 23-4
  buns 128
  pudding 303
honeycomb mould 268
House of Commons pudding 246
hygiene 10

ice cream 216-23, 226
  freezing 211, 212
  making 211-12

plombières 227
  vanilla 213, 216
  see also bombes
icing sugar 17
icings 57-60, 69
  chocolate 96-7
  fudge 57-8, 72-3
  glacé 59-60, 72, 87
  moulded 77-8
  royal icing 61-2, 79-81, 95
imperial measures 8-9
Indian fritters 322
ingredients
  basic 12-20
  choosing 10
  flavourings 20
  mixing 11, 42-3
    hints on 46
  specialist 21-4
Italian bavarois 266
Italian candied fruit gateau 162

jam
  baked roll *288*, 391
  decorations 82
  omelette soufflé 274
  sauce *264*, 402
  sponge pudding 387
  tart 354
Japanese plombière 227
jellies 191-2, 203-10
jelly cream 267
junket 237-8

kaiserschmarrn 311
kirsch, and pineapple salad 189, 194
kitchen hygiene 10
kiwi fruit 190
knickerbocker glory *144*, 233
knives 26, 29, 33
kumquats 190

l'ambassadrice pudding 255
lard 15
leaves, frosted 67
lemon
  and almond velvet cream 265
  butter 405
  buttercream 58
  cheesecake 184
  chiffon *260*, 290-1
  chiffon pie 294
  cream sponge 53
  cup custard 238
  custard 404
  diplomat cream 65
  fluff 270

glacé icing 59
ice cream 223
jelly 203
   clear 204
junket 238
meringue pie 352-3
omelette soufflé 274
pudding 336
   delicious 390
rice *261*, 300-1
rich cake 49
sandwich cake 51
sauce *288*, 395
smoothie 203
sorbet 215
soufflé 272
sponge pudding 387
water ice 212
Lexington apples 320-1
lime chiffon pie 294
linzertorte 369
liqueur
   custard 404
   diplomat cream 65
   and fruit pavlova 163
   glacé icing 59
   sauce 396
   soufflé 272
   velvet cream 265
liquidizers 30
Lockshen pudding 305
low-fat spreads 16
lump sugar 17
lunch cake 112

Madeira cake *113*, 156
madeleines *115*, 129
malakoff gâteau 167
malted wheat flour 13
Manchester pudding 368
mandarin water ice 214-15
mango 190
   mousse 291
maple
   mousse 291
   syrup 24
maraschino glaze 55
marble cake 157
marbled squares 131
margarine 15
marigold cheesecake 187
marmalade
   meringue pudding 383
   squares 131
   and wine sauce 403
Marquise Alice 248
marzipan 56, 74-6

decorations 82, 88-9
Mayfair cakes 132-3
measuring 8-9, 10-11, 26, 29, 33
melba sauce 398
melopita 187
meringue glacé Chantilly 233
metric measures 8-9
microwaves 9
   making custard 235
   making milk puddings 296
   making sauces 393
   making steamed puddings 327
   stewing fruit 191
Milanaise soufflé 276-7
milk jelly 206
milk puddings 295, 296
mille-feuille gâteau *284*, 367
mincemeat meringue pie 354
Miss Muffet cake 123
mixed peel 19, 20
mixed spice 20
mixing ingredients 11, 42-3
mocha
   bavarois 266-7
   fingers *116*, 132
   ice cream 221
   mousse 278
   sandwich cake 51
   sauce 400
   velvet 101
mock cream 65
molasses 17
moulds 27, 35
   coating with jelly 192
mousseline
   cake 170
   pudding 329
   sauce 396
mousses 278-9, 290-1
Mrs Beeton's
   apple flan 355
   bakewell pudding 352
   charlotte russe 180
   Delhi pudding 332-3
   Dutch flummery 268
   Manchester pudding 368
   tipsy cake 179
   traditional trifle *143*, 178
muscovado sugar 16-17
mushroom cake 84, 134

Neapolitan ice *144*, 226
nesselrode pudding 230
Newcastle pudding 339
Newmarket pudding 250
nutmeg 20
nuts 19-20

toasted 66
toppings 68
waffles 323

oatmeal flummery 307
oil wells 34
oils 16, 37-8
oldaya 319
omelette soufflés 274-5
   baked 275
   branded 275
   en surprise 230-1
   flambé 275
   surprise 275
   sweet 274
orange
   bavarois 267
   butter 405
   buttercream 58
   cake
      rich 49
      sandwich 51
   in caramel sauce 197
   chiffon pie 294
   chocolate chiffon pie 294
   chocolate mousse 279
   chocolate omelette soufflé 274
   chocolate split 103
   chocolate velvet 101
   coconut topping 68
   custard 240-1
   custard sauce 404
   diplomat cream 65
   fairy butter 406
   fritters 317
   glacé icing 59
   and grapefruit salad 194-5
   jelly 203
      baskets 205
   junket 238
   liqueur butter 406
   and pear cobbler 379
   praline mousse 290
   soufflé 272
      Milanaise 277
   sponge pudding 387
   walnut buns 126
   walnut roll 153
ortaniques 194
ovenproof dishes 27-8, 36
ovens
   cooking times 11
   preparing 11
   removing food from 11
   temperature 9, 43
   types of 9
   see also microwaves

Paddington pudding 336
pancakes *262*, 308-9, 312-13
  bunuelos 322-3
  freezing 309
  stack 314-15
papaya 190
paper cake cases 36
Paris-Brest 375
passion fruit 190
pastry
  brushes 28, 34
  cutters 34
  decorations 348
  making 345-50
  pies 347
patriotic pudding 339
pavlova 163
peaches
  bavarois 267
  in brandy 201
  and cream cake 53
  flan 356
  melba 231
    sauce 398
  omelette soufflé 274
  stewed 190
  trifle 177
pears
  and chocolate trifle 177
  fritters 317
  and orange cobbler 379
  poire belle hélène 229
  and rice meringue 302
  ring of 251
  stewed 190
  upside-down pudding 151
  in wine 200
pecan pie 358
pepper cake 122
peppermint cream pie 292
persimmon 190
petits fours 149
phylo pastry 349
picnic cheesecake 186
pies, pastry 347
pineapple
  buttermilk whip 269
  custard 239
  flan 356-7
  fritters 317
  jelly cream 267
  and kirsch salad 189, 194
  pancakes 313
  sorbet 213
  soufflé 273
  trifle 177

upside-down cake *119*, 151
piping
  bags 28, 36
  chocolate 98-100
pistachio
  bavarois 267
  velvet cream 265
plain cake 48
plombières 227
plum pudding 332
plums
  nutty crumble *286*, 381
  with port 193
  stewed 190
  upside-down cake 151
poinsettia cake 89
poire belle hélène 229
poor knights 319
port
  wine jelly 206
  with plums 193
praline 66
  custard 404
  orange mousse 290
  Paris-Brest 375
  soufflé 272
    Milanaise 277
preserving sugar 17
pressure cookers 31
  making custard in 235
  making milk puddings 296
  making steamed puddings 327
Prince Albert's pudding 342
profiteroles *284*, 374
prunes 19
puff pastry 346, 350
pumpkin pie 358

quark 24
queen cakes 49
Queen Mab's pudding 244, *257*
queen of puddings 252-3

raising agents 13-14
raisins 18
  rum and chocolate sauce 401
raspberry
  and almond pavlova 163
  buns 127
  jelly cream 267
  meringue roll 153
  omelette soufflé 274
  and redcurrant fool 202
  and redcurrant pie 351
  rosettes 361
  soufflé 273
    Milanaise 277

vacherin 173
water ice 214
yogurt cheesecake 185
  and yogurt delight 237
redcurrant
  and raspberry fool 202
  and raspberry pie 351
  sauce 393
rhubarb
  and banana fool 202
  cobbler 380
  pie 351
  stewed 191
ribbon bavarois 267
rice
  chilled mould 307
  paper 36
  and pear meringue 302
  puddings 296, 297, 300-1, 303
  rich cake 49
  types of 295
rich cakes 49
rich knights 319
rich pancakes 313
ring doughnuts 135
ring fritters 322
rock cakes 123
rolled cakes 152-3
Rothschild soufflé 273
royal icing 61-2, 79-81
  decorations 95
rum
  babas *142*, 175
  butter 405, 406
  and chocolate mousse 278
  and chocolate semolina 304
  junket 237-8
  omelette soufflé 274
  raisin and chocolate sauce 401

sabayon sauce 397
sacher torte 161
St Clement's
  roll 153
  sauce 395
salad, *see* fruit salad
Salzburger nockerl 391
sandwich cakes 44, 50-1
saucepan and steamer sets 325
sauces 393-403
  freezing 392-3
  making 392-3
  sweet white 394
savarin 174
  pudding a l'ambassadrice 255
Savoy pudding 251
Saxon pudding 252

scales 10-11, 28, 32-3
scone dough 344
scoops 29
scraper design 84
seafoam pudding 254
seed buns 126
seed cake 125
self-raising flour 13
semolina
    hasty pudding 303
    hot timbale of 304
    pudding 297, 298, 304
    soufflé 280
serving dishes 28-9
shahi tukra 244-5
shearing (Cacen Gneifio) cake 124
Sheer Khurma 305
sherry
    butter 405
    cream pie 293
    sabayon sauce 397
    sauce 402
short crust pastry 345, 349
shortcake 133
sieves 29, 33
Simnel cake *118*, 150-1
skewer pattern 86
skewer test 43
slow cookers 30-1
Snowdon pudding 335
sopaipillas 323
sorbet 213, 215
soufflés
    cold 276-7
    fruit *260*, 273
    hot 272-3, 280
    omelette 230-1, 274-5
Spanish fritters 322
spatulas 29, 33
spice buns 126
spice cake 110
spicy sponge pudding 387
sponge cakes 43, 44, 52-3
sponge pudding 337
    baked 387
spoon measures 8-9, 29, 33
spuma gelata angelina 228
star cake 84-5
steamed puddings 325-43
    microwave cooking 327
    pressure cooking 327
steamers 325-7
stewed fruit 190-1
stoneground flour 13
storing
    cakes 44-5
    chocolate decorations 96

dried fruit 19
eggs 18
flour 13
raising agents 14
sugar 17
see also freezing
strawberry
    blancmange 298
    butter 406
    and cheese pavlova 163
    cream cake 53
    dumplings 373
    ice cream 223
        layer gâteau 229
    jelly cream 267
    meringue torte *141*, 172-3
    omelette soufflé 275
    rosettes 361
    soufflé 273
striped-top cake 83
stuffed monkey 369
suet crust pastry 348, 350
sugar 16-17
    crystals 66
sugar paste 77-8
    decorations 90-5
sugared strands 67
sultana cake 111
sultanas 19
summer pudding 199
surprise pancakes 313
Swedish rice 303
Swiss cream 256
Swiss rolls 44, *137*, 152
Swiss shortcakes 133
syllabubs 270-1
syrup 17, 24

tangerine jelly cream 267
tapioca cream pudding 306
tea ice cream 217
temperature of ovens 9
toffee-topped grape cream 197
toppings 66-9, 344
    fruit 86, 89
torta di ricotta 188
tray bakes 131
treacle 17, 24
    layer pudding 334
    tart 355
trifle 164-5, 175-8
turnovers 347
Twelfth Night cake 150

utensils, *see* equipment

vanilla 20

bavarois 266
butter 405
buttercream 58
custard *281*, *288*, 403
ice cream 213
    rich 216
    plombière 227
    soufflé 272
velvet cream 256, 265
Victoria sandwich cakes 44, 50-1
    one-stage 50
vinegar cake 112

waffle irons 31, 309
waffles 309, 323
walnut
    and apple tart 378
    and banana cake 105
    buttercream 58
    and date cake 105
    and fruit pancake bake 314
    ice cream 217
    loaf 103, 104, *113*
    orange buns 126
    and orange roll 153
    topping 68
Washington ripple *281*, 338
water ices 212-15
wax paper 36
weighing 8-9, 10-11, 28, 32-3
West Riding pudding 352
Westmorland parkin 121
whisks 29, 30, 34, 42
white magic 222
wholemeal flour 12
Windsor pudding 301
wine
    and marmalade sauce 403
    syllabub 271
    trifles 178
wire racks 34

yeast 14, 174
    cake 107
yogurt 24
    fruit 237
    and fruit sauce 399
    grapefruit 236
    ice cream 226
    making 235-6
    and raspberry delight 237
Yorkshire pudding 316

zabaglione 239
    sabayon sauce 397